Intermediate Price and Income Theory

REVISED EDITION

INTERMEDIATE

PRICE and INCOME

THEORY *REVISED EDITION*

M. M. BOBER LAWRENCE COLLEGE

NEW YORK
W · W · NORTON & COMPANY · INC ·

To Dr. William A. McConagha

Library of Congress Catalog Card No. 61-7473

PRINTED IN THE UNITED STATES OF AMERICA
FOR THE PUBLISHERS BY THE VAIL-BALLOU PRESS

3456789

Contents

v

Preface to the Revised Edition

THIS BOOK is a revision of its predecessor published in 1955. The revision concentrates, in the main, on the first thirteen chapters. In the remaining chapters there have been minor changes, except for the last chapter, which is almost entirely new.

As in the first edition, the attempt is made to present a unified sequence of concepts and problems, and to stress alike step-by-step analysis and clarity of exposition. The concept of *equilibrium* is purposely introduced as early as the second chapter, to make the student aware from the outset of equilibrium as the central focus of the developing argument.

Specifically, the following changes may be regarded as of major character: Two introductory chapters, instead of one chapter, are offered on the nature of economics. The final chapter deals exclusively with aspects of equilibrium as the frame of analytical structure. The material given to the theory of production is put together in chapters V and VI, instead of chapters IV and XI, as in the previous edition. This change has been made in response to the urgings of many readers, including students in India, who wanted the full discussion of production theory treated in neighboring chapters.

More discussion is given to such problems as utility, elasticity, monopoly, indifference curves; and some new problems are introduced briefly, such as production planning in Russia. There is also a brief evaluation of price formation at the end of the discussion of each of the four structures of commodity markets (chapters IX to XII). This evaluation is borrowed from the last chapter of the first edition. This new edition occupies two more chapters, and has ten more diagrams and three more tables.

My sincere thanks are due to President Douglas M. Knight and to Dean

Marshall B. Hulbert, both at Lawrence College, for favoring me with a smaller teaching schedule for a couple of semesters. In this regard they followed the tradition stressed by President Henry M. Wriston and President Nathan M. Pusey, in their days at Lawrence College.

I am grateful to the following gentlemen and scholars for their friendly criticism and suggestions: J. F. Bell, of the University of Illinois; R. L. Darcy, of Oregon State College; J. E. Elliott, of the University of Southern California; L. B. Krause, of Yale University; D. A. Moore, of Michigan State University; J. C. Murdock, of the University of Missouri; C. R. McConnell, of the University of Nebraska; L. Nabers, of the University of Utah; Egon Neuberger, of Amherst College; and E. J. Stolnitz, of Indiana University.

I am under special obligation to Dr. E. C. Budd of Yale University, who gave generously of his time and whose acute insight combined with a whiplash style improved my discussion in more than one place. I owe a debt of gratitude to Professor Gunnar Myrdal and to Professor J. S. Duesenberry for a very useful quotation from each, specified in appropriate footnotes.

It is understood of course that I was a free agent in selecting, disregarding, or modifying the suggestions offered. Accordingly the blame for some weaknesses rests on me and not on those who tried to help me.

M. M. Bober

October 1961

Preface

THIS BOOK is meant for upper-class undergraduates interested in economics or business. It may also be helpful to the graduate student who has had no preparation in economic theory. It presupposes an acquaintance with elementary economics, but not a close acquaintance. It takes little for granted.

The book has been written in the conviction that economic facts, if approached as naked facts, are all things to all men. Facts assume meaning and pattern only when clothed in theory. Economic theory is vital in understanding economic realities and in solving economic problems. It is not an idle exercise in logic or geometry, but is an essential tool and weapon. Of course, what we need is better and better theory.

The prime purpose has been to prepare a teachable text. This book attempts to stress integrated organization of the material and careful explanation of the basic principles, with ample diagrammatic and arithmetic illustrations. It is hoped that teachers and students will like the result.

I am grateful to my colleagues, Professors Padraic P. Frucht and William A. McConagha, for having read various chapters and made valuable suggestions. My thanks are due to President Nathan Marsh Pusey and to President Douglas Maitland Knight, who reduced my teaching schedule for a while to help me make progress with this project. I am also indebted to Houghton Mifflin Company and to The Macmillan Company for permission to quote from their publications, as indicated in the footnotes.

M. M. Bober

Lawrence College
Appleton, Wisconsin

Intermediate Price and Income Theory

REVISED EDITION

1 The Nature of Economics

THERE ARE over two and a half billion people on this globe; and half of them are paupers. Many of them are hungry, and some of them, especially children, will die of starvation. Such circumstances exist particularly in India, China, the Middle East, and some communities in Africa. On the other hand, countries like the United States, Canada, and Great Britain, to mention only a few, maintain a much higher standard of living. In the underdeveloped countries, per capita annual income is around $100, whereas in the United States the average annual income of 180 million people is over $2,000.

We ask why some countries are affluent and other countries are on the list of the have-nots. The answer to such an overriding question contains a mixture of causes and considerations. But there is among them one factor, or a field of knowledge, that throws much light on this problem. This pre-eminent factor is economics. Adam Smith, usually called the father of economics, wrote a book on economics in 1776, which is still a classic, and which he appropriately titled *The Wealth of Nations*.

In each country, large or small, rich or poor, individuals vary in their capacities, earnings, and incomes. Why? Again economics can deal with this challenging question. The indispensable study of theoretical economic problems, and the application of economic principles in determining public policies and promoting social developments—these and other examples of economic influence make economics an interesting, useful, and rather difficult discipline.

We shall open our discussion with a study of what forms the central theme of this discipline. We begin with the time-honored beginning, the definition of economics.

I. The Scope of Economics

It is not easy to frame a definition of any science which will not lay itself open to objections. A good definition must satisfy two exacting requirements: (1) it must reveal the keystone idea, the common denominator, of all the many-sided problems and all the different elements in its field, and (2) it must fix the boundaries between the science defined and its neighbors. These requirements probably explain why definitions are often indefinite.

There are many definitions of economics. But common strands appear in most of them, and a classification of them is possible. Some definitions stress the content of economic inquiry. Such definitions state that economics is a study of the production, exchange, distribution, and consumption of wealth; or that economics is concerned with wealth-getting and wealth-using activities of man; or that it explores man's ways of making a living. The pronouncement of Alfred Marshall, the renowned British economist, is worth noting. He regards economics as "a study of mankind in the ordinary business of life; it examines that part of individual and social action which is most closely connected with the attainment and the use of the material requirements of wellbeing." [1]

Another group of definitions aims to characterize economics by one central idea which dominates and integrates all economic investigation. Economics is defined as a science dealing with wealth in its "value aspect." Or it is declared to be "the science that treats phenomena from the standpoint of price." Or economics is confined "to that part of social welfare that can be brought directly or indirectly into relation with the measuring rod of money" (A. C. Pigou).[2] That value, price, or money is a unifying element in economics ought to become clear before we are done with a few chapters.

It is not our purpose to catalogue, or classify, or discuss all definitions of economics. The examples cited above give us some idea of the character of the discipline. It is, however, significant to observe that there is no basic difference among the various definitions just cited. A common denominator is implied in all of them, namely the need to economize scarce resources. There is one other definition which deserves attention because it points to the heart of economics in a more revealing manner

---

[1] *Principles of Economics*, 8th ed. (New York, Macmillan, 1927), p. 1.
[2] *The Economics of Welfare*, 4th ed. (New York, Macmillan, 1932), p. 11.

than most of the other definitions. But before this definition can be introduced some preparatory remarks had better be made.

We begin with the proposition that human wants are extremely numerous. Most human beings desire more and more, and the more they have
the more they want. The appetite for wealth seemingly grows on what
it feeds upon. Many a college student is certain that he would be satisfied
with $10,000 a year. But let him reach this sum and he will strive for more,
or will envy those who make more; or else his wife will impel him to try
for more.

Our wants are satisfied by goods and services such as are rendered by
hotels, restaurants, railways, theaters, barbers, lawyers, and doctors. These
goods and services are produced by resources or factors of production,
like land, labor, capital, and management. Goods and services and the
resources used to produce the goods and services are the means of ful-
filling our desires. This truth is evident enough in the case of the wants
for food, clothing, shelter, and some amusements. But what about nonmaterial wants? A little reflection will suggest that even such wants cannot
be satisfied without benefit of goods and services. Religion needs churches,
hymn books, and preachers, perhaps also church bazaars trafficking in
sundry articles. Politics cannot live without meeting halls, printed material,
the radio, and loudspeakers. Music requires music sheets, saxophones, and
crooners.

The factors or resources which produce the goods essential to the fulfillment of wants exhibit two significant characteristics. In the *first* place,
quite unlike our wants, they are limited in quantity. There are not enough
natural resources and not enough labor, capital, and business ability to
produce per unit of time all the goods and all the services which the
people of our country, or anywhere else, could possibly desire. Accordingly there are not nearly all the houses, all the meats and drinks, and all
the trips to Florida that individuals would be disposed to enjoy. Our
wants are many, but the means of satisfying them are relatively scarce.
Obviously not all wants can be gratified. A choice must be made as to
which wants will be and which will not be gratified. If our resources could
provide all the goods and services needed to satisfy all our wants, there
would be no such science as economics. Economics as a science owes its
existence to scarcity.

The *second* feature of the means employed in producing goods and
services is expressed in the fact that they are capable of alternative uses.
Lumber can be used for houses, bookcases, hog pens, or sleighs. Labor of
a given kind can be set to produce food, to build factories, or to mix cock-
tails. Similarly with the varieties of tools and machines: each can be used
for different purposes, each purpose leading to the satisfaction of a different want. A choice must be made with respect to the particular use to

which each resource will be put.

The problem of making choices of the goods to be produced would be simplified if the resources employed in their production had no alternative uses. Then each type of land, of raw material, of tool or labor would be committed exclusively to one predetermined use. But even in such a case choice-making would not disappear altogether. We should still have to decide to what *extent* to employ each resource and how much of it to leave unutilized at a given time. If a particular type of tree is good only for making chairs, how many such trees shall we cut down each year for chairs? Shall we make as many chairs as will put to employment all the workers who are qualified only to make chairs, or shall we leave some such workers idle and support them out of public funds?

In the problem of making choices between one good and another, there is a difference between a situation of full employment and a situation in which some of the resources are idle. When all our labor is at work we can add to the output of one commodity only by producing less of another commodity and by switching labor from the making of this latter good to the making of the first. However, when business is slow and some labor is unemployed we can produce more of a given article not by surrendering another article but by putting to work the idle resources. In the first case the choice is between "guns and butter." In the second case we can have both "guns and butter." It is important to stress that the background assumption of all the discussions in this book, with the exception of the last three chapters, is that the economy runs at full employment.

To sum up, the fundamental problem of every economy is epitomized in the question: Given a large number of competing wants and relatively limited resources, versatile in application, how shall we maximize the fulfillment of our wants? Accordingly, among the many possible definitions of economics the following definition, pointing as it does to this problem, deserves attention: Economics is a study of the allocation of scarce means, capable of alternative uses, among competing ends for the attainment of a maximum result in the achievement of these ends.

Recently there has developed among some economists the disposition to put a new emphasis on the objective of economic inquiry and to define economics in the new perspective. Since the appearance of the influential and controversial book, *The General Theory of Employment, Interest and Money*,[3] written by the celebrated British economist John Maynard Keynes, there has been a growing concern with the problem of full employment; and economists began to look upon economics as pre-eminently a study of the forces governing the flow of expenditures in the economy, with emphasis on the interplay of consumption, saving, and investment

[3] New York, Harcourt, Brace, 1936.

in controlling the volume of employment. There is no conflict between the older views and this newer conception of the task of economics. There is no reason for objecting to the incorporation of both ideas into a broader definition of economics. Economics can then be briefly defined as *the study of the administration of scarce resources and of the determinants of employment and income.*

ECONOMICS AS A STUDY OF CHOICES

The satisfaction of wants constitutes a major segment of human activity and economics is occupied with a study of this segment. But apart from wants, there may be other situations and problems in which economics is involved. The end sought may concentrate on winning a war, when the satisfaction of only such civilian wants may be allowed as are essential to victory. The resources, here again, are limited and their uses multiple: steel can be used for tanks or airplanes or locomotives or knives; the mechanic can repair farm tractors to raise food or he can march in the infantry. How to apportion the resources between the military and the civilian needs, and secondly, how to distribute the resources within the various departments of the war effort and among the many civilian industries in order best to work for military power and victory are economic problems. Another example of achieving an end with scarce means, on a considerable scale, is the launching of a nation on a program of industrialization within a set period of time. Whenever the venture is to maximize a given goal with limited resources susceptible of varied application we are moving in the realm of economics. Economic analysis has been aptly described as "the logic of choice" (J. R. Hicks).

Towering above the choices of such particular individuals as the housewife and the businessman, and yet standing in close relation to them because in part composed of them, are three major types of choices, three questions, which every society, no matter what its basis of organization, must resolve.

The *first* question is: what goods are to be produced and in what amounts? Because of the relative scarcity of our factor resources, some wants must remain unfulfilled. Which ones? There must be a determination of the principle which will guide producers in the classification of wants from the highest to the lowest scale of preference. There must be a criterion in awarding some goods priority over others. Why are some goods produced in abundance, others sparingly, and still others not at all? Why are more resources expended annually on producing tobacco than on printing Bibles? Such questions are treated in Chapters III to XVII.

The *second* question confronting a society is: how shall the goods be produced? Goods are produced by factors, that is, by unique combinations of certain types of land, labor, capital, and entrepreneurship. One method of making goods reflects the combination of one set of resources used in certain quantities; another technique of making the same goods represents another combination of the same or other resources. A number of choices or combinations are open to the producers. Which choices are best? Why do we generally use more capital and less labor than the Chinese use in the processes of producing goods? This problem is explored in Chapters V, VI, and XIII.

The *third* unavoidable question is: for whom are the goods to be produced? This question would be pointless only in a society in which the overriding rule is to divide the annual total product equally for every man, woman, and child. But in no society today do we see such a rule in action. Some persons receive a large slice of the national output and have more goods and services to enjoy. Others have to content themselves with less. This third question can be paraphrased to run as follows: among the people contributing to the daily work of making goods and rendering services, who gets how much? On what basis is the annual, or weekly, national output shared by the people who contribute to the making of this total output? The answer is attempted in Chapters XIII–XVII.

SUBDIVISIONS OF THE SUBJECT MATTER OF ECONOMICS

We should not get the impression that economists are engaged exclusively in one pursuit: the accumulation of principles and theories. Theories are the heart of economics; but there is more to a body of knowledge than the heart. Economic discussion and exposition ramify into a variety of investigations, which may be grouped in four divisions.

(1) There are books and articles which deal with the *description* of existing institutions, organizations, movements, legislation, and the like. To cite a few examples, much labor is devoted to the exploration and description of trade-union organization, the financial structure of corporations, the banking system of this or that country, the tariff schemes against imports, the tax system, agricultural co-operatives, and antitrust legislation.

(2) Another branch of study is concerned with the *history*, evolution, or growth of such phenomena as were mentioned in the first division. Examples would refer to the history of factory legislation, of transportation and other means of communication like the telephone, of banking legislation, and of the national debt. Such studies are commonly called economic history.

(3) Much work is done with questions of *policy*—not from the angle of what is morally commendable, but for the purpose of exploring and

criticizing ways of solving important problems that face a community. Examples would be a consideration of our agricultural problems and ways of solving them; a study of the strong and weak elements in our banking system or in our tax system, and of measures of improving it; and an exploration of the ways of dealing with the problems of inflation or of labor monopoly.

(4) There is finally much exploration of a theoretical cast. Economic *theory* attempts to formulate hypotheses, generalizations, principles, and laws. This field may be broadly divided into two sectors. The *first* sector addresses itself directly and exclusively to two types of major problems: the administration of scarce resources for desired goals, and the determination of aggregate income and employment. This sector deals with the pricing of goods and of the productive services of the four factors of production. It attempts to explain the directive role of price in our economy. This sector also explores the principles underlying the behavior of total income, by tracing the effects of total spending, total saving, and total investing on total income and employment. This sector is the theme of this book.

The *second* sector of economic theory deals with the theories of direct concern in any one of the many large subjects of study in economics. The list of the subjects is familiar. It includes, in part, money, international trade, public finance, labor, public utilities, business cycles, and industrial organization. In these areas the theories will relate respectively to such problems as the value of money, the control of credit; foreign exchange, the movement of specie and capital, comparative advantage; the incidence of taxes, fiscal policy in relation to employment; the supply of labor, the guaranteed annual wage, labor monopoly; railway rate making, the valuation of property; public works, "underconsumption"; and the location of industry. The analysis of these problems is largely based on the theories presented in the first sector.

Often enough all these four approaches are combined in a many-sided treatment of a single subject. A treatise on business cycles, for example, (1) may offer a description of the typical behavior of our economy in the phases of depression, revival, prosperity, and decline; (2) may provide a historical account of the previous periods of prosperity and depression as experienced in our country and elsewhere; (3) may expound the theories of the causes of business fluctuations; and (4) may present an analysis of the strong and weak features of the various policies proposed to mitigate depressions if not to remove them altogether.

Even in the first three divisions of economic study we can discern underlying theoretical foundations. The *description* of economic institutions is largely a picture of arrangements and practices for the allocation of resources and for influencing, sometimes unintentionally, costs and prices.

For example, the description of trade unions indicates, among other things, how organized labor may affect wage rates, therefore cost of production, and therefore the price of goods and the distributive share of labor in the total income of the community. Similarly the *history* of economic units traces the evolving ways of affecting the use of resources, cost, and price. The history of many an industry, including oil, steel, railroads, and automobiles, illustrates the point. Finally, framing a *policy*, private or national, for the achievement of a certain economic objective entails aspects of economic theory. Examples: the policy of protective tariffs, the policy of unemployment insurance, bank policy to expand or restrict the volume of credit, and Treasury policy in raising money, in shifting accounts from commercial banks to the Federal Reserve Banks. Indeed, in the exploration of almost any economic phenomenon, theory can hardly be avoided. In his economic conduct the "practical" man is guided by some kind of theory, but he is not aware of it; his major premises are hidden.

II. The Method of Economics

We have an idea of what economics is aiming to do. We are interested now in the question of how economics is doing it. The theme of this section is that, since economics belongs to the social sciences, this status imposes limitations on the tools which it can use in its explorations.

THE NATURE OF SCIENCE

Economics is a social science. First, what is meant by science? The answer often given is that science is an organized body of knowledge. But such an answer seems to express an inadequate conception. "Organized" implies something that is not unorganized. If so, every field of knowledge, asserting that it is not unorganized, would lay claim to the rank of a science. Every course listed in the impressive catalogues of our big universities, from art to zoology, would be a science. A professor stating that some courses do not belong in the category of science would imply that such courses are not organized. He would invite the displeasure of his colleagues, who would warmly protest that their courses are all well organized. He would be a disturber of the academic peace.

Science is better defined as a body of principles, theories, generalizations, or laws. By a theory we mean a *causal* relationship between two phenomena, so that when we know the behavior of the antecedent phenomenon, the cause, we can predict the behavior of the consequent phenomenon, the effect. An example of a principle in physics is that, all other things equal, the volume of a gas is inversely proportional to the pressure exerted on it. This theory gives us the causal connection between two variables, the pressure on the gas and the volume of the gas. On the basis of this law, if we want the gas to occupy one-half of its present volume, we know that we must double the pressure on it. An example of a principle in economics is that, all other things equal, when the demand for a commodity declines its short-run price will drop. After World War I the demand for agricultural products grew smaller, because we no longer had to help feed our allies. The prices which the farmer was getting were often below his costs. For a long time many farmers were in distress (they are still in distress). The solution lies either in raising the demand for agricultural products, or in seeing to it that the "other things" are *not* equal: that, for instance, the amounts produced by the farmers become smaller, or the costs of improved methods of production descend to lower levels.

This concept and use of cause are of first importance in any analysis, be it in economics, history, physics, or ordinary conversation. To know the cause is to know the cure, in many cases, or to know what steps we must take next. Says Polonius to the Queen about "mad" Hamlet:

> "Mad let us grant him, then: and now remains
> That we find out the cause of this effect;
> Or rather say, the cause of this defect,
> For this effect defective comes by cause."

Often enough two related economic phenomena may not portray a case of cause and effect but rather a case of *mutual interaction*. By mutual interaction, or interdependence, or reciprocal relation, or interrelation, we mean that phenomena A and B are so related that A can be both cause and effect of B. Take two phenomena, savings and total income. A rise in savings (A) invested in additional capital goods may raise total production in the economy and thereby total income (B). In its turn, a rise in total income (B) may induce a larger volume of savings (A). Other examples of mutual interaction would be: the interrelation of wage rates and the marginal revenue product (MRP) of labor; the volume of money in the country and the price level; demand and supply; the standard of living in a country and the average amount of education obtained by its citizens; agricultural and industrial prosperity.

THE DIFFERENCE BETWEEN ECONOMICS AND NATURAL SCIENCE

In natural science the relationship between two phenomena can be expressed in exact terms, in most cases. We get a quantitative connection, an equation, a precise functional relation, between two variables. If one variable changes by a given amount, we know by *how much* the other variable will change. Given the magnitude of one variable, we can calculate the magnitude of the other variable. In physics, when the temperature of a copper rod is raised by one degree Centigrade, we can figure and predict the linear expansion of the rod. The relation between the increase in the length of the copper rod and the rise in its temperature is precise and can be expressed by the definite equation: additional length of the rod equals the original length times the rise in temperature times 0.00017. In astronomy, physics, chemistry, and often in biology, principles are of this nature. We know in a precise way in most cases what to do with the cause in order to obtain the desired effect.

Economic theories are not susceptible of this exact quantitative formulation. We cannot state that if a given industry raises its wage rate 5%, the number of workers applying for jobs will rise, say 7%; nor that if the price of a loaf of whole-wheat bread declines by 2¢, people will buy 1,000 more loaves a day in Chicago. There is a large body of generalizations and theories in economics, but all of them, or nearly all of them, are of the qualitative and not of the quantitative kind. They are not expressed by exact equations. They state, for instance, that, all other things equal, people generally buy more of a commodity when its price falls; that economic rent rises as the population of a country rises; that monopoly prices are very likely to range above competitive prices; that deficit financing in a period of prosperity will breed inflation; that when liquidity preference declines, the rate of interest on loanable funds may decline; and that if the demand for an article is elastic, the percentage rise in the amount bought will exceed the percentage drop in its price. In all these examples we do not have equations or definite functional relations describing the quantitative dependence of a given consequent phenomenon on the causal antecedent phenomenon. We see the *direction* of a change in *A*, and not the quantitative change in *A*, accompanying a change in the causal event *B*.

The consequence of this difference between economics or any other social science and the natural sciences is of pre-eminent significance. We develop a science for two purposes, to enrich our understanding and to control our environment by solving our problems. For thorough knowledge and effective control, we need to be in a position to *predict* precisely what happens to one phenomenon if we do something to another phenomenon which is found to be the cause of the first. In economics prediction is possible in many cases, but seldom quantitative prediction. We know that if the summer season is cool, the price of summer suits will sag. But the economist cannot predict by how much the price or the sales of a given kind of summer suit will drop. The economist could tell the maker of such suits to reduce his output, but not by how much.

Nevertheless, so striking is the significance of the knowledge of the causal connection between phenomena that it is a tool of great usefulness even if the connection can be expressed only qualitatively. Said J. S. Mill: "Knowledge, insufficient for prediction, may be most valuable for guidance." The mere knowledge that two events are related enables us to go a long way toward solving problems and toward the prevention of trouble in our social living. The knowledge of diminishing returns warns us that, unless there is progress in the efficiency of production, an increasing population in an old and well-settled country is likely to cause a lowering of the standard of living; and appropriate measures may be taken either to increase production or to discourage a high birth rate. Because in actual life other things do not remain equal, we cannot accurately predict how much inflation will be caused by deficit financing, but the knowledge of the connection between an unbalanced budget and possible inflation puts us on guard about fiscal and monetary policy in order to avoid the harmful effects of inflation. Although various principles of economics may not provide us with precise formulas for action, we derive from them valuable guidance to courses of action when we want to raise the wage of a given class of labor; when we want to lower the price of food; when we desire to gain more from international trade, or to frame an adequate system of taxation, or to mitigate the effects of a depression, and so on.

One is tempted to assert that if a given economic phenomenon or a given economic problem is a mere abstraction and bids fair never to materialize in reality, it (the phenomenon or the problem) should be ignored by economists. Why waste time on something nonexistent? Why not turn it over to the philosopher?

Such a view would not hold water. It is of prime importance to analyze the conditions under which the phenomenon *may* come into existence. It is equally important to learn the significance of the phenomenon from the social viewpoint; and we want to know whether or not it is desirable to incorporate this phenomenon in our economic system. For example, it is probably safe to venture the suggestion that free trade will not be adopted by us in the coming decades. And yet it is of great significance to study the economics of free trade and tariffs. Similarly, if pure competition were without a single example in the world of reality, it would still be eminently desirable not to draw the line on this subject, but to give it careful consideration, for reasons mentioned early in Chapter IX.

REASONS FOR THE DIFFERENCE BETWEEN ECONOMICS AND NATURAL SCIENCE

The chief reason for this difference between the social and the natural sciences rests on the difference in the nature of the subject matter under inquiry. The natural sciences deal with inanimate aspects of nature or with obedient rabbits or cats under chloroform. The social scientist studies that wayward, unmanageable material, the human being. We can *experiment* with natural occurrences and properties; we cannot experiment, on an effective scale, with economic occurrences and properties. Human beings will not submit, individually or collectively, to laboratory manipulation in the field of economics. Neither the individual nor society makes a good guinea pig.

The physicist comes upon the hypothesis that temperature may have something to do with the length of a copper wire. He knows that the length of this object is affected by pressure, by hammering, and by pulling and stretching. To test his hypothesis, he subjects the wire to a controlled experiment. He sees to it that all other things *are* equal: no pressure on the wire, no hammering, and no pulling and stretching. He isolates, abstracts the length of the wire from these other influences. Then he applies heat, and measures the wire. He finds that for each rise of one degree Centigrade in the temperature of the wire its length grows by 0.00017 units for each unit of its length. After several experiments with copper wires of different length and thickness he wins the generalization that the coefficient of linear expansion of copper is 0.00017. Such is the experimental way, the method of *induction*, the method of proceeding from the particular to the general, the method of distilling a theory from repeated observations of the same phenomenon re-created in the laboratory, or from a single "crucial" experiment on the phenomenon.

The economist is not so well off. Suppose he is interested in the possible connection between the volume of money in the country and the rate of interest paid by borrowers to lenders of funds. An experiment would decide. But he cannot perform an experiment. He cannot create a society (1) in which all the other factors that are assumed to influence the rate of interest stay unchanged, for instance, trade fluctuations, profit expectations, inventions, consumer tastes, or fiscal policies; and (2) in which he will change the volume of money in order to observe the behavior of the interest rate. Nor can we find in history two societies precisely identical in all economic respects but the total amount of money in circulation, so that we can note the level of interest in each society. Neither the laboratory nor history can assist in the formulation of the precise quantitative relation, if any, between these two variables.

There is another reason why the subject matter of economics is the villain of the piece. Economic phenomena are very complex. An economic event is ordinarily a compound of many features and many causes; and the event does not, as a rule, recur in the same compound and with the same pattern of causal conditions. History does not repeat itself. Each economic phenomenon, although referred to by the same name, is unique.

It exhibits different characteristics, it is set against a different background, and it carries different implications. There is less uniformity of sequence, less exact repetition and more variability in the flow of economic occurrences than in natural phenomena. The theory that A is connected with B in a certain way cannot easily be derived from observation or history inasmuch as, in repeated observations, either the antecedent A or the consequent B is not quite identical; nor is B in each case the resultant of the same aggregation of forces.

This circumstance breeds two difficulties for the economist. The *first* difficulty arises when, in the absence of experimentation, he turns to the next method, the plain consultation of facts. He finds that even if the causal phenomenon which he is studying happens to be substantially of the same nature at different times, the effect is apt to be in each case the product of a different combination of causes, apart from the cause under scrutiny. Suppose the economist wants to learn about the possible connection between free trade and the prosperity of a nation. He consults the national income of Great Britain before and after the 1840's when England adopted free trade. But the prosperity of that country in the second half of the past century was determined by a variety of factors, some of them different from those which determined her standard of living before the 1840's. The plurality of causation of her income and the difference in the causal factors before and after the introduction of free trade make the establishment of a relation between free trade and prosperity on the basis of historical observation an uncertain venture.

The *second* difficulty is of the same order. It appears when the economist wants to test a theory by turning to the facts. Again, because economic phenomena do not repeat themselves in all essentials, "disturbing" factors render verification precarious. Suppose the theory is that free trade raises the standard of living. The attempt to check the theory by consulting the history of England will be a difficult exercise. Many conditions are responsible for England's economic progress during her free-trade era. A protectionist may argue that England prospered then despite her free-trade policy. The facts will hardly resolve the dispute.

STATISTICS

The economist is urged in many quarters to show more respect for facts and to rely more on the world of reality in formulating his theories. He is advised to make more use of statistics. The study of economic phenomena by statistical devices is indeed very helpful and perhaps indispensable. But statistical calculation hardly offers the economist a source of supply of useful hypotheses and of quantitative connections between economic facts. In actual life we witness a great multitude of facts at play. We observe, for instance, that the volume of employment has considerably declined, and we want to know why. We cannot study the whole bewildering mass of available data in search of a hypothesis. The first task is to select "relevant" facts if our investigation is to be reduced to manageable proportions. But we must possess a hypothesis about the cause of low employment before we have a criterion for the selection of facts. Else we wallow in a mass of facts without a sense of direction. A hypothesis reduces chaos to order, an overwhelming task to a task of manageable size.

Suppose our hypothesis happens to be that the low employment is induced by the low rate of wages prevailing in a depression. Is this hypothesis correct? Statistics can hardly tell us. We see the coexistence of low wages and low employment; but coexistence, in itself, does not indicate cause and effect. It may be the other way around; the low wage rate may be the effect and not the cause of low employment. Or else, the reason for low employment may lie in circumstances apart from low wages. The low wages and the low employment may be the joint consequences of certain outside factors. Even if we decide to adopt the hypothesis that the reduced wage rates, by decreasing aggregate demand, contribute to the poor state of employment once unemployment sets in for one reason or another, statistics is not in a position to take charge of the further steps in the analysis of the connection between the two variables. It will be impossible to isolate statistically the effects of all the other forces contributing to unemployment and then establish a quantitative connection, so that we can tell, for instance, how many additional workers will lose employment if the wage rate declines further, say by 5%, or by a dollar a day.

Generally speaking, statistics can hardly promise to make substantial contributions to the accumulation of principles in economics. Rather, hypotheses and theories must be developed before we can employ statistics meaningfully, with a sense of direction. We need theory to guide us in selecting the relevant facts out of the enormous universe of facts about us, and in seeking a pattern in the facts selected. Facts in themselves do not pronounce their connotation and their significance. Facts do not speak for themselves. We see facts with our theories and not with our eyes. We must have theories if we are to find our way about among facts. Theories are generals, facts are soldiers. All this is not said to belittle fact-finding and statistics. Empirical investigation is invaluable in economics, and we must deal with facts diligently. But at the present state of knowledge the inductive method seems to labor under serious limitations in developing cause and effect generalizations in economics.

What Professor Gunnar Myrdal says on this problem is instructive: "Theory, therefore," he says, "must always be *a priori* to the empirical observations of the facts. Facts come to mean something only as ascertained and organized in the frame of a theory. Indeed, facts as part of scientific knowledge have no existence outside such a frame. Questions must be asked before answers can be obtained and, in order to make sense, the questions must be part of a logical co-ordinated attempt to understand social reality as a whole. A non-theoretical approach is, in strict logic, unthinkable." [4]

THE DEDUCTIVE METHOD IN ECONOMICS

With the door practically closed on experimentation with the phenomena under his inquiry, the economist turns, principally, to the deductive method for the framing of theories on causal sequences and interrelations. Is this method "scientific"? The answer depends on the meaning which we attach to the expression "scientific method." If we mean exclusively measurement and experimentation, the economist is not "scientific" in his thinking. No measurement, no science. But if scientific method refers to sound logical procedure in the cautious consideration of all the attributes and connections of the subject matter at hand, for the purpose of winning causal relations, the economist is scientific in his analytical work. The difference in the methods used does not reflect a difference in attitude or mentality between the economist and the natural scientist. The difference in method is imposed by the difference in the material handled. When an inventor like Edison discusses monetary standards, when the chemist Frederick Soddy, a winner of the Nobel Prize, writes on wealth, debt, and other economic questions, or when Einstein expounds on the workings of capitalism, he behaves mentally as economists do. On the narrow view of scientific method, these eminent scientists become "unscientific" as soon as they turn their minds to an economic problem. It may as well be added here that the deductive analysis is not a stranger in the study of many a problem even in the natural sciences.

The deductive method as used by the economist may be broken down into a number of steps. But before outlining the steps, it is important to stress that the indispensable preliminary to any investigation is the existence of a definite problem in the mind of the investigator. He must be aware of a particular question that seeks an answer. To perceive a problem is, moreover, as difficult as it is important. Says Einstein: "The formulation of a problem is often more essential than its solution. . . . To raise

[4] *Value in Social Theory* (London, Routledge and Kegan Paul, 1958), p. 233.

new questions, new possibilities, to regard old problems from a new angle, requires creative imagination and marks real advance in science." [5] A researcher motivated only by Veblen's "idle curiosity" is like a ship at sea without a steering wheel. We explore in order to solve problems.

(1) *Assumptions*

The first step in economic inquiry of a theoretical cast is the shaping of the background *assumptions* which form the starting point and the framework of the economist's thinking. Some assumptions are derived from observation. By introspection the economist examines his own motives and calculations when weighing choices of means and ends in buying, selling, investing, and the like. He also learns from the behavior of other people, by watching them or by talking with them, and by reading accounts of people's actions in different circumstances. Among the assumptions so derived are the premises that the firm is guided primarily by the profit motive but is not always in search for maximum profit, that the firm possesses fair knowledge of the conditions of the market, that the investor or the landowner ordinarily seeks pecuniary advantage, and that a higher wage may not tempt a worker to change residence on account of nonpecuniary considerations.

Other assumptions represent a modification of observed reality. In purchasing goods the consumer is moved by such forces as habit, ignorance, the impulse of the moment, imitation, emulation, as well as utility. However, the acknowledgment of all these forces would foreclose an analysis of consumer behavior, so unmanageable are these complicated and unmeasurable variables. The economist is accordingly led to adopt the simplifying assumption that, as a rule, the consumer seeks maximum total utility from a given total expenditure on a bundle of goods.

At times the assumptions made may deliberately diverge from the facts or may find no counterpart in reality. The economist may purposely assume competition for an industry which is known to have a strong element of monopoly; and he may assume monopoly where only competition rules. This is done because the analysis within the frame of the artificial assumptions may shed light on a problem of a more realistic order. The assumption of free trade provokes a useful analysis of important economic propositions. The assumption that men are born free and equal may produce an analysis throwing light on significant and realistic questions. The assumption of a Robinson Crusoe economy has not vanished from the pages of economic discourse because an unreal assumption may lead to the clarification of a complex reality. Fiction may be useful. Even in ordinary conversation, we often make fictitious assumptions:

[5] A. Einstein and L. Infeld, *The Evolution of Physics* (New York, Simon & Schuster, 1938), p. 95.

"If my sister Mary were a rich girl, she would have no difficulty in getting herself a husband."

Finally, some assumptions come in response to the requirements of the analytical process and vary with the particular problem at hand. When we examine the effect of a change in phenomenon A on phenomenon B, we necessarily assume that "all other things are equal," that all other phenomena *which can exert an influence on B* keep still; and what these other phenomena are depends on the nature of B. When we state that if the price of cotton rises, people will buy less cotton, we have in mind the following assumptions: (1) the price of related goods, like wool or rayon, stays the same; (2) consumer income remains unchanged; (3) the tastes and preferences of the buying public are not altered; (4) there is no rise in the population; and (5) the rise in the price of cotton is not regarded as a signal of further repeated price advances in the near future. It is not necessary, and it would make no sense, to assume that the production of cigars stays unchanged, nor that the price of elephant tusks rises by no more than 5%. The reason: the price of cigars and tusks does not affect the price of cotton.

It is accordingly of surpassing importance to keep in mind that in economics a certain truth, a given causal relation, holds only under given assumptions. The connection indicated is not necessarily falsified by an example from actual life in which the relation fails to show itself. The failure does not bear witness to the notion of a conflict between "theory and practice." The question is: does this fact from life reflect the influence of factors left out of the picture by the assumptions? If people buy more cotton despite the higher price, the reason may well be that some of the five assumptions enumerated in the previous paragraph are not fulfilled. Perhaps the price of wool or rayon moved up to prohibitive levels, and people turned to cotton because its price had increased to a lesser degree; perhaps a new fashion changed the preference of consumers in favor of cotton goods.

The assumptions must also be kept in mind when making predictions on the basis of economic principles. We are not sure that "all other things" will accommodate the prediction by staying unchanged, in obedience to the assumptions underlying the principles. If one of the factors put down as neutral in the assumptions undergoes a change, the predicted result will be nullified or modified. When the price of cotton is advanced—to go back to our example—the predicted decline in sales will not materialize if, for instance, a business boom develops and the higher incomes permit the consumer to buy more cotton goods even though the price is somewhat higher. In making a prediction it is better to stress the assumptions that go with it. He who is incautious about the assumptions may become a false prophet. There is truth in the legend that "An expert in economics is a man who knows tomorrow why the things he said yesterday did not happen today."

The assumption that "other things are equal" points to a transforming difference between the method used in natural science and the method used in economics. Suppose that elements a, b, c work together to produce changes in the phenomenon A, in physics. Suppose further that the physicist is interested in the particular causal connection between c and A. The physicist takes this problem to the laboratory. He sets up an experiment in which he eliminates the influence of elements a and b. He is left with A and c. Now he can vary element c and watch the effect on A. In due course he can develop a quantitative relation between A and c.

What can the economist do in a similar situation? Suppose phenomenon A is inflation, and the causal elements a, b, c are respectively a rise in the volume of money, a rise in the velocity of money, and a drop in production because of prolonged labor strikes. The economist desires to find the causal connection between inflation a and the fall in production c. He has no laboratory; so he does the next best thing. He *assumes* that "other things are equal," meaning that a and b stay unchanged. Then by a step-by-step analysis, based on relevant economic principles, he develops a rough connection between the two phenomena. Whenever a social scientist says "other things are equal," we are reminded of the factors that would be eliminated in the laboratory if there were a laboratory.

(2) *Hypotheses*

The next step concerns itself with the formulation of hypotheses. A hypothesis is a conjecture, a shrewd suspicion, of the possible connection between two phenomena. It is often suggested by the observation of the flow of events. But of equal importance with observation are insight and constructive imagination. The hypothesis may be (1) that there exists a relation between the variations in output on the one hand and on the other hand the applications of equal doses of one given productive resource to a fixed quantum of other resources; (2) that there is a connection between the utility of an object to the consumer and the amount of the object available to him for enjoyment, that, in other words, the utility of an object is a function of the quantity of it available to the consumer; or (3) that the level of income has something to do with the amount saved or with the amount of a good which the individual will buy. A hypothesis is an unverified hunch.

(3) *Theories*

Now comes the analysis of the nature and of the implications of the hypothesis; in other words, the framing of a theory or a principle. This part of the exploration is no milk-and-water procedure. It is a far cry from the time-honored but barren syllogism: "All men are mortal. Socrates is a man. Therefore Socrates is mortal." The formulation of a theory is often complex and demanding. The process is exemplified in almost each chapter that follows. For instance, Chapter V, parts of Chapter XIII, and Chapter XVI explore the theories bearing a relation to the first of the hypotheses mentioned in the previous paragraph, the hypothesis that there is variation in output as more and more units of a variable resource are applied to a fixed resource.

(4) Verification

The fashioning of theories does not constitute a finished product. It is of first importance to submit the theory to verification by an appeal to experience. But verification is often a difficult enterprise in economics. The phenomenon against which we want to test our theory ordinarily reflects a complex situation. Observation and statistical tools are commonly inadequate in face of the criss-cross interweaving of the various causes that produced the phenomenon to which we repair for verification. In many instances only a controlled experiment would make verification a convincing procedure. Nonetheless the attempt at verification is imperative. If anticipation based on a theory does not square with reality, a modification may be called for in the original assumptions which guided the inquiry: if the assumptions stand re-examination, the discrepancy between the expectation based on theory and the testimony of facts may be traced to an error in the chain of reasoning.

One theory becomes the steppingstone to, or a part of, the next theory. Thus a body of principles is developed, within the frame of a set of background assumptions, integrated by step-by-step links in the argument. An elaborate chain of deductions is forged and a coherent system of propositions is developed. The theories of demand, of production, of costs, and of supply are integrated into the theories of price determination, in various types of markets, of goods and of the services of the productive factors. Likewise, the theories of interest, of saving, of investment, of the productivity of capital, and of expenditures by consumers are combined to throw light on the size of the total income of the community. The structure of analysis is principally deductive in character. Economic reasoning does not remind us of the test tubes, the cyclotrons, and the cut-up frogs of experimental chemistry, physics, and zoology. It embodies the results of simple assumptions applied to simplified facts. Economic theory furnishes us a kit of tools for the analysis of approximations to the actualities of life. It has not as yet advanced far enough to give us a detailed understanding of all the complexities of the economic scene.

J. M. Keynes downgrades economic theory, unjustifiedly, I believe, when in his introduction to the Cambridge Economic Handbooks he states that "It is a method rather than a doctrine, an apparatus of the mind, a technique of thinking which helps its possessor to draw correct conclusions." [6]

THE GOAL OF ECONOMICS

The purpose of all inquiry in economics is, in common with all other human investigations, of a twofold character: (1) the acquisition of knowledge which gives us the satisfaction of understanding the economic world we live in; and (2) the control of our environment, the ability to solve our economic problems. We study in order to acquire light and fruit. To control our economic environment, we must be able to *predict* the result of a given policy or event; quantitative prediction is the ultimate test of science. If the event is a complex of several elements (and it generally is), the influence of each element is estimated and the total effect is compounded—taking care that the composition of forces is done properly, inasmuch as in economics two plus two does not always make four. Generalizations and theories enable us to anticipate the outcome of occurrences or of deliberate action, provided that there is in the meantime no intrusion of unexpected circumstances which interfere with the assumed conditions and falsify our expectations. We know then what to do in order to achieve a desired result. Knowledge is light and power.

It is not, however, the purpose of economics or of any other science, natural or social, to prescribe rules as to what *ought* to be done. Value judgments are outside the scope of economics. The discipline is not a dispenser of advice on proper economic conduct. It refrains from evaluating the merits of people's choices and the moralities of individual, group, or government behavior. Economics studies causal sequences; it is not the judge of ultimate goals. It states: "if *A*, then *B*"; if a certain step is taken, certain consequences will follow—provided that no modifying conditions intrude. If a duty is imposed on the importation of cheese, the economist will try to foretell the effect on the price of cheese to the consumer, on the price of related goods, on the income of certain groups, and on foreign exchange. Without advocacy of policy, economics aids in the choice of policy by indicating the consequences of given measures. Science is concerned with means and not with ends. Still, human beings are human beings. The element of value judgment dwells, unconsciously, in our minds.

[6] See, for example, his introduction to E. A. G. Robinson, *The Structure of Competitive Industry* (New York, Harcourt, Brace, 1932), p. iii. On the same page iii he himself mentions "economic science" and "general principles of thought." "Science" and "principles" are more than sheer "method."

Can we "break" economic laws? Yes, we can—but not without paying a price for the misbehavior. When labor wins in a strike for a wage rate higher than labor's marginal productivity, the cost of producing the commodities involved may rise and the price with it. Accordingly less of the commodity may be bought, with resulting unemployment. If, spurning free trade, nations build tariff walls against each other's imports, the punishment comes in the form of a lower standard of living for all of them. The same result would be inflicted on a community which breeds more and more monopoly at the expense of less and less competition.

In closing this chapter it may be well to point to another misconception of the nature of a generalization. The assertion is often made that "the exception proves the rule." But basically the exception does not make the rule; the exception *breaks* the rule, *tests* the rule. For example, it is established in economics that a lower price of an article will entice people to buy more of it, provided all other elements which influence the quantities of the article purchased stay constant. This proposition is based on human nature and conduct. Should we observe *one* case, one exception, in which a lower price generates smaller purchases, per unit of time, the established rule would go to the ashcan. We would suspect that there is something in our nature that negates the price-quantity relation, and we would seek for the elements that produce the exception. The result would stimulate the formation of a different theory which would not harbor a single exception.

SUGGESTED READINGS

See the list of readings on the last page of Chapter II which pertain to this chapter as well.

CHAPTER

11 Institutions. Concepts

I. Mixed Capitalism

ECONOMIC activity goes on within a setting of distinctive institutions in action. Institutions are expressed in organized group behavior, in established social usages, and in accepted ways of looking at things. Institutions mold the conduct of the individual; they form the coercive power over the member of society, pulling him to the line of conformity. If society is to endure, there must be a large degree of uniformity of conduct instead of chaotic diversity; institutions see to this. If society is to progress, there must also be a degree of nonconformity; pioneers and innovators, questioners and doubters perform this indispensable service. Almost every social advance is made either because existing conditions bring distress to an influential group of people, or because a nonconformist is dissatisfied with what is, and points the way to an improvement or else goads people to look for something better.

There are many institutions, as many as there are types of human interests. There are religious, legal, political, economic, esthetic, and other institutions, embodied in group organizations, in conduct, in tradition, and overlaid with emotion and compulsive authority. Economic institutions reflect our ways of doing things in the economic sphere and all the organizations and human groupings devised to help us provide a flow of goods and services to the members of the community. There are many economic institutions: for instance, farm co-operatives, trade unions, and the Federal Reserve Banks are institutions. But our focus here is on the outstanding institutions which uniquely characterize our economic system and which have most to do with answering the central questions of what to produce, how, and for whom.

1. PRIVATE PROPERTY AND PRIVATE ENTERPRISE

First on the list is private property. In nearly all known societies (except some very primitive) there has been private property in consumer goods: the loaf of bread on the table of the collective-farm peasant in Russia or the shirt on the back of the Russian factory hand is his own. But by private property as an earmark of our own economic organization we mean that the factors of production, the land and the capital resources used in making goods, are privately owned. The coal mines, the factories, the raw materials, the machines, and the farms are the property of individuals. The owners can dispose of them as it suits them, subject to the restrictive laws of the land. For instance, the owner of a house on a crowded street is not allowed to make a bonfire of his dwelling. Indeed, property is a bundle of rights hedged in by restrictions.

Not only is there private property in the productive resources; there is also private property of the individual in himself. The individual is free, and he can do with himself as he likes. He can apprentice himself to a trade of his own choosing and he can agree to work for whomever he pleases, as long as it is agreeable to the other party too. He can buy and sell goods and services from whomever and to whomever it is mutually desirable. People dispose of their work and their fortunes by free agreements and free relations with other people. These types of freedom are symbolized by the expression "freedom of contract."

It has not always been so, nor is it so everywhere today. In the Middle Ages the accident of birth in a particular group in the scheme of social stratification riveted the individual by law and custom to a given occupation or to a given type of existence and to a prescribed set of rights and duties. The serf was tied to the manor. If he wanted to loosen himself, he had to flee to the city, if he could. But the escape was much like jumping from the frying pan into the fire. The monopolistic guilds in the city barred newcomers with excessive fees, extended apprenticeships, and rules and regulations. Only those trades were open to a free person on which the exclusive guilds did not care to lay their restricting hand. Today in the Soviet Union not every boy out of school can choose his own career and his own place of work. The worker cannot readily move from town to town and from factory to factory in search of better wages and working conditions.

The one hundred and eighty-odd million inhabitants in the United States require an immense amount of food, clothing, shelter, and entertainment each day. The resources in land, labor, capital, and management called into use in producing the goods to satisfy these wants reach enormous dimensions. The responsibility of providing the goods and services and the job of co-ordinating the productive factors for this purpose are undertaken by the initiative of the businessman. Between four and five million farmers raise the food and the many raw materials for industry. Over four million other entrepreneurs engage in the infinite number of processes that produce the millions of commodities and in the art of retailing them to the consumer. Private enterprise takes charge of the task of satisfying the wants of the people. Private enterprise attends to this undertaking primarily for one reason, to secure a gain. The *profit motive* is the mainspring of this far-flung never-ceasing activity.

2. THE ROLE OF PRICE

Every day millions of individuals go to hundreds of thousands of stores and buy thousands of different articles. Every day sixty-odd million people work in field, in mine, in factory, in office, over the railway tracks, and in the waterlanes, harvesting, blasting, hammering, dictating letters, and hurrying themselves and goods from place to place, amid the clanging and screeching and hissing of tools, machines, and engines. The millions of buyers find the thousands of things that they want and in the amounts they want. There is rarely a perfect balance in the market between the amount of goods wanted and the amount available at a given price. The sixty-odd million people at their jobs make innumerable things of which scarcely anything is left unwanted and serving no purpose. Over our vast country, the astounding quantities of goods made in the numberless posts are sorted, assembled, and shipped to numerous places in such a coherent discipline that the fifty-odd million households can buy whatever they want and whenever they want it, nearly without fail. Only in depressions are things out of joint, dramatically and distressingly.

Such a multiplicity of processes of production and such a multitudinous diversity of wants require planning and co-ordination if they are to match each other and if the enormous activities are not to become log-jammed in turbulent confusion. The remarkable fact about our private-enterprise economy is that there exists no central agency which plans and co-ordinates economic activity into a coherent scheme. Nobody takes directions from a guiding national office presided over by a master mind. Each individual follows such a trade as he chooses and puts his property to such uses as he prefers. Each businessman produces goods of the type, quality, and amount that suit his own decision. Each consumer, each owner of a productive resource, each entrepreneur is guided by his individual calculations, without counsel or coercion from officials. Ours is a "free-enterprise" economy.

But planning there must be. And planning there is. It is done by *price*. Price is the planning agency in our economy. Price articulates the seeming chaos of individual actions into the essentially organized activity that actually exists. The businessman is commonly impelled by the profit motive; and every other agent, worker or owner of land or capital, is ordinarily motivated by the desire for gain. The prices offered for goods by consumers function as a guide to profitable enterprise by the businessman. In our economic organization the dollar spent by the consumer is a vote cast in favor of the commodity of his choice. This dollar voting steers economic resources into channels desired by the consumers. The businessman follows the election returns. He is, however, in no sense a mere bystander. By advertising and salesmanship he is engaged in considerable campaigning.

If consumers want more chairs, they register their preference by offering a higher price for chairs. The larger profit lures businessmen into producing more chairs. If consumers lose interest in horses and buggies in favor of automobiles, they indicate their preference by offering a lower price or none for horses and buggies. Those occupied in the trades of raising horses and making buggies seek other, profitable, occupations. Perhaps they open garages and gasoline stations. The relative prices offered by consumers for respective quantities of various goods and services compose (in the perspective of the cost schedules of the producers) the priority list of wants to be satisfied by business operations.

In general, the market price of an article is a warning and an invitation. A decline in the price of a good warns the producer to produce less and simultaneously beckons to the consumer to buy more of it. The low price of the good may spell a low profit, if any, to the firm. In the long run the producer will be induced to shift his resources to the production of another good, the price of which promises an adequate profit. As more and more firms shift to the production of this good, its price is apt to decline, on account of the larger amount of it that is available to the consumer. And as more and more productive resources shift out of the former low-priced article the price of it may tend to rise. The process of shifting stops when neither good is underpriced or overpriced, in the light of the cost of producing these two goods; when the profit made in both goods becomes about the same, in a given span of time.

Conversely, the high price of a commodity suggests to the consumer that he buy less of it, and at the same time gives the signal to the businessman to produce more of it per unit of time. The high price may breed prospects of attractive profits; and in the long run may lure new producers into the industry. More productive resources tend to be allocated to the production of this expensive good; and fewer resources remain in the comparatively low-priced industry. Again this long-run shifting will cease when in both industries the articles are so priced as to offer an equal profit.

Thus low prices insisted on by consumers may mean low profit to producers, therefore smaller quantities produced to meet the decreased demand. The consumer is "sovereign": his demand for a good sets the price, therefore the profit, therefore the shift of resources, therefore smaller quantities for sale. Similar steps are involved if the consumer offers a high price for a good. The consumer acts, the businessman reacts.

Thus is resolved the *first* major question before the community: what goods are to be produced and in what amounts? Too, in this manner is resolved the problem of the allocation of resources among industries (that is, among goods), pointing to the structure and the composition of our total national income in terms of the volume and the varieties of goods and services.

Price plays a leading part in shaping the answer to the *second* major question, namely, by what method shall the goods be produced? The function of price is broader than may appear at first. Price relates not only to goods but to factor-services as well. The wage received by labor expresses the price for the labor-service to production; so is interest the price paid for the services of capital, per unit of time; similarly with rent on land, and the profit of the businessman. The price of a good is, in the long run, composed of the prices paid for the factor-services hired to produce the good. The prices of these services compose the costs of production to the entrepreneur.

The aim of the producing firm is to make goods most efficiently, at the lowest cost: this is especially true when the firm is in a competitive industry. The prices of the diverse factor-services guide the firm in selecting the factors, in substituting one factor for another, and generally in allocating its expenditures among the factors in such a way that minimum unit cost is achieved. The expensive resources are used sparingly; the relatively inexpensive resources are used in larger quantities, as substitutes for the scarce factors. In China, road building uses vastly more labor than we do, and impressively less machinery and tools. China substitutes labor for capital; we substitute capital for labor, ordinarily. Contributing to least-cost in producing a commodity is synonymous with efficiency in production. The more efficient firm runs at smaller unit costs and is in a position to undersell less efficient firms. In this price struggle the outcome usually is the survival of the fittest, that is, of the most efficient producer. The inferior business units eventually fall by the wayside or else shift their resources to the production of another commodity.

Similarly with the role of price in the resolution of the *third* question:

for whom are the goods to be produced? What determines the distribution of income? People obtain goods in proportion to the amount of money they can afford to spend on goods. People have money to spend on goods in proportion to the price which they command for their service in producing goods. He who contributes more to the making of goods receives a higher price, earns more, and can claim more goods for enjoyment. Price is once more the key to the answer. If plumbers are scarce in relation to the call for plumbing, the price paid for plumbing service—the wage of the plumber—will rise; plumbers will receive more goods as their income. Should consumers' tastes shift from movies to prize-fighting exhibitions on television, the diminished attendance at motion-picture houses may lower the price, the earnings, of Hollywood actors. The Hollywood stars in their courses may have a less abundant life.

In this scheme of things the impersonal mechanism of the market organizes the separate individual activities of the economic agents into a coherent system of undesigned co-operation. In this scheme of things the consumer, casting his ballots with his price offers, induces the profit-motivated businessman to watch the vote for current goods and to anticipate the potential vote for new and different goods. This supremacy of the consumer, expressed and implemented by the interplay of prices, is a substitute for the planned production by government officials in a communist order. The strength and progressiveness of our economy rest on the arrangement which substitutes the actions of millions of business firms, the plans of millions of centers of deliberation and choice—with the spur of competition and the profit motive to assure efficiency—for the overwhelming task shouldered by a few official planners, liable to mischievous error no matter how brilliant and sincere they may be.

So vital is the role of price in our midst that we call our economic system a price economy. The analysis of the application of scarce productive resources to competing wants and goods necessarily centers on the exploration of the ways in which (1) price is determined for goods in the various markets; (2) the price or the earnings of the factor-services are shaped under various circumstances; and (3) price functions in the combining of resources into a given technique or method of production. These three problems are interrelated. It may be worth noting that the tools developed by this analysis are largely applicable in the investigation of the workings of other social orders, even socialism and communism. This analysis may bear the label of "value and distribution," or "value analysis," or "price analysis."

Production planning in Russia

The vitality of price as a guide to production can be underscored, by implication, when we briefly consider price and the allocation of resources in communist Russia. In our economy the prices and the quantities, of goods and of factor-services, are determined in the market by the forces of demand and supply and by adjustments and readjustments of millions of consumers and millions of producers day in and day out. The basic phenomenon of price functioning as a guide to production and other aspects of our economy seems to be absent in communist Russia. There, price is downgraded to a secondary position. The physical magnitudes of the multitudinous commodities are determined by the State Planning Commission, the Gosplan. This body serves, almost, as a substitute for the price mechanism in our economy. Of course, the communist economy faces the same central problems as arise in our economy, namely: What to produce and how much? How? For whom? But the resolution of these problems is different.

As the first step in the preparations for a Five Year Plan, the Planning Commission sends out detailed questionnaires to the top officials of the 1,500 industries (commodities), to plant managers, to the state banks, and to geographical areas. On the basis of the information received, principally from officials with experience in factory, shop, and office, and on the basis of the voluminous statistics derived from various reports, including the reports of the State Bank (the Gosbank), the Gosplan draws up a tentative plan in the form of separate "material balances" for the 1,500 industries. These balances indicate the expected output of each industry, for consumption, for export, for military use, and for inventory. On the other side, the "balances" specify the input in labor, in raw materials, and in tools; there is also prescription of technical standards and method of production. The recipient of this document may make suggestions or complaints, when he feels that too much is expected of him, or when he thinks that he has been allowed insufficient tools. These reactions go to the immediately superior bodies, ultimately reaching the apex, the Gosplan.

Each industry receives an account with the State Bank, which has over 6,000 branches and 150,000 employees. The account is drawn upon when a given industry needs to buy inputs, like tools, materials, machines, and labor-hours. As the account moves up (from the sales of its semifinished product to another industry), the *Bank* can form its opinion about the efficiency or inefficiency of a given plant. Ways are used to raise bank credit to the efficient plant and to make life unpleasant for the head of the inefficient plant. There is constant watchfulness over the work of each production unit; and perhaps the State Bank is the most energetic policeman: by examining the bank account of a given plant or industry, the inspector (the Gosplan field representative) can see how much was spent on inputs and how much it received from the sale of its output. He can see whether the production unit is moving along at a pace necessary to make the Five Year Plan a "great" success.

The final plan is not an ironclad creation. There are almost weekly checks and counterchecks, adjustments and revisions. The purpose is to avoid miscalculations and big errors; to see that there are no bottlenecks in the vertical flow of raw materials to the finished product; and to make sure that the input-mix is in proper proportions.

Price is not absent from this complicated picture. Arbitrary price-tags are put on each input and each output. Top officials regard physical planning, in terms of units of actual goods, as of backbone significance. Price is secondary: it is used for accounting purposes. It is therefore a *tag* and not quite the signal-giving and production-guiding *price*. If the tag proves to be too high, as would be shown by slow-moving inventory, measures are taken indirectly to reduce the price—for example, by lowering the sales tax. Conversely, if the tag is too low, if the shelves or storerooms are cleared too rapidly, so that shortages may develop in the sense that with the *given* tags, consumers are anxious to buy more than is offered for sale, the sales tax is moved up.

Despite the disposition of Russian officials and Russian writers to dwarf the importance of price, price is much more than a mere afterthought with the planners. As we saw, to reach equilibrium for any article, that is, to see that the shelves in the retail stores are bare after an expected period, the Gosplan must fix the appropriate tag-price, and must revise the price from time to time. The Planning Commission will not think of setting the price of a cake of soap as high as the price of a pair of shoes for a grown-up. The Commission is quite aware that at such a price very few cakes of soap will leave the store per unit of time. In most cases, the planners know from past experience which price will sell which quantities of a product. The quantities set by them for each commodity do not move in a vacuum: the quantities are tailored to price, but not directly and not at each step; and the price-quantity relation is not ignored. Too, without price-tags—and not only for the final product but also for raw materials, for semifinished goods moving up to another factory, for tools, and for the various types of labor used—without price tags no meaningful scheme of accounting is possible. Such considerations suggest that the directive function of price does enter into the calculations of the Gosplan; but not to the same extent and not as openly as in a free-enterprise society. Drive price out through the door and it will come back through the window.

3. A MIXED ECONOMY

We should not, however, form the impression that our economy is exclusively an economy of private, free, and competitive enterprise. Ours is a mixed system, mixed in two senses.

First, in the tasks of producing for our wants, the government is a partner with private enterprise, although a minor partner. The government runs the postoffice. It builds revenue-producing projects like the Tennessee Valley Authority. It controls the Federal Reserve System, which affects banking throughout the country; and through various agencies it lends money. In some cases municipalities own public utilities, supplying water and gas and electricity. The government is engaged in irrigation and flood control and in other projects of conserving our natural resources. It builds roads; sets price ceilings and price floors in some instances; prescribes minimum wage rates; and imposes pure food laws. It does considerable research and it publishes extensive statistical information, aiding industry and agriculture alike. In a depression the government may launch programs of public works to provide jobs for the idle and to stimulate private enterprise. By its fiscal and monetary policies it always affects business directly and indirectly. The scope of this government partnership with private business has been expanding. But there still exists an extremely large economic sector in which individuals act in accord with their own motivations and calculations.

Second, the price mechanism does not always work under conditions of pure competition. Our economy is preponderantly a blend of competition and monopoly. The many industries bearing the character of monopoly, oligopoly, and monopolistic competition contain varying degrees of monopoly elements. Monopoly elements contribute to generally undesirable pricing processes, to misallocation of resources, and to distorted division of income. On this account, our economy cannot get a clean bill of health. It is also well to keep in mind that the rugged individualism of the owner of the small establishment has given place in many instances to a sort of collective or co-operative endeavor typified by the large corporation with thousands of owners as stockholders, with huge aggregations of capital embodying, in part, the ownership claims of thousands of bondholders, and with multitudes of workers collaborating under one roof in an extensive scheme of division of labor.

II. Other Institutions and Concepts

Every science frames its concepts in unique terminology and develops its own vocabulary; and so does economics. Most of the concepts used in this book will be explained as they appear in connection with the argument. In this section, a number of general concepts are presented in the meanings commonly attached to them in economic discussion.

1. GOODS, SERVICES, WEALTH

Our wants are determined by our biological needs but perhaps to a greater degree by the cultural conditions of our society. Our wants are satisfied by goods and services. *Goods*, commodities, products, or articles refer to material objects. *Services* are nonmaterial; they represent the actions of individuals, like the examination of the patient by the doctor, the song of the crooner, or the lecture by the professor.

Some goods ready for use are supplied by nature in such abundance that no one thinks of exerting himself to make any more of them. These goods are not scarce in relation to wants; such goods are *free goods*. Free goods are not bought and sold; they have no price. They stir up no economic problems and they do not figure in economic analysis. Examples of free goods are air, sunshine, wild flowers in the woods. Most goods are *economic goods*, goods scarce in relation to human wants and therefore bought and sold at a price. Economic goods may be provided by nature, without effort on our part; examples are land, ores and oil underground, virgin forests, or the sea breeze blowing into the expensive rooms of a summer hotel. But most economic goods embody in them a good deal of human effort, as does coal in the bin of the coal dealer, ice cream, machinery, or houses. A good may be free when not scarce and it may become an economic good as soon as its amount becomes limited in relation to human wants. The free land occupied by the early pioneers did not wait long before it graduated to the rank of an economic good.

Some goods yield satisfaction directly as the consumer uses them, like bread or a family car. These are called *consumer goods*. Other goods help produce consumer goods. They are natural resources, raw materials, tools, machines, office buildings. Of these, the goods made by man are called *capital goods;* and those provided by nature, such as forests, minerals, and any other natural resources, are called *land*. The aggregate of economic goods in existence in a community constitutes its *wealth*. This concept does not include services.

2. PRODUCTION

Nearly all economic goods have to be produced. By *production* we mean any activity which adds utility to an object intended for exchange. Production involves the combination of resources or factors—land, labor, capital, and entrepreneurship. The keeper of a shoe store is engaged in the production of shoes; he does not make shoes, but he adds to their

utility for the consumer. He orders them from the wholesaler or manufacturer, unpacks them, and puts them on the shelves. He fits the shoes on
the customer, wraps them, and perhaps also delivers them to the customer's door.

Working around the house adds to the utility of one's dwelling. But
such activity is not classed as production if the purpose is to improve the
house for the owner's personal satisfaction and not to raise the price of
the house at a sale. Of similar status is the work of the housewife. Appreci-
ated as it is by young and old, such work is not production; it does not
relate to exchange and price. It may create domestic problems; it does not
form an economic problem calling for economic analysis. But the housewife's work done by a hired maid is another matter.

Note that production as a concept in economics does not extend into
the technological, physical, chemical, or engineering aspects. The concept
stands only for the nature of the combination of the factor-services which
adds to the utility of an object. Economics does not go into thermody-
namics, into the technicalities of the Bessemer process of making steel, or
into the biology of breeding minks.

The various agencies which collaborate in the processes of production
are called *factors of production*, productive services, inputs, productive
resources, or simply resources or factors. We have already classified these
factors in four categories: *land, labor, capital*, and the *entrepreneur*. *Land*
refers to all natural resources, to virgin forests, minerals underground,
and soil untouched by man. *Labor* designates all efforts, physical or mental,
exerted for compensation. *Capital* stands for man-made objects designed
to aid the other factors in producing goods and services. The pictures on
the walls of the office of the president of the corporation, the taxicab, the
monkey of the organ grinder, machinery, inventory, and raw materials
are capital. The automobile used by the physician in making his rounds is
a capital good. The same automobile when used by the physician to take
him to the theater is a consumer good. The *entrepreneur* is, briefly, the
businessman, who performs the special functions of organizing the productive processes and of assuming the risks associated with ultimate decisions and final responsibility in resolving problems created by dynamic
changes. The use of a given method of production implies a particular
combination of the factors; a change in the method of production expresses itself in a changed combination of resources, and is ordinarily made
possible or imperative by an improvement or an invention or a change in
factor-prices. These problems call for a choice-decision: they lie in the
province of the businessman's activity.

In normal times total production reaches its limits when all labor is
employed. In an emergency, like war, the limits can be stretched to the
boundaries of maximum possible employment. This maximum is attained

when children leave school, when the aged leave the rockers, when housewives leave the hearth—and join the ranks of labor. Add for good measure overtime work and scant absenteeism.

3. THE FIRM

The task of providing most of the goods and services for the population of a capitalist country is entrusted to private businessmen, in contrast to Karl Marx's teaching that goods for the public must be produced publicly, socially; for use and not for profit. The firm is the unit of production, whether it is a single proprietorship, a partnership, or a corporation; whether it is a one-man firm, like the independent plumber, the peanut vendor, the physician, or a giant organization, like the U.S. Steel Corporation, with thousands of employees and scores of thousands of stockholders. The firm is symbolized by and is presided over by one responsible manager at the top.

It is the firm which initially decides on the particular commodity it will produce, on the quality of the product, and on the method of production. The firm hires the services of the various factors of production and co-ordinates them in a manner calculated to bring about a maximum of output with a minimum of inputs or with minimum cost per unit of product. The firm buys factor-services in one market, transforms them into commodities, and sells these commodities in another market. In some cases, where the producer has a degree of monopoly power, the firm sets the price for the consumer; in cases of competition, the firm can do nothing but accept the price in the market for this commodity, and merely adjusts the quantity which it will produce in view of this market price against the backdrop of costs of production.

The guide to these and other decisions is chiefly price, the price which the consumer pays for the article and the price which the firm pays to the factors whose services are used in making the article. The first kind of price constitutes revenue or receipts by the firm; the second kind of price represents cost to the firm. The difference between total receipts and total costs forms the total profit per unit of time. Price and profit are of foundational significance in guiding production. In producing goods for society the firm is energized by profit and not by the "needs" of the community. The firm will make goods as long as it makes money; in the long run it will not if it does not.

The responsible manager in each of the plants in a *multiplant* firm does not function as an entrepreneur; nor is each plant a firm in itself. The reason is that neither in this manager nor in the single plant dwell the ultimate authority and responsibility of decision making. All the plants subordinated to one ultimate source of final choices and final risk taking compose one firm; and the final agents of decision above the plant managers constitute the entrepreneur.

The firm sells goods and services; the consumer buys goods and services. The term consumer is not confined to the one person who attends to the buying, but extends to the consuming unit, the household. The housewife makes the choice for the family when buying groceries and other articles. The household sometimes embraces only one individual, as in the case of the bachelor who manages his own purchases. There are more than 50 million households in the United States. The firms are the centers of decision with respect to production; the households are the centers of decision with respect to consumption. The firms are related to the supply of unfinished and finished goods; the households form the demand for finished goods. The firms produce for the households, the households labor and invest their savings for the firms. The firms have a demand for the factor-services, the households provide the supplies of the factor-services. For their productive services the households receive money income from the firms. The households spend the income, all or part of it, on purchasing the consumption products made by the firms. Thus the processes of production provide not only the goods but, in the main, also the money destined to buy the goods produced. This idea is called J. B. Say's law.

4. RATIONAL BEHAVIOR

The agents who participate in economic behavior may be divided into four groups: (1) the households or consumers; (2) the entrepreneurs; (3) the other factors, labor and the owners of natural and capital resources; and (4) the federal, state, and municipal governments which operate schools, libraries, hospitals, roads, the postoffice, and other undertakings. We shall omit from consideration the fourth group, inasmuch as the motives of the government in engaging in economic enterprise are at sharp variance with the predominantly pecuniary motives which inspire the other three groups.

Through what lenses one looks at the economic behavior of individuals in these first three groups is a question of foremost significance to economic analysis. The economist may decide to be thoroughly realistic and may adopt at the outset the premise that the consumer, the entrepreneur, and the other factors are actuated by many motives: by material, religious, political, social, ethical, altruistic motives, including for good measure imitation, emulation, habit, and ignorance. Unfortunately it is hardly an exaggeration to assert that a premise of such all-inclusive motivation, for all its realism, comes close to filing a petition in bankruptcy as far as the advancement of economic theories is concerned. Such a premise or assumption would launch the economist on the well-nigh insoluble task of isolating and evaluating a multiplicity of interwoven and tangled forces, intangible and intractable. Such an assumption would make the task of tracing cause and effect and forming generalizations too complex for appreciable achievement.

Most economists have decided to barter away this broad assumption, which almost blocks the road to analysis, for a simple assumption which opens the door to framing useful principles. The simple assumption is that, generally speaking, most individuals in the *economic* world are moved by self-interest, by the motive of personal gain. He believes that some few strive to be better; but that the majority strive to be better off. Individuals, it is assumed, behave rationally: they are bent on maximizing a certain magnitude. The consumer aims at maximizing the utility from his purchases of goods with a given amount of money. The firm seeks, usually, to maximize profit from its productive ventures. The worker will often choose the job with the highest wage rate; the landowner will put his natural resources to the uses which will bring him the greatest economic rent; and he who saves part of his income will place his savings where (risk being equal) he will reap the highest rate of interest. The economist assumes the rational calculus which seeks maximum returns.

Under the assumption that the individual acts rationally, as here defined, his choice of means and ends can be analyzed and his action can be predicted, more or less, by logical reasoning. We can discuss the behavior of the consumer in reaction to a change in the price of a commodity, the decisions of firms in hiring varying amounts of resources at certain prices, or the effect of a tariff on the imports and on the standard of living of the country that levies it. *Without* the assumption of the maximization principle, the economist lacks a basic guiding idea in his analysis. *With* such an assumption, he can move within the pattern of deductive analysis in which one step leads to the other, culminating, possibly, in a generalization.

The economist adopts this simplified assumption of economic motivation with eyes open and regretfully. He knows that consumers succumb to sales pressure, shop where they are in the habit of shopping, and buy what their friends are buying. He is aware that we save for a variety of reasons other than the interest received, and that some monied people buy worthless oil stock. He admits that the worker may forgo moving to a locality with higher wages because his children like their teachers, his wife loves her neighbor, and he hates to go to a strange place. The economist needs not to be told that ignorance and inertia or the desire for admiration may swerve a businessman from the geometric intersection of lines at the point of maximum gain.

Nevertheless, the assumption of rational conduct is not only closer to realities than any other simple assumption, but is also in itself and in fact a reasonable approximation of the actual behavior of the generality of people in many economic circumstances. Single individuals may act differently, but on the average the masses of individuals behave, in *economic dealings*, with a marked degree of closeness to the motives of self-interest. Moreover, the economist can attempt to match against actual events the result of his analysis as based on the simple assumption, and he can modify the conclusion by taking into account noneconomic motives. Of course he cannot frame the modification in quantitative terms. He cannot assert that because of charitableness or fear of punitive legislation the monopolist shades his maximum-profit price by $1.50. He can merely state that the monopolist is not apt to take full advantage of each fleeting favorable opportunity to squeeze the public with a higher price but will moderate the price in response to the stir of noneconomic motives.

5. MICROECONOMICS AND MACROECONOMICS

The many-sided conduct of the consumers, firms, and factors forms a picture of enormous complexity with intricate interrelations among such things as product prices, factor prices, inputs and outputs of firms, the behavior of industries, demands and supplies, and the flow of money in the various channels. How approach the analysis of this universe of facts? Two basic approaches are in practice.

The first is *microeconomics*. This approach confines itself to the study of a single phenomenon, like the price of an article, the behavior of one firm, or the adjustments occurring in one industry. The other elements in the economy—all the other prices, firms, or industries—are assumed to stay unaffected: they are impounded in the phrase "all other things are equal." We also see microeconomics when a system of *individual* prices, outputs, resources, and costs are connected by comprehensive equations, as is the case in general equilibrium analysis, to be explained presently.

Before 1936, the year of the appearance of J. M. Keynes' *General Theory of Employment, Interest and Money*, microeconomics constituted the main body of economic theory, and even today it exemplifies, perhaps, the major share of theoretical economic exploration. Realizing that many economists are preoccupied with newer phases of economic study, like econometrics, games, growth, activity analysis, Keynes' mutiny, linear programming, macroeconomics, and welfare, nearly all of them employing awe-inspiring higher mathematics, we may cultivate the impression that the new economics ought to be exalted above the traditional classical microeconomics, which dedicates its labors to the lowly problem of "the price of a cup of coffee."

Such a viewpoint scarcely does justice to microeconomics. Microeconomics has been and still is addressing itself to the investigation of economic problems of towering significance to the individual, to the nation, and to international dealings. It explores the behavior of the consumer, of the factors of production, and of the firm and industry. It studies the movement of factor-services into the market for productive resources, the allocation of these services among the vast realm of industries and firms, the combination of these services inside the firm, the flow of goods to the commodity markets, and the pricing of goods and services as well as the pricing of factor-services. Microeconomics studies the functioning of our economy in providing goods and services for 180 million people. It probes into the motivation, the efficiency, and the tendency toward equilibrium of over four million farmers as entrepreneurs and a like number of businessmen in industry. It studies ends and means over the vast panorama of economic problems thrust upon us by the scarcity of means in relation to culturally determined ends. All fields of economics, old and new, are of outstanding value in so far as they tend to throw light on what is going on about us; and in so far as they study such problems as the abolition of poverty and the attainment of higher standards of living, with the consequent possibility of greater leisure and deeper nonmaterial enrichment of the human being, they address themselves to the problems of the ages. We are using, Thoreau would say, improved means to unimproved ends.

Then comes *macroeconomics* or *aggregative analysis*. This approach stresses totals and their behavior. There are two spheres in which macroeconomics dwells. One is found in the study of any field in economics in which the attention centers at least in part on aggregate magnitudes. In the analysis of monetary problems, we consider the control of credit as a total for the country, or the effect of the total amount of money in circulation on the price level. In the study of business cycles, the concern is with the behavior of total output, total wage disbursements, or credit expansion, or with the effect on aggregate employment produced by investment or by a wave of technological innovations. In international trade, part of the inquiry deals with the movement of gold, with the balance of international payments, or with total borrowing and lending.

The other and better known sphere of aggregative analysis is of comparatively recent origin and is derived principally from the pioneering work of J. M. Keynes. It is occupied with the major question of the determinants of employment in the economy. The analysis explores the interaction of total consumption, saving, and investment in governing total employment, output, and income. This approach is exemplified in some places in this book.[1]

It may be of use to observe that in aggregative analysis we have to guard ourselves against the error called in logic the "fallacy of composition." In economics what is true of the parts is not necessarily true of the whole. The problem of the aggregate is not merely a composition, or a multiplication, of the problems of the component individuals; and we cannot generalize from individual experience to the aggregate as a whole. An individual who decides to save a larger part of his income will benefit himself in the end. But let many individuals launch on a program of increased savings, and the aggregate income may decline, a depression may be generated, and the end result may be smaller total savings. Beyond a certain point, a difference in degree begins to act like a difference in kind; at a certain stage, quantity transforms itself into quality. One tree cannot change the climate in the neighborhood, but a forest can.

6. EQUILIBRIUM

When we study an economic problem bearing on the adaptation of means to ends, what we are doing is exploring the conditions of equilibrium. Equilibrium is a term borrowed from physics. Simply put, in physics the concept means that a body is in equilibrium when the opposite forces acting on it cancel each other and sum up to zero. In economics equilibrium means that a position has been reached—by the individual, the firm, or the industry—in which there is no incentive to change: the position is nondynamic. The consumer is in equilibrium when he cannot gain in total utility by a change in the allocation of his total expenditure among his purchases. The firm is in equilibrium when it cannot raise its profit by changing its output or by changing the technique of its production. The industry is in equilibrium when there is no incentive for old firms to leave it and for new firms to enter it. A factor is in equilibrium when at the current compensation there is no incentive for it to offer more or less of its productive service, and no incentive to seek employment elsewhere.

When we examine the forces which tend to determine the price of a ton of steel, we are assuming rational behavior, that is, the search for maximum profit by the selling firm. When the analysis defines the elements which govern the price, it implies thereby the price which bears the firm the greatest profit. Once such a price is established the firm will have no inducement to change it: it cannot do better than to maximize its profit. The price of steel as finally shaped by the relevant determinants is accordingly an equilibrium price. Thus whenever we investigate the

[1] See Chapters XVIII and XIX, also Chapter XV.

determinants of a magnitude—utility, price, or wage rate—which maximize the return to the consumer, to the firm, or to the factors of production, we are investigating the conditions of equilibrium of this magnitude. The analysis of price becomes the analysis of price equilibrium, that is, of a price which offers no inducement to the agent concerned with it to institute a change.

The analysis of a problem conveniently proceeds by assuming first a given equilibrium situation and then by introducing a disturbing element: for instance, a change in one of the conditions affecting the demand or the supply of the commodity or the factor-service. Then we trace the effect of the changed condition on the relevant variables and on the firm, the industry, or the factor; and, finally, we examine the process by which a new equilibrium is established. In actual life the state of equilibrium is seldom reached; the reason is that economic life undergoes continual change. Before the determining elements succeed in shaping the final result, new disturbances arrive on the scene. Nothing is constant but change. In every segment of the economy there are ceaseless movements and tendencies toward equilibrium, but rarely the attainment of it.

There are varieties of phases to the concept of equilibrium and a number of classifications of it. We shall consider the three dominant types of equilibrium.

(1) There is first *particular* equilibrium analysis, the method most often used in microeconomics. We examine the determinants of one thing at a time and consider all other things as unaffected. An example is the equilibrium price and output of the firm in the short period or in the long run; another is the equilibrium wage rate of bus drivers, in a given city or in the country at large.

This method acknowledges the limitations of the human mind, which can grasp concretely the interaction of only a few variables, such as a given demand situation and a given supply situation. It is the position of those who favor this approach that if in analyzing, for instance, the effect of a sales tax on the price of bread we undertook to trace the impact of the tax on every nook and cranny of the economy, we should be overwhelmed by an endless network of repercussions, and the analysis would bog down instead of getting on with the job of supplying a specific answer to the problem at hand. Advocates of this type of analysis prefer therefore to isolate for examination a small segment, a single market problem. They believe in the motto, "Divide and conquer."

This method is linked with the name of Alfred Marshall and with the Cambridge School, in view of Marshall's influence on his followers in Cambridge University. This method is employed most frequently in economic exploration. It is used largely in this text.

(2) *General* equilibrium analysis embodies a more ambitious attitude.

Those who pursue this method prefer to take into account nearly all the phenomena and repercussions which are related to the specific problem under consideration. Ideally, an analyst using this method would strive to take into account the reactions of the whole economy to the event under inquiry. Where the attention in particular analysis would center on the relation, say, of cost and output of one commodity, in the general analysis one would examine the costs and outputs, the demand and supply, of all other commodities affected by what happens to the one initial commodity under investigation. This approach is commonly that of mathematicians, who find themselves at home with extensive arrays of lengthy simultaneous equations. The equations may embrace nearly all the variables involved in economic activity; they picture then the new equilibrium of the whole system. In such an equilibrium, no individual can improve his position by changing his purchases of goods or by changing his employment or investment; and no firm will reap greater gains by making a change in its price or volume of output.

Particular analysis is addressed to the clarification of a narrow problem, stressing cause and effect more than wide interrelations. Concentrated as it is on a limited number of data or variables, it loses in comprehensiveness but gains from focusing a sharp light on a small spot. It helps in prediction and control. General analysis is the survey of a panorama of the many far-flung variables related to those involved in the given problem. It brings intimations of the interweavings of prices and quantities, of goods and factor-services, and of firms and industries more than it stresses specific cause and effect sequences. It broadens our comprehension of how the economic system functions as a whole. The particular analysis is a worm's-eye view, the general analysis is a bird's-eye view.

This general approach is associated with the name of the French economist, Léon Walras, who taught at the University of Lausanne, Switzerland, and with the so-called Lausanne School.

(3) Finally comes *aggregative* equilibrium analysis. When the determinants of income and employment, namely total consumption, saving, and investment, bring about, after all adjustments, a given total of employment and output, this last total represents an aggregative equilibrium. This equilibrium is attained when savings and investment are brought into equality by adjustments in total income. As Keynes argues, this equilibrium may go hand in hand with full employment but more likely, in wealthy countries, with less than full employment.

An aggregative equilibrium may hide from view certain important elements which contribute to it. Totals conceal the relative shifts among the parts, and such shifts may be of central importance in shaping the tendency toward equilibrium in the economy or in disrupting the tendency. Aggregate consumption, saving, and investment are not the exclusive determinants of the level of output and employment. The interrelations of price, cost, and profit, in the firms of the many industries, play a powerful role in the course of prosperity and depression. But totals draw a curtain over the play and the transforming influence of imbalances among these strategic variables.

We have introduced equilibrium here since it is involved in almost all the discussions in the book and since, with this concept in mind, the reader can study economic analysis more fruitfully. We shall save a more detailed examination of the equilibrium concept until the final chapter (Chapter XX).

We are now at the end of the two introductory chapters. With the next chapter we begin the analysis of price formation and, later, of the determinants of total income. In traditional language we shall study value, distribution, and national income.

SUGGESTED READINGS

Enke, S. *Intermediate Economic Theory*, chap. 15. New York, Prentice-Hall, 1950.

Fraser, L. M. *Economic Thought and Language*. London, Black, 1937.

Hutchinson, T. W. *The Significance and Basic Postulates of Economic Theory*. London, Macmillan, 1938.

Keynes, John Neville. *The Scope and Method of Political Economy*, 4th ed. London, Macmillan, 1930.

Knight, F. H. *The Economic Organization*. New York, Augustus M. Kelley, 1951.

Lange, O. "The Scope and Method of Economics," *Review of Economic Studies*, III (1945–1946). pp. 19–32.

Machlup, F. *The Economics of Sellers' Competition*, chap. 1. Baltimore, Johns Hopkins Press, 1952.

Marshall, A. *Principles of Economics*, 8th ed., Book I. New York, Macmillan, 1927.

Papandreou, A. G. *Economics as a Science*. Chicago, Lippincott, 1958.

Robbins, L. *The Nature and Significance of Economic Science*, 2nd ed. London, Macmillan, 1938.

Ruggles, R. "Methodological Developments," *Survey of Contemporary Economics*, vol. II, Haley, B. F., ed., chap. 10. Chicago, Irwin, 1952.

Stigler, G. J. *The Theory of Price*, revised ed., chap. 2; pp. 290–295. New York, Macmillan, 1952.

III Demand: Utility Analysis

THE CHANNELING of the resources into the processes of producing the great varieties of goods for society is a function performed by the business firms under the guidance of the profit motive. Profit depends on the relation between the prices received from the sale of goods and the costs involved in producing the goods. By considering the prices and costs at various levels of output the firm can operate at a profit and provide employment, money income, and goods to the community.

But costs are prices too: the prices paid to labor, capital, land, and management for their part in the production of goods. The prices which consumers pay for goods and services are related to demand; the prices which firms pay to factors of production are related to supply. The two sets of prices are interdependent, and nearly all prices are shaped by demand and supply. No wonder we hear so much of "the law of demand and supply."

We shall begin our study of price by an analysis of the nature of consumer demand for goods and services. We shall examine in this chapter three prominent and related phases of demand: the kinds of demand; utility as the basis of demand; and elasticity of demand.

I. Three Kinds of Demand

Ultimately, all economic activity has its impulse in consumer demand. Production is the means; consumer's satisfaction is the end. The investments made by the firm in machinery and other equipment are made only for the purpose of producing consumer goods. Said Adam Smith: "Consumption is the sole end and purpose of all production; and the interest of the producer ought to be attended to only so far as it may be necessary for promoting that of the consumer. The maxim is so perfectly self-evident that it would be absurd to attempt to prove it." [1]

DEFINITION OF DEMAND

By demand we mean the various quantities of a given commodity or service which consumers would buy in one market in a given period of time at various prices, or at various incomes, or at various prices of related goods. The amount of a good or service which consumers would take depends on the price of the good or service, or on the incomes of the buyers, or on the price of related goods. There are accordingly three kinds of demand: price demand, income demand, and cross-demand.

That these three kinds of demand are of commanding interest to the firm in formulating its price and output policy needs no laboring. The firm wants to have an idea of the various quantities of its product which it could sell per unit of time if it were to charge one *price* or another price. Many a firm knows that its sales at given prices depend in large part on the preference which people have for its product; and that this preference must not cool off. Hence the advertising and sales campaigns to implant in prospective customers, and to fortify in old ones, the notion that without the article there is no well-being, physical, mental, or social. It is also important for the firm to know what fluctuations its sales will experience through the phases of the business cycle as customers' *incomes* move up and down. Finally, very few firms produce an article so remote from any substitute that the firm can set its price without regard for the reactions of other producers. Very often there are *related goods* ready to compete with the product of the given firm if it raises its price. What amounts it can sell as the prices of related goods rise or fall may become a question decisive for success or even survival.

Before taking a good look at each of the three kinds of demand, it is well to observe that price demand is pre-eminently the kind of demand with which people are concerned most of the time—so much so that economists generally think of demand as price demand, and define demand almost exclusively as price demand. In view of this circumstance, in the pages that follow price demand will be understood when demand is mentioned unless one of the other kinds of demand is directly specified.

Another observation: these three kinds of demand do not exhaust the determinants of demand. We can cite as additional determinants the *tastes*

[1] *The Wealth of Nations*, 1776, Everyman ed., Vol. II, p. 155.

of the consumer and his *expectation* that a falling or rising price of a given good will or will not continue to fall or rise. But in the following discussion we shall concentrate our attention on the three determinants of demand which we first enumerated—price, income, and the price of related goods.

1. PRICE DEMAND

Price demand refers to the various quantities of a good or service that consumers would buy in a given amount of time, and in a given market at various hypothetical prices. We assume of course that all other things are equal. This means that the other determinants of demand remain unchanged. We also assume that consumers' tastes stay the same, and that there is no expectation that the price will move up or down in the near future.

If we deal with the quantities purchased by one consumer at various prices, we face an *individual demand*; if we deal with the quantities purchased by all buyers of the commodity at various prices, we face a total demand for the good, or the *industry demand*. Each firm is of course interested in the various amounts of its output which it could sell to its customers at various prices. This we call the *firm's demand*, or the *individual seller's demand*.

When we put down the various hypothetical prices of a good in one column and in another column the corresponding quantities of the good

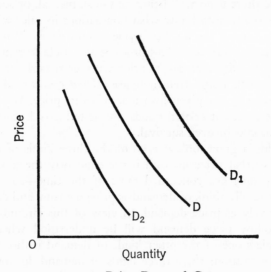

FIGURE 1. *Price Demand Curves*

which people would buy in a given period of time, we have a *demand schedule*. We can have the industry demand schedule, representing the purchases of a given article by all the buyers in the market at various prices; and the firm's demand schedule, or *sales schedule*, indicating the total purchases of the good by its own customers at various prices. If we plot the demand schedule on a graph, with the quantities of the good measured along the horizontal or x axis (the abscissa) and the prices measured off on the vertical or y axis (the ordinate), we obtain a *price demand curve*, like D in Figure 1. A demand curve pictures the relationship between price and quantity for a given article in a given period of time. Sometimes this relationship is linear, and the demand is illustrated by a straight line; and sometimes the relationship is more complex and is portrayed by a curve. As we have stated, it may be an individual demand curve, depicting the purchases of the individual as the price falls, an industry demand curve, or a firm's demand curve.

AN INCREASED OR DECREASED DEMAND

It is necessary to emphasize an exactitude of meaning: when we assert that the quantities of a given article demanded rise and fall as its price falls or rises, we are not at all dealing with an increased or decreased demand, but rather with one given demand situation for the article and with one given demand curve. It is incorrect to state that demand rises as the price falls or that demand falls as the price rises. If people buy in a given market 5 million packages of a certain brand of cigarettes a day when the price is 20¢ and 6 million packages when the price falls to 19¢, we are not witnessing an increased demand for this cigarette at the new price. These two sets of prices and quantities merely describe the demand for the article and are illustrated by two points on the same demand curve.

The commonly observed fact that, other things equal, people buy more of an article when its price is low, and less of it if its price is pushed up, is called the law of demand. This law will be amplified later in this chapter.

The situation is different when with the same array of various prices people buy at each price more of a good than before in a given unit of time. Now we deal with an *increased demand*. In this new situation the price column in the demand schedule remains the same, but each figure in the quantity column is larger than before. An increased demand is illustrated by a demand curve shifted upward and to the right, like curve D_1 in Figure 1. Similarly, if the figures in the quantity column of a demand schedule remain the same but each figure in the price column is larger than before, we face an increased demand. It means that people would buy more of the good were the price unchanged; and here too, the demand curve is shifted upward and to the right to illustrate the new demand schedule. Again, we encounter an increased demand when the prices and the corresponding quantities purchased are alike greater than before. The opposite situation exists when there is a *decreased demand*. Then the demand curve D shifts downward and to the left. Curve D_2 in Figure 1 pictures a decreased demand in comparison with curve D.

What induces people to increase or decrease their price demand for a good or service? The answer rests either on the change in the size of the other two determinants or on a change of consumer tastes. (1) A rise in their money incomes will, by and large, impel people to raise their demand for all kinds of goods. The expenditures and savings of people are closely related to their incomes. The larger their income the more they consume, although not necessarily in proportion to the advance in the income. As incomes go up, more goods are demanded at existing prices, even at higher prices. Conversely, the declining incomes during a depression compel the consumer to curtail his demand for goods. At current prices and even at sagging prices he will buy less of various commodities per unit of time. (2) As will be pointed out below, a change in the price of related goods will precipitate a change in the demand for the given commodity. (3) If on account of advertising or changed habits the consumer preference and taste for a good grows stronger, the price demand for it will rise. Since the discovery that calf's liver helps in curing anemia the demand for calf's liver has risen considerably. Calf's liver has climbed to a higher scale in social estimation.

A change in demand should not be confused with the law of demand. A few more examples may be of help. The following statements reflect a change in demand: there is a heavy demand for eggs; a rising population raises the demand for housing; intensive advertising sold more cigarettes and more fruit; there has developed a changed demand for olives; the demand for cars is strong this spring. The following statements illustrate the law of demand: the lower the price the larger the sales; with the rise in the price of the newspaper the number of subscribers fell off; the scarcity of milk pushed up the price of ice cream. Let the student point out the errors in the following: When the demand for a good rises its price rises; when its price rises the demand for it falls; when the demand falls its price falls; and when the price falls the demand rises.

2. INCOME DEMAND

Income demand refers to the various quantities of a good or service which consumers will purchase at various levels of income in a given unit of time. The assumption is made again that all other things are equal: that the price of the given commodity, the intensity of the desire for it, and the prices of related goods all stay the same. The demand schedule will indicate, in one column, the various hypothetical incomes of consumers, and in the other column, the corresponding amounts of bushels of wheat or of Ford cars that will be bought. Income demand expresses the relationship between income and the quantity of a good demanded, just as price demand expresses the price-quantity relationship.

The lower level of incomes during a depression is associated with a notable decrease in the purchases of such durable goods as automobiles, refrigerators, vacuum cleaners, and winter coats. When the consumer is compelled to become more cautious about spending a dollar, he will make the durable goods serve him a little longer. But nondurable goods, too, are subject to the impact of lower incomes. When incomes decline, the consumer hangs onto his cash balance and is less willing to convert his money into goods. In a given period of time he buys less of nondurable goods and still less of durable goods, at the same prices as before or even at lower prices. The picture is different when incomes rise.

The relationship between the amounts of a good demanded and the corresponding incomes depends on whether the good is superior or inferior. Superior or *normal goods* are those which are purchased in larger quantities as consumers' incomes rise. Such goods as the higher priced cars, furs, or the better cuts of meat may have brisk sales when the national income rises. For such goods the income demand curve has a positive slope, rising to the right, as does curve *DD* in Figure 2A.

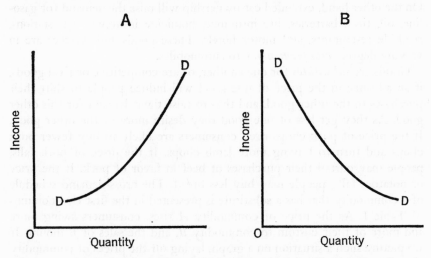

FIGURE 2. *Income Demand for* (A) *Normal and* (B) *Inferior Goods*

Inferior goods are goods of cheaper quality or goods not strongly desired for one reason or another. Purchased in larger quantities by those of lower income levels than by the well-to-do, these goods enjoy larger sales when consumer incomes run low than when they reach higher levels. Oleomargarine, cheaper meats, hand rug-cleaners, and perhaps potatoes are examples. When people reach higher income brackets they become reluctant, sooner or later, to purchase goods identified with the tastes of the poor if a more expensive substitute is available. In the days of the old model T Ford car the following statement would not have been far-fetched: "It is conceivable that should incomes rise sufficiently even such an institution as the Ford car may come under an eclipse, and the public may turn to more ostentatious vehicles as a means of expressing personality and of committing homicide on the highways." For inferior goods the income demand curve slopes negatively to the right, like *DD* in Figure 2B.

3. CROSS-DEMAND

Cross-demand refers to the various quantities of a good which consumers will buy in connection with the various prices, not of this good, but of a good closely related to it. We assume again that the other determinants of price stay unchanged. If the price of automobiles declines, and more automobiles are bought, the effect on some of the other goods would be negligible, if not nonexistent, provided they are definitely unrelated to cars, like apples or roses. But as more cars are bought, busses become less crowded. Car service to the owner of it is a *substitute* for bus service. On the other hand, extended car ownership will raise the demand for gasoline, oil, tires, batteries, life insurance, homicide insurance, gas stations, roadside restaurants, and motor hotels. These goods and services are in varying degrees *complementary* to automobiles.

Goods are *substitutes* for one another, or are competitive or rival goods, if an advance in the price of one good will induce people to shift their purchases to the other good, and thus to raise their demand for this other good. As they get less of one good they desire more of the other good. If the price of pork chops rises, consumers are likely to buy fewer pork chops and turn to buying more lamb chops. If the price of pork falls, people may curtail their purchases of beef in favor of pork. If the price of potatoes falls, people may buy less bread. The cross-demand schedule of a commodity that has a substitute is presented in the first two columns of Table 1. As the price of commodity *A* rises, consumers swing more and more of their custom to commodity *B*, and the sales of *B* mount. If we picture such a situation on a graph, laying off the prices of commodity *A* on the vertical axis, and measuring the resulting purchases of commodity

B on the horizontal axis, we get a positively inclined cross-demand curve, like *DD* in Figure 3A.

Complementary goods or joint-demand goods are goods so related that they are commonly used together in satisfying a given want. The more units the consumer buys of one commodity the more units of certain

TABLE 1. *Two Cross-Demand Schedules and One Unrelated Schedule*

Substitute goods		Complementary goods		Independent goods	
Price of *A*, cents	Quantity of *B* bought, units	Price of *C*, cents	Quantity of *D* bought, units	Price of *E*, cents	Quantity of *F* bought, units
10	20	10	20	10	25
11	22	11	19	11	25
12	25	12	15	12	25
13	30	13	14	13	25
14	36	14	12	14	25

other commodities will he be induced to buy. Else he will be in no position to enjoy the commodity already bought. Without gasoline or oil, of what use is the purchased automobile? In fact, the more we buy of

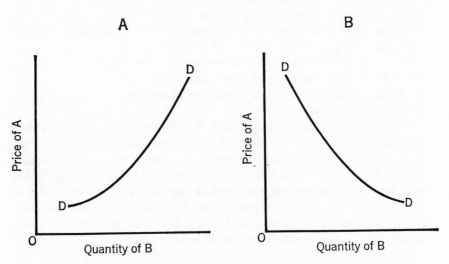

FIGURE 3. *Cross-Demand of* (A) *a Substitute Good, and of* (B) *a Complementary Good*

one article the greater the usefulness of the complementary articles. Examples: fountain-pen ink for a fountain pen that has been purchased; tea and sugar; and shaving cream and shaving blades. Some goods are strongly complementary: they are bought in a one-to-one ratio so that when 10% more is bought of one good 10% more must be bought of a certain other good—like right and left gloves, right and left shoes, or perhaps cups and saucers. However, most of the goods that are complementary are not strongly so. The demand for them moves in the same direction as for the given good, but not in a fixed ratio. Such is the case with automobiles and tires, bread and butter, trousers and belts, books and shelves, ham and eggs, cereal and milk, shirts and ties.

In the case of complementary goods, when the price of one good rises, less of it will be bought per unit of time and also less of the good associated with it; conversely when the price falls. The cross-demand schedule of complementary goods is illustrated in Table 1. The quantity acquired of a complementary good D varies inversely with the price of the other good C. On a graph, the cross-demand curve of a complementary good looks like DD in Figure 3B.

Independent goods are goods unrelated to other goods. The price of one good may keep on changing without affecting the quantities purchased of the other goods. A change in the price of a given kind of desk will not generate a change in the quantities bought of milk or of toothpicks. The last two columns in Table 1 illustrate the case of independent goods.

In a large sense, all goods no matter how unrelated are substitutes for one another. They all compete for the limited money income of the consumer. The more money we spend on one good the less money is left for other goods. However, a distinction exists between goods that are substitutes and goods that are not. If a person spends more on pork, he will have to spend slightly less on books and other things. If the money meant to be spent on the additional pork is lost, stolen, or taxed away, the purchases of books may be diminished to the same extent as when his money buys more pork.

Now let us consider pork and beef. If a consumer raises his purchases of pork, he is likely to buy less beef in consequence; not slightly less but noticeably less. If the additional money put aside for pork were stolen, the purchase of beef would fall off only slightly. He buys *noticeably* less beef *because* he buys more pork; and he buys slightly less beef when he does not buy more pork because he lost the money laid aside for more pork. Pork and books are unrelated goods. Pork and beef are rival goods or substitute goods in satisfying the want for meat.

II. Utility

All economic activity is undertaken for the sake of the consumer and is governed by consumer demand. What governs the consumer's demand? Why does he buy what he buys and in the amounts in which he buys? Since the 1870's and until recently the answer of the economist to these questions had been almost invariably one word: utility. That in recent years this answer has acquired a competitor will be indicated in the next chapter.

THE CONCEPT OF UTILITY

Utility is the power of a good or service to satisfy a want, to yield satisfaction. It is this power that makes an object a good and not rubbish or a nuisance, and makes an action a service and not a futile gesture—so much so that often *utility* and *good* or *service* are used synonymously in economic discussion. Utility does not mean that the commodity is necessarily useful in the ordinary sense of the word. The sheer nylon stockings in which women shiver in the cold will hardly stand comparison with woolen stockings for protection, but they satisfy a want because women prefer them as a decorative appliance. Nor does utility mean that the commodity does you good. The barfly may mutter that the stuff is killing him, but he keeps on buying the drinks because they give him satisfaction. Equally, utility is not charged with legal or ethical implications. Burglar's tools have a demand and command a price because they possess utility to certain characters.

Why people have certain patterns of wants and utilities depends on their culture and civilization, which are of interest to the anthropologist, historian, sociologist, and other scholars. The economist treats goods and utilities as given data. He does not probe into the question why people do not regard the automobile simply as a vehicle which can take them from point *A* to point *B*, but eye it instead with attachment as an extension of their personalities. The explanation of consumer attitudes toward utilities is apparently far from simple. Consider for example hunger, an elementary natural phenomenon. One should think that the ways of satisfying the want for food would be uniform among peoples. But we witness instead striking differences in the culinary arts, a profusion of customs, and a variety of taboos. The Chinese will not touch cheese and the Moslems recoil from pork, the British like plum pudding, and the Americans glorify the hot dog.

To induce the consumer to purchase larger amounts of a given article, the seller has to reduce the price. This fact is explained by the principle of diminishing marginal utility. But first it is necessary to clarify the concept. *Marginal utility* signifies the extra satisfaction obtained by a consumer from the use of an extra unit of a given commodity during a short period of time in which his tastes and habits of consumption remain unchanged. The marginal utility of n units of a good is the utility added by the use of the nth unit. But there is no one unit labeled as the nth unit; all units look alike. We therefore rephrase the idea by stating that the marginal utility of n units of an article is the utility lost when we consume one unit *less*; that is, when we consume $n - 1$ units of it. Or else, it is the utility gained when we consume one more unit after we have consumed $n - 1$ units. Still better, by the marginal utility of n units of a good we mean the utility of any one unit among these n units. Table 2 illustrates the idea.

TABLE 2. *Diminishing Marginal Utility*

Ounces of cheese	Total utility, in utils	Marginal utility, in utils
1	5	5
2	11	6
3	18	7
4	24	6
5	29	5
6	33	4
7	36	3
8	38	2
9	39	1
10	39	0
11	38	−1

DIMINISHING MARGINAL UTILITY

So far, no way has been found of measuring utility, of measuring the emotional or physiological reactions which register the amount of utility that a person receives from the consumption of a unit of an article. Let us, for the sake of illustration, call each imaginary degree of satisfaction a "util," and let us look at the utility schedule of a consumer as he enjoys, ounce by ounce, 11 ounces of a certain kind of cheese, at a given time or in a short space of time. The schedule is indicated in Table 2. The marginal utilities are specified in the last column. The marginal utility of 5 ounces of cheese is 5 utils, of 8 ounces 2 utils, and so on.

The up-and-down trend in the size of the marginal utilities is often characteristic when we consume several small units of a commodity. For the first few units the marginal utility may climb, reaching a maximum at a certain point; then the marginal utility begins a steady descent, illustrating the principle of *diminishing marginal utility*. We derive a degree of satisfaction from the first ounce of cheese. The next ounce may well give us greater satisfaction than the first ounce as the appetite is awakened for keener enjoyment. For the same reason the utility of the third ounce of cheese may exceed the utility of the second ounce. But beginning with the fourth ounce, each extra ounce of this cheese affords us less and less extra gratification until a point of satiety arrives with the tenth ounce at which marginal utility equals zero. Beyond this stage, each ounce causes increasing discomfort, or disutility, or negative utility.

There is a definite connection between marginal utility and total utility, and one can be derived from the other. When the total utility of n units is given, we find the marginal utility of n units by deducting the total utility of $n - 1$ units from the total utility of n units. When the series of the individual marginal utilities of n units is given, we obtain the total utility by adding all the marginal utilities. The total utility keeps on climbing up to the amount at which the marginal utility is zero; at this point the total utility is at its peak. With additional units beyond this point, marginal utility becomes negative and total utility begins to grow smaller.

APPLICATIONS OF THE UTILITY THEORY

It is the purpose of the utility approach to explain the behavior of the consumer in forming his demand for goods and services. This behavior is revealed principally in two ways: one, in the law of demand, to the effect that at low prices consumers demand larger amounts of a given good; and two, in the attempt of consumers to maximize their satisfactions with a given expenditure on goods and services.

(1) *The law of demand*

Why do consumers commonly buy more of a commodity at lower prices and less of it at higher prices? In other words, why does the price-demand curve slope downward from left to right? This behavior of the consumer, this price-quantity relation, as we have seen, is called the law of demand; there are two reasons for this law: (a) the income effect and (b) the substitution effect.

Before we discuss these causes we must take care of "other things equal." In considering the law of demand we keep in mind that certain variables are held constant: we assume that there is no change in consumer income; no change in the price of related goods, related as substitutes or complementary goods; no change in consumer tastes; and no expectation that the price of the good low (high) now, will continue to sink (rise). When a period of falling prices of the given commodity is expected, the consumers, far from buying a larger amount of it, may hold back with their purchases of it and wait for further price declines. On such occasions the price-demand curve for nonperishable articles may well slope upward to the right and look like curve *DD* in Figure 3A.

We can turn now to the causes behind the law of demand. First let us see about (a), the *income effect*. Suppose that the price of butter declines. After the weekly purchases of his groceries the consumer is left with more money in his pocket than before the price of butter stepped down. If the price of butter falls from 80¢ a pound to 60¢, the consumer has 20¢ more left. It is as though his income rose by 20¢ a week. He may decide to increase his weekly savings by 20¢, or he may spend this sum on an extra one-third of a pound of butter. In this second case we see the income effect in operation.

Collaborating with the income effect is (b), the *substitution effect*. As the price of butter goes down in relation to the price of other goods, the consumer is apt to substitute it for other goods; he will buy more butter and less of the other goods, the prices of which remain still. Conversely, if the price of butter rises, other commodities, relatively lower priced, may be substituted for butter: less butter will be purchased and more cream or bacon.

It is important to realize that the substitution effect will (almost) invariably induce larger purchases of the article the price of which went down, and compel smaller purchases of it if its price moved up. The income effect, however, will go in the same direction with the substitution effect only if we deal with a *normal* or superior commodity: more of such a commodity will be bought if the consumer's income rises, even as more of it is bought in the wake of a price decline. But if we deal with an *"inferior* good," like bread, potatoes, linoleum, or the cheaper cuts of meat, the income effect may go in reverse: the greater the consumer's income the less of such goods will he buy. In such a case the income effect works in opposition to the substitution effect. However, the substitution effect will do more than wash out the income effect inasmuch as the small drop in the price of one commodity is apt to produce a rather small equivalent rise in income. The result: a feeble income effect, easily overcome by the substitution effect.

The theory of utility helps resolve Adam Smith's famous paradox about the low exchange value of water although "nothing is more useful than water," and the high price of a diamond although "it has scarce any value in use." [2] If there were in existence as few cubic feet of water, because

[2] *Wealth of Nations*, vol. I, p. 25.

of the high cost of producing it, as there are of diamonds, the marginal utility of water would be fantastically high and its price enormous. (We are making the scarcely warranted assumption that society will remain essentially the same under conditions of a phenomenal scarcity of water.) But water is so plentiful because of the low cost of production that, although its total utility reaches great dimensions, its marginal utility is modest indeed. Total utility does not set the price; marginal utility does. If diamonds could be produced at a very low cost and were as abundant as water, they would be worth less, perhaps, than gravel. Children might play with them; but women would regard diamonds as unsuitable for their purposes.

(2) *Maximizing total utility*

The consumer with a given income faces a large number of goods on many or on some of which he will spend his money income per unit of time. We assume that the two or three commodities we talk about on these pages symbolize all the commodities on which he spends his income. We also assume that, by and large, when a person spends his money he allocates his spending among goods and services not in a thoughtless, haphazard manner but with a rough idea of maximizing his total utility. Ordinarily people mean to get the most for their money. If his money income were so large that he could buy all the goods and services he fancies, there would be no problem in converting his money into goods. But his income is limited.

Accordingly, as the consumer buys an assortment of goods and services in the categories of food, clothing, housing, medical care, amusement, and sociability, the more he gets of one good the less he can buy and enjoy of other goods. Too, the goods and services he may buy in large quantities would give him diminishing marginal utility; and the goods he may buy sparingly offer a higher marginal utility. Accordingly, to maximize his total satisfaction from his total income per unit of time, he matches one good against another, he substitutes one good for another good, and he gets more of one good and less of another, until he arrives at the optimum combination which gives him maximum utility, *provided* he spends his whole income. If he spends less than his whole income, we get involved in the problem of saving, and we do not want this complication as yet.

The consumer could not decide on these choices and substitutions if there were no price tag on each good or service. He considers the satisfaction derived from an additional unit of a good, not in a vacuum, but in relation to the market price which he would have to pay for it. Let us assume that the marginal utility of butter—the unit of butter he is barely willing to get—would give him twice as much additional utility as the level of additional utility offered by the extra amount of cheese he is barely inclined to acquire. To maximize his total utility in purchasing these two commodities, he will have to buy such quantities of butter and of cheese that the ratio of the marginal utility of butter to the price of butter equals the same ratio for cheese. If the price of butter is 80¢ a pound and the price of cheese is 40¢, the ratios would be:

$$\frac{2 \text{ utils}}{80} = \frac{1 \text{ util}}{40}.$$

These two fractions tell us that a cent's worth of butter gives the consumer as much utility as a cent's worth of cheese: two utils split 80 ways equal one util split 40 ways. In general, when we divide the marginal utility (in utils) of a good by its price in dollars or cents, we learn how much satisfaction we get from a dollar's worth or from a cent's worth of this commodity.

Our consumer will so distribute his expenditures among the various goods and services that the *last* dollar or dime or cent spent on each good or service brings him the *same* amount of satisfaction. If it were not so, he would find it to his advantage to spend a little less on the good that yields him less satisfaction for the last dollar's worth of it, and use the spared money to buy a little more of another good on which the last dollar spent brought him greater satisfaction. It would pay to transfer his purchases from the goods with a low marginal utility for a dollar's worth to the goods of which he has little and which therefore possess a higher marginal utility.

If, for example, the utility of the last dollar's worth (that is, the marginal utility of a dollar's worth) of the family's meat for the week is 20 utils, whereas the marginal utility of a dollar's worth of a minor article of clothes for Junior is, in the estimation of the decision maker of the family (the housewife) 30 utils, spending less on meat and more on clothes is in order. As this shift in expenditures from meat to clothes proceeds, the marginal utility of a dollar's worth of meat rises because less of it is bought and the marginal utility of a dollar's worth of clothes declines because more of it is bought, until the stage is reached at which the last dollar's worth of either meat or clothes offers a satisfaction of, say, 25 utils. At this stage the total utility obtained from the expenditure of one's income is at a maximum, since no additional utility can be gained by a change in the pattern of expenditures among the various articles and services. Such a stage is called the *equilibrium* position of the consumer, the optimum allocation of his expenditures, meaning that his total satisfaction is maximized. That there is a *second* condition for the maximization of consumer utility will be indicated below, in connection with Table 3.

The same considerations govern the allocation of a person's income between spending and saving. Both have their utility. Saving satisfies the desire to provide for emergencies, for old age, or for the education of the children. It gives one the utility of a sense of security and of a feeling of self-importance. The optimum division between consumption and saving is attained at the point at which a dollar spent on consumption gives as much satisfaction as a dollar laid aside for a rainy day.

Our discussion so far leads us to *one* condition of consumer equilibrium, namely that he must go on buying various goods in various quantities until he is brought to the stage at which the marginal utility of each good he buys bears the same ratio to its market price, so that

$$\frac{MU_a}{P_a} = \frac{MU_b}{P_b} = \cdots \frac{MU_n}{P_n},$$

where MU is the marginal utility; *a, b, n* are the various goods bought; and *P* stands for price. A *second* condition is that he spend his whole income. If he is involuntarily left with unspent money, he does not maximize the total utility from his total income. Besides, as has already been mentioned, the problem of saving would complicate matters. The following problem, in Table 3, will summarize our discussion and will also illustrate the second condition. In column 1 we have the various quantities of the respective goods which the consumer may buy; each of the three other columns indicates the diminishing marginal utility of each good as more and more of it is bought per unit of time, which is one day.

TABLE 3. *Consumer Equilibrium Attained by Maximizing Total Utility of Three Commodities Bought Daily*

Number of units consumed	MARGINAL UTILITY		
	Meat (60¢ a lb.)	Milk (30¢ a qt.)	Bread (20¢ a loaf)
1	130 utils	70 utils	51 utils
2	128	62	50
3	124	60	48
4	120	52	$41\frac{1}{3}$
5	112	45	40

Suppose our consumer buys 4 pounds of meat, 3 quarts of milk, and 5 loaves of bread. The first condition of consumer equilibrium is satisfied, inasmuch as the ratio of the MU to price is the same for each of the three commodities:

$$\frac{120}{60} = \frac{60}{30} = \frac{40}{20} = 2 \text{ utils}$$

for 1¢. To demonstrate that such a combination of purchases maximizes his total utility, let us deviate from this situation and see what happens.

Suppose he buys a pound less of meat and spends the 60¢ thus released on two extra quarts of milk. He loses 120 utils by giving up his fourth pound of meat, and he gains 52 utils from the fourth quart of milk and 45 utils from the fifth quart of milk, 97 utils in all. In addition, the new ratios of utils to price are distorted; they are not equal:

$$\frac{124}{60} \neq \frac{45}{30} \neq \frac{40}{20}.$$

The first condition for maximizing consumer utility is not satisfied.

Let us return to the correct combination. His total expenditure on the package will be:

$$(60¢ \times 4) + (30¢ \times 3) + (20¢ \times 5) = \$4.30.$$

If his daily money income were precisely this amount, the second condition would also be satisfied. The consumer maximizes the total utility from his *total* income. But suppose that his daily income is no more than $3.20?

The difficulty is resolved by trying a combination that will satisfy both conditions. Such a combination is 3 pounds of meat, 2 quarts of milk, and slightly over 4 loaves of bread. The ratios would now be

$$\frac{124}{60} = \frac{62}{30} = \frac{41+}{20} = 2\frac{1}{15}.$$

The total expenditure will be close to $3.20:

$$(60¢ \times 3) + (30¢ \times 2) + (20¢ \times 4) = \$3.20.$$

In actuality, the maximization of satisfaction from one's income often cannot be closely approximated in view of the fact that many commodities are not divisible. We can hardly transfer the purchase of a dollar's worth of house or car to a dollar's worth of radio or refrigerator. Nor can we shift from one type of house to another type or from one make of radio to another make which is superior or inferior in quality or style to the extent of only one dollar's difference in price. Perhaps in the case of a house the difference between one kind of paint and another may amount to one dollar for all the paint used. But the price differences in radios, fur coats, or violins scarcely run as small as one dollar; and nice adjustments in such purchases for the attainment of maximum utility may be out of the question.

(3) *Equal distribution of income*

The theory of utility is at times recruited into service in a realm outside consumer behavior. It is often asserted, on the basis of the principle of utility, that an equal distribution of income would raise the total satisfaction of society.[3] This assertion reflects the assumption that, in the main, people of various strata are much alike in their enjoyment of goods and services, and that with the consumption of several units of a good the marginal utility diminishes for all consumers by equal gradations (a hardly warranted assumption). Since the rich consume many more units of all kinds of goods than do the poor, the marginal utility of real income is much lower to the rich than to the poor. Equalization of income would diminish the consumption of the rich and add to the consumption of the poor. It would take away less satisfaction from the wealthy than it would add to the satisfactions of the poor. Thus in the calculus of marginal utility plus and minus do not cancel out, and the Robin Hood practice of taking from rich Peter to give to poor Paul would result in greater total utility from the same national income. The advocates of this scheme forget that the Peters may lose the incentive to produce much, so that, in the long run, the standard of living will go down for all, the Pauls too.

III. Elasticity of Demand

The demand for a good is a function of price, income, and the price of related goods; that is, the quantities bought will commonly change as the magnitudes of these three determinants change. It is important to the businessman, the statesman, and the economist alike to know what relationship exists between the change in the quantity demanded and the change in the size of the determinant. How responsive is the change in the amount of a good purchased to a change in its price, in incomes, or in the price of related goods? The degree of this sensitiveness the economist calls *elasticity of demand*. Accordingly there are three kinds of demand elasticity: price elasticity, income elasticity, and cross-elasticity.

1. PRICE ELASTICITY OF DEMAND

Price elasticity of demand hinges on the question whether the amounts purchased are very sensitive or only slightly sensitive to changes in the price of an article. A rough answer to this question could be: if a small change in the price of the article occasions a large change in the quantity bought, we have an elastic demand; and if a given price change is followed by a small quantity change, we have an inelastic demand. But what constitutes a small change, and what constitutes a large change? There is a

[3] For a detailed consideration of this question, see A. P. Lerner, *The Economics of Control* (New York, Macmillan, 1944), chap. 3.

reliable rule for the answer to this question. If the total revenue of the firm from the sale of the good after a price decline is larger than the total revenue obtained from the sale before the price decline, the demand is elastic; if the total revenue is smaller, the demand is inelastic; and if the total revenue stays unchanged, the demand has an elasticity of unity. Table 4 illustrates these three possibilities.

TABLE 4. *Price Demand Schedules of Three Commodities*

Commodity *A*, elastic			Commodity *B*, inelastic			Commodity *C*, unitary elasticity		
P	*Q*	*PQ*	*P*	*Q*	*PQ*	*P*	*Q*	*PQ*
10¢	1	10¢	10¢	24	$2.40	10¢	72	$7.20
9	2	18	9	25	2.25	9	80	7.20
8	3	24	8	26	2.08	8	90	7.20

In this table, *P* stands for price, *Q* for the quantity demanded, and *PQ* for the total revenue to the seller. For commodity *A*, the rising total revenue indicates that as the price drops the resulting increase in the amounts purchased more than makes up for the lower price; the change in price is associated with a still greater change in the quantity bought. For this price range, the demand for commodity *A* is therefore elastic. Similarly, the falling total revenue from the sale of commodity *B* as its price weakens, points to an inelastic demand; and the constant total revenue of $7.20 from the sale of commodity *C* tells us that its demand elasticity is unity.

The behavior of total revenue as the criterion of elasticity or inelasticity of demand can be illustrated graphically. Assume that in Figure 4A the price *BF* (= *OG*) *declines to EC* (= *OH*) and that as a result the quantity demanded is enlarged from *OB* to *OC*. At price *BF* and quantity sold *OB* the total revenue is the area of the rectangle *OBFG*. At price *CE* and quantity *OC* the total revenue is the area of the rectangle *OCEH*. The second area is larger than the former area, indicating that the demand is elastic between the points *F* and *E*, that is, between prices *BF* and *CE*. In Figure 4B the area *OCEH*, illustrating total revenue at the reduced price *CE*, is smaller than the area *OBFG*. This pictures an inelastic demand between prices *BF* and *CE*. If elasticity is unity at every price, the demand curve is an equilateral, or rectangular, hyperbola, as in Figure 4C. At every point on this curve the price multiplied by the corresponding quantity will give the same total revenue or area. Thus area *OBFG* is equal to area *OCEH*. To generalize, xy = constant; this is the equation of an equilateral hyperbola.

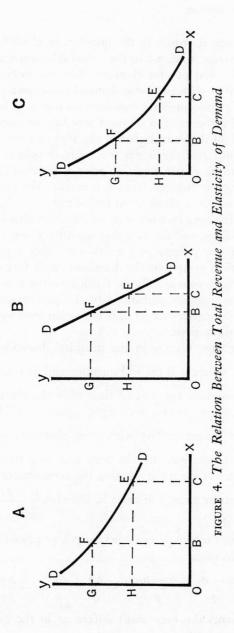

FIGURE 4. The Relation Between Total Revenue and Elasticity of Demand

POINT ELASTICITY OF DEMAND

The total-revenue approach to the question of elasticity is quite satisfactory if our interest is limited to the threefold classification of demand as elastic, inelastic, and of unit elasticity. But our interest goes farther. Among commodities with an elastic demand some have greater elasticity than others, and of two inelastic commodities one may be more inelastic than the other. Furthermore, a demand schedule or curve need not be, and usually is not, of the same degree of elasticity at each price. A demand curve may have different elasticities at its various points. The same commodity may be more elastic when its price is reduced from 90¢ to 89¢ than when its price is reduced from 87¢ to 86¢. We are interested in a measure of the *amount* of elasticity or inelasticity.

We shall look first for a measure of *point elasticity*, that is, of cases where both the price change and the resulting quantity change are very small. We shall achieve our purpose if we first formulate a precise definition of elasticity and then paraphrase the definition into a formula. The precise definition of elasticity runs as follows: elasticity is the ratio of the percentage change in the quantity demanded to the percentage change in the price charged. The paraphrase of this definition into algebraic symbols may proceed in three steps.

(1) The percentage change in the quantity demanded may be presented as $\frac{q - q_1}{q}$, where q is the old quantity and q_1 is the new quantity purchased by consumers per unit of time after the change in price. To obtain the percentage change, we might equally well have put down $\frac{q - q_1}{q_1}$, but since we are dealing with point elasticity, which, to repeat, involves very small changes alike in price and quantity, there is no appreciable difference in the result whether the denominator is q or q_1.

(2) The percentage change in price is, likewise, $\frac{p - p_1}{p}$, where p is the old price and p_1 the new price.

(3) The ratio of the two percentage changes, or price elasticity at point p, produces the formula

$$E = \frac{q - q_1}{q} \div \frac{p - p_1}{p} = -\frac{\Delta q}{q} \div \frac{\Delta p}{p} = -\frac{\Delta q}{\Delta p} \cdot \frac{p}{q},$$

where Δq represents the very small difference in the quantity, and Δp represents the very small difference in the price.

Consider two commodities. When the price drops for both from $12 to $11, the quantity purchased of the first rises from 9 pounds to 10 pounds, and the quantity of the second advances from 10 tons to 11 tons. For the first article we get

$$E = \frac{9 - 10}{9} \div \frac{12 - 11}{12} = -1\frac{1}{3}.$$

For the second article,

$$E = \frac{10 - 11}{10} \div \frac{12 - 11}{12} = -1\frac{1}{5}.$$

Both commodities are elastic, since for both the elasticity is numerically larger than unity; but the first is more elastic than the second because, disregarding the sign, $1\frac{1}{3}$ is larger than $1\frac{1}{5}$.

As we look at the formula

$$E = -\frac{\Delta q}{\Delta p} \cdot \frac{p}{q},$$

we notice that elasticity at a given point on the demand curve depends on the slope of this curve at the given point, or $\Delta q / \Delta p$, and also on the ratio of the old price to the old quantity, or p/q. This tells us that a given demand curve may have different degrees of elasticity at its various points (or prices) even if it has the same slope throughout its length, as it would if it is a straight line.

The measure of price elasticity has a negative sign because a *drop* in

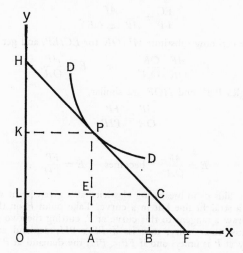

FIGURE 5. *The Geometrical Measure of Price Elasticity*

the price is associated with a *rise* in the quantity demanded, and a rise in the price is accompanied by a drop in the quantity demanded. If the formula for elasticity gives us a figure numerically larger than −1, like −2 or −5, the demand is called elastic; we know then, without stopping to compute, that at the lower price the total revenue obtained from the sale of the commodity rises, and that with a rise in price the total revenue will decline. If the formula gives a fraction of one unit for the answer, the demand is called inelastic; the total revenue from the sale of the good then declines with a decline in price, and rises with a rise in price. If the figure for elasticity is −1, elasticity is unity.

Alfred Marshall [4] suggested a geometrical measure of price elasticity which deserves attention. If we draw, he says, a straight-line demand curve, like *HF* in Figure 5, and consider the elasticity at any point *P* on it, the formula for elasticity at this point is $FP \div PH$, that is, FP/PH. The derivation of this formula is based again on the definition of elasticity, now cast in graphic terms, and on the properties of similar right triangles.[5]

[4] *Principles of Economics*, pp. 102–103, n. 1, and 839–840.
[5] In Figure 5, when the price declines from *AP* to *BC* the quantity demanded rises from *OA* to *OB*. The price change of *KL* (= *EP*) evokes a quantity change of *AB* (= *EC*). Our algebraic formula

$$E = \frac{\Delta q}{\Delta p} \cdot \frac{p}{q}$$

becomes

$$E = \frac{EC}{EP} \cdot \frac{OK}{OA}. \tag{1}$$

Since triangles *PEC* and *PAF* are similar,

$$\frac{EC}{EP} = \frac{AF}{AP \ (= OK)}.$$

In equation (1) we can now substitute *AF/OK* for *EC/EP*, and get

$$E = \frac{AF}{OK} \cdot \frac{OK}{OA}, \quad \text{or} \quad E = \frac{AF}{OA}.$$

Again, since triangles *PAF* and *HOF* are similar,

$$\frac{AF}{OA} = \frac{FP}{PH},$$

and

$$E = \frac{AF}{OA} \quad \text{becomes} \quad E = \frac{FP}{PH}.$$

This formula also aids us in measuring elasticity at a given point when the demand is reflected not in a straight line but in a curve. Take point *P* on the demand curve *DD* in Figure 5. Draw a tangent to this curve at *P*, cutting the two axes at *F* and *H*. If *FP/PH* is greater than unity, that is, if *FP* > *PH*, demand at *P* is elastic; if *FP* = *PH*, elasticity at *P* is unity; and if *FP* < *PH*, the demand at *P* is inelastic.

This brief footnote encounter with Euclid not only provides us with a simple measure of elasticity, but also tends to support the idea, already indicated, that unless it is an equilateral hyperbola a demand curve does not have the same elasticity throughout its length. As far as a straight-line demand curve, such as HF in Figure 5, is concerned, when we move up along this line the index of elasticity consistently rises, because in FP/PH the numerator gains on the denominator. Up to the midpoint of FH the demand is inelastic, inasmuch as $FP/PH < 1$. At the midpoint of FH the elasticity is unity since $FP = PH$. In the upper half of FH demand is elastic because $FP/PH > 1$.

It follows that when we compare the price elasticity of two demand curves we had better make the comparison for the *same* price range. If we compare on one demand curve a point close to the vertical axis (northwest) with a point close to the horizontal axis on another demand curve (southeast), the first curve will be more elastic than the second despite the fact that at the *same* price ranges the first curve is less elastic than the second curve.

ARC ELASTICITY OF DEMAND

Demand schedules with minute changes in prices and quantities are rarely available. Often we face data with appreciable gaps in these two variables; the points on the demand curve are somewhat apart. In such cases the elasticity of demand is not point elasticity but arc elasticity, for the segment of a curve between two points is called an arc. There are a number of formulas for the computation of arc elasticity.

Here too a good starting point for the derivation of a suitable formula is the definition of elasticity. However, figuring the percentage changes, in the price or in the quantity, presents a difficulty absent in the consideration of point elasticity. In point elasticity, q and q_1, the old quantity and the new quantity, and p and p_1, the old price and the new price, do not differ much from each other, and it matters little whether we figure the percentage change as $\Delta q/q$ or $\Delta q/q_1$, as $\Delta p/p$ or $\Delta p/p_1$; the answer will be nearly the same in either case. But it is different when these figures are considerably apart from each other. Suppose the data tell us that at the price of \$10 sales are 100 and at \$9 they are 125. It makes a difference whether we figure the percentage change in quantity as

$$\frac{100 - 125}{100} = 25\%, \quad \text{or as} \quad \frac{100 - 125}{125} = 20\%;$$

and whether we take the price change as

$$\frac{10-9}{10} = 10\%, \quad \text{or as} \quad \frac{10-9}{9} = 11\tfrac{1}{9}\%.$$

A good compromise is found in the use of neither the old nor the new price or quantity for the two denominators but the average of both the old and the new values. Accordingly, the arc elasticity is an *average* elasticity; it is essentially the elasticity of the midpoint between the two given points on the demand curve. Turning to our example, we get, then,

$$E = \frac{\dfrac{100-125}{100+125}}{2} \div \frac{\dfrac{10-9}{10+9}}{2} = -\frac{25}{225} \cdot \frac{19}{1} = -2\tfrac{1}{9}$$

Since in any example of arc elasticity the number 2 will always appear in both denominators and will always cancel out in the computation, the general formula for arc elasticity can be set down as

$$E = \frac{q-q_1}{q+q_1} \div \frac{p-p_1}{p+p_1}.$$

Before closing the discussion of price elasticity it is important to draw attention to two unique examples of it. There is on the one hand *infinite or perfect elasticity* of demand. An infinitesimally small percentage change in price will bring about an infinitely large percentage change in the quantity demanded. Such a demand is reflected in a horizontal straight line parallel to the x axis. It portrays the sales curve of the individual firm in a purely competitive market. At the other extreme is the demand curve of *perfect or infinite inelasticity*. Elasticity approaches zero in this case. Whatever the change in price, up or down, the amount purchased remains unchanged, provided that all the other factors are the same. Such a demand is graphed as a vertical line parallel to the y axis.

2. INCOME ELASTICITY OF DEMAND

Income elasticity of demand measures the responsiveness of the reaction in the quantity of a commodity demanded to a change in consumer income. The definition is the same as for price elasticity, and so are the formulas used; but now instead of price data we substitute income data. Since the differences in the magnitudes affected may be considerable, the arc elasticity formula is more appropriate than the point elasticity formula. If the commodity is "superior" and is purchased in larger amounts as incomes advance, the measure of elasticity is positive. If the commodity is "inferior" and less of it is demanded when income levels mount, the elasticity value will have a negative sign.

3. CROSS-ELASTICITY OF DEMAND

Cross-elasticity of demand resembles price elasticity of demand. We are seeking the ratio of the percentage quantity change of a given commodity A in reaction to the percentage price change of another, related, commodity B. The relationship between A and B may be, as we learned, substitutive or complementary. Suppose the price of butter rises from 80¢ a pound to 90¢. Some people will buy less butter or none at all and will divert their demand to oleomargarine as a substitute. The price of oleo is assumed to remain unvaried, but its sales may now mount from 1,000 tons a week to 1,500 tons. Here commodity A is oleo, and commodity B is butter. What is the cross-elasticity of oleo, the substitute for butter? How strong a substitute for butter is oleo, according to these figures?

The arc elasticity formula is again useful, but it will have a new look, namely

$$E = \frac{x - x_1}{x + x_1} \div \frac{y - y_1}{y + y_1},$$

where x is the old quantity of the given commodity A (oleo in our problem) sold while the price of the related commodity B (butter) was y; and where x_1 is the changed quantity of A demanded when the price of B changed to y_1. Substituting the figures, we get

$$E = \frac{1,000 - 1,500}{1,000 + 1,500} \div \frac{80 - 90}{80 + 90} = 3.4.$$

This value indicates that, all things equal, for the price range of butter from 80¢ to 90¢ a pound, a 1% rise in the price of butter may be expected to lead to a 3.4% rise in the quantity of oleo demanded. Oleo is a good substitute for butter.

If the cross-elasticity of a given commodity A in terms of the price of a related commodity B approaches infinity, it means that A is nearly a perfect substitute for B; that a slight rise in the price of B would cause an enormous swing of custom to A, while the sales of B would dwindle to almost nothing; and that A and B are nearly identical. On the other hand, if the cross-elasticity of oleo were less than 3.4, we would rate oleo as a poorer substitute for butter. Should the cross-elasticity of A in terms of the price of B approach zero, the indication would be that these two commodities are not at all related, that they do not belong in the same industry, and that the firms producing them need not eye each other as competitors. The cross-elasticity of substitute or competitive goods is always a positive value. The quantity of *A* rises and falls as the price of *B* rises and falls.

The same formula does service for *complementary goods*. The difference is that for such goods the cross-elasticity always comes out with a negative sign. As the price for fountain pens declines and more fountain pens are demanded, the sale of fountain-pen ink will mount even though its price is unchanged. Fountain pens and fountain-pen ink are complementary and the sales of the latter move with the sales of the former; and since both vary *inversely* with the price of the former, the cross-elasticity is negative.

Cross-elasticity is not a two-way street. The cross-elasticity of sugar with respect to coffee is not necessarily the same as the cross-elasticity of coffee with respect to sugar. Let the price of coffee decline 1%. More coffee will be drunk and more sugar will be consumed. Let us assume that the amount of sugar purchased rises 2%, hence that the cross-elasticity of sugar with respect to coffee is 2. Now let us assume that the price of sugar falls by 1%, the price of coffee staying unchanged. It does not follow that the amount of coffee enjoyed will rise 2%, giving us a cross-elasticity of 2 for coffee in relation to sugar.

Similarly with the cross-elasticity of substitutes. The cross-elasticity of oleo with regard to butter may not be the same as the cross-elasticity of butter in relation to oleo. When butter declines in price by 1% the sales of oleo may fall by ½%. But when the price of oleo declines by 1% the sales of butter may fall by only ⅓%.

THE IMPORTANCE OF PRICE ELASTICITY OF DEMAND

The problem of price elasticity of demand is of considerable significance in various situations, some of which we shall briefly summarize now.

(1) If a *sales tax* is levied on some domestic good with an elastic demand, the resulting higher price to the buyer may induce him to curtail drastically the purchase of it and thus may depress total revenue from the tax to the government and to the selling firm alike. In this case the incidence of the sales tax may be on the seller. But if the demand for certain goods is strongly inelastic, the sales tax may fall largely on the consumer, because the higher price will not, in this case, appreciably reduce the amount purchased by him.

(2) A successful *strike* for higher wage rates may result in a higher price to the consumer. If the demand for the product involved is elastic, sales may plummet downward, and some of the workers may lose their

jobs.

(3) We cannot stop here and try to analyze the complex problems of *international trade*, but we can state that elasticity of demand (also of supply) plays a heavy role in exports and imports, in terms of trade, in the effect of tariffs, and in the balance of payments.

(4) As we shall see when discussing *monopoly discrimination*, the degree of elasticity of demand is of substantial importance in pricing the same goods in two markets.

(5) Elasticity of demand is influential in the price-setting for the services of *public utilities*. The demand for electricity, for instance, by households is inelastic because convenient substitutes are scarcely available. The demand by business firms, however, is less inelastic: they can threaten to shift to coal power, water power, or oil. Accordingly the public utilities are allowed by the public utility commissions to charge the households a high price and set a lower price to business firms for a unit of electricity.

(6) If the demand for *corn* is inelastic, a large crop will dictate a precipitously reduced price to the consumer, so that total revenue to the farmers may be less than from a smaller crop. Not so if the demand for corn is elastic.

(7) One of the main objectives of *advertising* is to render the demand for the product less and less elastic with the consequence that if the price of the good is advanced, sales will not nose-dive punitively.

It may be worth while to close our discussion of elasticity of demand with an attempt at a few generalizations.

(1) A commodity will be of elastic demand if there are good *substitutes for it*. A small rise in the price of the given article will send buyers to the substitutes; a lower price will invite the patronage of the former buyers of substitute products.

(2) A *necessity* that has no substitutes will have an inelastic demand; the consumers will buy almost a fixed quantity of it per unit of time whether the price is somewhat higher or lower. But here, too, if there are substitutes the demand for the necessary good may be elastic. Bread is a necessity, but if the consumer can turn to whole-wheat bread, to oatmeal bread, or to corn bread, the demand for each of these kinds of bread is likely to be elastic.

(3) A commodity that constitutes a *small fraction* of a total expenditure on a rather expensive good is apt to be inelastic. Doorknobs are an example: a lower price of doorknobs will not stimulate more house-building or the demand for doors. However, if there is a variety of doorknobs, differing in the material that went into them or in their appearance, the demand for them may be less inelastic: here too, the demand for the object is governed in part by the availability of substitutes.

(4) *Inexpensive* goods, like matches, salt, toothpicks, needles, or a glass of beer, are apt to be inelastic; a lower price on these will not generate an impressive increment in sales; nor will a higher price shrink the sales appreciably.

(5) In the *long run* many a good may become more elastic than it is in the short run. If the price of the good goes up, the consumer needs time to change his habits, to make adjustments in his budget, and to find an acceptable substitute. If the price of the good is lowered, more people learn about this with the passage of time, and sales may be progressively enlarged.

(6) An object that has *several kinds of uses* is apt to be elastic. For each single use the demand may be inelastic, so that when the price of the object goes down, only a little more is purchased for each use; but when these small uses are added up they may constitute, percentage-wise, a substantial rise in the total amount demanded. A 5% fall in the price of water may be followed by increases in its use of 1% in cooking, 1% in drinking, 2% in the bathroom, 3% in sprinkling the lawn, and 1% in household laundering. The 5% drop in the price of water brought about an 8% rise in the amount of it purchased in a given unit of time.

(7) An article may be inelastic in face of a *small* drop in its price, but may become elastic in the wake of a *large* drop. When the price descends a little, none but the old customers may be in the market and they may buy a little more of the commodity. But when a serious dip in price takes place, new customers may appear to whom the marginal utility of this object is low, and who will step in as buyers only when the price becomes low enough to match their sluggish taste for it.

(8) In general, the *lower part*, the southeast part, of a price demand curve may be inelastic, whereas the upper part of it, the northwest part, is likely to be elastic. It is a matter of arithmetic. The lower segment of a demand curve represents low hypothetical prices associated with relatively large hypothetical quantities of a given article. Assume that the low price is a dollar and the related large hypothetical quantity of the article is 1,000 units. A small absolute change in the low price constitutes a large *percentage* change; an absolute change of, say, 950 units instead of 1,000 units stands for a relatively small change percentage-wise. We have then a small percentage change in quantity responding to a relatively large percentage change in price. Similarly with the demand-elasticity in the upper segment of a demand curve. A geometric demonstration of a case like this revolves around Figure 5, page 65.

We may close this discussion of price elasticity of demand with the observation that whenever we deal with two quantitative economic phenomena causally related, we may import the concept of elasticity to put a sharper edge on this causal relation. For example, we can state that savings are interest-inelastic; that sales of tobacco or of cosmetics are advertising-elastic; that the supply of labor in the coal-mining industry is wage-inelastic within a certain wage range, say, between 10 and 15 dollars a day.

SUGGESTED READINGS

Bain, J. S. *Pricing, Distribution, and Employment*, revised ed., chap. 2. New York, Holt, 1953.

Boulding, K. E. *Economic Analysis*, revised ed., chap. 29. New York, Harper, 1948.

Friedman, M. "The Marshallian Demand Curve," *Journal of Political Economy*, vol. LVII (December, 1949), pp. 463–495.

Leftwich, R. H. *The Price System and Resource Allocation*, revised ed., chaps. III and IV. New York, Holt, Rinehart and Winston, 1960.

Marshall, A. *Principles of Economics*, 8th ed., Book III. New York, Macmillan, 1927.

Morgenstern, O. "Demand Theory Reconsidered," *Quarterly Journal of Economics*, vol. LXII (February, 1948), pp. 165–201.

Norris, Ruby T. *The Theory of Consumer's Demand*. New Haven: Yale University Press, 1941.

Schultz, H. *The Theory and Measurement of Demand*. chaps. 2–6. Chicago, University of Chicago Press, 1938.

Stigler, G. J. *The Theory of Price*, revised ed., chap. 4. New York, Macmillan, 1952.

Viner, J. "The Utility Theory and Its Critics," *Journal of Political Economy*, vol. XXXIII (August, 1925), pp. 369–387.

IV Demand: Indifference-Curve Analysis

THE FORMULATIONS based on utility constitute one approach to the study of consumer behavior. Economics has developed a second approach, embodied in the framework of indifference curves. The first and traditional viewpoint stresses the utility which the consumer finds in the various units of a given commodity. The newer approach uses as its basis the consumer's preferences among various goods. One combination of goods is as satisfactory as, or is preferred to, another combination of goods.

The indifference theory neither denies the reality of utility nor refuses to bring utility into analysis. It merely frames the argument in a context that does not call for the measurement of utility. It does not ask how much utility the consumer sees in 5 apples. It asks instead which bundle of goods offers a greater total utility: a combination of 5 apples and 3 oranges or a combination of 4 apples and 4 oranges? We do not know how to express the utility of a good in *cardinal* terms (one, two, three) as so many units of utility. But, the new theory insists, the consumer can deal with *ordinal* (first, second, third) terms, by stating that 5 apples rank first in comparison with 4 apples and that one combination of apples and oranges has greater total utility than another combination of apples and oranges.

I. Indifference Curves

To understand the demand for goods and consumer equilibrium from this new viewpoint, it is necessary first to become acquainted with certain types of curves as tools of analysis.

ISO-UTILITY CURVES

A good starting point may be the concept of consumer indifference curves. Consider a consumer who wants to buy apples and oranges, commodities honored by usage as examples in economic literature. He is not set on buying arbitrarily a fixed amount of apples and a fixed amount of oranges. He knows that one combination of apples and oranges may give him as much total utility as another combination of fewer apples and more oranges, or yet another combination of more apples and fewer oranges. He cannot tell how much utility he obtains from an apple or from an orange but he has a scale of preferences as between apples and oranges, so that he can tell how the satisfaction derived from one bagful of apples and oranges compares with the satisfaction given by another bagful. He knows what substitutions of apples for oranges or of oranges for apples will leave him equally satisfied.

Our consumer, out to purchase fruit, has in mind an *indifference schedule*, a schedule of various combinations of apples and oranges which would yield him the *same* total satisfaction. Thus, in the schedule in Table 5,

TABLE 5. *Indifference Schedule of Apples and Oranges*

(1)	(2)	(3)	(4)	(5)
			Marginal rate of substitution, apples for oranges	Marginal rate of substitution, oranges for apples
Combination	Apples	Oranges		
1	15	0		1 : 5
2	10	1	5 : 1	1 : 4
3	6	2	4 : 1	1 : 3
4	3	3	3 : 1	1 : 2
5	1	4	2 : 1	1 : 1
6	0	5	1 : 1	

he obtains as much total utility from 10 apples and 1 orange as from 6 apples and 2 oranges, 1 apple and 4 oranges, and other combinations. From the standpoint of satisfaction, it is a matter of indifference to him whether he buys the first combination, the second, or any of the other combinations. Hence the name *indifference curve*. In the fourth combination, 3 apples and 3 oranges, the desirability of an apple is greater than the desirability of an apple in the second combination, 10 apples and 1 orange. But the total satisfaction is the same in both combinations.

If we plot the schedule in Table 5 we get an indifference curve, like curve 1 in Figure 6. On the *x* axis are measured the oranges and on the *y* axis the apples. Point *A* marks the second combination, 10 apples and 1 orange; point *B* illustrates the combination of 3 apples and 3 oranges; and so on. Any point on this curve represents a composite of so many apples and so many oranges which give the consumer the same total satisfaction.

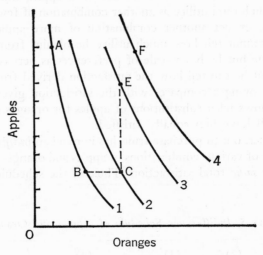

FIGURE 6. *A Map of Indifference Curves*

The curve is the locus of all combinations of two goods which provide a particular consumer with the *same* total utility per unit of time. It is a curve of equal utility, an iso-utility curve.[1]

Our consumer may want to increase his purchase of fruit because his tastes changed or for another reason. His first combination may then be 15 apples and 1 orange or 16 apples and no oranges or 16 apples and 2 oranges, and similarly with the succeeding combinations. When we plot such new indifference schedules we obtain new consumer indifference curves, like curves 2, 3, and 4 in Figure 6. Curve 2 pictures at each point a combination of either more apples or more oranges than a corresponding point on curve 1. Point *C* on curve 2 stands for the same number of apples but it represents more oranges. Curve 3 similarly portrays at each point a larger combination than either curve 1 or curve 2. Point *E* on curve 3 indicates as many oranges as point *C* on curve 2 but it designates

[1] *Iso* is a Greek word meaning "the same, equal."

more apples than point C. Any point on a curve to the right represents greater total satisfaction than any point on a curve to the left, inasmuch as any point on a curve to the right of a given curve represents more oranges, like point C; or more apples, like point E; or more of both apples and oranges, like point F on curve 4 in comparison with point E on curve 3.

We assume that consumers get more satisfaction from a combination in which there is the same amount of one good plus more of the other good. It follows that a curve to the right reflects a larger total utility than a curve to the left. It follows, too, that the curves cannot cross each other or be tangent to each other at a given point. If a curve were tangent to its neighbor on the left, it would represent at its various nontangency points more apples or oranges than at the point of tangency. It would mean then that a combination with a larger number of apples or oranges offers the same total satisfaction as a combination of a smaller number of apples or oranges.

Each iso-utility curve expresses three dimensions: so many apples; so many oranges; and the constant total utility along a given curve. Thus three dimensions are handled on a flat surface and not on a solid. Two dimensions, apples and oranges, are variable; the third dimension, total utility, is held the same *along* each curve. However, as we go from one iso-utility curve to another or as we look at the whole family of iso-utility curves, as in Figure 6, we comprehend variation in this dimension as well: each curve to the right has a higher total utility. A family of such curves reminds us of the weather maps showing the lines of equal pressure or the contour lines on a topographical map. It may be well to note that an iso-utility curve *close* to the origin deals with *small* amounts of apples and oranges, therefore with small total utility. Curves *distant* from the origin reveal the opposite: more apples and more oranges.

THE MARGINAL RATE OF SUBSTITUTION (MRS)

Let us take a good look at any indifference curve in Figure 6. We notice that it possesses two attributes: (1) it slopes to the right and (2) it is convex to the origin. Why? The answer in either case is traced to the concept of *substitution*.

(1) Why does the indifference curve slope to the right? When a consumer buys more oranges and fewer apples, without changing his total utility from these two fruits, he is substituting oranges for apples. When we are willing to part with 3 apples for 1 additional orange we can say that one orange is a substitute for 3 apples. Likewise, when we

state generally that oranges are a substitute for apples we mean that so many apples are given up in exchange for one extra orange. When we substitute commodity x (measured along the x axis) for commodity y we mean that without changing total satisfaction, we buy more of commodity x at the sacrifice of getting less of commodity y: we appoint x to substitute for y, to take the place of y.

We can now turn to the question put at the beginning of the preceding paragraph, namely: why does the indifference curve slope to the right? The different combinations represented by a given indifference schedule (Table 5) or indifference curve (Figure 6) are successive substitutions of oranges for apples. To get one more orange, the consumer diminishes the purchase of apples. With each additional orange there is associated a further drop in the number of apples, so that the same total satisfaction is maintained. To generalize, since with each extention of x (oranges) there is a drop in y (apples), the points on the curve simultaneously go down as they move to the right. The curve slopes to the right.

(2) Why is the indifference curve convex to the origin? To answer this question we need first to examine the rate of substitution of oranges for apples. As we read columns 2 and 3 in Table 5 we notice the following substitutions: to get one orange, the consumer is ready to part with 5 apples (15 — 10); to get a second orange, he is ready to part with another 4 apples (10 — 6); to get a third orange, he is willing to go without 3 other apples; and to obtain a fourth orange, he is forgoing 2 more apples. For each additional orange the consumer is willing to abandon a declining number of apples, and experience each time the same total satisfaction per unit of time.

This brings us to the concept of the marginal rate of substitution (MRS). The meaning of this concept depends of course on whether we substitute x (oranges) for y (apples) or y for x. If we substitute oranges for apples, MRS refers to the various quantities of apples that will be given up for each increment of *one* orange. In this case the MRS is identical with the slope of the indifference curve at a given point. We can therefore write

$$MRS = \text{slope} = \frac{-\Delta y}{\Delta x}$$

where y is apples and x is oranges. Column 4 in Table 5 illustrates this situation. However, if we are substituting y for x, apples for oranges, MRS means the number of oranges given up by the consumer for each *one* additional apple; in this case,

$$MRS = \frac{-\Delta x}{\Delta y}.$$

As we see, this last fraction is the reciprocal of the slope at the various points on the curve. Column 5, Table 5, illustrates this condition.

It is significant to observe that a given indifference schedule tells us not only about the MRS of x for y but also about the MRS of y for x. All we need to do is to read the schedule from the bottom upward. As we read in this order columns 2 and 3 in Table 5, we see that our consumer finds it equally satisfactory to gain one apple at the expense of one orange $(5 - 4)$; that he is willing to obtain two additional apples $(3 - 1)$ in exchange for 1 orange $(4 - 3)$, or 1 apple for $\frac{1}{2}$ orange; that beyond this stage he would barter 3 more apples for one more orange, or 1 apple for $\frac{1}{3}$ orange; then 4 more apples for another orange, or 1 apple for $\frac{1}{4}$ orange; and finally 5 apples for 1 orange, or 1 apple for $\frac{1}{5}$ orange. The MRS of apples for oranges ranges from 1 apple for 1 orange to one apple for $\frac{1}{5}$ orange, as is indicated in column 5. We understand of course that in all the above substitutions total satisfaction stays fixed.

This may be the proper spot to underscore once more the idea that if consumers could buy all the apples and all the oranges and all the other goods that their fancy suggested, there would be no such thing as an iso-utility curve: the consumer would not be compelled to sacrifice some units of commodity A in exchange for an additional unit of commodity B. The indifference curve is a phenomenon born of scarcity. No scarcity no economics, at least as we know it.

As we proceed with the successive combinations of apples and oranges in Table 5 we notice that the MRS (columns 4 and 5) keeps on declining; from 5 apples for the first orange the rate falls to 1 apple for the fifth orange (column 4); and from 1 orange for the first apple to $\frac{1}{5}$ orange for the fifth apple (column 5, read from bottom upward). As the consumer finds himself with more and more oranges and fewer and fewer apples he is willing to give up fewer apples for yet another orange; and equally, as he acquires more and more apples and finds himself with a smaller number of oranges he is inclined to surrender fewer oranges for an extra apple. This phase of consumer behavior is described as the principle of *diminishing marginal rate of substitution* (MRS).

We can now resolve the question why iso-utility curves are normally convex. The answer turns on the *diminishing* MRS. As x is substituted for y, x is extended by equal increments but y falls by ever *smaller* amounts. As the points on the indifference curve move to the right by equal distances they drop in height less and less. The slopes grow smaller toward the right; and tangents drawn to successive points on the curve become progressively less steep. As the consumer gains more and more units of article x he is inclined to part with less and less of article y in exchange for an additional unit of x. A curve of such attributes is a convex curve. When we draw a staircase descending to the right in which the steps are of equal width but their height diminishes from the top down, the curve fitting such a staircase is convex (seen from beneath), as in Figure 7A.

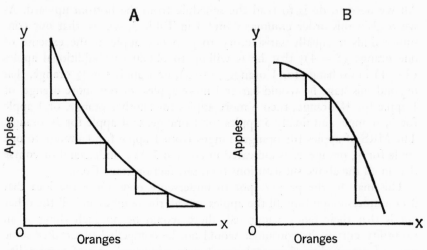

FIGURE 7. *Convex* (A) *and Concave* (B) *Iso-Utility Curves*

There are exceptions to this behavior of the MRS; but they are very scarce. When a stamp collector begins to near the point of possessing the largest collection of one certain category of stamps, say, a certain stamp issued by the Infracrania Kingdom in 1870–1880, he is ready to part with more and more of other things to acquire each stamp that brings him closer to the goal.

The indifference curve for such a consumer is concave to the origin, as in Figure 7B. Here, in the staircase, the horizontal lines are again all of the same length, representing equal increments of *x*. But the vertical bars grow longer as they go down to the right. The curve which connects the points is concave to the origin. Its slopes become greater as we move downward; and tangents to its points, as we move to the right, grow steeper. In contrast, the vertical bars in Figure 7A grow smaller. A curve like this is convex.

SUBSTITUTES AND COMPLEMENTARY GOODS

Let us tie together some of the elementary features of the slope of an indifference curve. The slope of a curve at a given point is either $-\Delta y/\Delta x$

or the tangent of the angle formed by the x axis and the line tangent to the curve at this given point. In Figure 8, the slope of curve DD at point

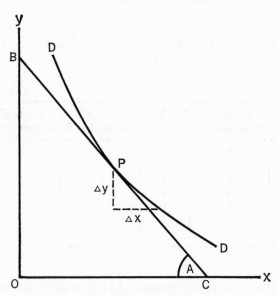

FIGURE 8. *The Relation Between MRS and the Slope of an Iso-Utility Curve*

P is $-\Delta y/\Delta x$ or else the tangent of angle A, namely BO/OC. We can see that $-\Delta y/\Delta x$ is the marginal rate of substitution of x for y: to acquire one more unit of x, we must give up a certain amount of y; y is the price of x, or the cost of x. When the slope of an indifference curve is steeper $-\Delta y/\Delta x$ is larger, disregarding the minus sign, pointing to a larger MRS: more of y will be given up for the gain of an extra unit of x; x substitutes for more y.

Contrariwise, the smaller the slopes of the indifference curve, or the flatter the curve, the lower is the MRS: to obtain one extra unit of x, we give up *little* of y; x substitutes for little of y; x is priced low in terms of y. This means that the two commodities forming the various combinations are good *substitutes* for one another. The limiting case of flat curves is a straight line, like BC in Figue 8. On a straight-line indifference curve, the slopes stay identical at all points and the MRS is constant for all the combinations of the two goods represented by the straight line. A straight-line indifference curve suggests that the two goods are perfect substitutes; and a straight-line indifference curve at an angle of 45 degrees with either

axis tells us that the two commodities consistently exchange for each other
in a ratio of one to one; that they are in fact one and the same commodity
in the thought of the consumer.

Table 6 illustrates this situation. We substitute commodity A for com-

TABLE 6. *Indifference Schedules of Two Commodities as Perfect
Substitutes for One Another*

(1)	(2)	(3)	(4)	(5)	(6)
Units of commodity A	Units of commodity B	MRS of A for B	Units of commodity B	Units of commodity A	MRS of B for A
0	7	1	1	6	1
1	6	1	2	5	1
2	5	1	3	4	1
3	4	1	4	3	1
4	3	1	5	2	1
5	2	1	6	1	
6	1		7	0	

modity B, holding total utility constant. As is seen in the first two columns,
we add one unit of A at the sacrifice (at the price) of one unit of B
(second row); then we add again one unit of A at the sacrifice of another
unit of B: we have now two units of A and 5 units of B; and so on. In
such a case the MRS of A for $B = \dfrac{-B}{A} = -1$. If we plot the indifference
curve as exemplified by the first two columns of Table 6, with units of
A along the x axis and units of B along the vertical, we get a straight line
sloping downward from left to right, similar to line BC in Figure 8. The
slope of this line stays unchanged throughout; it is -1. Accordingly
the MRS of A for B is constant; it is -1, consistently.

Now let us see what happens when we substitute article B for article
A; we are acquiring more and more of B at the expense of A. We derive
the new indifference schedule in columns 4 and 5 by *reading* respectively
columns 1 and 2 from the bottom upward and *transcribing* the figures
as usual, from top to bottom; the bottom figures go to the top, the figures
next to the bottom figures are transcribed next to the top figure, and so
on. The MRS of B for A is again 1: as we get one unit more of B (column
4, $2-1$) we go without one unit of A (column 5, $6-5$), and so on
down. We see, then, that the two commodities are not only *perfect* substitutes but, exchanging as they are doing on a one-to-one basis, they harbor an additional relation to each other. The straight line representing the

indifference curve expressed in the first two columns is a line making a
45 degree angle with either axis. It follows that commodities *A* and *B* are
not only perfect substitutes; they are *identical*.

Let us look into two unique-appearing types of curves.

(1) As was stated in the preceding chapter, two goods are complementary if the acquisition of more units of one good compels the consumer to purchase more units of the other good. For extremely complementary goods the indifference curves have a *unique* appearance. They
are straight lines with a right angle bent convex to the origin, as in Figure
9. In these curves, the vertical line tells us that no reduction in commodity

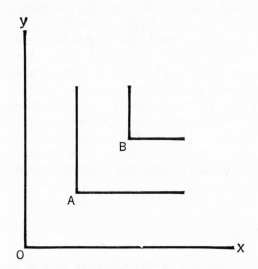

FIGURE 9. *Indifference Curves of Complementary Goods*

Y will encourage even a slight increment in commodity *X*: otherwise we
would have, not a vertical line, but a line sloping downward from left to
right. Similarly with the horizontal line. Only at point *A* are the two goods
bought in the given ratio. At point *B* more of each of these goods is
bought. If the two goods are not of extreme complementarity, the curves
in Figure 9 would have a sharp curvature near *A* and near *B*, instead of the
right angles (why?). A little more is said on complementary goods and
substitutes in the last page or two of Chapter IX.

Point *A* indicates complete complementariness of the two commodities
represented by the distances of point *A* from the two axes. Only at point
A will the two goods make a desirable combination—like the right and left

glove. Every point on the vertical line above point A has the same horizontal distance away from the vertical axis as point A has, but, of course, it is not at the same vertical distance as A is. Such a combination of two commodities would be ill-mated; and it would make no sense for the consumer to buy one right glove and, say, 5 or more left gloves, depending on the location of the point on the vertical line. The same reasoning applies with regard to any point on the horizontal line beginning to the right of point A and moving on to the right. We may come out with a combination of one left glove and 10 right gloves. Point B indicates a doubling of point A: 2 pairs of gloves.

(2) There is another type of indifference curves which can hardly lay claim to represent normal or typical behavior by the consumer. An example of this second type is a horizontal line *parallel* to the x axis. Such a line would indicate that the consumer has, to begin with, a fixed amount of commodity Y, equal to the height of this horizontal line. But he is completely indifferent whether commodity X (combined with this Y) amounts to zero, or to *any* small number of units, or to *any* large number of units. Similarly with an indifference curve in the form of a vertical line parallel to the y axis. Such a line would suggest that the consumer enjoys a fixed amount of commodity X, namely the amount equal to the fixed distance between this vertical line and the y axis. But he is completely neutral as to the amount of commodity Y that may be combined with the fixed commodity X: the amount may be zero, or any small number, or any large number.

THE TOTAL-OUTLAY CURVE

We shall now consider a second important type of curve, the total-outlay curve, which is also called the price line, expenditure curve, budget line, and line of attainable combinations.

By a total-outlay curve we mean a curve on which the points represent the various combinations of two goods, each bought at the market price, that can be purchased with a *given* amount of money. We assume (1) that the consumer spends on the two goods an invariable sum of money, and (2) that the prices of the two goods are given and remain uninfluenced by his purchases of these goods.

Suppose that a consumer wishes to spend 40¢ on apples and oranges, and that apples sell at 4¢ each and oranges at 5¢. What are the various combinations of these two fruits which he can buy? If he spends the whole sum on apples only, he can get 10 apples; if only on oranges, he can get 8 oranges. Let OA stand, in Figure 10, for 10 apples and OB for 8 oranges. The line AB represents all possible combinations of apples and oranges that can be purchased for 40¢ at the cited prices. Thus point C indicates 9 apples and 0.8 orange, point D represents 5 apples and 4 oranges. A combination suggested by any point not on this line would cost more than 40¢, or less.

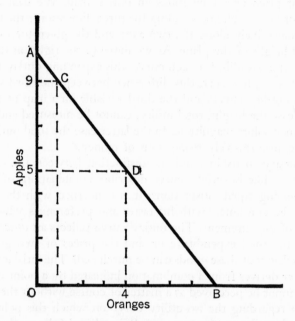

FIGURE 10. *Price Line Showing Various Combinations of Two Articles That Can Be Bought with a Fixed Outlay*

The idea that any point on line AB reflects a combination of apples and oranges which involves an expenditure of 40¢ is not self-evident. We are sure only that points A and B do so. That the other points on the line are of the same character needs to be demonstrated.[2]

[2] To generalize, we can write the equation

$$XP_x + YP_y = S,$$

where X and Y are the two commodities, P_x and P_y their respective prices, and S the total fixed sum spent on the various combinations of these two commodities. That this equation describes a straight line such as AB in Figure 10 can be seen from either one of the two following equations, derived from it. Solving for Y, we get

$$Y = \frac{S - XP_x}{P_y} = \frac{S}{P_y} - \frac{P_x}{P_y}X.$$

This equation is an equation of a straight line, with S/P_y as the y intercept and $-P_x/P_y$ as the slope.

If the consumer wishes to spend a larger sum on apples and oranges, and this normally occurs when his income rises, the total-outlay curve will shift to the right of AB and will be parallel to it. The same is true of a new outlay curve portraying the situation in which the total sum spent stays constant but the prices of apples and oranges drop by the same percentage. A family of price lines constitutes an outlay map. We deal once more with contour lines, each line standing for three dimensions: the two goods, measured respectively along the two axes, and the given total outlay, the unindicated height of the plane. As we move to the right on the map the total outlay rises steadily for each curve; this expanding outlay is the *third* variable. There is, however, this difference between the third variable on a map of iso-utility curves and the third variable on a map of price lines. In the first case the height, total utility, cannot be measured and is not expressed as an absolute magnitude. In the latter case the total outlays represent definite, progressively rising sums of money.

It is necessary to fix in mind the distinction between the two fundamental curves. The iso-utility curve describes combinations of two commodities yielding equal satisfactions. It is concerned with the *subjective* attitude of the consumer, with his tastes and preferences which are not susceptible of measurement. The outlay curve reflects an *objective* problem: given the total expenditure on and the prices of two goods, what different packages of these goods can be purchased? The satisfaction which the consumer derives from a combination indicated by a point on the outlay curve cannot be perceived as a matter of course without the additional information regarding the iso-utility curve on which this point lies. Let us look ahead to Figure 11 on page 88. Points F and C lie on the same outlay curve AB. But point F mirrors a greater total utility, inasmuch as it lies on the higher iso-utility curve 2, whereas point C belongs to the lower iso-utility curve 1. The different combinations on an outlay curve do not reflect the same total utilities; the different combinations on an iso-utility curve do not reflect the same outlays.

MRS AND MARKET EXCHANGE RATE

The steepness of a price line depends on the relation to each other of the prices of the two goods. In Figure 10, the slope of price line $AB = \tan B = OA/OB = 10/8 = 5/4$. The lower the price of apples or the higher

Solving for X, we get

$$X = \frac{S - YP_y}{P_x} = \frac{S}{P_x} - \frac{P_y}{P_x}Y.$$

We recognize that the intercepts S/P_y and S/P_x correspond respectively to OA and OB in Figure 10.

the price of oranges the greater the slope of line AB and the steeper AB is. From the given prices of these fruits, we see that 5 apples cost as much as 4 oranges; and that to acquire one more orange entails the surrender of $1\frac{1}{4}$ apples, if the total outlay of 40¢ is not to change. In the market, the exchange rate of apples and oranges is in inverse ratio to their prices. The *higher* the price of commodity A in relation to the price of commodity B, the smaller is the amount of A offered in exchange, in substitution, of A for a unit of B. By parting with $\frac{5}{4}$ apples the consumer spares enough money to acquire one more orange; 5 apples buy 4 oranges. The MRS of oranges for apples means, as we know, the ratio of apples given up $(-\Delta y)$ for one extra orange (Δx). To condense,

$$\text{MRS of oranges for apples} = \frac{-\Delta y}{\Delta x} = \frac{\text{price of } x}{\text{price of } y} = \frac{5}{4}$$

$$= \text{market exchange rate.}$$

The concept MRS applies to both types of curves, the iso-utility curve and the outlay curve; and in both it equals $\Delta y / \Delta x$, minus sign disregarded. For the outlay curve,

$$\text{MRS of oranges for apples} = \frac{\text{price of } x}{\text{price of } y}.$$

Since the outlay curve is a straight line, the MRS is constant; it is always 5 : 4 in our example of apples and oranges, priced at 4¢ and 5¢ respectively. Should the price of apples and oranges be identical, the outlay curve would be a straight line making with either axis an angle of 45 degrees; the exchange rate in the market would be one apple for one orange; and the MRS would be the constant 1 : 1 ratio. The MRS of the iso-utility curve, however, changes, as we have seen, from point to point; we deal with a diminishing MRS.

II. Analysis of Demand

So far we have been preparing the tools for the new approach to consumer behavior. We are now ready to use them: indifference curves can be applied in the exposition of various phases of demand without the need to measure utility.

The first problem is to explain price demand, which was explored in the preceding chapter in the perspective of utility theory. This job involves two steps: (1) the maximizing of satisfaction with a given total expenditure on two commodities the prices of which are specified; and (2) the nature of the price-consumption line.

Assume, as before, that the consumer wants to spend a total of 40¢ on apples and oranges priced, respectively, at 4¢ and 5¢ each. The question is: what combination of apples and oranges will give him maximum satisfaction? In Figure 11, the total-outlay curve *AB* tells us that a combination

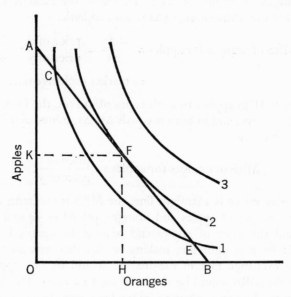

FIGURE 11. *The Optimum Combination of Two Commodities Purchased with a Given Outlay*

suggested by any point on it will cost 40¢. The indifference map, that is, the iso-utility curves 1, 2, and 3, tells another story. Any combination of apples and oranges on curve 1 offers less total satisfaction than any combination on curve 2; and similarly as we move to curve 3. The consumer, to repeat, is supposed to seek the highest satisfaction for his 40¢. Which combination he can *afford* to buy is indicated by the total-outlay curve *AB*. Which combination he will actually *choose* is indicated by the point common to both an iso-utility curve and the given outlay line.

Such a point is the point of tangency of the indifference curve 2 and line *AB*; it is point *F*. This point indicates that the combination of *OK* apples (5 apples) and *OH* oranges (4 oranges) will give him the greatest satisfaction. Why point C or E (both of which are points of *intersection* of the outlay line and curve 1) is not the best choice will be explained shortly. Curve 3 traces combinations of apples and oranges yielding greater total utility than the combination symbolized by point F; but any combination on curve 3 costs more than 40¢. Point F represents the optimum purchase, the equilibrium position of the consumer. At this point the consumer maximizes his satisfaction. Any other choice is either less desirable or more costly.

It is important to notice that this explanation of how a consumer maximizes his total satisfaction rests on his *relative* preferences for various units of goods, and not on the idea of marginal utility which cannot be measured. It is one thing to *compare* utilities; it is another thing to try to measure an absolute utility. To repeat, ordinal utility is easier to get at than cardinal utility.

Since the indifference curve 2 and the total-outlay curve AB are tangent to each other at F, point F is common to both of them. The slopes of these two curves at point F are identical; and this common slope can be measured in two ways. *First*, as the slope of *indifference* curve 2 at point F, it is the MRS of x for y; and like any slope on a negatively inclined curve, it (MRS) equals $-\Delta y/\Delta x$. This slope can be measured numerically from an indifference schedule which provides the data for iso-utility curve 2. See, for instance, Table 5, at the beginning of this chapter, where the MRS is indicated in the last two columns. *Second*, the slope of the *outlay curve AB* at F (as at any other point on AB) equals the market exchange rate of the two goods, oranges for apples, or the ratio

$$\frac{\text{price of } x \text{ (oranges)}}{\text{price of } y \text{ (apples)}} = \frac{5}{4}$$

or 5 apples for 4 oranges. We arrive at the general proposition that the maximum consumer satisfaction from a given expenditure on two goods is attained when

$$\text{MRS (of } x \text{ for } y) \text{ on the iso-utility curve} = \frac{\text{price of } x}{\text{price of } y};$$

when, that is, the MRS on the iso-utility curve equals the exchange rate, or the price ratio, of the two goods in the market. With his tastes given, the consumer will tend to substitute goods for one another until their ratio is brought into accord with the ratio at which these goods exchange in the market on the basis of their respective prices. When these two ratios are equal the consumer is in equilibrium. Point F, the point of *tangency* of the two curves, is the point of such equality.

We are now ready to see why the points of intersection C and E in Figure 11 are disqualified as indicators of the optimum combination of goods for the consumer. There are two explanations, a simple one and a more sophisticated one. The simple explanation rests on the fact that these two points of intersection lie on the indifference curve 1, which represents a lower total utility than the higher curve 2 on which point F lies.

There is another explanation. At the point of *tangency* of two curves their two slopes are equal, but not at the point of *intersection*. At point C or point E, in Figure 11, MRS does not equal the ratio $\dfrac{\text{price of } y}{\text{price of } x}$. Stated generally, at any point common to two curves which is not a tangency point, the marginal rate of substitution, which expresses consumer preferences between two goods, differs from the market exchange rate, which expresses the relative prices of these goods. Suppose that MRS (the slope of the indifference curve 1) at point C is greater than the market exchange ratio (the slope of AB) at point C. This may mean, for instance, that $\text{MRS} = 3 : 1$, whereas $\dfrac{\text{price of } y}{\text{price of } x} = 2 : 1$. The MRS tells us that, to our consumer, the surrender of $3y$, 3 apples, is compensated for by the gain of $1x$, 1 orange. But the market exchange ratio tells us that in actuality he can gain $1x$ by forgoing the purchase of only $2y$. At point C, it follows, the consumer's purchase is not at equilibrium; point C does not suggest the best combination of commodities x and y. He will move away from point C and get to a combination at point F on curve 2 which will consist of more x and less y and which will give him more satisfaction. Similar reasoning will show that if MRS is less than the market exchange ratio the point of intersection is not an equilibrium point; and that it will serve the consumer to move to a combination of goods with more y and less x. In this case as well as in the previous case the consumer will be under the incentive to move to a higher indifference curve.

(2) THE PRICE-CONSUMPTION CURVE

We can now look at demand with new spectacles. Assume, as in Figure 12, that the price of apples remains constant but the price of oranges is falling. We get then a series of outlay curves AB, AC, AD, and AF meeting the horizontal axis respectively at the distances OB, OC, OD, and OF. These distances measure the increasing quantities of oranges that our consumer can purchase with a given sum of money and in a given period as the price of oranges continues to fall. Thus

$$OB = \frac{\text{total outlay}}{\text{highest price of oranges}}$$

and

$$OF = \frac{\text{total outlay}}{\text{lowest price of oranges}}$$

Each of the total-outlay lines fanning out from A has a point of tangency with an iso-utility curve in the indifference map including curves 1, 2, 3, 4. The points are K, L, M, and N. They specify the various equilibrium combinations of apples and oranges which the consumer can buy at the de-

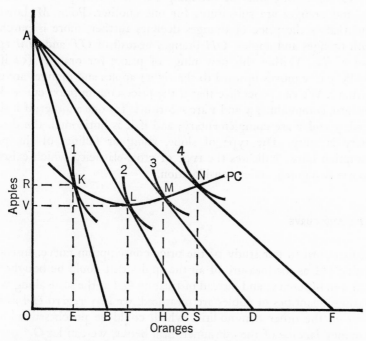

FIGURE 12. *Various Combinations of Two Goods Bought with a Fixed Outlay*

clining price of oranges. The curve PC, connecting these points, is called the price-consumption curve. This curve is the locus of the points which indicate the various combinations of two goods that can be bought with a fixed sum when the price of one good is constant and the price of the other good is going down. If we fix our eye on the oranges, curve PC traces the price-consumption curve, the counterpart of the price demand curve for oranges. But this is getting somewhat ahead of the game.

It is well to pause here for a moment to draw attention to something that a price-consumption curve PC can tell us but which a demand curve based on the utility analysis cannot. The declining part of curve PC, on its left (or if the *whole* PC curve slopes steadily downward) tells us that as the price of oranges sags and more oranges are bought in consequence, the quantity of apples purchased diminishes. Thus point L on curve PC represents a combination of more oranges and fewer apples than the combination specified at point K; namely, a combination of OT oranges and TL apples instead of OE oranges and EK apples. Within this range of prices (or throughout the declining PC—if PC keeps on declining), apples and oranges are substitutes for one another. Point M, however, tells us that as the price of oranges declines further, more is purchased of both oranges and apples: OH oranges instead of OT and HM apples instead of TL. Within this new range of prices for oranges (or if the *whole* PC curve moves upward to the right) apples and oranges are complementary. We can generalize that if the price-consumption curve slopes downward, commodities y and x are substitutes for one another; if it slopes upward, y and x are complementary; and if it is horizontal, the demand elasticity is unity. The type of slope, rising or falling, of the price-consumption curve indicates the type of cross-elasticity which exists between the two goods under consideration.

PRICE DEMAND CURVE

Let us return to our study of the price-consumption curve. Instead of regarding OA as the measure of all the apples that could be bought with a given sum of money, and instead of treating OA as the scale along which the various quantities of apples are measured, we may regard OA as symbolizing *all* the other commodities which could be purchased with the total money *income* of the consumer. Still better, we can let OA portray his whole money income and make certain that OA is divided into the parts spent on oranges and on all the other goods, as is done in the next paragraph. In these circumstances, an indifference curve, instead of expressing the various substitutions of oranges for apples, specifies the substitutions of oranges for all the other goods. As increments of oranges are acquired less purchasing power is left to the consumer for other goods.

Under these assumptions, the price-consumption curve has a different tale to tell. Thus curve PC (Figure 12) becomes a one-commodity price-consumption curve. As far as price line AB is concerned, the distance OB indicates, as before, the amount of oranges that can be bought with the total income. But the vertical distances along OA measure the amount of money income left for all other goods *after* the given amount of oranges has been purchased. Point K on price line AB indicates, as before, that OE units of oranges have been bought; but KE $(= OR)$ no longer points to the number of apples bought; it stands, rather, for the amount of money available for other goods. Similarly with price line AC, the distance OC and point L on AC: point L specifies that OT oranges are bought and that the purchasing power possessed by our consumer for all the other goods is OV. Similarly with price lines AD and AF, with the distances OD and OF, and with the points M and N. In brief, consumers buy OE units of oranges and pay for them with EK or OR in goods. Goods pay for goods.

In other words, under our assumptions, the curve PC becomes a price demand curve not unlike the one which we studied in the preceding chapter. The horizontal distance of point K on it indicates that OE oranges are bought at a given price; the horizontal distance of point L shows that more oranges are bought at a lower price. The distances OB, OC, OD, and OF give us an idea of the respective prices of oranges. When we divide the consumer's total money income OA by these distances we obtain the successive market prices of oranges: OA/OB becomes the highest price indicated in Figure 12, OA/OC is a lower price. The price demand schedule and some of the points on the price demand curve PC for oranges will be as in Table 7.

TABLE 7. *Price Demand Schedule for Oranges*

Price of oranges	Quantity of oranges bought	Point on demand curve
$\dfrac{OA}{OB}$	OE	K
$\dfrac{OA}{OC}$	OT	L
$\dfrac{OA}{OD}$	OH	M
$\dfrac{OA}{OF}$	OS	N

As was pointed out in a recent paragraph, the price-consumption curve can give us an idea of the type of cross-elasticity that exists between the two commodities involved. It can now be shown that when we assume that the vertical axis measures income or purchasing power, this curve can also indicate the price elasticity of demand. Let us look again at the price demand curve or price-consumption curve PC in Figure 12. As was already mentioned, point K on it, like any other point on a curve, suggests two things: its horizontal distance measures the number of oranges bought (namely KR or OE units); its vertical distance $KE = OR$ tells us how much income the consumer has available to spend on other goods. Since OA stands for the total money income and OR stands for what is spent on other goods, the sum spent on oranges is AR $(= OA - OR)$. As the price of oranges drops, point L shows that OV $(= LT)$ is spent on all the other goods; AV is then the total expenditure on oranges. Inasmuch as AV is larger than AR, it signifies that when the price of oranges drops the consumer spends a greater amount of money on this fruit. In other words, where the price-consumption curve slopes downward the demand is elastic. It can be shown in similar fashion that when the price-consumption curve slopes upward to the right the demand for the commodity is inelastic; and when it is horizontal the commodity has a demand elasticity of unity.

INCOME DEMAND

In the preceding chapter we learned a little about income demand. We can now present this kind of demand by means of indifference curves. In Figure 13, the parallel lines AE, BF, and CH are a map of price lines representing the rising outlays of a consumer on two goods, apples and oranges,

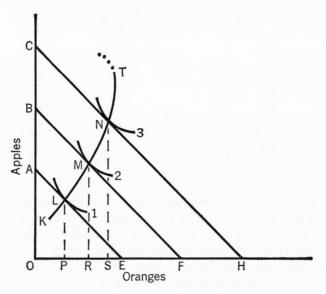

FIGURE 13. *The Income-Consumption Curve*

induced by a larger and larger income. The map of indifference curves 1, 2, and 3 tells their usual story. The points of tangency of these indifference curves and the price lines, namely points L, M, and N, specify the optimum combinations of apples and oranges which the consumer can obtain for each outlay, corresponding presumably to each income in the progression. Curve KT, the locus of such points of tangency, is the *income-consumption* curve. With advancing incomes there is alike an advance in the expenditure on fruit and in the enjoyment of larger combinations of apples and oranges. In general, the influence of the size of the income on the size of the purchases of the two commodities is termed the *income effect of a price change.*

The price relationship between apples and oranges is the same for all the price lines involved in income demand: the price of apples and oranges is assumed to stay unchanged as the income mounts, because we are interested in the income effect alone. Accordingly, the rate of exchange of the two goods in the market, or the ratio of the price of x to the price of y, remains constant as outlays and incomes climb. Since at the point of tangency between an iso-utility curve and an outlay curve,

$$\text{MRS of } x \text{ for } y = \frac{\text{price of } y}{\text{price of } x},$$

it is clear that at such points as L, M, and N the MRS is identical. We can generalize: the income-consumption curve is the locus of points indicating the *same* marginal rate of substitution on the various indifference curves which are intersected by this curve.

Now let us assume, as we did in connection with the price-consumption curve, that the distances OA, OB, and OC along the y axis represent the total money *income* of the consumer; and that the distances along the x axis measure the quantities of oranges, as before. Then the points L, M, and N refer to the increasing amounts of oranges which our consumer would buy as his income is raised. Then KT is a one-commodity income-consumption curve, or simply an income demand curve. The income demand schedule would then appear as in Table 8.

TABLE 8. *Income Demand Schedule for Oranges*

Income	Quantity of oranges purchased	Points on demand curve
OA	OP	L
OB	OR	M
OC	OS	N

As we should expect, normally the income demand curve rises to the right; with increasing incomes people buy more of almost any commodity. It is necessary to say "almost" because of the possible presence of "inferior" goods discussed in the previous chapter. At a higher income the consumer is apt to favor less and not more of "inferior" goods. For such goods the income demand curve *KT* will sooner or later curl back on itself, as is indicated by the dotted segment in Figure 13.

INCOME AND SUBSTITUTION EFFECTS OF COMMODITY PRICE CHANGE

Various economic problems can be solved with the subtle apparatus of the indifference curves. Some of these problems can be analyzed and graphically illustrated more clearly, and perhaps more simply, by this approach than by the classical utility method. To see this new method in action, let us address ourselves to the idea of the law of demand. This principle, we recall, deals with the response, in terms of quantity purchased by the household, to a change in the price of one given commodity. We know that, other things equal, a drop in the price of a commodity is usually followed by larger purchases of it. The reason for this behavior of buyers is twofold: the income effect and the substitution effect.

The traditional attitude saw no particular difficulty in these two effects, although it did not stress their connection with the price-quantity relations. The old attitude concentrated on diminishing marginal utility: the price of oranges fell because at the price offered by consumers the sellers would be left with big stocks of oranges. The old view was simply that marginal utility prescribed a lower price to the buyer of these fruits on the market and warned the producer to curtail production. The issue between the two views is not, however, whether or not the two effects throw the necessary light on a problem but whether the one influence can be *separated* from the other, so that the influence of income can be seen apart from the influence of substitution. The utility approach could not separate the two; the new approach could. Let us see how the new approach handles this problem.

Our frame of reference will be Figure 14. The horizontal axis indicates the quantities of a given commodity X, or oranges. The vertical axis is versatile. It may register the money income of the consumer or the several other commodities in his weekly budget, or just one other commodity, like apples. For simplicity, we assume that our consumer is allowed a definite sum and that he is to spend it on two commodities, oranges and apples, at market prices. We assume that, as usual, he is bent on maximizing his satisfaction in the manner (which manner?) detailed on these pages. We assume finally that the buyer of the articles is in the vicinity of consumer equilibrium.

Comes a drop in the price of oranges. The older view would explain this occurrence in terms of diminishing marginal utility. The newer school goes farther: when the price of an article declines we witness two forces in operation to induce this result: the income effect and the substitution effect. These concepts were discussed in the preceding chapter.

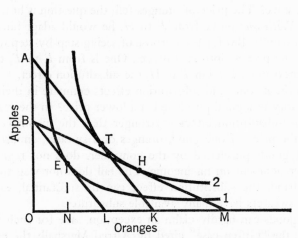

FIGURE 14. *Separation of Income Effect and Substitution Effect*

Let us turn to Figure 14. Before the price decline for oranges, the consumer's position is at E, on price line BL. He can buy, then, ON units of oranges and NE units of apples. His total satisfaction is not high; it is indicated by the comparatively modest indifference curve, or iso-utility curve, number 1. *Two* lines or curves are of special significance because they mirror the new situation facing the buyer of the fruit.

(1) At the lower price for oranges, he can buy more of them; it seems that the price line BL rotates, with B as the pivot, and gains the new position of BM. This movement of BL toward BM is counterclockwise, just as in the case of a *rise* in the price of oranges the movement of BL would be clockwise. Now he can buy OM units of oranges without lessening the purchase of apples; or he can buy more units of apples, or more of both fruits.

(2) The rise in our consumer's income, expressed by the drop in the price of oranges, puts him in a new position. His old position represented by E is obviously no longer adequate as a description of his new situation. Accordingly he moves from E to T. Point H is a point on the new price

line *BM* representing the new income level; it is also a point on indifference curve 2, representing a higher level of satisfaction.

But we cannot stop here. The fact that oranges fell in price means that there is a discrepancy between the market rate of exchange for the two fruits and the personal rate of exchange. To remove such a discrepancy, the buyer substitutes one fruit for the other, that is, he moves along iso-utility curve 2 from *T* to *H*, where the consumer finds his equilibrium as far as these two fruits are concerned.

Where are we? The price of oranges fell; the question is how the buyer will react. With *one* move from *E* to *H*, he would adapt himself to the new circumstances. But for the purpose of seeing step-by-step movements, we resolve the process into *two* moves. One is from *E* to *T*, the income effect; the next move is from *T* to *H*, the substitution effect.

How do the income and substitution effects compare in their influence on the quantity of a good purchased at a lower price? In the vast majority of cases the substitution effect is stronger than the income effect. The change in the price of one good, oranges or a sweater, amidst the many varieties of goods purchased by the consumer, does not register a sub-stantial encroachment on his income. The tail does not wag the dog. On the other hand, the substitution effect can be substantial, especially if oranges or sweaters have many available substitutes.

Inferior goods can hardly claim an exception, save for such an unusual situation as the "Giffen case" cited by Alfred Marshall: the expenditure on bread may use up a large proportion of the very poor man's income and a rise in the price of bread may bite into his budget to such an extent that he has less money left for other somewhat more expensive foods; the consequence is that, despite the higher price, he consumes more bread to make up for the deficiency.[3] Conversely, when the price of bread goes down he may expect to spare enough money to come within reach of some meat; he therefore buys less bread at the lower price.

But such exceptions are exceedingly rare even for inferior goods. The poor are always with us. When the price of an inferior good declines, some consumers may well turn away from it. But the majority of those in the low income brackets are apt to be attracted by the favorable price into buying larger quantities of the inferior goods per unit of time. In the market as a whole a higher price is generally accompanied by reduced sales. In technical terms, the price rise of a good alters the market exchange ratio between this good and other goods. This upsets the equality between the exchange ratio and the marginal rate of substitution. The equality, and consumer equilibrium, are re-established as the relatively lower priced goods are beginning to serve as substitutes for relatively dearer goods.

[3] A. Marshall, *Principles of Economics*, 8th ed. (New York, Macmillan, 1927), p. 132.

Before we turn to the next topic, a footnote comment may be in order. We carry our exposition of a problem by such statements as follow: the buyer moves from point E to point H; the buyer indicates a rise in his income by a line parallel to his initial budget line; the seller desires a lower cross-elasticity for the goods he sells. The economist does not assume such knowledge on the part of the typical consumer, producer, buyer, and seller. Sending the buyer on a trip from E to H is merely a pedagogical device of clarifying and vivifying the argument. The economist, as a teacher, seeks ways of holding his students' attention in the discussion of a problem.

III. Shortcomings of the Analysis of Demand

We may close our discussion of demand by pointing out some weaknesses alike of the utility and the indifference-curves approaches. Some shortcomings are unique to the one or the other conceptual frame; other shortcomings are common to both.

A SHORTCOMING OF THE UTILITY ANALYSIS

The basic difficulty with the utility theory derives from the fact that no way of measuring utility has yet been discovered. In the exploration of utility the economist has to improvise an imaginary yardstick like a "util." Although the motto of the natural scientist—"no measurement, no science"—has lost some prestige in recent days when immeasurables have made their appearance in the laboratory, it tends to underscore this difficulty.

A UNIQUE SHORTCOMING OF THE INDIFFERENCE-CURVES ANALYSIS

The indifference-curves theory seeks to steer clear of the need to measure utility by substituting new concepts for old and new equations for the traditional equations. It substitutes the idea of preferences for the idea of utility. Instead of cardinal numbers, like one, two, three, which would presume to measure the strength of the consumer's desire for a good, it employs ordinal numbers, like first, second, third, to indicate his preferences. It replaces the concept of marginal utility with the concept of marginal rate of substitution; and for the principle of diminishing marginal utility it offers the principle of diminishing marginal rate of substitution.

For a guide to maximum consumer satisfaction, it abandons the equations

$$\frac{\text{MU of } A}{\text{price of } A} = \frac{\text{MU of } B}{\text{price of } B} = \ldots,$$

where A and B are commodities and MU is marginal utility, and proposes the equation of the marginal rate of substitution of one commodity for another to the price ratio of these two commodities in the market.

But the new theory jumps from the frying pan of the difficulty of measuring utility into the fire of the difficulty of assuming consumer familiarity with preference schedules. The theory visualizes a consumer who carries in his head varieties of columns of figures. He is assumed to be familiar with combinations and substitutions of apples and oranges, of shoes and shirts, of gasoline and motion pictures, of saxophones and mandolins. For each pair of such commodities the indifference curve portrays a long string of combinations; and an indifference map brings into play a large number of indifference curves. The combinations of pairs of goods out of the large assortment of goods which the ordinary consumer or household is in the habit of buying during a week constitute arrays of figures involving many preferences, substitutions, total utilities, total outlays, and incomes.

We can hardly assume such knowledge on the part of the consumer. He may be expected to know what substitutions he is ready to make among commodities that play their part in his frequent experience. He may discern whether 3 pairs of shoes and 4 shirts would give him as much satisfaction as 2 pairs of shoes and 5 shirts. But he may be at a loss to compare the desirability of 12 pairs of shoes and 1 shirt with the desirability of 10 pairs of shoes and 2 shirts. Of course it is very rare when the consumer has to make such extreme choices. While it may be mathematically useful to consider a combination of 15 shirts and no shoes, such a combination has no counterpart in actuality. How many shirts can make up for the discomfort and distressing eccentricity of making an appearance in bare feet on the street or in the office? Shirts are scarcely a relevant commodity to contemplate for a scheme of life in which shoes are absent. Bedsheets and bedroom slippers would be more to the point.

SHORTCOMINGS COMMON TO BOTH ANALYSES

Some blemishes are shared by both formulations. In the *first* place, some commodities (a house, an automobile, or a refrigerator) are indivisible; and, moreover, people normally buy only one such commodity. Only for a millionaire who owns several dwellings, pianos, or vacuum cleaners can there be mention of diminishing marginal utility with respect to such objects. To the ordinary consumer the idea of the marginal utility of washing machines or house furnaces has scant application. True, some of the indivisible goods are to a certain degree an assembly of parts which can be enjoyed in varying dimensions. Houses essentially alike in all other regards may differ in the number or size of rooms, in the number of windows or bathtubs, or in the size of the back yard; and houses with more and more of such items offer diminishing utility. However, when considering the parts which identify a commodity we must bear in mind that diminishing marginal utility always refers to increasing units of the *same* commodity. Two Chevrolet cars, one with and one without a heater, a defroster, a clock, or a radio, may not exemplify one identical commodity with diminishing marginal utility as the string of gadgets is lengthened; they may rather exemplify different cars competing with each other as substitutes.

In the *second* place, the assumption of consumer choice among units of the *same* good, as the price falls, is not always warranted. The well-to-do persons who buy cars and diamonds will not buy more of the same cars or diamonds at lower prices. The reason for this behavior is twofold. One is what Veblen calls "conspicuous consumption." The wealthy derive satisfaction from advertising their capacity to spend money by displaying a variety of costly possessions. But two cars or two evening gowns alike in all respects will impress neighbors no more than only one such article; the two units will be mistaken for one unit. But apart from the desire for ostentation, the rich consumer seeks self-expression in variety. The millionaire will consult an architect about a type of house and grounds in Florida different from those in the suburb of New York. Two diamonds of the same cut and size and mounting will not appeal to the wearer even though the combined glitter will duly impress the onlookers. The lady will prefer to mirror herself in two different pieces of jewelry.

The ordinary consumer even in ordinary purchases is not of a different breed in regard to these motivations. He cannot indulge in "conspicuous consumption," but he likes display and variety. When the price declines he will buy more units of precisely the *same* article only when there is a unique reason for not turning to something different, or when the commodity is homogeneous, as are water, electricity, or fuel oil. Sold on a particular kind of motor oil or gasoline, cigarette or coffee, he may be disinclined to experiment with other varieties and is likely to buy more of his favorite brand when the price falls. But when the consumer's preference for a given differentiated product has not solidified into a habit or when his vanity is served by a display of variety, a price decline, far from inducing him to purchase more units of one specific make of the article, may send him to other varieties of it. Rare is the housewife who will buy two identical hats or three identical kitchen aprons at a bargain counter.

These considerations suggest that the analysis of demand is not a closed book. Some corners of the problems await further exploration. Two noteworthy attempts in this direction may be cited in closing: *Income, Saving, and the Theory of Consumer Behavior,* by Professor J. S. Duesenberry,[4] and *The Theory of Consumer Demand,* by Professor Ruby T. Norris.[5]

SUGGESTED READINGS

Duesenberry, J. S. *Income, Saving, and the Theory of Consumer Behavior.* Cambridge, Harvard University Press, 1949.

Enke, S. *Intermediate Economic Theory,* Appendix D. New York, Prentice-Hall, 1950.

Friedman, M., and Savage, L. J. "The Utility Analysis of Choices Involving Risk," *Journal of Political Economy,* LVI (1948), 279–304. Reprinted in *Readings in Price Theory.*

Hicks, J. R. *Value and Capital,* Part I. Oxford, Oxford University Press, 1946.

Leftwich, R. H. *The Price System and Resource Allocation,* revised ed., chap. V. New York, Holt, Rinehart and Winston, 1960.

Norris, Ruby T. *The Theory of Consumer Demand,* 2nd ed. New Haven, Yale University Press, 1952.

Stigler, G. J. *The Theory of Price,* revised ed., chap. 5. New York, Macmillan, 1952.

Weintraub, S. *Price Theory,* chap. 1. New York, Pitman, 1949.

[4] Cambridge, Harvard University Press, 1949.
[5] New Haven, Yale University Press, 1952.

CHAPTER

V   The Theory of Production

AFTER chapters on demand, a discussion of supply is expected to follow, since in nearly all cases the price of goods is governed by demand and supply. But supply is intimately connected with costs; and an understanding of the various types of costs is incomplete and inadequate without an acquaintance with some of the principles of production. In the next two chapters the theory of production is examined in detail as a prelude to the subsequent discussion of costs and supply. We may as well add here that production theory also throws light on the allocation of factor-services among their many possible employments; that it helps explain the choice made by the businessman of the particular combination of factors in the production of a given commodity; and that by exposing the productivity of factor-resources it lays the foundation for the theory of distribution of the total income per unit of time among the four factors that produce the commodities and services. The theory of production is, finally, prominently connected with population problems, with some aspects of international trade, and with other questions outside the scope of this book.

The theory of production explores the relation between the inputs of the services of land, labor, capital, and management, on the one hand, and the output of goods and services, on the other hand. It examines the behavior of output in response to a change in inputs; it co-ordinates these two variables.

The theory of production is occupied with at least three types of problems. *First* is the examination of input-output relations in the *short-run* period, that is, when the change in the demand for goods and services is expected by the entrepreneurs to rule only over a short period of time. An example of such a situation is provided by the outburst of demand, after a war, for durable consumer goods, such as automobiles, rugs, winter overcoats, mechanical dishwashers, frigidaires, electric ranges, and vacuum cleaners, the last few items serving to transform the kitchen from a penal institution for the housewife into a realm in which she is the mistress of obedient mechanical servants. The demand for such goods is expected to swing back to the vicinity of the prewar condition before very long. The adjustment of production in this short period is reflected in the law of variable proportions. The dominant fact or idea in this law is the principle of *diminishing returns*, a concept laden with enormous consequences to backward and advanced countries alike, to "capitalist" societies as well as to socialist and communist societies.

The *second* problem in the theory of production deals essentially with the same idea of input-output relations, but from the angle of *long-run* adjustments. In the case of short-run developments, some input can be profitably varied whereas the other inputs stay unchanged because they cannot be varied in the short run, and because it would not be profitable to vary them even if they could be varied. But in the long-run situation the change in demand is expected by businessmen to stay with us for a long time, so that *all* inputs can be profitably varied—not only the flexible inputs, like raw materials or ordinary labor, or power, that are varied in the previous problem, but also the size of the physical plant, the number of machines, and the amount of other kinds of heavy equipment. Such long-run expectations may be fostered when the population is rising and bids fair to keep on rising in the future; when new substantial foreign markets have been developed; and when the government establishes itself as a big spender, on defense or on projects of social welfare, like schools, hospitals, research centers, and roads.

When all inputs, fixed and variable alike, can be changed up or down, we deal with the *scale* of the firm. The central concept in this second case is *returns to scale*, which refers to the change in the total output of an industry in response to a long-run change in the demand for its product. In the short run only the change in the variable resources can be used to meet a new short-run demand. In the long run all resources become variables: to meet a change in demand destined to govern for a long time, the adjustment takes the form principally of the entry of fresh firms, thus enlarging the industry. An industry is the composite of *many* firms producing the same homogeneous article; in monopoly the industry embraces *one* firm; in monopolistic competition the industry stands for *many* firms each producing a different variety of one commodity; in oligopoly the industry is the sum of a *few* firms.

The *third* segment of the theory of production deals with the crucial problem of determining the imputed productivity of labor, land, and capital, as well as the problem of determining the optimum mix of productive resources which would produce a given output at *least cost*. The central principle in this sector is the ramifications of the law of *marginal productivity*.

It will readily be admitted that marginal productivity is essentially the theme of the law of variable proportions centered on the law of diminishing returns. However, there is more to the pricing of factor-services and there is more to their combinations for least-cost production than is contained in the principle of variable proportions. The attempt to clarify the elaborations and the implications of this principle may as well be regarded as a separate sector in the theory of production.

This third segment of production theory can be treated at this stage only in part, chiefly because marginal revenue, marginal cost, competition, monopoly, and monopsony are involved, and we are not yet familiar with these problems. A full-dress discussion embodying these concepts will have to wait until we come to Chapter XIII.

I. The Law of Variable Proportions

The first problem in the theory of production is embodied in the law of variable proportions. This law is also identified as the law of returns, as the law of diminishing productivity, and as the law of nonproportional returns. As a phase of the theory of production, this law deals with the connection between input and output in the short run. We assume a given state of technology, that *one* and only one resource collaborating with the other resources keeps on increasing unit by unit, and that all the other productive resources are kept constant. The question is: how does the output of a given product behave, in the short run, as more units of one variable resource, say, labor-hours, are added, in order to meet a short-run increase in the demand for the product in question?

By output or product we may mean *three* things: total output produced; average output per unit of the variable resource; or the marginal output, that is, the increment in total output per unit of time caused by the employment of an extra unit of the variable agent. Accordingly the answer to our question can take three directions. It can examine the behavior of the *total* output produced as more units of one variable resource are used. It can study the behavior of the *average* output per variable as more and more units of the variable factor are employed. It can examine the course of the *marginal* outputs in response to the use of progressively more units of the flexible agent. In this section, we shall try to acquaint ourselves with all the three approaches.

THE PRODUCTION FUNCTION

Before we proceed with the discussion of the law of variable proportions it may be well to project it against its background. This law is a phase of the production function. First of all, what is meant by "function"? When we state that one variable y is the function of another variable x we mean that y depends on x and is related to x, in such a way that when we assign a certain value to x we can thereby determine the corresponding value of y. For every value of x we can compute the associated value of y.

In many instances of economic study we come face to face with functional relations. Thus, parallel to the production function, we have the consumption function, or the relation between total national consumption and the corresponding total national income, in the same interval of time. We can set down $C = f(y)$, where C refers to aggregate consumption, y refers to aggregate income, and f stands for "function." This equality states that total consumption is a function of total income.

As was stressed in Chapter I, relations in economics differ from relations of magnitudes in physics. In physics we have quantitative relations expressed by equations. If we could quantify relations in economics, we could change the consumption function just mentioned as follows: $C = f(y) = 100 - y + y^2$. (This equation is a fictitious illustration.) But we cannot quantify the relation of variables in economics; we have to be satisfied with a general expression like $C = f(y)$.

Two more examples: (a) As we know, the price demand for an article depends on a variety of conditions. We can therefore write, for pure competition, $q = f(p, y, e)$, where q stands for the quantity of a given article demanded in a given market, in a unit of time; p is the price of the article; y is the total income of the buyers; and e denotes the expectation about the stability of this price in the future. If the commodity in question resides in a market of monopolistic competition, three additional variables would be enclosed in the above parentheses: the quality of the article, the advertising activity of the producer, and the price of related goods.

(b) A simple production function may take the form of $P = \sqrt{ab}$, where a and b symbolize respectively the number of machine-hours and the number of labor-hours, and P stands for the size of the output per unit of time. This function suggests that these two resources can be substituted for one another: more machines and less labor, or fewer machines and more labor. This equation summarizes the possible combinations. For example, to produce 20 units of a certain article (P) we may use 8 machine-hours and 50 labor-hours, or 10 machine-hours and 40 labor-hours, or 20 machine-hours and 20 labor-hours, and so on. We get $P = 20 = \sqrt{8 \times 50} = \sqrt{10 \times 40} = \sqrt{20 \times 20} = \sqrt{1 \times 400}$, and so on.

More general and more comprehensive than the law of variable proportions, the production function indicates what quantities of various kinds of natural resources and of labor and capital will have to be employed in order to produce one unit or any other amount of a particular good or service in a given interval of time. It points to the variety of resources and the unique combinations of them which can be transformed into desired products and services. The production function reflects the state of the arts and the technological possibilities of the production processes. The production function changes under the impact of innovations. It indicates the multitude of possible combinations of factor-services which can produce a given article or several in a unit of time.

Concerned with the physical aspects of production inside the plant and synonymous with the technique and organization employed, the production function is external to economics and lies in the realm of production engineering. The engineer or technician can tell us that the use of such and such varieties of natural resources, of labor, and of capital goods will result in a specific output of a given commodity per day or week. Which particular combination the entrepreneur will single out from the many possible combinations will be governed principally by the market price of the various factor-services that could be employed, as well as by the sales price of the resulting output. The engineer is interested in physical combinations; the businessman is interested in the monetary elements of such combinations. In the entrepreneur's choice of the appropriate quantities of the variable resource to collaborate with the fixed resources we see exemplified the law of variable proportions, also the law of diminishing returns. Should the price of labor rise, there will begin the gradual substitution of other resources for labor; in time the firm may have a combination entailing fewer labor-hours and more of other variables, like tools. Dominating these and other relevant short-run choices by the firm is the overshadowing search for minimum unit costs and for maximum aggregate profit.

TABULAR PRESENTATION OF THE LAW OF VARIABLE PROPORTIONS

Let us start our detailed study of the law of variable proportions with the aid of Table 9. This table gives hypothetical figures of the output of a business firm's product as resource combinations are varied—specifically, the output of wheat on a 100-acre farm as annual experiments are performed in which varying numbers of workers are set to raise the grain. The assumption is that while these eleven experiments are carried on all other things are equal: there is no change in the art of cultivation; all the workers are of the same normal efficiency, and similarly with the tools they use; there is no change from experiment to experiment in the number of hours each worker puts in during the year; and the fertility of the farm and the weather conditions undergo no alterations. Only one factor changes: the number of workers employed. Thus the difference from experiment to experiment consists solely in the number of labor-hours

TABLE 9. *Output from 100 Acres of Land with Varying Amounts of Labor*

(1)	(2)	(3)	(4)	(5)
Amount of land (acres)	Number of workers	Total product (bu.)	Average product per worker (bu.)	Marginal product of labor (bu.)
100	1	820	820	820 ⎱
100	2	1,720	860	900 ⎰
100	3	2,640	880	920 ⎬ Phase 1
100	4	3,600	900	960
100	5	4,500	900	900 ⎰
100	6	5,340	890	840 ⎱
100	7	6,090	870	750
100	8	6,640	830	550 ⎬ Phase 2
100	9	6,930	770	290
100	10	6,930	693	0 ⎰
100	11	6,820	620	−110 ⎰ Phase 3

applied to the 100 acres of land, and this difference is determined only by the variation in the number of workers from experiment to experiment —the number of workers is the variable factor.

We shall now study Table 9 column by column. In column 2, the number of workers rises from 1 in the first experiment to 11 in the eleventh experiment. First, in column 3, the resulting *total* output or product is registered. The total output keeps on rising, fast (or steeply on a graph) where the marginal outputs in column 5 are large; and slowly (or less steeply on a graph) where the marginal outputs in column 5 grow smaller, as in experiments 7, 8, and 9. The total output reaches a maximum in experiment 10 where marginal output equals zero; thereafter total output declines as marginal output becomes negative. The total output when n units of the variable resource are employed equals the sum of the marginal outputs of these n units; and when the total outputs are indicated, the marginal output of n units is found by subtracting the total output of $n - 1$ units from the total output of n units.

Second, *average* output or product per worker, in column 4, rises to a maximum and then falls steadily. Average output will reach zero only when total output is zero; and total output dwindles to zero when so many workers are crowded onto this farm that the mounting negative marginal outputs (column 5) build up a total of 6,930 bu., completely wiping out the maximum total output attained in experiment 10. The relationship between the average output and total output is the usual one between an average and a total quantity. When total output is given, the average output is found by dividing the total output by the number of workers employed in the experiment; and when average output is known, total output is obtained by multiplying the average output by the corresponding number of workers. It is important to note that as long as the rate of increase in total output is, say, 10% greater than the rate of increase in the variable factor, say, 8%, the average output will continue to rise.

Third, column 5 is concerned with the *marginal* product of labor on this farm; that is, with the extra output emerging when one extra worker is taken on. This marginal product traces a characteristic curve. At first it rises and then it falls, reaching zero and negative magnitudes beyond zero. As additional units of the variable factor are combined with the constant factors the resulting increment in product, or the productivity of the variable factor, sooner or later begins to fall off. As long as total product rises at an *increasing rate* marginal output will keep rising; as soon as the *rate* of increase in total output begins to decline marginal output falls. Let the student compare these rates of increase for the first four experiments, then for the later experiments, in columns 3 and 5. The principle of diminishing returns or diminishing productivity reveals itself chiefly in marginal output and average output. It can be noticed also in the behavior of the total output: see column 3, experiment 11. However, the most telling aspect of the law of returns lies in the eventually declining marginal product, or in *diminishing returns*. The primary question to the firm in employing and allocating resources is: how much increment of output will accompany the use of an extra unit of a resource? That is, what is the marginal productivity of the resource?

It is to be observed here that the point of falling output is not identical for total, average, and marginal output. Total output begins to fall "latest," with the largest input of the variable resource. Average output begins to decline sooner, that is, with a smaller input of the variable resource. Marginal output begins to diminish even sooner than average output, while the average output is still climbing to its peak; this can be seen better on a graph than in columns of figures.

(1) *Relationships between average and marginal quantities*

For a better understanding of the principles back of the results of our 11 experiments, it is well to stop (1) to consider some of the relationships between the average output and the marginal output, and (2) to explore some geometric connections between average and total output curves, and also between average and marginal output curves. Diagrams A and B of Figure 15 come to our aid. In both diagrams the number of labor-hours

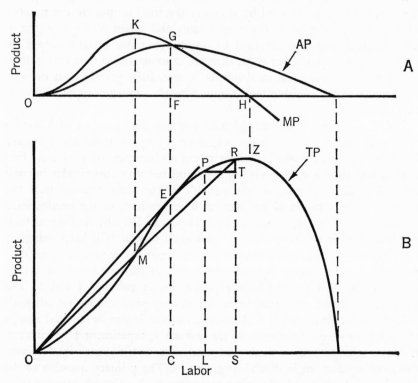

FIGURE 15. *Relation Between Product and Input, Short Run*

is marked off on the horizontal line and the output on the vertical line. In Figure 15A curves AP and MP represent average product and marginal product respectively. In Figure 15B curve TP traces total product.

Whenever we deal with average and marginal variables it is important to realize that certain unique relations exist between them. These relations are often briefly identified as the "average-marginal" relations. To bring out these relations, let us attend to column 5 and then go back to columns 3 and 4. By adding the figures in column 5 we get the figures in column 3; then we divide the totals in column 3 by the number of workers and get column 4. In other words, we can regard the average product as derived from the marginal product figures: we begin by adding the marginal products to get the totals needed for the computation of the average products.

It follows then that as long as the marginal output *exceeds* the average output each new average output will be larger than its predecessor: the average product will keep on rising. In Table 9 average output (column 4) is rising up to and including experiment 4. In these four experiments the marginal output (column 5) is greater (except for the initial experiment) than the average output. As long as the marginal output is larger than the average output a larger ingredient is added to form the next average output. The larger ingredient pulls up the new average. It follows, too, that as long as the average output is moving up it is safe to infer that the marginal output is above it in magnitude. In Figure 15A, where the MP curve is above the AP curve, AP is on a steady rise—up to point G.

Similarly, as soon as the marginal output declines *below* the average output, average output begins to drop. The addition of a new marginal figure to compose the new average pulls down this new average. This is seen in columns 4 and 5, Table 9, beginning with the sixth experiment; also in Figure 15A, beyond point G, where MP is consistently less than AP.

This relationship between average and marginal quantities may be easier to perceive if we turn to an example of some personal interest to the student. Suppose that a student's average grade on the first two written quizzes in economic theory is 80 and his grade on the third quiz is 86. His new average grade will rise above 80 because his third grade pulls up his average, to 82. Suppose that his fourth quiz is returned with a grade of 84. This grade is poorer than on the third quiz, but it exceeds his average for the first three quizzes. It therefore pushes up his new average above the old average, to 82.5.

Now let the grade on the fifth quiz (we assume that the professor pelts his students with quizzes, unwisely) stand below this last average; let it be 80. The student's average for the five quizzes will decline. As long as the grade on a new quiz is above (below) the average for all the preceding quizzes his average will keep on climbing (sinking). By the same token, if his averages are steadily rising (falling), they tell us that his quiz grades stay each greater (smaller) than his previous average grade.

It will be noticed that the average output (Table 9) stays at 900 bu. when 4 workers as well as when 5 workers till the land. This situation is inherent in the arithmetic involved. To reach the average product for 5 workers, the output contributed by the fifth worker, or the marginal output of 5 workers, is added to the total output of 4 workers; to get the new average, 900 bu. are added to the total for 4 workers. Since the previous average was 900 bu. the addition of another 900 bu. will not change the new average. In fact, we can make the generalization that whenever the marginal output equals the average output, average output stays *constant*; and, conversely, if the average output is constant, it is a sign that the marginal output is constant, too, and, moreover, *equals* the average output. Graphically, in such cases the average and marginal curves are horizontal, are parallel to the *x* axis, and they coincide into *one* line.

The point at which the average product curve and the marginal product curve intersect (point G in Figure 15A), or the point at which average output equals marginal output, is significant. It is the point of maximum average output. Conversely, when the average output is at its maximum it equals marginal output. The reasoning is as follows. As the average product curve is rising the marginal product curve lies above it; and as the average product curve is falling the marginal product curve lies below it. It follows that the point where the average output curve is neither rising nor falling is the point at which the marginal output curve is neither above it nor below it but coincides with it. Such a point on the average product curve, at which the curve no longer rises and beyond which it falls, is obviously the point of *maximum* height; at this point the two curves must meet, since the marginal curve is neither above nor below the average curve. We note that the point of maximum average output does not coincide with the point of maximum marginal output. The point of maximum marginal output lies to the left of the point of maximum average output; in Figure 15A, point K is to the left of and above point G.

(2) *Some geometrical relations between total, average, and marginal output* [1]

We are familiar with certain relations between total output and average output, and between total output and marginal output. We know how to find total output when either average or marginal output is given, and how to find either average or marginal output when total output is given. We know, too, that total output is at its maximum when marginal output is zero, and that the total output curve is steepest where the marginal output is largest. We shall now explore some further relations, of a geometrical nature, between total output on the one hand and either average or marginal output on the other hand. Figure 15B will be drawn into service for this purpose.

---

[1] This topic may be omitted by those to whom the mathematics involved is a barrier and not an aid. They can go directly to the topic "The Three Phases of the Law of Variable Proportions," p. 115.

TOTAL PRODUCT AND AVERAGE PRODUCT

From the total product curve TP (Figure 15B) we can get an idea of the behavior of the average output. Take any point R on TP. Connect R with the origin by a straight line OR; we get angle ROS. When OS workers cultivate our 100-acre farm the total output is RS, and the average output per worker becomes RS/OS. This ratio is the tangent of the angle ROS, by definition in trigonometry. This ratio is also the *slope*, or gradient, of the line OR. The tangent varies in magnitude with the angle ROS; so, of course, does the slope of the line OR. We can generalize and state that the larger the angle formed with the x axis by a line *from* a point on the total output curve *to* the origin, the larger is the tangent of this angle; the larger, in other words, is the average output at that point for the number of workers indicated by that point. A similar generalization holds for the slope of a straight line from any point on the total product curve to the origin. The larger the slope of the line from this point the larger the average output.

By comparing such angles, we can tell with which number of workers the average output is large or small. As the number of workers increases from zero, and as we move from point to point on the total product curve TP, the angles grow larger, until the largest angle is reached for point E, namely angle EOC. Line OE is tangent to the total product curve TP at E. Of all the lines from points on the total product curve to the origin the line *tangent* to this curve makes the largest angle. Point E, or rather the abscissa OC of point E, indicates the number of workers who will produce the maximum average output. Point E in Figure 15B corresponds to point G in Figure 15A, so that $EC/OC = GF$. As more workers are employed than are specified by point E, the average output will drop consistently; and the angles, and the slopes of the lines forming the angles, will keep on falling.

TOTAL PRODUCT AND MARGINAL PRODUCT

We can likewise learn from the total product curve about the marginal output. The marginal output, on our farm, can be defined as the ratio of a very small increment in output to a very small increment in labor. The marginal output is a slope, too; but not a slope of the *line* joining the origin and a point on the total product curve, as is the case with average output in the preceding two paragraphs. The marginal output is the slope of the total product *curve* itself. A large slope will designate a large marginal output, and conversely. In Figure 15B, the marginal output of *OS* workers, or 9 workers, is $(RS - TS)/PT$. This is the slope of the curve of total product TP over the distance $PT = LS$; it pictures the extra output induced by the addition of the last extra worker to the labor force. The units of the variable factor, namely workers, in column 2 of Table 9, are discrete; the number of workers can be increased in our experiments on the farm, or anywhere else, by one worker and not by less. (For simplicity, we ignore labor-hours.) But since the total product curve is drawn as a continuous curve the measurements on the horizontal axis can be made very small. Accordingly, as a very small increment of labor is added to *OL* units of labor the total product will rise by such a minute quantity that point *R* is very close to point *P*, and a straight line connecting *R* and *P* becomes a tangent to curve TP at *P*.

The marginal product is indicated by the slope of the curve of total product. This means that it is indicated by the size of the angle formed by the horizontal axis and the tangent to the output curve, at its various points. A large angle will portray a high marginal product, and a small angle a low one. It is to be noted that the tangents to the various points on the total product curve will almost invariably meet the horizontal axis either to the right or to the left of the origin, like tangents *KC* and *AB* in Figure 16. Only in one case will the tangent meet the horizontal axis *at* the origin; namely, the tangent we already discussed, tangent *OE* in Figure 15B. The tangent to the total product curve at the point of

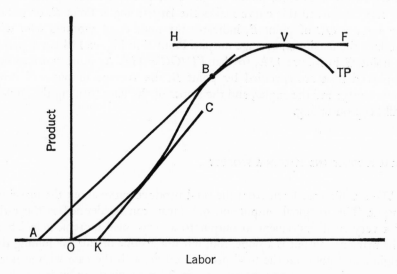

FIGURE 16. *Total Product Curve and Tangents to It*

maximum average output is the tangent at the point at which average and marginal output coincide. Thus we see geometrically that when maximum average product is attained, average product equals marginal product. It is also interesting to observe that at the point of maximum total output V, in Figure 16, the tangent HF to the total product curve TP is parallel to the horizontal axis. At this point V, marginal output is zero and the slope is zero.

The steeper the total product curve at a given point in its course, (1) the greater the slope of the curve at this point, (2) the greater the angle made by the horizontal axis and the tangent to the curve at this point, and (3) the greater the marginal product. When for a given point on the total product curve the marginal output is large the inference is that a large addition has been made at this point to the total output; the total product curve, in response to a small increment in the variable resource at this point, takes a big climb and becomes steep. Where the total product curve is steep the marginal output must be large. The maximum marginal output in Figure 15B is at point M, where the TP curve is supposed to look steepest—if well drawn. Point M corresponds to point K in Figure 15A. Point M appears when the fourth worker is added and the total output gains the maximum *increment* of 960 bu., as in column 5 of Table 9. Point M is the *point of inflection* of curve TP: curve TP is convex to the horizontal axis up to point M and concave beyond point M.

The relations discussed in this section are not unique to the behavior of the output or the productivity of a variable resource. They hold whenever we encounter total, average, and marginal values. They hold in connection with utility, with costs, with revenue, and with other situations.

THE THREE PHASES OF THE LAW OF VARIABLE PROPORTIONS

It is scarcely necessary to discuss in turn the rising, the stationary, the falling, the zero, and the negative phases of the total, the average, and the marginal outputs. But there are three phases of the law of returns which are charged with prime significance and which accordingly deserve attention.

The first phase: increasing average returns

The first phase of this law is exemplified by the situation in the first five experiments on the 100-acre farm. It begins with the application of the first unit of the variable resource and ends at the stage at which the output per unit of variable resource, or the average product of the variable resource, is at a maximum, as in experiment 5 (column 4), Table 9. Graphically, the first phase is portrayed, in Figure 15A, by the curves AP and MP from their beginning up to point G where they meet. In this phase, the upward climb of the total output exhibits a twofold behavior. At first total output climbs at an *increasing rate,* and the marginal product of labor keeps on climbing, too. Curve TP behaves this way up to point M (Figure 15B), and MP rises up to point K (Figure 15A). Then the total output begins to *rise* at a *declining* rate but still at a rate greater than the rate of growth of the variable resource, labor; with the consequence that marginal output falls beyond point K, whereas average output AP continues to rise up to point G.

At the end of this phase, the product or the efficiency of the variable resource, labor, reaches its peak, GF (Figure 15A). But it is best to stop cultivation at this point of highest return per man only when land is free, when no return is imputed to land, as in a new colony. In such a case the best way to use the land is to employ labor on it until the most is derived per man. This goal is reached, in our example, when 5 men are employed on the farm, each one averaging 900 bu. The most economical use of labor, when land is free, is to employ labor up to the end of this first phase: 5 men and no more on our 100-acre farm. Instead of using 6 men on this farm and raising a total of 5,340 bu., we can reach a better result if we set the sixth man to work on an additional plot of 20 acres. He will then add 900 bu. to the total output, and the 6 men together will produce 5,400 bu. (4,500 + 900), as against 5,340 bu. (column 3). More land will be used: 120 acres instead of 100. But land is free.

Since the ownership of *free* land commands no income, the 5 workers are the only claimants to compensation. The total product belongs to them and each one gets 900 bu. This reward of labor squares with the principle that the wage of labor equals its marginal product. In the present instance the marginal physical product, identical with the average product, is 900 bu.

In this first phase, land is superabundant in relation to the workers who till it. There is too much land per worker and he cannot handle it well. As the number of workers applied to the farm rises, the tilling is done better, and increasing returns per man may result. We see here exemplified the basic idea that the law of variable proportions is associated not with absolute numbers—so many acres and so many workers—but with ratios of variable resources to fixed resources.

The second phase: diminishing returns

The second phase begins right after, or with, the point at which average output is at a maximum; or after, or with, the point at which the average output and the marginal output curves intersect. This phase ends at the stage at which total output reaches its peak, 6,930 bu. in our examples. In Figure 15A, this phase is pictured by the marginal output curve MP, beginning with point G down to where it meets the horizontal axis. In Figure 15B, it is portrayed by the total product curve TP from point E, which marks maximum average output, to point Z, which represents the maximum total output. In this phase, the rate of growth of the total output is not only continuing to decline, reflecting the steady fall in marginal output, but begins to become smaller than the rate of growth of the variable resource, initiating a steady decline of average output.

In this phase, average output begins to fall and keeps on falling; marginal output, which began to fall during the first phase, continues to fall in this phase; and the total output is moving to its maximum. In this first phase, the marginal output data and the marginal output curve are above the average output data or curve. In the second phase, the marginal output figures and curve are below the average output figures and curve.

In the first phase, land is used lavishly per worker. In the second phase, land is relatively scarce and has to be economized. It is used intensively by the application of more and more labor to it. The scarcer a productive agent the more it is economized: more of the less scarce agents will be employed in conjunction with it in order to raise a greater output. In the first phase, land is substituted for labor; a good deal of land is used per unit of labor. In the second phase, labor is substituted for land; more and more labor is used per unit of time on a unit of land. If *labor* were free and not land, it would be most profitable to carry production up to the end of the second phase, where the marginal productivity of labor is zero.

DIMINISHING RETURNS

The second phase ought to be called diminishing average returns. But the transforming importance of diminishing marginal returns is so impressive that economic analysis refers to this phase as the phase of diminishing marginal returns; the adjective "marginal" is usually omitted, but is always implied. The definition of this principle runs as follows: when we apply more and more units of one given variable resource to a fixed amount of other productive resources, the total product will keep on rising, but after a certain point the rise will proceed by smaller and smaller increments. We see the illustration of this principle in Table 9, column 5. Some elements of this principle invite comment.

(1) The variable resource may be labor, tools, fertilizer—any resource commonly engaged in production.

(2) The variable resource is applied *unit* by unit; each unit is identical in amount and quality.

(3) All the resources, apart from this one variable, are held unchanged in quantity and character.

(4) This principle refers to a short-run situation; in the long run all resources serving in the production of a commodity are variable. In the long-run situation we deal with the *scale* of the firm.

(5) This principle applies wherever we see short-run variable factor-services co-operating with short-run fixed factor-services in producing a good or service. It applies, accordingly, not only in agriculture, as the classical economists (Adam Smith, Ricardo, J. S. Mill) taught, but also in manufacturing, retailing, advertising, railroading, mining, and street cleaning.

(6) In some discussions of the problem of returns there is mention that chemical alloys and compounds are not subject to the law of variable proportions and therefore to diminishing returns, on the ground that their composition is prescribed by chemical formulas and admits no variation. This view will not stand examination. In the making of chemical compounds the production function dominates, as usual: the compounds may be produced with more labor and less machinery; with less skilled labor and more mechanical devices; with small containers or a few giant containers; with retorts, heating schemes, burners, or hoods of one kind or another. The fixed chemical formulas do not dictate to the firm one fixed technique of production, just as the fact that each ordinary kitchen table must have a flat top and four legs does not thereby prescribe one unchangeable way of making kitchen tables.

If not for the law of diminishing returns, many economic phenomena would bear a different stamp; economic theory would be changed in face of new overmastering realities; and the fortunes of nations would be different. England, Japan, or India could feed their populations by the intensive cultivation of a few acres. The daily bread could be won with much less sweat. The other necessities of life, and luxuries too, could be produced in large volumes by crowding more and more variable resources into plants of given size. Without a law like this, nations would perhaps not be plagued with dictators shrieking for *lebensraum*.

The third phase: negative marginal returns

This phase begins where the second phase leaves off; where total output begins to decline and marginal output becomes negative. In Figure 15A this phase is represented by the part of the marginal product curve MP which is *below* the horizontal axis. In Figure 15B it is pictured by the total product curve TP *beyond* its maximum height at point Z, to the right. This phase is not earmarked by any uniqueness in the average output, which just keeps on declining.

Obviously this phase cannot be expected in practice. In the first phase, there is too much land per worker and he cannot cope with it well; so that as more workers are employed there is desirably and manageably less land per man, and the return per man rises. In the third phase, there are too many laborers swarming the land and the more laborers the less the total product. Too many cooks. Now the marginal productivity of labor is negative. In the first phase, land is wasted that could be put to use for some other purpose; in the third phase, workers are wasted who could be used to advantage in another occupation. Only in the second phase are there returns to both fixed and variable resources; both are productive. Accordingly the firm will operate only somewhere within the second phase.

RETURNS FROM THE FIXED FACTOR

So far we have occupied ourselves with the behavior of output in relation to changes of one variable input. That is, we have studied the productivity of the variable factor, labor, co-operating with all the other factors which are held constant in quantity and quality. We shall now briefly summarize the answer to the associated question: what about the productivity of the fixed factor?

In the *first* phase the contribution of the fixed factor, land, is a negative magnitude which becomes a smaller and smaller negative magnitude until, at the end of the first phase, it registers zero. Let us see why.

As we study Table 9, column 4, experiment 5, we observe that 5 men produce the highest average product, that the optimum acreage per man is 20, if we assume, as we do here, that one man alone can do as well on 20 acres as 5 men do together on 100 acres. For example, in experiment 3 the optimum acreage would be $20 \times 3 = 60$ acres. Since each worker can produce 900 bu. on 20 acres (column 4, experiment 5), we multiply 900 bu. by 3 and get 2,700 bu. The actual output by 3 men is 2,640 bu. (column 3, experiment 3). We come upon the interesting result that when 3 men cultivate the whole 100 acres they produce a *smaller* total of bushels than when they cultivate only 60 acres. The product in experiment 3 is 60 bu. less when they cultivate 40 acres more $(100 - 60)$. The productivity of the fixed factor, land, is negative, which means that the return in bushels can be greater when less land is used by the same number of laborers.

Let us look at the situation at the end of the first phase, namely at experiment 5. The 5 workers produce a total of 4,500 bu. The contribution of land is zero. Thus we see that throughout the first phase the contribution of the fixed factor is improving: the negative product becomes smaller and smaller, for example, -10, -4, tending toward zero at the end.

During the *second* phase both the variable and the fixed factors are productive. Take, for instance, experiment 6. If each of the 6 workers had 20 acres to take care of, total product would be $900 \times 6 = 5,400$ bu. The actual product is 5,340 bu., or 60 bu. less. The reason is that the 6 workers had 100 acres and not 120. This means that more land than 100 acres would produce more product; land is productive. In fact, the marginal productivity of land rises during this second phase, whereas the marginal productivity of labor is declining, reaching zero at the end of the second phase.

During the *third* phase, we have too many workers; land is scarce in relation to labor. In consequence, arithmetic can show that the productivity of land is rising and the productivity of labor is negative, with the negative quantities rising with each additional laborer: for example, -100 bu. becomes -110 bu., -125 bu., and so on as additional workers join the force.

In closing our discussion of the short-run relationships among the factor-services, it may be advisable briefly to summarize one more set of relationships. There is a relationship between the average product of labor and the marginal product of land. This relationship, from the nature of the mathematics involved, can be generalized as follows: when the average product of labor rises, the marginal product of land is negative; when the average product of labor stays constant, the marginal product of land is zero; and when the average product of labor is declining, the marginal product of land is positive and is rising. It can be shown that the same relation exists between the average product of land and the marginal product of labor. Accordingly the relation can be further generalized to read: when two factors collaborate in the production of a commodity, if the average product of one factor is rising, is constant, or is falling, the marginal product of the other factor is correspondingly negative, zero, or positive as well as increasing.

REASONS FOR THE LAW OF VARIABLE PROPORTIONS

The basic reason for the phenomenon of variable returns rests on the short-run *internal economies and diseconomies*. Superior efficiency is achieved in production as we apply, up to a certain point, progressively more units of the variable factor in a plant of given size or scale. Greater division and specialization of labor are possible, and more effective use can be made not only of the given amount of materials, tools, and other variables but also of fixed resources. One worker tending to a big and complicated machine is at a loss where to turn and what to do. But let two or three additional workers appear on the scene and much more will be accomplished with this machine. In general, a larger aggregate of the variable factor permits a more effective organization of the production processes resulting in increasing total product. Net internal economies prevail, so that a 10% rise in the input of a variable resource may result in a 14% rise in product. The total product (TP) curve is rising.

But only up to a certain point. Beyond a certain point the further dosing of the fixed factors with the variable resource may breed internal diseconomies: the plant becomes crowded with laborers. Moreover, the vigilant eye of the entrepreneur cannot discern every detail in every process and every misstep of crowded labor. For a while the internal economies and diseconomies cancel each other and the total product curve, rising in the *first* stage, flattens out and stays horizontal in the *second* stage. Then if still further units of the variable resource are applied, net internal diseconomies may begin to assert themselves. The TP (total product) curve declines: additional labor is accompanied by negative additions to total product. In this *third* stage, the marginal productivity of the variable is negative.

Then there is another consideration related to internal economies and diseconomies. When fixed and variable resources co-operate, one resource aids the other. How much aid one resource, land, can offer to the other resources, like labor, depends on how much there is of it and how many there are of them. In the *first* phase, the fixed factor, land, is plentiful in relation to the units of the variable factor and they receive much aid. In the *second* phase the tables are turned. As the units of the variable resource multiply they obtain less and less aid from the unvarying resource, land. Each extra unit of the variable resource adds less and less to total output. In the *third* phase, there is such a clutter of variable units that aid from the fixed factor, land, becomes insignificant. The marginal product of the variable factor turns negative.

SUGGESTED READINGS

Carlson, Sune, *A Study on the Pure Theory of Production.* London, P. S. King & Sons, 1931.

Cassels, J. M. "On the Law of Variable Proportions," *Explorations in Economics,* pp. 223–236. New York, McGraw-Hill, 1936. Reprinted in *Readings in the Theory of Income Distribution,* pp. 103–118.

Chamberlin, E. H. *The Theory of Monopolistic Competition,* 6th ed., Appendix B. Cambridge, Harvard University Press, 1948.

Due, J. F. *Intermediate Economic Analysis,* 4th ed., chap. 7. Homewood, Ill., R. D. Irwin, 1961.

Leftwich, R. H. *The Price System and Resource Allocation*, revised ed., chap. VII. New York, Holt, Rinehart and Winston, 1960.

Lerner, A. P. *The Economics of Control*, chaps. V–XVII. New York, Macmillan, 1947.

Stigler, G. J. *The Theory of Price*, revised ed., pp. 111–121. New York, Macmillan, 1955.

VI   The Theory of Production (Continued)

IN THIS chapter we complement and substitute. We add first the theory of the scale of the firm, which forms an integral part of the principles of production. Then we present vital aspects of the theory of production in the perspective of the indifference-curve method.

I. The Scale of the Firm

The theory of the scale of the firm runs along two channels. The traditional approach emphasizes indivisibilities as the root explanation of the fluctuating relation between the returns in output and the size of the firm. The other, newer, approach sees the explanation in the economies open to the large firm and in the diseconomies afflicting the firm as it extends its scale beyond a critical size. In this section we shall outline the first view; then briefly present the second; and finally indicate the author's preference, in compliance with requests of readers of the first edition of this book.

THE PROPORTION AND THE SCALE

The combination of a fixed factor with a complement of variable resources is a *proportion*. The plant constitutes an aggregate of proportions.

Inside the plant are machines with laborers around them, with tools and raw materials; offices with desks, typewriters, telephones, and filing cabinets; storerooms holding materials and appliances; and many other proportions. Any resource in the plant is either a variable co-operating with a fixed agent or a fixed agent co-operating with a variable. And there are wheels within wheels: variables co-operating with a fixed agent which in its turn is a variable in relation to another fixed agent. The floor space in a given plant is fixed, and the number of rooms is variable in relation to this floor space. In its turn, the room is fixed in relation to desks, the variable.

The plant as a whole is one large proportion. Over the short normal period the plant is constant in size; and the number of plants and firms in the industry is unchanged. Inside the plant, over the short period, the machines are fixed in size and number; or the chain belts; or the blast furnaces. Over the long normal period the plant and these other fixed factors alike can be varied. However, even then, in the opinion of most economists, one fixed factor endures: the top management. On this reasoning the firm functions in the long run as one great proportion between management and such variables as the physical plant, machines, and labor.

Now we come to the concept of the *scale* of the firm. In the customary analysis a clear-cut distinction is made between the proportion and the scale. The number of times all proportions are reproduced, that is, the number of times the fixed, and therefore also the variable, resources are multiplied, establishes the scale of the firm. Small scale means a small family, a small multiple of proportions; large scale means a large family of proportions. The proportions in a small firm are necessarily of a different nature from the proportions in a large firm; so that the large firm is not merely the small firm with all its proportions multiplied by a constant.

In a small firm, the proportions consist of simple machinery and of equipment modest in size and complexity. In the large firm, proportions refer to the co-operation of more complex and more specialized aggregates of equipment, with variables of materials and labor different in amounts and quality from their counterparts in the small firm. Changing the scale of the firm implies changing all the fixed factors, and in the same proportion. Raising the scale by 10% means raising each fixed factor by 10%— and therefore using more variables by 10%. To repeat, in the short run, we increase output by applying more and more units of the variable factor to the existing fixed factors; in the long run, by increasing the size of the firm, that is, by installing additional fixed factors.

RETURNS TO SCALE

The central problem in the economics of scale is "returns to scale." This phrase refers to the behavior of output of the firm as its scale is increasing in response to a growing industry. The decisive question is: when the scale is raised by 10%, what will happen to output?

When *all* productive resources, fixed and variable alike, are increased in the same proportion and the scale of operations is thus enlarged, the resulting output displays three stages. At *first* there is increasing return to scale; the total product rises more than in proportion to the increase of all the inputs; it rises, that is, at a greater rate than the rate of growth of all the productive services. Raise the scale by 10%, and output rises by 15%. *Next*, in many cases, as the scale of the firm continues to grow, the disproportionate climb in total output ceases, and instead a constant rate of growth in production is observed; the total output mounts in proportion to, or at the same rate as, the rise in inputs. Beyond a certain point, a rise in scale by 10% is followed by a 10% rise in output. This is the stage of constant returns to scale. *Finally*, with the still further growth of the scale of the firm, decreasing returns emerge. The total product indeed becomes larger but it does so at a lower rate than the rate of growth of all the factors used in production. A 10% rise in scale may go with only a 7% rise in total output. The returns to scale trace, then, a curve ⌐‾, like a dish bottom up (the x axis for this curve being output, the y axis, input).

THE TRADITIONAL EXPLANATION: INDIVISIBILITY

Why do returns to scale behave in this manner? The answer generally given rests on the conception of indivisibility of certain resources in the categories of equipment and labor.

A linotype machine, a locomotive, or a blast furnace comes in a small variety of sizes. Suppose that of two machines the smaller one can, with the best proportion of variable resources, produce a maximum of 100 units of an article per day and the larger machine can turn out 250 units. A small firm with a call for 140 units a day cannot make the most economical use of these machines, either two small or one large. Part of the time, in either case, a machine will stand idle. If machines were divisible and came in many sizes, the small firm would have no problem on its hands. It would acquire one or two machines which would turn out the daily product of 140 units. (The newer view would not build the analysis on indivisibility:

it would stress that the *large* firm would have no difficulty in acquiring machines of the desired size.)

Furthermore, even if there is a degree of divisibility and machines come in many sizes and the small firm uses them, diseconomies are inevitable. The large motor delivering twice the power of a small motor does not generally occupy twice the floor space or twice the cubic space, and does not require for its operation twice the number of workers nor twice as much light. A plant five times the size of a small plant does not demand five times the lighting and heating. In other words, when units of equipment are available in various sizes and *seem* divisible, the efficiency of the small unit often is not equal to the efficiency of the large unit. The reason back of these shortcomings of the small firm is lodged in one fact: insufficient divisibility of the resource involved; insufficient to the traditional eyes. (Again, the *size* of the firm, and not the fiction of *divisibility*, is the governing element.)

In the view of traditional theory, indivisibility may also apply to *workers*. A small firm cannot employ one-half of a night watchman, one-third of an engineer, or one-fourth of a statistician. Many a small store could do with less than one hired clerk. It may need a clerk for half time. The result is that the returns per unit of labor and other resources may be smaller for the small business firm than for the large one. (The large firm has no trouble with such fractions; it does not run into them.)

Another aspect of the indivisibility of labor expresses itself in marketing. Quantity buying of needed materials and quantity selling of the finished product are more economical to both buyer and seller. It takes only a little more of the time of responsible officials to correspond about a large order than about a small order. The loading and unloading and the packing and unpacking of a large consignment does not require labor and equipment in direct proportion to the small consignment. The buying or selling effort is not so finely divisible that handling half a ton of merchandise entails half the resources needed in handling one ton. (Again, the *size* of the firm wins over divisibility.)

Note should be made of the fact that the traditional analysis recognizes that with the enlargement of scale the proportions themselves become different. Larger enterprises can use specialized skills, an elaborate division of labor, and a superior equipment which small firms cannot afford. Thus size by itself affects the variation of output with scale. However, this *independent* significance of size is not stressed but is, moreover, subordinated to indivisibilities.

These indivisibilities of equipment and labor help explain why output at first rises more than proportionately to inputs (and why unit cost declines) as the scale of the firm is enlarged. (Returns to scale are involved here and not divisibility.)

We now come to the other question: after a certain scale has been reached, why does the total output begin to rise less than proportionately to inputs, and why does average unit cost begin to mount? Put differently, the question is: why do net diseconomies appear beyond a certain critical scale?

The answer to this question, too, is found in indivisibility, the fixed factor of management which we have already mentioned. The top administration of a firm is the bearer of ultimate responsibility in all matters involving co-ordination, risk taking, innovation, and decision making. As the scale of the firm expands, some of the managerial functions are delegated to various top-flight officials. Nonetheless there remains the single brain, or the combined brains of a small group of persons, at the top of the pyramid, as the one principal and final co-ordinator and decision maker. Herein resides the fixed, indivisible factor. Beyond a certain scale the firm becomes an intricate domain of plants and branches; of departments and offices; of junior heads, experts, and foremen; of reports upward and instructions downward; and of rules, checks, and balances. Management necessarily becomes less efficient. Impersonal relations, inflexible routines, divided responsibility, and lack of initiative are apt to develop along the line. The result expresses itself in less than proportionate returns to scale. The limited number of hours available for work each day sets a limit to the entrepreneur's scope of activity in hiring upper officials, in attending conferences with his chief subordinates, in adjusting differences of opinion among the top-flight specialists, in reading final reports or summaries of them, and in formulating basic policy. The limits to the entrepreneur's activities in, say, an 8-hour day govern the limits to the size of the firm. (The source of trouble here is the *oversized* firm.)

The assumption basic to the concept of divisibility of resources is that no loss of efficiency is sustained when we postulate miniatures of a factor of fixed size. When we suppose that our small firm producing 140 articles per day solves its problem by installing one machine putting out 100 articles and another machine two-fifths its size, we assume that the smaller machine will operate at an efficiency exactly equal to two-fifths the efficiency of the standard machine: that it will produce 40 articles per unit of time. The assumption is made that the ratio of total cost to output, the unit cost, is the same for the imaginary diminutive models as for the machines in actual operation. Indivisibility thus means the presence of lumpy factors which cannot be acquired in smaller sizes of *proportionate* efficiency; with the consequence that the output of the small-scale firm cannot be produced as cheaply per unit as the output of the large-scale firm. (The issue centers once more on size or oversize of the firm.)

With unlimited divisibility of all resources, economies and diseconomies of scale disappear; there is no such phenomenon as nonproportional returns to scale and no such thing as falling and then rising unit costs as the scale of the firm is extended. With the growth of the scale, the output curve and the long-run average cost curve trace horizontal lines. The large firm has no advantage over the small firm. Says Professor F. H. Knight in expounding the principle of indivisibility: "*If* the amounts of *all* elements in a combination were freely variable without limit and the product also continuously divisible, it is evident that one size of combination would be precisely similar in its workings to any other similarly composed." [1]

THE NEWER APPROACH TO THE THEORY OF SCALE

As was already mentioned, the second theory of scale stresses the economies of size as reflected in greater division and specialization of labor and equipment alike. Prominent among the proponents of this thesis is Professor E. H. Chamberlin.[2] What follows is a brief summary of some of his views.

(1) The economies and diseconomies of scale are the combined expression of proportion *and* size. The best proportions and the best scale are determined simultaneously. Size, as such, is responsible for economies to the firm at least on two grounds: as more resources are used there is opportunity for greater specialization; also, the larger firm can choose superior techniques and better machines from among the techniques and machines available at a given state of knowledge. The proportion, far from being sovereign and autonomous, may depend for its character upon the scale of the firm; and the scale cannot be dissociated from the proportions. The two are interdependent.

(2) The indivisibilities are not as prevalent as is assumed. Labor can be made divisible on the time basis. Half a statistician does not exist, but a statistician can be employed for half-time. The laborer cannot be divided, but his time can be. Labor can also be made divisible by qualitative variation. Fewer or more workers of smaller or greater skill can be used. A worker and a half of one type may be replaced by one worker of a superior type or by two workers of a different type. Similarly with machines. They can be made divisible on the basis of time by leasing or sharing; and by varying their qualitative elements.

(3) The accepted doctrine that larger firms can command superior

---

[1] *Risk, Uncertainty and Profit* (Boston, Houghton Mifflin, 1921), p. 98. Italics in the original.

[2] "Proportionality, Divisibility and Economies of Scale," *Quarterly Journal of Economics,* Vol. LXII (February, 1948), pp. 229–262; comments by A. N. McLeod and F. H. Hahn, and reply by Chamberlin, *ibid.,* Vol. LXIII (February, 1949), pp. 128–143. This article is reprinted in E. H. Chamberlin, *The Theory of Monopolistic Competition,* 6th ed. (Cambridge, Harvard University Press, 1948), Appendix B.

resources and proportions moves on the right track. But the failure to give this idea sufficient emphasis in the full-dress discussion of scale is a grave error. At least size ought to be made co-ordinate with the proportion in the explanation of the behavior of returns to scale. Instead, this effect of *size* is recorded and then ignored. Often enough it is presented as an illustration of the indivisibility of the fixed factor.

Even if the basic proportions remain unchanged and even when indivisibility is not a problem, size alone may cause nonproportional returns. Ten woodworkers, all of the same capacity and each with the customary kit of tools, set to making chairs will introduce division and specialization of tasks and will produce more than ten times as many chairs per week as will one of these woodworkers, with his kit, working alone.

(4) Professor Chamberlin is far from turning his back on the fixed-factor analysis. He denies, however, that there is validity in the assertion that the indivisibility of the constant factor is responsible for nonproportional returns. He sees no meaning in the argument that if the fixed resource were perfectly divisible, then returns per unit of variable resource would stay uniform and the average output curve would be horizontal. We do not know how efficient a divisible agent would be if a nondivisible agent were to become divisible. "In the same way, if horses cannot fly, there is no way of finding out how high they could fly, if they could." [3]

(5) The economies and diseconomies of scale are not to be charged to management as a *fixed factor*. Management is divisible, by delegation of responsibility and in other ways. After a critical scale has been attained management becomes too complex and bureaucratic, therefore inefficient and costly. Such is the fate of too large an enterprise no matter how divisible management may be.

If entrepreneurship is divisible, the question may arise why a giant firm does not split itself into separate units each with its own management, thus removing the inefficiency of complex administration. To this query, Professor Chamberlin says: "The question is whether the firm, as the 'control unit,' can divest itself *completely* of control over its component parts; . . . yet there must always be a residue of authority in central hands." There is a limit to decentralization, and ". . . the [unit-cost] curve does turn up somewhere." [4]

(6) The definition of divisibility framed to include the proviso of no loss in efficiency is question begging. "To assume that factors are 'perfectly divisible' carries with it no implication whatever as to how their efficiency will be affected in the process." [5] Divisibility ought to be defined

[3] *The Theory of Monopolistic Competition*, Appendix B, p. 244, n. 1. Italics in the original.
[4] *Ibid.*, p. 248, n. 1. Italics in the original.
[5] *Ibid.*, p. 238.

without such a proviso; then, in the perspective of the definition, the effect of divisibility on efficiency ought to be subjected to examination. There is no warrant for ruling out economies and diseconomies of scale simply because divisibility is assumed. Resources may be finely divisible and yet a small firm will be restricted in the possibilities of division of labor and equipment, whereas a large firm will not be.

SCALE AND INDIVISIBILITY

If a choice is to be made between these two theories, the Chamberlin approach seems to be more acceptable, and for the following reasons.

In the *first* place, the idea of divisibility of a factor is a blurred idea. What is meant by half a worker or half a machine? by one-fifth of a scientist or one-third of a night watchman? What do we see in our mind's eye as we talk about such fractions?

In the *second* place, even if we adopt, for the sake of the argument, the concept of divisibility, we come face to face with another difficulty. As was already stated, the assumption basic to the concept of divisibility of a factor necessarily implies that there is no loss of proportionate efficiency when we deal with a fraction of a factor. The indispensable assumption claims that one-tenth of a horse will raise total output by one-tenth of the increment in output brought in by a full-bodied horse; that half a machine will add to the total product one-half of the amount of product added by a whole machine. It is mere conjecture, however, to affirm that, for example, one-third of a businessman in one-third of a factory with machines one-third in size will produce one-third of the output which could be produced by one full unit of the same factors. We do not know how much output imaginary fractions of factor-inputs can turn out per unit of time.

In contrast, the new approach to the theory of returns to scale does not rest on wayward, far-fetched assumptions. It moves on the foundations of economies and diseconomies of scale. As the scale of the firm expands, in response to the expanded scale of the industry, the advantage of size asserts itself in long-run internal economies, economies of scale, which are now even greater than the short-run internal economies. In the short run, we recall, one certain resource is variable unit by unit and the other resources are held constant. But in the long run all resources are variable. There are accordingly greater flexibility and more play in substitutions, in combinations of factors, in specialization of labor and machines alike, in division of labor, and in superior, and therefore more expensive, mechanical appliances and devices. The result is that, as the scale of the firm is enlarged, internal economies help in producing a more than proportional return to scale.

This is not all. As an industry gains in scale it does so primarily by the entry of new firms into this industry, attracted by the long-run rise in the demand for its product, which is the original stimulus back of the rising scale of the industry. With the enlarged size of the industry, external economies make an appearance.

By *external economies* we mean that because of its large size the industry invites certain developments outside the firms, which breed economies to the firms in the industry. Laboring people become interested in the industry and move to the areas where the plants are located. Manchester and other towns in the British textile center are the magnet, the workers are the iron filings. Recruiting the *labor* force becomes less expensive in labor-hours of the recruiting agent. Trade journals appear which help in spreading *knowledge* of better ways of doing things. *Subsidiary* and correlated firms spring up which provide the expanding industry with accessories. New *intermediate* industries and a diversification of processes insert themselves between previous stages of production. Thus grows up a greater specialization on fewer processes, with benefit to the firms in a longer chain of vertical disintegration; that is, an important process may be splintered off from the chain of processes and turned over to an outside firm which learns to specialize in such a process. Also, jobbers, wholesalers, brokers, and *bankers* attach themselves to the industry, offering expert knowledge and varieties of accommodations. The large-scale firm reaps long-run internal economies, or economies of scale; the large-scale industry brings to the firm external economies.

But there is the other side of the coin: external diseconomies, the diseconomies of scale. The chief diseconomy of scale is reflected in the deterioration of management, as we pointed out earlier in the present section when discussing indivisibility of management. By external diseconomies we mean that the entry of new firms into an industry generates intensive bidding among the firms for labor of rare skill and for special high-priced raw materials, with the consequence that the prices for these productive agents is driven up too high in the market. This situation is referred to as external diseconomies because, far from developing inside the plant, these agents and the price for their services are market phenomena, outside the firm; but they move *into* the firm, raising costs, and bringing about other changes.

In the perspective of these economies and diseconomies the varying returns to scale can be explained without importing questionable assumptions. Suppose the scale of the firms is increased by 10%. The returns in product may rise by 15%: the internal economies, bred by the size of the plant, combined with the external economies, bred largely by the size of the industry, do more than overcome the corresponding diseconomies.

Result: at first the larger scale of the firm asserts itself by a rising total-output curve, running steeply at the beginning and then less steeply. (Why?) At the other extreme, expanding the scale of the firm may evoke net internal and external diseconomies, so that doubling the scale of the firm may be accompanied by an 80% rise in output and not by 100%, or by 110%. The total-output curve is declining. Between these two extremes there may be a region in which economies are neutralized by diseconomies; the total product curve flattens out then and runs parallel to the x axis. For an illustration we can consult the total product (TP) curve in Figure 15 or in Figure 16, in the preceding chapter. In both figures the flattening part of the TP curve is omitted in the diagrams.

The issue tends to crystallize when questions are raised. Why is it uneconomical for the small firm to use a large machine? Why is it wasteful to have a high-rank officer to attend to a small order? The old answer is: indivisibility; the new answer is: small-size firm. The large firm can afford to use the big machine; it can also afford a division of labor in which a junior officer attends to the many small orders. The small store needs half a clerk, the large store employs two full-bodied clerks. To expect the small firm to operate generally like a large firm is to have Hercules try to clean the Augean stables with a toothbrush—to exaggerate a bit.

OPTIMUM, OR LEAST-COST, COMBINATIONS OF RESOURCES

In the opening pages of the previous chapter, we mentioned three segments or sectors in the theory of production. We have already encountered the first two; the third sector brings into view the relationship among the four types of factor-services. This sector gives room to four problems: (1) the marginal revenue product (MRP) of a factor, that is, the increment of dollar output contributed by one extra unit of a factor barely worth using in production; (2) the nature of the demand for a factor-service; (3) the determinants of the price paid by the firm for a unit of input, like the wage rate or the interest rate; and (4) the optimum allocation of productive resources. Of these problems the last one is examined here; the other three will be merely referred to as needed. They will receive attention in Chapter XIII, after the treatment of certain antecedent concepts and problems.

The optimum combination of resources is responsible for two outstanding results: the least-cost or most efficient production of a given output, and maximum profit to the firm. The businessman tends to combine a variety of resources in such a proportion that a given amount of a product will be made most efficiently, that is, at least cost. One way of calculating the least cost is to figure the cost of all possible combinations suggested by the production function. For each technical combination of factors we multiply each input by its market price and add these sums. The *least-cost* combination wins.

This method of getting at the least-cost combination is too laborious. Besides, we are interested in generalizations and not in the arithmetic of multiplication and addition. The problem at hand is essentially the first cousin of the problem faced by the consumer who allocates his money income among various commodities with the end in mind of obtaining maximum satisfaction.

With competition ruling in the factor-market, the entrepreneur achieves the least-cost combination for the production of a given output by substituting inexpensive inputs for the costly inputs, until the following equations emerge:

$$\frac{\text{MPP of } A}{\text{Price of } A} = \frac{\text{MPP of } B}{\text{Price of } B} = \ldots$$

It would hardly be premature to elaborate a little on the meaning of these numerators and denominators. We shall begin with the assertion that MPP (the marginal physical product) represents the increment in physical output which an extra unit of a given input, just worth hiring, adds to the total output—other things equal. Let A and B stand for two types of factor-services. The prices of A and B symbolize two types of compensation, in wages to labor and in interest to the bondholder whose money purchased capital goods for the factory. We assume that the market price for factor-services is not deranged by the hirings and firings of our firm.

Such equations as the ones above tell us that the last dollar's worth of each factor hired will bring the same amount of MPP, marginal physical product. Should the first of the above two fractions be larger than the second fraction, the firm will begin to substitute factor A (labor units) for factor B (units of capital). As the firm does this, the first fraction becomes progressively smaller because as the firm buys progressively more of A the marginal physical product of A grows less and less. Similarly as the amount of B grows smaller (because of the substitutions of A for B) the MPP of B mounts. The substitution goes on until the two fractions are equal. Thus we attain the least-cost combination of the factor-services.

The businessman does not stop with the type of behavior which the *economist* describes by these equations and which the *economist* regards as a guide to the businessman in the production of goods most efficiently, at least cost. What he is after is maximum profit from the production and sale of the output. This goal is achieved by employing each factor's service up to the point at which the marginal revenue product (MRP) of the extra unit of the factor-service (labor or capital) equals the price (wage or interest) paid for it by the firm per unit of time—until the MRP of the extra unit covers its cost to the firm. At this point the worker is worthy of his hire; capital, too.

Related to these aspects of production theory is the significance of the connection between any two resources used in production. If factors A and B, labor and capital, are substitutive, an increment in A (labor units) will lower the marginal productivity of B (given units of capital), other things equal. The reason is not far to seek. An increment in A (labor units) has the same effect as an appropriate increment in B (units of capital), for the reason that A and B are substitutes, and a rise in units of A is like a rise in units of B. Likewise an increment in B will, other things equal, depress the marginal physical product (MPP) of A. Since A and B are substitutes the increment in B acts like an increment in A; and an increment in A, other things equal, will tend to depress the MPP of A.

Not so if A and B are complementary. A rise in the hired units of A will by itself fail to add to total output, inasmuch as, in order to produce, A needs the aid of B. Empty-handed labor (A) cannot produce goods: a rise in A calls for a corresponding rise in B. Result: the more we hire of A the greater the MPP of B. Without the additional B the increment of A contributes little to total output; but with the additional B there can be a rise in total product per unit of time.

II. Indifference-Curve Analysis of Production

In Chapters III and IV we discussed the behavior of the consumer whose objective is maximization of total utility from the expenditure of his money income on goods and services per unit of time. In the preceding chapter and in this present chapter we are examining the behavior of the producer whose objective is the maximization of profits from producing and selling given articles or given services per unit of time. The indifference-curve technique contributes to the analysis of consumer reaction. This technique can likewise contribute toward the clarification of the conduct of the producer. In the remainder of this chapter the purpose is to present the theory of production by the indifference-curve approach.

The student will do well first to review Chapter IV. He will notice quite a number of parallels in the concepts and procedures pertinent to the study alike of consumer and producer reactions. The stepping stones in our traditional exposition of the principles of production, in the previous chapter and so far in this developing chapter, have been: substitution and complementariness of productive resources; the law of variable proportions, especially diminishing returns; returns to the scale of the business firm; the optimum combination of factor-services, technically and cost-wise, in producing an article; and the least-cost or the greatest efficiency in production. Now we face the same job, only it will be done differently. We shall not strain ourselves to produce each parallel nor to set the parallels in the same sequence. Our job is to discuss the theory of production from the indifference-curve viewpoint; this job has prior claim on the relevant ideas and the order of their appearance.

ISOQUANTS

First we have to acquaint ourselves with a prominent tool of analysis, the isoquant. An isoquant is a curve on which every point indicates a different combination of *two* types of factor-resources, like units of labor, or the labor-hour, and units of capital, but represents the production of the *same* total output per unit of time. The units of capital may refer to a machine or to a kit of tools required in the production, for example, of plain wooden chairs. Hence the name isoquant, "equal quantity" (produced). An isoquant to the right of another isoquant indicates a higher uniform total product for any factor combination suggested by a point along its path. The farther up to the right an isoquant is, the greater this total product becomes at each point on it. There is a small variety of isoquants each distinguished by the telltale slope which it has. We shall confine ourselves to some typical variants of isoquants and to some nontypical variants.

Some typical and nontypical isoquants are illustrated by Figure 17. Labor units are measured on the horizontal axis and units of capital on the vertical axis. The product is wooden chairs. The total product stays constant on each isoquant: 100 chairs at each point on the lowest isoquant, 500 chairs on any point on the topmost isoquant. For the moment we leave aside the dotted arcs.

The isoquants are based, in our discussion, on a combination of two factors, as if only two types of resources collaborate to produce the article. This simplification is due to the difficulty of comprehension, and presentation, of the relations between more than two factor-resources. To include a third factor-resource means three dimensions on the flat page; getting into space is also difficult in economics. In the production of most commodities many discrete resources are employed: skilled, semiskilled, and unskilled labor; capital in the form of varieties of raw materials, tools, machines, trucks, computers, chain belts, construction, and inventory. Then in almost each case of production we deal with possible substitutions among them; then subvarieties of the varieties of labor: some are skilled in handling raw materials, others are adept with tools only, or with machines only, or with one type of machine and not with another type.

A commodity may therefore be produced by 20 "factors." How capture all their relations, all the possible substitutions until we are sure that we have reached the optimum, the least-cost, combination for the production of a given number of chairs per unit of time? What we can do is to study the various relations that govern two types of resources, like land and labor, again on the assumption that the production of a commodity requires no more than two kinds of resources.

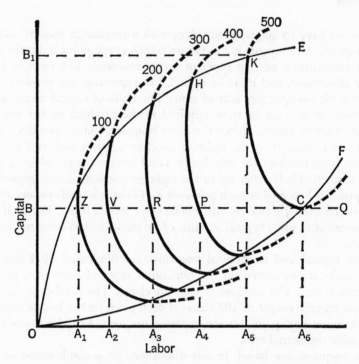

FIGURE 17. *Typical and Nontypical Isoquant Segments*

The anatomy of a typical isoquant is revealed by a number of characteristics, including causal connections. We shall take up some of them.

We note two differences between the isoquant and the iso-utility curve: (1) The third dimension of an iso-utility curve, namely total utility, cannot be measured, whereas the total produced by the various combinations of the two resources along the isoquant curve is definite—in our example, 500 chairs for resources along the isoquant curve at the top, 400 chairs for the isoquant next on the left. (2) The expenditure of the consumer is more or less limited by his money income in a unit of time, but the businessman can vary, within limits, his expenditures on the factor-services hired to produce chairs.

Just as an iso-utility curve cannot be tangent to its neighbor curve, so a given isoquant cannot be *tangent* to its neighbor isoquant. If one isoquant were to touch another, the point of tangency would belong to two isoquants. As a point on the lower isoquant, it would stand for a small total of chairs; but as a point on the next upper isoquant, the tangency point would have to stand for a larger number of chairs. But one given point cannot represent *two* different combinations of the two resources; nor can this point blow hot and cold and claim two different quantities of chairs. In such a case tangency makes as little sense as a "white blackbird."

Similar reasoning would argue against the proposition that one isoquant can *intersect* another isoquant.

The typical isoquant slopes to the right. The reason is that, beginning with point K in Figure 17 and ending with point C, we witness a steady substitution of labor for capital: more labor, less capital.

At point K on the top isoquant, 500 chairs could be produced by the combination of KB_1 units of labor and KA_5 or OB_1 units of capital. At point C the same 500 chairs could be produced by the combination of CB units of labor and CA_6 or OB units of capital. In the process of making a given number of chairs, labor units may be extended from OA_1 to OA_6, but the need for capital is stubborn. As additional labor is hired, it serves to displace some capital. As we move along an isoquant, we go to the right and downward: the isoquant slopes to the right. In this movement we note the reality, and the concept, of the *marginal rate of technical or physical substitution*, the MRS of labor for capital. The succession of points along an isoquant represents the substitution of x for y: more x, less y. By this concept of MRS we mean the amount of capital that can be spared by the last extra units of labor, put by the businessman into the combination to displace some of the capital. The MRS of labor for capital is, to remind ourselves, the *slope* of the isoquant at any point. It is $-\Delta y/\Delta x$: in this case y is capital and x is labor. We move down $(-y)$ and forward (x).

The isoquant is *convex* to the horizontal axis. As more units of labor are put into the factor-combination to produce chairs, the drop in the capital used becomes smaller and smaller. It takes progressively more units of labor to substitute for capital if the total production of chairs is not to decline below 500 per unit of time. Once more, we come upon the concept of the *diminishing marginal rate of technical substitution*.

There is a relation between the marginal rate of inputs-substitution (MRS) and the marginal physical product (MPP) of these inputs. Let us consider any point in Figure 17. If in the combination at the chosen point an extra unit of capital adds 50 chairs to the total output, and if an extra unit of labor adds 30 chairs per unit of time, the MRS (the marginal rate of substitution of labor units for capital) means that adding one unit of labor raises the total product by 30 chairs per unit of time; giving up $\frac{3}{5}$ unit of capital depresses total output by 30 chairs. Thus,

$$\text{MRS of labor for capital} = \frac{-\Delta y}{\Delta x} = \frac{-3}{5} = \frac{\text{MPP}_r}{\text{MPP}_1};$$

in the last fraction of this equation the numerator designates the marginal physical product of labor and the denominator reflects the marginal physical product of capital. In building a road we may employ more and more capital like mixers, trucks, tractors, steam-shovels as a substitute for labor. With the first units of capital, say steam shovels, much labor can be displaced, perhaps 20 coolies. With additional amounts of capital, less labor will be displaced, until no further displacement is economical, for the reason that road-building capital appliances are not (yet) robots; they are useless without the guiding hand and mind of labor. A minimum of labor is indispensable.

THE WASTE-BEARING SEGMENTS OF AN ISOQUANT

By "waste-bearing" we mean that the marginal combination of inputs is partly or wholly accompanied by zero or negative output. First of all, the *dotted* segments of an isoquant invite attention. The fundamental fact is that not all the points on an isoquant mean the same thing. Some segments tell one story, other segments are supposed to tell another story. To distinguish one story from the other, we draw the isoquant curve in part solid and in part dotted. The features of the *central* part KC of isoquant 500 in Figure 17 were discussed in previous paragraphs. The striking novelty about the *dotted* segments derives from the fact that they portray a rise in *both* resources: the dots move *upward* to the *right*. The movement upward boosts the amount of capital, the movement to the right means that more labor units (labor-hours) are employed. The dotted segments illustrate nontypical, non-serviceable segments of an isoquant.

A study of points K and C may not be without reward. Point K is the upper terminal of the solid part of isoquant 500. (1) At point K this isoquant is vertical and parallel to the vertical axis. (2) There is no slope and no substitution of capital for labor—as is the case with any vertical (and horizontal) line. This means that K indicates the irreducible minimum of capital needed in the production of 500 chairs. (3) The marginal physical product of capital amounts to zero; in other words, the last extra unit of capital adds nothing to the previous total output of chairs by the firm, in a unit of time. (4) If we also employ a larger amount of capital than OB, the productivity of capital goes negative. In order to counteract this negative tendency and produce the uniform number of chairs, 500 of them, per unit of time, we need more labor units to match the larger amount of capital and to make it productive. This is why the dotted part of an isoquant moves up to the right. A businessman guided by self-interest will not consider combinations suggested by the *upper* dotted segments. He can do better by selecting a combination of the two resources as suggested by a point along segment KC: the input will be smaller and yet the product will be 500 chairs.

Nor will the firm be interested in the *lower dotted* segments. Point C, like point K, is the terminal of the economical production of chairs. At C the isoquant is flat, parallel to the horizontal axis. Again, no slope; no substitution of labor for capital; no increment of product is made by the marginal unit of labor: the marginal physical productivity of labor is zero. Again, the combination of the two types of inputs, labor and capital, is larger and more costly than the combination reflected by a point on KC; and yet the product is no more than 500 chairs per unit of time. The businessman will not be foolish enough to use more input and obtain no larger an output. The "invisible hand," sponsored by Adam Smith, will refuse to guide the foolish entrepreneur. Thus curves OE and OF touch each isoquant at points at which the same situation develops as around points K and C just discussed. What is true of K and C is true of H and L and of the terminal points on the other isoquants. Curves OE and OF are the boundaries beyond which it is poor economics to use any combination of labor and capital suggested by the *dotted* segments. Curves OE and OF are called *ridge lines*. Economic combinations of resources in the production of an article are lodged between the two ridges.

It is not surprising to discover that the law of variable proportions is no stronger to the indifference-curve approach. We recall that we keep one of the two variables constant in quality and amount, and apply more and more units of the other variable resource to collaborate with the fixed. We turn once more to Figure 17.

Assume that in making chairs the amount of capital used is fixed at OB and forms therefore a line BQ parallel to the horizontal axis. Collaborating with this steady amount of capital are quantities of labor coming in succession and measured by OA_1, OA_2, OA_3, OA_4, OA_5, and OA_6. As we apply doses of the variable resource the total product grows, first more than in the proportion of the variable; for example, the variable, labor, may rise 10% in quantity and the resulting output may rise by 15%. In Figure 17 the number of workers producing 100 chairs is OA_1 or BZ. To produce 200 chairs per unit of time, OA_2 units of labor co-operate with the OB units of capital; OA_2 is less than twice OA_1. The reason is internal economies. As more labor is introduced in the chair factory a better organization of the enterprise can be attained.

In the *first* phase of the law of variable proportions there is too much capital in *relation* to labor—we are dealing with ratios and not with absolute magnitudes. As the number of workers grows, the productivity of the fixed capital becomes less and less negative (for example, —10, —4, —1) until it reaches zero at the end of the first phase. The first phase is not economical; and this phase is the realm of the dotted segments above the ridge line $OHKE$. But sooner or later, as more units of labor appear on the scene, the *second* phase begins. In this phase both resources become productive. This phase is exemplified by the solid segment, like KC on the topmost isoquant; by the solid segment HL of the next isoquant to the left; and so on with the other isoquants to the left. In this phase we observe the phenomenon of diminishing returns exemplified by isoquant 300. To produce, for example, 300 chairs instead of 200 per unit of time, the number of workers has to be more than proportionate to the rise in output; 300 chairs constitute 150% of 200 chairs; but the rise of labor units from OA_2 to OA_3 is more than 150% of the rise of labor from OA_1 to OA_2. The dotted segments below ridge line OF display the *third* phase of the law of variable proportions. Now, in relation to the fixed capital there is too much labor. The productivity of capital is negative.

Once more the business firm will find it wasteful to operate in accord with the first phase or the third phase. It is more economical to make chairs by a combination of the two resources suggested by the proper point between K and C if 500 chairs are to be produced, between H and L if the firm decides to produce 400 chairs.

OUTLAY LINES

Technically each isoquant represents an indifference curve to the firm. Technically it does not matter to the firm which combination of inputs it may use inasmuch as they all result in a uniform total output per unit of time. But as soon as we turn from physical inputs to their dollar-costs, only one combination of resources is the least-cost, the most efficient, combination. To incorporate the dollar sign, we have to deal with outlay lines.

This type of curve goes by various names in addition to outlay line: price line, factor-cost line, isocost curve, factor-price line, and outlay contour. Each line represents various combinations of two inputs which can be hired for a *given* total amount of money. The price of each unit of factor-service is known; and the assumption is made that the factor market is competitive, so that the input prices, like the wage rate, remain constant as the firm calls for varying amounts of a service. This curve is of the same order as the outlay curve indicating the combinations of goods which the consumer can purchase with a given amount of money and derive maximum satisfaction.

Figure 18 illustrates outlay lines. The axes measure labor and land. The

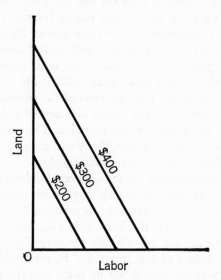

FIGURE 18. *A Map of Outlay Lines*

first outlay line sums up the various combinations of land and labor which, at their market prices, could be hired for $200. Again, as we move to the right the lines represent larger total outlays: the third dimension grows. If land can be leased for $5 a unit and labor can be hired for $3 a unit, the equation of an outlay line takes the form of $5d + 3r = c$, where d and r signify the amount of the inputs (land and labor) in the combinations and c designates the total expenditure. Such an equation is the equation of a straight line. The outlay lines are straight lines: we assume fixed factor-prices, so that the equation is always of the form just indicated.

The slope of an isocost line indicates the marginal rate of outlay substitution between the inputs. If the slope is steep, an extra unit of labor can replace a good deal of land without affecting the total expenditure. If the outlay line descends gradually, the addition of a unit of labor requires the abandoning of but little land in order to maintain the level of total outlay.

The marginal rate of outlay substitution of labor for land equals the ratio of their prices; it equals, that is, the ratio of the price of labor to the price of land:

$$\text{MRS (of labor for land)} = \frac{\text{price of } x \text{ (labor)}}{\text{price of } y \text{ (land)}}.$$

If the land costs \$5 a day and the wage rate is \$10 a day, the MRS of labor for land will be two units of land for one labor-day, without change of total expenditure on these inputs. The outlay forgone by giving up two units of one input is expended on the extra unit of the other input. Since the price of the inputs in our assumed *competitive* factor market is identical with their marginal costs (the additional costs incurred as additional units are produced) we can also write: $\text{MRS} = MC_x/MC_y$. That is, the slope of an outlay line is equal to the ratio of the marginal costs of inputs y and x. With the prices of the inputs constant, the slope of an isocost line remains unchanged from point to point. This indicates once more that an outlay line is a straight line. Since the slopes are identical for all isocost lines, these lines are parallel to one another.

If the two inputs command the same price, the slope of the outlay line will be unity. The line then forms a 45° angle with either axis. If the price of the input plotted along the vertical axis is higher (lower) than the price of the input measured along the horizontal axis, the isocost line will be less (more) steep than the isocost line forming the 45° angle. In each combination less (more) of one input will be used with one unit of the other input than was the case when its price was the same as the price of the other service. The more expensive input is economized; the cheaper input tends to replace the dearer input in each combination. The slope of the isocost line will change similarly if the price of the y input rises or falls more than the price of the x input.

THE LEAST-COST COMBINATION: THE EFFICIENCY OF THE FIRM

With the aid of isoquants and isocost lines various problems can be resolved. One of them is finding the least-cost or optimum combination of factors for a given output. The production function tells us that the same output can be produced by various combinations of factors. The isoquant portrays the array of such combinations. But, given the market prices of the productive services, only one of these combinations costs the firm the least amount of money to produce the given output per unit of time. When the firm wishes to spend a certain sum on production, only one combination will yield the largest output of minimum average cost; only one combination will reflect the optimum allocation of the firm's given expenditure and will exemplify maximum efficiency. Which combination is it?

Assume that the firm plans an expenditure of $400 on inputs. We draw one such outlay line and a map of isoquants (Figure 19). The maximum-

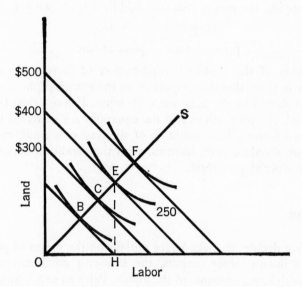

FIGURE 19. *Equal-Cost Lines and Least-Cost Combinations*

profit position, and therefore the equilibrium position, of the firm is at point *E*, where the given isocost line is tangent to one of the isoquants. The third dimension of this isoquant indicates that the maximum output which can be obtained with the outlay of $400 is 250 bu. The co-ordinates of point *E* give us the optimum combination of labor (*OH* units) and land (*HE* units). This is the least-cost and the most efficient combination. It is also a position of stable equilibrium. With any other combination the output for the outlay of $400 would be smaller than 250 bu.; or else, to get a yield of 250 bu., the expenditure on factor-services would have to be larger than $400.

At point *E* the slope, and therefore the MRS, is identical for both the isoquant and the outlay line. On the isoquant, at this point MRS (of labor for land) $= MPP_r/MPP_d$, where, again, the numerator and denominator refer to the marginal physical product of labor and land, respectively. On the outlay curve, at the same point, again in a competitive factor market,

$$\text{MRS (of labor for land)} = \frac{MC_r}{MC_d} = \frac{\text{price of labor}}{\text{price of land}}.$$

It follows that

$$\frac{\text{MPP}_r}{\text{MPP}_d} = \frac{\text{price of labor}}{\text{price of land}}.$$

By interchanging the means (the two middle terms), we get

$$\frac{\text{MPP}_r}{\text{price of labor}} = \frac{\text{MPP}_d}{\text{price of land}}.$$

The condition of the least-cost combination of factors for any given total output is, then, that the proportion of the marginal physical product to the price should be the same for each input. If more than two inputs are employed, the proportions and the equations are extended to include the additional factors. This condition of the least-cost equilibrium of the firm is, as we should expect, identical with the condition derived by the marginal-productivity method.

THE SCALE LINE

As the firm decides to make larger outlays on the means of production in order to obtain larger outputs, the least-cost combinations will be associated with larger amounts of the inputs. With an expenditure of $500 (Figure 19) the least-cost combination, indicated by point F, entails more labor than OH and more land than EH. With smaller outlays than $400 the optimum combinations are smaller than at point E. They are as indicated by points B and C. When such points are connected we obtain line or curve OS, called the *scale line* or *expansion path*. This line does not suggest the actual course taken by a firm in its career of growth. It traces only the optimum combinations of inputs associated with a larger and larger scale of operations. The scale line is the locus of points at which the marginal rate of factor substitution equals the marginal rate of outlay substitution, for the reason that it is the locus of points of tangency of isoquants and isocost curves.

Each point on the scale line specifies the proportion or combination of inputs which will cost least to produce the output in question per unit of time. Thus, as we saw, point E (Figure 19) suggests the combination of OH units of labor and HE units of land as the cheapest way, the most efficient way, of producing 250 bu. of wheat. It follows that the slope of the scale line at a given point gives us an idea of the ratio of land to labor at that point. If the scale line rises steeply, the indication is that in the various combinations the amount of land used is relatively large in proportion to the amount of labor; conversely, if the scale line rises gradually.

SUGGESTED READINGS

Bain, J. S. *Pricing, Distribution, and Employment,* revised ed., chaps. 11, 12. New York, Holt, 1953.

Boulding, K. E. *Economic Analysis,* revised ed., chap. 31. New York, Harper, 1948.

Cassels, J. M. "On the Law of Variable Proportions," *Explorations in Economics,* pp. 223–236. New York, McGraw-Hill, 1936. Reprinted in *Readings in the Theory of Income Distribution,* pp. 103–118.

Chamberlin, E. H. *The Theory of Monopolistic Competition,* 6th ed., chap. 8, Appendix B. Cambridge, Harvard University Press, 1948.

Enke, S. *Intermediate Economic Theory,* chap. 26. New York, Prentice-Hall, 1950.

Lerner, A. P. *The Economics of Control,* chap. 13. New York, Macmillan, 1945.

Machlup, F. "On the Meaning of the Marginal Product," *Explorations in Economics,* pp. 250–263. New York, McGraw-Hill, 1936. Reprinted in *Readings in the Theory of Income Distribution,* pp. 158–174.

Machlup, F. "The Common Sense of the Elasticity of Substitution," *Review of Economic Studies,* Vol. II (June, 1935), pp. 202–213.

Marshall, A. *Principles of Economics,* 8th ed., Book VI, chaps. 1, 2. New York, Macmillan, 1927.

Weintraub, S. *Price Theory,* chap. 3. New York, Pitman, 1949.

CHAPTER

VII Cost of Production

DEMAND is concerned with the behavior of the buyer of goods. The buyer may be the ultimate consumer of the finished product or the industrialist in need of the semifinished product, like raw materials, to carry on. Supply is concerned with the behavior of the firm, the producer, and the seller of goods; but supply very often depends on costs. Cost, in relation to price, guides the firm in its decision to offer for sale certain quantities at certain prices; to expand or to contract output; and to enter or leave an industry.

The law of variable proportions throws light on the behavior of costs. For this reason we discussed this law before taking up costs. Costs shed light on many situations affecting supply. This is why it is better to examine costs before bringing supply into consideration.

I. Four Concepts of Costs

It is the purpose of this chapter to touch first on four phases of costs (money costs, real costs, opportunity cost, and private and social costs), and then to explore the various types of cost and cost curves governing the conduct of the firm in short periods. Long periods will be studied in the next chapter.

1. MONEY COSTS

The concept of costs that readily comes to one's mind relates to the money outlays of a firm on the processes of producing a good: the wages and salaries paid to labor; the expenditures on machinery and equipment and the needed repairs; the payments for materials, power, light, fuel, and transportation; the disbursements on rents, patents, advertising, and insurance; and the inevitable taxes. A firm is obliged to pay the going wage for labor, the market rate of interest on its borrowings, the customary rents, and so on. Cost of production also embraces items which are not paid out to others. The building may be owned by the individual proprietor of the business, the capital may be contributed by the partners in the enterprise, and the owner of the firm may work like the hired hand and commonly longer hours. The interest, rent, and wages in such cases ought to be included in the costs of production; if the firm does not earn the customary market returns on its own capital or land or labor, it would do better not to use these resources in its own business but to hire them out to others. To add to the list of items composing the cost of production, we can mention depreciation, obsolescence, and an allowance for bad debts and uninsured contingencies.

The above enumeration of the components of cost begins to suggest some of the difficulties involved. First, there is the problem of allocating the costs among the various products. The firm which produces only one commodity is rare; most firms turn out a variety of similar or even very different articles. A meat-packing concern is responsible for the output of varieties of fresh meat and cured meat and of chemicals, fats, soaps, cosmetics, and condiments. This list is far from complete. How much of the president's salary in such a corporation, how much of the night watchman's wages, how much of the outlays on research is to be charged as the cost of making one of the various kinds of soap? In some way, the cost accountant reaches a figure representing the cost of producing the soap; but the way is not without some arbitrary calculation.

Then there is the difficulty of determining the amounts to be allowed for such items as depreciation, obsolescence, and bad debts. Depreciation may be reckoned on the straight-line method, the sinking-fund method, the reducing-balance method, or the unit-of-production method. Bad debts may be estimated as a certain percentage of all sales, of charged sales alone, or of accounts receivable. Each method gives a different answer.

2. REAL COSTS

The employer's primary concern is with the monetary costs which he has to incur in order to obtain the services indispensable to production. But many economists, notably among them Alfred Marshall, are inclined to go further. From the social viewpoint, they claim, there arises the important question of what lies beneath these monetary expenses of production. Precisely for what are these payments made? The answer is: the disutilities of rendering the services. Says Marshall: "The exertions of all the different kinds of labor that are directly or indirectly involved in making it; together with the abstinences or rather the waitings required for saving the capital used in making it: all these efforts and sacrifices together will be called the *real cost of production* of the commodity." [1] It is uncomfortable, even somewhat painful, to work a given number of hours each day. The first few hours of work may bring pleasure but the strain begins to tell as the hours wear on. The disutility at the margin is what counts; and the marginal disutility of labor rises as the hours go by. It is similarly irksome for the businessman to bear responsibility and risk. It means worry and nervous wear although some businessmen, or many, "enjoy the game."

Capital, too, symbolizes a real cost. It is unpleasant to save, that is, to postpone the enjoyment of consumption for the future. Some savings offer the satisfaction of the sense of security and of the peace of mind that goes with the provision for a rainy day, for old age, or for the education of the children. But as more and more is saved there is greater encroachment on present consumption; and the marginal utility of saving becomes less than the marginal utility of present consumption.

Nor do we see real cost evaporate when we consider J. M. Keynes' emphasis on liquidity preference as the source of interest. People *prefer* their savings in liquid form, in the bank or in the strongbox. When buying a bond the saver parts with liquidity, and the rate of interest functions as compensation for the irksomeness involved.

No real cost is ascribed to the services of land. Superior or inferior in quality, the land is there; its services are fixed. Neither labor nor saving will, generally, increase the quantity of natural resources.

There is no unique correspondence between monetary expenses and real costs, in the long run, even if the purchasing power of money is assumed to stay unchanged. If the price of goods is to reflect, for example, the disutility of the various kinds of labor with the various degrees of unpleasantness of the effort involved in production, other conditions besides the constancy of the value of money will have to be satisfied. The wages of labor will have to be determined by, and will have to be proportional to, the marginal disutility of labor. Such a determination of wages does not commonly square with the prevalent theory of marginal productivity as the regulator of wages. The section hand laboring on the roadbed in the blazing sun would, in accordance with the disutility idea, receive a higher wage than the research scientist or the college professor or the crooner. Such a theory of wages would seem to postulate that all

[1] *Principles of Economics*, p. 339. Italics in the original.

workers in a homogeneous group of trades, which pay the same wage rates, have such disutility schedules that their marginal disutilities for a working day of the same length are all alike. Similarly, theories will have to be tailored for the other components (interest, for example) of unit costs or of price in terms of the marginal disutility of saving. Such theories may stress partial truths, but on the whole they would be at variance with prevailing comprehensive theories.

3. OPPORTUNITY OR ALTERNATIVE COST

A widely held concept of costs is embodied in the idea labeled *opportunity cost* or *alternative cost*. Opportunity cost can be seen in the consumer's purchase of one article rather than another, in the laborer's choice of the firm in which he will work, in the businessman's choice of the product which he will produce, in the investor's choice in placing his savings, and in various other connections. Choices imply alternatives. Choice means that something is given up in favor of something else. What is given up forms the cost of what has been chosen.

Consider the consumer. When he pays a dollar for an article the cost of the article is not the dollar nor the labor expended to earn the dollar. The cost lies in the sacrifice of doing without another article which ranks next in his scale of preferences but which was displaced by the article actually purchased. If I am wavering between a pocketknife and a book of famous sayings, both selling for $2, and I buy the pocketknife, then the cost of the knife to me is the loss of the enjoyment which owning the book could give me. The basic measure of the significance of the pocketknife to me lies in the importance of the next most desired article given up, the book of famous sayings. The cost of the knife, to me, is the book; the cost is what I must do without.

When workers choose employment in an auto factory the cost to them of working there is not the marginal discomfort of eight hours of exertion per day, but the wage they can get in the steel mill in the same locality or elsewhere. We assume mobility of labor, that a given worker can handle either kind of job, and that both employments are equally safe, steady, and pleasant or unpleasant. The management of the auto factory will have to pay, then, the same wage that workers receive in the steel mill, else he will not keep his labor force. At the margin, labor will get the same return in both mills. Should somebody be so foolish as to hire a house painter as baby sitter during the day, he would have to pay him something in the neighborhood of a house painter's wage. This wage is the alternative earning of the painter, therefore it defines the cost of baby sitting to him. To those hiring baby sitters, of course, baby sitting is not worth a painter's wage. The marginal productivity of baby sitting is lower than the marginal productivity of house painting. For this reason, house painters paint houses and schoolgirls do the baby sitting.

Similarly with capital. The cost of lending or using capital is the interest which it can earn in the next best use of equal risk. The alternative uses of capital measure the marginal cost of capital to a given borrowing or lending concern. In the same fashion, the economic rent earned by land growing wheat becomes a cost of growing oats when turning the land to oats is contemplated. The rental cost to a person occupying his own house equals the rental he could get by leasing it to a tenant. The reason a warehouse it not located, generally, on the busy street corner in the shopping district lies in the fact that the service of the warehouse is not valued highly enough to enable its management to pay the rental which is offered by the storekeepers. It is no different with management's choices. What a businessman can earn as a restaurant keeper becomes the cost, to him, of running a grocery store; and he will not set up in storekeeping unless he can earn as much profit as in the restaurant business.

Whatever the factor, it expects as much compensation in one employment as it can obtain in the alternative employment. Whatever the resource, the employer of it, having to pay as much for its services as any other employer of it, will use it in such quantity and in such manner that it, the factor-service, will earn for him as much as it earns in any alternative use. In response to consumer demand for various goods and to changes in consumer demand, there is an ebb and flow of the productive resources among the various industries, so that in the long run each service finds its place in the line of production in which it earns most.

Opportunity cost is, in some phases, no respecter of economic systems. The alternative forgone constitutes a cost whatever the nature of the economy. If Robinson Crusoe faces the choice between fishing and repairing his hut and decides on the latter, the cost of improving his shelter is measured by the loss of the fish he could have caught. Corresponding to the asset of a better hut is the liability of less food for his table. If the overlords of Soviet Russia decide on building tanks instead of tractors, the cost of the tanks to the people is their loss of the services of the tractors in increasing the amount of food. In any society, if—under full employment—the choice is between guns and butter, the cost of the guns is the butter lost to the people. However, as far as the factors of production are concerned, opportunity cost is relative to the social organization. For instance, where, as in Russia, there is little free choice of a trade and even of the place of work, opportunity cost has little meaning to the worker but is of decisive significance to the economy. Yet even in Russia, wherever choice is involved, opportunity cost applies in one sense or another.

Assume a depression and much unemployment. It seems that the employed workers ought to receive a wage barely above the starvation level, inasmuch as the alternative to the worker is complete idleness. Such would indeed be the case if the choice before the worker were between starvation and work at an extremely low wage. But the idle workers are supported by public relief if not by unemployment insurance. The cost of working is reflected, to the worker, in the relief or insurance allowance which he would get even when idle. Other factors enter into the picture, as they usually do in social phenomena: inertia, custom, miscalculation, inflexibilities, not to speak of labor monopoly setting minimum wages.

The work done by the unemployed in the early days of the New Deal in improving parks and "manicuring" the roadside was considered by many as sheer waste. Sheer waste this work would have been, or nearly so, if the same labor would otherwise have been employed in making shoes or in building houses. But in that severe depression the alternative open to these workers would have been complete idleness, or zero production; in addition, they would have been placed on relief. The utility of the improved parks and roads was a gain. The monetary cost of improving the grounds in this manner contained much waste, inasmuch as it may have been more than the service was worth. But from the angle of opportunity cost the public can afford such undertakings in bad times although it cannot afford them in good times. (Why?)

Specialized and unspecialized agents

In significant affiliation with opportunity cost is the conception of specialized and unspecialized productive agents or resources. An unspecialized agent or resource is one that can serve in several lines of production—in the production, that is, of various goods. The specialized agent can render the best service only in one particular field. There is a considerable gap between the values of its use, marginally, in the best field and in any other.

Let us assume that the unspecialized agent can contribute in producing commodities and services A, B, C, and D—respectively as motorman on a bus, as truck driver, as janitor, or as attendant in a gasoline station. If we center our attention on A, which is the cost of a motorman's work to the public utility company, we can state that this cost will be governed by his cost in B, as truck driver, in C, as janitor, or in D, as gasoline station attendant. The agent will not accept measurably less in A than in B, C, and D. If we focus our attention on B, the cost of a truck driver, we can see that this cost will be controlled by the wage of this worker in A, C, and D. Similarly with this agent as used in C or D. We visualize here a case of mutual determination, the interaction of elements, where X can be both cause and effect of element Y; and element Y can be both cause and effect of X.

Opportunity cost asserts itself differently in relation to a *specialized* agent or resource. The chosen occupation of the agent is without a close alternative occupation. The movie star earning $150,000 a year may qualify as a model, a receptionist, or a sales girl, at $5,000 a year; or as a schoolteacher for less. The opportunity cost to the actress is only $5,000. The cost of the actress to the firm engaging her services is not affected by the price she commands in an alternative employment. The price of the specialized agent's service is derived from the consumer demand for the service; in our example, from the prices which can be charged to the public for the picture featuring the star, and from the increased attendance in the theater at these prices. The increased gain to the firm employing the actress sets the limit to the compensation which will be offered her. The motion-picture producers, calculating this gain, compete for her services. The competition for her services does not come from other types of service, from other industries, but from the various firms in the same industry.

The unspecialized service is a price-determining service; it helps determine the price of the product of the service. The specialized service, on the other hand, is a price-determined service; the price, or cost, of this service hinges on the price of the product. In the case of an unspecialized service, the *industry* that can pay the most sets the price of it; and this price becomes the opportunity cost to the agent in considering employment elsewhere. In the case of the specialized service, the most efficient *firm* in the same industry governs the price of the service; and this price becomes the opportunity cost to the agent in considering employment in another firm in the same industry.

4. PRIVATE AND SOCIAL COST

Maximum satisfaction necessarily implies a proper allocation of resources, a proper composition of total output. Whenever we see a misallocation of resources we see a deviation from maximum satisfaction; and the other way around. Income inequality reflects one source of misallocation of resources. The gap between marginal private cost and marginal social cost is another source. By marginal social cost of producing a good we mean the increment to the total cost of the economy; that is, essentially the sacrifice of the production of other goods incurred while producing the good in question, or the loss of satisfaction caused. This type of cost figures largely in the analysis of welfare economies.

In some industries the firm does not bear all the costs incidental to the production of the article; some costs are borne by others. A tavern does not fully pay for the additional police force needed to take charge of drunken people; nor does it carry insurance to make good the damage caused by drunken drivers. If the tavern or the liquor manufacturer were to meet such costs, the price of intoxicants would rise and there might be less drinking. Some of the resources used in producing such beverages would be diverted to the making of other goods. Other examples of marginal private cost falling short of marginal social cost are found in the pollution of water by mining and industrial wastes; the impairment of health and property values by the air pollution from the fumes and smoke of slaughterhouses and factories; the noise caused by juke boxes in restaurants; the crowded parking and other inconveniences caused by dance halls and by motion-picture houses; incomplete private compensation for injuries at work or for occupational diseases; and soil erosion, deforestation, and wasteful depletion of oil and coal reserves.[2]

On the other hand, there are cases in which marginal private cost exceeds marginal social cost. The production may bring unpaid-for advantages to other producers or to the economy at large. If these beneficiaries were to reimburse the producer fully, the marginal private costs would decline and the price of the article with it; more of the article would be produced. The private business and technological colleges, usually meeting in the evening, may serve as an illustration. When a public utility builds a dam, neighboring farms may find their irrigation problems less costly: the public utility pays for the dam more than does society at large. Excise taxes on gasoline, cigarettes, furs, and railroad tickets contribute more than their proportionate share of tax revenue. If all or most of the other commodities were to contribute such revenue, the price of the currently taxed articles would be lower and more of them might be consumed by the public. Despite patents, private research by one producer cannot help, in some cases, giving free hints to other producers on how to improve their products or their method of production. The mere appearance of the new article reluctantly offers instruction to the scrutinizing eyes of competing sellers.

II. Cost and Output in the Short Run

It is the task of the economist to probe into the nature of costs, as was indicated in the preceding section. But the businessman is pragmatic. In his daily decisions he confronts the conspicuous influence of costs as monetary outlays on the productive services bought or hired. Accordingly,

[2] W. Kapp, *The Social Costs of Private Enterprise* (Cambridge, Harvard University Press, 1950).

when we explore the behavior of the firm in reaction to costs we shall treat costs as the firm does, chiefly in terms of monetary expenditures.

The cost of production is closely associated with, and depends upon, three variables: (1) the period of *time* available to the firm in which it can profitably make adjustments to a change in the demand for its product; (2) the *output* of the firm: a firm of a given size may produce varying outputs by applying more or fewer units of a variable resource, that is, by running part time, full time, or overtime, and on holidays in response to a short-run change in demand; and (3) the magnitude of the components of *cost*, or the price paid for the services of the productive agents. The cost behavior is not related to each of these variables separately and independently but to all of them in interaction. When we speak of the unit cost of the product (that is, of the average cost per unit of product), we refer simultaneously to a given period of time, short run or long run; to a given rate of output by the firm; and to given factor costs. The first two elements will be discussed together in this section and in section III of this chapter; the third element, in section IV.

THE THREE PERIODS

When there is a change in the demand for a given product, the firm, under the spur of self-interest expressed in the desire for maximum profit or minimum loss, attempts to make price-output adjustments to the new situation. The type of adjustment and the degree of its completeness will depend on the length of time available to the firm. If the change in the demand is expected to be of short duration, there will be one kind of adjustment. If the change in the demand promises to last for a long time, the firm will meet the situation with a different policy. With regard to the behavior of costs and especially with regard to pricing, there are three periods of time to consider: (1) the market period; (2) the short-run or short normal period; and (3) the long-run or long normal period.

(1) *The market period*

This is commonly the shortest period. During this period the goods have already been produced and are in stock available for sale. If there is a drop in the demand for the product, the amount already in the storerooms or on the shelves cannot be shrunk; it is there, fixed in quantity. If there is a flare-up in demand, but for a very short time, it can affect only the existing stock of goods. In agriculture, for instance, an increased demand lasting for nearly a year will bring its influence to bear only on specific delimited quantities of goods yielded by the recent crops. The market period cannot be as long as the amount of time required to produce more goods; it must be shorter. The essential point is that, in view of the temporary character of the change in demand, the firm finds it either unprofitable or impossible to change the amount of goods available for sale.

(2) The short normal period

Next comes the short-run or short normal period. This period is not long enough to permit a variation in the size of the plant. But it is long enough to allow the firm to increase or decrease the flow of output per unit of time by changing the quantities of the variable agents of production applied to the fixed agents. During this period fixed costs cannot be changed and accordingly they exert no influence on the pricing of the goods produced, but total variable costs can fluctuate. It is necessary to pause here and explain these two kinds of cost.

Fixed costs are costs which the firm incurs even if the plant is idle and output is zero. Whether the firm produces nothing, little, or a good deal, total fixed costs remain the same. Examples of fixed costs are the salaries of the permanent staff, except in a depression when salaries are cut; the interest charge on the bonds sold to raise money for the buildings, machinery, and other heavy equipment; such depreciation of the capital goods as would take place even when they stand idle, from sheer deterioration through time; rentals on leased properties; property taxes; and the night watchman's wages. Fixed costs are commonly the fruit of contractual commitments, like the obligation to pay interest on bonds or to pay the stated salary to the manager hired for five years.

The shorter the period of time under consideration the more instances of fixed costs there are. If a laborer is hired by the day, his wage is a fixed cost for the day, whether he is kept busy the full hours or is idle part of the time for lack of something to do. A man hired by the week is a fixed cost for the goods, few or many, produced during the week. But in the perspective of a month's production, the wages of both this day laborer and this man hired for a week are variable costs. Fixed costs are not all fixed for the same length of time even in the same firm. The interest charge on the plant may be fixed for forty years, the interest charge on machinery for ten years.

Variable costs are costs the totals of which vary, in the short run, when the volume of output per unit of time varies. As can be seen from the law of variable proportions and as will be indicated shortly, total variable costs do not rise and fall in direct proportion to the volume of output. In other words, average variable costs are not constant. Examples of variable costs are materials, wages of labor hired for short periods, transportation costs, power, sales taxes on materials purchased, and depreciation due specifically to the use of the equipment. Apart from the depreciation which takes place even when machinery stands idle, there is the additional depreciation from the wear and tear of use. This extra depreciation is termed *user cost* by J. M. Keynes.

Often a fixed resource, a resource that does not vary in size or quantity in the short run, will stand for fixed costs, and variable resources for variable costs. But it is of some importance to stress that there is no necessary connection between the technical nature of the agent and the type of cost which its service means to the firm. The distinction between fixed and variable costs lies in the circumstances attending the *use* of the agent rather than in the physical character of the agent. Telephone service is a fixed cost to the firm for local calls; there is a fixed monthly charge whether the number of local calls per month is large or small or nil. But long-distance calls are a variable cost, in the sense that more business entails more such calls and less business entails fewer calls and the cost varies with the calls.

(3) *The long normal period*

This period is long enough to enable the firm to make adjustments to a changed demand by varying the scale of the plant. It is an interval of time in which, if the demand falls, plants can wear out without being replaced by new ones or can be adapted to other uses; or, if the demand rises, new plants and more machinery can be built and existing buildings can be enlarged. In this period the change in the demand is expected to last long enough to make it possible and profitable to vary even the fixed resources in order to produce the changed volume of output. In this period all resources are variable, and accordingly the costs of all the resources affect the price of the product. This period is commonly marked by the entry or exit of firms.

Neither the short-run nor the long-run period refers to a clock-time interval; the period is rather an "operational" concept. It refers to the unique interval required by the given firm to make the appropriate adjustment to a rise or fall in the demand for its product. The interval will vary with the nature of the processes and the kind of equipment used. In some cases one or two years will describe a short normal period, in others a long normal period. If the increased demand for a good promises to last only a short time, the adjustment will take the form of dosing more variables like labor and raw materials. If the increased demand bids fair to last a long time, the adjustment will be made by raising the scale of the plant—by installing more machines, assembly lines, and buildings.

Let us summarize the salient points about the three time periods. (1) The market period relates to a given *stock* of goods for sale. (2) The short period deals with a *flow* of output from a fixed stock of fixed resources, permitting this flow to change appreciably in response to changes in the earnings. In this period the output can be varied in quantity by fluctuation of the *variable* factors but not of the scale of the firm. (3) In the long period there is enough time for the changed earnings of the fixed resources to influence the quantities of these resources.

COSTS IN RELATION TO THE OUTPUT OF THE FIRM

Let us turn now to the behavior of costs in response to the changes in output which the firm can make in the short run. In this short period, fixed costs (and total costs in so far as they include fixed costs) have no influence in forming the price of a commodity. However, our concern in this section is the behavior of the various types of cost in relation to the *output* of the firm, without regard to their impact on the pricing of goods, which is the theme of other chapters. We shall therefore allow fixed costs and total costs to join the family of costs and cost curves relevant to the short normal period.

It is a complex family. The firm deals with three types of aggregate costs: total fixed, total variable, and total costs of both types. It deals as well with three kinds of average costs: average fixed cost, average variable cost, and average total cost.

It is well that we explore the nature of these costs arithmetically and graphically. Let us return to Table 9 illustrating the law of variable proportions. In that table we examined the physical product of a business firm—the total, average, and marginal quantities of wheat produced on a farm as operations on it were extended by increasing the amount of labor. To translate these physical data into costs, we shall have to take into our reckoning the fixed cost of the farm as well as the wages of the workers employed. Let us assume that the annual fixed outlays on the farm, in the shape of interest charges, depreciation of improvements, and the like, are $1,000; and that the wage of each worker for the season is also $1,000. We assume, too, that in bidding for workers our farm does not make enough of an impact upon the labor market to raise the wage of the hired men. The farm can employ any amount of labor of this type at the going wage, $1,000. With these figures in mind, we derive the cost data in Table 10.

THE THREE TYPES OF TOTAL COSTS

In Table 10, columns 2 to 4 refer to physical output, in bushels, as in the original Table 9 in Chapter V. (1) In column 5 is recorded the total *fixed costs*, TFC. This figure stays unchanged as output rises. In the short

TABLE 10. *Costs and Output*

(1) Number of workers	(2) Total product (bu.)	(3) Average product per worker (bu.)	(4) Marginal product of labor (bu.)	(5) Total fixed costs, TFC	(6) Total variable costs, TVC	(7) Total costs, TC (5) + (6)	(8) Average fixed costs, AFC	(9) Average variable costs, AVC (6) ÷ (2)	(10) Average costs, AC (8) + (9)	(11) Marginal costs, MC $1,000 ÷ (4) *
0	0	0	—	$1,000	$ 0	$ 1,000	∞	—	∞	—
1	820	820	820	1,000	1,000	2,000	$1.22	$1.22	$2.44	$1.22
2	1,720	860	900	1,000	2,000	3,000	.58	1.16	1.74	1.11
3	2,640	880	920	1,000	3,000	4,000	.38	1.14	1.52	1.09
4	3,600	900	960	1,000	4,000	5,000	.28	1.111	1.39	1.04
5	4,500	900	900	1,000	5,000	6,000	.22	1.111	1.33	1.11
6	5,340	890	840	1,000	6,000	7,000	.19	1.12	1.311	1.19
7	6,090	870	750	1,000	7,000	8,000	.16	1.15	1.313	1.33
8	6,640	830	550	1,000	8,000	9,000	.15	1.21	1.36	1.82
9	6,930	770	290	1,000	9,000	10,000	.14	1.30	1.44	3.45
10	6,930	693	0	1,000	10,000	11,000	.14	1.44	1.58	—

*Each increment in total cost is $1,000 (column 7). To get MC, we divide this increment in total cost by the corresponding increment in output (column 4).

run, fixed cost is independent of output; this is why fixed cost is not a price determinant. In the long run, this type of cost becomes a variable cost; this is why it becomes a component of price. (2) Total *variable cost*, TVC (column 6), is obtained by multiplying the units of the variable factor (column 1) by $1,000. This figure rises consistently with output, but not in direct proportion to output. The reason is that the number of variable agents does not rise in direct proportion to output, as we know from the principle of variable proportions. At first we may get increasing returns in output, then diminishing returns. (3) *Total costs*, TC (column 7), are composed of both total fixed costs and total variable costs; the figures in column 5 are added to the figures of column 6: we see here an example of vertical addition.

The graphic picture of the three types of total costs is given in Figure 20. As usual, the horizontal axis measures the product and the vertical axis indicates the total costs.

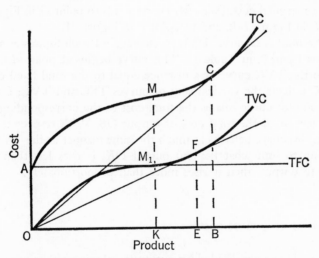

FIGURE 20. *The Three Types of Total Cost*

(1) Total *fixed costs*, represented by line TFC, trace a horizontal line at a distance from the *x* axis equal to the magnitude of total fixed costs. In Figure 20, distance *OA* equals the total fixed costs, or $1,000.

(2) The total *variable costs* curve TVC is derived from such data as in columns 1 and 6 in Table 10.[3] It begins at the origin. Each point on

---

[3] The columns are specified merely to indicate how the curves are derived. The curves in Figures 20 and 21 are not plotted exactly from the data of Table 10, because these data would not display to advantage their typical appearance.

this curve indicates the total variable cost involved in producing the given output. Thus EF is the total variable cost of producing OE units of the commodity.

Throughout its course, the behavior of the TVC curve exemplifies the law of variable proportions. During the first phase, up to the product OE, we recall, the total output on the farm rises more than in proportion to the rise in the variable resource, the men employed on it. The output, that is, rises more than in proportion to the rise in total variable costs. The total variable costs rise less than in proportion to the rise in output. All this means that up to output OK the average variable cost is falling steadily, and that therefore curve OM_1 is concave to the horizontal axis. The opposite is true during the second phase, from point M_1 on, for outputs beyond OK. Total variable costs mount in greater proportion than output; average variable cost rises.

It is for this reason that TVC beyond M_1 for output beyond OK is convex to the x axis. Point M_1, the point of inflection, harbors accordingly the lowest marginal cost. Point M_1 corresponds to point G in Figure 15A, to point E in Figure 15B, and to point P in Figure 21.

(3) The *total cost* curve TC is plotted against such figures as are given in columns 1 and 7, in Table 10. This curve begins at point A and stays parallel to the TVC curve at a distance equal to the total fixed cost OA. Curve TC reflects the vertical sum of curves TFC and TVC; each point on the total cost curve relates the total cost to the corresponding output. For instance, BC is the total cost of output OB. With respect to growth of output, this curve behaves in much the same manner as the TVC curve. At first, up to somewhat beyond output OK, it rises less than proportionately to output, then it rises more than proportionately.

THE THREE TYPES OF AVERAGE COSTS

When total costs are divided by output we obtain average costs. Parallel to the three types of total costs are three types of average costs. These average costs are shown in tabular form in Table 10, columns 8, 9, and 10 and illustrated in Figure 21.

(1) *Average fixed costs*

Average fixed cost AFC (column 8) is obtained by dividing the total fixed cost (column 5) by the total product (column 2). The result is a steadily declining average fixed cost. At first this average drops considerably. The second average (column 8) is less than half the first, inasmuch as at first total product becomes more than twice as large when the variable factor is doubled. As total product continues to rise, however, the average costs drop more and more slowly. When graphed, as in Figure 21, the AFC curve is a rectangular hyperbola with the equation $xy =$ constant.

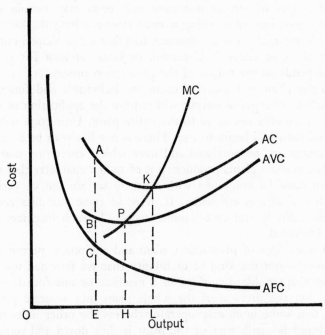

FIGURE 21. *Three Average Costs and One Marginal Cost*

(2) *Average variable costs*

The average variable costs are found by dividing total variable costs TVC (column 6) by the total products (column 2). The results are recorded in column 9. These averages are pictured diagrammatically in Figure 21 as the U-shaped curve AVC.

The column of figures, as well as the graph, display results to be expected from the law of variable proportions. In the first phase, the output rises faster than the input of variable resources; faster, that is, than variable cost. Average variable cost declines. In the second phase, as the output continues to rise it does so at a slower rate than the input of variable agents or than total variable costs. Accordingly unit variable costs mount. The point of separation of these two phases is the point of minimum average variable costs, or the point of optimum rate of output in the firm of a given scale, or the point of maximum efficiency. It is represented by point P (Figure 21), which is the lowest point on curve AVC. The AVC curve in Figure 21 is the cost counterpart of the average output curve AP, in Figure 15A.

Empirical investigations of the cost-output relation in some industries suggest that perhaps not infrequently the cost function is linear: [4] for extended ranges of output minimum unit costs may remain constant. The cost curve, instead of rising at once after reaching the lowest point, may stay horizontal for some distance, forming a dish-shaped curve ⌣ . Whether the cost curve is U-shaped, or linear at least for part of its course, depends on the nature of the production process.

When the plant and the equipment are indivisible and function as a unified whole, changes in output will require the application of different amounts of variable resources to the entire plant. Unit costs will decline at first and then will begin to rise. There is not likely to be a range over which returns are proportional and over which, therefore, cost is constant. Also, in some plants production is of such a character that the fixed equipment must be combined with a nearly set amount of variable resources for maximum efficiency. If more of these variables are added, output rises slowly and costs mount steeply. In such instances the cost curve is U-shaped.

But in some lines of production, plant and equipment permit a degree of *divisibility*—not the kind of divisibility that we frowned upon in the preceding chapter, like one-third of a machine or one-fourth of an accountant, but the division of the whole plant into separate production units, so that some units may operate whereas the other units stay idle. When output is small, part of the plant is shut down and some of the machines are kept idle. When production rises, more of the plant and more of the machines are put into operation. Over a certain range of output total variable costs are accordingly nearly proportional to the volume of output and there is no appreciable deviation from the minimum average variable cost level. Cost stays linear for wide limits of output.

In addition to this kind of divisibility of the plant, there is another measure for maintaining linear cost curves, depending on the possibility of introducing built-in *flexibility*: plant and equipment are designed to accommodate varying outputs and to make different types of products. In a shoe factory identical machines can be set up to fill expanding orders. In a paper mill or steel mill machines may be used which can turn out several widths, thicknesses, lengths, and types of material and which can operate at several different speeds. In the production of only one designated amount per unit of time or of only one specific kind of article, the

---

[4] *Cost Behavior and Price Policy*, National Bureau of Economic Research. Committee on Price Determination; E. S. Mason, chairman (New York, 1943), chap. V.

use of flexible resources is very likely to be more costly than the use of specialized resources meant exclusively for this particular output or this particular make of commodity. But for the production of varying amounts and different varieties of products the unit cost of applying versatile resources may be lower than the unit cost of applying specialized resources. Finally, the unit cost of flexible resources is apt to display a flat, nearly linear cost-output relation for a considerable range of production.[5]

(3) *Average total costs*

Average total costs, or briefly average costs, are computed by dividing total costs, column 7 of Table 10, by corresponding total outputs (column 2), with results as in column 10. Average total costs can also be obtained by adding average fixed costs (column 8) and average variable costs (column 9).

Average total costs are pictured graphically by the AC curve in Figure 21. This is the U-shaped or dish-shaped average cost curve. At each point, it lies above curve AVC at a distance equal to the corresponding height of curve AFC: thus $AB = CE$. It is important to note that the point of minimum average cost is reached for a *larger* output than the point of minimum average variable cost: in Figure 21, point K is to the right of point P. The reason is not far to seek. For each output, the average cost is compounded of average fixed and average variable costs. Beyond output OH, the average variable cost, having reached its minimum level, is beginning to move up. But the average fixed cost continues to decline. For some output beyond OH, the falling average fixed cost may outweigh the rising average variable cost, with the net consequence that the average total cost is declining. However, as the output grows, the fall in average fixed cost becomes smaller whereas the average variable cost is apt to climb more and more impressively. Sooner or later average total cost will begin to rise.

As can be seen from Table 10, with given costs of the fixed and variable resources employed, certain combinations of these resources and the resulting outputs entail lower average costs to the firm than other combinations. One combination, or several combinations in the case of the dish-shaped average cost curve, gives the lowest short-run unit cost. This combination indicates the short-run stage of optimum output and minimum unit cost to the firm. In our table, this optimum stage is reached when 6 men are employed. Then the output is 5,340 bu., and the unit cost is $1.311. On a diagram, the least-cost combination is indicated by the lowest point on the average total cost curve. In Figure 21, KL is the lowest unit cost and OL is the optimum output.

[5] *Ibid.*, pp. 111–113.

At which volume of output the lowest-cost point will be located depends on the prices of the fixed and the variable resources alike. We saw in the discussion of the law of variable proportions that in the first and third phases respectively the contribution of the fixed and the variable factors is negative, and that only in the second phase do both factors make a positive contribution to the total output. The point of maximum efficiency (or of minimum unit cost) attained by the combination of both the fixed and the variable factors is located somewhere within the second phase. The more costly the services of the fixed factor are in relation to those of the variable factors, the more intensively will the fixed factor be used; the more will the variable factors be substituted for the fixed factors before the minimum average cost stage is achieved; and the farther along in the second phase will minimum unit costs emerge. In a firm with large fixed costs and small variable costs, the fixed costs have the lion's share in shaping average total costs. The average variable costs may be rising, but for a wide range of output the falling average fixed cost will overbear them to result in declining average total costs. The firm will strive for "capacity" output to reduce the "overhead." The average cost curve will keep on declining for a long distance on the horizontal axis; and minimum unit costs will be reached at a stage of considerable output. Mass production industries illustrate such a situation.

MARGINAL COSTS

The costs and cost curves discussed so far are important to the firm and in analysis. But they are not sufficient. For the determination of the exact output which a firm will try to produce, in the short run and the long run alike, under given demand conditions, it is important to introduce the idea, and the fact, of marginal costs.

Parallel to the concept of marginal utility and marginal output, marginal cost refers to the additional cost incurred by the firm when it produces one additional unit of a commodity. It is the ratio of a small increment in total cost to a small increment in output. By total costs, in this connection, we may mean total *variable* cost or total *fixed and variable* cost: it does not matter, as will be seen in the next paragraph. Often we deal, as in Table 10, column 4, with increments of output larger than one unit. In such a case marginal cost is roughly, but not exactly, the increment in costs divided by the increment in product. The marginal costs in column 11 are estimated by dividing the cost increments of $1,000 (column 7) by the marginal outputs (column 4). When graphed, marginal costs trace a curve like the MC curve in Figure 21. The MC curve is apt to rise steeply to the right for the reason that, beyond a certain point, as we feed the fixed resources of the firm with more and more variables, marginal product grows only slightly and accordingly MC shoots up almost perpendicularly.

We have three total costs and three average costs, but only one marginal cost. Why? *First,* there is no such thing as marginal fixed cost: there is no increment in fixed costs accompanying an increment in output. *Second,* as far as total costs and total variable costs are concerned, they are both associated with the same marginal costs. All along the line, the total costs exceed the total variable costs by a constant quantity, namely the total fixed cost of $1,000. Accordingly, for an increment of output, the increment in total costs is identical with the increment in total variable costs. We can generalize as follows: if a fixed quantity is added to or subtracted from a series of total costs, or total utilities, or total revenues, or total output, the marginal magnitudes remain unaffected. The outcome is that we have only one set of marginal magnitudes.

It follows that marginal costs depend on the size of the variable costs and not on the size of the total fixed costs. Whatever the total fixed costs are, they cancel out as we subtract the total cost of $n-1$ units from the total cost of n units of the commodity in order to get the marginal cost of n units, or the cost of the nth unit. It follows, too, that when we add all the marginal costs for n units we obtain the *total variable* cost of n units. In Table 10, when we multiply each marginal cost in column 11 by the corresponding output in column 4 and add the products (which are $1,000 in each case), we get total variable cost, as in column 6.

RELATIONS BETWEEN AVERAGE AND MARGINAL COSTS

After the discussion of the relations between average and marginal output in Chapter V, the connection between marginal costs and average variable costs, between the MC curve (Figure 21) and the AVC curve, ought to be clear enough. As long as the marginal costs are lower than the average variable costs, the average variable costs are "pulled" down and continue to decline. When marginal costs exceed average variable costs, the latter begin to rise. It follows that the MC curve crosses the AVC curve at the minimum point of AVC. At this minimum point the AVC curve neither rises nor falls. At this point the slope of this curve is zero.

The marginal cost curve MC also crosses the average total cost curve AC at its minimum point.[6] But this proposition is not so easy to perceive, and needs demonstration. The algebraic proof is perhaps the simplest.[7]

Should average *variable* cost stay constant for given outputs, the infer-

---

[6] This relationship is not pinpointed in Table 10 because the figures are not continuous.

[7] Let $a =$ average cost of q units, and $a_1 =$ average cost of $q-1$ units. Then

ence is that the marginal cost is also constant for these outputs and is, moreover, equal to this average variable cost. Both kinds of costs will be represented by the same horizontal line. A constant average variable cost indicates that the marginal cost neither pulls it up nor down, but is equal to it.

The situation is no different if the average *total* cost stays unchanged for a given range of output. Such a fact would tell us that an extra output entails an extra cost equal to the preceding average total cost. Should the extra output involve an extra cost larger, or smaller, than the previous average total cost, the new average total cost would not stay constant but would correspondingly rise or fall. (To refer to the algebra used in the footnote, when average total cost remains fixed, $a = a_1$. Then q $(a - a_1) = 0$, and marginal cost equals a_1.)

RELATIONS AMONG THREE TYPES OF COST

The relation between total cost TC on the one hand and average cost AC or marginal cost MC on the other hand can be presented graphically, as in Figure 22. Let us examine first the relation between TC and AC. In Figure 22A we see that for product OQ the average cost is HQ/OQ; for product OQ_1 the average cost is BQ_1/OQ_1. The average costs are falling; angle BOQ_1 is smaller than angle HOQ. The angles HOQ, BOQ_1 keep on diminishing until we reach angle FOQ_2. Beyond this angle, the angles, formed by a line from O to a point beyond point F on the TC curve, begin to rise. This behavior of the angles is reflected in the behavior of the AC curve in Figure 22B: the AC curve keeps on descending up to output Q_2 (or up to output L) and keeps on rising for outputs beyond Q_2 or beyond L. Angle FOQ_2 is significant for another reason. It is the smallest angle formed by a line from O to any point on TC. Accordingly point L represents the lowest average cost AC. But this is not all. Line OF is tangent to TC—and a tangent at point F indicates marginal cost for output OQ_2: the slope of a TC curve at any point along its course indicates the

---

$aq =$ total cost of q units, and $a_1(q-1) =$ total cost of $(q-1)$ units. The marginal cost of q units will then be

$$aq - a_1(q-1) = aq - a_1q + a_1 = q(a - a_1) + a_1.$$

If average cost *falls* as output is increased, $a < a_1$. Then $q(a - a_1)$ is a negative quantity. Then marginal cost, which is $q(a - a_1) + a_1$, equals a quantity smaller than a_1. This signifies that when average total costs are falling, marginal costs range below these average costs.

Similarly, if average total cost *rises* as output is extended, $a > a_1$. Then $q(a - a_1)$ becomes a positive quantity; and then marginal cost, or $q(a - a_1) + a_1$, has a value larger than a_1. This means that as soon as average cost begins to rise, the marginal cost exceeds average cost. It follows that the marginal cost curve MC cuts the average total cost curve AC at its minimum.

marginal cost of output corresponding to the point we choose. We see, then, that for output OQ_2, MC = AC. Thus in Figure 22B, MC cuts AC at output OQ_2, which is the same as output L.

Now let us examine the relation between TC and MC. We see that up to point M the TC curve is concave to the origin, and that beyond point M curve TC is convex to the origin. Up to point M the slope of TC is

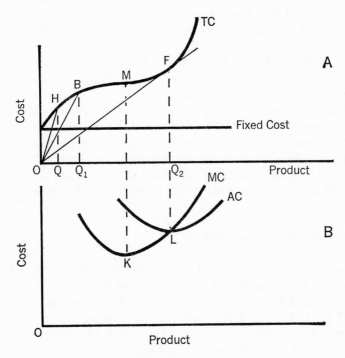

FIGURE 22. *Relations Among Three Types of Cost*

declining: TC becomes less and less steep. With each additional unit of a variable resource applied in a plant of a given scale, the marginal physical product rises and marginal cost falls; this behavior of TC corresponds to the declining left wing of the MC curve down to point K. Beyond point M, diminishing marginal returns set in, marginal product moves downward, and marginal cost spurts upward. This part of TC has its counterpart in the rising right wing of the MC curve beyond point K. Point M is the point of inflection on TC; that is, it is the dividing point between the concave and convex curvatures. Its counterpart on the MC curve is point K, the lowest point on MC.

III. Cost and Output in the Long Run

In the long run, the firm is in a position to vary its fixed resources. Over short periods the firm's adjustment to a change in the demand for its product will take the path of employing more or less of the variable resources within the plant of a given scale. But if the demand for the firm's product is expected to stay changed for a long time, the adjustment in output and costs will be achieved by changing the scale—by changing the size of the buildings, the number of machines, and the amount of entrepreneurial activity. Once the new plant, larger or smaller in scale, is in operation, short-period fluctuations in demand for the firm's product will be met, as usual, by changing the quantity of the variable resources used. The new larger or smaller plant will deal with the customary *short-run* costs: total, average, and marginal costs. The point to stress is: the change from one scale of the firm to a higher scale—from SAC_1 to SAC_2—depicts a long-run adjustment. But once the change has been made, we see before us a short-run average cost curve of a higher scale, like SAC_2.

THE LONG-RUN AVERAGE COST CURVE

These ideas can be portrayed graphically as in Figure 23. Along the horizontal axis is measured the output of the firm. Costs are measured along the vertical axis. Curve SAC_1 traces the short-run average total costs of the firm when it is of small size and adjusts its output over the short period. Similarly with curve SAC_2 which pictures the firm as of larger scale, and with SAC_3 and SAC_4 which represent the same firm as of still larger size. The minimum point of average costs on SAC_1 is relatively high. But as the firm is enlarged to SAC_2 the minimum grows lower. As long as this minimum continues to grow lower, the inference is that the larger scales of our firm are more efficient. This minimum is lowest when the firm reaches the scale depicted by SAC_3. But beyond this scale the minimum begins to rise, as in SAC_4, pointing to the inefficiency of a larger scale than the scale implicit in SAC_3.

Perhaps we can now put a sharper focus on the long-run average cost curve (LAC). For each successive output the corresponding point on LAC is the least cost per unit of such an output, provided that the firm enlarges its scale by gradations suitable to the slightly increased output. In other words, each point on LAC is a point of some SAC curve touching it (*forming* it is better!). To each successive point on LAC corresponds a larger and larger scale of our firm, and each scale gives us an optimum, a least-cost combination of resources. And, we recall, the least cost of an output is attained when the marginal physical product (MPP) of a dollar's worth of one resource equals the marginal physical product of a dollar's worth of any other resource. A dollar spent on any one productive resource gives as much increment in output as a dollar spent on any other input.

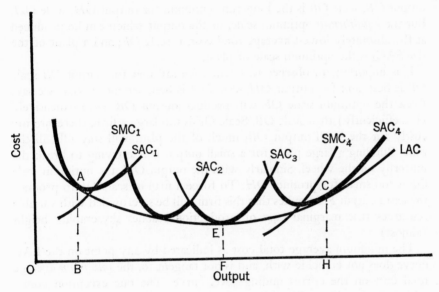

FIGURE 23. *The Long-Run Average Cost Curve*

If the firm expands its scale by the four definite stages in Figure 23, the fat wavelike curve portrays the LAC curve of the firm as it raises its output by enlarging its size. The smooth continuous LAC curve is fitted to the four SAC curves so that it is tangent to each of them at some one point. This LAC curve is called the *envelope*.

Assume, however, that the firm can vary its scale, not by discrete large jumps, as in Figure 23, but by minute gradations. Then instead of four U-shaped short-run SAC curves we would have a succession of a multitude of such curves crowding one upon another. Then the LAC curve would not be formed by fitting it to these curves, but would emerge as a curve *ready made* by the closely crowded appropriate points on the numerous U-shaped SAC curves, each point on the LAC curve being at the same time a point, and only one point, on some SAC curve—a point at which the LAC curve is tangent to some SAC curve. The SAC curves are called *plant curves*; the LAC curve is often referred to as the *planning curve*.

In this instance, the envelope LAC traces the relation between output and minimum average total cost, in the long run, as the plant varies its scale by small gradations. Each point on this envelope curve indicates the lowest average total cost and therefore the most efficient scale at which the corresponding output can be produced in the long run. Output *OB* can be produced at the lowest unit cost of *AB*; output *OH* at *CH*. For output *OB*, scale *OB* is the long-run optimum; for output *OH*, scale *OH*. But the *equilibrium* optimum scale, or the output which can be produced at the absolutely lowest average total cost, is scale *OF*; and a plant of the size SAC$_3$ is the optimum scale of plant.

It is important to observe that when we say that for output *OB* scale *OB* is best, and for output *OH* scale *OH* is best, we mean what we say. Even the optimum scale *OF* will produce output *OB* more expensively (less efficiently) than scale *OB*. Scale *OF* is too large a firm, therefore too costly for the small output *OB*; much of the plant will stay idle all the time. Building a large plant for a small output is like trying to break the butterfly on the wheel. Similarly with the output *OH*, the optimum scale *OF* is too small for product *OH*. To force a firm of scale *OF* to produce the extra output *FH* implies that this firm will be so crowded with variable resources that marginal cost of production reaches skyscraping height (almost).

The minimum average total cost as indicated by any point on the LAC curve does not coincide with, and is not tangent to, the *minimum* average total cost on the corresponding SAC curve. The one exception comes with the average cost *EF* at the optimum scale *OF*. For instance, the long-run minimum average cost *AB* and the point of short-run minimum average cost on SAC$_1$ are two separate things. The short-run variations of output in SAC$_1$ move along the marginal cost curve SMC$_1$ in accordance with the principle of equating marginal cost and marginal revenue, to be discussed in the next chapter. But the long-run variations in output move along the curve LAC. From the viewpoint of long-run average costs, the minimum short-run average cost on a given SAC curve is of no unique significance.

For outputs smaller than the optimum output *OF*, the LAC curve is tangent to the individual SAC curves at points to the *left* of the minimum average costs on these SAC curves; for outputs larger than *OF*, at points to the *right*. Only for output *OF* is the LAC curve tangent to the SAC curve at the point of both short-run and long-run average cost *EF*. Accordingly tangents to points on the falling wing of LAC, to the left of point *E*, slope negatively; and tangents to points on the rising wing, to the right of point E, have a positive slope. *Sloping* tangents indicate that the points of tangency are not minimum points on the SAC curve nor on the LAC curve. A tangent at the minimum point of a curve is parallel to the horizontal axis. Such a tangent comes at point E. This is the only point at which LAC is tangent to the *minimum* point of the SAC curve.

We can look at the proposition from another angle. On our diagram, output OB can be produced at the long-run minimum unit cost AB. Should the output be extended in the long run, the new minimum cost will not be at the lowest point of the SAC_1 curve. It will be at the point of tangency of the LAC curve with the *next* SAC curve, portraying the short-run average costs of the next larger firm. This new point of tangency is below the lowest point on SAC_1. Similarly with the next larger outputs. The lowest points on the various SAC curves play no particular part in forming the LAC curve; again, except for point E.

All this means that at any scale *less* than the optimum scale OF it is cheaper for the firm to produce the given output in a somewhat larger plant (that is, in plant SAC_1) but to operate it only up to A, than it is to produce the same output in a smaller plant at its minimum unit cost. It is cheaper to get economies of scale than the economies of optimum production in a smaller scale firm, that is, at minimum average cost. For scales *larger* than OF, the lowest unit cost is attained by crowding a smaller plant, like SAC_4, beyond its lowest-unit-cost stage, and not by building a larger plant and using it only up to its minimum unit cost. It is cheaper to avoid the diseconomies of a larger scale than the diseconomies of crowding a plant of smaller scale. The minimum unit cost of a new larger plant would be greater than the average unit cost of the same output produced in plant SAC_4 pushed beyond the point of its lowest average cost.

LONG-RUN MARGINAL COST

The short-run variations in unit costs in response to changing output are represented by the three average cost curves discussed in the previous section. Since in the long normal period fixed costs become variable, the long-run average cost curve LAC is the only average cost curve involved. Left for consideration are marginal costs. The data for the long-run marginal cost curve are different from the data underlying the short-run marginal cost curve, inasmuch as an increment in output is now associated not only with an increment in costs treated as variable in the short run but also by an increment in the costs entailed in enlarging plant and equipment. It is for such reasons that the long-run marginal cost curve LMC in Figure 24 is different from any of its short-run counterparts, like curve SMC.

The "average-marginal" relations between the long-run marginal cost curve and the long-run average cost curve are the same as the relations between the corresponding short-run cost curves, and for the same reasons. The long-run marginal cost curve LMC intersects the long-run average cost curve LAC at the minimum point P on LAC. Since at its minimum point the LAC curve is tangent to the short-run average cost curve SAC at the minimum point of the latter curve, the two marginal cost curves, SMC and LMC, are equal at their common point P; they are both equal to PA.

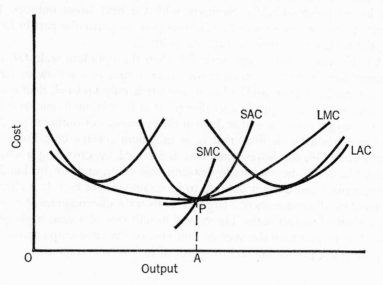

FIGURE 24. *The Relation Between Long-Run Marginal and Average Costs*

There is no ironclad direct connection between these two marginal cost curves. For a given output, except output OA, the one can be larger or smaller than the other, depending on the balancing of the following considerations: Short-run marginal costs are controlled only by the short-run variable costs; whereas long-run marginal costs embrace in addition the costs of resources considered fixed in the short run. On the other hand, short-run marginal costs grow rapidly as the firm strains its fixed resources to obtain a larger output, and beyond a certain output marginal costs rise almost perpendicularly. But the expansion of plant avoids this overutilization of the smaller plant, and provides the flexibility of a larger aggregate of resources which permits lower long-run extra costs with extra output: the SMC is steeper than the LMC.

ECONOMIES AND DISECONOMIES OF SCALE

The question why long-run average costs at first decline and then rise, why the LAC curve is U-shaped and not horizontal, is related to the economies and diseconomies of the scale of the firm. This question received attention in the first section of the preceding chapter. In some instances after the firm has reached the size of lowest minimum cost, with further expansion of scale the economies and the diseconomies may balance each other for a certain range of output. In such cases the falling wing of the LAC curve, instead of terminating in a *point* of minimum cost, flattens out into a horizontal segment before taking an upward course. This horizontal segment illustrates the fact that in some instances the minimum average cost applies not just to *one* given output, but over a certain stretch of larger and larger outputs, before this cost begins to rise. Let the student explain why both SAC and LAC curves have a descending left wing and a rising right wing.

IV. Costs and Factor Prices

As was mentioned early in section II of this chapter, costs are related to three elements: the *time* period; the *output* of the firm, of a given scale, per unit of time; and the prices paid for the *factor-services* which go into the making of a commodity. In sections II and III we examined the first two elements. We now turn to the third.

CHANGE IN PRICE OF VARIABLE FACTORS

Let us assume that because of a minimum wage law or because of a strike the rates per labor-hour rise, or that on account of a general industrial expansion the price of raw materials has advanced. The impact upon unit costs to the firm will depend upon the time period and on whether or not the change in the factor prices induces a change in the technique.

Let us consider first the *short run*. We assume that there is no change in technique, that the production function remains unaltered. In such circumstances, the average costs as well as the marginal costs may rise for each level of output. The cost curves will move upward, as in Figure 25, where the average cost curve AC_1 shifts to AC_2 and marginal cost curve MC_1 assumes the position MC_2. These new cost curves trace the relation of cost to output, in the short run, after the advance in wages per hour or in the price of materials, or in both. These new curves are parallel to the old ones.

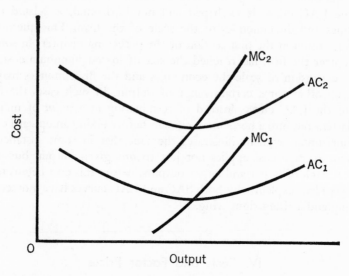

FIGURE 25. *Effect of Factor Prices on Cost of Production*

Sometimes a change in the price of a variable service will induce the firm to adopt a new technique, a new combination of productive services. The result in such a case is somewhat different. Suppose that raw materials rise in price while wage rates stay constant. The firm may find it economical to substitute labor for raw materials: it may use a little more labor and a little less of raw materials, since, with additional labor, greater care can be taken of the materials in order to reduce waste. This substitution may prevent the rise in the price of materials from registering its full effect on average and marginal costs. Higher costs may not be avoided, but the change in technique may keep the costs from advancing as much as they otherwise would. The AC_1 and MC_1 curves will shift upward, but not to positions as high as those of the AC_2 and MC_2 curves.

In the *long run*, a rise in the price of the variable resources is apt to produce results similar to those in the forgoing paragraph, because there is time to change the technique. As the old fixed factors, like plant and equipment, are worn out they are replaced by similar fixed factors which embody a larger aggregate than before, in proportion to the relatively more expensive variable resources. In the long run, that is, formerly fixed factors can be substituted for the variable factors. The cost curves will rise, but not as much as they would if the long-run process of substitution were not available.

CHANGE IN PRICE OF FIXED FACTORS

Let us assume now a rise in the costs of fixed resources—in rentals, property taxes, or interest rates on bonds. Here, too, we have to distinguish between the short run and the long run. In the short run, (1) the variable costs are not affected; (2) marginal costs remain the same, since they depend on the variable cost alone; but (3) average total costs may tend to rise. In Figure 26, curve AC_1 will shift to AC_2: these two curves are

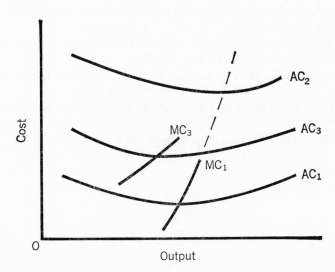

FIGURE 26. *Effect of a Price Change of Fixed Factors*

not parallel because when the total rise in the cost of the fixed factor-service is spread over larger outputs it boosts the average cost (AC_1) by smaller and smaller magnitudes. The MC_1 curve (Figure 26) will stay unchanged; if extended upward, it will cut AC_2 at its minimum point.

The effects are different in the long run. The firm will strive to substitute the relatively cheaper variable services for the fixed agencies. As the old plant is worn out it can be replaced by a less expensive plant. Average total costs, which had risen in the short run, may now decline to some extent from this higher level. Curve AC_2 may drop to AC_3. The opposite happens to marginal costs. With *smaller* fixed factors, as successive doses of variable agents are applied, the variable agents are likely to yield smaller increments of output. Marginal costs are apt to rise; and the new marginal cost curve shifts above and to the left of MC_1. The long-run situation is exemplified by curves AC_3 and MC_3.

SUGGESTED READINGS

Bain, J. S. *Pricing, Distribution, and Employment,* revised ed., chap. 3. New York, Holt, 1953.

Boulding, K. E. *Economic Analysis,* revised ed., chap. 22. New York, Harper, 1948.

Clark, J. M. *Studies in the Economics of Overhead Costs,* Chicago, University of Chicago Press, 1923.

Conference on Price Research, *Cost Behavior and Price Policy.* New York, National Bureau of Economic Research, 1943.

Leftwich, R. H. *The Price System and Resource Allocation,* revised ed., chap. VIII. New York, Holt, Rinehart and Winston, 1960.

Stigler, G. J. *The Theory of Price,* revised ed., chaps. 6, 7. New York, Macmillan, 1952.

Weintraub, S. *Price Theory,* chap. 4. New York, Pitman, 1949.

CHAPTER

VIII Revenue, Supply, and the Market

THE PRECEDING chapters, dealing with demand, production, and cost, prepared some of the tools of price analysis. Before we take up the problem of pricing, a few more tools are needed. To the firm involved in pricing, demand presents itself as *revenue* or receipts from the sale of quantities of goods at certain prices. Furthermore, by offering goods for sale at given prices the firm is actively engaged in forming the *supply* of the commodity. The specific aspects of supply are best explored when examining the specific problems of price formation. However, some general conceptions of supply are necessary preliminaries. Lastly, the determination of the price of goods and services takes place in a *market*; and the particular character of the market structure puts a stamp on the manner in which the price of the article is established.

Accordingly this chapter will examine three related problems: the demand for a good as revenue to the firm; the general conception of supply; and the various types of markets.

I. Average, Marginal, and Total Revenue

To the firm the demand of the consumers for its commodity means revenue. To the firm the sales schedule is a revenue schedule; the sales schedule outlines average prices or average revenues. When we say that a producer could sell 1,000 hats per week if the price were $5 a hat, and

900 hats if the price rose to $6, the price in each case is an average price; so much per hat. To the firm, the demand curve for the product of the firm is an average revenue curve.

But when a firm aims to sell additional units of an article it is interested not only in the average receipt per unit of the larger amount sold but also in the marginal revenue which it can expect from larger sales. With an eye on profit, the firm must match the additional receipts against the additional cost of the extra output in order to decide whether or not it pays to expand production and try to sell more.

The concept of marginal revenue is of the same cast as the concept of marginal utility, marginal output or product, and marginal cost. It is the ratio of a small increment in revenue to a small increment in output; it is $\Delta R/\Delta P$, where R is total revenue and P is total product. The marginal revenue of a number of units sold is the revenue obtained from the sale of any one unit in this number. It is the revenue lost when the sale is smaller by one unit.

RELATIONS AMONG THE THREE TYPES OF REVENUE

We face three types of revenue: average revenue, marginal revenue, and total revenue. Their relationships can be conveniently sketched by reference to Table 11. The first four columns picture the demand situation or sales schedule confronting a firm with a degree of *monopoly* power over the price of its product. The last four columns describe the demand as it looks to a firm in a purely *competitive* industry.

TABLE 11. *Three Types of Revenue of Two Commodities*

Monopoly Product				Competitive Product			
(1)	(2)	(3)	(4)	(5)	(6)	(7)	(8)
Number of units sold	Average revenue (price), cents	Total revenue, cents	Marginal revenue, cents	Number of units sold	Average revenue (price), cents	Total revenue, cents	Marginal revenue, cents
1	10	10	10	1	10	10	10
2	9	18	8	2	10	20	10
3	8	24	6	3	10	30	10
4	7	28	4	4	10	40	10
5	6	30	2	5	10	50	10
6	5	30	0	6	10	60	10
7	4	28	−2	7	10	70	10

The same relation exists between marginal revenue and total revenue that exists between any other marginal and total magnitudes. One determines the other. Given column 3, in Table 11, we can find column 4; given column 4, we can fill in column 3. Total revenue reaches its maximum when marginal revenue becomes zero. Compounded as it is of the marginal revenues, total revenue will not rise when zero is added.

There is also the usual connection between average revenue and marginal revenue. In Table 11, columns 1 and 2 present a demand or average revenue schedule; and columns 1 and 4 outline a marginal revenue schedule. To derive column 4 when columns 1 and 2 are known, we first find column 3, and then we obtain the figures for column 4. If columns 1 and 4 are given and column 2 is the unknown, we again find column 3 first, by summing the figures in column 4, and then we obtain column 2 by dividing the totals in column 3 by the corresponding number of units in column 1.

But let us consider a less obvious arithmetic relation between average revenue and marginal revenue. Let us look at the average revenue figures in column 2 and the marginal revenue figures in column 4. We see from column 2 that the firm can sell more and more units only when it cuts its price. If the firm sells two units instead of one unit, it receives 9¢ in new revenue but simultaneously reduces by 1¢ its revenue from the sale of the first unit. The net gain in revenue, or marginal revenue, when two units are sold becomes $9¢ - 1¢ = 8¢$. If average revenue (or the price) declines as more output is offered for sale, when one additional unit is sold the gain in revenue is equal to the price of this extra unit, diminished by the reduction in price of all the previous units which are now sold at the lower price. Thus when the firm sells 5 units instead of 4 units the average price of 5 units is 6¢, whereas the average price of 4 units is 7¢. On these 4 units it loses $4(7¢ - 6¢) = 4¢$. The marginal revenue from the sale of 5 units is accordingly $6¢ - 4¢ = 2¢$.

From the above arithmetic and from our knowledge of the "average-marginal" relations we can generalize that as long as the average revenue declines with growing sales the marginal revenue is smaller than the average revenue; and, likewise, a marginal revenue smaller than the associated average revenue suggests that the average revenue is declining as more units are sold. In column 4 the marginal revenue figures become consistently smaller, after 10¢, than the corresponding figures in column 2. In graphic presentation this means that if the average revenue curve slopes downward to the right, the marginal revenue curve lies below it, to the left. See Figure 27, below.

The same average-marginal connections hold for the situation depicted in the second part of Table 11. But the results are different. Columns 5 to 8 refer to a firm producing under conditions of pure competition. The firm's sales schedule is given in columns 5 and 6. The firm can sell varying amounts of its product at the unvarying market price of 10¢. When it sells an extra unit the extra revenue gained coincides with the unvarying price: there is no loss item to subtract from the sales of the previous units. This means that if the average revenue figures remain the same when more units are sold, the marginal revenue figures will undergo no change either, and will, moreover, coincide with the average revenue figures. Columns 6 and 8 are identical. We reach the same conclusion if we focus our attention on column 8 and try to deduce from it the behavior of the

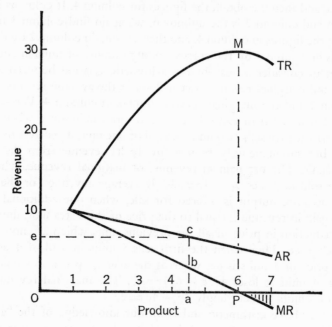

FIGURE 27. *Three Types of Revenue*

average revenues in column 6. Since the marginal revenue figures are not smaller than the average revenue figures, they will not pull down the averages in column 6. If our student invariably gets 90 on each quiz, his average grade for any number of quizzes will stay at 90. If the average revenue curve is horizontal, the companion marginal revenue curve is also horizontal and of course it coincides with this average revenue curve.

We do not concern ourselves with a *rising* demand curve and the appropriate marginal revenue curve hovering above it. Such a curve is rare indeed. When the price of a commodity drops the total sale of it rises.

The "inferior" commodity is no exception. The poor are compelled to patronize the cheaper goods. Let the price of oleomargarine or linoleum decline: some consumers may well turn away from these goods; but many of those in the low income brackets are very likely to be attracted by the favorable price into buying larger quantities per unit of time. The *total* amount bought may well increase.

The "Giffen case" cited by Marshall in this connection is as rare as it is interesting. The expenditure on bread, he tells us, may use up a considerable proportion of a poor man's income, and a rise in the price of bread may make such an inroad into his budget that he has little money left for other somewhat more expensive foods. In consequence, he consumes more bread to make up for the deficiency.[1] Conversely, when the price of bread goes down he may expect to save enough money to come within reach of, say, more meat. He therefore buys less bread at the lower price in order to divert money to meat.

By plotting the figures in columns 1 to 4 in Table 11, we can depict graphically average, marginal, and total revenue. In Figure 27, the number of units sold are laid off on the horizontal axis and the revenue on the vertical axis. When the figures in columns 1 and 2 are plotted and the points connected, we get the average revenue curve AR. Plotting columns 1 and 3, we obtain the total revenue curve TR; and plotting columns 1 and 4, we trace the marginal revenue curve MR. We note that TR is at a maximum (at point M) when MR is zero (at point P).

It is worth noting that graphically total revenue can be presented in three ways. *One*, by the total revenue curve TR, in Figure 27. *Two*, by the area of the rectangle the sides of which represent respectively the number of units sold and the average price charged for them. To picture the total revenue for units *Oa* in Figure 27, we multiply *Oa* by *ac* and get the rectangle *Oace*. *Three*, total revenue can be depicted as the area under the marginal revenue curve. The total revenue from *Oa* units is the area under MR, in the range beginning with the point at which MR touches the vertical axis (as it does, if we deal with minute fractions of units) and extending to the point where it touches the perpendicular above *a* (at *b*). This area is merely the result of adding, graphically, the succession of marginal revenues. We are adding, that is, very narrow columns adjacent to one another, beginning at the origin and ending at point *a*. The height of these columns is limited by the height of the corresponding points on MR. The total revenue of all the seven units considered in Table 11 (in other words, when $Oa = 7$) would be the area under MR *minus* the small shaded area under the horizontal axis, to the right, which pictures the negative marginal revenues of all the fractional units between 6 and 7 units.

[1] A. Marshall, *Principles of Economics*, p. 132.

FITTING THE MR CURVE TO A STRAIGHT-LINE AR CURVE

The geometric relationships of the marginal and average revenue curves are such as to permit us to construct the particular marginal revenue curve which goes with a given demand curve. We have to make a distinction between a demand curve which is a straight line and a demand curve which is not. We shall try only the first case.

Fitting a marginal revenue curve to a given straight-line demand curve is based on the following geometric connection between the two. A perpendicular drawn from a point on the straight-line average revenue curve to the vertical axis is *bisected* by the marginal revenue straight-line curve.[2] Suppose we have, as in Figure 28, the demand curve *BC*, and our problem

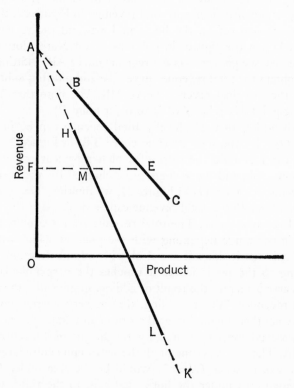

FIGURE 28. *The Derivation of the MR Curve from the AR Curve*

[2] For proof, see Joan Robinson, *The Economics of Imperfect Competition* (London, Macmillan, 1948), p. 30.

is to draw the appropriate marginal revenue curve. (1) Prolong *BC* until it meets the vertical axis at *A*. Inasmuch as the initial price or average revenue is identical with marginal revenue, point *A* is also the starting point of the marginal revenue curve. (2) Draw from any point on *BC* a perpendicular *EF* to the vertical axis. (3) Bisect *EF* at *M*. Points *A* and *M* are the two points which determine the straight-line marginal revenue curve *AK*. The marginal revenue curve for *BC* is *HL*.[3] Point *H* is directly below point *B*, and point *L* is directly below point *C*.

RELATIONS BEWEEN MR AND ELASTICITY

The derivation of concepts is important enough. Just as important are the relations among the concepts derived. It puts a sharper focus on a concept when we see how the given concept is related to other concepts. In this case, the relation can be presented by (1) tables, (2) algebra, and (3) graphs.

(1) *Tabular presentation*

At the beginning of our study of elasticity of demand it was stated that if we are interested to know whether demand for a commodity is elastic, inelastic, or of unitary elasticity, it is sufficient to compare total receipts from the sale of the commodity after the price change with total

TABLE 12. *Relationships Between Marginal Revenue and Elasticity*

Demand elasticity	Size of marginal revenue (MR)	Position of MR curve
1. Perfectly elastic	MR = average revenue, or price	Coincides with average revenue curve
2. Highly elastic	Somewhat less than average revenue	Lies slightly below average revenue curve
3. Somewhat elastic	Much less than average revenue	Lies much below average revenue curve
4. Unitary elasticity	MR = zero	Coincides with x axis
5. Inelastic	MR is negative	Lies below x axis

receipts before the price change. Since a change in total receipts is identified with marginal revenue, we can see that a connection exists between marginal revenue and demand elasticity.

The general relationship may be indicated as follows: if the marginal

[3] For fitting the marginal revenue curve to a curvilinear demand, see *ibid.*, pp. 31–32.

revenue is *positive* as one more unit is sold, the demand is elastic at the price range involved. In column 4 of Table 11, marginal revenue is positive up to the sale of the fifth unit; the demand is elastic for the price range from 10¢ to 5¢. If marginal revenue is *zero*, the demand has an elasticity of unity; with the price change from 6¢ to 5¢ the total revenue stays at 30¢. If the marginal revenue is *negative*, the demand is inelastic; such is the case with the price reduction from 5¢ to 4¢ (Columns 2 and 3 of Table 11).

Table 12 is a summary of the connections between marginal revenue (MR) and the elasticity of demand. In case 2, to induce larger sales, the price needs to be cut, percentagewise, very little; MR is only somewhat below its possible maximum, which equals price. In case 3, to encourage greater sales, the price must be lowered, percentagewise, a good deal; MR drops considerably below average revenue. In case 5, total revenue declines as more units are sold; MR is negative, and the MR curve is therefore below the horizontal.

(2) *Algebraic presentation*

The connection between revenue and elasticity may be stated more precisely, by a formula. It can be shown [4] that

$$E = \frac{P}{P - \text{MR}},$$

where E is elasticity of demand, P is average revenue (AR), or price, and MR is marginal revenue. From this equation we can derive the following two equations:

$$P \text{ (or AR)} = \text{MR} \frac{E}{E - 1}, \quad \text{and} \quad \text{MR} = P \text{ (or AR)} \frac{E - 1}{E}.$$

More algebra could be introduced at this stage, but it is hardly advisable to make a display of it. In some cases diagrammatic presentation of a complicated situation is more effective in revealing the basic elements involved than other means of explanation. Such a case is before us now, in the form of Figure 29.

(3) *Graphic presentation*

Along the horizontal axis of Figure 29 we lay off the amounts of the commodity which the single firm puts on the market for sale. The vertical distances measure the three kinds of revenue—average, marginal, and total.

Line *AR* is the *average* revenue curve or the demand curve confronting the firm which possesses a degree of monopoly power and consequently

[4] *Ibid.,* p. 36.

a price policy: if the firm were in a competitive market, the demand for its product would graph a horizontal line. Let H be the midpoint of AR. The lower half of the demand curve AR has an elasticity less than one (why?); at point H the elasticity would be unity; the upper half is progressively elastic, so that at point R the elasticity of demand would be infinity. Line MR is the marginal revenue curve associated with and derived from AR. As we know, the marginal revenue curve bisects a perpendicular from any point on AR to the vertical axis. Let us consider

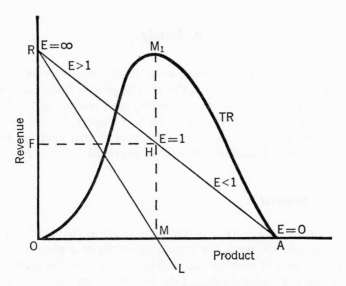

FIGURE 29. *Three Types of Revenue (AR, MR, TR) and Elasticity (E)*

horizontal OA as such a perpendicular from point A to the vertical axis at zero. Point M is therefore the midpoint of OA. Point M specifies that the marginal revenue of output OM is zero. It follows then that total revenue MM_1 is at its maximum for output OM. Beyond this output, that is, for outputs larger than OM, marginal revenue is negative: it descends below the horizontal axis toward L. It is this negative part of the marginal revenue curve that sends total revenue (TR) downward, for production greater than amount OM.

The TR curve begins at the origin; rises up to its peak at M_1; then moves downward until it reaches the horizontal axis at A (zero). Maximum total revenue is reaped by our monopolist when he sells OM units at the price $HM = OF$. How do we know? When we start with a triangle like ARO, the largest rectangle that can be inscribed inside it is a rectangle whose sides are one-half of two sides of the triangle. Thus H is the midpoint of the AR side in the triangle; and M is the midpoint of OA, the other side. A rectangle like $OMHF$ seems to be the answer. A monopolist must ignore his cost of production of a given commodity primarily because the cost of production has been sunk and cannot be revoked. In general, the monopolist will do best to sell OM units of his output at the price OF—and drown the rest.

II. Supply

As has already been mentioned, some of the vital aspects of supply cannot be expounded apart from the pricing process under competition, so interwoven are the two, that is, supply and pricing under competition. Such aspects will be unfolded in the next chapter; it is for this reason that this section contains so many references to that chapter. But first a few introductory fundamentals must be examined.

THE MEANING OF SUPPLY

The definition of supply is of the same order as the definition of demand. By supply we mean the various quantities of a given commodity which producers will offer for sale during a given period at various corresponding and hypothetical prices. Like demand, supply reflects a relationship between two variables, quantity and price. Most frequently the relationship is direct: at a lower price smaller quantities of goods are offered, at a higher price larger quantities, in a given unit of time. In decreasing-cost industries, however, the long-run supply situation reveals an inverse relation between quantity and price: in decreasing-cost industries larger quantities offered for sale and lower prices go together, in the long run. Supply pictures the behavior of the seller. Except for the very short market period, the motive force of this behavior is the level of costs.

A *supply schedule* is presented by a column of prices and another column of corresponding quantities of a given commodity which would be offered for sale per unit of time. A *supply curve* is a curve or a straight line, with the horizontal axis indicating the quantities that would be sold and the vertical axis measuring the corresponding prices. The supply curve has a positive inclination, as in Figure 30. Its slope is positive; it slopes upward to the right, indicating that as the price rises, larger quantities are offered for sale. Supply may refer to the individual firm or to the industry. An industry supply curve mirrors the horizontal addition of the supply schedules of the individual firms operating in the industry: at each given price the offerings of the individual firms are summed up.

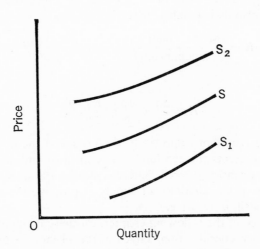

FIGURE 30. *A Change in the Supply*

By an increased supply we mean that at various prices sellers are willing to sell larger quantities of a good than before, in a unit of time; or that they would offer the same quantities as before, at lower prices; or both. We deal with a decreased supply when, at a given series of prices, firms would offer for sale smaller quantities of an article than they did before; or that the same amounts would be offered as before, but at a corresponding array of higher prices; or both. Graphically, an increased supply is portrayed by the supply curve shifted to the right of S and below S, like S_1 in Figure 30; a decreased supply, by a curve shifted to the left and upward, like S_2.

Supply is governed by costs, and, to repeat, costs are related (1) to the time period, short run or long run, (2) to the volume of output of the firm, and (3) to the price of the productive factors which compose the cost of making the good. These aspects of supply will be considered in the following chapter.

ELASTICITY OF SUPPLY

The concept of elasticity in connection with supply is similar to that concept in connection with demand. Elasticity of supply refers to the ratio of (1) the percentage change in the quantity offered for sale in response to (2) the percentage change in the price; or to what is numerically equal, the percentage change in quantity in reaction to a 1% change in price. Elasticity of supply measures the degree of responsiveness of sellers to changes in the price of the commodity which they sell, per unit of time. The formula is familiar. It is

$$E = \frac{\text{rise in amount supplied}}{\text{amount supplied}} \div \frac{\text{rise in price}}{\text{price}},$$

or

$$E = \frac{\Delta q}{q} \div \frac{\Delta p}{p} = \frac{\Delta q}{\Delta p} \cdot \frac{p}{q},$$

where p and q represent respectively the price and the quantity offered for sale, Δp represents the absolute change in price, and Δq the absolute change in the quantity offered. Since, typically, the quantity varies directly with the price, elasticity of supply is positive. Price elasticity of demand, we recall, is negative.

As will be seen in the following chapter, elasticity of supply varies with the period under consideration. Given a 1% change in price, the percentage change in the quantity offered by sellers in a given period will

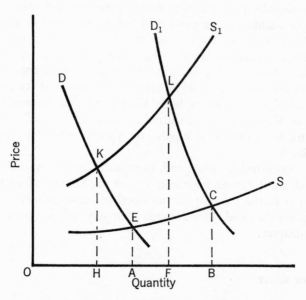

FIGURE 31. *The Effect of Elasticity of Supply on Price*

be smaller in the short run than in the long run. In the short run, the reaction of the producers is confined to the variation of output by changing the variable resources within the fixed plant. In the long run, however, the same change in price will evoke a larger change in the quantity offered for sale than is evoked in the short period, by virtue of the fact that there is time to change output by varying the output of the firm. Supply elasticity increases with the time period.

The significance of the elasticity of supply is many-sided. To give only one example, with a rise in the demand for a commodity, the effect on the price will depend, among other things, on the elasticity of supply. The more elastic the supply the smaller the rise in price needs to be, in order to induce sellers to offer a good deal more for sale. In Figure 31, supply S is generally more elastic than supply S_1 for the same price ranges. Assume that demand rises from D to D_1. The small advance in price from AE to BC evokes a relatively large increment (from OA to OB) offered for sale. But the big rise in price from HK to FL induces a rise in offerings of only HF.

A tangent drawn at a point on the supply curve can tell us whether, at that point, supply is elastic, inelastic, or of unitary elasticity, according

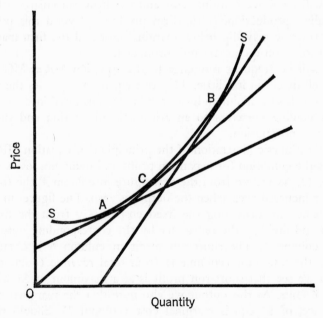

FIGURE 32. *The Relations Between Tangency and the Elasticity of Supply*

to whether the tangent cuts respectively the vertical axis or the horizontal axis, or goes through the origin.[5] In Figure 32 the supply curve *SS* is elastic at point *A*, inelastic at point *B*, and of unitary elasticity at point *C*.

THE RULE OF MAXIMIZING PROFITS

What is the final purpose of the firm in estimating revenues and in contributing its portion to the total supply of a good? The answer is that the firm seeks to maximize profits or minimize losses. As was indicated in Chapter II, section II, the economist is aware that other motives may animate the entrepreneur, examples being the desire for power or prestige, the quest for security, emulation, or altruism. But these other motives are not measurable and are uncertain in their effects; and they are less perseverant in their influence than the motive of gain. Moreover, and this is very important, in so far as they operate they render prediction of the firm's behavior impossible. We are lost in a sea of potentialities.

The desire for maximum profits is realized when the firm carries production to the volume of goods at which marginal cost equals marginal revenue. Such is the rule of maximizing profits. If the firm stops short of this optimum output, it fails to realize *all* the potential gains; the marginal revenue will be above marginal cost and the firm can enlarge its profits by extending production. If the firm produces beyond this point, the marginal revenue may dip below marginal cost and the firm may suffer mounting losses on each extra unit produced.

There will be frequent reference to the equation $MR = MC$ and we may as well dwell on it a little. That this equation expresses the rule for maximum profits or minimum losses can be demonstrated in various ways. We shall confine ourselves to an arithmetic illustration and then to a geometric demonstration.

For the arithmetic illustration of the principle that equation $MR = MC$ represents the condition for maximum profit and minimum losses we shall use Table 13. As we see from the first figure in column 4, the fixed cost is $10; it is incurred even when the output is zero. The figures in column 8 are obtained by deducting the fixed cost of $10 from the figures in column 4 and dividing the remainder by the corresponding output indicated in column 1. The short-run profit in column 6 is obtained by deducting the total cost (column 4) from total revenue (column 5). In column 6 we see that short-run profit is at a maximum of $5 when the output is 6 units. At this output we also note that the marginal revenue, or the price, of $7 equals marginal cost (column 7). Should the firm

[5] For proof, see K. E. Boulding, *Economic Analysis*, revised ed. (New York, Harper, 1948), p. 138.

TABLE 13. *Illustration of the Principle that Maximum Profit Is Obtained when MR = MC*

(1)	(2)	(3)	(4)	(5)	(6)	(7)	(8)	(9)	(10)	(11)
Output, units	MR or price	Average total cost	Total cost (3) × (1)	Total revenue (2) × (1)	Profit (5) − (4)	Marginal cost	Average variable cost	MR or price (alternative)	Total revenue (9) × (1)	Profit (10) − (4)
0	$7	∞	$10	$ 0	−$10			$5	$ 0	−$10
1	7	$14	14	7	−7	$4	$4	5	5	−9
2	7	8	16	14	−2	2	3	5	10	−6
3	7	$6\frac{1}{3}$	19	21	2	3	3	5	15	−4
4	7	6	24	28	4	5	$3\frac{1}{2}$	5	20	−4
5	7	6	30	35	5	6	4	5	25	−5
6	7	$6\frac{1}{6}$	37	42	5	7	$4\frac{1}{2}$	5	30	−7
7	7	$6\frac{3}{7}$	45	49	4	8	5	5	35	−10

191

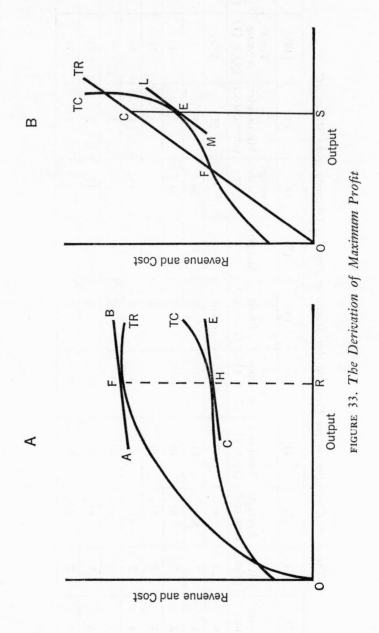

FIGURE 33. *The Derivation of Maximum Profit*

produce 7 units it will lose money on the additional unit, for the reason that additional receipts are $7, whereas the additional cost (column 7) is $8. If it stops production with only 4 units, it does not maximize its gains, inasmuch as the production of unit 5 entails an extra cost of $6 but brings an extra revenue of $7.

In column 9 we change the price to $5, which is above the average *variable cost* (column 8) or equal to it. If the price were below average variable cost, the firm would close down. At this price of $5 short-run losses (column 11) are sustained for all outputs, since in each instance the price is below average *total* cost (column 3). However, the short-run loss is smallest, namely $4, at an output of 4 units. Again at this output the marginal cost of $5 (column 7) equals marginal revenue (column 9).

We shall now turn to the geometric demonstration. We shall involve two situations, monopoly (Figure 33A) and competition (Figure 33B). In Figure 33A, let TR stand for total revenue and TC for short-run total costs, both measured along the vertical axis; since profit equals TR — TC, the vertical axis also shows total profit as the firm sells progressively more goods. Output is scaled along the horizontal axis. The slope of the TR curve is marginal revenue and the slope of the TC curve is marginal cost. The tangent AB to TR at point F is parallel to CE, which is the tangent to TC at point H. This indicates that at points F and H the slopes of the two respective curves are equal, and that for output OR marginal revenue equals marginal cost.

For this output OR the total profit is also the greatest. The distance FH between the total revenue and the total cost curves, which measures the total profit, is greater than any other distance between these two curves. To the left of point F the slope of TR is steeper than at F: TR drops fast to the left of F. To the left of point H the slope of TC is less steep than at point H. Accordingly to the left of FH the distance between the two curves is narrower than distance FH. Similarly, to the right of point F the slope of TR becomes less steep, but this is not important; what is important is the fact that TR is moving downward and is narrowing the gap between TR and TC, and that to the right of point H the slope of TC is rising: to the right of FH the distance is again smaller than FH. The output for which marginal revenue equals marginal cost brings to the firm maximum total profit.

As can readily be perceived, the problem portrayed by Figure 33A and the discussion centered on it refer to a monopoly market for the product made by our firm. Curve TR (total revenue) is characteristic of monopoly pricing of goods. The more the monopolist desires to sell per unit of time the lower must be his price or average revenue (AR). Sooner or later the TR curve reaches its peak beyond which it would steadily decline.

In Figure 33B we deal with a commodity produced and sold under pure competition. Now the total revenue (TR) looks different. Inasmuch as the competitive price of the article sold by our firm stays unchanged, the more units of the commodity the firm sells the higher is the total revenue which it gathers, as is illustrated by line TR in Figure 33B. This TR curve is a straight line beginning at zero (at the origin) and steadily rising to the right as more and more units of the article are sold by the firm at the unvarying competitive price, as established in the market. The total revenue obtained from the sale of two units of its article will amount to double the revenue received from the sale of only one unit. Graphically, both the horizontal and the vertical distances will be twice the corresponding distances for the sale of one commodity; similarly with, say, ten units sold. Let us draw the one line which is simultaneously parallel to the total revenue (TR) curve and tangent to the total cost (TC) curve. This is ML tangent to TC at point E. The biggest spread between the TR and TC curves comes between points E and C. At point E the slope of the TC curve equals the slope at point C on the TR curve (or to any other point on TR). Output OS is the equilibrium output, the most profitable output by the firm per unit of time, for the simple reason that profit = TR — TC.

Why is equilibrium for some output to the left of point F in Figure 33B ruled out? This is an important question. The answer is: any point to the left of point F depicts an output at which total cost exceeds total revenue; the firm would be losing money. It would cut production; it would move farther away to the left. Losses do not inspire extension of output. To the left of F the biggest spread between TC and TR, with TC above TR, would only measure the greatest total loss to the firm. Stated differently, when the cost curve is above the revenue curve so that it comes to meet the revenue curve from *above*, the point of meeting (point F in Figure 33B) is an unstable equilibrium.

III. The Nature of Markets

By a market we do not mean the stores where buyers buy and sellers sell. The essence of a market is lodged in the total interrelations between buying and selling, in demand and supply, and in the approximation of a uniform price of a given good. It is assumed that the sellers of a particular article are in contact with each other and that the buyers, too, have an idea of how much buying goes on per unit of time. At a higher price for a good, buyers purchase less and sellers offer more for sale; the converse, if the price is low. The result is that sooner or later a uniform price is formed, with known deviations to account for quality variations, insurance, and cost of transportation.

Organized markets are of two kinds: in some there are buying and selling of securities, like stocks and bonds. The New York Stock Exchange comes to mind as an outstanding example. In this market almost each minute the forces of demand for and supply of shares of common stock to the U.S. Steel Corporation may forge one uniform price. We visualize the brokers at the steel post on the floor of the Exchange transacting purchases and sales; representing many buyers and sellers, possibly in many countries, and forming one price per share, which becomes the ruling price for any unit of time—minutes, hours, days—and not only in our country but also in other countries where there are people interested in buying or selling U.S. Steel Corporation shares. The transatlantic cable brings people from across the seas into the New York market.

Then there are markets for commodities, like the Chicago Board of Trade, handling corn, wheat, cotton, and other goods; the New York Coffee and Sugar Exchange, and the New Orleans Cotton Exchange. In principle there is little difference between a stock exchange and a commodity exchange. At a given moment the price of a given grade of wheat is the resultant of bids and asks, of supply and demand, by brokers executing orders given them by manufacturers who use commodities like soybeans, cotton, and wheat as raw materials, and by speculators bent on amassing fortunes (or destined to lose their shirts). If the price of a given kind of wheat is higher in one market than in another market, brokers and speculators will buy low and sell high, until a uniform price for this kind of wheat is established in each wheat market, here or abroad: we omit the cost of transportation.

An organized commodity market demands certain qualifications in the commodity traded. The commodity must be standardized, so that when there is reference to it everybody in this game knows precisely which type of commodity is involved. Further, almost each commodity is classified into varieties, known to the brokers and other buyers and sellers. Too, the commodity must be nonperishable in storage.

A third type of market, not "organized," is the ordinary market for a commodity, like shoes, furniture, milk, textbooks, automobiles, and so on. There are no brokers nor speculators nor buildings, nor pits where brokers ply their trade. The market may be local, like fresh apple pie; regional or national, like an Elgin watch, or the automobile; and international, like gold, diamonds, or Wedgwood china. Every commodity which is bought and sold has a market of one kind or another.

Let us be specific. The calculations of the firm and its resultant behavior in setting the price of its product will depend on the particular situation in which it finds itself in the market for its commodity; that is, on the market structure for this commodity. The market structure, in its turn, is characterized primarily by two features.

One feature relates to the number of producers of the article. The paramount question is: is the firm the only producer, or one of a few producers, or one among very many? This condition will indicate whether or not the single firm is compelled to take notice of the possible reactions of other firms to its own policies. The *second* feature points to the type of commodity produced by the firm. The commodity may have perfect substitutes in the goods produced by other firms, or it may have close or very remote substitutes. This characteristic will decide whether or not the firm has monopoly power in shaping its price. The substitutability of one good for another, the degree of cross-elasticity of the products of various firms, determine whether or not the individual firm can impress its will upon the price of its output.

THE CLASSIFICATION OF MARKETS

The classification of market structures is not a settled question. There has been controversy about it. The classification used in this book is the one generally adopted in textbooks. It is based on the two criteria mentioned above, and it leads to the conception that our economy exhibits the following four types of market structures:

1. Pure competition (many sellers; many buyers; homogeneous commodity)
2. Absolute or pure monopoly (one seller; sharply differentiated commodity)
3. Monopolistic competition (many sellers; differentiated commodity)
4. Oligopoly (few sellers)
    (a) Pure oligopoly (homogeneous commodity)
    (b) Differentiated oligopoly (differentiated commodity)

Each of these four types of markets will form the subject matter of a separate chapter. But it is well to describe them briefly here, so that we may gain a bird's-eye view of the chief markets before we begin the exploration of the pricing process in any one of them.

1. PURE COMPETITION

The backbone of pure competition rests on the fact that no one seller exercises control over the supply and therefore over the price of the commodity. This implies that the two criteria of this market are as follows: (1) the number of sellers and buyers is very large; (2) the commodity produced by the firms is regarded by the buyers as homogeneous.

The *first* criterion signifies that the most profitable output of each of the numerous sellers constitutes a very small fraction of the total volume of the commodity on the market. This circumstance breeds two consequences. In the first place, the single firm is in no position to influence the price of the product by enlarging or shrinking its output. In the second place, *each* firm feels that by shading its price it can increase its trade without drawing away appreciable custom from any of its many rivals, and for that reason without provoking retaliation. The result is that *each* producer adjusts his price to the lowest level consistent with his costs. Moreover, because the number of buyers is considerable, no one buyer is large enough to dictate to the seller a price below the prevailing level. It is important to anticipate and mention that involved here are Chamberlin's *dd'* and *DD'* demand curves.

The *second* criterion implies that the buyer has no preference respecting the seller with whom he will deal. In the mind of the buyer, the article sold by one firm is identical with the article sold by any other firm. The goods are perfect substitutes for one another; their cross-elasticity is infinite. It follows from this that if a firm raises its price slightly above the current level, it may lose all its customers to its rivals. Since it can sell its maximum production at the prevailing price, it has no incentive to lower it. Without inducement to raise or cut the price, the firm is content to accept the price formed in the market as its own.

Once the market price has been established, each single firm accepts it as a given datum and regulates its output accordingly. The outstanding feature of pure competition is reflected in the fact that the individual firm has no price policy. To the individual firm the sales schedule looks like a horizontal line. The firm can sell at the market price any amount which it may produce. The demand for its product is perfectly elastic.

No concept in our economy is hailed so warmly as competition. From editorial pages to legislative halls comes the chorus of praise of competition as the foundation of our economy. The striking fact is, however, that examples of pure competition are rare. In real life there are few industries which fulfill the two basic preconditions of pure competition. The classic example is the production and sale by farmers of certain grain crops like wheat and corn, and of some other commodities like cotton and hogs. Outside of agriculture, examples may be found in the mining and sale of bituminous coal and in such organized commodity markets as those for wool.

It is essential to keep in mind that most of the examples of pure competition refer to raw materials and not to the final product made of these materials. The classic example of pure competition is wheat. But people do not munch on wheat. They eat what is made of wheat: loaves of packaged bread, varieties of cake, and brandy.

Perfect competition

British economists are apt to choose for their anaysis perfect competition, whereas American economists are very likely to deal with pure competition. Pure competition and perfect competition have their separate meanings. Pure competition refers only to one perfection in the market: the complete absence of monopoly power in forming the price. Perfect competition implies pure competition and adds other perfections. It implies perfect mobility of resources, labor, and capital, in any economic adjustment: there is no cost of movement nor restraining habits, preferences, or inertia. It also implies perfect knowledge on the part of buyers and sellers. As Professor F. H. Knight states: "They are supposed to know absolutely the consequences of their acts when they are performed, and to perform them in the light of the consequences." [6] Other elements of perfection may be introduced, to suit the requirements of a particular analysis; for instance, perfect divisibility of equipment or effort.

The perfection of the market does not by itself indicate competition; nor does competition imply perfection. A monopoly market may be perfect or imperfect. There may or may not exist mobility of resources and perfect knowledge as to demand and costs under monopoly, monopolistic competition, or oligopoly. Likewise, competition may be pure and perfect or pure and imperfect; the absence of any monopoly element may or may not be associated with perfect mobility and perfect knowledge.[7]

2. ABSOLUTE MONOPOLY

The single-firm monopoly, or absolute or pure monopoly, stands at the other extreme of pure competition. One seller produces an article for which it is difficult to find a substitute. The one firm constitutes the industry; and the demand for its output is at once the demand for the total product in the market. The cross-elasticity between the monopolized good and its nearest substitute is small. Because the most available substitute may be viewed by the consumer as highly unsatisfactory, the monopolist has wide latitude of choice in his price policy without being

---

[6] *Risk, Uncertainty and Profit* (Boston, Houghton Mifflin, 1921), p. 77.
[7] E. H. Chamberlin, *The Theory of Monopolistic Competition*, 6th ed. (Cambridge, Harvard University Press, 1948), p. 26.

obliged to mind the policies and reactions of other firms. A company can charge a good deal for water, telephone service, or perhaps even railway or bus service before the hard-pressed consumer will turn to such corresponding substitutes as digging a private well, gossiping only across the fence, or traveling long distances by car.

3. MONOPOLISTIC COMPETITION

Like pure competition, monopolistic competition involves many sellers and buyers. But the product is differentiated. What one firm produces is not quite like what any other firm produces. The products are, however, close substitutes, as a rule. The differences which separate one variety from another in a given family of similar goods, which make their cross-elasticities rather high, are numerous. They may be differences in quality, style, color, size, packaging, container, trade name, brand, type of service, location of the store, credit terms, and other considerations. All the firms producing the closely related goods compose one industry. Examples are toilet articles, articles of clothing, coffee, breakfast cereals, and the objects generally sold in retail stores in good-sized cities. Between the products of one given industry, say, toilet articles, and those of another industry, perhaps brands of coffee, there is a considerable gap; such products are very remote substitutes and their cross-elasticity is minute: the price of article A may decline appreciably, and yet the quantity sold of article B may move up but lazily.

The presence of many sellers suggests that the price policy of a given firm in this type of market is of little concern to the other firms since the effect on their sales will be inconspicuous. A reduction in price will enlarge a firm's trade, but the sales of any one of the numerous other firms in the industry will experience a negligible decline.

However, the fact that the commodities are not identical and are not perfect substitutes for one another gives the seller a measure of discretion in setting the price for his product. Some buyers are attached to his variety of the good as against other varieties; and to maximize his gains, he can charge a little more. Within a certain range of prices he enjoys a monopoly situation and can have a price policy. He can charge less and sell more, or charge more and sell less. But his independence is limited. Should he raise his price above a certain level, a shift to substitutes may be induced and he may face losses.

Thus in so far as monopolistic competition is characterized by many sellers and *close* substitutes the mass result of the individual behavior of the firms forms the market price level or range of prices as a datum confronting the individual firm, almost as in pure competition. But in so far as the varieties, close substitutes though they may be, are not *perfect* substitutes, there are pockets of monopoly control, and individual prices vary from one another, depending on whether the nearest substitute is or is not very close.

4. OLIGOPOLY

In many instances the market for a commodity, homogeneous or differentiated, is dominated by a few firms each of which is producing a considerable proportion of the total output of the industry. If the product of these firms is homogeneous, we call it pure oligopoly; if different, differentiated oligopoly.

Producing a sizable fraction of the total, each oligopolist can, by withholding or enlarging his offerings, raise or lower the price for the whole industry and affect the fortunes of the other firms. It follows that in shaping its price policy each firm must take into consideration the reaction of the few other producers and then his possible reaction to their reactions. There is thus a unique interrelationship among the few sellers with respect to their price and output policies. This interrelationship is inseparable from oligopoly.

This interrelationship and its consequences are not susceptible of simple classification, much less of convenient generalization. What price will result, and by what steps, will depend on unique elements in the situation and in the assumptions made. The price may be competitive, monopolistic, or one which oscillates between set limits. There may be independent pricing by each large firm, price leadership, price wars, varieties of collusive agreements, and other types of conduct by the few sellers.

SURPLUS AND SHORTAGE

Before we undertake the more or less detailed and "technical" analysis of price formation, in the next four chapters, it may be well to close this chapter with a brief illustration of what the market does in the realm of price, and of the difficulties inseparable from government interference with the price as determined in the market.

Our economy is predominantly a market economy. The price of goods, especially under pure competition, is established in the market by the pre-eminent effects of supply and demand, culminating in the equilibrium of the seller and buyer of the goods. Very largely, the price of a factor-service (wages, interest, rent, and profit; particularly the first three) is formed in similar manner in similar markets.

What happens when the government thrusts on us price control as a substitute for the workings of the market? We begin to appreciate the significance of the market as we try to answer this question. A prominent writer (John Ruskin) stated in a moment of temporary (we hope) aberration that a parrot can become an economist. All you have to do is to teach the bird to pronounce three words, "supply and demand."

To answer the question raised in the previous paragraph, let us avail ourselves of Figure 34. The horizontal axis measures the quantity of corn

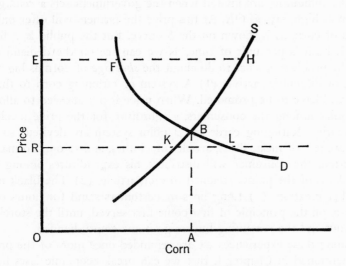

FIGURE 34. *Surplus and Shortage*

and the vertical axis measures price. Curve *S* is a supply curve and curve *D* is a demand curve. The equilibrium price is *AB*. At this price consumers are ready to buy *OA* units of corn and sellers are willing to offer *OA* units for sale.

Assume now that the government puts a *floor* price *OE* below which the price of corn is not to decline. Unpleasant adjustments begin to trouble us. At price *OE* the producers of corn are willing to sell *EH* bushels, as we see on the supply line *S*. But the consumers would buy only *EF* bushels in a given period of time, as can be seen on the demand line *D*. Line *FH* measures the resulting *surplus* of corn; *FH* is being produced but is not being sold.

We have on our hands the problem of disposing of the surplus created by the government disequilibrium price; or else, we shall have to bring about, somehow, an increased demand for corn (a dubious possibility), so that the new demand curve for corn will shift upward to the right, intersecting the S curve at point H. This surplus, cumulating each year, becomes a deluge harassing the government and the citizen alike. Various schemes have been designed to take the surplus of corn off the market: free school lunches; throwing corn on foreign markets to make enemies of our friends; foreign aid with corn; storage of corn in the colossal metal containers pockmarking the countryside; and of course the variety of devices of paying the farmer for curtailing his production of corn. The problem has not been solved yet. Let Mr. Ruskin consult his parrot.

Similar difficulties are invited when the government sets a *ceiling* price on corn as high, say, as OR. At this price the farmers will offer only RK bushels of corn, as is shown on the S curve. But the public is willing to buy RL bushels per unit of time, as we can see on the demand curve. Now the problem is what to do about the *shortage* of corn as big as KL. A host of difficulties arrive. (1) A system of rationing corn to the consumer will have to be promoted. When price is not allowed to allocate a commodity among the consumers, a substitute for the price mechanism is imperative. Rationing cards and a point system are devised: so many points are set for meat, shoes, articles of clothes, and so on. To maximize satisfaction, the consumer will distribute his expenditures among goods on the basis of the points attached to each article. (2) The black market is another creation. (3) Long lines of customers stand for hours outside the store, on the principle of first come first served, until the storekeeper is sold out and the remaining buyers go home empty-handed.

Scanning these experiences we are reminded once more of the proposition, mentioned in Chapter I, that we can break economic laws but not with impunity.

SUGGESTED READINGS

Bain, J. S. *Pricing, Distribution, and Employment*, revised ed., pp. 58–75, 199–203. New York, Holt, 1953.

Machlup, F. "Monopoly and Competition: a Classification of Market Positions," *American Economic Review*, Vol. XXVII (September, 1937), pp. 445–451.

Machlup, F. *The Economics of Sellers' Competition*, chap. 4. Baltimore, The Johns Hopkins Press, 1952.

Robinson, Joan. *The Economics of Imperfect Competition*, chap. 2. London, Macmillan, 1948.

Rothchild, K. W. "Price Theory and Oligopoly," *Economic Journal*, Vol. LVII (September, 1947), pp. 299–320.

CHAPTER

IX   Pure Competition

WE NOW begin the study of the pricing of goods, which forms the theme of this chapter and of the three chapters to follow. We recall that the conditions of pure competition are: many sellers, many buyers, and a homogeneous product. As was stated in the preceding chapter, cases of pure competition are rare in our economy. They are confined to agricultural products, to bituminous coal, and to materials bought and sold in organized commodity markets like hides, tin and zinc, and other raw materials that go into the making of final *products* which may not represent pure competition at all. Wheat is bought and sold in the competitive organized market; but loaves of bread and varieties of cake sold by bakeries may form a market of monopolistic competition or local oligopoly.

The question may be raised at this point: why *study* pure competition at all if we come upon it so rarely in actual circumstances? Moreover, why *begin* our analysis of pricing with pure competition? There are at least two persuasive answers.

First, agriculture, the classic example of pure competition, is a huge industry involving an enormous number of producers and the total population as consumers. The four million producers (farmers) compose nearly as many entrepreneurs as are counted in our total economy outside agriculture. The four million farmers and their families, under twenty million in all, constitute a high percentage of our total population. It is important to understand the workings of this sector of the economy in order to perceive the good and bad fortune affecting so many people in our midst. In addition to providing us with food and clothes, agriculture supplies the raw materials for an enormous variety of industries. Besides, there are many industries which do not exemplify pure competition but nonetheless exhibit varying degrees of approximation of it. There is more competition in our economy than is sometimes realized. We cannot therefore by-pass such a big and significant sector when price analysis is undertaken.

Second, in its various aspects, pure competition may function as a *norm* with which we may fruitfully compare the processes in markets which deviate from pure competition, like monopoly, monopolistic competition, and oligopoly. Price, output, cost, equilibrium, efficiency, least-cost, progress, profit, growth, and other elements of the economics of competition can be matched against their counterparts in noncompetitive markets. When we are familiar with the basic aspects of competitive price, we may gain in evaluative comprehension of our fundamental laws against monopoly, namely the Sherman Act of 1890, the Clayton Act and the Federal Trade Commission Act, both of 1914, and other legislation against monopolistic practices. A study of competition may throw light on Supreme Court decisions. A member of this Court will do well to learn about such problems as monopsony and oligopoly.

The formation of a competitive price depends on supply and demand; but the nature of supply changes with the time period in which the firm can make adjustments in order to realize maximum gains or minimum losses. As was mentioned in Chapter VII three time periods are involved in the problem of price determination: the market period, the short-run period, and the long-run period. Accordingly our study of competitive price will concern itself with price formation in each of these periods.

I. Market Price

THE MARKET PERIOD: THE VERY SHORT RUN

We are now concerned with market price or very short-run price. This period embraces a span of time during which the amount of goods available for sale is fixed. This period is longer in some instances than in others. The amount of wheat in the world market varies from year to year, but during the year it is so much and no more, except for holdovers from the past, which are commonly of little significance in comparison with the size of the crop yields of the year. In manufacturing, the period in which the amount of the homogeneous good is well-nigh invariable may be short indeed—a few days. The dealers in wheat, the retailers with homogeneous goods on the shelf, and the manufacturers with stocks in the warehouse at times face very short-run price situations. There are other instances of fixed stocks: end-of-season standardized goods cluttering the shelves of many stores; stocks of homogeneous goods the further production of which is shut off by war; or particular articles in sudden demand in a local market because of an unexpected heat wave, a spell of inclement weather, a flood, or some other such occurrence.

The total amount available may have to be sold almost immediately, as in the case of perishable produce brought to market by many competing farmers, or in the case of numerous dealers caught with inventory when the season for the particular homogeneous commodity is over. In such a contingency the supply is infinitely inelastic and the supply curve is a vertical line. In Figure 35, the fixed amount which must be disposed

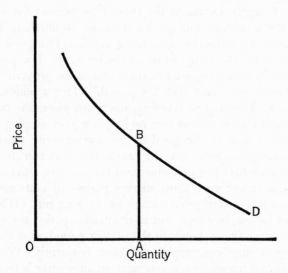

FIGURE 35. *Market Price with Supply Completely Inelastic*

of by the sellers for whatever it will bring is *OA*. The supply curve is *AB*. As the price climbs above *AB* the amount offered for sale does not stir; it stays at *OA*.

Ordinarily, however, the firm is not compelled to sell its total stock in short order. The amounts which it will offer for sale may vary with the price which the buyers are willing to pay. If the price is low, the offerings will be scant: the seller may hold back a large part of his stock for the time when the price will be more attractive. In some cases he will consume more of the good himself, since the low price may match his own marginal utility when he considers greater personal use of the commodity. In such instances it is said that the seller has a *reservation price,* a price below which he is not disposed to make any sales. The reservation price will, at a given time, be high if the seller thinks that the ruling price is too low and promises to take a turn upward, if the storage costs are low, if the goods do not deteriorate fast, and if he is not hard pressed for cash. His reservation price will be low in contrary circumstances. At a given price, each seller may offer a different amount for sale, depending on his reservation price. When these amounts are added to one total for each price—this process is called horizontal addition—we obtain the supply of the homogeneous good in the market, the various quantities offered by the sellers at various corresponding prices. The supply curve has the usual positive inclination: it slopes upward to the right.

The supply situation in the very short market period is unique within the family of supply curves in the three time periods because it is not related to the monetary outlays incurred in production. There is no monetary cost of production governing supply. The good has already been produced by the many firms and is on hand. The past monetary costs involved in its making are like the water in the proverb "you cannot grind flour with the water that has passed." Once a middle process of production, say irrigating or weeding, has taken place, the costs of these processes are, in the very short run, no longer a price-shaping force. Only when there is a flow of the good to the market, only when there is a rate of producing the good, as is the case in the short run and in the long run, is there a tie between unit costs and the amounts offered for sale at various prices. In the very short market period all costs are fixed; and fixed costs do not govern price, except in the long run. (Why?)

It does not follow, however, that in the market period the supply curve is not a cost curve in any sense. In the market period, as in the other two periods, opportunity cost applies, at least frequently. When a given amount is offered for sale at a given price an alternative is forgone by the selling firm: the alternative of consuming it or the alternative of holding it for a possibly better price in the future.

PRICE DETERMINATION

If for one reason or another the many sellers of a given standardized product must dispose of the whole amount almost at once, the price will be determined by the demand and by the demand alone. In Figure 35 the amount for sale is OA; and, according to the demand curve D, such an amount will sell at price AB per unit, the price which the consumers are willing to offer. The seller is at the mercy of the buyer. If only one or only a few sellers possessed this amount, they could behave like monopolists. They could sell *part* of OA at a higher price than AB, and destroy the remainder; their total revenue would be larger than $OA \times AB$.

When reservation prices are possible and the offerings are variable, depending on the sales price, the market-period price will be determined by the equilibrium of supply and demand, by the intersection of the supply and demand curves S and D, as in Figure 36. At the price AB, the

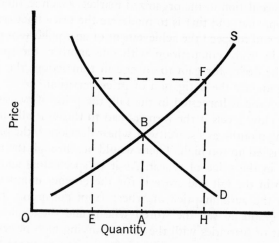

FIGURE 36. *Market Price with Reservation Prices*

sellers are willing to offer OA units of the good and the consumers are likewise willing to buy OA units. No other price is the equilibrium price; and no amount other than OA is the equilibrium amount. For instance, at any price above AB, say, FH, the sellers would be willing to offer OH units, as is seen from the supply curve S, but the buyers would be willing to take only OE units, as is seen from the demand curve D. Rivalry among the sellers will lower the price in order to raise sales, until the equilibrium price AB is reached. Similarly with a price lower than AB: the buyers would be ready to take a larger quantity than the sellers would be willing to offer at such a price. Now rivalry among the buyers, ready to purchase more than is offered, will push the price up, until again the equilibrium price is established. Since knowledge is not perfect and reactions are not lightning-swift, the equilibrium price does not emerge instantaneously. It is, however, approximated by successive adjustments by the buyers and sellers.

SPECULATION AND RATIONING

To round out our discussion of price determination in the very short market period, we touch on two relevant problems: *one* problem deals with the influence of speculation on the market price of a commodity; and the *other* problem concerns the function of the market price as a rationing device, as an allocator of the fixed amount of a good among the consumers who have a demand for it.

Since J. S. Mill,[1] economists have generally been of the opinion that the role of speculation in the organized markets (such as those for wheat, coffee, cotton, zinc, and tin) is to moderate the price fluctuations of such commodities and to speed the achievement of an equilibrium price. Skilled traders and in lively competition with one another, the speculators are moved by the desire for gain to engage in transactions the net result of which is commonly the mitigation of price variation.[2]

When the crop is harvested in the fall, the price of wheat would sink to extremely low levels if the farmers had to throw it all on the market. In succeeding months, as a scarcity of wheat developed, the price of wheat would be pushed up too high. There would be, through the months, wide fluctuations in the price of wheat. As it is, speculators and dealers buy up the crop in the fall and store it for the coming months. These purchases keep the autumn price of wheat from collapsing. Later on, the speculators gradually sell the stored wheat; and these sales prevent the development of scarcities with the accompanying high prices.

Thus through the year (and even from year to year) the price of wheat fluctuates less on account of the speculators, the wheat is "rationed" to the consumer in an orderly manner without gluts and dearths, and a closer approximation to an equilibrium price is attained. Of course, even at best, the price of wheat cannot be constant. With the passage of the months, the price must rise enough to compensate the speculators for the cost of storing and holding the commodity in stock. In addition, the motive of the speculator is to make a profit by "buying cheap and selling dear."

It is to be understood, however, that such procedures will tend to stabilize the price of the commodity only if the speculators are correct in their estimates of future supplies. Suppose that the September crop of wheat is large but speculators expect a small harvest of May wheat and a much higher price then. They will buy September wheat to sell high in May. But if the crop in May turns out to be larger than was anticipated, the operations of the speculators aggravate the price differences of wheat instead of mitigating them. The enthusiastic buying in September tends to support the autumn price, and the unloading of the accumulations on the market in the spring adds to the large crop and sends the price plum-

[1] J. S. Mill, *Principles of Political Economy*, 1848 (Ashley ed., New York, Longmans, Green, 1909), Book IV, chap. 2, sections 4 and 5. Cf. A. Marshall, *Principles of Economics*, p. 332.

[2] For a dissenting view, see E. H. Chamberlin, *The Theory of Monopolistic Competition*, 6th ed. (Cambridge, Harvard University Press, 1948), p. 29.

meting down.[3]

We turn now to the theme of market price as the *rationer* of goods. When the amount of a given product stays fixed for a while, two problems may emerge and urge a solution. *One*, how will this fixed quantity be rationed among the consumers who have a demand for it? *Two*, if the amount stays constant for a week or a year, how will the commodity be rationed throughout the period so as to avoid a glut early in the year and a shortage at the end of the year? The allied question is how to avoid the violent up-and-down fluctuations in the price of wheat during the year between harvests. Briefly, the two problems are: rationing among consumers at a given date, and rationing over time.

As to the first problem. Suppose many farmers bring to market baskets of blueberries, a perishable product, and they aim to sell the total amount during the day. In such a case the sellers can have but little influence over the price of the berries. The price is governed mainly by the demand curve of the buyers. The resulting price functions as the rationing agency. The consumers with a high utility for berries will pay the price and obtain the amount of berries they wish to enjoy at this price. At this price some will buy several baskets, others a basket or two. Those having a comparatively low utility for berries may buy no berries and may instead spend the money on grapes.

The situation is illustrated by Figure 35, early in this chapter. The amount that must be sold during the day is OA baskets; the supply curve is AB, completely inelastic: whatever the price, the amount offered for sale is AB, invariably. The demand curve D shows the various quantities that consumers will buy at various hypothetical prices for a basket of berries in a period of time. If the sellers of the berries guess correctly this demand, the equilibrium will be reached without ado. The equilibrium price will be AB cents a basket; the amount sold will be OA baskets. The market would be cleared. If the sellers mistakenly expect a demand curve above and to the right of D, the price set will prove higher than AB. Sales will be sluggish; the farmers will be compelled soon enough to reduce the price. If the demand as figured by the sellers is below the D curve, and the price chosen by them is lower than AB, sales will run so briskly as to foreshadow a shortage of berries at this low price before long. The sellers will raise the price and the market will be cleared. Price is the allocator, the rationer.

The problem is more complicated when the fixed supply (in the sense of a given quantity) rules for a relatively long period, say, one year between harvests of wheat, corn, or cotton. If the whole crop should be brought to the market, the price of wheat would be disastrously low for

---

[3] This presentation of speculation is elementary indeed, to avoid the technicalities of "futures" contracts and hedging.

the farmers. Moreover, toward the end of the year there might be a severe shortage of wheat, with resulting skyrocketing prices. From the viewpoint of the consumers, there would be feasting early in the year, after the harvest, and fasting late in the year before the new crop appeared.

The wheat is in the hands of speculators, dealers, and other sellers. It is being sold by them, not in periodic or sporadic outbursts but rather continuously, for consumption and industrial uses. In the early months of the year the price is developed by buyers and sellers. If productive rains are reported over the wheatfields of Canada or Argentina, as fore-runners of big crops, and accordingly the price of wheat on hand is low, more wheat will be offered for sale at this low price. If the war lords of a belligerent country make a threatening move or declaration, and the prospect of a good price of wheat seems to be justified in a setting of more strenuous preparations for war, less wheat will be offered for sale at this low price.

As the year is getting old, two opposing situations may develop. The cost of holding wheat becomes heavier because of storage and the interest charge on the investment over more and more months. The price of wheat tends to rise on these accounts—other things equal. But a countervailing consideration joins the picture as the months go by. If for one reason or another the price of wheat goes down, the sellers will offer more wheat for sale in the late months of the year than in the early months. The later it is in the year the less time is left for the vagaries of the market to bring an opportunity to sell at a compensating price. Accordingly in the region of very low prices the amounts offered for sale are larger late in the year than when the year is young.

At around the end of the year the sellers of wheat may find themselves in the position illustrated by Figure 35. The sellers are not anxious to carry over unsold wheat into the next year, adding old wheat to the crop of new wheat. They may prefer to dispose of most of their holdings at a price matching the marginal utility of wheat to the consuming public. As we see, in rationing over time, price is again the functioning agency.

II. Short-Run Normal Price

Let us state, or restate, our assumptions. (1) We are dealing with static conditions: we assume a given technique of production and given tastes and preferences of consumers. (2) As the firm employs changing amounts of the variable resources, the prices of these resources, like wages, interest, and rent, in the general market remain unaffected. (3) The firm produces only one homogeneous commodity, and so do the many other firms.

NATURE OF THE SHORT-RUN PERIOD

In the short normal period the firm faces a given or changed demand for its product, which demand is expected to last long enough to permit an adjustment of the rate of output by employing different amounts of variable resources. In this period the scale of the plant, symbolizing all the fixed resources, remains unchanged. The length of this period depends on the nature of the commodity and the method of production. Typically, the firm can vary the quantities of ordinary labor, raw materials, simple tools, power, and light in a shorter period than it can vary *skilled labor*, complicated machinery, large buildings, and top management.

In the very short market period, except for carrying charges, money cost is not a determinant of price; only opportunity cost is usually involved. In the short run, however, the outlays on the services of the variable factors are a first consideration; and opportunity cost finds expression chiefly in these prospective outlays. What is true of *all* past costs in the market period holds only of the *fixed* costs in the short period. The cost of the plant and equipment cannot affect the alternative of currently producing more or less. In this short period the price and output policy of the firm facing a given demand hinges on the behavior of its variable costs.

PRICE DETERMINATION IN THE SHORT RUN

Let us consider now how the firm decides on the price and the allocation of resources in this short period. In Figure 37, the diagram on the right represents the industry, on the left the firm. The vertical scale, that is, the price and cost scales, are the same for both diagrams. But a distance along the horizontal axis on the industry diagram measures many more units of the commodity than the same distance on the diagram on the left. Suppose that the price in the market for the industry is Q_1H_1 as a result of the supply and demand situations pictured by S and D_1. Having no price policy of its own, the firm will accept this price. It will charge the price $OP_1 = Q_1H_1$; and in view of this price it will decide on the amount which it will produce. The demand for the product of this firm is pictured by the horizontal line P_1d_1. This line P_1d_1 is at once the sales curve, the demand curve, the price curve, the average revenue curve, and the marginal revenue curve, to the individual firm.

At this price how much will the firm produce? Our firm is operating at a loss since the demand line P_1d_1 is below the average cost curve AC.

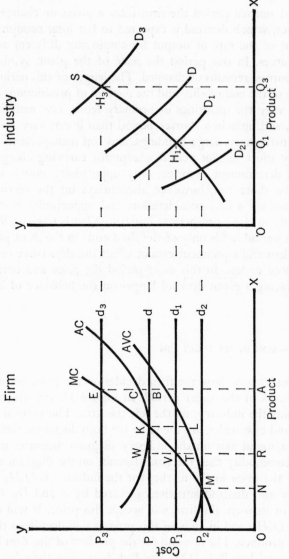

FIGURE 37. *Price Determination in the Short Run Under Competition*

The price OP_1 does not completely cover the fixed cost. To minimize its losses, the firm will produce up to the point at which the price, or marginal revenue, equals marginal cost. It will produce P_1V (or OR) units. If it produces less than P_1V units, it does not take full advantage of the situation, as is indicated by the fact that to the *left* of point V on line P_1V the price OP_1 is above marginal cost, so that by producing up to P_1V the firm gains, on each unit, more in revenue than the marginal cost amounts to. But if it produces beyond P_1V it loses on each extra unit, since to the *right* of V the marginal cost curve is above the marginal revenue curve P_1d_1. It is worth noting that a price such as OP_1 may well occur in a depression.

As long as the industry demand is D_1 the firm, charging the price OP_1 and producing OR units, is in equilibrium. Its price, or marginal revenue, equals marginal cost. It minimizes its losses. In the short run it can do no better. Should it close the plant its losses will be greater, extending to the full amount of fixed costs. When producing OR units the firm realizes toward fixed expenses an amount equal to VT on each unit; the total amount realized toward fixed costs is $OR \times VT$. This amount falls short of covering the fixed costs completely by VW on each unit or by $OR \times VW$ on the whole output. But "half a loaf is better than none."

Now let us assume that the industry demand rises to D_3, as it is apt to do in prosperity. Our firm will raise its output to OA units, charging the price $OP_3 = Q_3H_3$. In this situation its marginal revenue AE equals its marginal cost AE; the firm is in equilibrium once more. In response to the increased demand, our firm raises its output by RA units. The industry—that is, all the firms—increases production by Q_1Q_3 units per unit of time.

QUASI-RENT

At the price OP_3 the firm is making a unit profit of EC, inasmuch as the average cost curve AC, representing outlays on labor, capital, land, and wages of management, contains no profit. This profit will appear in the short run because the number of firms in the industry stays the same. In the long run such profits would invite the entry of new firms with a gradual decline in profits and eventual disappearance of profits. The opposite situation emerges if demand declines *below* D_2. The demand curve facing the firm would fall then below the AVC curve. In such a circumstance it would be better for the firm to close, because if it operates it loses not only all the fixed expenses but part of the variable outlays as well. If the firm does not close, it may be because of such considerations as developing good-will among its employees, or preventing its skilled labor from getting employment far away. As long as the industry demand for the good is not lower than D_2 and the sales curve for the firm's product is correspondingly not below the minimum average variable cost, it is to the advantage of the firm to keep producing.

All this means that the unit revenue OP_2, equal to the minimum average variable cost NM, is a revenue which firms can *insist* on obtaining; but any unit revenue above OP_2, like OP_1 or OP_3, is price determined, depending on the demand. In other words, the firms can force the price OP_2 into being, because at any lower price each firm is induced to withdraw from production to avoid losses on the variable outlays; but each firm accepts any market price above OP_2 and merely adjusts its output to each price. Any unit revenue above OP_2 is, to repeat, a reflex of the demand situation, is price determined. Such revenue is called *quasi-rent*. It is a short-run price-determined return on the fixed factors; it is a return above the variable costs and is available for fixed charges and profit. In the short run an increased demand for an article is met by the intensive use of the fixed resources for the purpose of getting more output; and by the law of variable proportions, after a certain point or output, marginal costs rise. They rise above average variable costs. Since the average revenue, or price, is equated to marginal costs and not to the lower average variable costs, a surplus revenue, a quasi-rent, results. When the demand is D_3 the quasi-rent per unit is EB, and the total quasi-rent on the output of OA units is $EB \times OA$. When the demand is D the unit quasi-rent is KL; when it is D_1 the quasi-rent is VT per unit; and when it is D_2 there is no quasi-rent.

It is necessary here to get ahead of ourselves a bit and refer to the long-run period. In the long run, there is no quasi-rent. The return above the AVC curve and up to the AC curve becomes wholly a return on variable outlays, since in the long period the plant and equipment are variable resources. Price determined in the short run, quasi-rent is price determining in the long run—except for the quasi-rent, like EC, which exceeds the total average cost AC. This EC element of quasi-rent disappears altogether in the long period. If the demand is as high as D_3 the entry of firms will, in the long run, wipe out the quasi-rent EC. In sum, in the long period a return above AC is wiped out by entry; a return below AC is raised to AC by exit; and the return equal to AC tends to endure.

SUPPLY

Let us look once more into the adjustments of the firm to given prices in the industry market. At each new price in the market as a whole, the firm faces a new horizontal demand curve for its product (like Pd, P_1d_1, etc.); and this new straight line intersects the firm's marginal cost curve. The point of intersection tells us two things: the price which the firm will charge and the corresponding quantity which it will offer for sale. Thus point K tells us that the firm will sell PK units at the price OP. Every point on the marginal cost curve indicates the quantity which the firm is ready to sell, in the short run, at the corresponding price, because at every such point MR $=$ MC. The marginal cost curve is the firm's supply curve, in the short run.

But not the whole marginal cost curve. To the left of point M where the AVC curve intersects the marginal cost curve, any output would be associated with a marginal cost below the average variable cost. Accordingly, if the demand price is less than NM—that is, if the horizontal demand line is below the AVC curve—no output would cover the *variable* cost, and the firm will not produce at all. It follows that the supply curve of the firm moves along its marginal cost curve *beginning* with the point (M) of intersection of the MC and the AVC curves; that is, beginning with the point of minimum average variable cost (AVC).

The supply curve for the industry as a whole is the horizontal addition of the supply curves of the individual firms. At any given price exceeding the minimum average variable cost, the various firms will offer their various quantities for sale. When we add these quantities for each corresponding price we obtain the industry supply curve S (Figure 37). Curve S is the sum of the abscissas of the individual marginal cost curves (each curve beginning with a point like M) of all the firms in the industry. Since the individual marginal cost curves move upward to the right, the industry supply curve will behave likewise; curve S has a positive inclination.

As is often the case with economic phenomena, the pricing process exhibits an interaction between the individual firm, on the one hand, and all the firms in the industry market, on the other hand. In the light of a given demand for the product of the industry, all the firms taken together, but each acting independently, form the price in the market as a whole. Each firm alone, however, accepts this price and adjusts its output to it. We may visualize all the firms as adjusting their output to a given expected price P_1. Their total offerings may, however, turn out to be too large for the amount which buyers are willing to purchase at this price P_1. The price drops to P_2. Each firm will now revise its calculations and by restricting its employment of variable resources will produce less, in the attempt to get an output for which marginal cost will equal the lower price P_2. In their retrenchment the firms may go too far, and the aggregate offerings may be so low that the price rises to P_3. Now the firms will readjust their production to this price. Thus the many small output adjustments and revisions ebb and flow until a price is reached at which there is an approximate equality between the amount offered for sale and the amount which buyers are willing to take off the market. This will be the short-run equilibrium price for the industry market, that is, for the product of all the firms.

CONDITIONS OF EQUILIBRIUM IN THE SHORT RUN

It may be well to conclude this section with a summary of the conditions of equilibrium, for the firm and for the industry. The *firm* is in equilibrium when it cannot improve its position by a volume change in the allocation of resources, that is, by enlarging or diminishing its output. The condition for equilibrium is that marginal revenue, which in pure competition is identical with price, equals marginal cost—with the proviso that total revenue is not below total variable cost. This equation may entail losses for the firm, in the sense that it does not cover its fixed charges. But when losses are in prospect, the best the firm can do in the short run is to hold them to a minimum.

There is seemingly another condition of short-run equilibrium of the firm, which will be developed in Chapter XIII and which can be stated here only categorically. The firm produces an output by hiring the services of various agents. The firm will be in equilibrium when it employs as much of each *variable* factor as will yield a marginal revenue product equal to the marginal cost of the factor-service. When this equation holds for each type of variable (not fixed) factor in the realm of labor, capital, and land alike, the firm is in short-run equilibrium. These two conditions of equilibrium do not clash with each other. When one of them is fulfilled the other one is, too.[4] Strictly speaking, these two conditions are, more or less, identical propositions.

The condition of equilibrium of a competitive *industry* in the short period can be stated simply: when each firm is in equilibrium, the industry must be in equilibrium. No separate condition is needed. If each firm offers at the market price the amount that buyers wish to purchase at this price, the total of the amounts which buyers buy will equal the total amount offered by the firms for sale. The market is cleared. An equivalent condition is that there is no incentive for firms to enter or to leave the industry.

The allocation of resources has been adjusted by the firms in the industry to fulfill the demand of the consumers. This condition is briefly stated as $S = D$: the quantity supplied equals the quantity demanded at the given price. (Why not so in Russia?) It seems like the same condition

[4] For a proof of this, see S. Weintraub, *Price Theory* (New York, Pitman, 1949), pp. 112–113.

that is laid down for equilibrium in the very short market period.

But there is a difference. In the market period, equilibrium is reached when at a certain price the buyers are willing to purchase the whole existing stock of a perishable good; or else, when the buyers are purchasing at a given price that portion of a stock already produced which sellers are willing to offer at a given time. In the short-run period, however, equilibrium is attained when at a certain price the rate of consumption and purchasing approximates—each day, week, or month—the rate and *flow* of production, variations in which are accomplished by changes in the variable resources employed. In the first case, we witness a *stock* of goods, in the second case, a *flow* of goods into the market.

III. Long-Run Normal Price

NATURE OF THE LONG-RUN PERIOD

If a given demand or a given change in demand is expected by the firms to last a long time, they will adjust their output by varying the scale of all the plants operated by the firm. The long normal period is long enough to permit new firms to enter the industry and to give businessmen already in the industry ample time to increase the service of the fixed agents, either by enlarging the given plant or by building new plants to accommodate more machines. Contrariwise, it is a long enough period to enable the firms to leave the field altogether or to diminish the fixed agencies by allowing them to wear out without replacement. This period is apt to be shorter when expansion is in order than when contraction is involved. New plants can be built and new machines can be installed in a year or two or three. But when demand is declining, many years may elapse before firms will withdraw from the field. They are apt to cling hopefully to the sinking enterprise for a long while.

In this long period, the AVC curve is of no particular relevance. Of determining importance is the AC curve, which may now be regarded as a long-run average variable cost curve, LAC. In this period, all costs incurred by the efficient firm are price determining. To be precise, the minimum average cost of the optimum-scale firm dictates the long-run price. In Figure 23 (Chapter VII), this price-determining cost is FE; and the optimum scale firm is SAC_3. If the price is above or below this level, the adjustment will take place principally by the entry or exit of firms into the industry and out of it, enlarging the industry or shrinking it, but also by the expansion or contraction of the scale of the old firms as they change their fixed resources, plant and machines. When the adjustments are complete, the new price of the commodity once more equals the long-run minimum average cost of the optimum-scale firm. But—and this is important—whether this new minimum average cost is equal to, or is higher or lower than, the *previous* minimum average cost will depend on whether we deal with a constant-cost, increasing-cost, or decreasing-cost industry. We shall examine such adjustments and such industries presently.

It is necessary to stress that the three periods during which adjustments are made do not display themselves in separate compartments, nor one after another. The adjustments go on in interaction and simultaneously. If, for instance, to the minds of the entrepreneurs the demand for a commodity bids fair to stay low for many years, we may witness the following developments: (1) The plants may be allowed to depreciate or may be gradually remodeled to other uses. (2) Against the background of the declined demand as a trend there may be a temporary upswing of demand, inducing a short-run increase in output by a larger employment of the variable resources in the plants of existing scale, until $MC = MR = P$ (price).

An example of such simultaneous adjustments would be a decline in the farming population coupled with an expected long-range reduction in demand for agricultural machinery. Over a short period, however, there may arise an increased foreign demand for farm equipment, occasioning a short-run adjustment. Then an unexpected poor crop may cause a sudden drop in the demand for the regular inventories of agricultural implements in dealers' storerooms in various regions.

The long-run minimum average costs tend to become identical for all the firms in the industry. True, not all the firms are of the same efficiency in producing a commodity. Some firms have superior management; other firms enjoy an advantageous location; still others have in their employ special agents of unique skill. The superiority of these services expresses itself in greater output for a given aggregate outlay, or in lower average costs. However, the possessor of these services will not make a gift of them to the firm. Firms will bid for them; the opportunity cost of the favored resources will rise; their services will command a higher price in the competitive market, a higher price equal to their marginal revenue productivity. The superior factor receives superior compensation, and when these extra costs are added to the ordinary costs the minimum long-run average cost LAC becomes identical for all firms in the industry.

But whereas the lowest point of unit cost is the same for all producers, the optimum level of operation is not the same for all of them. The firm with superior resources will utilize them more intensively and, before reaching the optimum size, will obtain more output than other firms will at their optimum level. Also, entrepreneurs differ in their methods, which may lead to different optimum levels of production.[5]

EXTERNAL ECONOMIES AND DISECONOMIES

When discussing the shape of the long-run average cost curve LAC in Chapter VII, it was pointed out that as the firm extends its output certain internal economies and diseconomies emerge; economies because a larger aggregate of resources permits better combinations and lower costs, diseconomies because a larger organization may suffer from inefficient management. Alfred Marshall,[6] who elaborated on internal economies, also drew attention to another category of economies, which he called external. External economies and diseconomies are faced by each member firm as a consequence of the expansion of the size of the *industry*.

With the growth of an industry certain circumstances develop which tend to reduce the average costs for each firm in it. The short-run average cost curve AC is lowered. We discussed the nature of external economies in Chapter VI, section I, in connection with the newer theory of scale. The examples of external economies cited there are: greater ease of recruiting labor; helpful trade journals; subsidiary firms aiding the growing industry; and specializing brokers, wholesalers, and bankers.

External economies are a definite possibility when a new industry enjoys a career of growth. But it is doubtful whether new economies emerge or old economies continue to expand when a well-established good-sized industry experiences further enlargement. We cannot assume as a matter of course that external economies are the steadily growing companions of an expanding industry.

However, the skepticism attached to external economies does not attend external diseconomies. When an industry is enlarged in size as its constituent firms become more numerous, there appears a more intensive bidding for the services of agents needed in production. The nonspecialized agents are elastic in supply, in the long run. But specialized factors, like highly skilled labor or highly specialized machinery, may be relatively scarce. Moreover, the procurement of varieties of raw materials is subject to rising costs. The outcome is that as more and more firms bid for such resources their prices rise to all the firms using them. The average cost curve is raised for all the firms.

The combined result of external economies and diseconomies may display itself in three ways. *First*, the economies and diseconomies may cancel

[5] E. H. Chamberlin, *op. cit.*, p. 20; G. J. Stigler, *The Theory of Price* (New York, Macmillan, 1946), p. 161, n.

[6] *Principles of Economics*, 8th ed. (New York, Macmillan, 1927), pp. 266, 277, 318.

each other, so that the constituent firms of an enlarged industry do not face a change in average costs. Such an industry is called a *constant-cost* industry. An industry may belong to this category if it makes so little impact on the market for productive services that its expansion breeds neither external economies nor external diseconomies.

Second, the end result of a growing industry may be reflected in net external diseconomies. Such are *increasing-cost* industries. Since external economies find limited exemplification in the world of actuality and since raw materials are indispensable in all lines of production, increasing-cost industries are more typical than constant-cost industries.

Third, it is conceivable that net external economies characterize a young industry in its early stages of growth. It is then a *decreasing-cost* industry. But there are at least a few examples of industries with consistently falling average cost curves for their member firms as the growth of these industries continues. Public utilities may be one example.

Constant-cost industries

We shall examine the pricing process in each of these three types of industries. Assume a constant-cost industry in long-run equilibrium, as in Figure 38, where once more the diagram on the right refers to the industry and that on the left, to the firm. Again, the vertical distances stand for the same measurements in both diagrams, but not the horizontal distances. The industry supply curve S represents the horizontal sum of the short-run marginal cost curves SMC of the individual firms. With demand D the long-run equilibrium price for the industry is OP and the equilibrium output is PA. For the firm, also in long-run equilibrium, the demand line or sales line is pd, the price is Op, and the output is pa at long-run minimum average cost ab. At the optimum output pa the following are equal to one another: long-run minimum average cost, short-run minimum average cost, long-run marginal cost, short-run marginal cost, and average revenue or price. In addition, the average revenue line pd is tangent to both the LAC and SAC curves. Whenever a firm is in long-run equilibrium these equations and properties hold for the point of equilibrium, whether we deal with constant-cost, increasing-cost, or decreasing-cost industries.

Assume now that the demand for the product has risen to D_1 and is expected to stay there for a long time. Short-run and long-run adjustments will be set in motion simultaneously. The short-run industry price will be OP_1, a height at which the new demand D_1 intersects the short-run supply curve S. In the short run, the firm will increase its output until its SMC will equal price Op_1 at c. The horizontal sum of the quantities corresponding to p_1c for all the firms equals P_1C. In the long run, the unusual profit will lure new firms into the industry; the industry will grow

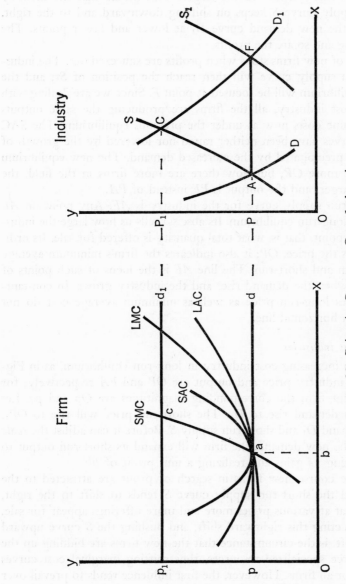

FIGURE 38. *Price in Constant-Cost Industries*

in size. As new firms enter production, more units of the commodity are offered at various prices than before; the horizontal sums of the short-run marginal cost curves become larger. This means that the industry short-run supply curve S keeps on shifting downward and to the right, intersecting the new demand curve D_1 at lower and lower points. The price is falling and so are the profits.

The entry of new firms stops when profits are squeezed out. The industry short-run supply curve will then reach the position of S_1; and the long-run equilibrium will be focused at point F. Since we are dealing with a constant-cost industry, all the firms are producing the same outputs and at the same costs now as under the previous equilibrium. The SAC and LAC curves have been neither raised nor lowered by the growth of the industry precipitated by the increased demand. The new equilibrium price is once more OP; but now there are more firms in the field, the industry is larger, and the output is PF instead of PA.

The long-run supply curve for the industry is AF. Any point on AF is a point of long-run equilibrium. Its abscissa tells us how large the industry is at that point, that is, what total quantity is offered for sale. Its ordinate indicates the price, OP; it also indicates the firm's minimum average cost, long-run and short-run. The line AF is the locus of such points of equilibrium when the demand rises and the industry grows. In constant-cost industries long-run price as well as minimum average cost do not vary; AF is a horizontal line.

Increasing-cost industries

Assume an increasing-cost industry in long-run equilibrium, as in Figure 39. The industry price and output are OP and PA respectively; for the constituent firm the corresponding magnitudes are Op and pa. Let the long-run demand rise to D_1. The short-run price will rise to OP_1, equating demand D_1 and short-run supply S. Before it can adjust the *scale* of plant to the new demand, the firm will expand its short-run output to p_1b, maximizing its gains and realizing a unit profit of bh.

(1) In due course new firms in search of profit are attracted to the industry, and the short-run supply curve S tends to shift to the right, signifying that at various prices more and more offerings appear for sale. (2) Counteracting this rightward shift, and pushing the S curve upward and to the left, is the circumstance that the new firms are bidding up the price of scarce specialized resources, thus shifting marginal cost curves to the left, for all firms. However, the first influence tends to prevail over the second, and for the following considerations. The supply of most of the factor-services needed by the new firms is generally elastic in the relevant range of prices; it is inelastic only in comparatively few instances. Accordingly the new firms contribute more to the output of the industry

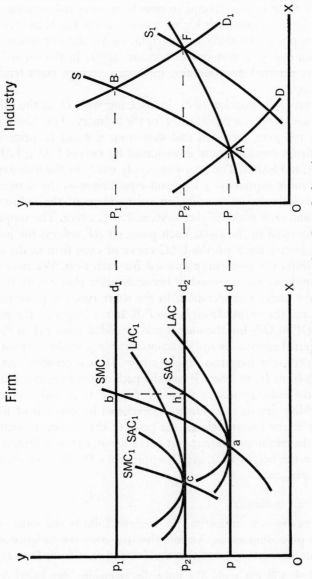

FIGURE 39. *Price in Increasing-Cost Industries*

than the diminished output caused in the old firms by the loss of some of the few scarce resources bidden away from them. Then there is the consideration that the specialized factors are now utilized more intensively by all firms in the attempt to raise their marginal revenue productivity to make them earn their higher compensation. On balance, then, the short-run supply curve shifts to the right, to S_1; the horizontal sums of the short-run marginal cost curves become larger. In the meantime, as a result of net external diseconomies, minimum average costs tend to rise for each firm.

When S takes the position of S_1, intersecting with D_1 at the price OP_2, we reach a new long-run equilibrium for the industry. The minimum average cost to the *firm*, long-run and short-run, is equal to price Op_2, or OP_2. The firm's costs are now as indicated by curves LAC_1, LMC_1 (absent), SAC_1, and SMC_1. The long-run supply curve of the industry is AF. Each point on it represents a long-run equilibrium as the demand shifts to the right, inducing, ultimately, an enlargement of the industry, with more firms and each with a higher LAC and SAC curve. The supply curve AF moves upward to the right. Each point on AF reflects the horizontal sum of the lowest point on the LAC curve of each firm as the entry of new firms shifts the cost curve upward for each firm. We note that the industry supply of the commodity becomes more elastic with the length of the period under consideration. In the short run, the price rose from OP to OP_1 and the output from PA to P_1B. In the long run, the price rose only from OP to OP_2 but the output was extended from PA to P_2F.

Since external economies and diseconomies hinge *exclusively* on the size of the industry, the long-run supply curve AF is reversible.[7] As the demand drops from D_1 to lower levels, the path of the long-run equilibrium points for the industry moves along AF from F to A and beyond. With the diminishing size of the industry occasioned by the exit of firms, the bidding for scarce factors relaxes, the price of the service of such factors drops, and the minimum average cost curve drops, for each firm, to smaller heights than the height of c. As D_1 approaches D, the short-run supply curve S_1 approaches S.

Decreasing-cost industries

For decreasing-cost industries, the analysis follows the same course as in the two preceding cases. Assume that the industry (Figure 40) is in long-run equilibrium at A and that the demand rises from D to D_1. In the

[7] This analysis will not wash. We make the assumption that knowledge gained from large-scale operation is not applicable, generally, to small-scale operation. If it were applicable, it would, in the main, be acquired under the small scale, without the need of the large scale as a tutor. By definition, external economies are the adjunct of a larger and larger industry; external economies do not go with a smaller and smaller industry.

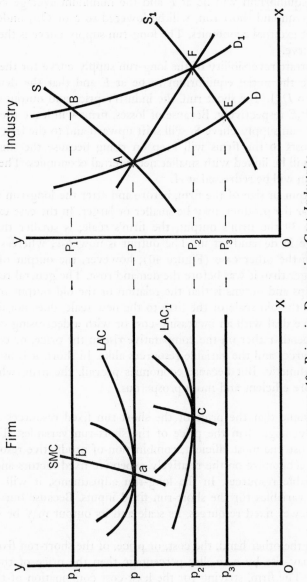

FIGURE 40. *Price in Decreasing-Cost Industries*

short run, the industry price and output rise to OP_1 and P_1B respectively. The corresponding figures for the firm are Op_1 and p_1b. Eventually the long-run equilibrium will be at F and the minimum average cost to the firm, long-run and short-run, will be lowered to c or Op_2 under the impact of net external economies. The long-run supply curve is the descending AF curve.

To illustrate reversibility of the long-run supply curve for the industry, we assume the initial equilibrium to be at F and that the demand falls from D_1 to D. In the short run, the industry price and output decline to OP_3 and P_3E respectively. Because of losses, firms will leave the industry. The short-run supply curve S_1 will shift upward and to the left; minimum average costs to the firms will keep on rising because the smaller sized industry will be linked with smaller net external economies. The long-run equilibrium will be redressed at A.

The output or size of the firm, before and after the long-run rise in the demand for the product, may be smaller or larger. In the case exemplified by Figure 39 the firm's output, the firm's scale, is smaller than before the change in demand set in. The output is now p_2c, whereas before it was pa. In the other case (Figure 40), however, the output of the firm is now larger than it was before the demand rose. The general reason back of these ups and downs is that the relation of the old output to the new output, of the old scale of the firm to the new scale, does not depend on whether we deal with an increasing-cost or with a decreasing-cost industry; it depends rather on the comparative rise in the price, or cost, of the fixed resources and the variable resources alike. In short, it is more a matter of arithmetic. But because economies prevail, the firm, whatever its size, is more efficient and more prosperous.

(1) Assume that the price of the short-run fixed resources rises by a larger percentage than the price of the short-run variables. To achieve the least-cost, the most efficient, combination of productive resources, the firm may economize on the relatively expensive fixed factors and will use more variable resources. In the long-run adjustments, it will substitute short-run variables for the short-run fixed inputs. Because our firm now employs fewer fixed resources, its scale and its output may be somewhat *smaller*.

(2) On the other hand, the cost, or price, of the short-run fixed factor-services may rise by a smaller percentage than the price of the variable resources. The firm, striving for the least-cost combination of the inputs, will substitute short-run relatively inexpensive fixed resources for the variables. The relatively larger use of the short-run fixed resources means a somewhat larger size of the firm and a larger output by the firm. But perhaps these paragraphs carry the case to too many decimals.

CONDITIONS OF EQUILIBRIUM

We are ready to draw up once more the conditions of equilibrium. A *firm* is in long-run competitive equilibrium when price equals long-run minimum average cost (LAC). The entry or exit of firms will produce a situation in which this equation rules. At the output for which this equation holds, the average revenue curve, or the horizontal sales curve, is tangent to the LAC curve at its lowest point; and both short-run and long-run marginal cost equals price, that is, both marginal cost curves meet at the point of tangency. All this is seen in Figures 38, 39, and 40. In fact, the tangency of the horizontal average revenue curve with the LAC curve depicts the condition of the long-run equilibrium of the firm. If the average revenue line lies below LAC, firms will withdraw from the industry. If the average revenue line intersects the LAC curve, profits exist, and the entry of firms will remove them. We observe that when the firm is in the long-run equilibrium it is simultaneously in the short-run equilibrium.

The long-run *industry* equilibrium is once more attained when $S = D$, when the quantity supplied equals the quantity demanded at a given price. But here, too, there is a difference. In the short run, the industry is in equilibrium when the amounts purchased are matched, more or less, by the flow of production which is regulated by changes in the employment of *variable* factors. In the long run, the flow of production is made to match demand by varying the *size* of the industry, that is, by the entry or exit of firms; so that when the industry is in equilibrium the number of firms in it is fixed. There is no incentive for exit or entry. Of course we can state that when each firm is in long-run equilibrium, the whole industry is.

IV. Interrelated Supplies or Demands

In the typical price analysis, such as given in this chapter so far and in the chapters to follow, the assumption is consistently made that the firm produces only one commodity. In reality, however, firms often make a variety of related goods; and the pricing of such goods calls for some unique considerations. The purpose of the present section is to sketch briefly two types of interrelations on the side of supply and two types of interrelated demands.

It is well to observe at the outset that the fact that a firm produces several commodities does not always imply that they must be related. They may be independent. They may be produced with separate equipment, with separate labor and other resources, even in separate plants. An example may be the pharmaceutical products and plastic materials made by subsidiaries of the well-known dairy concern, the Borden Company. Another example is seemingly furnished by the extensive printing activity of many of our universities. In the case of independent multiple products the usual price analysis applies without special modification.

1. JOINT OR COMPLEMENTARY SUPPLY

At times a given sequence of processes of production results in the output of more than one commodity. When the amount of one product rises, the amount of the other product is apt to rise also. Such products are called complementary or joint in supply. As we shall see soon, the making of one such product lowers the marginal cost of making the other product and therefore shifts downward the supply curve of this other product. We get mutton and wool from raising sheep; beef and hide from cows; grain and straw from wheat; gasoline, lubricating oil, fuel oil, and kerosene from refining crude oil; and the coke and gas from distilling coal. Such goods may come in fixed proportions, like so many pounds of straw from each bushel of wheat; or in variable proportions, like wool and mutton when sheep are raised experimentally for their meat and not for the wool—or the other way around, as with Merino sheep, which are raised primarily for their wool.

To indicate the nature of the relationship between joint products as well as the pricing problem involved, let us refer to Figure 41, A and B, where A pictures supply and demand for mutton, and B for wool. But first it is necessary to pause and explain the nature of the supply curves. When the proportions in which joint products come are variable, as is assumed in our case of mutton and wool, the determination of the marginal cost of either product is as follows. The output of wool per sheep is kept constant, and the experiment is directed toward getting more meat per sheep. Dividing the extra expense of raising the sheep by the extra mutton obtained, we arrive at the marginal cost of mutton. It follows that if more wool results instead of the assumed constant amount, the marginal cost of producing mutton declines, because the extra expense of raising the sheep, far from being charged to the extra mutton alone, is now shared between the extra mutton and extra wool.

To return to our diagrams. Representing as it does the horizontal summation of the marginal cost of mutton, curve Sm pictures the supply of mutton only on condition that the output of wool stays fixed, at OW. Similarly the supply curve Sw is linked with the amount OM as the con-

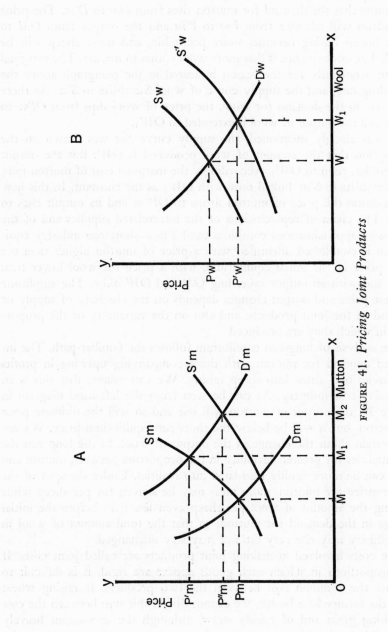

FIGURE 41. Pricing Joint Products

stant output of mutton.

Assume that the demand for mutton rises from Dm to $D'm$. The price of mutton will advance from Pm to $P'm$ and the output from OM to OM_1. Sheep raising becomes more profitable, and more sheep will be raised. The consequence is that more wool comes to market. The marginal cost of wool falls, for the reason indicated in the paragraph above the preceding one; and the supply curve of wool Sw shifts to $S'w$. As there is no rise in the demand for wool, the price of wool dips from OPw to $OP'w$ and the output of wool is extended to OW_1.

As was already mentioned, the supply curve Sm was drawn on the assumption that the amount of wool produced is OW. But the output of wool has risen to OW_1. Accordingly the marginal cost of mutton falls, and Sm shifts to $S'm$, linked now with OW_1 as the constant. In this new repercussion the price of mutton drops to $OP''m$ and its output rises to OM_2. The chain of repercussions of the interrelated supplies and of the successive approximations continues until a new short-run industry equilibrium is established, identified with a price of mutton higher than the OPm price of the initial equilibrium, with a price for wool lower than OPw and with an output exceeding OM and OW alike. The amplitude of these price and output changes depends on the elasticity of supply or demand of the joint products, and also on the variability of the proportions in which they are produced.

The analysis of long-run equilibrium follows the familiar path. The increased demand for mutton with the accompanying upswing in profits will invite new firms into sheep raising. We can assume that this is an increasing-cost industry. As can be seen from the left-hand diagram in Figure 39, the output of mutton will rise and so will the ultimate price of mutton, but it will be below the short-run equilibrium price. We are less certain about the change in the output of wool. In the long run the potentialities for greater flexibility in the proportion between mutton and wool can be more readily translated into realities. Under the spur of the higher price for mutton, more meat may be striven for per sheep while keeping the amount of wool per sheep even less than before the initial change in the demand for mutton; so that the total amount of wool in the industry may rise very little or may stay unchanged.

The costs involved in making joint products are called joint costs. If the proportions in which such goods appear are rigid, it is difficult to allocate the common cost between the two products. If raising wheat costs the farmer $2 a bushel, we cannot divide this sum between the cost of raising grain and of raising straw, although the accountant bravely tries to do so. In this case wheat and straw are treated as one composite commodity. The equilibrium of the firm producing such complementary goods is reached when the marginal cost of producing both of them equals their combined marginal revenue, which under competition equals the sum of their prices. Symbolically, $MC_{1+2} = MR_{1+2} = P_1 + P_2$, where the subscripts 1 and 2 refer to the respective commodities and P refers to price.

The familiar condition for the long-run equilibrium of the firm is that price equals long-run minimum average cost (LAC). But the average cost of two complementary goods has no significant meaning. The condition of equilibrium becomes therefore the equation of total costs and total revenue, $TC = TR$.

If the proportions in which the joint products come are variable, the marginal cost of each can be found by the procedure indicated on page 228. The short-run competitive equilibrium for the firm rests therefore on the equality of marginal cost and price for each of the complementary articles. The condition is once more embodied in the equation $TC = TR$. If this equality is deranged, the exit and entry of firms will re-establish it.

2. RIVAL OR COMPETITIVE SUPPLY

Goods are in rival supply when a greater output of one necessarily entails a smaller output of the other. This relation exists when either good is made by the same resources. The resources employed to produce one good are not simultaneously available for the production of the other good. If the same kind of land can grow oats or barley, the more land is turned to oats and the more oats are raised, the less land is left for barley and the less barley is offered for sale. During World War II, when women readily got jobs in factories, domestic help became scarce. Certain kinds of factory work and housework are services in rival supply. At full employment, goods and services are generally in rival supply. Then we can hardly have more guns *and* more butter.

Alfalfa and clover are grown on the same type of land and in the same climate. Assume a rise in the demand for alfalfa with the consequent rise in the price of this product. Land given to alfalfa earns more economic rent, and more land is turned to alfalfa. Less land is available for raising clover. Less clover goes to the market for sale; the supply schedule of clover shifts to the left. Thus the rise in the price of alfalfa brings about a rise in the price of clover as well. The prices of competitive goods move in the same direction.

3. JOINT OR COMPLEMENTARY DEMAND

Some goods are bought together because they jointly satisfy one given want: they are complementary goods. Automobile driving involves a demand for cars, gasoline, oil, tires, sundry accessories, and life insurance.

A greater demand for one of the joint products induces a greater demand for its companions. The proportions in which the joint goods are bought may be fixed, as with cups and saucers, by and large; or variable, as with tires and gasoline. With the former the cross-elasticity is higher than with the latter.

Suppose that because of improved methods on coffee plantations the cost of growing coffee and therefore the price of coffee go down. The supply of coffee is increased; at each price more coffee will be offered for sale than before; the supply curve shifts to the right so that with the same demand for coffee, more coffee is sold. Many people drink coffee black, unsweetened, or both; but many do not. On the whole, the demand for cream and sugar rises; the demand curves for these articles shift to the right. The prices of cream and sugar go up. (1) For goods in joint demand the prices tend to move in *opposite* directions—*if* the equilibrium is upset by a change in the *supply* of one of them. (To be precise, the change in supply has to occur in the good that requires the other good as its companion: coffee goes with sugar, but sugar is not joint with coffee alone, inasmuch as sugar has a variety of uses.) (2) The prices of goods in joint demand move *together* if the change occurs through an increased or decreased *demand* for one of them; again with the proviso as given in the parenthetical sentence in the present paragraph: an increased demand for coffee may raise the demand for sugar, but an increased demand for sugar may not register in an increased demand for coffee, because the increased demand for sugar may stem from a greater consumption of cake or breakfast cereal, or from canning a greater amount of peaches.

4. RIVAL OR COMPETITIVE DEMAND

Often a given want may be satisfied by one of several goods. Such goods are substitutes for one another, so that if more is bought of one of them less is bought of the other. Bread and rolls, lumber and brick for housebuilding are examples. We discussed substitute goods earlier.

Consider the relation between lamb chops and steaks. If because of improved methods of raising sheep the cost of lamb chops falls, the supply curve of this commodity will shift downward and to the right. With the demand for chops unchanged, there will be a greater consumption of chops, and at the expense of steaks. The demand for steaks drops; the demand schedule shifts to the left; the price of steak sags. Some of the resources used to raise cattle for steaks will be transferred to raising lambs. When goods are in competitive demand their prices tend to move in the same direction. In this case, as in all the other cases of interrelated products, the magnitude of the shifts and of the adjustments is contingent on the elasticities of supply or demand.

OBSERVATIONS OF PURE COMPETITION

At the end of a chapter on pure competition it is fitting that we ask: what are the potential achievements and what are the shortcomings of pure competition? We shall ask such a question toward the end of each of the three following chapters, dealing with the three other types of markets. A question like this can be answered only in the light of a given criterion. Our criterion is maximum satisfaction of the consumer, or maximum total utility.

(1) First of all, the important task of optimum *allocation* of resources is almost ideal under competition, ideal in the sense that total consumer satisfaction would shrink if there were a meddling reallocation of resources. Assume (a) that the utility of a good to one person is the same as the utility of this good to any other person; (b) that there is perfect mobility of the factors of production, so that the remuneration for a given factor-service is the same in all its occupations; and (c) that full employment prevails. Then under conditions of competition, in the commodity (and factor) markets alike, ideal allocation is attainable.

The reasoning behind this proposition runs as follows. The price offered by the consumer measures the marginal utility which he derives from the commodity. This price, charged by the selling firm, reflects the cost to the firm.[8] Each factor in each employment contributes a marginal revenue product which holds the same ratio to the price received by the factor-service. It follows that in each sphere of production the consumer satisfaction from goods made by the marginal unit of a factor, or by the marginal dollar's worth of a factor, is the same. Assuming, as we are, that a dollar represents the same satisfaction to all individuals, we see that an hour's labor stands for the same satisfaction wherever used. The arbitrary diversion of a unit of factor-service from one line of production to another would then result in a smaller total of satisfaction.

In sum, under competition, which enforces an equality of price and marginal cost, the *allocation* of resources in harmony with consumer preferences, on the one hand, and the distribution of factor-income in accordance with marginal productivity, on the other hand, constitute two aspects of the same process of attaining equilibrium or optimum use of resources.

To put the matter symbolically, the consumer will allocate his expendi-

[8] *Cf.* J. S. Bain, *Pricing, Distribution, and Employment,* revised ed. (New York, Holt, 1953), pp. 165–166.

ture on various goods in such a manner that the ratio of the marginal utility (MU) to price (P) is the same for all goods (a, b, c, · · ·):

$$\frac{MU_a}{P_a} = \frac{MU_b}{P_b} = \frac{MU_c}{P_c} = \cdots .$$

Likewise, under competition, the prices charged for the goods by the industries will bear the same ratio to the marginal costs:

$$\frac{MC_a}{P_a} = \frac{MC_b}{P_b} = \frac{MC_c}{P_c} = \cdots .$$

It follows that

$$\frac{MU_a}{MC_a} = \frac{MU_b}{MC_b} = \frac{MU_c}{MC_c} = \cdots .$$

(2) Competition also tends to assure *least-cost* combinations of resources in the production of a commodity; thus maximum *efficiency* may be uniformly approximated. In the long run the competing firm may produce goods at optimum scale and long-run minimum average cost. The price for the consumer coincides with minimum long-run unit cost (LAC).

(3) In addition, pure competition constitutes a market with a built-in propensity to *improve* the product or the method of production. The firm is well aware that sooner or later its improvement may be paralleled by other producers. But in the interval it expects to reap a profit, either because at the going price the improved article sells more briskly, or else because the improved technique permits a lower cost of production. To stay in the race, our firm must stir itself out of the beaten path.

(4) With its low unit cost and the potentially low price, and with profits squeezed out by entry of firms, competition tends to mitigate *inequality* of income, and with less inequality of income, total utility may rise (why?).

(5) Competition stands for many entrepreneurs, therefore for many centers of decision. It is supposed to offer rewards to the efficient and punishment to the inefficient, leading to the survival of the fittest in the economy. A regime of competition attracts the venturesome, the innovators. It tends to limit economic power. It is self-regulatory, to a large extent, making it unnecessary for the state to interfere.

(6) But it is necessary to stress that all these good marks are subject to a heavy discount if we assume, as assume we must, that, in general, industries cannot accommodate many large-scale firms producing a homogeneous product; and the condition of many sellers is inseparable from pure competition. For a purely competitive market in steel we shall need, say, thirty large producing units; but can the steel industry accommodate so many without cut-throat competition and without a disastrous market

price? The same question may apply to the automobile industry, to the oil refining industry, to the cigarette industry, to breweries. True, many an industry can contain a large number of small firms, but small firms can hardly reap the full advantages of the internal economies of large output. We are running into a dilemma: either we have pure competition with numerous small and high-cost firms, or we have a small number of large firms—and this spells oligopoly and not pure competition.

Still because of its advantages, from the social viewpoint, competition is generally favored by economists and statesmen alike. Competition delivers the goods. Whether the businessman favors competition, with its rigors and uncertainty, and dislikes the other three types of markets, is an open question.

SUGGESTED READINGS

Bain, J. S. *Pricing, Distribution, and Employment*, revised ed., chap. 4. New York, Holt, 1953.

Boulding, K. E. *Economic Analysis*, revised ed., chaps. 3–8, 23. New York, Harper, 1948.

Chamberlin, E. H. *The Theory of Monopolistic Competition*, 6th ed., chap. 2. Cambridge, Harvard University Press, 1948.

Ellis, H. S., and Fellner, W. "External Economies and Diseconomies," *American Economic Review*, Vol. XXXIII (September, 1943), pp. 493–511.

Leftwich, R. H. *The Price System and Resource Allocation*, revised ed., chap. IX. New York, Holt, Rinehart and Winston, 1960.

Meriam, R. S. "Quasi-Rent," *Explorations in Economics*, pp. 317–325. New York, McGraw-Hill, 1936.

Stigler, G. J. *The Theory of Price*, revised ed., chaps. 9, 10. New York, Macmillan, 1952.

Wilcox, C. *Competition and Monopoly in American Industry*, chap. 2. Temporary National Economic Committee, Monograph No. 21. Washington, D.C., 1941.

Young, A. A. "Increasing Returns and Economic Progress," *Economic Journal*, Vol. XXXVIII (December, 1928), pp. 527–542.

CHAPTER

X Monopoly and Monopsony

THE PRECEDING chapter dealt with a phenomenon rare in our economy. Pure competition finds exemplification in very few industries. In most industries there prevails, typically, a blend of competition and monopoly. The admixture of monopoly, sometimes very prominent and sometimes very moderate, brings new sets of considerations into the problem of pricing and generally contributes toward the determination of a price different from a competitive price. The element of monopoly presents itself in different guises in various markets. We shall deal with three types of markets in which the monopoly element is present: monopoly and monopsony, monopolistic competition, and oligopoly. These types will be examined in three separate chapters.

PART 1. MONOPOLY

DEFINITION

By pure or perfect or absolute or single-firm monopoly we mean that one firm is the only seller or the dominant seller of a given article for which it is difficult to find a substitute. In setting its price-output combination the firm is not constrained to concern itself with the possible reactions of other producers of the same article or of the producers of any other article.

One point in this definition needs underscoring. The commodity must not have a close substitute. The cross-elasticity between the product of the monopolist and the product of the closest rival must be low. If many substitutes made by many firms exists, we deal with monopolistic competition. If there are a few substitutes made by a few firms, we face oligopoly once more, but now what is called differentiated oligopoly. The privilege of being the only seller of a product does not by itself make one a monopolist in the sense of possessing the power to set the price. As the one seller, he may be a king without a crown. His power over prices depends on whether or not close substitutes are available for his commodity. A large share of the market does not necessarily point to a corresponding degree of monopoly strength. Said an official of the Standard Oil Company before an investigating commission long ago (before the automobile had emphasized gasoline): "The Standard Oil Company can never afford to sell goods dear. The people would go to dipping tallow candles in the old fashioned way if we got the price too high." [1] The official evidently assumed that tallow candles were close substitutes to kerosene lamps.

Cases of pure monopoly are rare. In the field of public utilities, water supplies and railway service have already been cited. Until World War II, the Aluminum Company of America was the only producer of aluminum ingots; and magnesium metal was produced by one firm, the Dow Chemical Company. The United Shoe Machinery Company and the International Business Machines Corporation had, for a while, nearly full sway respectively over machines for certain processes in shoemaking and over certain calculating devices. Also, in many an isolated locality the one hotel, general store, bank, or newspaper may command a sizable measure of monopoly power over the customers in the community.

I. Monopoly Price

BARRIERS TO ENTRY

In the examination of monopoly price it is essential to keep in mind that the existence of monopoly is invariably associated with a barrier to the entry of rivals. In general, the *persistence* of profits of a more than ordinary level reveals the lack of freedom of entry. The monopolist maintains his position as the one seller of a product or service only because circumstances keep other firms out of the field of production. These cir-

[1] Ida Tarbell, *History of the Standard Oil Company* (New York, Macmillan, 1933), Vol. II, p. 201.

cumstances create barriers that fall into two categories.

Barriers of the *first category* are economic in nature. In a given industry or in a given area the consumer can best be served by a single firm; and the profit motive does not attract additional firms. As the one firm enlarges its output the internal economies continue to overwhelm the diseconomies. The left wing of the U-shaped or dish-shaped ($\smile$) average cost curve keeps on declining for a large range of output. Even the large city can be served more economically by one water company than by several. Service by two or more water companies would involve the cost of duplicating plant and equipment, imposing higher costs of supplying water and higher prices to the consumer if the additional output of water is to be sold. One firm can make a profit, two firms may incur steady losses. The would-be newcomer is not anxious to enter the business. It would likewise be uneconomical to have two railways with tracks, bridges, tunnels, and depots paralleling and duplicating each other over the same route between Chicago and San Francisco. Such industries are called "natural monopolies." To prevent their exploitation of the consumer, public commissions watch their conduct. The Federal Trade Commission is supposed to be the vigilant watchdog.

The *second category* of barriers to entry is institutional or else artificial in nature. (1) A firm may enjoy exclusive ownership of indispensable *resources*. By the legalities of ownership it may withhold these resources from a rival. The Aluminum Company of America was for a long time the sole possessor of bauxite, out of which aluminum is made. (2) The possession of a *patent* of strategic importance in the production of an article confers a monopoly privilege on the owner. The United Shoe Machinery Company is an example. (3) Entry can also be blocked by the *fighting* tactics of a monopolist, who will not be indifferent to the intrusion of rivals into his preserves. The would-be entrant will think twice before deciding to risk a large investment, and a reputation, in the battle with a giant grown strong in the business. He fears the familiar fighting devices: ruinous local price cutting; disparagement of the product; pressure on banks not to grant credit and on business concerns not to sell materials; spurious and exhausting lawsuits; misrepresentation or disparagement of a competitor's character; bidding away of key employees; and spying and sabotage.[2] (4) The demand for a product may be too small to support more than one, or more than a few, firms.

It is important to note that since oligopoly is a much more frequent phenomenon in American industry than monopoly, these barriers to the entry of new firms, with the possible exception of the barrier protecting "natural monopolies," are encountered more frequently in the oligopolistic industries.

---

[2] Some of these devices are illegal, but they are practiced nonetheless.

In exploring monopoly pricing it is also important to realize that the monopolist, far from being a figure ruled by the sinister desire to exploit the buyer, is a person actuated by the same motive as the entrepreneur in a competitive market: the motive, namely, to maximize profits or minimize losses. The difference lies in the greater opportunity open to the monopolist. The competing firm is compelled to accept the price in the market as an external fact and to adjust its output to it. The competing firm cannot impress its will on the price. The monopolist can. He has a price policy. By producing more or less, he can bring on a lower or a higher price for the product. To the firm in a competitive field, the sales curve looks horizontal. To the monopolist, the sales curve slopes to the right and therefore has an elasticity less than infinity. The monopolist can choose on this curve a point which promises him the optimum combination of quantity and price.

In the discussion of competitive price we saw that when, in the short run, an increased demand favors the industry, the short-run profit reaped by the firms may reach an impressive level. Such a profit may well be above the level enjoyed by a monopolist. This is one of the reasons why it is incorrect to assert that a high profit invariably reveals the presence of monopoly.

MARKET-PERIOD PRICE

In the determination of monopoly price the same three periods are involved as in the analysis of a competitive price, namely the market period, the short normal period, and the long normal period.

In the market period, it is assumed that the monopolist has already produced a certain amount of a given article, represented by OA in Figure 42, and is compelled to sell it. He cannot withhold any of it by storage. In his calculations regarding the price to be set, the cost incurred is not of determining influence. In this period, we recall, all costs are like fixed costs and therefore are of no effect in shaping the price. The price which the monopolist will charge depends on the demand situation. The only producer of the commodity, he represents the whole industry; and his sloping sales curve ED is the total industry demand. To sell a larger proportion of the amount OA, he has to charge a lower price.

Since costs are out of the picture, any amount of revenue obtained from the sale is that much velvet to our seller. The price that maximizes total revenue is the price which he would like to choose. In the search for this price the marginal revenue curve EM is helpful (Figure 42). It indicates how much extra revenue is obtained from each extra unit sold. When marginal revenue is zero, total revenue reaches its maximum size, since the sale of additional units beyond this stage will diminish total revenue instead of increasing it. Marginal revenue is zero at point M on the horizontal axis and negative for outputs beyond M. The monopolist maximizes his revenue, and his firm is in equilibrium, when he sets his price at MF and sells OM units. The unsold part MA may as well be

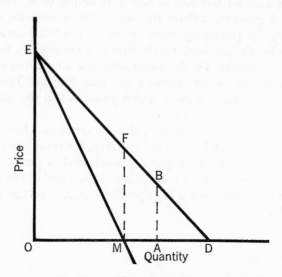

FIGURE 42. *Very Short-Run Monopoly Price*

cheaply destroyed. Under competition, in similar circumstances, the price would be AB and the amount sold would be OA, the total amount on hand. It will do no harm to remind ourselves that point M is the midpoint of OD: a straight-line marginal revenue curve bisects a perpendicular drawn from a point on the straight-line demand curve to the y axis. And OD is such a perpendicular.

SHORT-RUN MONOPOLY PRICE

In the short normal period, the monopolist, like the competing firm, has to keep an eye on the variable costs. His price cannot go below his average variable costs. In Figure 43 AD is the demand curve, AM is the marginal revenue curve, AC is the curve of average total cost, AVC the curve of average variable cost, and MC is the curve of marginal cost. The monopolist will produce an output at which marginal revenue equals marginal cost. He will produce OQ units. The equation MR = MC is the condition of short-run equilibrium for the monopolist as it is for the competing firm. As we see from the demand curve, for output OQ he can charge the price QP. This price is not only above the average variable cost NQ but also above average total cost RQ. His average monopoly profit is PR, and his aggregate monopoly profit is portrayed by the rectangle BPRC. With a low short-run demand, the monopoly price may fail to cover *total* cost; it may equal variable cost or it may exceed it to some extent.

Let us examine the characteristics of this equilibrium monopoly price QP. We shall refer to Figure 43A. *First*, it is not the highest price. A monopolist will not necessarily charge the highest price possible. Any price to the left of P on AD is a higher price. But at a higher price he may sell less and will reap a smaller total profit. *Second*, the price QP does not bring the seller the highest average profit. To the left of P on AD are prices farther above AC than the distance PR. What the monopolist is aiming for is not a maximum unit profit but a maximum total profit. *Third*, monopoly price is often associated with an output the average cost of which is still falling. Often the marginal cost curve cuts the marginal revenue curve to the *left* of the point of minimum average costs. In this respect our diagram is typical. The minimum unit cost is at F. But marginal revenue coincides with F, the lowest point on curve AC; curve MC cuts curve AC at the lowest point of AC. (This is more or less familiar material.) The equality of MC and MR is indicated by L. This limits the output to OQ. The chief reason for this limitation of output is that as output is expanded the unit price falls, and marginal revenue drops below this declining price, whereas marginal cost is likely to rise. Under competition, it pays the firm to expand production while average costs are falling inasmuch as the price and marginal revenue both stay as high for a large output as for a small output: both are depicted by a horizontal line.

Fourth, it is important to notice that, whereas in competitive equilibrium the price charged by the firm equals its marginal cost, under monopoly the price set is above marginal cost. The price QP exceeds marginal cost QL by LP. That such must be the situation can be seen from the following line of thought: The condition for the equilibrium of the firm, in both a competitive and monopoly market, is that marginal cost equal marginal revenue. In competition, marginal revenue is identical with price. In a monopoly market, however, the demand curve, as seen by the single seller, slopes to the right. Marginal revenue no longer coincides with price or average revenue, but lies below it. In Figure 43B AM (marginal revenue curve for AD) lies below AD. Since for the equilibrium output (OQ) marginal cost equals marginal revenue, and since marginal revenue is below price, it follows that marginal cost too is below the equilibrium price. When the firm is in competitive equilibrium we have the trinitarian

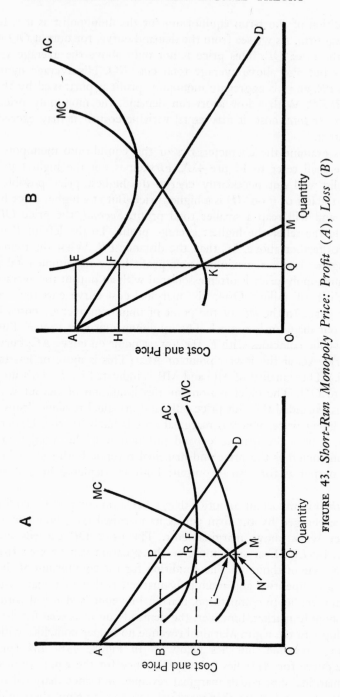

FIGURE 43. Short-Run Monopoly Price: Profit (A), Loss (B)

equality P (price) $= MC = MR$. Under monopoly, when the single firm is in equilibrium, $P > MC = MR$. Herein lies an outstanding difference between the monopoly price and the competitive price.

It follows from the forgoing paragraph that the marginal cost curve, which functions as the supply curve of the competitive firm, performs no such service for the monopolistic firm. To the competing firm in equilibrium, marginal cost equals price and the marginal cost curve pictures the various quantities offered by the firm at various corresponding prices. However, the price set by the monopolist is not equated to marginal cost, but stands above it. In monopoly, marginal cost associates cost and quantity, not price and quantity.

To proceed, as we know, monopoly not only tends to maximize its profit but also strives to minimize its losses when losses may be unavoidable, as in a serious depression. This case is exemplified in Figure 43B. Here marginal revenue AM, as usual, is brought into equality with marginal cost MC, at point K. Accordingly the monopolist produces OQ units of the given article. For *this* output OQ, the average revenue $AD = QF$, and the average cost is QE, with point E lodged on curve AC. The vertical distance FE indicates average *loss*; average revenue at F fails to catch up with average cost at E. The discrepancy between receipts and cost amounts to EF. Rectangle $HFEA$ defines the total loss. It is the minimum loss; let the monopolist produce more than OQ or less than OQ units of the article, and his potential loss will be greater. (Why?)

LONG-RUN MONOPOLY PRICE

In the long run the monopolist can change the size of his plant in response to a change in long-run demand or in long-run costs. In the long run he can so adjust the size of all resources, fixed and variable, that marginal revenue equals not only short-run but also long-run marginal cost. In the short run *only* the equality of marginal revenue and short-run marginal cost can be achieved. The equality of marginal revenue and short-run marginal cost signifies, as we know, that with the firm of a *given* size production is pushed up to the most profitable stage. The equality of marginal revenue with long-run marginal cost reflects the fact that the *scale* of the whole firm has been adjusted for maximum profit to the monopolist. Figure 44 portrays the long-run equilibrium position of the monopolist facing the demand AD, the marginal revenue AM, and the four cost curves familiarly labeled. With the long-run equilibrium output of OQ, both short-run and long-run marginal costs are equal to marginal revenue; the size of each of these three magnitudes is QN. The equilibrium price QP is above marginal cost; the unit monopoly profit is *PR*. The condition for long-run equilibrium is of the same cast as for the short-run period; namely, marginal revenue must equal marginal cost. Only now marginal cost refers to both short-run and long-run marginal cost.

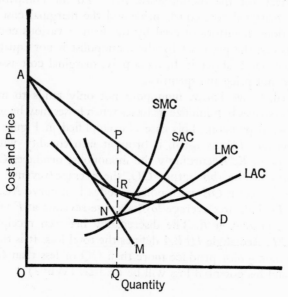

FIGURE 44. *Long-Run Monopoly Price*

A monopolist reaps excessive profits by reason of his power to restrict output and to equate marginal cost with marginal revenue and not with price. If he were to produce more goods for the community, his price would have to come down and his excessive profit would dwindle. He can impressively restrict output because other businessmen are kept from entering his field of production. One might say that the monopolist makes a monopoly profit for not producing; that as a monopolist, he does not produce goods—he produces profits.

II. Price Discrimination

DEFINITION OF THE CONCEPT

One of the practices open to monopoly but unknown to pure competition is price discrimination. We have price discrimination when different prices are charged for different units of the same product. The "same product" implies, as usual, the same quality, packaging, service, credit terms, and so on. There is no discrimination if the price differential is merely the measure of the difference in the cost of handling, shipping, or servicing the order. We may also define price discrimination as treating buyers differently in price, quality, service, and credit terms when the difference is not accounted for by a difference in costs. By the same token we face price discrimination when customers are treated alike in all these particulars although there is a cost difference in filling their orders. It is to be stressed that price discrimination is found not only in single-firm monopoly but also in markets with an admixture of monopoly: in oligopoly and monopolistic competition.

There is no want of examples of price discrimination. *First*, discrimination is sometimes based on the *size* of the purchase. In a drugstore an 8-ounce bottle of mouthwash may go for 32¢ and the "economy size" 2-pound bottle for 99¢. Of course, even under competition the large bottle will sell for less than $1.28, inasmuch as the large container does not cost proportionately more than the small one. The gas and electric company makes high charges per cubic foot or kilowatt-hour for a stated minimum amount, less for certain amounts beyond the minimum, and still less for maximum volumes. Manufacturers and wholesalers have been known to favor the large buyer, pricewise, beyond the limits justified by the economy of handling large consignments.

Second, some kinds of discrimination are related to the *location* of the buyer. There are many varieties of this type of discrimination, and we can mention only one or two. Many a nationally advertised article sells at the same price all over the country despite the differences in freight costs to the seller. This is equivalent to a price concession to the remote customer. The most interesting type of spatial discrimination is the former Pittsburgh-plus basing-point pricing system for steel, under which no matter where the seller was located, the buyer was charged for transportation from Pittsburgh. A Chicago buyer of steel from a mill in Gary, Indiana, paid more for his steel than a Detroit buyer from the same mill because the freight cost more from Pittsburgh to Chicago than from Pittsburgh to Detroit. After the freight deduction, the price obtained by the Gary seller—called the mill net price—was greater on the sale to the Chicago customer than to the Detroit customer.

Third, there are instances of discrimination based on the *income* of the consumer. Doctors and lawyers get a larger fee from the rich than from the poor for the same kind of service. A public speaker receives a larger check for reading a set of typed sheets to a convention of industrialists than he receives for reading the same sheets to a gathering of schoolteachers. In this kind of discrimination a distinction is to be made between a service and a good. The service cannot be resold. The extraction of a poor man's wisdom tooth cannot be resold to the rich patient. But the low-priced good sold to the poor can be resold to the rich. Middlemen can buy up low-priced books from those of low income levels for resale to the rich. To defeat such a practice, the goods are somewhat differentiated. Two types of the good are marketed, the standard type and the "de luxe" type. The two makes are, of course, no longer the "same product." But the point is that the charge for the "de luxe" article exceeds the added cost; and the monopolist makes more profit on it than on the standard model. The "de luxe" edition of a book may differ from the popular edition only in the color of the cover.

Fourth, there is price discrimination based on the *time* and the *type* of use of the service and the age of the user. Motion-picture houses charge less in the afternoon than in the evening; long-distance telephone rates are higher during daytime than in the evening; week-end and holiday prices are higher in theaters, in summer resorts, and on golf courses. Barbers, railroads, and theaters charge less to children than to adults. Telephone, gas, and electric service is more costly to the domestic users than to industrial users. In charging what the traffic will bear a railroad obtains different prices from different uses of its space, so that more is paid for the carriage of a pound of butter or silk than for the transportation of a pound of coal or lumber.

Fifth, in some public utilities discrimination is based on *use*: household and commercial, wholesaler or retailer.

PRECONDITIONS OF PRICE DISCRIMINATION

The practice of price discrimination is made possible and profitable under two conditions. *First*, the seller must be a monopolist or must, at least, possess a degree of monopoly power. Else the customer who faces the higher, discriminatory price will shift his patronage to another firm.

Second, there must be at least two separate markets for the commodity or service. This implies two circumstances. (1) The demand for the commodity must have different elasticities for at least two separate sets of consumers. A higher price can be charged for a small bottle of lotion or for the minimum amount of gas or electricity because the demand for the smaller quantity is less elastic than for the larger quantity, within the same price ranges. The doctor can charge the well-to-do patients a higher fee because their demand for his services is much more inelastic than is the demand of those with low incomes. Similarly, the demand for telegraph and long-distance telephone service is more elastic to those ready to postpone till evening than to those who must communicate at once; and the demand for theater tickets and the golf course is more insistent on week ends than on weekdays.

(2) There must be no opportunity for those who pay the low price to resell to those who are charged the high price. Else, a group of middlemen would develop who would traffic in buying from the former and selling to the latter, and the high-price market would be lost to the monopolist. If, at a certain cost, intercommunication and resale can be established between the separate markets, this cost must be at least as great as the price differential between the two markets. Roughly speaking, if the domestic consumer is charged $10 for an article which is dumped on the foreign market for $8, the cost of reshipping the good must be $2 at the least.

TWO-MARKET DISCRIMINATION

Various types of discrimination are possible in various monopolistic situations. We shall discuss the kind that involves the strategy of price and output fixing in two markets.

A monopolist may face two markets for his commodity: the demand situation is different in each market, and there is no resale between the two. In market 1 (Figure 45) the demand curve is D_1 and the marginal revenue curve is R_1; in market 2 the corresponding schedules are D_2 and

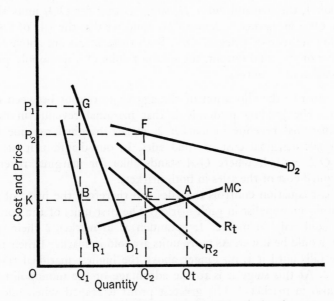

FIGURE 45. *Two-Market Price Discrimination*

R_2. The monopolist will gather more profit if he charges a different price in each market than if he charges one price in both markets. What price and what output will he set for each market?

(1) First, he will determine the size of his output for both markets put together. He may be guided by the equation of marginal revenue and marginal cost. The marginal cost curve is MC. The marginal revenue curve for both markets is the horizontal addition of R_1 and R_2, or the curve R_t. The point of intersection of these two curves is A. He will choose the aggregate output OQ_t.

(2) Next comes the problem of allocating this output between the two markets. In each of these he will dispose of an output for which the marginal revenue obtained equals the marginal cost of the total output, namely cost AQ_t. At once it is necessary to stress that sales in market 1 are not governed by the intersection of R_1 and MC, and sales in market 2 are not governed by the intersection of R_2 and MC. What counts is the point on R_1 with a height equal to AQ_t and the point on R_2 with a height likewise equal to AQ_t. To get such a point on R_1 and on R_2, we draw from point A a line AK parallel to the horizontal axis. Line AK meets R_1 at B and R_2 at E. Accordingly the sales in market 1 amount to $KB = OQ_1$, and sales in market 2 are $KE = OQ_2$. The sales in both markets will be $OQ_1 + OQ_2 = OQ_t$.

(3) With the output in each market ascertained, we can tell from the demand situation in each of them which price the monopolist can charge. In market 1, the demand curve D_1 suggests that for OQ_1 units the price will be OP_1; in market 2, demand D_2 indicates that the sale of OQ_2 units will bring an average price of OP_2. Both these prices are above the marginal cost of the total output, the signpost alike of a monopoly price and misallocation of resources.

To return to the allocation of the aggregate output between the two markets: The guiding principle is that marginal revenue in market 1 equals marginal revenue in market 2, equals marginal revenue of total sales, equals marginal cost of total sales. In our diagram, it means that $Q_1B = Q_2E = Q_tA$, where Q_tA stands alike for marginal revenue and for marginal cost of the sales in both markets.

This last equation controls the sales and therefore the price of the discriminating monopolist in each market. The first units of the commodity will be sold only in market 1, inasmuch as in market 2 their marginal revenue would be lower. As more units are sold in market 1 their marginal revenue falls until it is no longer above the highest marginal revenue in market 2. At this stage it is to the advantage of the monopolist to start selling also in market 2. His greatest profit is reaped when sales are so distributed between the two markets that marginal revenue is the same in both. Should the monopolist refuse to discriminate between the two markets and behave like a *simple* monopolist with a *single* price, marginal revenue in the two markets will not be equalized and he will not gather the most profits. The discriminating monopolist makes more profit than the simple monopolist. Herein lies the incentive for the monopolist to discriminate, if he can.

According to the diagram (Figure 45), the demand in market 1 seems to be generally less elastic than in market 2 for the same price ranges. We know that for a given output the marginal revenue is farther below the average revenue where the demand is inelastic than where it is elastic. Conversely, in the first instance the average revenue or price is farther above marginal revenue than in the second instance. With the same marginal revenue Q_1B and Q_2E, accordingly, point G on D_1 directly above point B on R_1 will be higher than point F on D_2 directly above point E on R_2. We can generalize that in discriminating monopoly the price in the market with the less elastic demand will be higher than the price in the market with the more elastic demand, in the given price range. To put it differently, it will pay the monopolist to sell less of his output in the market where the demand is less elastic, in the relevant price range, and the marginal revenue drops considerably for a small sales volume, and to shift his sales to the market with the more elastic demand, in the given price range, where marginal revenue stays at a comparatively high level as sales are extended. It follows that if demand is of the same elasticity in both markets, the price will be the same and discrimination will be absent.

COMPARISON OF SIMPLE AND DISCRIMINATING MONOPOLY

The problem of how price, output, and the allocation of resources under discriminating monopoly compare with those under simple monopoly is full of intricacies. The pioneers in this field are A. C. Pigou and Mrs. Joan Robinson.[3] We shall close our discussion of discrimination by citing a few cases in which discriminating pricing is not without its good points.

We may generalize that if the single price of the simple monopolist is so high that many a consumer finds the service beyond his reach, the introduction of price discrimination may lower the price to these consumers in the weaker and elastic market. The output of the discriminating monopolist may then well exceed the output of the simple monopolist. This may be especially true if the expansion of output is associated with declining average and marginal costs and (or) if the sales are scant at a

[3] A. C. Pigou, *The Economics of Welfare*, 4th ed. (London, Macmillan, 1932), chap. 17 and pp. 810–812; J. Robinson, *The Economics of Imperfect Competition* (London, Macmillan, 1948), chaps. 15 and 16.

high price but conspicuously larger at a low price.

Consider the practice by the railroads of charging what the traffic will bear. If the price were uniform for the transportation of jewelry and gravel, silk and coal, the traffic in the heavier commodities would nearly be lost to the railroads, whereas the carriage of the lighter and more expensive articles would hardly be extended. Railway service would thus be curtailed and the profits of the industry would suffer. In addition, the roads might even charge more for jewelry and clothing than under discrimination.

There are other examples. The high single price for all the patrons of the motion-picture houses may practically exclude children. To get rid of Junior, parents may coax him to seek adventure in the backyard instead of sending him off to the show. Discrimination lowers the price of admission to children, greatly increasing their attendance. Similarly, if a doctor were to set a uniform fee to all patients, he would receive no additional calls from the rich and the visits of the poor to his office might drop off considerably. Thus in many a community the doctor might not make ends meet, and medical service there might become inadequate. Of course the question may be raised whether the poor should not be aided in some other manner and by some other agency.

III. Monopoly Power and Restraints on Monopoly Power

When considering the degree of monopoly power enjoyed by the seller of a commodity, we do not deal with pure monopoly alone but also with other markets in which there is a monopoly element, namely with monopolistic competition and oligopoly. By monopoly power we mean the amount of discretion which the seller possesses, or the amount of competition which governs the seller, in shaping his policy with regard to the output and price of his product and to the differentiation of his product by quality and service. In general, monopoly power indicates the scope of deviation from competitive behavior.

LERNER'S MEASURE OF MONOPOLY POWER

Two problems compose the theme of this section: the measure of monopoly power and the possible restraints pressing on the monopolist seller in shaping the price of his output.

Among the measures suggested, Professor A. P. Lerner's is of the longest standing and the most widely cited.[4] His measure is based on the difference between the price charged by the monopolist and his marginal cost. The formula is $P - MC/P$, where P is price and MC is marginal cost. Under competition, $P = MC$ and this formula gives zero, indicating no monopoly power. If the monopolized product is a free good, $MC = 0$ and the formula registers unity. The index of monopoly power can thus vary from zero to unity. Inasmuch as free goods are seldom among those monopolized, the monopoly index will ordinarily not be as high as unity.

In monopoly equilibrium marginal revenue (MR) equals marginal cost. The formula becomes $P - MR/P$. Since (as was indicated near the end of section I, Chapter VIII),

$$MR = P\frac{E - 1}{E},$$

where E is price elasticity, the formula can be written

$$\frac{P - P\frac{E - 1}{E}}{P} = \frac{1}{E}.$$

The result indicates that the degree of monopoly varies inversely with the elasticity of the demand for the commodity. It suggests that to measure monopoly power it is sufficient to obtain an indication of the elasticity of the demand for the commodity. We note that whereas the original formula $P - MC/P$ can yield a maximum figure of no more than unity, this last formula can give a much larger result. If, for example, the price elasticity is $\frac{1}{5}$, the formula will indicate a monopoly power of 5. This measure also implies that the limiting case of pure monopoly is a demand elasticity of zero for the product offered.

This measure seems to have a number of shortcomings. Foremost among them is its inability to measure nonprice competition in cases of product differentiation, as in monopolistic competition and differentiated oligopoly. Suppose the index for a firm selling a differentiated commodity is high. This can hardly establish a high degree of monopoly and a low degree of competition for this firm. The sellers of the variants of this commodity may choose not to compete in price but rather to wage intensive competition in product variation and in the selling effort. Two firms may show the same index, but one firm may sell a product of superior quality, may offer better service and better credit terms, and may spend more on marketing activity than the other firm. We can hardly ignore these competitive elements and conclude that the two firms reveal identical propor-

[4] A. P. Lerner, "The Concept of Monopoly and the Measurement of Monopoly Power," *Review of Economic Studies*, Vol. I (June, 1934), pp. 157-175.

tions of competition and monopoly.

Even for a homogeneous product, though it is obvious that when the firm's sales curve is nearly horizontal the monopoly price will not depart much from the competitive price; and though it is equally obvious that a substantial departure is generally possible when the sales curve is of low elasticity; it is nevertheless going too far to claim that all the small gradations in the elasticity of the sales curve point to parallel gradations in the monopoly power of the firm, and that accordingly the limiting case of pure monopoly is the vertical sales curve of zero elasticity.

In the third place, it is important to stress that monopoly power does not express itself exclusively in the departure of price from cost. It also asserts itself in restriction of output. Restriction of output may be the sequel of two policies: underutilization of plant capacity already in existence, or outright underinvestment by the firm or by the industry, as through the prevention of entry. The Lerner formula hardly throws light on these vital aspects of monopoly power.

For example, with a given investment in the firm possessing a monopoly element, if the demand for its product is inelastic, the departure of price from cost may be *large*, but the restriction of output required to force this result may be *small*. Nor can we tell from the formula whether in a given case we deal with underutilization of existing investment in plant, or with underinvestment in the first instance. Is public policy to strive in this case for more adequate use of available capacity or for expansion of investment? Again, two firms may exhibit the same index of monopoly power. Yet one firm may exemplify underinvestment, perhaps because it is in a new industry and faces the related uncertainties; whereas the other firm may be overinvested, possibly because of exaggerated estimates of a steady growth in demand.

RESTRAINTS ON MONOPOLY POWER

A monopolist is not likely often to exercise his power to the limit. He will ordinarily not be inclined to exploit fully a short-term advantageous situation and charge the price which will always fetch the highest possible profit. There are a number of long-run considerations which tend to moderate his appetite and to keep monopoly prices below their temporary maximum possibilities.[5]

(1) The monopolist may fear potential *competition*. True, we define monopoly as a type of market in which the product has no close substitute, and the single seller of it need not reckon with the reactions of other sellers. However, the definition does not imply that the monopolist has

[5] See the same topic in Chapter XII, section IV.

an ironclad guarantee that this situation must endure, come what may. The definition does not imply that the monopolist has no reason to fear that if his profits are enormous they may, in time, excite human ingenuity into contriving a closer substitute than is currently available. High profits may not stimulate a substitute, but tremendous profits may lure new entrepreneurs into the attempt to break through the barriers to entry.

Nor is this restraint weakened by the monopolist's speculation that the newcomers will behave "well" and will not undersell—that you can do business with them. Even at the undisturbed monopoly price, the existing market will have to be shared with the new members of the club. The aggregate profit of the monopolist will shrink and his scale of operations will be reduced. Such adjustments are painful. There is also the question of sharing power with others. Power and prestige are among the motive forces back of monopoly, nearly as potent, probably, as the desire for large gains. A monarch does not contemplate with indifference the possibility of a demotion to membership in an oligarchy. In order not to attract rivals, the monopolist may prefer to shade his price.

(2) There is also the fear of *public reaction*. Despite their high-powered public-relations officers who know how to make friends and influence people, monopoly firms fear that high prices and huge profits may provoke unfavorable editorial comment, may raise protests from consumers, may stir unrest among the employees, who will demand a share in the melon, and may induce agitation for stronger antitrust legislation. To let sleeping dogs lie, the monopolist is apt to moderate his price.

(3) Another restraining influence lies in the difference in *elasticity of demand* between the long run and short run. In the long run, the demand can be more elastic than in the short run. If the price is raised, the consumer needs time to change his habits, to make adjustments in his budget, to find an acceptable substitute, and to curtail the purchases of the commodity affected. If the price is lowered, more people learn about it with the passage of time and sales may be progressively enlarged. The firm may therefore refrain from a grasping price policy because the losses in the future may overshadow the temporary gains, and a steadier adherence to a lower price may in time attract more and more customers. With an eye on the good-will of customers and on the security of good profits, the monopolist may be disposed to moderate his price instead of pushing to the limit the fleeting potential of greater profits.

(4) *Taxation* is a further curb on monopoly. Restraints on monopoly price may be instituted by the government, which can frame antimonopoly legislation, like the Sherman Act (1890), the Clayton Act (1914), and the Federal Trade Commission Act (1914). The state may regulate monopoly price directly by setting ceilings on the price of a monopolized article, or indirectly through taxation. The tax levied may

be proportional to the output, so that as output rises the tax rises. Or the tax may be a given fixed lump sum no matter how big the annual output is. Let us examine first the influence of the *lump-sum* tax as in Figure 46.

Before the lump-sum tax appears, marginal cost (MC) cuts the marginal revenue curve (MR) at H; accordingly OQ and the monopoly price QK become, respectively, the output of the monopoly and the monopoly price QK charged for a unit of its product. The lump-sum tax is in its nature a fixed cost. It lifts the whole AC curve upward into the position of the curve AC_1. The lump-sum tax has no effect on marginal cost. The marginal cost of any output, we recall, equals the total cost of N units minus the total cost of $N - 1$ units. The lump-sum tax is canceled out. We are left with marginal cost undisturbed. Price and output also stay put. The lump-sum tax comes completely out of monopoly profit. Even

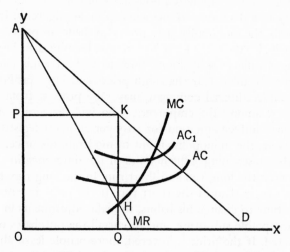

FIGURE 46. *Effect of a Lump-Sum Tax on Monopoly*

if the lump-sum tax took annually the whole monopoly profit, there would be no way for the monopolist to shift the burden to his customers. To begin with, monopoly profit is a surplus above costs, and the monopolist already *maximizes* this surplus: A change in price or output would only bring him losses.

The government may levy a *variable* tax on a monopoly; such a tax is also known as a specific tax per unit of product. Figure 47 presents the usual picture as it appears before this tax is imposed: AC and MC stand for average cost and marginal cost; and MR (marginal revenue) cuts MC (marginal cost) at point H. Accordingly the price of the product is QK and the associated quantity is OQ.

The variable tax functions to raise all costs, average and marginal: AC shifts into AC_1 and MC becomes MC_1. Figure 47 indicates what happened: MC cuts MR at point H; this means quantity OQ and price QK. After the tax, MC_1 cuts MR at a higher point than H (because of crowded space, this point is not labeled in the diagram). The new price becomes Q_1L, and the new and corresponding quantity is OQ_1. The consumer pays a higher price and obtains a smaller amount of the article purchased. The monopolist has shifted part of the burden to the public; but just the

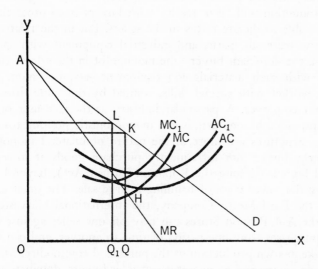

FIGURE 47. *Effect of a Variable Tax on Monopoly*

same, the monopolist carries part of the burden. Should the government levy a much higher variable tax, the reaction of the monopolist would be to lessen production more drastically and to raise the price above previous heights. A brief footnote: this is a case where a diagram is more effective in exposition than verbal discourse.

PART 2. MONOPSONY

Monopsony is comparatively rare in our economy. The colonial companies of centuries past, against whose "monopolizing spirit" Adam Smith argued so eloquently, were in many cases the only buyers of certain types

of native labor or native products in isolated areas. Nowadays the buyer
for a large chain store can influence the price of the produce obtained
from farmers in a given region who through years of association with
him have lost contact with other buyers. Not many years ago concerted
action by the few large meat packers produced an oppressive monopsony
in the purchase of livestock from the numerous cattle dealers. The large
canning companies have monopsony power in buying up peas and other
vegetables in a given area during the canning season.

In most instances materials and equipment can be used in any number
of industries; and the buyer representing even a major segment of one
field of production will be in rivalry with buyers from other fields and
will not be able to dictate terms to the sellers. But in the relatively few
cases of raw materials, parts, and industrial equipment with specialized
application, the dominant buyer—the monopolist in the sale of the product made with such materials and equipment—acquires monopsonistic
power. A worker with special skills, wanted by only one firm, faces a
monopsonist employer. A particular industry as the sole user of certain
resources provided by one firm is in a monopsonistic position toward this
firm. Such structures are more in the nature of bilateral monopoly. In
general, large buyers not infrequently purchase goods at lower prices
than small buyers (despite the Robinson-Patman Act), beyond what is
justified by the lower costs of handling a large sale. The great establishment like the Ford Motor Company, the International Harvester Company, or the A & P Food Stores can play off one seller against another,
can shift purchases from one period of time to another, and can threaten
to undertake its own production of the purchased commodity. Mail-order
houses, chain stores, and co-operatives may, as buyers, dominate the markets where consumer goods are sold.

Parallel to the types of markets distinguished by the kind of monopoly
element possessed by the seller is the classification of markets according
to the kind of monopsony on the buyer's side. Corresponding to duopoly,
oligopoly, and monopolistic competition is the array of duopsony, oligopsony, and monopsonistic competition. These are not all. We can visualize hybrid markets exemplifying permutations and combinations of the
above categories on the buyer's and seller's side. We can have a monopsonist buying from an oligopoly or from firms producing under conditions
of monopolistic competition. Then there is the combination of oligopsony-
oligopoly, or bilateral oligopoly; of buyers under oligopsonistic competition purchasing from a monopolist or from an oligopolist. In what follows
we shall be interested only in monopsony; a few words will also be said
about bilateral monopoly.

The list of parallels between monopoly and monopsony is not easily
exhausted. Like monopoly, monopsony implies barriers to the entry of

other buyers. The monopsonist may insist on a contract with the sellers binding them not to traffic with other buyers. Like monopolists, monopsonists may not exploit to the full the advantage of the moment and squeeze the seller with the lowest price possible. Long-run considerations, not unlike those motivating the monopolist, may stay the hand of the monopsonist, inducing him to offer a "fair" price to the sellers. The monopsonist may fear that offers of an exceedingly low price may foster hostile public opinion or government interference. He may be interested in the certainty of a steady supply of raw materials or of labor over the years to come. Given time, the sellers to a monopsonist may try to escape the dominance of a close-fisted buyer by developing connections with other buyers, or by shifting to the production of another commodity or to a less handicapped occupation. The monopsonist may strive to prevent such behavior by offering reasonable prices for what he buys. Finally, nonpecuniary motives may actuate the monopsonist as they actuate the monopolist.

MONOPSONY PRICING

The analysis of price under monopsony is fundamentally similar to that applied in pure competition or monopoly. The relevant forces turn around the conditions of supply and demand as seen through the glasses of the monopsonist.

The supply situation

Let us consider first the supply situation in Figure 48. We shall assume

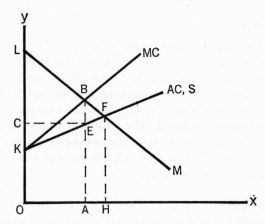

FIGURE 48. *Monopsony Price: Increasing-Cost Industry*

that the industry selling to the monopsonist is subject to increasing cost and a rising supply price. Increasing-cost industries are probably typical in our economy. Accordingly, when the monopsonist bids for more units of what he is purchasing he is compelled to offer a higher price, as is indicated by the rising average cost curve AC or S in Figure 48. This curve depicts the supply situation as it looks to the monopsonist. It represents the various amounts of the article which the many sellers are willing to offer to the monopsonist at various prices.

But it is not this curve alone which is important to the monopsonist. What he is also interested in is the marginal cost of his increased purchases. These costs rise and stay above the AC curve, as is illustrated by the marginal cost, or the marginal outlay, curve MC. When he buys one additional unit the price which he has to offer rises not only on this extra unit but also on all the other units already purchased. The cost of the extra unit is not only its price but also the accompanying additional expenditure on *all* the preceding units. Assume that he can buy 10 units at 10¢ each and 11 units at 12¢ each. For the 11th unit,

$$\text{cost} = 12¢ + (2¢ \times 10) = (12¢ \times 11) - (10¢ \times 10) = 32¢.$$

The marginal cost of 11 units is thus 32¢. The purchase of the 11th unit sets him back 32¢.

Both the relation between the two rising curves AC and MC and the above arithmetic are merely exemplifications of the "average-marginal relation" discussed in previous chapters. When the average quantities rise, the associated marginal quantities also rise and stay consistently above the average quantities. To refer again to our student and his grades, if his average quiz grade is rising as the new quizzes come along, it means that his grade on each new quiz beats his average on the preceding quizzes.

The demand curve

The demand situation is portrayed by curve LM (Figure 48). This curve represents the marginal utility of the various amounts of the good, or the utility of each successive unit, to the single buyer. If he buys the commodity, not for personal consumption, but for resale, this curve pictures the additional benefit or revenue which he expects from the resale of the additional units purchased. The total utility or total revenue from a given quantity purchased by the monopsonist is depicted by the appropriate *area* underneath LM. In brief, the demand curve LM is in the nature of a *marginal revenue* curve.

Monopsony equilibrium

The equilibrium monopsony price and output are focused at point B in Figure 48, where the demand curve and the marginal cost curve intersect. The monopsonist will realize his greatest advantage when he buys the quantity *OA* at the unit price *AE*. Point *B* lies on both *LM* and MC; at the equilibrium combination of price and quantity the monopsonist equates *AB* as his marginal utility or marginal revenue with *AB* as his marginal cost.

When in the equilibrium position the monopolist maximizes his total profit, that is, the excess of his total revenue over his total cost. Likewise with the monopsonist: he attempts to maximize the excess of his total utility or total revenue over his total outlay. The total utility or total benefits which he derives from the *OA* units is represented by the area *OABL*. The total outlay is rectangle *OAEC*. At the equilibrium price *AE*, he maximizes the difference between these two totals: the area *CEBL* represents his maximum gain.

To compare the equilibrium price-output situation under monopsony with that under competition, we have to assume comparable demand and supply conditions, an heroic but perhaps useful assumption. Let us assume that under competition the demand and supply curves are likewise *LM* and AC respectively.[6] The equilibrium position will then be indicated by the intersection of these two curves: the amount purchased by the many buyers would be *OH* and the price *FH*. Under monopsony, as we see, the output is smaller and the price (*AE*) obtained by the firms selling to the monopsonist is lower. The advantage goes to the monopsonist. He owes this advantage to the fact that the commodity which he is buy-

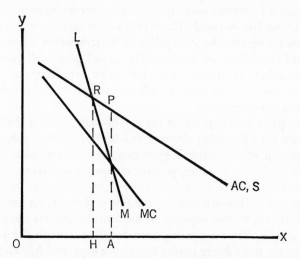

FIGURE 49. *Monopsony Price: Decreasing-Cost Industry*

[6] J. S. Bain, *Pricing, Distribution, and Employment*, revised ed. (New York, Henry Holt, 1953), pp. 383–384, 392; Joan Robinson, *op. cit.*, pp. 216, 219.

ing comes from an industry with an ascending supply price. By buying less than *OH* units he can offer a lower price. Being the only buyer, he buys less. The monopolist curtails output in order to raise the price to the buyer; the monopsonist curtails purchases in order to lower the price to the seller.

However, in the rare case when the many sellers are in an industry with a decreasing cost curve the results are partly different. Then the MC curve lies below the AC curve, as in Figure 49. The amount purchased, *OA*, exceeds the competitive amount *OH*; but the price *PA* paid to the sellers stays lower than the competitive price *RH*. If the industry is subject to constant costs, the AC curve will be horizontal, and the MC curve will coincide with it. The amount purchased by the monopsonist and the price he offers to the sellers are then identical with those under competition. As we see, the quantity purchased by the monopsonist may at times exceed the quantity purchased under competition, but the price offered by the monopsonist may never rise above the competitive price.

BILATERAL MONOPOLY

Sometimes Greek meets Greek; the monopsonist meets not many sellers but only one seller. This type of market is called bilateral monopoly. The monopsonist is interested in offering a low price for a limited amount of the commodity. The monopolist, on the other hand, aims to charge a high price and sell a restricted output, but the output is different in size from what the buyer has in mind. These two prices constitute the upper and lower limits which may be susceptible of determination when the supply and demand conditions are known. The actual price will commonly be a compromise between these limits. This price is indeterminate. Analysis assuming self-interest and the principle of maximizing gains cannot locate precisely the resulting price.

The final price will depend on the tug-of-war between the buyer and the seller, on the bargaining strength and skill of the two sides. The bargaining position of the seller is governed by such considerations as the future demand for his product, possible competition from new sellers, the cost of carrying inventory, and financial resources needed to hold on in the waiting game. The strength of the buyer depends on the alternative sources of supply, on the urgency of his demand, and on the prospect of obtaining supplies after a waiting period. Often enough the public attitude toward the contending parties exercises a degree of influence.

Examples of bilateral monopoly of goods are not abundant. There is an instance of it when a farmers' co-operative association sells milk or fruit or produce to the large buyer in a given area. Not many decades ago the tobacco growers learned to unite and face as one seller of tobacco leaf the one buyer, the American Tobacco Company. Examples are more frequent in wage determination when the big employer meets the representatives of the big union to negotiate a wage contract. We shall study this case in the chapter on wages.

PART 3. OBSERVATIONS ON MONOPOLY

We conclude this chapter with a discussion of the implications of monopoly and monopsony for society as a whole. We saw that monopoly and monopsony alike are objective elements clothed with human destinies, and that in many respects they are parallel phenomena. When the buyer or the seller is *one* entity the resulting behavior is damaging to society.

We have been talking about single-firm monopoly as it exists side by side with other enterprise structures, not about a "world of monopolies." It is evident that under monopoly the *allocation* of resources is not contributive to maximum output and satisfaction. The price set for the commodity stands above marginal cost: the last dollar's worth of a factor-service produces an output with more than a dollar's worth of satisfaction, as shown by the price paid by the consumer. When the resources used in producing a unit of a good are reflected in a marginal cost of $5, whereas the consumer's utility from this unit is reflected in a price of $6, total utility would gain if more resources were used to produce more of this good, to the stage at which the marginal cost of making the good would rise to, say, $5.50, and the price to the consumer would step down to this sum in face of the increased output. Under monopoly, moreover, the limitation of output and the correlative underemployment of resources tend to force fixed and variable factors alike to overflow into competitive fields with resulting congestion and misdirection of resources there.

Misallocation of resources marks any form of single-seller or single-buyer dominance. The monopoly of a labor union may push the wage rate above the level of marginal revenue productivity. Employer monopsony pulls the wage rate below marginal revenue productivity. In either case there is underemployment of the given type of labor. In general, where competition and monopoly exist alongside each other we cannot expect commodities to exhibit the same ratio between marginal utility or price, and marginal cost; nor can we expect resources to exhibit a uniform ratio between marginal revenue productivity and factor price.

As far as *efficiency* of scale, or of a larger output by the firm, is concerned, the picture is blurred. The profit-maximizing price is very likely to be set at a level of production below the optimum possible for the monopolist. This means that monopoly does not exploit to the limit its potential internal economies and low unit costs. But the interesting question is: does a monopoly operate at a lower scale and at a higher cost than a firm in a competitive industry? It is difficult to answer this question because it is difficult to compare the two firms. The competitive firm, one among very many in the industry, may operate at a modest output with fewer than the maximum internal economies. The monopoly firm may, despite its restriction of output, run on a larger scale and with greater efficiency than each of the competing firms. On the other hand, a competitive industry may, in some cases, accommodate numerous large firms, whereas the one monopoly firm may be overextended in size and may therefore suffer from net internal diseconomies. It is perhaps not incorrect to assert that with respect to efficiency of scale the monopoly firm is hardly in a position to score against the *large* competitive firm.

Nor is it easy to strike a balance among contending considerations when we think of *progressiveness*. The monopoly profits provide the firm with financial resources to engage in a program of research. The firm's benefit from an innovation is longer-lived and more secure than under competition. On the other hand, if an improvement in the product renders its sale less profitable, it may not be adopted although it would add to consumer utility. A monopolist may not be quick to introduce a more durable tire or flashlight. He may be slow in introducing an innovation; he will wait until the depreciation of the old fixed equipment proceeds far enough. The spur of competition and the survival incentive are not available to force him to make greater use of the scrap heap. On the whole, there is reason to believe that an entrenched monopoly is not conducive to progress.

Generally speaking, competitive industry provides more output and employment than monopoly does: unless competition inevitably implies many small firms with high production costs. With the absence of large profits, competition tends to lessen inequality of income. On the other hand, moderate profits provide a smaller pool of savings and investment so essential to capital formation and the greater production of income.

Monopoly of the single-firm variety tends to contribute, more than competition, to income *inequality* and instability. In the main, profits are greater in monopoly than in the competitive sectors. The restriction of output, or the scarcity economy characterizing monopoly, reflects itself in a reduced demand for factors, with the end result of lower incomes to households generally. Enhanced income inequality may lower aggregate consumption, may raise the volume of savings, and may create the necessity of greater investment as an offset to these savings, if total income and employment are not to tend downward. Moreover, the comparative rigidity of prices in monopoly and particularly in oligopoly tends to concentrate on the level of output the burden of adjustment to changes in demand. Although mitigating inflationary pressures, such rigidity is calculated to intensify booms and depressions, aggravating the instability of incomes. Thus in a depression the restriction of output to keep the prices of equipment and materials from declining may hold back investment and retard recovery. Likewise, monopolistically set high interest rates may discourage investment with similarly frustrating effects on the development of a business revival out of a depression.[7]

Let us finally sum up the desirable and the undesirable implications of monopoly. Monopoly breeds a faulty allocation of resources; permits a departure from least-cost production (maximum efficiency); and fosters a sleepy attitude toward improvements. Monopoly stands for a scarcity economy: limited output and high prices. Monopoly creates rigid prices, which preclude flexible price adjustments; and it may accentuate inequality of income with its undesirable consequences to the economy. Of no small account is the fact that monopoly and its occasional abuses invite the intrusion of government in the free-enterprise system, with additional regulations, a development that can hardly be applauded by the student of monopoly. Nearly two centuries ago Adam Smith pointed out that monopoly thrusts a double tax on the economy: (a) monopoly does not allow entry and robs the would-be businessman of the freedom to choose his trade; and (b) it afflicts the community with high prices and scant production.

But monopoly is not without friends. The most noted modern economist who has defended monopoly, the late Professor Schumpeter, argued that a new investment needs protection: patents, insurance, secrecy, or hedging. Monopoly provides the necessary protection. High prices and large profit serve as stimuli for improvements and innovation. Monopoly can be predatory and cut-throat, so can competition, he would say. Monopoly does develop rigid prices, but in the long run the rigidity vanishes. One wonders why he invites monopoly as the bodyguard of innovations, and not, say, a revision of the patent system. When we extend the power of monopoly we are giving hostages to fortune. However, in some cases monopoly status is won and kept by a succession of innovations. Examples are the Du Ponts and the General Electric Company. Moreover, monopoly has money for heavy research, more than the single firm in pure competition. But the monopolist nonetheless makes insufficient use of the scrap heap. Toward the end of the chapter on oligopoly we shall enumerate various measures designed to abolish or to diminish the power of monopoly.

[7] D. H. Wallace, "Monopoly Prices and Depression," *Explorations in Economics* (New York, McGraw-Hill, 1936), pp. 346–356.

SUGGESTED READINGS

Bain, J. S. *Pricing, Distribution, and Employment,* revised ed., chaps. 5, 8, 9. New York, Holt, 1953.

Boulding, K. E. *Economic Analysis,* revised ed., chaps. 25, 26. New York, Harper, 1948.

Burns, A. R. *The Decline of Competition,* chap. 6. New York, McGraw-Hill, 1936.

Leftwich, R. H. *The Price System and Resource Allocation,* revised ed., chap. X. New York, Holt, Rinehart and Winston, 1960.

Machlup, F. *The Economics of Sellers' Competition,* chap. 17. Baltimore, The Johns Hopkins Press, 1952.

Marshall, A. *Principles of Economics,* 8th ed., Book V, chap. 14. New York, Macmillan, 1927.

Robinson, E. A. G. *Monopoly.* London, Nisbet, 1941.

Robinson, Joan. *The Economics of Imperfect Competition,* Books II, VI. London, Macmillan, 1948.

Stigler, G. J. *The Theory of Price,* revised ed., chap. 12. New York, Macmillan, 1952.

Wilcox, C. *Competition and Monopoly in American Industry,* chap. 3. Washington, Temporary National Economic Committee, Monograph No. 21, 1941.

X I Monopolistic Competition

THE THEORY of price formation in a market with a differentiated product is chiefly the fruit of Professor Chamberlin's work. Before the appearance of his *The Theory of Monopolistic Competition* in 1933 the different varieties of a given commodity were commonly treated in economic literature as though they were units of a homogeneous article. A Ford, a Buick, and a Cadillac were usually regarded as automobiles with one equilibrium price. A Camel, a Lucky Strike, a Chesterfield, and all the other varieties of cigarettes were merged in economic analysis, into one cigarette industry with one set of supply and demand curves, the intersection of which determined the price of cigarettes.

I. Product Differentiation

THE CHANGED VIEWPOINT

This way of looking at things no longer prevails. Economic analysis no longer considers the variants of a given article sold by the same or different concerns at identical or different prices as examples of the same commodity. The various makes of cars, radios, cosmetics, or silverware are not treated in the same way as all the wheat in the country, or in the whole world, is treated in a chapter on pure competition. Instead, the investigation addresses itself to the study of the price of a Ford apart from a Chrysler or a Rambler, or to the price of an Emerson radio sold in a shop in a side street as distinct from the price of the Emerson radio sold in an attractive store on a busy block.

In this chapter, and in this book generally, the term monopolistic competition is used somewhat differently from the way Professor Chamberlin uses it. He designates by this term both (1) a market with a differentiated product offered by many sellers, each with his unique variety of it, and (2) oligopoly, pure or differentiated, that is, a market with a small number of sellers of a homogeneous or of a differentiated product. He employs the term monopolistic competition to stand for any blend of competition and monopoly whether the blend is the outcome of product variation or of a small number of selling firms in the market.

The term monopolistic competition as used in this book will refer only to a family of related articles sold by *many* sellers, each one offering a somewhat different make of it. Oligopoly, or a small number of sellers, will be treated as another type of market. This difference in the classification of markets is only a matter of convenience for purposes of exposition. The realities and the analysis are alike unaffected.

Examples of industries characterized by monopolistic competition are far from rare. In any good-sized city there are many small-scale establishments making or distributing articles of the same category or rendering personal services of the same category. The product or service varies from concern to concern but ordinarily not to a considerable extent. The makers of women's dresses and hats, the small restaurants, the small dry cleaners, the shoemakers, and the barbers are examples. The field of retailing offers the widest scope. The grocery store, the drugstore, the clothing store, the dry-goods store, the soda and candy store require a comparatively small investment and little experience and knowledge. This may account for the high birth rate of these enterprises and for the parallel of a high death rate.

NATURE OF PRODUCT DIFFERENTIATION

Under pure competition we are dealing with a homogeneous product. Number 2 red wheat produced by any farmer in Kansas or Nebraska or anywhere else in the world is wheat of the same type and it sells at the same price everywhere. But customers do not consider the many brands of coffee on the market as precisely the same commodity. They do not regard Chase & Sanborn coffee as identical with Manor House coffee or Simon Pure coffee or A & P coffee. Even at the higher price charged for Chase & Sanborn coffee many prefer it to other brands which sell at lower prices. The varieties of a commodity offered by different firms are treated by consumers as almost different articles.

Many are the ways of making products different from one another.

There can be a difference in the materials, workmanship, strength, and durability; in size, style, brand, color, and packaging; in the convenience and prestige of the location of the business; in the appointments in the store or office and the attitude of the personnel attending to customers; and in the terms of trade, such as cash or credit, acceptance of returned goods, and guarantee of service and repairs. In addition, advertising claims may press on the buyers notions of spurious differences among articles by using catchwords like "the schoolgirl complexion" and by playing on such motives as fear, pride, and emulation.

More articles are diversified than is realized at first thought. Wheat is a standardized commodity; but the loaf of bread sold in the bakery or grocery is differentiated by the devices cited above. The same holds of other goods dealt in organized markets. Coffee and sugar are homogeneous goods when bought and sold in such markets, but not when sold in packages in the retail store. The raw wool or cotton is standardized, but not the dresses or sweaters. Even eggs in the chicken coop are not a standard commodity. For one thing, the owner does not pursue a laissez-faire policy toward the hen. By subjecting the hen to different amounts and types of food, chemicals, heat, and light, the eggs can be made to differ in size, color, quality, hardness and porousness of shell, and durability of freshness. Further variation can be achieved by packaging, service, and advertising claims.

Consider semifinished products, which are usually made to specifications. The buyer is commonly an industrial user of the product who subjects it to further processing. A manufacturer who uses steel as material in his factory will specify to the seller the exact shape, size, type of surface, degree of hardness, durability, and tensile strength which he requires. The big buying firm is, moreover, armed with testing devices, engineers, and statisticians to examine samples of the materials received in order to make certain that there has been strict compliance with specifications. Technologically, every steel mill will turn out precisely the same steel materials as long as the specifications are identical. However, even here variation of product may appear. There may be a difference in the service attending the sale as offered by the various mills. In the buyer's estimation steel firms, and other firms producing semifinished capital goods, make almost a different product although they all fulfill the specifications. The producers of such materials advertise in business journals and send out batteries of salesmen to solicit trade for a product differentiated, not by workmanship, but by the type of service promised.

As will be seen in greater detail in section III of this chapter, the differentiation of products is achieved in ways which can be grouped under two heads: (1) quality variation and (2) promotional or selling effort. The objectives of these two activities are different.

(1) The purpose of quality changes in the product is to adapt the product to the latent demand of prospective buyers, to fashion a variant of the article that will appeal more strongly and more widely. One variant of the good may enlist the loyalty of more consumers than another variant. By changing the materials, the workmanship, the service, or the credit terms associated with the commodity, the producer expects to face a demand different from the demand for his previous type of commodity. In doing this he is not changing the demand for the article; he is not shifting the demand curve for it. Changing the demand or shifting the demand curve implies that something has been done to the buyers' attitudes to cause them to change their previous price-quantity reactions to the *same* article. But the different demand for a new variety is essentially the demand for one product as distinct from the demand for another product. By experimenting with quality variation the seller is seeking the variant of the product for which the latent demand of the customer is most advantageous to the seller.

The purpose of quality changes is to adapt the commodity more sensitively to the tastes and preferences of consumers. With the new make on the market, the producer hopes to face a more inelastic demand as well as a demand curve farther up and to the right with respect to the origin on the graph. With the other price determinants (income and the price of related goods) unchanged, he can charge a higher price than for the old brand, without losing customers to a marked extent, in view of their greater attachment to what he is offering them now: his sales curve is less elastic. Or else he can charge the same price and enjoy a considerable rise in sales: his sales curve is farther to the right. The purpose of quality differentiation is to reap what quality differentiation has to offer—a degree of monopoly power over the price by widening the gap between his type of product and somebody else's offerings in the vicinity.

(2) It is different with product variation by means of advertising and salesmanship. The variety of the article stays the same. There is no change in the materials, style, service, or terms of sale. But advertising, by puffing the distinctive features of the article, real or imaginary, aims to implant in the buyer a greater desire for the object, as well as to inform a wider public. The purpose is alike to make the demand less elastic for the existing unchanged article and to shift the demand to the right. Quality variation addresses itself to the product; it manipulates the product. Sales promotion addresses itself to the customer; it manipulates the customer. The former process makes a product; the latter makes a demand. The one process seeks to adapt the product to the expected demand; the other process strives to influence the demand for the given product.

Differentiated products may be close substitutes for one another, with a high cross-elasticity, or remote substitutes, with a low cross-elasticity. It seems reasonable to believe that when there are many sellers and accordingly many types of a given product the chances are that for a given variety of the article there may be found other varieties which are close substitutes. Thus it may be easy to obtain a close substitute for a given make of soap, inasmuch as numerous kinds of soap are to be found on the market. In the large array of soaps there may very likely be a gradual dispersion of the elements which go to form a buyer's preferences. It is for this reason, chiefly, that in the discussion of monopolistic competition, where many producers are implied, the reference is commonly made to close substitutes and small differences in price from one make to a neighboring make. Should a commodity face remote substitutes, it may be classed as an example of monopoly.

DEMAND FOR A DIFFERENTIATED PRODUCT

The demand for a particular brand of an article produced in monopolistic competition is different from the demand for a given firm's commodity in pure competition. In both cases we are dealing with the sales curve of one firm among many firms. But in this instance the product of each seller is different. At a given price for its variety of product the firm may not sell any amount which it can possibly produce because many consumers are attached to other varieties. To increase its sales, our firm will have to lower the price and attract customers away from these rival varieties. In other words, the demand curve confronting the firm is not horizontal. Likewise, because some buyers are loyal to the given variant, the producer of it can within narrow limits raise his price without fear of losing many customers. Besides, each producer feels that since he is one among many sellers, the trade which his price reduction will attract from each of his rivals will not be appreciable and will not provoke retaliation on their part. All this suggests that he is not in complete isolation, pricewise, from his companions. He must keep an eye on what his rivals in his neighborhood charge; and he can deviate up or down.

In the light of these considerations, the demand curve for the differentiated article of a given firm is very elastic, in some price ranges, but not horizontal. If the firm raises the price substantially, it may lose a great deal of patronage because the varieties sold by the other firms are commonly not remote and not undesirable substitutes. The price is not apt to be far away from the price which would rule under pure competition; that is, if the articles sold by the various firms were homogeneous.

But the fact that the sales curve of a given make of product does slope to the right signifies that the producer possesses a degree of monopoly power over his price. (Why?)

II. The Equilibrium Price

The analysis of price formation in an industry exemplifying monopolistic competition may follow two roads. One approach leans on adjustments through the entry or exit of firms. The other approach reaches equilibrium primarily by the price adjustments of existing firms. The first road takes us along more or less familiar territory; the second road involves such vehicles as Professor Chamberlin's demand curves dd' and DD'.

A. Pricing: The First Approach

Let us be clear first about our assumptions. We assume numerous firms, each producing a somewhat different variety of the product. There is no barrier to the entry of new firms. The given pattern of product differentiation among the producers is assumed to be unchanged, so that adjustments are not made by product variation. Sales costs are left out of consideration. For the sake of simplicity, we assume that all firms are nearly alike with respect to their demand and cost curves, and that the price and output changes made by one firm may affect many other firms to a more or less equal degree. We assume finally a constant-cost industry, so that the appearance and exodus of firms and the correlated enlargement or shrinking of the industry leave unchanged the external economies and therefore the cost curves of the firm.

In order to arrive at the equilibrium price, let us assume that each firm in the industry is in the position portrayed in Figure 50. By industry we mean the large family of firms producing the many varieties of one given article, with high cross-elasticities. The demand curve D represents the various outputs which any firm can sell at various prices. Related to this average revenue curve is MR, the marginal revenue curve. We may as well admit that both the D and the MR curves ought to be much less steep than they are in this diagram as well as in Figures 51, 52, and 53. But this steepness of curves simplifies our discussion. The two cost curves are familiar; they are the short-run average and marginal cost curves for each firm. As usual, the producer has adjusted his price-output combination so as to equate marginal revenue and short-run marginal cost. The profit-maximizing output is OA and the price is AB.

The firm and the industry are in short-run equilibrium, but not in long-run equilibrium. When entry is free, long-run static equilibrium is established when pure profits are squeezed out, that is, when price is brought into equality with short-run and long-run average costs. In the situation at hand the firms reap a unit profit of *BC*. This situation is symbolized by the fact that the demand curve *D* *intersects* the short-run average cost curve SAC, instead of being *tangent* to SAC.

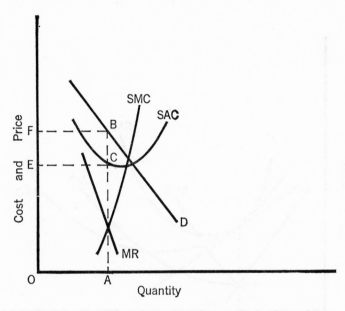

FIGURE 50. *Short-Run Price in Monopolistic Competition*

The reason for the high price and excessive profit is the fewness of sellers. In the long run, the corrective can take the form *either* of the entry of new firms *or* of independent price reductions by the firms, each seeking to enlarge its sales at the expense of its companions. The second corrective (price reduction) must, generally, be ruled out. When there are few firms in the industry, each one is reluctant to lower its price—knowing that it may gain little by the move, since its rivals will, in self defense, follow suit with similar price cuts. But, in our assumption, there is no barrier to the first corrective, entry.

In the long period these profits will invite new firms into the industry, each producing a make different from the varieties already on the market. We notice that the concept of entry is somewhat strained here. By entry we mean customarily that the newcomer is reproducing the commodity. But when product differentiation is involved, be it in monopolistic competition or differentiated oligopoly, entry designates the appearance of a new firm with an article different from the variants already in existence in the industry.

As new firms invade the field the existing custom is roughly divided among more sellers, so that at various prices each firm will sell smaller quantities of its particular make in a given period of time. The demand curve *D* shifts down and to the left, as in Figure 51. If new firms keep

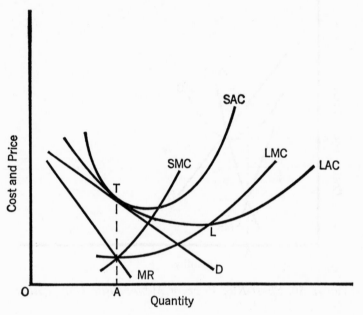

FIGURE 51. *Long-Run Price Formation by Monopolistic Competition*

on entering, it may happen that the *D* curve will descend *below* the average cost curve. This would mean that the market is so crowded with firms that sales are insufficient to cover average costs. In time, some firms will leave the industry. Equilibrium will be reached, by both the firms and the industry, when no pure profit is obtained and when, therefore, the entry and exit of firms cease. The earmark of such a situation is that the demand curve *D* is *tangent* to the LAC and SAC curves, and does not intersect them. In Figure 51, the point of tangency is *T*; it lies directly above the intersection of the marginal revenue curve MR and the long-run and short-run marginal cost curves LMC and SMC. The equilibrium price and quantity are respectively AT and OA. As in the competitive long-run equilibrium of the firm, price or average revenue equals long-run (and short-run) average cost; only now it is not minimum long-run average cost: point T is higher up than point L.

Our assumption of essential similarity, with respect to demand and cost, among the firms in the industry can be dropped without appreciably affecting our conclusions. In reality, firms differ. Some have more monopoly power than others. Some have many attached buyers, others few. With the entry of a new variety of the product some of the existing firms are injured more than others. When demand rises some make substantial profits, others earn little above the competitive level. But these considerations will generally induce only minor deviations from the results of the forgoing analysis.

MONOPOLY AND EXCESS PROFITS

Let us take another look at the long-run equilibrium price AT. It is higher than the competitive price would be. Like a monopoly price, it is above marginal cost. And yet it contains no profit above the ordinary competitive return. Price AT is a monopoly price without a monopoly profit in it. This unique long-run equilibrium price is characteristic of monopolistic competition. It contains no pure profit because of the freedom of entry. It stays above the competitive price because the product of each firm is differentiated and consequently harbors a monopoly element.

This unique price points a moral. The absence of a profit is no sign of the absence of a monopoly element. As we saw in Chapter IX, the presence of profits or of abnormal profits does not necessarily point to the existence of monopoly power. Under pure competition, in the short normal period, an increased demand for the product may breed considerable profit. He skates on thin ice who identifies profits with monopoly and monopoly with profits.

"WASTES OF COMPETITION"

It is well to notice another peculiarity of monopolistic competition. The equilibrium output OA is smaller than the optimum output which rules under pure competition. In monopolistic competition the equilibrium of the firm is established, not at the minimum long-run average cost, but at a point where the long-run average cost may still be declining. Other things equal, under pure competition each firm may yield a larger output and accordingly fewer firms may satisfy the demand. Under monopolistic competition we are apt to witness too many firms, all running under optimum capacity, all charging a higher than competitive price, and all exercising their art of advertising against each other in the effort to retain customers and to take them away from each other.

It looks like duplication of plant and selling effort. In many a sizable city there are many underutilized grocery stores, drugstores, clothing stores, gasoline stations, small restaurants, small laundries, and barber shops. Waste and maldistribution of resources are involved in this duplication and underutilization. The "wastes of competition" that we hear about are in reality the wastes of monopolistic competition. These wastes, it may be observed, have at least one redeeming feature: satisfying our desire for variety. Fewer styles and makes can bring the economies of large-scale industry. But the customer will be restricted in his choices, and innovation may become less frequent. Besides, there is the danger of jumping from the frying pan of monopolistic competition into the fire of oligopoly.

B. Pricing: The Second Approach

The second approach to the analysis of price determination under monopolistic competition imports the use of Professor Chamberlin's two types of demand curves dd' and DD'.

THE dd' AND DD' DEMAND CURVES

Let us consider an industry producing portable radios. We assume that there are many firms in this industry, each firm making its own brand. A given seller in this group may feel that he can vary the price of his type of radio without provoking the other firms into reacting with a price change of their own. Let us assume that the other firms keep on charging the constant price of $40 for their brand of portable radio, indifferent to the fact that our firm is indulging in price changes. The demand for its type of radio may then be represented by the first two columns in Table 14 and by the top dd' curve in Figure 52. Both this demand schedule and this demand curve outline the various price-quantity combinations for our firm's product on the assumption that the rival firms continue to charge the fixed sum of $40 for their makes. The dd' curve is apt to be rather elastic and almost horizontal. By lowering the price a little our firm can succeed in detaching many customers from rival brands since the other sellers have not chosen to match our firm's price reduction. Conversely, if our firm raises its price somewhat above $40 as the other firms hold fast to the price of $40, it may lose a good deal of patronage to its rivals.

Suppose that the unvarying price charged by the other firms is not $40 but $30. How will our firm's *dd'* curve look then? The answer is provided by columns 1 and 4 and by the second *dd'* curve. Column 4 in Table 14 indicates the number of radios which our firm can sell at the corresponding prices specified in column 1 on the assumption that the rival firms in the industry stick to the price of $30. Now at each price our firm will sell fewer radios; the figures in column 4 are smaller than in column 2. The reason for the drop in the demand is that now the other

TABLE 14. *Two Types of Demand Schedules*

(1) P	(2) Q (d)	(3) Q (D)	(4) Q (d)
$50	750	900	600
45	850	925	700
40	950	950	800
35	1,050	975	900
30	1,150	1,000	1,000
25	1,250	1,025	1,100
20	1,350	1,050	1,200
15	1,450	1,075	1,300

sellers hold to a price of $30 instead of $40. At this lower price more customers will stay loyal to the old firms and will not switch to our firm as it reduces its price. At a price of $25 our firm will sell 1,250 radios per unit of time when the price of the rivals is $40, but it will sell only 1,100 radios when their price is $30. The second *dd'* curve therefore lies to the left of and below the top *dd'* curve.

Assume now that our firm expects all the other firms to react to its every price move with a corresponding price change of their own. A lowering of its price can hardly be expected to swing customers away from the rivals when the rivals too reduce their price. The sales will rise for each firm simply because at a lower price, other things equal, radios sell more briskly. This type of demand is illustrated by columns 1 and 3, and by curve *DD'*. Curve *DD'* is less elastic than curve *dd'* for the same price ranges. It represents a demand schedule as it looks to each firm when all firms behave alike pricewise: when no one can steal a march on the others.

For each firm there is only one *DD'* curve; but many *dd'* curves are possible. With each fixed price assumed for the other firms, our firm faces a new *dd'* curve as its demand schedule. Thus the bottom *dd'* curve in

Figure 52 may fit the case when the constant price of the rival firms is $15. Each *dd'* curve has one point in common with the *DD'* curve. The top *dd'* curve has point *A* in common, corresponding to $40; the middle *dd'* curve meets *DD'* at *B*, corresponding to $30; and the bottom *dd'* curve

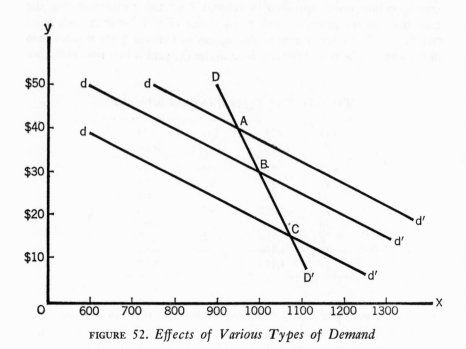

FIGURE 52. *Effects of Various Types of Demand*

cuts *DD'* at point *C*. We can imagine the *dd'* curve sliding down the *DD'* curve and intersecting it at lower and lower points.

THE EQUILIBRIUM PRICE

We are now ready to consider price formation under monopolistic competition by the second approach. We begin with the portable-radio industry in disequilibrium. For one reason or another an excessive price rules the market. But this time the number of firms is not small; it approximates the number proper to ultimate equilibrium. The corrective of the maladjusted situation will seek its way through price reductions.

Let us assume that the price is as high as *A*, which stands for $40 (Figure 52). It seems to our firm that if it reduces its price it will sell more radios without provoking retaliatory price cutting by its many companions in the industry because it will lure only a little trade away from each one of them. The sales schedule will appear to our firm like *dd'* pass-through point *A*.

Here we come upon the usually simple and interesting circumstance. The anticipations, calculations, and behavior of our firm are not unique to it. The thoughts guiding our firm are the thoughts motivating the other firms too. The firms are not far apart with respect to their demand and cost situations; their conduct is therefore not dissimilar. Our firm is not the only one that lowers the price. *All* the other firms *cut* the price, each one counting on the others *not* to do so. This behavior is of the same order as the price cutting of each seller in pure competition, as was noticed in Chapter IX.

Accordingly, as our firm reduces the price from $40 to $30 it does not find itself moving along the *dd'* curve; and $30 is not a point on this *dd'* curve to the right of point *A*. All the other firms have also reduced the price to $30, roughly speaking. The outcome is that our firm, in common with all the other firms, finds itself at point *B* on a *DD'* curve. The situation is similar when the firms reduce the price below $30. Each firm keeps on lowering the price in the expectation that its demand curve is like *dd'*. But the effect of this behavior, when *all* the firms are considered together, is to nullify this expectation and bring about the reality of a curve like

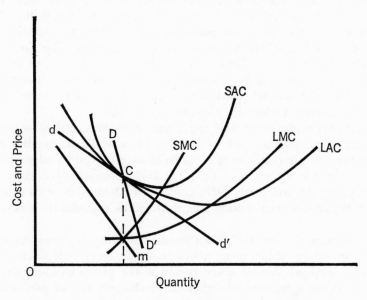

FIGURE 53. *Interrelations Among Types of Demand*

DD' for each firm. The behavior prompted by the prospect of the dd' curve eventuates in a DD' curve. Not retaliatory reaction of the other firms to our firm's price reduction, but *independent* motivation and calculation bring about this result.

How far will the price cutting go? It will continue until the price is low enough to cease being out of touch with cost. The equilibrium of the firm is attained when the dd' curve is tangent to the average cost curve. Assume that the point of tangency is C (Figure 52). At point C average revenue will equal average cost, short-run and long-run.

The equilibrium situation can be better pictured on a separate diagram. Let us turn to Figure 53. Curve m is the marginal revenue curve for dd'. The other curves are familiar. Point C is common to dd' and DD'; and since dd' touches the LAC curve at C it follows that DD' cuts the LAC curve at point C.[1] Except for the demand curves, this diagram does not differ from Figure 51, which portrays the equilibrium position of the firm as viewed by the first analytical approach. Nor are the equilibrium equations in this situation different from the equations indicated there. It is not necessary to recite them again.

THE dd' AND DD' CURVES IN OTHER MARKETS

The student no doubt has begun to suspect that these two types of curves have their relevance in other markets as well. Under *pure competition*, the horizontal demand curve facing each individual firm is of the dd' type, since no seller is compelled to take into account what the reaction of the other sellers will be to his price changes. The single-firm *monopolist*, not having effective rivals, can treat his demand curve as of the dd' kind. Also, since he practically constitutes the whole industry for his product, the demand schedule can appear to him at the same time as DD' in character. To him, the two curves coincide.

These curves also make their appearance in various cases of *oligopoly*. In independent pricing, each of the few firms would be mindful in its calculations of the reactions of rivals to its own moves. Its sales schedule will seem to it in the nature of DD'. The *kinky demand* curve, as we shall see, is partly dd' and partly DD'. Under *price leadership*, with collusive action, the demand confronting each firm will be regarded by it as of the DD' kind.

The concept dd' and DD' is not an idle plaything. It draws our attention to an influential human trait. The trait may assert itself when a large group is involved. Almost every person in the group will secretly bolt away from the agreement to curtail the production, say, of potatoes. He

---

[1] R. Triffin, *Monopolistic Competition and General Equilibrium Theory* (Cambridge, Harvard University Press, 1940), p. 32, n. 27.

expects that the others will not be as smart as he is. So he behaves in accordance with the dd' path and produces more potatoes than ever, expecting everybody else to curtail production and drive up the price for him, so that his large crop will bring him a fortune. The trouble is that everybody else makes the same assumption—and next year, despite the agreement, the overproduction of potatoes will be astonishing; prices will collapse. Each individual was thinking on the basis of dd', but the result was DD'.

III. Nonprice Competition

The discussion of price determination in the preceding section assumed that competition among the many sellers of a diversified product took the form of price change alone. But when the product, whether offered by many sellers or few, is not homogeneous, another type of competition almost invariably comes into existence. It is nonprice competition, a type of competition which ought to be familiar to the consuming public at large because it affects mostly final consumption goods. Before 1933, the date of the appearance of Chamberlin's classic, this type of competition was scarcely known in the literature of economic analysis.

A. Types of Nonprice Competition

The phases of nonprice competition almost coincide with the different ways of achieving product variation. If we assume that each seller offers only one brand of a product instead of several brands of it, nonprice competition among sellers and product differentiation become identical. Be that as it may, the many kinds of nonprice competition can be classified under two heads: product competition and promotional competition.

(1) PRODUCT COMPETITION

First comes the type of competition which concentrates on the *quality* of the article itself. The effort is made to tailor the commodity to suit the taste of the buyer, so that he will develop a strong preference for the particular style of the merchandise and confer on the seller a degree of monopoly power over the price to be charged.

By quality variation and quality competition we mean two things. (a) One type refers primarily to the physical aspects of the commodity; to changes in the materials, workmanship, durability, style, size, shape, color, packaging, and the attractiveness and separate usefulness of the container. Two dresses may be identical with respect to all of these elements except one, say, color. They may compete with each other for patronage and they may command different prices.

(b) The other type of quality variation or product competition relates to differences in the service associated with the sale. The convenience of the location of the store, its furnishings and general atmosphere, and the personality of the people attending to the customer are examples. To these must be added a list of items called terms or conditions of sale: promptness of delivery, readiness to accept returned goods, willingness to make alterations, the guarantee of service and repair for a certain length of time, the trade-in allowance, and the credit facilities. A variation in one of these considerations may make a difference between two otherwise identical goods.

(2) PROMOTIONAL COMPETITION

Second comes a category of nonprice competition which relates to the *promotional* activity aimed to increase the demand for a given product. The purpose is to modify the buyer's preferences, so that more of the good will be sold at the going price or nearly the same volume of it at a higher price. The attempt is to instill in the customer the belief that the given brand possesses desirable qualities distinct from and superior to those of other brands in the chain of related articles. Wherever quality variation is possible, promotional activity is most likely to make an appearance. The consumer must be informed about the unique features of the commodity and he must be properly impressed by them.

The means used in promotional ventures constitute the legend-charged professions which capture the imagination of the young people in our schools—advertising and salesmanship. By constant repetition in such advertising media as newspapers, popular journals, radio, television, handbills, and billboards, the consumer is sprayed with adjectives in praise of each offering. Salesmanship by personal contact, public-relations outlays, labels, brands, and trade-marks work in the same direction; also window displays, show cases, demonstrations, free samples, and door-to-door canvassing.

Not all producers advertise. In cases of pure competition, where the product is homogeneous, the claim that the output of one concern is different from the output of another concern will serve no purpose. The wheat raised by farmer Black would, despite advertising representations, be regarded by the buyer as identical with the wheat raised by farmer White. Moreover, it would not occur to either farmer to advertise since he can sell at the prevailing price all the wheat that he can efficiently produce. Without influence over the price in the market, he knows that an advertising venture would be a total loss. It is not necessary to advertise; nor does it pay.

Conversely, if firms do not advertise, the inference is safe that their product is homogeneous. It must be mentioned, however, that in various instances of pure oligopoly or even pure competition the group of producers as a whole may advertise their product in order to increase the demand for it by capturing trade away from the sellers of other goods. A fruit growers' association may advertise its commodity to inform and impress people into using more of it.

It is not always easy to distinguish between quality competition and promotional competition. Packaging an article in loud-colored paper may express the desire of the firm to cater to a latent demand for the article generally. But this may also be a step to change the demand of consumers by drawing their attention to the object with a more striking and more appealing exterior. The kind of wrapping paper used may thus constitute a selling cost. Paper mills specializing in making paper for packaging experiment with the appearance of their product as to color, texture, and the like, in the belief that attractive and striking wrapping paper advertises the product inside.

NONPRICE COMPETITION AND THE ALLOCATION OF RESOURCES

In the evaluation of nonprice competition, especially of advertising, various questions can be raised which would take us far afield with protracted discussions. Here we shall deal briefly with one question.

Nonprice competition introduces a new aspect into the problem of the allocation of resources. It can be argued that some or much of the so-called quality variation indulged in by many firms and some or much of the resulting multiplicity of brands are of spurious, fictitious character; that often product variation exemplifies a distinction without a difference. Moreover, the consumer is confronted with diverse claims, varieties, sizes, and prices for a given product, and he cannot easily reduce these elements to a comparable basis for an intelligent choice. The consumer must rely on what he is told over the advertising channels; and he pays accordingly. A much-advertised inferior product may sell for more than a less-advertised superior product.[2] Among essentially similar goods those nationally advertised may command a higher price than those less well known.

Often the customer would buy not at all or only at a lower price if he knew that there was only a remote resemblance between what the article

[2] M. M. Bober, "Price and Production Policies," *American Economic Review*, Supplement, Vol. XXXII, no. 2 (June, 1942), pp. 45–46.

was represented to be and what it actually was. The result is a maldistribution of resources toward making goods which the consumer would decline to buy at ruling prices if he were more adequately informed. This serious defect may be remedied as the consumer is better educated about his purchases and as a greater insistence on less extravagance and more truth in advertising develops.

It may be contended, as a corollary, that advertising and salesmanship, having for their function the creation and modification of demand, have dethroned the consumer, who, through his initial demand for goods, is supposed to rule as the sovereign regulator of production. Instead, the firms produce the articles of their own choice and then they proceed to work on the buyer to make him like what they want him to buy. The producer makes the article first; then by an advertising campaign he makes a demand for it also. Thus where nonprice competition prevails, the *producer* is apt to be the sovereign.

There is a measure of validity in this line of thought, but it is of limited applicability. It would apply more extensively, in the area of nonprice competition, if the firm were in the habit of deciding on the article which it will make without reference to the desires of the consumer and in full confidence that it can manipulate the buyer into favoring its particular creation. But this version does not square with the facts. The producer of one variant of a commodity knows that there are in the field many other producers making other variants and that they will all advertise and compete for the consumer's patronage. Confronted though he is with confusing claims, it is nonetheless the consumer alone who ultimately makes the choice of the variant on which he will spend his money. Aware of this fact, the producer cannot completely ignore the tastes and preferences of the consumer and try to beguile him with empty words. Thus, despite examples of spurious variation in quality and exaggerated and misleading claims, there is a substantial residue of real product improvement. When thinking about such a question it is steadying and instructive to look about us and consider the changes in the commodities and in the service going with them which have been made in the recent past. We shall be impressed by the fact that improvements are in evidence almost wherever we look, at least in service if not in quality.

B. Selling Costs

PRODUCTION COSTS AND SELLING COSTS

When the product is homogeneous, competition among firms can only take the route of price reduction; producers undersell each other until the equilibrium price is reached. The problem of the firm is to choose the price-output combination which will maximize gains or minimize losses. But when the product is susceptible of differentiation, two additional competitive weapons are forged—quality variation and selling activity. The competing firm can then employ three methods: price reduction, product improvement, and the attempt to reshape the demand of the buyer.

When the product can be differentiated, the firm is concerned with two types of costs, production costs and selling costs. Production costs are those incurred in making a given variety of a commodity. They embrace quality variation as defined above and they include workmanship, packaging, service, and the terms of sale. Selling costs represent the costs of all the activities directed to persuading the buyer to change his standard of valuation so as to raise his demand for the given article. To repeat, these costs include such outlays as those on advertising, salesmen, samples, and premium coupons. Like production costs, selling costs can ultimately be resolved into the outlays on the services of the four factors of production, land, labor, capital, and entrepreneurship. As has already been mentioned, at times no sharp line of division can be drawn between production costs and selling costs.

It is not easy to generalize about the responses of consumers to repeated stimuli administered by advertising or any kindred effort. But it is probably reasonable to expect that in many instances selling costs are subject to something in the nature of diminishing returns.

With a product of a given quality selling at a given price, successive doses of selling outlays will raise the total sales, at first by larger and larger increments but after a certain point by progressively diminishing increments. The reason is that there are two sets of forces involved which work against each other; some tend to cause increasing returns in response to selling outlays, and others tend to bring about decreasing returns. Up to a certain volume of selling expenditures the first set of forces overcomes the effect of the second set. Beyond this point the net effect is the other way around. The outcome is that up to a certain output the unit selling cost falls and beyond this critical output it rises.

Let us consider briefly these two sets of forces. (1) Two factors tend to account for increasing returns as outlays on sales promotion expand. *One*, consumers are in the habit of buying a certain variety of a given product; they become attached to this variety. Advertising another variety attempts to break the habit and dissolve the attachment. A small selling effort may scarcely make an impression on the buyer. But larger expenditures, permitting repetitive and intensive impingements on his consciousness, may succeed in turning the buyer to the new brand of this product. When they do, its sales become much larger. *Two*, as a more ambitious selling program is undertaken, the usual internal economies make an appearance in the promotional activity. Greater administrative skill, better salesmen, and more popular comedians may be recruited to work on the buyer. Up to a certain point, as the volume of advertising is increased the sequel is lower advertising rates per page or per minute.

(2) Then there are the counteracting factors. An extended sales campaign strives to achieve two results: to sell more to customers already well disposed toward the given merchandise and to reach out for customers loyal to other brands. Each additional sale to either of these two categories of customers entails a progressively mounting promotional expense. To sell more to an old customer, rising increments of pressure and therefore of expense are required to induce him to relinquish desirable alternative expenditures in order to release purchasing power for the extra units of the product urged on him. Similarly, to reshape the desires of a widening circle of new customers, more outlay is needed to overcome their resistance to the substitution of a new brand for an old one. Thus both the intensive and the extensive cultivation of buyers involves rising selling costs per unit of the commodity sold.

THE OPTIMUM COMBINATION

In the search for maximum gains the firm in a market under pure competition has to contend with a restricted number of variables. Accepting the ruling price for his commodity, the seller consults his costs and adjusts his output to equate marginal cost and marginal revenue. Not so with the seller in a market under monopolistic competition. He can compete by varying the price, by varying the quality of his brand of the product, and by changing the promotional program. He has to choose that combination of these three elements which, in the perspective of his costs (production costs and selling costs combined), will yield a maximum profit. The problem is now more complicated. Several combinations are possible.

(a) In pure competition, the firm will sell its output at the market price. No choice of any other price is fruitfully open. But in monopolistic competition, a given output of a given type of product can be disposed of at a variety of prices, depending on the size of the *selling effort* directed at the buyers. The greater the selling activity the higher can be, within limits, the unit price of the given output. Given the product and given the output, the question facing the firm is: which selling expenditure will permit charging a price at which, in the light of costs, including the projected selling costs, maximum profits can be attained?

(b) Likewise, in pure competition, at a given price the firm will tend to sell one definite output, governed by equating price to marginal cost.

But under monopolistic competition the volume of a given brand which can be sold at a given price will depend again on the selling expenditure. There is an optimum selling cost which will make possible a sales volume likely to provide the highest aggregate gain.

What has been said in the above two paragraphs about the influence of selling expenditures applies to the role of quality variation: (c) With a given selling outlay and a given output, the price charged can be higher as the *quality* of the product is improved. A certain combination of outlay on the change in quality and the correlated price which can be charged for the article will yield a maximum profit. (d) Similarly, given the unit price and given the promotional outlay, sales can rise with the improvement in the product.

Two further profit-seeking combinations may be mentioned: (e) The price and the corresponding output can be decided upon; and the choice is to be made with regard to the quality change and the selling effort. These last two variables are in inverse relation to each other. Thus the largest gain may be derived when the quality is permitted to deteriorate somewhat but a greater effort is made to push the product. (f) Lastly, there may be the decision to fix the quality of the product as well as the aggregate selling expenditure, and to treat price and output as variables with which to experiment. However, in view of these two constants, a degree of freedom is hardly left for experiments. The choice of product and promotional expense governs the demand and the marginal revenue schedules. With a given product facing him and a given sales pressure exerted on him, the consumer will react in a given manner. Likewise, the decision regarding the quality of the product to be made and the selling outlay will define costs. There is only one way, then, in which to derive the optimum profit; namely, by equating the predetermined marginal revenue to the predetermined marginal cost.

It is important to stress that ordinarily the firm is compelled to choose the best combination of all three elements—price, product, and promotion—simultaneously. The problem before the firm is: which product variety, at which price, and with which selling cost will be most promising of profits? In some comparatively rare instances one of these elements may be kept fixed and the choice can be centered on the other two elements. The public may be strongly habituated to a 5¢ bottle of soft drinks. The firm may decide to keep the price constant and concentrate on changing the quality of the product (or the size of the bottle) and on varying the selling program.

But ordinarily the firm has to reckon with all the three variables; and the analysis of the situation is complex. Even the use of the indifference-curves approach or of tabular presentation does not make it convenient to take into account the three elements at once. At least one variable must be assumed as being given. This variable is usually the particular quality of the good. Given the product, that is, the brand of it, the choice is made with respect to (1) the selling expense and (2) either the size of the output to offer for sale or the price to charge. The indifference-curves analysis is rather complicated.[3] We shall present the tabular exposition of the problem.

Table 15 illustrates the determination of maximum profit from the sale

TABLE 15. *Relation Between Output, Selling Cost and Price—and Maximum Profit*

Selling Cost		Output, units						
		5	10	15	20	25	30	35
$100	Unit price	$ 25	$ 20	$ 15	$ 10	$ 5	$ 3	$ 2
	Total receipts	125	200	225	200	125	90	70
	Aggregate outlays	105	110	112	115	120	130	145
	Total profit	20	90	*113*	85	5	−40	−75
$200	Unit price	26	24	20	18	15	10	5
	Total receipts	130	240	300	360	375	300	175
	Aggregate outlays	205	210	212	215	220	230	245
	Total profit	−75	30	88	145	*155*	70	−70
$300	Unit price	30	28	25	20	18	15	10
	Total receipts	150	280	375	400	450	450	350
	Aggregate outlays	305	310	312	315	320	330	345
	Total profit	−155	−30	63	85	*130*	120	5
$400	Unit price	35	30	26	22	20	18	12
	Total receipts	175	300	390	440	500	540	420
	Aggregate outlays	405	410	412	415	420	430	445
	Total profit	−230	−110	−22	25	80	*110*	−25

of one given variety of a product out of several varieties open to the firm. The top row indicates a succession of outputs ranging from 5 units to 35. The first column on the left shows selling outlays, growing from $100 to $400. In each box are four figures. The top figure specifies the unit price at which the corresponding output can be sold. The second figure stands for total receipts, obtained by multiplying the price by the relevant sales volume. The third figure refers to the aggregate outlays on the particular output, which depend on the production function, the law of variable proportions, and the cost of the factor-services, including selling

[3] See K. E. Boulding, *Economic Analysis*, rev. ed. (Harper, 1948), pp. 717–726; S. Weintraub, *Price Theory* (Pitman, 1949), pp. 211–215.

costs. The bottom figure indicates the total profit, derived by deducting the third figure from the second figure.

As the selling expenses are extended, the unit price at which each volume is sold can be raised. The total cost, of production and of selling combined, also rises and by the amount equal to the increase in the selling cost. Thus when the selling expenses increase by $100 (as from $200 to $300), the first two figures become larger and the third figure rises by $100, in each box. Obviously the unit price, and accordingly the total revenue, depend on the demand schedule as influenced by the size of the promotional activity. Since total costs rise concomitantly with the selling effort, it does not follow that largest profit will appear in one of the boxes corresponding to the largest promotional program.

In each of the four rows of boxes corresponding to the four selling costs there is one maximum profit. Thus the four large profit figures are $113, $155, $130, and $110. The firm will obtain the largest profit of $155 when it spends $200 on promotional activity and sells an output of 25 units of the one particular variety which it had chosen to produce. At this stage marginal revenue $\left(\dfrac{375 - 360}{25 - 20}\right)$ ought to equal marginal cost $\left(\dfrac{220 - 215}{25 - 20}\right)$. There is no equality in this instance because the figures in the table are not continuous. The gap between neighboring quantities in each row is considerable.

Similar tables can be constructed to find the largest profit from the sale of each of the other varieties of the product which the firm may intend to make. From the series of maximum figures so derived the firm will choose the combination which promises the largest profit. Thus the variety of the product, the selling cost, the output sold, and the price charged can be roughly decided upon by the firm.

SELLING COSTS AND FINAL PRICE

In the previous section we studied price determination on the assumption that selling costs are ruled out. We reached what is called a "tangency" solution. With many sellers of a diversified commodity the equilibrium price of the firm is located by the point of tangency of the average revenue curve and the average cost curve. The solution suggests a "profitless" monopoly price. (See Figures 51 and 53 in this chapter.)

What happens to this equilibrium price when selling costs are taken into consideration, as they must be? The equilibrium price becomes higher, at least in many cases. The considerations leading to this conclusion are as follows: When we deal with many sellers of a differentiated article, and leave selling costs out of account, the resulting price, or the point of tangency, is not far to the left of the lowest point of the average cost curve. In Figure 51, point T is not far to the left of point L. In the neighborhood of the point of tangency the average cost curve is not likely to fall steeply; it usually flattens out as it approaches its minimum height at point L. This means that in this range the economies of larger output are not apt to be considerable. Accordingly when we add selling costs to the production costs the combined average cost curve is lifted, so that the point of tangency to this new higher curve is very likely to be above the point of tangency obtained when selling costs are ignored. Suppose that advertising activity does not merely resolve into the firms' taking trade away from each other but stimulates sales for each concern and, inducing internal economies, lowers the cost of *production*. Even then it may be doubtful that the lower cost will, except occasionally, cancel out the promotional outlays and result in a lower price to the consumer.

IV. Observations on Monopolistic Competition

The many firms in this market produce at a rate less than optimum and charge a price higher than under pure competition; there is a discrepancy between price and marginal cost. The efficiency of larger output by the firm may fall short of that attained in pure competition. Also, the number of firms in a given industry, comprising the family of related goods, exceeds the number that would prevail in a purely competitive market.

As regards the magnitude of these differences between the two market structures, two positions are entertained by economists. Some hold that these differences are minor and that in these respects monopolistic competition closely resembles pure competition. They hold, then, that the *allocation* of resources, the *efficiency* of scale attending the growth of the industry, and the price situation do not depart significantly from the expected performance of pure competition.[4] Other economists take the view that the differences are substantial and that production in the monopolistically competitive market is associated with noticeable waste. The rise in output is too small, the price is too high, and there are too many firms, with the consequence that the allocation of resources is distorted and the efficiency of long-run scale is appreciably below optimum.[5]

Both camps agree, however, that monopolistic competition stresses prod-

[4] For example, J. S. Bain, *Pricing, Distribution, and Employment,* revised ed. (New York, Holt, 1953), p. 373; M. J. Bowman and G. L. Bach, *Economic Analysis and Public Policy,* 2nd ed. (New York, Prentice-Hall, 1949), p. 396.
[5] For example, E. H. Chamberlin, *The Theory of Monopolistic Competition,* 6th ed. (Cambridge, Harvard University Press, 1948), chap. 5; K. E. Boulding, *Economic Analysis,* revised ed. (New York, Harper, 1948), pp. 578, 595, 664.

uct variation and advertising activity. It is agreed that some advertising conveys information to the consumer about products, varieties, and qualities, and makes him better acquainted with the ways of satisfying his wants effectively. It is equally agreed that advertising makes possible the low-priced newspaper and popular journals, and provides much entertainment and instruction in the form of radio and television opera, plays, music, round-table discussions, and news reports.

But most economists have question marks about excessive advertising and excessive product variation. As has already been mentioned, the case is inconclusive. Take, for instance, the oft-repeated claim that advertising breeds large-scale production with the accompanying greater efficiency, lower costs, and lower prices to the consumer. Let us examine such claims.

(1) In the first place, advertising does not always lead to large-scale production. When some firms expand their promotional activity other firms may follow suit, in self-defense or in retaliation. An advertising war may break out; and the effect may be self-canceling. If the demand for the product of the industry as a whole fails to rise appreciably, we witness a situation in which all firms advertise, all have spiraling selling costs, and none has enlarged its rate of output. The consumer pays a higher price; but be it noted that the higher price may be matched by the higher utility of the article *induced* by the advertising hubbub.

(2) Assume that on account of combative advertising one or several firms manage to gain in output. They may do so, however, at the expense of other firms whose sales diminish. If the injured firms stay on in business, their costs are high because of the reduced output, and their efficiency in the allocation of resources goes down. It is also conceivable, as Pigou hesitatingly suggests,[6] that a firm inferior in production proper may be more efficient in selling effort than the firm superior in production. If the inefficient firm is enabled by the art of advertising to stay in business or to take custom away from the more efficient firms, there is waste in the economy.

(3) If advertising succeeds in raising the demand for the industry product, thus enabling some firms to grow in size, they may do so at the expense of firms in other industries. The allocation of resources in the injured industries is inadequate. If these injured industries respond, in their turn, with larger promotional programs, the advertising-war theater spreads. Firm takes trade away from firm, industry from industry. Only if, as in times of unemployment, the increased selling effort tends to raise the volume of aggregate spending, are such unfavorable effects of advertising mitigated.

(4) Finally, even if advertising should raise the demand for the product of some firms without encroachment on the sales of other concerns, the

[6] *The Economics of Welfare*, 4th ed. (London, Macmillan, 1932), p. 199.

net result does not necessarily favor the consumer. The promotional effort may have created in the mind of the buyer a wider gap between the product of the successful firm and the rival product; the successful firm may emerge with a wider margin of monopoly power, and a stronger monopoly position suggests little assurance of lower prices to the consumer. The seller may choose to press, by means of continued promotion, the larger output into the market at high prices. Or he may decide to shade the price but to lower the quality of the article at the same time. In fine, all these considerations tend to throw cold water on the unqualified proposition that advertising is the passkey to large-scale production and lower prices.

In economic analysis, the consumer is expected to divide his total expenditure among the various purchases in such a fashion that for each good the same proportion holds between marginal utility and price. It is doubtful, however, that the consumer always behaves this way. First of all, the consumer must be bent on maximizing utility, and he must possess knowledge of the relative attributes of the numerous goods available to him. In reality the consumer is hardly a rational agent pursuing the greatest satisfaction as his prime purpose. He is more a creature of habit, custom, conformity, and inertia, swayed by fleeting emotions and impressions and prone to follow the crowd. He is inadequately informed about the materials, ingredients, workmanship, and durability of goods. He is manipulated by misleading advertising claims which often stress the superficial aspects of goods, irrelevant brand names, and spurious catchwords.[7]

However, in evaluating the behavior of the consumer certain considerations tend to give us pause. In some instances the disutility of stopping to investigate the competing commodities and to ponder over the possible choices may outweigh the increment in utility brought by the wiser choice. It is painful to think, and not to move in the established groove. Again, things are not what they are (whatever this means in philosophy) but what people think they are. If the consumer is influenced by what the radio jingle tells him about the particular cigarette, he derives more satisfaction from the smoke than he would without benefit of jingles. Consumer demand does not spring up in any case by spontaneous generation. It is bred in the consumer by a variety of social factors, including

[7] Perhaps Francis A. Walker, a prominent economist of a former generation, is still not far from the truth when he states: "On the other side is the 'customer,' a creature of custom, as the term implies; often ignorant in the widest sense of the word, unintelligent and untrained; always and necessarily ignorant in the special sense of being unacquainted with the conditions which should determine price, not knowing what a commodity ought to cost, and, in the case of many classes of commodities, unable to judge of the quality of the goods offered, perhaps at the mercy of the dealer in the matter of the measure or the weight." *Political Economy* (New York, Holt, 1888), p. 109.

group attitudes and scales of value. It is difficult to discern which of these factors molding consumer demand are to be set down as legitimate, and which as manipulative.

Nonetheless it is to be admitted that much of the salesmanship that envelops the consumer is not calculated to inform him about the want-satisfying attributes of an article, but is meant to appeal to his irrational impulses, to his emotions, ignorance, vanity, and emulation. Much advertising presses on the consumer flimsy gadgets, trifling improvements, shoddy merchandise, and adulterated goods. Such goods the consumer would buy not at all, or at a much reduced price or in considerably smaller quantities, if he knew the truth about them. If consumers were better educated about consumption, they would make choices more conducive to maximum satisfaction from the disposal of their money income.

SUMMARY

Let us sum up the gist of monopolistic competition. The strongest point in favor of this type of market is variety of product. It offers the customer a choice of quality, color, size, and other attributes, instead of the homogeneous standardized product under pure competition. It is difficult, however, to think of other advantages.

The shortcomings are substantial. Free entry breeds, sooner or later, a multiplication of firms, each running a smaller output per unit of time than the output of pure competition, each charging a somewhat higher price than in pure competition, but without reaping a profit. (Why?) Easy entry normally squeezes out the potential profit. Entry stops when the profit of the existing old firms has dwindled to next to nothing. Then the industry is in equilibrium. Should firms insist on entering the field, the equilibrium will be deranged, and losses will begin to develop. Firms will leave the formerly green pastures, and equilibrium will be redressed, more or less. When the industry is in long-run equilibrium it means that the number of firms stays fixed. The waste of excessive advertising is compounded with the waste of undersized firms.

The following statement is no doubt a gross exaggeration but it is worth thinking about: a salesman is a person who has what it takes to take what you have.

SUGGESTED READINGS

Abbott, L. *Quality and Competition.* New York, Columbia University Press, 1955.

Bain, J. S. *Pricing, Distribution, and Employment,* revised ed., chap. 7. New York, Holt, 1953.

Borden, N. H. *The Economic Effects of Advertising.* Chicago, Irwin, 1942.

Boulding, K. E. *Economic Analysis,* revised ed., pp. 570–580, 717–726. New York, Harper, 1948.

Brems, H. *Product Equilibrium Under Monopolistic Competition.* Cambridge, Harvard University Press, 1951.

Buchanan, N. S. "Advertising Expenditures: A Suggested Treatment," *Journal of Political Economy,* Vol. L (August, 1942), pp. 537–557.

Burns, A. R. *The Decline of Competition,* chap. 8. New York, McGraw-Hill, 1936.

Chamberlin, E. H. *The Theory of Monopolistic Competition,* 6th ed., chaps. 4–7. Cambridge, Harvard University Press, 1948.

Gregory, P. M. "Fashion and Monopolistic Competition," *Journal of Political Economy,* Vol. LVI (February, 1948), pp. 69–75.

Leftwich, R. H. *The Price System and Resource Allocation,* revised ed., chap. XII. New York, Holt, Rinehart and Winston, 1960.

Lever, E. A. *Advertising and Economic Theory.* Oxford, Oxford University Press, 1947.

Machlup, F. *The Economics of Sellers' Competition,* chap. 6. Baltimore, The Johns Hopkins Press, 1952.

Nelson, S., and Keim, W. G. *Price Behavior and Business Policy,* Part I, chaps. 3, 4. Washington, Temporary National Economic Committee, Monograph No. 1, 1941.

XII Oligopoly

THE PRICE problem of oligopoly is a price problem peculiar to small numbers. A few firms dominate the industry because each firm produces a considerable percentage of the total industry output. The product may be homogeneous, in which case we have pure oligopoly; or it may display a family of varieties, in which case we deal with differentiated oligopoly. Responsible for an appreciable fraction of the output of the industry, each firm can exercise some control over the market by its price and output policies. What is of direct significance is not the absolute size of the concern so much as its position in the industry when measured by the ratio of its production to the total output of the industry. The ratio ought to be high enough to give the firm influence over the price of the article in the market. Beside the few dominant firms, a number of small units may exist. So long as they do not account together for a considerable part of the total output, or so long as they do not combine to influence price, the oligopolistic character of the market is not disturbed.

I. General Features of Oligopoly

BASES OF OLIGOPOLY

The circumstances which tend to create oligopoly are varied in character and are not unlike those which foster the one-firm monopoly. Perhaps foremost among them are the economies of scale. In various industries, especially those with much mechanization, the minimum long-run average costs are attained by the firm only when it reaches such great size that its output constitutes an impressive portion of the whole industry.[1] A few such firms can produce the major part of the total in the market. Thus the optimum scale of production of the firms may very well lead to oligopoly in such industries as agricultural machinery, heavy electrical equipment, rayon, steel, and automobiles. We should not infer, however, that only in mechanized industry can economies of scale beget an oligopolistic industry. In local markets, like small or even sizable towns, a few efficient business units may be all that are necessary to satisfy the demand. Hence the local oligopoly of hardware stores, building-materials dealers, or plumbers.

The government also aids in the growth of large business units, by tariffs and by defective patent laws. The Supreme Court's long-standing declaration (modified in 1945 and 1946, in the Aluminum case and the Tobacco case) that size or the existence of unexerted power is no offense,[2] coupled with its almost uncompromising decisions against price agreements among small dealers, indirectly suggested until recently the formation of mergers as an inoffensive way of limiting competition. The softness of this Court toward "good" trusts, like the United States Steel Corporation and the International Harvester Company; its stress, until recently, on the actual intent of large units and not on the possible consequence of their presence; its "rule of expediency" which feared the disruptive effect of the dissolution of an empire like the United States Steel Corporation—these and other basic attitudes of this tribunal have lent comfort if not aid in the building of huge concerns.

In addition, ordinary business motives, human motives, play a part. There is the desire for large gains, for power and prestige, for leadership, and for attaching fame to the family name. Such desires find expression in an aggressive policy of forming large concerns, by hastening natural growth, by ruthless competition which forces rivals to the wall, and by mergers and holding companies. Ready to implement such desires and to aid such ambitions are promoters and bankers in search of the windfalls of the high finance of consolidating firms into massive units. A prominent early example is the promotion in 1901 of the United States Steel Corporation, a billion-dollar holding company, which netted J. P. Morgan and his syndicate millions of dollars in fees.

Finally, small numbers of firms in an industry can be traced to the difficulty of entry. The enormous requirements of capital outlay in many an industry give the businessman pause before he will venture his fortunes and those of others,[3] especially when the addition of output to that

[1] J. W. Markham, *Competition in the Rayon Industry* (Cambridge, Harvard University Press, 1952), pp. 50–55.

[2] V. A. Mund, *Government and Business* (New York, Harper, 1950), pp. 175–179.

[3] J. W. Markham, *op. cit.*, pp. 21, 39, 56–57.

of the existing firms may depress the price to a level of slim prospective profits. The would-be newcomer may also fear provoking a price war by the firms established in the market, which may render his intrusion suicidal. Moreover, once several brands have entrenched themselves in popular favor, the entrant faces an expensive task to win a following for his new variety. It will require perseverant advertising to build a demand for the new product by pulling away buyers from the popular brands to which they have grown attached. We are told of the maker of a high-quality and low-priced toothpaste who discovered that he would have to spend fabulous sums on advertising in order to induce customers to ask for his product, before retailers would consent to carry his toothpaste along with the well-known brands.[4] The modern oligopoly, especially differentiated oligopoly, with firms of enormous capital, has introduced a change in the traditional concept of free enterprise as the freedom to enter a business. Such freedom is more characteristic of an economy where small business units are pre-eminent. No wonder the appearance of the Kaiser-Frazer company in the automobile industry was regarded as a singular business event! (The event did not last long.) More successful was the entry of Proctor & Gamble, a soap-products empire, into the baking-goods field—a move which cut severely the sales of such entrenched milling firms as Pillsbury.

THE UNIQUENESS OF OLIGOPOLY

The price analysis of commodities in an oligopolistic market introduces an element not encountered in the analysis of pricing in the other three types of markets. This new element also applies to oligopsony, where a few dominant buyers deal with many sellers; to bilateral monopoly, where a monopolistic buyer faces a monopolistic seller; and to bilateral oligopoly, where a few large buyers obtain goods from a few large sellers. In this chapter we are concerned with oligopoly alone.

In the markets characterized by pure competition or monopoly, the individual seller, in considering his policy for the attainment of maximum profit, is not compelled to take into account the effect which his price-output behavior may have on other sellers of the same or similar goods. He does not have to worry about the steps, and their consequences to his own fortunes, which may be taken by his rivals in response to his own conduct.

The situation is essentially similar in monopolistic competition. There

---

[4] *Hearings before the Temporary National Economic Committee*, Part 8, p. 3398; W. H. Nicholls, *Price Policies in the Cigarette Industry* (Nashville, Vanderbilt University Press, 1951), p. 198.

the individual firm, one among many, knows that its price policy would be of little consequence to the other firms—thus as in pure competition. In varying the quality of the product or in fashioning a selling program, he will keep in mind and will learn from what others are doing. But because *many* others are involved, he makes his moves without fear that they are constantly eyeing his steps with calculations of defensive or punitive reactions—thus as in pure monopoly.

It is different in *oligopoly*; and the difference arises from the circumstance that sellers are few. Each produces a large share of the industry; therefore his moves affect the other producers. The individual seller has to contend with the conduct of the other few sellers in response to his own action. He must evaluate the combined effect of the rivals' adjustments precipitated by his own initial move. He may need to compose, so to speak, a list of his own possible policies and of the total effect in each case on his profit. From this list he may select the price and output policy which will stimulate such mutual reactions as will promise to yield him the greatest gain. The other firms behave similarly. Thus all firms act and react to each other's expected reactions. In oligopoly much hinges on what a given firm thinks the other firms will do. The implicit interlocking of the calculations of the few sellers is an ever present and dominant fact. It is this interlacing of policy that constitutes the *unique* character of an oligopolistic market. The background of the reactions of buyers and sellers partakes of the nature of "I know that he knows that I know."

It is easy to perceive a family resemblance between the moves and countermoves of the oligopolist, on the one hand, and, on the other hand, the strategy and tactics of the player in a game of poker or a general in war. Small wonder that economics has become interested in the nature of "games." Note is to be taken of an important pioneer study in this area by two scholars, one a mathematician and the other an economist, von Neumann and Morgenstern.[5]

It is not surprising therefore to find that the *demand* curve for the product made by an oligopolist is not easy to trace. In fact, the demand curve cannot be drawn, more or less accurately, unless there is a *known* pattern of behavior among the firms in the industry. In *pure competition*, the demand curve for the output of one given firm is horizontal; however, the demand curve for the whole industry is, as usual, a curve sloping to the right. In *monopoly*, the demand for the product is the demand for nearly the whole industry; here too the demand curve slopes to the right. In *monopolistic competition*, the demand for a given article departs to some extent from the horizontal demand curve in pure competition. How

---

[5] J. von Neumann and O. Morgenstern, *Theory of Games and Economic Behavior* (Princeton, Princeton University Press, 1944).

does the demand curve for the product of *oligopoly* look? It is difficult to say. We put down a curve sloping to the right, hoping that back of this curve reside the moves and the countermoves of the few firms in this type of market.

In the rest of this chapter we shall occupy ourselves first with pure oligopoly, turning to phases of independent pricing and collusive pricing; then some distinctive features of differentiated oligopoly will be sketched; and finally, the kinky demand curve will be introduced.

II. Pricing by Pure Oligopoly

There are many instances of pure oligopoly in our economy. Pure oligopoly has been found in the recent past—and the picture is probably not much different today—in the following fields: industrial alcohol, aluminum, ball bearings, beet sugar, cement, anthracite coal, copper, fixed-nitrogen fertilizer, natural gas, iron ore, incandescent lamps, mineral wool, magnesium, pipe lines, potash, shoe machinery, cane-sugar refining, surgical supplies, electron tubes, commercial wheat, and many nonferrous metals not already cited.[6]

Oligopoly pricing may be grouped under three heads, beginning with no collusion and ending with strong collusion. We shall accordingly study the problem of pricing in three sectors: A, independent pricing; B, price leadership or tacit agreement; and C, price agreements.

A. Independent Pricing

FIRMS WITH THE SAME COSTS AND MARKET SHARES

For simplicity we shall assume only two firms in the industry, with identical cost curves and equal shares in the market. For each firm (Figure 54) the demand is AD, the marginal revenue equals marginal cost at point E, each firm maximizes its profit with an output OQ_1, and a price Q_1C. We may generalize that when the demand and cost situations are nearly alike for the few firms producing a homogeneous commodity, the *independent* behavior by the constituent members of the industry may often result in an identical price for the product.

Nor is this generalization all. This identical price may be a monopoly

[6] *Economic Concentration in World War II: Report of the Smaller War Plants Corporation* (Washington, 1946); Clair Wilcox, *Competition and Monopoly in American Industry*, Temporary National Economic Committee, Monograph No. 21 (Washington, 1941), pp. 113–118.

price. It may be a price that would be charged by a single-firm monopoly formed by combining our two identical firms into one unit. To demonstrate this assertion, let us see how this monopolist would set his price (Figure 54). We assume that by replacing the two smaller units he realizes neither net economies nor diseconomies, so that his costs stay unchanged.

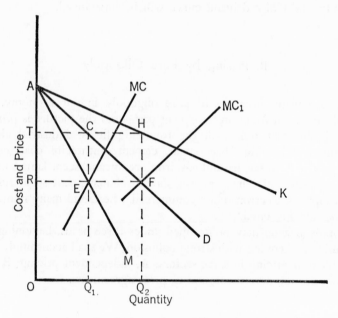

FIGURE 54. *Independent Oligopoly Pricing*

The monopolist faces the following demand and cost situation: (1) His sales curve is AK, which is derived by the horizontal addition of AD and AD, that is, by doubling AD. On AK at each price twice as much can be sold as on AD. Each point on AK, with the same ordinate as a point on AD, has an abscissa twice as large. Thus TH is twice TC. (2) Curve AD is the *marginal revenue* curve for AK inasmuch as AD bisects a perpendicular erected from any point on AK to the vertical axis. (3) The marginal cost curve facing the monopolist is MC_1. It is derived in the same way as curve AK: it is double the MC curve. Every point on MC_1 is twice as far along the horizontal line as a point of the same height on the MC curve; for instance, $RF = 2RE$.

The monopolist will produce an output at which MC_1 intersects AD. From the relationship between MC and MC_1 and between AM and AD

we can see that MC_1 will intersect AD at a point F of the same height as point E but twice as far removed from the vertical axis. In other words, $FQ_2 = EQ_1$ and $RF = 2RE$. His output will be OQ_2; and for this output the price HQ_2 that would be charged by the monopoly is the same as the price CQ_1 charged by each of the two firms.

It is well to stress that this monopoly price is the sequel of small numbers and not primarily of the assumption that oligopolists seek maximum profit. The assumption of maximum profit is not unique to oligopoly. It governs in any other market structure. But where sellers are numerous each firm considers the effect of its price policy as too negligible to be noticed by its rivals. Each firm therefore cuts its price in order to enlarge its sales by drawing expectedly slight patronage away from each rival firm. Even when the number of sellers is small, if each producer chooses to neglect the effect of his price reduction, a competitive price will result. However, realistically speaking, when sellers are few, such a neglect cannot be assumed as a matter of course; whereas when sellers are many, such a neglect can confidently be expected.

It is necessary to express doubt that independent price setting can often endure in oligopoly. It may last when there are very few firms in the industry; but hardly if there are, say, ten or more firms. A sense of uncertainty and insecurity regarding each other's behavior may hang even over a market with only three or four firms; it is well-nigh inseparable from a market with a dozen firms. An ambitious firm may decide to enlarge its share of the market by reducing its price, which step will simultaneously enlarge its output and lower its costs. The temptation to reach for a larger share is always present; so is the fear that a struggle for it may be unleashed. In general, with the passage of time firms come to vary in size; they do not grow in goose-step fashion. Nor do the costs stay alike for all the rivals through the years. With different costs and different shares in the industry, different price policies are likely to develop. A large firm may decide to remove uncertainty by seeking a position of price leadership, or it may attempt by price wars to weaken the smaller concerns as potential rivals. Independent pricing when firms differ in size and costs leads to uncertainty and insecurity. The effort to escape these outcomes commonly leads to price leadership or outright collusion.

Sometimes the *tangency* condition, so characteristic of monopolistic competition, is encountered in oligopoly, pure or differentiated. The tangency condition is apt to appear in instances in which impediments to entry are not very effective, with the consequence that, although the number of firms in the industry is small, it is not small enough. Five or six hardware stores in a small town instead of two or three, fifteen large steel corporations in the country instead of ten, may exemplify the situation. As the trade is divided among more firms the demand for each shifts to the left until it is tangent to the average cost curve. The result is a monopoly price in the sense that it is above a competitive price: the demand curve is tangent to the average cost curve to the *left* of the point of minimum height of the latter curve; and the price is above marginal cost. But since the price coincides with average cost there is no monopoly profit in it. Figures 51 and 53, in the forgoing chapter, can serve as illustrations.

PRICE WARS

Often the object of an oligopolist's ambition is increased sales and a more impressive position in the industry. In pure oligopoly, because of the sophistication of the industrial buyer, puffing one's wares by advertising and salesmanship may be an ineffective method of achieving such a goal. The outstanding method which the firm is tempted to use is price reduction. It is a method to which the firm turns with reluctance. It "spoils the market"; it provokes retaliation; and it violates business "ethics." But price reduction is likely to be used if the firm is driven by ambition; if it has only a temporary interest in its business and disregards long-run effects; if it has reason to believe that the rivals will not react to a price cut or will react only after a considerable interval; or if it is ignorant.

Such ordinary price reductions in oligopoly are not price wars. All price wars are price reductions, but not all price reductions are price wars. The earmark of a price war, an earmark not easy to recognize, is the intent to force the rival to the wall or at least to injure him seriously. The price cut strikes below the rival's cost—below his total or even his variable cost. The motive of the "warmonger" may be to obtain a larger proportion of total sales, to increase his monopoly power after he wins his victory, or to intimidate rivals into submitting to his leadership in the market. Victory usually goes to the firm of greater efficiency and lower costs as well as greater tenacity vitalized by liquid assets and the power to borrow. The loser may turn his capital to another industry, or may sell out to the victor on the victor's terms. But it may happen that victory turns the vanquished into a stronger rival. Bankruptcy may be followed by reorganization which reduces the claims of bondholders and preferred stockholders. The losing firm may emerge with rejuvenated management and lower fixed costs. As among nations, a corporation may lose the war and win the peace.

A price war is not always beer and skittles to the attacking firm. It has to reckon with its costs, with the market demand for its product, with the extent of its advantage over the intended victim, and with the strategy of the attacked firm. As the aggressor lowers the price, consumers' purchases of the article become larger than before. If the attacking firm attempts to accommodate them, its enlarged output may run into costs rising above the price. In general, the costs of the attacking firm must be much lower than the costs of the rival firm if the reduced price is not to inflict much damage on the attacker. The victim firm may make the war still more exhausting to the aggressor by adopting a "scorched-earth" policy and announcing that it intends to produce a certain amount, thus adding to sales and pushing the price down below the attacker's cut price, and causing greater losses to both firms.

B. Price Leadership; Tacit Agreements

NATURE AND SCOPE

Independent pricing in oligopoly is probably less frequent than a form of mutual understanding among the producers. Collusion may exhibit itself in two ways: in tacit agreements and in formal agreements or cartels. There is a tacit agreement when, without face-to-face contact and without correspondence, a unity of behavior with regard to policy develops among the member firms.[7] A formal agreement is the result of consultation by the parties involved. It may imply a written compact with rules of conduct and fines for "misbehavior."

The most frequent example of a tacit agreement is probably price leadership, which is probably also the most prevalent form of controlled prices in the markets for goods. Involving no agreement and no formal organization, it is not open to the charge of conspiracy to restrain trade and is beyond the reach of antitrust laws. It commends itself to those who do not wish to leave the question of price to independent action or to direct agreement. At times, however, price leadership may be the fruit of a formal meeting and a definite agreement with a chosen leader. The price leadership of the United States Steel Corporation or of other companies in the iron and steel industry was the outcome, at one time or another, of formal conferences and discussions.[8]

Many industries have now, or have had in the past, one scheme or another of price leadership. Examples are: agricultural implements, anthracite coal, biscuits and crackers, canned salmon, cement, cigarettes, copper and lead, corn products, fertilizer, flour, glass containers, industrial alcohol,

---

[7] For example, the cigarette industry. See W. H. Nicholls, *op. cit.*, pp. 201, 396.
[8] *Hearings before the Temporary National Economic Committee*, Part 18, pp. 10294–10355; D. Lynch, *Concentration of Economic Power* (New York, Columbia University Press, 1946), pp. 178, 182 ff.

milk, newsprint paper, nonferrous metals, petroleum and gasoline, rayon, steel, tin cans, and tin plate.[9] These examples obviously refer to pure and differentiated oligopoly alike.

Price leadership varies in character. (1) There is, for instance, the price leadership of the *dominant* firm or the partially monopolistic price leadership. One of the few firms in the industry may produce a sizable proportion of the total output and may dominate the market almost with the power of a monopolist. The small producers ignore the effect which they individually may exert on the market, nor do they choose to join forces to challenge the large producer.

(2) Then there is *barometric* price leadership. The largest firm—or the old, experienced, and respected firm—assumes the task of evaluating the changing market conditions with regard to demand, costs, competition of related products, and the phase of the business cycle. In the perspective of such changes it fashions a new price, with an eye on the interests of all the constituent firms. The "official" price is commonly agreeable to the followers. In the rayon industry, the American Viscose Corporation was a price leader of the first type before 1931 and of this second type after 1931.[10]

(3) A third kind is the *exploitative* or aggressive price leadership. The powerful firm may decide to crowd out some of its rivals; or it may desire to force the other firms into acquiescing in its price leadership. A price war initiated by a producer may be an aspect of this type of leadership.

PRICE AND OUTPUT

The analysis of price leadership, in common with the analysis of other types of oligopoly, does not follow a time-honored set pattern. Various assumptions can be made, and each case must be probed specifically. One can assume, for instance, that the member firms do or do not differ in size, costs, and share of the market; that the entry of new firms is or is not effectively blocked; and that the leader looks uncompromisingly to his own advantage, or is willing to hold a protective umbrella over the smaller or less efficient producers.

Many of these cases involve complicated diagrams or mathematics. We shall consider two simple cases, one as connected with Figure 55, and the other without benefit of diagrams. Let us consider the first case.

We assume that there are only two firms, *A* and *B*. Since the product

[9] Clair Wilcox, *op. cit.*, pp. VI, 123; A. R. Burns, *Decline of Competition* (New York, McGraw-Hill, 1936), chap. III.
[10] J. W. Markham, *op. cit.*, pp. 102–104.

is homogeneous, buyers have no preference between these firms. Each firm faces therefore the same demand curve D, which is half of the total demand curve for the commodity. That is, at *each* hypothetical price the quantity purchased is one-half of the usual quantity. The marginal revenue curve is M. But the marginal costs differ. For firm A it is MC_a, higher than MC_b for firm B. Firm A would prefer price AK and output OA; but firm B finds its equilibrium in price BL and output OB. Firm B "wins" and sets the price. Firm A is compelled to follow. Both firms sell the quantity

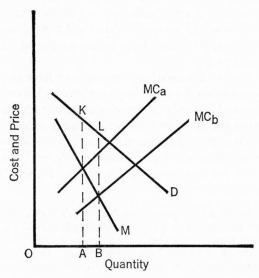

FIGURE 55. *Price Leadership by Dominant Firm*

OB, but producer B makes more profit than producer A: the price is farther above his marginal cost than A's marginal cost. The case is much more complicated if firm B's superiority over firm A is so great that its optimum position calls for a price which is *below* MC_a along curve D.

Now as to the other case of price leadership by the dominant firm. It is assumed that this firm is roughly acquainted with the total demand for the product made by the oligopoly; and that it is also acquainted with the marginal costs of the small firms. From the total amounts demanded at various prices, the dominant firm deducts the totals which the small firms are ready to sell in view of their marginal costs. The rest, the large firm itself will offer for sale: it is in this fashion that this large firm derives its own sales schedule. Then it sets the price which equates its own marginal revenue with its own marginal cost. The small firms will not charge more for their product than this set price lest they lose all trade. Nor will they cut this price of their product inasmuch as they can sell what they produce at the announced price. Each small firm regards its sales curve as horizontal at the price set by the leader.[11]

C. Formal Agreements (Cartels)

The formal agreement among oligopolists is a method of behavior of long and dramatic standing. It has become customary to refer to any type of such agreements as a *cartel* although originally and technically the term had been confined to agreements that had for the central feature a sales agency which alone handled the selling of the product for all the parties to the compact.

Since the purpose of the cartel agreements is to limit competition, they run afoul of our antitrust laws. But apparently these laws are not barriers; they are only hurdles. The urge for monopoly profit breeds secret devices for circumventing the laws; and the refined ways of evasion manage to stay ahead of the law, even as the electrical jackrabbit is ahead of the racing hounds. The members of the legal profession help in the art of inventing ways of honoring the antimonopoly laws in the breach. The following testimony is suggestive:

A friend of mine in a very prominent New York [law] office said: "Yes; I am almost certain that our trade practices are illegal, but we can keep the matter in court for at least 5 years before we get an ultimate judgment on that matter, and at the end of 5 years I am not worth my salt unless I have thought up a new set of trade practices which will accomplish the same thing." [12]

It is impossible to estimate the extent of collusive practices, and many of the examples given in the succeeding paragraphs refer to instances of a bygone day. But from such evidence, direct or circumstantial, as comes to light it is reasonable to assume that such practices continue in vogue. Says D. Lynch: "Despite the policy to hold only 'informal meetings,' to 'keep no minutes,' to 'destroy all letters,' and to 'write no memos,' tell-tale evidence is frequently left behind, some of which eventually falls into the hands of investigators." [13]

---

[11] For a diagrammatic presentation of this case see G. J. Stigler, "Notes on the Theory of Duopoly," *Journal of Political Economy*, Vol. XLVIII (August, 1940), pp. 522–523.

[12] *Hearings before the Subcommittee on Study of Monopoly Power*, 81st Congress, first session, Serial No. 14, Part 1, p. 291.

[13] *Concentration of Economic Power* (New York, Columbia University Press, 1946), p. 193; Thurman Arnold, *Bottlenecks of Business* (New York, Reynal and Hitchcock, 1940), pp. 26–28, 38 ff., and chap VIII; Alfred R. Oxenfeldt, *Industrial Pricing and Market Practices* (New York, Prentice-Hall, 1951), pp. 289 ff.

PRICE-FIXING AGREEMENTS

Despite their illegality, price agreements do not seem to be extinct. In food products alone, during the period 1935–1940, the Federal Trade Commission issued orders against price fixing in nearly 20 different cases.[14] Between 1920 and 1940, cease-and-desist orders or complaints were issued by the FTC, decisions were handed down by courts, or suits were initiated

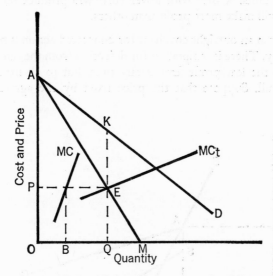

FIGURE 56. *Price-Fixing Agreements in Oligopoly*

by the Department of Justice in cases involving viscose rayon yarn, pin tickets, flannel skirts, turbine generators and condensers, liquid chlorine, medical cotton goods, calcium chloride, corncribs, silos, certain types of waterworks and gas-system fittings, fire-fighting equipment, pulverized iron, rubber heels, music rolls, lithographed labels, plumbing supplies, fertilizer, metal lath, gasoline, brushes, foreign-type cheese, erasers, milk, newsprint paper, tobacco products, typewriters, ophthalmic lenses, hardboard, mineral wool for home insulation, and aircraft fabric.[15] Since the end of World War II we have been reading in the newspapers about suits against agreements in a dozen or more industries.

[14] Thurman Arnold, *op. cit.*, p. 231.
[15] Clair Wilcox, *op. cit.*, pp. 132, 235–240.

Let us consider a strong price agreement among oligopolists of different sizes and costs, producing a homogeneous article. The aim is to maximize joint profits. Together they face the market demand *AD* for the product as a whole (Figure 56). By horizontal addition the individual marginal cost curves are combined into the total marginal cost curve MC_t. This curve intersects the industry marginal revenue curve *AM* at point *E*. The price fixed by the agreement may be the monopoly price *KQ*, and the output set for the industry will be, roughly, *OQ*. The output of a constituent firm will be governed by the point at which its own marginal cost equals the marginal cost *EQ*. A firm with marginal cost MC will produce *OB* units. A firm with lower costs will produce more than *OB*. Some firms will make more profit than others.

(1) But even an outright covenant for concerted action is not a guarantee of stability. There is temptation for defection from the ranks, attractive especially to the low-profit firm at any time, but to all firms also when business is dull. Suppose that the price fixed by the agreement is *OP*,

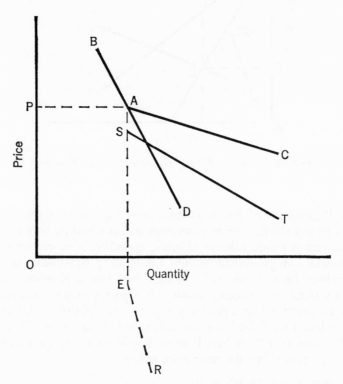

FIGURE 57. *Possible Instability of Price Agreements*

as in Figure 57. At this price one of the firms may sell PA units of the article; and its sales schedule will appear to it like the horizontal line PA.

If all parties to the agreement were to follow with a price change as soon as any firm initiated one, the demand curve for the initiating producer would be BD (Figure 57). In such a case a price cut below OP would raise its sales only slightly because the AD part of the sales curve BD is of low elasticity. Still worse, the cut would bring losses, since the marginal revenue for AD is the array of negative quantities pictured by line ER. But the result is different if the other firms do not react to a price reduction by this one firm, or if they react gradually, or after an appreciable interval of time—which may well be the expectation of the "misbehaving" firm if its price concessions are secret. Then its demand curve will be, not AD, but the more elastic curve AC (in the price range of OP or less), with its accompanying positive marginal revenue curve ST. The student, it may be remarked parenthetically, will recognize in curves BD and AC Chamberlin's DD' and dd' curves, explained in the preceding chapter, section II. Since AC is relatively elastic, in the neighborhood of price OP and less, a small price reduction may induce a large advance in sales. Moreover, with a rise in industry output, further long-run economies of scale may follow and lower unit costs may result. Thus one firm or another is tempted to try secret price cutting.

(2) This is not the only difficulty. Recurrent changes of demand and cost conditions induced by the business cycle and other circumstances may bring distress to some members of the cartel and impel them to violate the agreement. A single-firm monopoly can make short-term adjustments to new conditions. But for a cartel to attempt an adjustment means to open the door to lengthy sessions potential of declarations of grievances, and quarrels, and possibly ending in upsetting results. To avoid such conferences, the cartel may set an initial price which is a compromise fitting a variety of conditions and which is only a loose approximation of a single-firm monopoly price.

(3) The desire for maximum joint profit is always strong. But this desire is at odds with a satisfactory division of profits or of sales, as is stressed by Professor Fellner in his notable study of oligopoly.[16] If all firms are to earn an equal total profit, the high-cost firms and low-unit-profit firms will have to sell more than the low-cost firms; this condition is inconsistent with maximum industry profit, which would require the opposite situation with respect to sales. If the agreement is to divide sales equally, again maximum joint profits will not be attained. Unique arrangements will be required to supplement a price cartel if the difficulty is to be resolved: there may be a pooling of profits; the high-cost firms may pay

[16] W. Fellner, *Competition Among the Few* (New York, Knopf, 1949), chaps. IV and VI.

smaller dues to the cartel; the low-cost firms may help their less favored companions to reduce costs. But there are objections to these and other devices. The life of a cartel, like that of a covenant among nations, is a series of squabbles, violations, and revisions.

OTHER AGREEMENTS

Many are the varieties of cartels, and a few more will be briefly mentioned.

One is the *quota* agreement, which seeks to limit competition by assigning to each firm a fixed proportion of the total production of the cartel. This total is first restricted after the manner of a monopolist. The firm's share in the output depends on its size, its past sales, its argumentative power, and its capacity to make trouble for the group. Usually, the lion's share goes to the lion or to him who can roar like a lion. In the past, output agreements have been known in anthracite coal, cotton, meat packing, gunpowder, steel rails, structural steel, tin plate, wallpaper, whisky, and wire nails.[17]

Then there is the market or *territorial* agreement. The market is divided among the member producers; and in its own territory the firm rules like a monopolist, fixing the price without interference. Sometimes the territorial division provides for a no-man's land where the members can dispose of surplus output at a competitive price. In this kind of cartel the bone of contention is the amount and quality of territory allocated to the firm. Geopolitics takes the place of the *Quotenkampf*. Such cartels have allegedly been in existence in meat packing, anthracite coal, window glass, cement, textile refinishing, oil refining, certain types of containers, lumber, rice, gunpowder, steel rails, sulfur, thread, and tobacco.[18]

Some agreements provide for a *sales agency* which takes charge of selling the product for all the parties to the agreement. Underlying this scheme is the desire to prevent underselling. The classic habitat of this type of agreement is Germany, where it is known as *Kartell*. In this country such an arrangement was practiced by firms in oil, salt, wallpaper, and window glass.[19] There have been agreements on formulas to be used in pricing, such as markups, zone pricing, or the basing-point system which as recently as 1950 was in vogue in nearly twenty industries.

[17] E. Jones, *The Trust Problem in the United States* (New York, Macmillan, 1924), chap. 2.
[18] A. R. Oxenfeldt, *op. cit.,* p. 312; E. Jones, *op. cit.,* pp. 12–13.
[19] A. R. Burns, *op. cit.,* p. 151.

III. Differentiated Oligopoly

Differentiated oligopoly is a cross between pure oligopoly and monopolistic competition. As in the former, the number of sellers is small; as in the latter, the product is not homogeneous. In pure oligopoly the element of monopoly derives from small *numbers*; in monopolistic competition it derives from the differentiation of the *product*. Differentiated oligopoly contains both of these monopoly elements. Although differentiated, the products of the several firms are not very remote substitutes for one another. If they were, each seller would be a monopolist. Much of what has been said on product differentiation in sections I and III in the preceding chapter applies in this section.

Abundant as may be the examples of pure oligopoly, those of differentiated oligopoly are equally numerous. They were found in agricultural machinery, automobiles, bread, biscuits and crackers, chewing gum, cosmetics, dairy products, electric refrigerators, fountain pens, gasoline, glass containers, ink, insurance, liquor, meat packing, motion pictures, oil, oleomargarine, optical instruments, radios, rayon, rubber tires, soap, soft drinks, tobacco, typewriters, and washing machines.[20] There are local oligopolies, as in banking, bakeries, milk delivery, groceries, plumbing supplies, and retail stores of other descriptions.

INDEPENDENT AND COLLUSIVE PRICING IN DIFFERENTIATED OLIGOPOLY

The basic analysis of price formation in differentiated oligopoly follows lines similar to those in pure oligopoly. Some of the outstanding differences will be outlined presently. Assume a few producers, each making a variety of a given product. Each producer seeks maximum gain and takes into account the reactions of the rivals to his price moves. The price set independently by each seller may well be a monopoly price. The optimum price charged may differ from firm to firm because their products differ in one respect or another.

A result similar to such independent pricing may emerge if there is collusion on price. The cartel may fix for each firm a price in the neighborhood of a monopoly price. Or else the cartel may set a given price as a frame of reference, with fixed differentials for each member, reflecting

[20] *Economic Concentration and World War II: Report of the Smaller War Plants Corporation* (Washington, 1946); Clair Wilcox, *op. cit.*, chap. IV.

the uniqueness of his product and the special demand and cost conditions.

If the entry of new firms is not successfully barred and more producers appear with new brands of the product, the demand curve for each firm may shift to the left as the trade is shared by more sellers, until it is tangent to the average cost curve. As in pure oligopoly, we obtain then for each firm a separate monopoly price which contains no monopoly profit. The few gasoline stations, grocery stores, or barber shops in a small town may serve as examples.

PRICE LEADERSHIP IN DIFFERENTIATED OLIGOPOLY

Price leadership probably occurs with the same frequency in differentiated as in pure oligopoly. Examples were cited in the discussion of price leadership in pure oligopoly. One firm sets the price and the others follow, with the same price or with customary differentials. At some time one firm assumes the role of leader, at another time another firm, with or without a struggle for the position. The following paragraphs, relating to the tobacco oligopoly, tell, very likely, a typical story.

For many years, the actual prices were determined by Reynolds. As the largest cigarette producer, that company was in a position to enforce its will on the other companies. In 1918, an attempt was made by American [Tobacco Co.] to lead a large price rise. Reynolds refused to follow, and American was forced to retract. In 1921, American cut its price, but Reynolds seized the initiative by cutting still further. Thereafter, Reynolds made the important changes with Liggett setting an identical price and American setting a related but slightly higher price. . . .

In 1928, Reynolds led a price cut from $5.64 to $5.29 per thousand net. . . . The cut had the effect of reducing the advertising funds . . . and was probably designed to hobble the successful American advertising campaign. . . .

In 1931, Reynolds led a further price rise to $6.04. . . . This interesting experiment in extreme monopoly pricing . . . did make possible the rise of new competition. . . . A number of brands were introduced, of which "Wings" . . . and "Twenty Grand" . . . were the most important. . . .

In January, 1933, American cut the price of "Lucky Strikes" to $5.29 net, and the others followed. In February, there was a second cut to $4.85. . . . The 10¢ brands wilted under the attack, and their sales fell. . . . During the price war, both "Lucky Strikes" and "Camels" were sold at a loss, and when the enemy was under control, Reynolds—in January, 1934—led a rise back to $5.38. . . . Since the end of OPA, the American Tobacco Co. has led two price rises to a present [1950] level of $6.86 net, while Reynolds has adapted to the American lead with a net price 3¢ per thousand lower.[21]

[21] W. Adams, ed., *Structure of American Industry* (New York, Macmillan, 1950), pp. 249–251; W. H. Nicholls, *ibid., passim.*

PRICE DIFFERENCES IN DIFFERENTIATED OLIGOPOLY

In differentiated oligopoly, independent pricing, price leadership, or joint action exhibits at least two features absent in pure oligopoly: *price differences* among the constituent firms and *nonprice competition.*[22]

When the article is homogeneous the prices charged by the firms must be identical. A price difference of a cent or two on a barrel of cement may shift buyers to the low-price seller. A price cut by one producer will ordinarily precipitate a price cut by the rival producers. When the United States Steel Corporation announces a price reduction on cold-rolled sheet steel it does not take long before the newspapers report a similar reduction by other steel companies.

But no identity of price is necessarily established when the few firms make different varieties of the product. The differences in price can be wide if, in the buyer's estimation, wide differences exist in the design, quality, or size of the various brands. The price gaps must be narrow indeed if the varieties are strongly alike. The price differentials can be substantial with automobiles or refrigerators; not with gasoline.

Two results may follow in the above situation. *First,* in differentiated oligopoly the demand for the product of a given firm is apt to be more uncertain than in pure oligopoly. It is difficult for the seller to estimate the relative attachment of the buyers to the several makes of the article, or the response of rivals to his price cut. There is therefore greater uncertainty about the increment in sales which will accompany a decrease in price. Cross-elasticity is not a figure which he who runs can read.

Second, price cartels are more difficult to organize than in pure oligopoly; and once organized are likely to be less stable. There can be enough wrangling before one price is established for the homogeneous article in pure oligopoly. Even more squabbling can develop before the several prices are fixed for the several brands; and more dissatisfaction can arise after they have been fixed, especially as market conditions change.

NONPRICE COMPETITION

By and large, of the three types of competition—in price, in product adaptation, and in promotion—price cutting is the most unpopular among oligopolists. The other two types of competition, both in the nature of nonprice competition, are held in much greater favor, and are widely

[22] Even in pure oligopoly there may be a good deal of informational advertising.

practiced, even by the members of a price cartel. For this preference there are at least two reasons.

First, businessmen feel that there is a difference between price and nonprice competition in the sharpness of the impact upon the consumer. Consumers are impressed by an appreciable price difference between essentially similar goods. A price cut by one firm may make a serious raid on the trade of the other firms. The raided firms must respond with defensive price reductions. The fear prevails that at best nothing is gained from the all-round price cut and that at worst a price war may be precipitated.

On the other hand, nonprice competition lacks the directness of impact upon the customer. Nonprice competition does not express itself in the language which the consumer readily understands, the language of the price tag. The consumer may be impressed by the difference between 20¢ and 24¢ for a pack of cigarettes. But the effect upon him is less penetrating when one billboard tells him "I'd walk a mile for a Camel" and another billboard boasts "Not a cough in a carload."

Second, a price cut can ordinarily be matched by rivals almost immediately. But a new wrinkle in the product or a new strategy in the selling effort is not so easy to initiate and cannot be introduced without a lapse of time. The innovator can expect at least a temporary advantage. For these reasons price competition is regarded as a hot war, and nonprice competition as a cold war.

In oligopolistic industries the stress on nonprice competition is greater than in industries under monopolistic competition. Disinclined to use the weapon of price cutting, oligopolists, whether independent in conduct or collusive, lean more heavily on product variation and selling activity. Since their volume of operations is larger and their resources are greater, generally, than those of firms in monopolistic competition, they can afford research departments for the improvement of the product. Greater still, seemingly, is the emphasis on advertising and salesmanship. Except for those in small local oligopolies, the firms are apt to be nationally or regionally known and with a far-flung clientele. Advertising becomes an enormous enterprise. Campaigns are carried on with the loud paraphernalia of blindfold tests, testimonials by movie starlets, an assortment of jingles, and generally much sounding brass and tinkling cymbals.

Nonprice competition is contagious, probably more so in oligopoly than in monopolistic competition. A firm stressing product improvement or advertising activity may succeed in diverting patronage away from the other firms. At least the other firms fear such a result. They follow suit in self defense. Sometimes the race, costly as it may be, is to little purpose. All introduce innovations, mythical or real, all puff the unique features of their brands, all take away trade from each other, and none is better off. The situation is not unlike an armament race among nations. The rivals run fast in order to stay in the same place. It is important to add, however, that at least the product improvements constitute a benefit to the public, if prices are "reasonable."

The discussion of price determination in this section has ignored selling costs. When these costs are introduced the picture becomes more complicated. The oligopolist deals with a *triple* problem: At what price, with what change in the product, and with what selling cost can maximum profits be reached? The situation is analogous to the position of the firm in monopolistic competition, discussed in the preceding chapter, section III, B. But in oligopoly the problem presents greater difficulties: the price, product, and promotion policies of one establishment may exert a direct and substantial effect on the fortunes of the other firms. Their reactions must be weighed before a choice is made. The interdependence of oligopolists, troublesome when only price policy is considered, is more troublesome still when choices regarding product variation and selling effort are added. An appreciation of the problem involved can be gained by consulting, in the preceding chapter, Table 15 and the associated discussion.

IV. Price Rigidity. The Kinky Demand Curve

NATURE AND CAUSES

A price is said to be flexible when it is sensitive to changes in supply and demand. In pure competition price adjusts itself to shifts in these determinants. We deal with price rigidity when in face of changing conditions there is no disposition on the part of the sellers to vary the price. The price may stay fixed amidst fluctuating circumstances that affect demand and supply.

Some oligopoly markets are often associated with sticky prices, and for a number of reasons. *First*, instead of reducing the price in response to a declining demand, the firms may choose to intensify their sales effort in order to win customers at the prevailing price. *Second*, after having spent a large sum to make a particular brand a household word and to identify it with a particular price, the oligopolist is reluctant to change the price and break the established association of price and product in the mind of the buyer. In a period of rising prices the 5¢ candy bar stays with us although in reduced size. *Third*, the parties to a cartel-determined price are not anxious to move for a new price agreement and open a Pandora's box of conferences, bickerings, and maneuverings. *Fourth*, oligopolists are often content to leave well enough alone, and with an eye on forestalling the entry of new firms, they may be satisfied with a markup which gives good long-run profits, and which is not changed, except under drastic circumstances.

Fifth, contributing to price rigidity, but rendering service in various analytical connections, is the so-called kinky demand curve. A kinky demand curve is a straight-line demand for a commodity which abruptly changes its slope. The demand curve *BPD* (Figure 58) is an example.

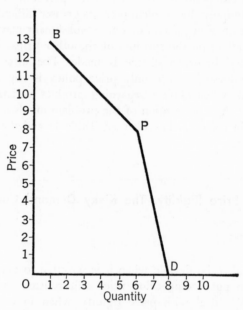

FIGURE 58. *The Kinky Demand Curve*

The kink comes at a point *P*. Point *P* splits the demand curve in two segments, *BP* and *PD*. Each segment has its own uniform slope. But the slope of *BP* is different from the slope of *PD*. In both cases if we advance *one* unit, we move downward more on *PD* than along *BP*. The lower segment *PD* is steeper than *BP*.

It is relatively easy to observe that price rigidity exists in oligopoly, but it is hard to tell to what extent the rigidity results from the monopoly power of the firms and consequently from such reasons as have been mentioned in the forgoing paragraphs, and to what extent it flows from reasons having no connection with the monopoly element in oligopoly. There is an extensive literature on price rigidity, but this question remains unresolved. One theory which attempts to demonstrate deductively that an oligopoly price is likely to be rigid is based on the kinky demand curve facing an oligopolist *after* the price of his product has been determined.[23] We shall now examine this theory.

Assume, as in Figure 59, that the established price for the product in

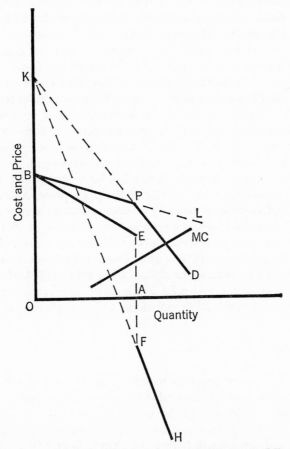

FIGURE 59. *The Kinky Demand Curve; Rigidity of Oligopoly Price*

the oligopoly market is *AP*; imagine a straight line from *A* to *P*. If we are dealing with pure oligopoly, *AP* is the price for all the firms; if with differentiated oligopoly, *AP* may stand for the price of one firm while the prices of the other firms differ by prescribed amounts.

[23] P. M. Sweezy, "Demand under Conditions of Oligopoly," *Journal of Political Economy*, Vol. XLVII (August, 1939), pp. 568-573.

At any price *above* AP the demand for the product of the firm is pictured by the very elastic curve BP. This means that should the firm raise the price above AP, the other firms are not likely to follow its lead. It will lose considerable trade to its rivals, and its sales will be greatly diminished. Our firm will therefore think twice before raising the price. Now suppose that the firm considers a price *below* AP. It can expect to do a land-office business only if it thinks that the other firms will hold their prices fixed. Then our firm's sales curve would look like the elastic curve PL (Figure 59). However, there is much reason to believe that the other firms are not ready to lose trade to our price cutter and may respond with price cuts of their own. When all the firms are expected to move together on price reductions, the demand curve of the firm in question is not PL but PD. In such a case the gain in sales to our firm is negligible and the gain in revenue is precarious, since segment PD is of lower elasticity than segment PL, and its companion marginal revenue curve FH is very low or negative.[24] Our firm will accordingly neither raise nor lower the established price. Price AP stays rigid.

Once the market price of the article has been determined, the demand curve to the individual firm is kinky at the price point. At the price AP and output OA (that is, at point P) its slope makes an abrupt change and the marginal revenue becomes discontinuous, dropping from E to F. The kink is at P: the average revenue curve is elastic for a price above P and inelastic for a price below P. The more elastic the sales curve is to the left of P and the more inelastic to the right of P the greater the kink at P and the larger the gap or discontinuity EF in the marginal revenue curve. To put it differently, as the angle BPD approaches a right angle the gap EF widens.

CHANGE IN COSTS OR IN DEMAND

The oligopoly price promises to stay rigid, in some instances, even if changes occur in cost or demand. Consider a fall in *cost* for all firms, occasioned by a reduction in the wage rate or in the sales tax on raw materials. The average cost and the marginal cost curves will alike shift to the right and downward. Before the change in cost, the marginal cost curve was MC, as in Figure 59, and it met the marginal revenue curve somewhere in the gap, between points E and F. Now the marginal cost curve is lower than MC; but it is still likely to intersect the marginal revenue curve in the gap, above point F, even if the old MC curve meets the marginal revenue curve at a point *close* to F. The reason is that the gap

[24] Again, the student will recognize in BP (or BPL) and PD (or KPD) Chamberlin's *dd'* and *DD'* curves. The dotted segments KP and KF serve to indicate how the marginal revenue FH is obtained: KH is the marginal revenue curve for the average revenue curve KD, and FH is the segment of KH corresponding to PD.

EF widens. First, the *BP* curve becomes more elastic because, in view of the lower cost, there is greater certainty that a price advance by one firm will not be matched by its rivals and will cause the firm great losses in sales. Second, the *PD* curve becomes more inelastic because, with the drop in cost, a price reduction by one firm is more certain to be followed by the other firms. The result: angle *BPD* at point *P* approaches a right angle and the gap *EF* is wider. With a wider gap, the lower marginal cost curve is likely to intersect the marginal revenue curve *inside* the gap, pointing to the same output *OA* as before the decline in cost and to the old price *AP*. The firms clear more profit.

However, if there is a rise in unit cost, the price is not apt to stay inflexible. The new marginal cost curve rises above the MC curve; and it is very likely to cross the marginal revenue curve above point *E* (that is, somewhere along *EB*), indicating a higher price and a smaller output. The reasoning is similar to that in the preceding paragraph. Since cost has risen for all producers, each firm expects that if it leads off with a price above *AP* the other firms will not hold back but will follow. This means that *BP* becomes less elastic. Each firm expects to lose less trade by raising the price since trade will not be shifted to the other sellers. With *BP* less elastic, the angle *BPD* is more obtuse and farther away from a right angle. The gap *EF* is smaller; and the higher marginal cost curve is apt to go above point *E*. All firms are likely therefore to raise the price.

Similar considerations govern price determination when there is a change in *demand*. Consider a decreased demand from BD_1 to CD_2, with the respective broken marginal revenue curves *LFKM* and *REHM'* (Figure 60). With a decreased demand, there is more likelihood that if one firm initiates a price cut the other firms will follow. This circumstance renders CD_2 more inelastic than the previous BD_1. The angle at *C* is accordingly apt to be less obtuse than the angle at *B*. Gap *EH* is apt to be larger than gap *FK*. The marginal cost curve is likely to cross *REHM'* somewhere inside the gap, signifying no reduction in price.

But an increased demand may result in a higher price. Each firm knows that if it raises the price its companions will hardly refrain from doing likewise. The upper part of the sales curve, to the *left* of the old price, will now be less elastic than the corresponding part of the previous sales curve, forming a more obtuse angle. The gap will be smaller; and the marginal cost curve is apt to cut the marginal revenue curve at a point above the gap, indicating a correspondingly higher price.

In sum, the kinky-demand-curve analysis points to the likelihood of price rigidity in oligopoly when a price reduction is in order and of price flexibility when conditions warrant a rise in price. There is hardly a disposition to lower the price when there is a decline in demand or in costs; but the price may be raised in response to an increased demand or to rising costs.

The theory of the kinky demand curve is probably of limited application in explaining price inflexibility.[25] In cases of price leadership or price
cartels there is concerted behavior with respect to price changes: there
is no kink in the demand curve in these instances; and they probably
compose a large proportion of oligopoly markets. The relevance of the
theory in the whole area of differentiated oligopoly is dubious. When

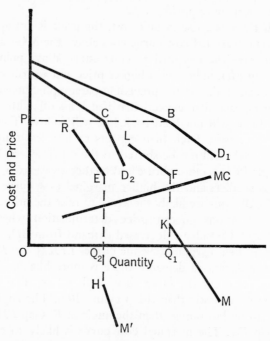

FIGURE 60. *Oligopoly Price with a Change in Demand*

the products are not homogeneous it is precarious to generalize that a price
cut by one firm will be matched by the other firms, and a price advance
will not. Even if such a generalization can be made, the gap or discontinuity in the marginal revenue curve is likely to be too narrow to account
for price rigidity, especially when costs decline.

In independent pricing, there may be no kinky demand curve when the
number of sellers is either very small or rather large.[26] Professor Stigler

[25] G. J. Stigler, "The Kinky Oligopoly Demand Curve and Rigid Prices," *Journal
of Political Economy*, Vol. LV (October, 1947), pp. 432–449.
[26] *Ibid.*, p. 435.

found no such demand curve in cigarettes, automobiles, anthracite coal, steel products, dynamite, potash, and, in the areas studied, gasoline. As we see, some of these industries exemplify differentiated oligopoly, and the others may be under one type or another of price leadership and collusive pricing, in which cases there is presumably no deviation from the set price change.

Certain facts, moreover, suggest the inference that there must be explanations of price stability beside the thesis of the kinky demand curve: we witness rigid prices where this type of demand curve does not exist. For instance, a monopoly price will often be rigid, at times more so than in oligopoly. Also, stability of price and collusive oligopoly often go hand in hand. Professor Stigler gives several examples of price collusion associated with relatively inflexible prices. They are: rayon, copper, pineapple (the leading growers and canners), typewriters, and oil in the Midwest. Other explanations of price rigidity are available; some of them are mentioned at the beginning of this section.

RESTRAINTS ON HIGH PRICES IN OLIGOPOLY

We shall now consider the factors which tend to moderate the oligopoly price. In the chapter on monopoly it was indicated that the monopolist may be disinclined to exploit a temporary advantage and charge a price that would yield the largest profit per unit of time. It was indicated that the monopolist would try to avoid potential competition by forgoing extraordinary profits; that he would fear unfavorable public opinion and legislative reaction; and that long-run calculations would overcome the temptations of the moment.

These considerations apply with much force to oligopoly as well.[27] There are, moreover, some further circumstances which would keep the oligopolistic producer from a grasping price policy. Some of these conditions may also apply to *monopoly*.

(1) There is, for instance, the desire for security. The oligopolist may want to assure for his firm a continued existence and may seek to maintain its position in the market in volume of output, financial strength, and customer good-will. At times maximum profit and the desire for security may go hand in hand, but not infrequently they part roads. The producer may tone down the price in the belief that the policy will win or preserve the good-will of the buyers.

(2) Where the numbers are small, a sense of group loyalty and a spirit of live and let live may develop. Contending with similar problems and experiencing similar fluctuations of fortune imposed by external condi-

[27] See, for example, W. H. Nicholls, *op. cit.*, pp. 193-195.

tions, the oligopolists may develop sympathy for each other. The outcome may be that the seller may not be disposed to seize upon each temporary possibility suggested by the conditions of demand and cost, but may rest satisfied with a steady policy of reasonable markups and moderate profits.

(3) Out of a variety of other factors one more may be mentioned. As between the stockholders of a corporation and the top management, a divergence of motivation and interests may develop. If the corporation is not prospering, both these parties suffer. But if a given policy succeeds, the benefit to the stockholders may exceed the benefit to the chief managers. The owners are therefore apt to be more venturesome in policy, whereas the top officials are apt to display conservatism. Managers may decide on prices which will not bring the most attractive profits to the owners, but which promise greater security and stability to the firm and therefore greater security to their own position and reputation in the business world. "Management is becoming professionalized, and leadership is being divorced from profit-receiving if not from profit-making." Thus speaks an acute student of the problem.[28]

There is another angle to the divergence of interest between managers and owners. The managers at the head of a corporation are apt to develop a loyalty to it as a specific entity. They may identify themselves with it as a vital reality in their lives and careers. The stockholders, on the other hand, may exist in the minds of the chief administrators as an anonymous mass of strangers, sometimes quarrelsome, short-sighted, and demanding. To protect the position of the firm and to do what is best for its continued career are objectives which often dominate the attitude of management more than the desire to please the stockholders with large dividend checks.

V. Observations on Oligopoly

If for the moment we disregard promotional costs, oligopoly with strong collusion among its constituent firms may approximate the misshapen *allocation* of resources characteristic of monopoly. If there is some price rivalry or if the collusive understandings lack discipline, so that the discrepancy between marginal cost and price is minor, the misallocation may be moderate. If entry is blocked, too few resources may be used in the industry; if entry is comparatively free, too many resources.

As to the level of production, at least in some cases the size of the firm may reach the optimum range more readily than in the case of the possibly oversized monopoly firm and the possibly undersized purely competitive firm. However, as a rule, oligopoly may stand for a few over-

[28] R. A. Gordon, *Business Leadership in Large Corporations* (Washington, Brookings Institution, 1945), p. 312.

sized firms.

But we cannot neglect *promotional* costs. When these are taken into account, the infirmities of oligopoly may be substantial. Nonprice competition in oligopoly is very apt to stress combative, expensive, and self-canceling advertising, swallowing resources which could be used to produce goods of greater total utility than the increment of utility imparted to the intensively advertised goods. Soap operas do not make soap wash things whiter. Enough has already been said on this question.

If the oligopoly is strongly collusive, the incentives to product improvement may be of the same order as those ruling under monopoly. There may be less emphasis on useless refinements than in monopolistic competition. But if the oligopoly is weak, product variation may be carried to extremes. The automobile industry, with the annual outburst of features, gadgets, and other talking points, may be an example. Nonprice rivalry stirs *progress* in product variation, but in some or many instances too much progress.

In any but the strongly collusive oligopoly there is keen incentive to improve the technique of production, but it is doubtful whether the consumer always benefits. With the kinky demand curve in mind, we can see that an innovation will have to reduce marginal cost substantially before a larger output and a lower price will develop. If the cost reduction is not great, the marginal cost curve may cut the marginal revenue curve within the range of discontinuity; and the innovation may merely fetch a higher profit.

The most stubborn problem in the effort to remove monopoly is encountered in oligopoly. In some industries the member firms in this type of market closely approximate optimum size and efficiency. The solution is not to atomize such industries into purely competitive structures with numerous small firms, but rather to see to it that the existing firms share the benefits of their efficiency with the consuming public in the form of low prices. Often, however, the large oligopolistic concerns are not marked by great efficiency: they develop as the result of unfair business tactics, of mergers with other units, or of the possession of exclusive patents. In such cases, the problem is to decentralize existing giants of doubtful efficiency, and to prevent oligopoly-breeding practices in the future. A very large order!

Various measures have been suggested in dealing with oligopoly. They embrace a stricter enforcement of antitrust laws; greater vigilance against mergers, holding companies, and unfair competition; government-owned yardstick plants to ascertain and publicize costs of production and to compete with the oligopolists; government price regulation; the reduction of tariffs on imports; the adoption of national charters for corporations engaged in interstate commerce; taxation of excess profits; a scheme of taxes and subsidies for large and small firms; encouragement to co-operatives and to the entry of entrepreneurs into oligopoly industries; limitation of the size of the firms; and the reformation of our patent laws. There is also the advocacy of government ownership of all stubbornly oligopolistic industries.

It would take us too far afield to try to scrutinize each remedy suggested for oligopoly (or for monopoly power). It can be readily seen that it is not easy to uproot the monopoly element in oligopoly. How regulate prices? How enforce truth in advertising? What size-limits shall we prescribe for firms in various industries? How many firms can we tolerate in each industry? Nearly all the measures listed call for conspicuous and persevering government intervention, with the concomitant limitation of individual freedom and stubborn ramifications injurious to the economy. Perhaps the root difficulty of dealing with oligopoly lies in our search for four irreconcilable prime objectives: the economies of the large firm; the passing on of the benefit of these economies to the consumer; the preservation of producer incentives to be efficient and to innovate; and yet to maintain the freedom of the individual from undue state interference.

Nonetheless, as we reconsider the four types of commodity market structures which we have examined in this and the previous three chapters, we must assert that, despite all the reservations which we have noted, time has proved the astonishing success of our economy. The incontrovertible fact stands out that during the past two centuries capitalism has shown remarkable progress in volume of output, in variety and quality of goods, in techniques of production, and in raising the standard of living of a constantly growing population.

APPENDIX: The Theory of Countervailing Power

As an appendix to our discussion in Chapters IX–XII, we shall consider briefly a topic that bears on aspects of some of the problems discussed in these four chapters. It is as interesting as it is irritating for its failure to take seriously a serious problem.

In the past decade there has appeared a theory which asserts that the processes of our society tend to generate their own antidote to monopoly power. It is the theory of countervailing power, propounded by Professor J. K. Galbraith.[29] Monopoly or oligopoly on the buying or selling side of the market begets a restraining organization on the other side. Oligopoly in the steel, automobile, or metal-mining industry brings into being the big labor union to curb the power to push down wages. The big seller of goods faces the big buyer like the chain store, the department store, the mail-order house, or the farmer's co-operative. The steel com-

[29] *American Capitalism* (Boston, Houghton Mifflin, 1952).

pany as a seller is restrained by the motor company as the buyer; the Goodyear Tire and Rubber Company has to contend with Sears, Roebuck and Company. The solution of monopoly is not to be sought in archaic competition, incompatible with modern technology necessitating the large firm, but in the counteracting large organization: fight fire with fire. Instead of fighting monopoly with antitrust laws, let the government offer encouragement to the neutralizing work of countervailing forces. In short, the answer to monopoly is bilateral monopoly.

Professor Galbraith is too optimistic. First of all, his theory does not demonstrate the inevitable emergence of a countervailing power. We do not notice, for instance, the presence of such power in the markets for calculating machines, cement, cigarettes, insurance, liquor, motion pictures, optical instruments, pipe lines, plumbing service, or shoe machinery. The public utilities failed to generate counteracting agencies; the solution in this area had to come from government regulation.

Nor does the presence of two large units on the opposite sides of the market necessarily guarantee compensatory action. Bilateral monopoly does not necessarily result in a low price. In addition, both units may operate under the financial control of bankers, insurance companies, or interlocking directors; or else they may combine by collusive agreements or as a vertical merger or holding company. If the field is magnetized by prospects of larger profits, the two units will be drawn together; instead of profit-reducing antagonism we may witness co-operation in exploiting the consumer.

Even when there is an active countervailing agency it does not always follow that all consumers will benefit. Macy's buys tires at low prices and charges less than the going price for them to its customers. But not all buyers of tires can shop at Macy's. Mail-order houses sell durable household equipment, and tires too, at comparatively low prices; but not all consumers can and will trade in mail-order houses. A farmers' co-operative can obtain and sell lubricating oil cheaply; but this advantage does not extend to city people. Furthermore, not all large buyers of such materials as steel, aluminum, or manganese transmit the advantage to the buyer of the finished commodity.

Says Professor Galbraith: "The operation of countervailing power is to be seen with the greatest clarity in the labor market where it is also most fully developed."[30] It is not clear, however, that the countervailing function of the union always contributes to maximum welfare. Galbraith himself acknowledges that his theory is not exemplified in times of inflation when the high wages wrested by the strong union are shifted to the consumer in the high prices charged by the strong company; and he admits that we have inflation nearly half of the time. Moreover, once the union establishes a wage rate exceeding the marginal revenue productivity

[30] *Ibid.*, p. 121.

of labor in an oligopolistic industry, the same grade of labor will tend to obtain the same rate in other industries with less monopoly power to incorporate the high wage in high prices. In general, the excessive wage may set off processes of substitution of labor-saving devices for the high-cost labor, pushing the released workers into crowded employments. Thus labor monopoly, instead of diminishing the infirmities of business monopoly, may add to them.

This theory visualizes an economy with static giants on both sides of a market, with inflexibility of adjustment to change, with insufficient incentive to inventiveness, and with relatively few avenues for new talent. This implies a denial that competition may stimulate efficiency, flexibility, and innovation; that it generally holds open the door of opportunity to the able but venturesome newcomer; that by providing many centers of decision it tends to decentralize economic power; and that by inviting government intervention less, it preserves personal freedom more.

SUGGESTED READINGS

Boulding, K. E. *Economic Analysis*, revised ed., pp. 580–591. New York, Harper, 1948.

Burns, A. R. *The Decline of Competition*, chaps. 3–5. New York, McGraw-Hill, 1936.

Coppock, J. D. *Economics of the Business Firm*, chap. 15. New York, McGraw-Hill, 1959.

Fellner, W. *Competition Among the Few*. New York, Knopf, 1949.

Hamilton, W. *Price and Price Policies*. New York, McGraw-Hill, 1938.

Leftwich, R. H. *The Price System and Resource Allocation*, revised ed., chap. XI. New York, Holt, Rinehart and Winston, 1960.

Machlup, F. *The Economics of Sellers' Competition*, chaps. 11–16. Baltimore, The Johns Hopkins Press, 1952.

Markham, J. W. *Competition in the Rayon Industry*. Cambridge, Harvard University Press, 1952.

Nicholls, W. H. *Price Policies in the Cigarette Industry*. Nashville, Vanderbilt University Press, 1951.

Rothchild, K. W. "Price Theory and Oligopoly," *Economic Journal*, Vol. LVII (September, 1947), pp. 299–320.

Stigler, G. J. *The Theory of Price*, revised ed., chap. 13. New York, Macmillan, 1952.

Wilcox, C. *Competition and Monopoly in American Industry*, chaps. 4, 5. Washington, Temporary National Economic Committee, Monograph No. 21, 1941.

XIII   The Price of a Factor-Service: General Principles

So FAR our concern has been with the formation of the price of *goods*. Involved were two out of the three basic questions mentioned in Chapter I. The *first* question was: *what* to produce and how much? The underlying assumption of our previous discussions has been that factor-prices were *given* data impounded in "other things are equal," when discussing, for example, the cost of production.

We now release from this impounding one highly important element, namely factor-prices; and we turn to the problem of pricing the factor-service. This kind of pricing has long been known as the *factoral* distribution of income: distribution in accordance with the earning, MPP (marginal physical product) or MVP (marginal value product), of each factor per unit of time. But of late the word "distribution" has gone under a cloud and equivalent expressions like "pricing" the productive resources, or the "compensation" of the factors of production, or "factor-pricing" have taken over. The chief objection to the traditional use of "distribution" stems from the fact that the determination of wages, interest, rent, and profit is far away from the idea of percentage *share* of the total national income per unit of time claimed by each participant in the production of this total income. The aim of the economist is to analyze the determinants of the wage of labor, the rent on land, etc. However, the use of the traditional phrases is not to be condemned, provided we know what they mean in economics.

The *second* problem, of *how* to produce, has been discussed in the chapters on the theory of production, Chapters V and VI.

The *third* question, which dominates the present chapter, is: how much compensation does each factor earn for the contribution imputed to him in the processes of production per unit of time?

It will take five chapters to answer this last question. The present chapter will look into some general ideas on the problem of factor-compensation; then a separate chapter will be devoted to the discussion of the determinants of the price of the service of each of the four production factors per unit of time.

In the study of the prices paid for factor-services our prime interest is in *functional* distribution as distinguished from personal distribution. By *personal* distribution is meant the total income and wealth of individuals no matter from what sources derived. The main question is: how much income and how much property do the various households have? The answer may include inherited property, a time deposit in the bank, gains in the stock market, and stocks and bonds of various corporations. *Functional* distribution refers to the distinct shares of the national income which people receive per unit of time as compensation for the unique functions which their services or the services of their property perform in the processes of production. These shares are, to repeat, the prices of the four productive factors, familiar as wages, interest, rent, and profit.

The importance of the price problem under consideration hardly needs emphasis. The level of wages governs the income and the well-being of the laboring millions. The wage rates affect costs of production and commodity prices. The wage earnings of the working population largely determine the aggregate consumption of a country, therefore a large part of the effective demand for goods and correspondingly the volume of employment. The level of the other prices, interest, rent, and profits, accruing chiefly to the wealthier order, has much to do with saving and investment and consequently once more with general employment and the prosperity of the economy as a whole. So important is the problem of distribution that the penetrating British economist David Ricardo said in 1817: "To determine the laws which regulate this distribution is the principal problem in Political Economy." [1]

The prices commanded by the services of the productive resources are, like Janus, two-headed. (1) To the firm paying these prices when hiring the services, the payments constitute the cost of producing goods. As costs of production they play a prominent part in governing the prices of such goods. Prices determine prices: the prices of factor-services determine the prices of goods. The long-run price of a good can be resolved into the prices paid for the productive services which went into the making of it. (2) To the recipients, these prices constitute income. Wages,

[1] David Ricardo, *Principles of Political Economy and Taxation*, 1817 (New York, Everyman ed., 1912), p. 1.

interest, rent, and profit are the functional income, respectively, of labor, the owner of capital, the owner of land, and the businessman. People sell productive services in order to obtain an income. Some sell personal services, as do the laborer and the entrepreneur. Others sell the services of the property which they own, as do the owners of land and money capital.

We see a complex of reciprocal relationships in the pricing mechanism of our economy. The firm hires productive services and pays for them. These payments are a cost to the firm and income to the factors of production. In return, the factors produce goods, which the firm sells. The buyers of these goods are these very factors of production (or their wives); and the purchase price offered comes from the incomes received. The firm buys factor-services and sells goods; the factors sell services and buy goods. Thus money leaves the firms and goes to the productive agents, then it leaves the agents and returns to the firms. The flow of money and goods and the allocation of resources move in this unending circle, now at a level of nearly full employment and then, as in a depression, at a level far below full employment. Our economy is a panorama of circular interdependence. It is also erected on two pillars, on two penetrating principles, marginal utility affecting the consumer, and marginal productivity centered on the producer. (Of course, the physicist will tell us that *three* pillars are needed.) Price is the language of both these forces; and profit and gain are the energizers to greater effort. A rising price is an invitation to the producer to produce more and a warning to the consumer to consume less.

I. The Marginal-Productivity Theory

The pricing process affecting productive services is similar to the pricing process in the markets for commodities. Human beings are not commodities and are not for sale; but their services are. By a market for a productive service we mean the area in which the factor is free to choose among alternative employments. The governing forces are demand and supply. But, as we have had occasion to learn, these two versatile conceptions, indispensable tools in any price situation, vary in content and in attending circumstances in nearly each type of pricing problem. In some of the coming chapters the task will be to explore the unique conditions of demand and supply of the factors of production. There is, however, a principle already somewhat familiar to us which sheds light on important ground common in various degrees to the four types of distribution. This principle can be briefly called marginal productivity. The center of it can be summed up as distribution according to contribution. What governs the nature of contribution?

The marginal-productivity theory gives the answer, and it runs as follows: When we employ successive *units* of one given variable resource, say labor-hours, in conjunction with the fixed amounts of all the other resources, the behavior of the resulting output will exhibit three phases. At first the total product will rise at an increasing rate; then the total output becomes flat; and then, as we keep on feeding the fixed resources with units of this one variable resource, the total output keeps on rising but now at a diminished rate. It is this third phase that contains the heart of the marginal-productivity theory.

A direct corollary of this principle states that, to maximize its profits, the firm will hire units of productive resources up to the point at which the marginal outlay in purchasing the service is equal to the marginal value product, to the contribution of a unit of this service to the total output that had been attained before this unit was hired. This principle is in large measure an aspect of the law of nonproportional returns, a phase of the theory of production. In fact, this chapter may be regarded as a supplement to Chapters V and VI.

Lest we forget. The marginal-productivity idea back of, say, wages is not the only causative element. As we were warned in Chapters I and II, other forces play a part in the determination of, for example, wages or interest: the significance of property; economic power; a surplus, as in agriculture; historical, social, psychological, and other forces. But we impound (why?) these elements in "ceteris paribus"—"other things equal."

PRICING A FACTOR-SERVICE

The price of the unit service of a factor implies the partnership of two markets: the market in factor-services, where the businessman buys or hires production factors which will produce his goods, and the market for the finished goods which this businessman produces and sells. It is not difficult to perceive that these two market structures can combine into many patterns. Thus we may have (1) competition on both markets, in the purchase of materials and in the selling of the finished product; or the two markets may be: (2) competition-monopoly; (3) monopsony-monopoly (a single buyer of, say, raw materials, and a single seller of the resultant commodity in a monopoly market); (4) monopoly-competition (monopoly in the possession of raw materials and competition in the market for the finished product); (5) oligopsony-oligopoly (an oligopsony in buying the raw materials and oligopoly in selling the finished product); and various other market configurations. We must realize, however, that we cannot put down any pair of markets that irresponsibly come to mind. Some market combinations do not make sense; for example, monopsony and pure competition, or oligopsony and monopolistic competition.

We shall not attempt to analyze all these market situations; we shall confine ourselves to a few remarks on the first three cases: (1) competition-competition; (2) competition-monopoly (many producers of the raw materials selling to one manufacturer who is the only seller of the resulting commodity); and (3) monopsony-monopoly. Table 16 on the next page may help us with these first three cases.

Let us become acquainted with this Table 16. We start with the *first* situation (competition-competition), which is portrayed in columns 1 and 2. The demand for the product is perfectly elastic and would trace a horizontal line. As the first two columns indicate, the firm can hire any relevant amount of, say, labor-hours, at the steady price of $12 a unit. In this situation the price of $12 is also the marginal cost of the factor-service (why?) and column 2 may be identified as the column of marginal cost. Columns 3 and 4 outline the variations in the total and in the marginal physical outputs as more and more units of the service are set to work with the other, fixed inputs, like plant and machines. These two columns (3 and 4) exemplify the law of returns.

Beginning with column 5, Table 16 deals with the revenue from the sale of output. The product may be sold by the firm in a competitive market at the invariant unit price of 50¢, as in column 5a. Or the firm may sell in one of the three types of monopoly situations: single-firm monopoly, monopolistic competition, or oligopoly. The sales schedule is then assumed to be as in column 5b. Columns 6a and 6b indicate the total receipts from the sale of the various outputs in the competitive and in the monopolistic markets respectively. The two sets of totals are obtained by multiplying the figures in column 3 by 50¢ (for 6a) and by the prices in column 5b (for 6b). We are now in the *second* situation with regard to the market structure: we introduce a monopoly element into the market.

The final two columns, 7a and 7b, in Table 16, give us the marginal revenue or marginal value product, MRP or MVP, that is, the increments in net revenue contributed to the firm by each additional unit of the service hired. For instance, the second unit of factor-service accounts for an increment in net receipts equal to $65 — $30 = $35; or to $117 — $60 = $57, depending on whether the firm sells the output in a competitive or in a monopoly-element market.

The behavior of the marginal revenue product is of the same character as the behavior of the marginal physical output. Both exemplify the law of nonproportional returns. Underlying the calculations of marginal revenue product are the marginal physical output and the unit price at which the various outputs sell.

TABLE 16. *Marginal Revenue Product with Competition and Monopoly*

Units of factor-service hired	Price of factor-service: Marginal cost	Total physical product	Marginal physical product	Price of the product		Total receipts		Marginal revenue product	
(1)	(2)	(3)	(4)	(5a)	(5b)	(6a) (3) × (5a)	(6b) (3) × (5b)	(7a)	(7b)
1	$12	60	60	$0.50	$1.00	$ 30	$ 60.00	$30	$60.00
2	12	130	70	.50	.90	65	117.00	35	57.00
3	12	210	80	.50	.80	105	168.00	40	51.00
4	12	280	70	.50	.70	140	196.00	35	28.00
5	12	340	60	.50	.65	170	221.00	30	25.00
6	12	390	50	.50	.60	195	234.00	25	13.00
7	12	430	40	.50	.55	215	236.50	20	2.50
8	12	460	30	.50	.50	230	230.00	15	−6.50

(1) Accordingly, the marginal revenue product may rise at first, especially if the product is disposed of in a competitive market and therefore at a constant price such as the $.50 in column 5a, Table 16. As the marginal physical output rises and is sold at this unvarying unit price, a rising marginal revenue product may well appear at first. This rise is noticed in column 7a for the first three units of service.

(2) But sooner or later, primarily because of diminishing marginal physical output, the marginal revenue product will begin to fall even if the firm sells the product competitively; so we notice in column 7a, beginning with the fourth unit of service. With each extra unit of service hired the extra revenue to the firm is falling off. When the output is sold monopolistically the trend of diminishing marginal revenue productivity is aggravated by the fact that diminishing increments of product are sold at a declining price. In column 7b the diminishing trend is not only immediate but also more pronounced than in column 7a. When the output is sold in a competitive market, the marginal revenue product is also called, and for an obvious reason, the marginal value product. In general, the marginal revenue product curve of a factor slopes downward more rapidly to a monopolistic seller of the product than to a competitive seller.

The marginal revenue product determines the optimum number of units of a service which the firm can employ at a given market price for this service. The guiding formula is, to repeat: marginal factor cost equals marginal revenue product. As is seen in the first two columns, in Table 16, for each unit of service hired the firm pays $12. The marginal factor cost is $12. If the firm sells its output competitively, the optimum number of productive units which it can hire is 8, with a marginal revenue product of nearly $12 ($15, to be exact). A firm selling its product as a monopolist will find it most desirable to hire 6 units. As was already observed, if the factor-services are offered in a competitive market, the price of the factor-service and the marginal cost of the factor-service are identical. We can therefore generalize for such a case that whether the firm is a competitor or a monopolist in disposing of its product it will do best by employing each factor-service up to an amount at which the marginal revenue product of the service equals the price, the cost, of the service. Roughly, the cost of the service to the firm is to be balanced by the product contribution of this service to the firm.

A few words about the *third* situation for consideration, namely monopsony in one market and monopoly in the second market; one buyer of materials is also the one seller of the product. As a big firm hires more and more units of a service, like labor-hours, it may make a large inroad on the total amount of the service available in the area, so that the monopsonist firm is compelled to offer increasing compensation for the factor-

service if the factor is not to be drawn away to other locations and occupations. To the monopsony firm the supply curve AC or S of the
service rises to the right; this AC or S curve has a positive inclination.
The monopolist, in selling the finished product, may get the most profit.
He will curtail, if necessary, his purchases of the raw materials in order
to make the maximum unit of profit as he sells the finished product as
a monopolist.

TWO NAMES FOR MARGINAL PRODUCTIVITY: VMP AND MRP (OR MVP)

It is well to stress that in the discussion of the concepts of marginal
productivity we are dealing with two aspects of the concept; if the finished
product sells in a *competitive* market, the value of the marginal product
(VMP) equals the marginal physical product (MPP) times the unvarying competitive price. The second case involves a degree of *monopoly*:
as more and more of the finished product is sold, the price declines and
is not uniform as under competition. Now we no longer deal with VMP
but with MRP or MVP (marginal revenue product or marginal value
product). The formula now is MVP (or MRP) $=$ MPP $\times$ MR, where
MR is the marginal revenue brought in by the sale of the finished product.
When we employ, for example, 4 units of the factor-service instead of
3 units, the output of the article rises by 70 and MPP $=$ 70 (column 4,
Table 16). Total revenue rises by $28 (column 7b).

This rise in revenue *per unit* of additional output sold is MR $=$ \$28 $\div$
$70 = 40¢$. We get marginal revenue product (MRP or MVP) $=$
$70 \times 40¢$.[2] In sum, the price of a factor in a competitive market is VMP;
the price in the market with a small or large element of monopoly is
MVP or MRP. Only in a competitive market is VMP a usable concept:
as output rises, we multiply the marginal, the extra amount of the product,
by the unvarying price per unit. The other symbols, MRP or MVP, apply
not only if there is an element of monopoly in the market for the finished
product, but even when this market is competitive. Accordingly MRP
or MVP is a more general concept than VMP.

Some of the other cases in which the concept of "marginal" is involved
are certain *pairs* of market structures—in buying materials and selling
the finished product in the appropriate market. Examples are: monopoly-
monopsony, monopoly-oligopoly, oligopoly-monopsony, oligopoly-oli-
gopsony; and these markets are not all.[3]

Before leaving the theory of marginal productivity, we must record

[2] For a brief demonstration of this formula, especially the MR in it, see G. J. Stigler,
The Theory of Price (New York, Macmillan, 1946), p. 244.
[3] J. D. Coppock, *Economics of the Business Firm* (New York, McGraw-Hill,
1959), chap. 21.

an inborn vexing difficulty. In the discussion of marginal productivity of a factor-service we mean that, say, 50 workers are employed, in factory or field, and that marginal productivity refers either to the *loss* of output of chairs, for example, when one worker is shifted to another job in the firm, or to the *increment* in output resulting from hiring one additional worker. We choose the first meaning: the analysis has a clearer complexion in the light of this first meaning.

The question arises as to what this additional worker will do, day in and day out. We have 50 machines and 51 laborers. This additional man may earn his keep by running errands for the original 50; by buying for them cigarettes or ice cream during working hours; by collecting and using waste materials; by keeping the 50 machines in good order, thus helping the 50 other men to raise total output in a unit of time from 200 chairs to 203. But if this is how the newcomer is occupied, we can scarcely class him with the other 50 workers; rather, we witness 50 workers and one handy man. If we assume that the marginal man comes furnished with the necessary tools and raw materials, then marginal productivity refers, not to one new worker alone but to the productivity of *two* factor-resources, labor and capital. Without the aid of the new capital, the productivity of the additional worker may be zero.

THREE RELATIONSHIPS

As we stand off and look at the processes pictured in Table 16 we see three interdependent relations.

First comes the purchase schedule or supply schedule of the factor-service. This schedule relates the purchase price and the various units of the service hired by the firm. If the factor market is competitive, this schedule will be perfectly elastic to the firm. The supply curve is horizontal. The situation is illustrated in the first two columns of Table 16. However, if the firm is a monopsonist in the factor market, the supply schedule of the service will trace a positively inclined curve. The average factor-price rises; and, as we know from the average-marginal relationship, the marginal outlay on the service exceeds the average price paid for it in the market.

Second comes the input-output relationship, exemplifying the law of returns. Columns 1, 3, and 4 of Table 16 give the data. The given hired service is treated as the variable. The other resources are regarded as constant.

Third is the sales schedule, the relation between magnitudes of output and the prices at which they can be sold. If the firm sells in a competitive market, the sales schedule is, pricewise, of infinite elasticity, as is indicated in Table 16, columns 3 and 5a. If the firm, as a seller, enjoys a degree of monopoly power, the sales schedule will be as given in Table 16, columns 3 and 5b.

The first and third relationships translate the second relationship, the physical-production function, into monetary terms. The first relationship monetizes the inputs and provides the calculations of the marginal outlays on a factor-service. The third relationship monetizes the outputs and specifies the marginal revenue product, or the marginal revenue productivity, of units of service as these units keep on rising.

In closing this sector we may allow ourselves a serious digression. The theory of marginal productivity does not attempt, and wisely so, to square itself with a large *ethical* question. For instance, the initial inequality of opportunity among the poor condemns some people from the start, on account of a skimpy education, to contribute less product than others, and accordingly to earn a small wage. Not every individual has what it takes to become a doctor or a mechanic. Even with equality of opportunity some people will earn more because of their greater inborn capacity; not all lawyers, or carpenters, or mechanics are equal in capacity, in ambition, and in the propensity to work hard. But even then the question may arise why income distribution must be ordered on the basis of marginal productivity and not on the basis of the size of the family of the worker, or of his needs generally, or of flat equality. Why should society reward the natural accident of greater ability in some individuals, instead of making amends for this natural unfairness to those with only average endowments?

As things stand, the ethics of capitalism seems to be, in this particular domain, utilitarian and pragmatic. The principal considerations in production in modern societies are efficiency in production; progress in the arts of production; a high standard of living; moderation of toil by the growing use of tools and machines, our modern slaves; and a large degree of freedom. The income incentive playing on private initiative in a setting of scant government interference is a basic formula in our economy. But enough of philosophizing. Let us return to the theme at hand, namely the price of the factor-service.

II. The Demand for a Factor-Service

The demand for a factor-service may refer to the demand by the firm, by an industry, or by the economy as a whole. In each case demand signifies the various amounts of a factor which could be hired at various corresponding prices charged for it, other things staying constant. The series of price-quantity combinations forms a demand-schedule; the graph of this schedule gives us a demand curve. That this conception needs modification will be indicated before long. What marginal utility is to the price of a consumer good, marginal productivity is to the price of a unit of factor-service per unit of time.

THE FIRM'S DEMAND CURVE FOR A FACTOR-RESOURCE

The price offered by a firm for a factor-service is governed by the marginal revenue productivity (MRP) of the factor. It is poor business practice to pay the worker $50 a week when his contribution to the gains of the firm is only $40 a week. To refer to the situation illustrated in Table 16, if the firm sells its product as a competitor and hires 5 units of service, it can afford to pay for each unit no more than $30 (column 7a); were it to sell in a monopolistic market, no more than $25 (column 7b). The price column of the demand schedule for a factor-service is to be sought in the column of the marginal revenue product (MRP). In Table 16 the demand schedule is composed by columns 1 and 7a. Not quite, as will shortly be shown in discussing the industry's demand for a factor-service.

For a clearer comprehension of the principles involved, let us present a separate Table 17 illustrating the firm's demand for a factor-service, like labor-hours, under competition in the sale of the product. We borrow from Table 16 all the data we need. Inasmuch as we are dealing with competition and not with monopoly, we use column 7a rather than column 7b. In the last column of Table 17 we compute the average productivity

TABLE 17. *The Firm's Demand for a Factor-Service*

Units of factor-service	Marginal revenue product of factor-service *	Average product of factor-service under competition
(1)	(2)	(3)
1	$30	$30.00
2	35	$32.50 = (30 + 35) \div 2$
3	40	$35.00 = (30 + 35 + 40) \div 3$
4	35	$35.00 = 140 \div 4$
5	30	$34.00 = 170 \div 5$
6	25	$32.50 = 195 \div 6$
7	20	$30.70 = 215 \div 7$
8	15	$28.70 = 230 \div 8$

* Column 7a of Table 16.

of the factor-service, in the usual way: We obtain first the marginal revenue product of the factor from Table 16; add up these marginal revenues; and divide the total by the relevant figure in column 1. Thus if we seek the average productivity of a factor-service when we employ 3 units of this service, we add the marginal revenue products $(30 + 35 + 40)$ in column 2, Table 17, divide the sum by 3, and get $35 (column 3).

It may be desirable to use a simple table to illustrate the problem at hand. Table 17 will do. Column 1 indicates the number of units of a factor-

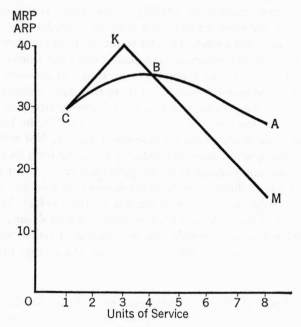

FIGURE 61. *The Firm's Demand for a Factor-Service*

service. Column 2 gives the marginal revenue of the factor hired as more and more of such a service is hired. Column 3 accounts for the average product of a factor-service as more of it is employed: as more of this factor-service is employed. Columns 2 and 3 in Table 17 give us the marginal and the average quantities with the usual marginal-average relations.

We can generalize now that a firm's demand for a factor-service refers to the units of the service hired at prices equal to the marginal revenue products—beginning with a point like B in Figure 61 at which the average revenue product coincides with the marginal revenue product. Figure 61 illustrates the demand for a factor-resource according to the data in columns 1 and 7a of Table 16. The horizontal axis measures the units of the service. The vertical axis measures the marginal (MRP) and average (ARP) revenue productivity. Curve *CBM* reflects the marginal revenue products as given in column 7a. Curve *CBA* pictures the average revenue products, as shown in Table 17, column 3. The point of intersection of the two curves is *B*, which corresponds to nearly four units of service; from the relations between average and marginal quantities we know that point *B* is the highest point on curve *CBA*. The demand curve for the service is *BM*.

THE INDUSTRY'S DEMAND FOR A FACTOR-SERVICE

It appears, at first, that nothing new is introduced when we consider the demand for a productive resource by a group of firms. It seems that the horizontal addition of the demand curves of the individual firms—the addition of the quantities of the service hired by each firm at each price—will give us the composite demand by industry as a whole. But as is often the case in economics, what applies to parts does not apply to the sum of the parts. The "fallacy of composition" is involved here.

The outstanding difficulty arises from the difference in the impact upon the commodity price between the firm and the industry. In considering the competitive firms' demand for a service we treat the sales curve for its output as horizontal. Thus column 5a, Table 16, specifies the constant price of 50¢ for the increasing amounts in column 3. Assume now that the wage rate of a particular kind of labor has declined. If only one firm reacts by hiring more of this labor and by extending its output, the price of the article will not be affected. The price will not dip below 50¢. However, if all the firms in the industry hire more of this labor and expand production, the combined increase in sales will tend to depress the price of the article.

The one firm hires more labor in the expectation that the price of the commodity will stay at 50¢ and that the marginal revenue product of this labor will be higher than it actually becomes when the impact of the similar behavior of *all* the firms in the industry pushes the price of the article down below 50¢. However, with the lower price for the output, the marginal revenue productivity of this labor falls and the firm's demand schedule for labor shifts downward and to the right. With each drop in the wage rate we witness the same chain reaction: a lower price for the article produced resulting from the increased production by all the firms in the industry; a lower marginal revenue productivity schedule and therefore a lower demand curve for labor; and, in the end, the hiring by each firm of less *additional* labor at the lower wage rate than was anticipated by each firm in the expectation of a constant unit sales price of 50¢. In such circumstances, the horizontal summation of unadjusted demand curves for labor by the firms in the industry, plausible at first sight, is inadequate.

The preliminary modification, for each firm, of the demand curve for labor, to render it suitable for horizontal addition, involves much calculation. The process follows, in seven steps, with the assumption that the wage rate of a given type of labor has declined, say, because of immigration. (1) The supply curve of the product of the industry employing such labor is shifted to the right and downward, owing to the induced lower cost of production. (2) The intersection of the consumer demand for this product with this new and lower supply curve will give a lower equilibrium price for the product and larger sales, pointing to a larger employment of this labor. Also, because this labor is cheaper, it will in part be substituted for other factor-services. (3) This lower commodity price shifts the firm's marginal revenue product schedule to the left and downward, inasmuch as the physical products are lower priced than before the change in the wage rate. This in itself means that the firm's demand for this labor will decline. The net result of (2) and (3) is that at the lower wage rate more of this labor will, very likely, be employed.

(4) The supply schedule of the labor-service to the firm is indicated, for example, in the first two columns of Table 16. The intersection of the firm's demand curve for labor as arrived at in (3) above with this supply schedule will give us the *second* point for this firm's revised demand curve for labor. The *first* point is given by price-quantity data for this labor as they existed before the change in the wage rate. (5) In a similar manner we obtain more such points, by assuming successive declines in the wage rate, until we are ready to draw through them this firm's revised demand curve for labor. (6) Such revised demand curves are then obtained for each firm. (7) The horizontal addition of the revised demand curves of all the firms will give us the industry demand curve for the type of labor in question.

It may be noted that it is equally inadequate to obtain the demand of the *whole economy* for a resource-service by the horizontal addition of the demand curves of all the industries using this service. It is necessary to take into account such interactions among industries as produce mutually canceling effects. Suppose, for instance, that a lower price for cotton goods results in increased sales. This fosters an increased demand for a given category of labor employed in the cotton industry or an increased demand for steel used in the machines in the cotton industry. However, we cannot without ado add this new demand for labor or steel to the old demand for labor or steel in all the other relevant industries. The increased use of cotton goods may be in part at the expense of the use of woolens.

The woolen industry requires steel for its machines. It may even employ the same category of labor. The demand for steel or for this kind of labor suffers a decline in the woolen industry at the time when it enjoys an upswing in the cotton industry.

III. The Conditions of Equilibrium

Given the demand schedules for the various resources, how much of each resource will the firm employ? This question relates to the equilibrium of the firm. In previous chapters we explored the equilibrium of the firm as a seller of output. We can now examine the equilibrium of the firm as a buyer of inputs.

THE OPTIMUM ALLOCATION OF INPUTS

We raise the questions: What is the best allocation of the resources used by the firm? When is the firm in equilibrium as regards its employment of the various productive factors? The answer to such questions involves two problems, both of which are part of the theory of production.

(1) The first problem deals with the following questions: With *any* given total expenditure by the firm on inputs, which is the most efficient distribution of this outlay among the several inputs? Which is the least-cost combination of factors in the production of *any* given output? Which is the cheapest way of producing goods as far as factor combination is concerned?

The answer to these questions does not break new ground. We dealt with a question of similar character in Chapter III when discussing the optimum allocation of a consumer's outlay among a variety of goods. A firm will achieve the best combination of inputs when for the last dollar spent on one factor the increment in physical output is the *same* as the increment in output brought by the last dollar spent on any other factor. The increment to the total physical product obtained from the last dollar spent on a factor is measured by dividing the marginal physical product (MPP) of the factor (for example, column 4, Table 16) by the marginal cost (MC) of the factor (column 2, Table 16). The answer to our question can be formulated by the following equations:

$$\frac{\text{MPP of factor } A}{\text{MC of factor } A} = \frac{\text{MPP of factor } B}{\text{MC of factor } B} = \frac{\text{MPP of factor } C}{\text{MC of factor } C} = \cdots$$

If the factors are hired in a competitive market, the denominators can be changed to read: price of A, price of B, and so on. If we are dealing with the short run, factors A, B, C may refer to the variable resources alone; if we are dealing with the long run, "factors" refer to formerly fixed but now variable resources.

The equality of these ratios is brought about by the substitution of one factor for another. If the ratio for factor A is greater than for factor B, we face disequilibrium. A dollar's worth of A yields more marginal physical product than a dollar's worth of B. The firm will do better by employing more of A and less of B; by substituting A for B. As it does so, the marginal physical productivity of A falls and that of B rises until the two ratios are in balance. If the ratio is less for tools than for unskilled labor, the firm will get more output, without an increase in its money outlay, by merely shifting dollars from the purchase of tools to the hiring of skilled labor, until the two ratios are equal.

The equality of the above ratios will be disturbed if the price of one of the services changes; the equality is restored by the process of substitution. Assume, for example, that in a given industry unskilled labor becomes more expensive in relation to its efficiency than skilled labor. All the firms in the industry will tend to use less unskilled and more skilled labor. The MPP of unskilled labor will tend to rise, whereas its price (wage rate) falls; the MPP of skilled labor will fall, whereas its price rises. The substitution of skilled labor for unskilled will go on until the ratios are in balance. Underlying this adjustment is the principle of elasticity of substitution.

(2) The second problem deals with the question: of all possible factor-combinations, which combination can bring maximum profit to the firm? The answer to this question has been shaped in previous discussion. The firm attains maximum profit if it employs each factor-service up to the point at which the marginal cost, or marginal outlay, on the service equals the marginal revenue product of the service. If it employs the various services short of this stage, even though it keeps on maintaining for all factors the equality of the ratios MPP/MC, it will not reap maximum profit. The marginal revenue product of each service will exceed the marginal outlay on it, and in the long run the firm will improve its profit position by hiring more of each service, that is, by enlarging its output. If it uses each service beyond the point of this equality, it sustains a loss on each extra unit of each service taken on. What this equation means is that it is most advantageous for the firm to stop hiring the inputs when the last dollar of expenditure on each input brings precisely a dollar in additional net revenue. In long-run equilibrium, the firm produces at least cost, or minimum average cost, or maximum efficiency, and reaps a maximum gain. The least-cost combination of inputs is obtained by substitu-

tion among inputs; the maximum gain, by adjusting the level of output.

We have now two separate conditions or equations for the equilibrium of the firm. One was derived in Chapter IX. It is the equation $MC = MR$ (the marginal cost of the article equals its marginal revenue or price). The other condition is stated in the previous paragraph: it is $MRP = MO$ (the marginal revenue product of each service equals the marginal outlay on it). The first condition focuses on the output, the second on the input. These two conditions are not at odds with each other. So interdependent are the firm's calculations and choices, and so interwoven are the mathematical variables and equations involved, that when the firm attains a position of equilibrium portrayed by one of these equations the other equation is simultaneously satisfied. However, the demonstration of this thesis would take us into complicated algebra or the differential calculus.[4]

ELASTICITY OF SUBSTITUTION

Occupied, on the production side, with combinations and proportionalities of factors, the firm is perennially considering the substitution of one factor for another. In Chapter V and in this chapter alike, the principle of substitution appears and reappears. Faced with varieties of factors, with fixed and variable resources, and with changes in the prices of goods and factors, the firm has to make choices, usually, in substituting one resource for another.

The limitation to these choices is set by technology of production and the stimulus is provided by changes in the prices of factor-services. Sometimes technology prescribes fixed proportions. If a machine requires precisely three attendants, it will not be plied with more than three attendants even when their wage rate declines or when the cost of such machines rises. The elasticity of substitution of attendants for such machines is zero.

At the other extreme is the example where technically factor A is almost a perfect substitute for factor B. The two factors are nearly identical. With a slight drop in the charge for A's service, A will crowd B out of employment. The elasticity of substitution of A for B is almost infinite. In most cases, factors are not nearly identical, but differ in varying degrees; and technology permits a range of substitution. In such cases, how far the substitution of one factor for another may go depends on technology and on the relative prices of the factors under consideration.

Broadly speaking, elasticity of substitution refers to the extent to which a relative change in the prices of two factors will induce a replacement of one by the other. We are dealing with eight magnitudes: the given price

[4] See, for example, G. J. Stigler, *op. cit.*, p. 185n.; S. Weintraub, *Price Theory* (New York, Pitman, 1949), pp. 112-113.

and quantity of one factor and the changed price and quantity of this factor; then the similar four variables for the other factor. It may be wise to stop here with the scrutiny of this difficult concept.

IV. Indifference Curves

In the discussion of demand and the behavior of the *consumer* we applied at first the marginal-utility idea, and then we turned to the indifference-curves technique. We can do likewise in our discussion of the behavior of the *firm* with respect to production. So far, in this chapter, we used the marginal-productivity theory. We can now apply the indifference-curves method.

We do not expect clear sailing in the presentation of the case. The villain in the piece is *repetition*—verbal and diagrammatic repetition. The indifference-curves approach in the treatment of the theory of production was presented in the last section of Chapter VI. In general, repetition of analysis and of tables and of illustrative figures ought to be avoided.

We turn to a compromise. Some aspects of the indifference-curves analysis will not blink at the double exposures; for example, the isoquant and the MRS (marginal rate of substitution). Other aspects need not indulge in duplication, like outlay lines, the least-cost combination, and the scale-line. We shall deal with the first two, and omit repetition of the last three.

ISOQUANTS

In our first study of isoquants (Chapter IV) we centered our attention on typical and nontypical *segments* of a typical isoquant, as depicted by Figure 17. Now we shall study briefly typical and nontypical isoquants. The concept of the isoquant is vital enough to justify modified repetition of its nature. The isoquant in production is the counterpart of the iso-utility curve in consumption. There are at least three varieties of the isoquant: the typical isoquant (Figure 62A); the nontypical isoquant (Figure 62B); and the exceptional isoquant (Figure 62C). A few words about each of these varieties.

In Figure 62A we lay off labor units on the horizontal axis, and units of land on the vertical axis. Each curve mirrors a succession of combinations of land and labor which can produce equal quantities of a product per unit of time. The first isoquant on the left in Figure 62A traces various combinations of the two inputs (land and labor) which can produce 100

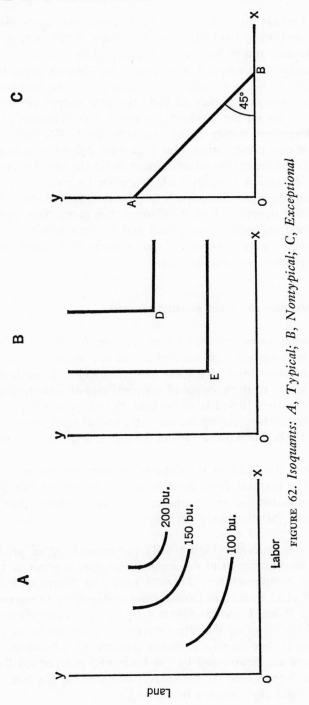

FIGURE 62. Isoquants: A, Typical; B, Nontypical; C, Exceptional

bushels of wheat. In each given isoquant curve the inputs vary, but the output is uniformly 100 bushels or 150 bushels or 200 bushels, depending on the isoquant and its location on the map of isoquants.

Technically each isoquant represents an indifference curve to the firm. Technically it does not matter to the firm which combination of inputs it will use, inasmuch as they all yield the same output per unit of time. Thus *any* point on the 200-bushel curve is a combination yielding 200 bushels. But when *money* outlays are considered, only one combination is the least-cost combination. One important difference between a consumer indifference curve and an isoquant lies in the fact that in the former the third dimension is utility (which cannot be measured), whereas in the isoquant the third dimension is total production (which is represented by a definite figure). Another difference lies in the fact that the consumer's total expenditure on goods and services is necessarily limited by his income minus his savings, if any, whereas the businessman can vary his total spending on factor-services.

THE MARGINAL RATE OF FACTOR SUBSTITUTION (MRS)

The combinations mirrored by an isoquant function as substitutions: the combinations represent less and less of one input (y) and more and more of the other input (x). How much less and how much more? The answer takes us to the concept of marginal rate of substitution. Suppose we talk about the MRS of labor for land. We mean by this the amount of land which may be given up for one extra unit of labor, output remaining unchanged. The MRS is the slope of the curve; it is $-\Delta y/\Delta x$; more labor, less land.

How does the MRS or the slope of an isoquant behave as we move along on the isoquant from point to point? To answer this question, it may be sufficient for our purposes to consider three situations: two extremes and variations between them.

(1) At one extreme (Figure 62B) the technology of production is such that no substitution of one input for another is possible. The inputs are rigidly complementary. There is only one "correct" combination which will yield an output. Double this combination and the output may be doubled. Points E and D (Figure 62B) illustrate correct combinations. Any combination other than the correct one produces no output of the desired nature but merely a useless mixture of substances. Incorrect combinations are represented by the horizontal and vertical lines of the isoquant in Figure 62B. At the correct combination the isoquant bends to form a right angle convex to the origin.

(2) The other extreme (Figure 62C) is exemplified when the two inputs are perfect substitutes for one another. The MRS is constant; the slope is the same from point to point. The isoquant is then a straight line, but neither vertical nor horizontal: in these two kinds of lines, no substitution is going on at all. If the inputs are identical, MRS = 1; and the isoquant makes an angle of 45° with either axis, as does line AB in Figure 62C. But inputs of different categories are not identical; and the typical lines will be steeper or flatter than AB, the line forming the 45° angle.

(3) Between these two extremes (Figures 62C and 62B) many midway positions are possible. The isoquant of Figure 62A may have a small curvature; then the curve roughly approximates a straight line. The MRS and the slope change gradually as we move along *on* the isoquant from point to point. The two inputs are good substitutes.

These midway situations are typical. Inputs are commonly to some degree substitutes and to some extent complements, like land and the workers on it in our example of isoquants, Figure 62A. As the substitution of labor for land proceeds and as more labor is taken on, less and less land can be given up for each extra unit of labor without lessening total output per unit of time. There is a diminishing marginal rate of substitution. As x is extended, y drops; the isoquant slopes to the right. Moreover, as x is extended by *equal* distances, the y drops by smaller and smaller amounts; the isoquant is convex to the origin. (Why?)

It is necessary to stress the relation between the marginal rate of inputs substitution (MRS) and the marginal physical product (MPP) of the inputs. Consider any point on isoquant 100 bushels in Figure 62A. If in the combination at this point an acre of land adds 50 bushels to the total output and a labor-month adds 30 bushels, the marginal rate of substitution of labor for land is $\frac{3}{5}$ acre of land for 1 labor-month: adding one unit of labor contributes 30 bushels to total output; giving up $\frac{3}{5}$ acre of land depresses total output by 30 bushels. The firm can maintain the output at 100 bushels by giving up $\frac{3}{5}$ acre of land and acquiring 1 labor-month. The marginal productivity of land and of labor is such that $\frac{3}{5}$ acre of land and 1 labor-month can replace one another without affecting total output. The slope of the isoquant, or the MRS of labor for land, represents the reciprocal of the ratio of the marginal products of labor and land. We can write, then: MRS of labor for land $= \text{MPP}_r/\text{MPP}_d$, where the numerator and the denominator designate the marginal physical product of labor and land respectively. That is, at the given point on the isoquant, MRS (of labor for land) $= \frac{3}{5}$: add one unit of labor-months and give up $\frac{3}{5}$ unit of land.

We come now to the elements of the problem of production which need no duplication—namely, outlay lines, the least-cost combination, and the scale line. These three aspects are discussed in Chapter VI, and the reader can turn to that chapter.

SUGGESTED READINGS

Bain, J. S. *Pricing, Distribution, and Employment,* revised ed., chaps. 11, 12. New York, Holt, 1953.

Boulding, K. E. *Economic Analysis,* revised ed., chap. 31. New York, Harper, 1948.

Chamberlin, E. H. *The Theory of Monopolistic Competition,* 6th ed., chap. 8. Cambridge, Harvard University Press, 1948.

Due, J. F. *Intermediate Economic Analysis,* revised ed., chap. 12, pp. 159–172. Chicago, Irwin, 1950.

Enke, S. *Intermediate Economic Theory,* chap. 26. New York, Prentice-Hall, 1950.

Leftwich, R. H. *The Price System and Resource Allocation,* revised ed., chaps. XIII, XIV. New York, Holt, Rinehart and Winston, 1960.

Lerner, A. P. *The Economics of Control,* chap. 13. New York, Macmillan, 1945.

Machlup, F. "On the Meaning of the Marginal Product," *Explorations in Economics,* pp. 250–263. Reprinted in *Readings in the Theory of Income Distribution,* pp. 158–174.

Marshall, A. *Principles of Economics,* 8th ed., Book VI, chaps. 1, 2. New York, Macmillan, 1927.

CHAPTER

XIV Wages

THE CENTRAL theme of this chapter is the theory of wage determination. But before we go directly to this problem it is necessary to clarify the concept of wages.

I. Wages and Wage Differences

THE MEANING OF WAGES

The word wages may refer to a number of things: to piece rate, time rate, payroll, take-home pay, money wage, and real wage. In this chapter, and elsewhere in the book, we mean by wages the wage rate per hour, the payment for the hour-unit of physical or mental service hired by the firm. Wages include salaries, fees, and commissions. We mean, moreover, real wages; that is, the amount of goods which the monetary wage rate commands. In the discussion of a money wage we shall assume that the price level is constant. It can readily be seen that the worker is vitally interested in earnings over an extended period, say, a year. But in economic theory the wage rate per hour is of unique significance. It measures the compensation for a unit of effort; and it constitutes the basis of the firm's calculations of the labor cost of production.

Wages are the price of the service of labor. They are a very important set of prices in our price economy. Around 65% of the personal income in our country is derived from wages and salaries. The percentage becomes much higher when we consider that a large part of the income of the farmer, the businessman, the professional man, and other self-employed people is essentially a wage for labor. Economic systems are evaluated by the level of wages of the multitudes of those whom Adam Smith called "the laboring poor." Nowadays social systems are threatened with dissolution where the wage level is too low.

THE WAGE LEVEL

The concept of the wage level in a country is of the same nature as the concept of the price level or the production level. It is a general concept compounded of the wage rates of the many kinds of labor in the numerous trades and pursuits. Some wage rates in the United States, for those not covered by the minimum-wage law, are still below $1.00 an hour, even in these days of a high cost of living. The wage level is a concept symbolizing a heterogeneous mass of items. Vague as it is, it is on occasion a useful and even an indispensable concept, as when we compare the wages of one country with those of another, or the wages of a given country at two different times.

General wages are higher in the United States than in nearly all other countries. The laboring population is better off, in the satisfaction of necessities and comforts, here than elsewhere. Why? Because the marginal productivity of labor is generally higher here than abroad. For this fact a number of circumstances are responsible. *First*, in proportion to the population we possess abundant natural resources such as fertile land, ores, coal, oil, and timber. *Second*, our labor is aided by more capital facilities. In manufacturing trades a worker receives the help, on the average, of over $15,000 of capital. In our civilization man has machine-slaves working for him, far exceeding in productive power the slaves of ancient Greece. *Third*, the American businessman is, by and large, more daring and enterprising and more single-minded in the pursuit of gain than his counterpart in many other lands. *Fourth*, universal general education and the wider spread of higher education have made our labor more efficient in production.

In sum, the people of the United States are more productive than others, in part perhaps because its labor generally possesses greater energy and dexterity, but in greater part because the factors collaborating with the American worker are strikingly more abundant. The combination of productive resources inside the firm is markedly effective in making goods. But these two reasons do not suffice for all the productivity difference. There are conditions in the United States society at large which contribute enormously to a high degree of productivity and have their impact on the efficiency of the business concern.

First among these is the absence of the remnants of feudal institutions and the strong sense of social equality in the United States. The feeling that one man is as good as another sharpens incentives, fires ambitions, and generates a restless striving for the good things of life. The few want to be better, the many want to be better off. *Second,* United States businessmen enjoy free trade over a vast continental area. The absence of internal tariff walls gives a huge national market which breeds division of labor and mass production with the many associated economies in making goods. *Lastly,* there is apparently less monopoly in the United States than abroad, where a business may be regarded as a private preserve, often producing on a small scale and thriving on high prices, low wages, and scant taxes. There is accordingly less of a scarcity economy in the United States than in many a community abroad.

However, when we investigate wages in a given country at a given time it is inadequate to treat wages as a comprehensive entity standing for the general level of returns to labor. Labor does not present itself as one large mass of identical units; it is not a homogeneous factor. In a specific discussion we cannot use "wages" to mean at once the compensation of the bus driver, the welder, the chemical engineer, and the janitor. We must confine the discussion to a narrower category of wages. Accordingly, the laboring population and the multitudes of jobs are divided on the basis of more or less characteristic wage differences. We shall note here three types of differences: among noncompeting groups, among jobs within a noncompeting group, and among geographical areas.

1. NONCOMPETING GROUPS—REAL WAGE DIFFERENCES

First we shall consider noncompeting groups. The laboring population may be classified into separate large divisions. Within a division there is a substantial degree of homogeneity of labor and of mobility from trade to trade. But crossing the boundary from one group to another is not an ordinary occurrence. It is not important to decide here precisely how many such groups a society exhibits. The decision is largely a matter of classification. We may distinguish three categories.

(1) *The unskilled and semiskilled.* At the bottom of the ladder are the workers who perform tasks which call for little knowledge, skill, and training. The vanishing pick-and-shovel laborer and the run-of-the-mill factory hand are examples.

(2) *The skilled workers.* On a higher rung of the ladder are workers whose trades call for lengthy training, special capacities, and substantial skills. The plumber, the mechanic, and the bookkeeper belong here. The

variation in ability and performance per hour is greater among members of this group than among the members of the lower group.

These first two groups of labor do not move in tight compartments. The elasticity of substitution is not zero. A firm may consider hiring more or less skilled labor in combination with less or more semiskilled labor. Should the price of unskilled labor rise, say, because of a minimum-wage law, the tendency will develop to replace unskilled by skilled labor. There is some competition between these two "noncompeting" groups.

(3) *The professional group.* At the top we find the professional people like the dentist, the lawyer, the scientist, the high-grade actor, or the prosperous businessman. Part of the income of such individuals is profit because their functions are in part entrepreneurial. But part is a salary for rendering a service requiring training, experience, general ability, and other qualifications of a more than ordinary caliber. Here is where individual differences are pronounced and prevalent. But even this group does not live on a social mountain peak in splendid isolation. The children of artisans can become lawyers or professors. Conversely, should a skilled trade command a considerable income, even established professionals, let alone their children, may turn to it. Many a small-town lawyer is more a real-estate agent or an insurance man than a lawyer.

Groups within groups. There are noncompeting groups within noncompeting groups. Because of racial prejudice and because of a considerable residue of discrimination against women—a Negro, a Mexican, a Jew, or a woman within each noncompeting group is not hired as readily as the other workers. In many localities the opportunities for employment of such unfavored individuals are limited. Such people crowd into occupations and areas where discrimination is less prevalent or nonexistent, and where they compete for the available openings. In such instances, their marginal productivity is lower and their compensation is below what it would otherwise be, or else their jobs are inferior in comparison with the jobs of those not in disfavor.

It is not necessary to explore here the complex question why the laboring population finds itself in these more or less distinctive compartments. One reason commonly cited is the difference in the natural endowments of people. Not all individuals possess the ambition, the patience, and the ability to master a calling which requires long training and mental alertness. Another reason is the difference in environment, which exercises an overshadowing influence in shaping the inclinations of a young person. The home atmosphere, the neighborhood associations, and educational opportunities are not equal for all people. Even in our prosperous democracy it requires the uncommon combination of ambition, will power, good health, mental capacity, and fair luck for the son of a poor man to become a doctor. Very few born to families with an income of $3,500 a year go to college; very few whose fathers make $12,000 do not.

The outcome is that in relation to the demand there has been so far in the United States an abundance of unskilled and semiskilled labor, a smaller pool of skilled labor, and a still more limited number of people offering professional service. It is this circumstance which largely accounts for enduring differences in the wages of these categories of labor. Sometimes these differences are called *real differences*. It is to be expected that with less immigration from abroad and with greater educational opportunities beyond the grammar school, the ranks in the lowest group will grow thinner in the United States. Conversely, the shift which we have witnessed in recent decades to the varieties of white-collar occupations may eventuate in relatively lower wage rates for them, unless the demand for clerical work and the like surges upward.

2. "EQUALIZING WAGE DIFFERENCES"

Within a given noncompeting group all the occupations ought to command the same wage rate in a given region. But this is not the case. Here we come upon the *second* type of wage differences, called *equalizing differences*. Within the given group, some trades are more pleasant and less dangerous, and offer better opportunities for advancement, more regular employment, and a longer working life than other trades. At the same wage rates these favored callings would be crowded, whereas the less advantageous pursuits would be sought by small numbers. Under competitive conditions, the consequence is that the marginal productivity of labor in the less desirable trades is higher and the wage rate is greater than in the other trades. And so it comes about that a coal miner gets a higher wage than the farm hand; at the same wages, there would be a shortage of coal miners and a superabundance of farm hands. A clerk in the office receives less than the man in overalls at the lathe. And the college professor earns less than the doctor or lawyer: he pays dearly for the attractions of his occupation.

3. GEOGRAPHICAL WAGE DIFFERENCES

We now come to the *third* kind of wage differences. In different areas the wages earned by the same grade of labor vary considerably. A carpenter receives a smaller wage rate in the South than in the Northeast, a higher rate in Montana than in Wisconsin. We mean, of course, real wages; money wages may diverge more or less than real wages do since the cost of living varies. It costs less to get on where the climate is mild and expenditures on clothing and house-heating encroach less on the family budget. Living costs are higher in large cities than in small towns where rentals are lower, where it is less expensive to move about, and where the temptations to spend are fewer.

A prominent cause of regional wage differences lies in the immobility of labor. Workers often lack knowledge regarding better jobs in other places. Workers become attached to the community in which they live. There is reluctance to break camp and to go to unfamiliar surroundings. Leaving an old post often means surrendering the privileges of seniority and the chance of promotion. It costs money to move; and there is the inevitable loss of working time. It can therefore happen that in some areas a given trade may be relatively crowded and the workers may be subject to a low marginal revenue productivity, whereas in other localities in the same trade the job seeks the man.

To these three classes of wage differences (real, equalizing, and regional) may be added a *fourth* class; namely, personal differences. Some workers are more capable, more alert, and more reliable than others. Ordinarily, under competitive conditions, they are paid more, are laid off latest in slow times, or are given more pleasant jobs.

SUMMARY

The four types of wage differences touched on above possess one common quality. They are all barriers to a worker's movement from a low-paid to a high-paid position. The barriers prevent workers from being interchangeable. Remove the barriers—(1) let people be equal in endowment and opportunity, (2) let all tasks be equally pleasant or unpleasant, and (3) let distance present no impediment—and the wage rates of all people would be identical. Assume, however, the second of these barriers and remove the other two, and apart from the expense of medical training, the ditchdigger will receive more pay than the doctor. His job is less attractive than the doctor's; and doctors would not shift to the ditchdigger's job and wipe out his equalizing wage differential. But in the world of reality, with all these barriers in existence, we see the window cleaner get more than the ordinary factory hand, but less than the surgeon, even after allowance has been made for the cost of a medical education. The window washer retains his differential because the factory hand will not become a window washer; and the surgeon will continue to earn more per hour although the window cleaner's job is more hazardous, because window cleaners do not apply for admission to medical schools.

There are more wage differences than have been cited. Each plant in a given city may offer different rates for the same general type of work because of the uniqueness of attending circumstances. Jobs of the same general category may display differentiation akin to product variation in monopolistic competition in the markets for goods. We shall slur, however, such minor wage differences. In our discussion we shall mean by a wage the rate of pay in a given trade in a given locality; for instance, the wage of a carpenter or bookkeeper in a city or in a larger more or less homogeneous area.

II. The Demand for and the Supply of Labor

Like any other price, the wage of a particular kind of labor is governed by the conditions of demand and supply in a given labor market. We shall now look into the nature of these conditions. We begin with demand.

A. The Demand for Labor

By the demand for labor we mean the various amounts of, say, labor-hours of a given grade that may be hired by the firm at various corresponding prices of labor, that is wage rate per unit of time. The demand for labor or any other factor-resource can be condensed into two columns: the first column registers an array of labor units applied. The second column indicates the marginal revenue product (MRP or MVP). What the marginal unit of resources contributes to the output defines the limit of its contribution and therefore its wage—other things constant.

The schedule of wages offered by the firm per unit of time depends on the marginal revenue product. The labor-wage sets the limit to the number of workers to be employed. The limit is expressed by the equation $MR = MC$. Thus in Figure 63 back of the D curve is the marginal productivity principle. The marginal labor unit earns a weekly wage which constitutes the weekly cost to the firm. It is not necessary to repeat and belabor what has been said about these aspects of production theory, especially in Chapter XIII and Table 16.

The simple curve in Figure 63 *looks* like the demand for a commodity. True, but we are dealing with a demand curve much more complicated: by demand here we involve the marginal productivity of a factor. The vertical line in Figure 63 measures the marginal revenue productivity (MRP) or the marginal value productivity (MVP); the horizontal axis registers the number of labor units. Each point on the demand curve stands for the number of labor-units employed and the corresponding contribution to output, MRP or MVP. Like the demand curve for com-modities, the *D* curve for factors slopes downward to the right. In both cases an increased demand will shift the curve upward. In both cases the elasticity of demand plays a part.

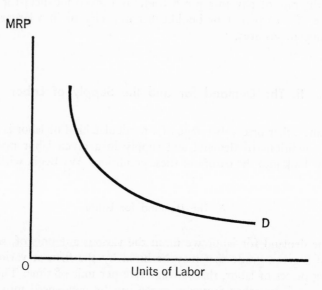

MRP

D

O   Units of Labor

FIGURE 63. *The Demand for a Factor-Service.*

The marginal productivity theory stands pre-eminently as the founda-tion of wage theory. However, to become better acquainted with this theory, let us touch on some significant aspects of it: technology; the nature of the demand for the article being produced; the price of other inputs; and the elasticity of the demand for labor. We shall make brief remarks about some of these causative elements, that is, some wage determinants.

(1) One such determinant is *technology*, or the input-output relations in the firm. As more units of labor are set to work the behavior of the marginal physical outputs will ultimately affect the marginal revenue products. Suppose the proportions of the fixed resources and the variable labor units are by the technology of the processes of production so in-flexible in range that beyond an early stage additional labor will contribute little to the total output. The precipitous drop in the marginal output will register in low marginal revenue productivity of labor. The price of labor will have to fall sharply before the firm will employ additional amounts

of it per unit of time. On the other hand, if the technique employed is associated with a gradual decline in marginal physical returns as more labor is taken on, this fact contributes to gradually diminishing marginal revenue products. A slight drop in the wage may be sufficient to induce the firm to hire more labor. In brief, the argument of this paragraph merely suggests that in Table 16, in the previous chapter, column 7a or 7b is partly affected by what is going on in column 3 or 4.

The technology of production also stamps the relation of a given kind of labor to another kind of labor or to other resources as complementary or substitutive, thus affecting the demand for labor. The machine needs a complement of attendants. Or, the technique may permit the substitution of some skilled labor for some unskilled labor, or the other way around. On the technique often depends whether the elasticity of substitution is high or low.

(2) A second determinant of the demand schedule for labor is found in the nature of the *demand for the commodity* produced. The demand for labor is a *derived* demand, as is the demand for any other factor-service; it is derived from the demand for the output. The greater the consumer demand for the product the greater the producer demand for the labor involved in making it. All other things equal, the higher the prices offered for the various amounts of output the higher the marginal revenue products. Functioning as the agent of the consumers, the firm translates their demand for the output into its own demand for labor input.

(3) The demand for labor depends, in the third place, on the *prices of other inputs* related to labor in terms of substitution. Suppose, for instance, that the price of machinery rises. Two opposing effects on the demand for the labor in question may emerge: the substitution effect and the output effect. The net impact on the demand for labor will depend on the relative strength of these two counteracting forces.

Because, in our assumption, machinery has become relatively more expensive, firms will acquire a tendency to substitute labor for it. At given wages more of this labor will be employed. This is the substitution effect. How much more labor and how much less machinery will be used? The answer is: up to the point at which a dollar's worth of labor will yield as much marginal physical product as a dollar's worth of machinery.

But this substitution effect is not all the story. Because some of this more expensive machinery must continue in use—since the labor in question is not a perfect substitute for it—the cost of producing the commodity rises. To equate marginal revenue and marginal cost, the firm may reduce its output. The demand for this type of labor, and for other factors as well, will decline. Such is the output effect.

These determinants of the demand for labor have much to do with the degree of *elasticity* of the demand for labor. Our brief discussion above of the *first* determinant (technology) indicates its relation to demand elasticity; and no more needs to be said here.

As for the *second* determinant (the nature of the demand for the article produced), it can be broadly stated that the elasticity of the demand for a firm's input will depend, roughly, on the elasticity of the demand for the output. When the demand for the output is elastic, the unit prices in the sales schedule of the article decline slowly as more of it is offered on the market; and in their turn, the marginal revenue products are likely to descend gradually. This means that as the wage rate falls by 1% the rise in the amount of labor hired may be greater than 1%. But we should not infer that the elasticity of demand for *labor* is identical with the elasticity of demand for *output*. The demand for the output of the firm may be infinitely elastic, but the demand for labor will be much less than infinitely elastic. Compare columns 5a and 7a in Table 16. However, it is safe to generalize that the firm's demand for labor is more elastic when it sells its product in a competitive market, and therefore enjoys a perfectly elastic demand for its output, than when the market for the article is monopolistic and the demand for it is less than infinitely elastic.

The elasticity of demand for labor may depend, in the *third* place, on the degree of substitution possible between labor and the other resources. If substitutes are readily available, that is, if the elasticity of substitution is considerable, the elasticity of the demand for labor may be high. With a small advance in wages, the firms will tend to turn to substitute factors. Conversely, a small drop in the wage rate may encourage the use of labor as a substitute for other factors, if it is a good substitute for them. Of course, if the bidding for substitute resources tends to drive up their price to a high level, they will not readily be used to replace labor as its price rises. The demand for labor will then be inelastic. This situation is equivalent to one in which labor does not face readily available substitutes. The alternative factors must be cheap substitutes to be good substitutes.

Reinforcing the effect of *factor* substitution is the correlative *commodity* substitution. As the price of labor declines it is substituted for other inputs. But in addition, under competition, all the goods in the making of which this kind of labor is involved become cheaper, and consumers will favor them as substitutes for other goods the price of which has not moved down. This commodity substitution contributes to the elasticity of the derived demand for the labor affected. (Why?)

One additional observation on the elasticity of the demand for labor may be worth recording. We learned that in an oligopoly market price rigidity is not uncommon. Inflexibility of product prices implies that, for a certain wage range, the demand for labor is inelastic. The wage may rise, but since the price and the associated volume of sales may stay unchanged, the oligopoly firm has little inducement to discharge some of its labor. Similarly, a decline in the wage rate, and in the unit cost of production, may scarcely invite the firms to hire more labor. In these various considerations the element of short run or long run must be distinguished.

DEMAND FOR LABOR BY THE INDUSTRY AND THE ECONOMY

A consideration of the demand for a particular grade of labor by a whole industry imports the same complications as were indicated in the previous chapter, section II, where we sketched the adjustments necessary to arrive at the industry demand for a factor-service. We saw there that the simple expedient of the horizontal addition of the demands for labor by the constituent firm is unsatisfactory.

In dealing with the demand for labor by the economy as a whole we come upon new pitfalls. How many skilled workers will be employed in the country when their wages are lowered or advanced? If the national income were to stay unaffected, the concept of the demand schedule for skilled labor in the economy would not introduce unique difficulties. But the earnings of the millions of skilled workers form a substantial component of the national income; and changes in such a prominent magnitude cannot be ignored. Suppose there is an advance in the wages of these workers, at a time when the economy is not fully employed. With their relatively high propensity to consume, the workers will spend a good part of the additional earnings, swelling the aggregate demand and consequently the national output. The volume of employment of skilled labor, far from falling because of the higher wage rates, may thus experience an upswing. Conversely, a falling money wage rate for a considerable number of workers may occasion a smaller national income and less employment instead of more.[1] The wage rate is not only a cost or a price to the firm but also an *income* to the recipient. As an income, it does not keep still, when we deal with large numbers, but reacts on the demand for labor.

TRADE UNIONS AND THE DEMAND FOR LABOR

Organized labor does not leave alone the demand for labor. The trade union is inclined to render the demand inelastic, by preventing substitutes for labor. Often it attempts to raise or to maintain the demand when the

[1] On this question, see J. M. Keynes *The General Theory of Employment, Interest and Money* (New York, Harcourt, Brace, 1936), chap. 19.

demand would otherwise decline. The worker regards his job with an emotional sense of proprietorship and as an inalienable right which he must defend against the inventor, the legislator, and the usurper hailing from another trade. The protective attitude toward his job shows itself in a number of ways.

Like the businessman, the worker is apt to be a supporter of tariffs on imports of goods. In some vague manner he feels that an imported article competes for his job. During the Senate hearings on the Smoot-Hawley tariff of 1930 many a union urged import duties on goods in the production of which its members had a share.

Organized or not, a worker often eyes with suspicion the introduction of improvements into his round of tasks. The trade union often merely formalizes or intensifies this attitude. A boon to society at large, and to labor too in the long run, technical improvements often reduce the skilled worker in earnings, social position, and self-esteem. They add to his feeling of insecurity. Workers are also given to the "lump-of-work" theory. They believe, wrongly, that there is a given quantum of work available in the community and the sooner it is done the sooner is the worker out of a job. However, in the short run, and with the individual worker, the "lump-of-work" idea is hardly a fallacy.

Accordingly organized labor is often inclined to obstruct new and better ways of doing things and is apt to sanction "make-work" devices —openly or indirectly, although sometimes with indifferent results. Painters' unions, in various localities, have resisted the use of paint sprayers and limited the width of the paintbrush. Carpenters have often persisted in the use of handsaws and other hand tools instead of portable power equipment. Some of these practices aim to lighten the burden of heavy work and to prolong the earning life of the worker. But many other such practices, while occasioning higher costs of production, carry no mitigating justifications.

B. The Supply of Labor

By the supply of labor we mean the various amounts of hours of a given type of labor which will be offered for hire at various wage rates. Given the efficiency of workers, the supply of labor is a function of two variables, the number of workers presenting themselves for work and the number of hours they are willing to work per day or week.

Let us remind ourselves that an increased supply of labor for a firm or an industry means that the supply curve shifts to the right signifying that more labor-hours are offered at the *same* wages. Such a situation may be exemplified during the demobilization of soldiers after a war or when there is an influx of immigrants. We do not, however, face an increased supply of labor if, in response to a higher wage rate, more workers apply for employment or those already engaged are willing to put in more hours per day. In such a case we are merely moving along the same upward-sloping supply curve.

If the *firm* is of *small* size, so that its labor force forms only a small fraction of the total labor pool of the particular grades available in the locality, it tends to regard the curve of its labor supply as a horizontal line. At the current wage it can obtain varying amounts of labor; if it desires to employ more labor, it need not raise the wage rate.

The situation is different with the *large* firm. The number of additional workers needed may constitute a considerable fraction of the total number in the area available for the given type of job. The large employer may have to advance the wage if he is to attract workers from their jobs in the given area or from other areas. This situation reminds us of the monopsony demand for labor. It will be discussed in the next section.

Firms in a given *industry* can draw laborers away from their current posts in other industries by matching the opportunity cost facing the workers who consider a change of employment. The opportunity cost involves the wage received in the old job as well as the cost and inconvenience of making the shift. Note that as the given industry attracts labor away from the other industries the marginal revenue productivity of this type of labor in these latter posts is apt to rise, for the reason that fewer workers are left there. We assume here a state of full employment. When there is underemployment an industry may obtain additional labor on easy terms. The supply of labor to the industry is then of considerable elasticity: a small advance in wage rates may draw an impressive number of workers into the industry.

THE SUPPLY OF LABOR TO THE ECONOMY

What aggregate amounts of labor-hours will offer themselves in the *economy* as a whole when wage rates move up all along the line? Assume that, on account of a depression, wage rates are generally low, but that they are beginning to rise to level *OA*, as in Figure 64, where the amounts of labor are measured along the horizontal axis and the wage rates along the vertical axis. At the higher wage rates more and more labor will present itself for work. Since family earnings are still low, more women may appear on the labor market. In a low but rising range of wages, the supply of labor will be upward sloping, like segment *EF*.

As the wage rates advance to substantial heights and workers feel much better off, we come upon a unique turn in the supply curve. Married women will abandon their outside employments; and children will return from the factory to school for a little more education. Even the breadwinner may begin to play truant. At a comparatively high level of income the worker begins to value added leisure more than added work. The earnings from extra hours of work are balanced against the attractions of a fishing trip. At higher than customary wage scales many a worker puts in fewer hours per week. During World War II absenteeism reached considerable proportions in some factories. For a certain wage range the supply curve curls back on itself, like *FH* in Figure 64.

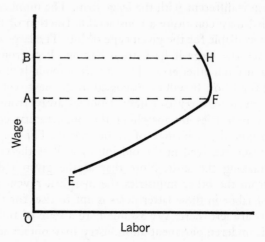

FIGURE 64. *The Supply of Labor to the Economy*

It is charged by some critics of economic theory that the supply schedule of labor is formed on the assumption that the worker is bent exclusively on maximizing his money return. It is argued that the worker is motivated by nonmonetary considerations in his job preferences and that he may not move to a better-paying job because of inertia, attachment to his surroundings, and fear of the unknown. It is objected that since the supply schedule of labor associates the amounts of labor with the wage rate alone, it falsifies the supply situation.

The charge exaggerates. The supply schedule of labor does take into account the reluctance of a laborer to give up the old for the new. The wage rates in the supply schedule are assumed to match the opportunity cost involved in changing jobs: the schedule monetizes the nonmonetary motives. If workers were assumed to be creatures devoid of habit and sentiment, their mobility would be regarded as much greater, and the supply curve of labor, at given wage rates, would be presented as farther to the right and closer to the x axis, and as more elastic. The smaller elasticity of a supply curve is the objective pecuniary measure of the pull of habit and emotion.

TRADE UNIONS AND THE SUPPLY OF LABOR

The trade union is as active in tampering with the supply of labor as it is in interfering with the demand for labor. Like the commodity monopolist, the trade union is prone to restrict the amount of its service in order to attain a higher wage rate. Some unions, especially the industrial unions and unions of the unskilled or in mass production industries, are not interested in the limitation of membership. The unions in the automobile, rubber, and steel industries see safety in numbers. But many of the strongly organized skilled trades commonly limit the number of apprentices and put barriers against entrance into the union by requiring severe tests, large initiation fees, and heavy monthly dues. Not every limitation of apprenticeship is to be laid at the door of the union. The inefficient novice represents a high cost of production; and even when allowed a free hand, the employer will not fill up his plant with apprentices. However, unions in such trades as building and printing specify in the contracts with employers a fixed low ratio of apprentices to journeymen, or else insist on wages for apprentices high enough to discourage their employment.

The effect of a shorter working day, on which unions have a tendency to insist, is to limit the supply of labor. A given labor force with a shorter average working day represents a smaller amount of labor at given hourly wage rates. Where the work is heavy or requires concentrated effort, shorter hours may induce a higher marginal productivity of labor; they may also prolong the working life. But a general indiscriminate reduction of hours, not bred by improvements in production, reflects a limitation of the labor available at given wage rates, and it lowers the national income.

Implementing and supplementing restrictive practices are the closed shop and the union shop. Under the closed-shop agreement, the employer is confined to hiring only union members. The union shop permits a nonunion worker to be employed, but after a brief period he must join the union if he is to stay in the shop. On the demand side, the closed shop and the union shop render the demand for union labor inelastic by barring the substitution of cheaper nonunion labor. On the supply side, these two devices restrict the numbers available for hire so that wages can be forced up.

III. The Determination of Wages

How a wage rate is established for a particular kind of labor depends on the market structure for labor. A variety of markets can be explored. We shall examine three types of markets which are in varying degrees illustrative of actual conditions in our economy. They are the competitive market, employer monopsony, and bilateral monopoly.

A. The Competitive Wage

By a competitive wage we mean a wage determined in a market in which the demand and supply of labor of a given kind are without a monopoly element. In a given area, accordingly, there are many employers of this labor acting independently in their demand for it; and there are likewise many workers of this type and they are not organized. Within the area there is easy mobility of labor from firm to firm. It is not implied that jobs must not differ in pleasantness, safety, and the like; equalizing differences take care of such variations. If there were perfect mobility from area to area, the market would become a competitive

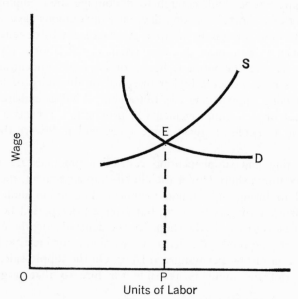

FIGURE 65. *Formation of the Competitive Wage*

market on a national level.

In such a market the *demand* of the firms for a given grade of labor is expressed by the marginal revenue product of this labor. More workers can be hired only as the wage rate declines. The *supply* curve of this labor for all the firms slopes upward to the right. As more workers are called for, the wage will have to advance if workers are to be attracted from similar occupations in other regions or from somewhat similar jobs in the same region.

As we know, the intersection of demand (D) and supply (S) curves (Figure 65) gives us the equilibrium wage rate PE. Once this market wage rate has been established, the supply curve of labor to the individual firm is horizontal, like OP. (Why?) It is also to be noted that in a competitive market the wage of the worker tends to coincide with his MRP (marginal revenue productivity). In earlier days in the United States, when labor was generally unorganized, competitive labor markets existed in many trades and in many regions. Such markets are more limited today; but they are not extinct.

B. Employer Monopsony

THE NATURE OF THE MONOPSONY MARKET

This type of market may exist in industries in which labor is not organized and the geographical mobility of labor is limited. One big employer may hire a large proportion of a given kind of labor in the area. Or else several outstanding employers may have an understanding not to compete for labor. Thus one employer, or several employers acting as one, face many unorganized workers whose mobility is not pronounced.

Immobility of labor is an essential condition of a monopsony market. If labor is ready to move to greener pastures, the single large employer will possess no unique power in hiring labor. Let him offer a lower wage than is customary elsewhere and the fluid labor force may melt away from his plant. Some economists are impressed by the wanderlust of the American people and are inclined to stress the mobility of labor in our economy. But many students of labor problems are of a different mind.[2]

THE DETERMINATION OF THE WAGE RATE

The formation of the wage rate in the monopsony market is illustrated in Figure 66. Curve D is the demand curve of the large buyer of the labor

[2] E.g., G. F. Bloom and H. R. Northrup, *Economics of Labor and Industrial Relations* (Philadelphia, Blakiston, 1950), pp. 241, 268; L. G. Reynolds, *Labor Economics and Labor Relations* (New York, Prentice-Hall, 1949), pp. 344–352.

service. (We treated it as the demand curve of all the firms in the previous market.) The average cost curve AC is the supply curve of labor as it appears to this buyer. It is the average cost schedule or the price schedule of labor to the one large firm. The fact that the supply curve to the *individual* hirer of labor is not horizontal, as in the competitive market, but slopes upward as AC does, introduces the peculiar feature of the monopsony labor market. In this market, the marginal outlay or the marginal cost (MC) of labor rises above the average cost curve. This means

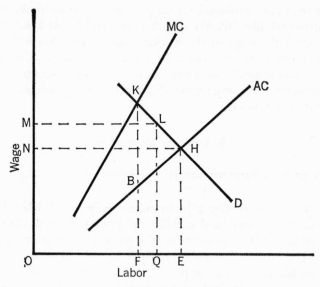

FIGURE 66. *Monopsony Pricing*

that the hire of an additional worker costs the firm more than the wage paid him, inasmuch as the wage rate of all the workers already in the plant must be raised to the level of the new worker.[3]

The monopsonist will employ labor up to the point at which the demand curve *D* intersects, not the supply curve AC, but the marginal cost curve MC. There is nothing new in this behavior. The only difference is that in a competitive labor market the MC curve facing the individual firm coincides with the horizontal curve *HN*, whereas in a monopsony market the MC curve is above the supply-of-labor curve AC. The number of workers hired by our monopsonist will be *OF*; and the wage rate can be as low as *FB*. This wage falls short of the worker's marginal revenue

[3] The arithmetic of this point is given in Chapter X, p. 258.

productivity by the amount *BK*. Employing *OF* units of labor, the monopsonist can afford to pay the wage rate *FK*, the marginal revenue product. Paying only *FB*, he reaps the extra gain *BK*, often referred to as "monopsonistic exploitation," because of his monopoly position as a buyer of labor service.

Under monopsony the amount of labor employed is less than under competition and the wage is lower. In a competitive market the equilibrium wage would be *HE* and employment would rise to *OE*; in a monopsony market the corresponding magnitudes are *FB* and *OF*. The focus of the difference between the two situations may be said to lie in the fact that under competition the supply curve and the marginal cost curve to the *individual* firm is the horizontal *HN*, whereas to the monopsonist the supply curve is the rising AC curve, with the diverging marginal cost curve MC. Thus under monopsony the workers are subjected to the double disadvantage of lower wages and less employment; and society gets less output.

If the workers hired monopsonistically become organized, the new union can improve the position of these members. Suppose that by collective bargaining the new union pushes the wage rate up to *OM*. The supply schedule of labor to the monopsonist becomes *now* the horizontal line *ML*: whatever the amount of labor he hires, up to *ML* units, he pays the uniform union wage *OM*. As before, and as usual, he will hire labor up to the stage at which the marginal revenue product equals the marginal outlay on the labor service, which now coincides with the average wage *OM*. He employs *OQ* units of labor instead of the former *OF* units and at the wage *OM* which is above the former wage *FB*. Observe that the monopsonist pays now a wage (*OM*) equal to the marginal revenue productivity of labor (*QL*).

C. Bilateral Monopoly

The view is sometimes held that the coming of the labor union symbolizes the intrusion of the monopolistic unions into the realm of competitive wage formation. This view is hardly realistic. Before the development of strong labor organizations there was much monopsonistic wage setting by the employer. Monopsony governed wages in the textile mills of Passaic and Paterson; in the steel plants of Pittsburgh and Youngstown; in the coal mines of Illinois, the copper mines of Montana, and the iron mines of the Mesabi region; in the shoe industry of New England; in the paper mills of Wisconsin; and in many other places.

Often the union compounds a labor monopoly with monopoly on the side of the employer as a buyer of labor service. This remark should not be interpreted as approval of labor monopoly. Like other types of monopoly, the monopoly of labor can do harm to our economy. Bilateral monopoly is gaining ground as a type of labor market in industry. In many an industry the big union bargains with the big employer or a combination of big employers. Coal mining, steel, automobiles, meat packing, rubber, tobacco, farm machinery, and shipbuilding are some of the examples.

In the bilateral monopoly labor market the wage is governed by social, psychological, and political influences, as well as by the economic considerations motivating the contending personalities. Economic analysis cannot offer a precise determination of the wage. Collective bargaining is a tug-of-war in which some factors are of ruling importance to both sides at the bargaining table. Both parties are affected, for instance, by public opinion, the attitude of the government, the capacity to wait while the factories are idle, and the loss of customers to substitute products. In addition each side is swayed by its own unique calculations.

The employer would like to offer a wage no higher than the monopsonistic wage which he would set if the labor in question were not organized. This is his lower limit. The upper possible limit is generally a wage which would leave the employer with enough revenue to cover variable costs in the short run and total costs in the long run. How far above the lower limit he will go depends on the factors just mentioned and on others besides. He will be inclined or compelled to make concessions, for instance, if there is the apprehension that key laborers may drift away to other occupations or areas; if a wage increase has been granted in other sectors of the economy; if the cost of living is rising; and if it is feared that a strongheaded attitude will rear into prominence a more radical union leadership.

THE MOTIVATION OF UNION LEADERS

The motivation of union officials is complex. If wages are pushed up beyond a certain scale, the union cannot have both high wages and high employment. The two variables stand in inverse relation to one another. A wage policy chosen by the union is, broadly speaking, at the same time an employment policy and a union-membership policy.

Labor leaders are not always conscious of the inverse relation between wage rates and employment. The reason for this unawareness probably lies in the fact that the connection between the two variables is commonly obscured by the slow operation of causation and by the confusing intrusion of outside circumstances. Social phenomena do not display cause-and-effect sequences. The adverse effect of an artificially high wage rate may be overlaid with modifying and beclouding situations. A growing industry may merely retard its growth on account of excessive wage costs; instead of discharging workers, the firms may only fail to hire more. The effect may be merely to keep new firms from entering the industry which would otherwise enjoy a career of expansion. Smaller sales and layoffs of labor occasioned by the high price of output, brought on by the high wages, may be blamed on general conditions or on some irrelevant but talked-about occurrence in the economy, or on politics.

Some unions follow the liberal policy of admitting to membership all qualified workers who care or can be made to join. The principal purpose of the union may be to limit the monopsonistic power of employers in various localities. In such cases the wage rate won by collective bargaining may depart only little from the competitive wage. The union sees to it that the wage does not fall, roughly, below the marginal revenue productivity of the labor involved.

Other unions adopt an aristocratic attitude and seek benefits for a limited membership. None but skilled trades can venture such a policy. The union may aim at an arbitrarily high wage scale, at which only limited employment can be available. In Figure 66, if the union wage rate rises above FK, employment will shrink below OF. The union may let the unemployed sink or swim. It may limit entry into the club by the usual devices already mentioned. It may choose to widen its membership somewhat and provide work by an energetic policy of restriction of output per man-hour; by featherbedding, that is, by insisting on the assignment of more men to a job than efficiency requires; and by other make-work schemes.

Which wage policy the union will decide upon and how militantly it will press it upon the employer will depend on a variety of elements. Foremost among them are, for example, the resources of the union treasury; the morale of the rank and file; the cost of living in relation to the current wage; the profit record of the employing firm; the level of aggregate employment in the economy; and the estimated unity and stubbornness of the employer group. Two potent forces are molding the sentiment of the union membership: (1) what is a "fair" wage, and especially (2) the wage current among workers in comparable occupations. Not to be neglected in this connection is the personality of the union officials. There is rivalry among labor leaders for prestige and power, for the admiration of their followers, and for publicity. The labor official keeps an eye on his chances of re-election at the next union convention. Far from functioning as the servant of his fellow workers, he may develop into a "political" figure with wayward ambitions. Ego, desire for victory, and inflamed emotions may sway leaders on both sides of the bargaining table.

As we see, in bilateral monopoly in the labor market we move in the realm of economics, sociology, psychology, politics, leadership, and crowd behavior; and also in the realm of diplomacy, tactics, and strategy. Where so many intangible factors are involved on both sides to the bargain, economic analysis, with its stress on maximizing something, cannot deliver a definite answer on the equilibrium wage rate. The collective bargaining in such instances is indeterminate. The outcome is ordinarily a compromise, but the "stronger" side will come more closely to its objectives. The settlement is not confined to the wage scale. It tends to be a resultant of forces affecting such questions as working conditions, shop rules, seniority privileges, promotions, dismissals, vacations, the handling of grievances, and many other problems and details of serious significance to hundreds or thousands of people thrown together during many hours almost daily in the tasks of earning their bread. Often the wage rate is of pre-eminent importance in the negotiations; and sometimes it is submerged by other acute issues. But seldom is the wage rate settled in isolation from the other considerations. The bargaining union ordinarily aims to maximize a bundle of objectives, not solely the wage rate.

IV. Wages and Depressions

The prevention of mass unemployment such as afflicts us in a depression is probably the outstanding domestic problem of the age. But, as was remarked at the end of the preceding chapter, the problem of depressions is too large a domain and we cannot stray into it. We shall take up only one question, which is of the same order of analysis as the problems explored in this book: namely the proposition of curing a depression by cutting wages. This is a complex question [4] and it has generated a good deal of discussion among economists. We shall here confine ourselves to the bare outlines of two dominant views, the classical view and J. M. Keynes's.

To the classical economists the volume of employment is a function of the wage rate, just as the volume of purchases of any commodity depends on its price. The assumption is that competition and flexible wages and prices prevail. To obtain full employment, it is enough to reduce

[4] G. Haberler, *Prosperity and Depression*, 3rd ed. (United Nations, Lake Placid, 1946), pp. 237–244, 395–405, 491–503.

the money wage rate. When unemployment develops this reduction is achieved automatically: the pressure of the unemployed brings down the wage. As wages fall, marginal costs fall. Prices decline, but not in the same proportion in which wages fall, since wages are not the only cost. In consequence, real wages come down. Lower costs and the associated lower prices induce larger sales. Lower real wages raise profits and stimulate investment. The rise in sales and in investment boosts employment.

It should be noted that classical economists do not necessarily urge wage cutting as a policy or as the only policy in a depression. They are aware that such a policy may involve practical difficulties; and they are generally inclined toward such measures as monetary and fiscal schemes and programs of public works.

J. M. Keynes raises objections to this type of analysis, principally because it correlates employment with the wage rate whereas, to him, the prime determinant of the volume of employment is aggregate demand. Since aggregate demand is a function of three variables—the marginal propensity to consume, the marginal efficiency of capital, and the rate of interest—the line of analysis which Keynes favors is an examination of the impact of a wage reduction on each of these variables. His argument runs as follows.[5]

The reduction in money wages and consequently in prices produces a redistribution of income, chiefly from the working people to the entrepreneurs and in general from the poorer to the wealthier groups. The latter have a lower propensity to consume; and the net effect is apt to be reduced consumption, a smaller effective demand, and an adverse repercussion on employment.

Next he considers the impact on the marginal efficiency of capital. If one decisive wage cut is made across the whole economy, so that no further wage lowering is anticipated, the effect will be a rise in the expected marginal efficiency of capital and consequently greater investment and more employment. But if the drop in wages is moderate and if for this and other reasons the drop is regarded as a prelude to further cuts, investment will be postponed and an incipient depression may well gain headway. Only an authoritarian government, however, can undertake a sudden, large and over-all downward wage revision. In a democratic society a drastic wage amputation is unthinkable. Only a gradually declining wage can be envisaged, with aggravating results for employment.

What is left is the effect of the wage reduction on the interest rate. The lowering of wages and prices will entail smaller requirements of cash for transaction purposes and will release cash for speculative purposes. With a given liquidity function, the greater amount of cash will tend to depress

[5] *The General Theory of Employment, Interest and Money* (New York, Harcourt, Brace, 1936), chap. 19.

the rate of interest and will encourage investment and employment. But there is a fly in the ointment. The initial downward movement of wages may stir labor unrest and impair general confidence: the schedule of liquidity preference may therefore rise sufficiently to produce the net effect of a mounting rate of interest.

Keynes also examines the influence of wage cutting on business optimism and pessimism. The cutting works on both sides. It may engender optimism in the entrepreneurs toward expected marginal efficiency of capital and investment. On the other hand, the labor discontent spread by the fact that wage reductions are neither simultaneous in all industries nor of uniform proportion for all workers may neutralize the incentive to enlivened activity. He also adds the consideration that the lower prices associated with wage reductions render the business debts burdensome enough to dampen all optimism, especially when we add the equally increasing weight of the national debt.

Keynes concludes [6] that if a wage reduction is to bring greater employment, the route to this result can lie only in the induced lower rate of interest which would encourage investment. But he does not rest his case at this stage. There are two ways of lowering the rate of interest. To attempt it by an all-around decisive wage cut is to use a clumsy and painful method, fostering labor troubles and the imbalances associated with price declines. It is much wiser, he argues, to leave the manipulation of the interest rate to the monetary authorities. In time of developing unemployment, keep the wage level unchanged and let the banks expand the monetary medium sufficiently to bring the interest rate down to the point at which encouraged investment will reinforce effective demand and restore full employment.

SUGGESTED READINGS

Bain, J. S. *Pricing, Distribution, and Employment,* revised ed., pp. 552–560. New York, Holt, 1953.

Bloom, G. F. "A Reconsideration of the Theory of Exploitation," *Quarterly Journal of Economics,* Vol. LV (May, 1941), pp. 413–442. Reprinted in *Readings in the Theory of Income Distribution,* pp. 245–277.

Bronfenbrenner, M. "The Economics of Collective Bargaining," *Quarterly Journal of Economics,* Vol. LIII (August, 1939), pp. 535–561.

Chamberlin, E. H. *The Economic Analysis of Labor Union Power,* Washington, D.C., American Enterprise Association, 1958.

Due, J. F. *Intermediate Economic Analysis,* revised ed., chap. 13, Chicago, Irwin, 1950.

[6] *Ibid.,* pp. 267–270.

Dunlop, J. T. *Wage Determination under Trade Unions*. New York, Macmillan, 1944.

Enke, S. *Intermediate Economic Theory*, chaps. 27, 28. New York, Prentice-Hall, 1950.

Hicks, J. R. *The Theory of Wages*. London, Macmillan, 1935.

Lester, R. A. "Shortcomings of Marginal Analysis for Wage-Employment Problems," *American Economic Review*, Vol. XXXVI (March, 1946), pp. 63–82.

Marshall, A. *Principles of Economics*, 8th ed., Book VI, chaps. 3–5. New York, Macmillan, 1927.

Reynolds, L. G., and Taft, C. H. *The Evolution of Wage Structure*. New Haven, Yale University Press, 1956.

Robertson, D. H. "Wage Grumbles," in *Economic Fragments*, pp. 42–57. London, King, 1931. Reprinted in *Readings in the Theory of Income Distribution*, pp. 221–236.

Robinson, Joan. *The Economics of Imperfect Competition*, chaps. 23–26. London, Macmillan, 1948.

Rothschild, K. W. *The Theory of Wages*. New York, Macmillan, 1954.

Stigler, G. J. *The Theory of Price*, revised ed., pp. 251–259. New York, Macmillan, 1952.

Taylor, G. W., and Pierson, F. C. *New Concepts in Wage Determination*. New York, McGraw-Hill, 1957.

CHAPTER

XV   Interest

THE THEORY of interest draws into its sphere many vital problems of our economy. The nature, source, and function of capital; saving and investment; employment, output, and income; business fluctuations; and many monetary questions are bound up with aspects of interest and interest theory. Up to a few decades ago the ruling theory of interest was what is called the *time-preference theory* or the *real theory*. Money and monetary policy were then customarily not projected into the analysis of interest; nor was interest regarded as a prominent weapon of policy in our economy. But views are different now. The two theories of interest widely held today, the *liquidity-preference theory* and the *loanable-funds theory*, are at least partly monetary theories of interest. For a comprehensive understanding of the problem of interest, we shall discuss in this chapter these three theories. But first a few words about the nature of interest.

The definition of interest depends on the theory which one accepts. To the follower of the real theory, interest is the payment for the service of capital goods; it is also the payment necessary to induce people to save. The upholder of the liquidity-preference theory treats interest as the reward for parting with the liquidity of the funds saved. Those accepting the loanable-funds theory view interest as the price paid by the borrowers to the lenders for the use of the money—as the price formed in the credit market by the interaction of the supply of and the demand for funds.

THE STRUCTURE OF INTEREST RATES

When we refer, in discussion, to the interest rate, we do not imply that there prevails in the market only one definite rate. There exists, rather, a family of different rates determined in a number of independent but connected loan markets. There are rates for government bonds, real-estate mortgage bonds, industrial bonds, bank loans, call loans in the stock market, and so on. These rates vary over time, not necessarily in identical proportions but often in the same direction. If there were perfect mobility of funds from market to market, the rates on all types of loans would be identical. But a number of factors tend to render each of the above categories of loans more or less distinct. Let us consider some of them.

One factor is *risk*. With some securities there is no fear of default on interest or principal; with others there is. The type of property pledged behind the security and the credit standing of the borrower are governing considerations. The bond involving risk will carry a higher rate. A government bond will offer a lower rate than an industrial bond of the same maturity. The difference in the rate is the premium for the risk taken. The interest rate minus the premium is the pure rate of interest. When we discuss interest we have in mind the pure rate.

A *second* factor is *liquidity*. By liquidity we mean the ease of selling an asset, and without loss, when the holder of it needs cash. The sale of some assets may involve delay, cost, and capital loss; other assets can be readily disposed of. The more liquid securities will carry a lower rate.

A *third* element is the *maturity* of the loan. A long-term bond will have to offer a higher rate than a short-term bond, in the same circumstances. On a long-term loan there is the risk of a drop in the value of the security. A $1,000 bond with a long life, paying 3%, will drop, roughly, to $750 if the rate of similar bonds advances to 4% and if the bond has a good many years to run before it matures. The lender may also fear a possible rise in the general price level. Furthermore, the short-term lender has a more frequent opportunity to study afresh the market situation and prospects. A lender is more confident of his calculations when he commits his funds for five years than when he commits them for thirty years.

Finally, there is the *monopoly* factor. In a given locality the few commercial banks may constitute an oligopoly with a degree of monopoly behavior; for short-term commercial loans their interest rates are then likely to stand above those which would rule under competition. Their rates may vary almost from customer to customer. Similarly with the personal-loan company offering hard terms for the consumer anxious to buy a television set. On the other hand, the large nationally known corporation appearing on the market as a long- or short-term borrower may enjoy a more competitive situation. Not confined to a locality, it can shop around. It can borrow by selling commercial paper in the open market; it can sell bonds on favorable terms, with the services of the best bidder from a number of investment companies—if these companies are in rivalry with each other.

There is thus a complex of interest rates, each depending on marginal lending and marginal borrowing in its particular market. The markets have common frontiers and there will be crossing of borders if the differential between two neighboring rates departs from the usual magnitude. When we talk of the interest rate we do not refer to the whole list of rates in the various markets, but to one particular rate with the other rates standing above it or below it with more or less consistent gradations, governed by such factors as have been cited. In a discussion of interest we usually have in mind a government bond or perhaps a first-mortgage bond of a concern like the American Telephone and Telegraph Company.

I. The Time-Preference Theory

The time-preference theory of interest also goes by the name of the time-preference-productivity theory and the real theory. It is called the real theory because it is not monetary in character and has as its frame of reference real goods—the productivity of capital goods and the saving, essentially, of goods. The theory is based on productivity and thrift. Like any other pricing problem, and like the other two theories of interest, this theory is a demand-and-supply theory, with interest as the price which equilibrates demand and supply. The difference among the theories of interest lies in the answer to the question: demand for what and supply of what?

The term "capital" has no universally accepted meaning. For our purposes it is sufficient to regard capital as produced instruments of production. Capital stands for objects which man produces for the purpose of using them as an aid in making goods. Capital refers to raw materials, machines, apartment houses, and pictures on the office wall; to inventories and to finished goods on the shelves of the retailer; and to such animals as the old-time peddler's horse or the cows on the dairy farm. Land is not capital because it is not man-made; it is a natural resource.

The question arises why capital is elevated to the rank of a distinct factor of production. Is it not merely the product of land, labor, and management? What is uniquely involved in capital to make it a separate factor? The answer of many economists is that capital does not reflect merely the handiwork of the other three factors, but embodies in *addition* a special entity, the *time* element. The time element appears in the concepts, and in the facts, of roundabout production and of saving.

THE DEMAND FOR WAITING OR SAVING

The demand for capital goods comes from firms which desire to invest, that is, to purchase capital goods or to apply land, labor, current capital, and management toward the making of new capital goods. Firms seek capital because they prefer to engage in the roundabout process of production. Producing goods with simple tools is almost a direct process. Producing goods by first taking time to prepare the factory, the machinery, and elaborate tools is a roundabout process.

One of the significant facts about the formation of capital and roundabout production is that they involve time. Land, labor, existing capital, and management are directed toward the making of railroads, factories, machines, and materials. Before consumer goods result from the use of such facilities a year or more may pass. In the meantime, as the various factors are at work producing this capital, unfit for consumption, somebody has to make advances to them in the form of consumer goods to keep up their real income and to compensate them for their services. Put differently, the factors have to be released from the production of consumer goods so that they can turn to the building of capital. In any economy with full employment, before new investors can employ resources, somebody has to make the resources available.

The resources are made available by those who save. By postponing consumption, they release consumption goods which become available to feed and clothe the factors busy manufacturing nonconsumption goods, capital. Relieved of the necessity of making consumer goods for their livelihood, these factors are made ready to devote themselves to the formation of capital. Another way of looking at the situation is to consider the goods not consumed by the savers as goods which do not have to be made. The factors which would otherwise be occupied in making them are now released to do something else—to produce capital. Thus saving in its turn involves the element of time, the element of waiting for the future enjoyment of the savings.

The roundabout way of making goods is preferred for the reason that it is more efficient. With the aid of capital facilities we turn out more goods per man-hour than when we produce with bare hands or with scant tools. Capital is productive. After allowance is made for the maintenance or replacement of the capital from the sale of the increased output, there is a surplus left for each $100 worth of capital goods. This surplus constitutes the productivity of capital as a percentage of its cost. If a machine which costs $100 raises the annual revenue of the firm by $25 and the annual repairs and replacement amount to $15, the productivity of the machine is 10%.

The demand for capital is the demand for its marginal revenue productivity. It is essentially a demand for saving or waiting. The demand is illustrated by the marginal revenue productivity curve D in Figure 67, in which the amounts saved are on the horizontal line and the interest rates on the vertical. It is a demand schedule relating the savings borrowed by the firms to the rates of interest charged by those who save. The horizontal

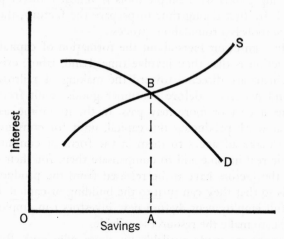

FIGURE 67. *Supply of and Demand for Capital*

distance of a point on D indicates the amount borrowed; its vertical distance measures the corresponding expected marginal revenue product, therefore the interest rate which the borrower can afford to pay for that amount. If an improvement in the arts comes, calling profitably for more capital, the demand curve shifts to the right and upward.

THE SUPPLY OF WAITING OR SAVING

Whether an economy is capitalist or communist, if its resources are fully employed, the limit to the volume of new capital that can be built is set by saving, by lowering the level of consumption. Assume that saving is spontaneous and costless to the saver. The supply curve of savings would then coincide with the x axis; and the investment in capital goods would proceed until the D curve reached the x axis; that is, until the marginal revenue product equaled zero.

But saving is not spontaneous. The position of the *real* theory of interest is that, at least beyond a certain point, the cost of saving reflects itself in the unpleasantness of postponing consumption, in *time preference*. People prefer the present enjoyment of goods and services to the future enjoyment of them. The enjoyment of spending $100 today is normally preferred to such an enjoyment a year from now. For this attitude there are a number of reasons. A person is not certain that he will be alive later; the price level may rise; and people are generally so constituted that prospective enjoyment is generally not valued as highly as present enjoyment. An object or an enjoyment far away from our eyes looks smaller.

To make people overcome their time preference, inducement must be offered them in the shape of interest. The real or time-preference theory argues that a person, with a given income, may save $100 if he sees the prospect of getting $104 at the end of the year. His time preference is 4%. If the person is to save more and more, the premium must rise to overcome his increased marginal time preference. As he saves more, the marginal utility of what he has left for consumption grows, whereas the present marginal utility of the cumulating funds for the future declines. To induce him to save more, a higher rate of interest must be offered. Accordingly the horizontal addition of the individual savings curves gives us a supply schedule of savings which rises to the right, like curve S in Figure 67. The real theory assumes that, by and large, the prime incentive back of saving is the receipt of interest and that savings are not hoarded. Savers invariably become lenders. The real theory also assumes that incomes stay constant.

THE EQUILIBRIUM RATE OF INTEREST

The rate of interest is determined by the interaction of the demand for investment and the supply of savings, by the expected productivity of capital and time preference. In Figure 67 the equilibrium rate is *AB*. At this rate, investing firms are ready to borrow, and households are willing to save and lend, the amount *OA* at the rate *AB*. It is a basic thesis of the time-preference theory that the equilibrium rate of interest brings savings and investments into equality. If more were saved than the equilibrium quantity *OA*, the rate of interest offered by prospective investors would drop below *AB* inasmuch as the marginal productivity on curve *D* would sag below *AB*. At this lower rate of interest, people will save less, as is seen on curve *S*; and the rate will begin to move up. The equilibrium is finally redressed when the rate *AB* is re-established.

This theory of interest treats the two determinants of the rate, investment (curve *D*) and savings (curve *S*), as independent of one another.

The theory teaches, for instance, that if an invention increases investment activity and shifts the D curve to the right, this new demand curve will intersect with the given supply curve at a higher point and will raise the rate of interest. The invention is not assumed to increase the supply of savings (by virtue of the increased income induced by the greater investment activity) and thus shift the supply curve to the right and downward. Similarly, according to the theory, if increased thriftiness brings the S curve farther to the right and downward, the intersection with the unchanged D curve will bring the rate down. The theory is not inclined to inquire whether increased thrift would not diminish aggregate demand for goods, would not reduce income and employment, and would not cause the D curve to move to the left and downward. Thus the supply and demand schedules are treated as independent: with a change in one of them the other is assumed fixed. The effects of a change in investment on saving and of a change in saving on investment are ignored.

II. The Liquidity-Preference Theory

The liquidity-preference theory of interest is the brain child of J. M. Keynes. Keynes does not see in productivity of capital and thrift the ingredients which can form a theory of interest. He says: ". . . the response of investment and the response of the amount saved out of a given income to change in the rate of interest, do not furnish material for a theory of interest." [1] The liquidity-preference theory treats interest as a monetary phenomenon. Interest is the price paid for borrowed money, and is governed by the demand and supply of money or liquidity. What is liquidity?

LIQUIDITY PREFERENCE

Our money consists of coins, paper bills, bank deposits. The total amount of money in this country these days (the early 1960s) is around $140 billion. It is held by households, firms, and government units, principally by the first two classes. Why do all these people and institutions keep all this money idle, in the pockets and in the banks, in preference to converting it into other forms of wealth which would bring an income? The answer is simple. Wealth can be held in three ways: in ownership of goods,

[1] *The General Theory of Employment, Interest and Money* (New York, Harcourt, Brace, 1936), p. 181.

such as machinery or real estate or shares of stock; in money claims against others, in the form of bonds, notes, and the like; and in money. The most liquid form of wealth is money. The holding of money provides convenience and satisfactions, and above all the advantage of having ready at hand a medium of exchange whenever the need arises for nonliquid assets —say groceries, or the service of the garageman.

People hang onto their money because of their preference for liquidity. In technical language, people have a demand for money to *hold* as a store of value. This demand, we shall see, is related to the rate of interest. To induce people to give up liquidity and to lend their idle cash, the borrower (the seller of a security) must offer a reward. The reward is the rate of interest.

Unlike the real theory, this theory holds that savings do not automatically become lendings. In disposing of his income, says Keynes, the individual is confronted with two decisions. The first concerns how much of his income he will consume and how much he will save. The second decision concerns the form in which the savings will be held, in liquid cash or in securities. This choice is prompted by the liquidity preference of the individual.

To understand better why people prefer to hold liquid cash, why they have a demand for money to hold, let us look into the motives back of this desire for liquidity. Keynes cites three motives.

(1) First comes the *transaction* motive. Households keep money in order to make the ordinary purchases, from the butcher and the baker, in the periods of time between receipts of the pay envelope. It is embarrassing to run out of cash and put friends to the test. The business firm too must keep a cash balance in the bank to meet expenses. The inflow of revenue from the sale of the product does not coincide with the stream of disbursements.

(2) The second motive is called *precautionary*. Individuals desire to hold cash balances for incompletely insured contingencies. Accidents, prolonged illness, or the loss of a job must be provided for. In business it is necessary to retain funds to cope with an unfavorable turn of affairs without soliciting the aid of a possibly unsympathetic banker. There may emerge an unexpected slump in the demand for the product; a large credit account may go sour. A profitable bargain may have to be forgone if there is no command over immediate funds.

(3) Third is the *speculative* motive. Some individuals and firms, after setting aside what they consider sufficient funds for transaction and precautionary ends, may have resources left which can be converted into earning assets such as bonds. To improve our understanding of the con-

nection between the demand for money and the speculative motive, it is advisable to pause and consider the relation between interest rates and bond prices.

A bond brings a fixed annual income. A bond paying 6% on the maturity value of $1,000 earns $60 a year. Because the income is fixed, as the bond fluctuates in its market price the interest rate which it earns holds an inverse relation to the changed price. If the bond is purchased when its price has advanced to $1,200, the $60 fetches only 5%. In addition, when this bond matures, there is a capital loss of $200. If the bond matures in 10 years from the date of purchase, the annual capital loss is $20, or ($20 ÷ $1,200) = 1⅔%. Without considering compound interest, the per cent yield on this bond is $5 - 1\frac{2}{3} = 3\frac{1}{3}$. Suppose the same bond is bought at $900. The interest earned on it rises to ($60 ÷ $900) = 6⅔%. Besides, at maturity, say 10 years hence, the capital gain is $100, or $10 a year. This gain amounts to ($10 ÷ 900) = 1⅑%. The per cent yield on the bond rises to $(6\frac{2}{3} + 1\frac{1}{9}) = 7\frac{7}{9}$.

We can generalize that the price of a bond and the rate of interest which it earns stand in inverse relation to each other. High bond prices reflect low interest rates; low bond prices reflect high rates. Similarly, low interest rates in the loan market are indicative of high bond prices, and high interest rates go hand in hand with low bond prices.

THE DEMAND FOR MONEY AND THE SPECULATIVE MOTIVE

Let us consider now the speculative motive in relation to the demand for cash. Suppose some of the potential lenders or purchasers of securities are of the opinion that existing bond prices are too high and that the rate yielded is consequently too low. Suppose, too, that they expect the opposite situation in the future. These people diverge from the consensus of the majority of borrowers and lenders as expressed in existing bond prices in the market. The individuals who think that they know better than the market will hold onto their cash, waiting for the bond market to drop. If they possess bonds, they will sell them; they will shift from bonds to cash. It is to their advantage to sell the bonds at the current high prices and, when the market turns, be ready to purchase the lowered-price bonds and earn higher rates on their investment. Conversely, if some individuals expect interest rates to tumble and securities to advance in price, they will lose little time in shifting out of money and into bonds.

For example, if bonds yield at present 4%, the possessor of cash will hold it and will refrain from buying bonds priced at $1,000 if he expects the interest rate to move up to 5% and the bonds to drop, in consequence, to $800 (roughly)—if these bonds do not mature before long. If he buys the bond at present, he earns $40 a year on his expenditure of $1,000. If he waits until the market behaves as he expects it to behave, he reaps $40 on the investment of $800. Likewise, the holder of a bond will prefer to sell it now at $1,000 and repurchase it later at $800.

If the prevailing interest rate is low, people will feel there is a strong likelihood that it will rise. They will shift from income-bearing assets to money; they will attempt to hold more money. Conversely, if existing interest rates are high, preponderant opinion may be that they are bound to decline. People will convert money into bonds; they will attempt to hold less money. The demand for money to hold suggests the same conception as the price demand for goods: at low rates of interest people hold more money, at higher rates less money. What is crucial is not that all people shift from money to bonds or from bonds to money, but that the shift takes place for marginal funds.

M_1 AND M_2

Of the three motives for liquidity preference, Keynes lays particular stress on the speculative motive. The cash balance held for the other two motives is commonly a stable quantity. Households and businessmen alike are accustomed to an even flow of expenditures on transactions. And, guided by their experience, they set aside definite sums for contingencies. The amount of money reserved for these two purposes is governed chiefly by the level of one's income. The liquidity preference inspired by these two motives is almost completely interest-inelastic, except when interest rates are very high. (Explain.)

It is different with the speculative motive. The strength of this motive is sensitive to gradual changes in interest rates. Accordingly Keynes puts liquidity preference for the other two motives into one category and designates the amount of money held for these two purposes as M_1 which he regards as a function of income. The funds held for the speculative motive he symbolizes by M_2 and treats it as a function of the rate of interest. The total amount of money in the country is then $M = M_1 + M_2$. It may be convenient to call M_1 active balances and M_2 passive balances.

THE DEMAND FOR MONEY TO HOLD

We can now sum up the conditions of demand and supply which determine the rate of interest. The demand for money to hold is a schedule of the various aggregate cash balances demanded by the public at various rates of interest. In Figure 68 the total volume of money in the economy is indicated along the horizontal axis and the interest rates along the vertical axis. The vertical line L_1M_1 represents the unvarying amount held by the public for transaction and precautionary ends. Since this demand for money is interest-inelastic, it is pictured as perpendicular to the x axis. This demand is controlled by the size of the national income. We assume one given total income for the situations depicted by the diagram.

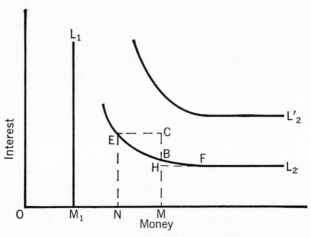

FIGURE 68. *The Demand for Money*

Curve L_2 pictures the relation between the rates of interest and the corresponding amounts of money which people desire to hold for speculative purposes. When the rate of interest is, for instance, as high as NE, the total amount demanded for speculative reasons is $ON - OM_1 = M_1N$. When the rate is lower, people will wish to hold more money; at rate MB the quantity demanded will be M_1M. At a high rate of interest the penalty for holding cash, instead of lending it, is great—it costs much money to hold money. Therefore less money is held. At a lower rate the opportunity cost of liquidity is small. More precisely, as we saw above, when the rate of interest is high, potential lenders expect it to go down, and lenders shift from money to bonds. When the interest rate is low, there is less marginal shifting from money to bonds; there is a desire to hold more money.

If for some reason the liquidity preference for the transaction and precautionary ends becomes stronger, so that at the same aggregate income people mean to hold more money, the line L_1M_1 will shift to the right. Similarly, if the preference for liquidity to satisfy the speculative motive becomes more intense, the demand curve L_2 shifts to the right and up-ward, to the position of L'_2. This means that the community will try to hold more money at the same rates or the same volumes of money at higher rates.

In connection with the elasticity of the demand curve or the liquidity-preference curve, Keynes advances an interesting proposition. He argues that at a certain low rate, say 2%, the demand for money to hold becomes *perfectly* elastic. To the right, curve L_2 becomes horizontal. At 2%, people will hold onto any new amounts of money that may be forthcom-ing. People do not expect the rate of interest to sink below 2%; they are accordingly not inclined to shift from money to bonds. On the con-trary, they anticipate a rise in the rate; and they fear that if they purchase bonds they will sustain a capital loss as soon as the rate begins to advance and the price of the bonds takes a downward course. The striking infer-ence is drawn that the rate of interest is not apt to sag below a certain low figure, and that there is no way of depressing it below this figure even if public policy demands such a result.

THE SUPPLY OF MONEY

The other determinant of the rate of interest is the amount of money in the economy. In the United States the amount depends chiefly on the central banks and the treasury. By their credit policy the Federal Reserve banks can regulate the reserves of the commercial banks and thereby their lending power and the volume of bank deposits. We are dealing with the large province of money creation and we cannot venture into it here. Involved are, among other things, the credit controls by central banks, such as the discount rate, open-market operations, and changes in the re-serve requirements; the factors which supply reserves to the commercial banks and the factors which use up these reserves; and the credit expan-sion possible on the basis of a given reserve. In Keynes's view, the volume of money supplied to the economy is, at least over short periods, a given stock, independent of the interest rate in the loan market.

THE EQUILIBRIUM RATE OF INTEREST

The rate of interest is governed by the interaction of the forces of de-mand and supply—by the liquidity function and the stock of money sup-plied by the monetary authorities. Let us refer again to Figure 68. With the liquidity function L_2 and the stock of money OM, the rate of interest will be MB. It is an equilibrium rate. Suppose the rate is MC instead. At this higher rate people will try to hold—so the L_2 curve tells us—not the amount of money OM but ON, less than OM by the amount EC. In other words, they will try to shift from money to bonds to the extent of EC dollars. But all attempts to hold only ON dollars and all the exchanges of money for bonds cannot reduce the total amount of money in the economy; the quantity of money is not changed by such transactions. This total remains at OM. The outcome of the attempt to get rid of cash in favor of bonds is to raise the price of bonds and to lower the rate of interest. The shifting from cash to bonds will proceed until the rate of interest is re-established at MB.

Should the rate happen to be HM, individuals will strive to hold more money than OM by the amount HF. They will unload bonds for cash. The total stock of money in the economy (unless changed by the monetary authorities) remains, however, OM and no more. What happens is that, on account of the conversion of bonds into cash, the price of bonds will drop and will keep on dropping until the rate of interest is moved up to MB. At this rate the volume of money in the economy equals the volume which the public is content to hold, without the incentive to sell bonds or to shift to bonds. It follows that, given the liquidity function or schedule, the rate of interest will depend on the amount of money made available by the authorities—up to the amount at which the rate reaches the "floor" level of, say, 2%. Given the liquidity function, the rate of interest is the creature of the monetary authorities.

The idea which will bear repeating is that with all the exchanges of bonds for cash or cash for bonds the total amount of money in the economy stays what it is. And it is all held by somebody. There is no unowned money. If Mr. A sells bonds, he holds the money received. If Mr. A shifts to bonds, Mr. B, the seller, holds the money. The total amount of money stays at the size which the monetary authorities have provided. What the shifting into and out of money accomplishes is to move the rate of interest into consistency with the amount of money available, in the perspective of the given liquidity function. (How?)

We should not form the impression that in the determination of the rate of interest the liquidity preference for the transaction and precautionary motives is of no account. It does exert an influence, but the influence is indirect. Assume that incomes rise. The demand for cash to hold as prompted by these two motives will be increased and the vertical line L_1M_1 in Figure 68 will move to the right. If the banking system does not inject more money or sufficient money into the economy, M_1 grows at the expense of M_2. Less money is available for speculative purposes, and the rate of interest rises. Conversely, when incomes fall the interest rate will decline. Less cash is needed for the first two purposes and more money spills over into speculative channels (we assume that the banks do not shrink sufficiently the volume of the circulating medium). Thus M_1 may be a contributing factor in the formation of the interest rate.

III. The Loanable-Funds Theory

The loanable-funds theory holds that interest is the price paid for the use of borrowed funds; that the interest rate is determined by the equilibrium of the demand and supply of loanable funds in the credit market; and that several sources of both demand and supply exist. Incorporating elements of the other two theories, this is an eclectic theory; and it can be shown that it can be reconciled with the liquidity-preference theory.[2] There are variants of this theory and a typical version is presented below.

A. The Supply of Loanable Funds

The supply of loanable funds is derived from a number of sources, chiefly from saving, dishoarding, bank credit, and disinvestment.

(1) SAVINGS

The savings of individuals constitute a prime source. Saving may be defined as the difference between income and consumption per unit of time. However, for certain purposes of analysis it is necessary to define saving more precisely. There are two approaches. *One* approach views savings as *ex ante* or *ex post*. *Ex ante* savings are savings planned by individuals at the beginning of a period in the perspective of expected incomes and anticipated expenditures on consumption. *Ex post* savings refer to savings as they have actually developed in view of the actual income, price level, and the like. Obviously *ex post* savings may diverge, and usually do, from *ex ante* savings.

Another approach to savings brings in the time lag. It stresses that income earned today is not disposed of today. A short period elapses—a day or two, perhaps a week—before earnings are translated into expenditures and savings. Savings may then be regarded as the income of the *previous* period minus the expenditures on consumption in the *current* period.

[2] W. Fellner and H. M. Somers, "Alternative Monetary Approaches to Interest Theory," *Review of Economic Statistics*, Vol. XXIII (February, 1941), pp. 43–48; A. P. Lerner, "Alternative Formulations of the Theory of Interest," in *The New Economics*, S. E. Harris, ed. (New York, Knopf, 1947), pp. 634–654.

In the loanable-funds theory, savings may be regarded from either of these two angles—as planned, *ex ante*, savings; or as the difference between the income of the preceding period and the consumption of the present period. In either case we deal with a schedule of savings at various interest rates. In the main, personal savings depend on the size of the income. But it is assumed that given the income, savings are responsive to the rate of interest. A higher rate will generally elicit more savings. In the analysis of personal saving, the loanable-funds theory may not diverge from the approach of the time-preference theory: the emphasis may fall on time preference.

Some individuals save, others *dissave*; these others spend on consumption in a given period some of the savings accumulated in the past. Their current consumption exceeds the income of the previous period. For the nation as a whole, then, aggregate personal saving in a given period is total saving minus total dissaving.[3] Dissaving hinges, to some extent, on the rate

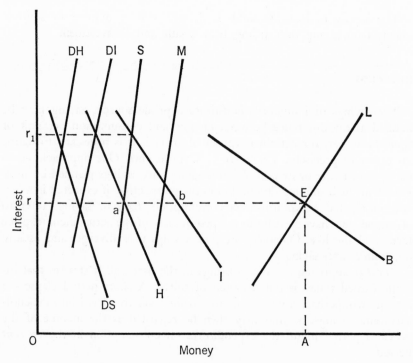

FIGURE 69. *The Loanable-Funds Theory*

[3] When the result for the nation is net dissaving, it means that the nation is consuming its capital, by allowing the equipment to wear out without replacement, or by depleting inventories.

of interest. At lower rates the opportunity cost, the income forgone by eating up the savings, is small, and dissaving may be greater than at higher rates when the penalty is greater. In Figure 69, below, the curve or schedule of dissaving DS slopes downward to the right, like a demand curve, and is treated as a demand curve. There is nothing strange in this. The addition of dissaving to the elements composing the demand for funds and the deduction of the same dissaving from the sources of supply produce the same effect on the interest rate, and can be treated as equivalent procedures.

A second source of savings is traced to the firm. Part of the earnings of a concern is consumed as declared dividends; the undistributed part constitutes *corporate* saving. Such saving depends in part on the prevailing rate of interest. A high rate is likely to encourage corporate saving as a substitute for corporate borrowing to obtain capital. Like individuals, a corporation can dissave. It can declare a dividend out of the savings of the past.

When we add personal and corporate savings at the various interest rates, we obtain the savings curve S in Figure 69.

Hoarding

Individual and corporate savings are only the first step toward forming part of the supply of loanable funds. There is no warrant for the assumption, implicit in the real theory of interest, that savings automatically go to the loan market. There is hoarding to reckon with.

In a broad sense all money is hoarded: all the money in the community is *held* by somebody. Broadly speaking, the deliberate holding onto cash for the transaction, precautionary, and speculative motives constitutes hoarding. Narrowly conceived, hoarding may signify that people desire to hold, for a while, their savings as idle cash balances; this conception of hoarding stresses the speculative motive alone. Hoarding is akin to the velocity of circulation of money. If people want to hang onto their money a while longer before spending it or converting it into securities, hoarding rises and the velocity of money slows down.

In dealing with hoarding, the loanable-funds theory may walk in the path of J. M. Keynes and analyze the problem from the angle of liquidity preference. There is one seeming difference. In the liquidity-preference theory hoarding plays its part on the side of the demand for money to hold, whereas in the loanable-funds theory hoarding makes an appearance in the discussion of the supply side. But, as we saw in connection with dissaving, the difference is only on the surface. Hoarding may be viewed as a deduction from the supply of funds or as an outright demand for money to hold. In Figure 69 the hoarding curve H is treated as a component of the demand for funds. Hoardings are sensitive to the rate of interest; they are interest-elastic. At a high rate of interest less idle cash will be kept, in view of the large penalty for liquidity.

(2) DISHOARDING

Dishoarding is the opposite of hoarding. Cash balances idle in a previous period become active balances in the present period and are available as loanable funds. At higher rates of interest, would-be hoarders are impelled to offer part of their cash balances to borrowers. At lower rates, there is greater inclination to hold onto money. Essentially, dishoarding is reflected in a greater velocity of the circulating medium. To current savings we can add dishoardings as a component of the supply of funds on the loan market. In Figure 69 the dishoarding curve is marked DH.

(3) BANK CREDIT

The banking system provides a third source of loanable funds. Banks create credit money, and they increase the stock of money in a given period when they extend new loans or make investments by purchasing securities and paying for them with deposits credited to the sellers. Banks can diminish the volume of money by diminishing their lending or by selling securities to individuals and deducting the price from the deposit balances of the buyers. This component of the supply of funds bears a relation to the rate of interest. In many localities banks exemplify oligopoly, with rigid interest rates charged their customers. At one given time the rate may vary with the character of the borrower, the size of the loan, and other considerations. The pattern of rates does not sensitively move up and down as the volume of bank credit grows or shrinks. Generally, however, rates of interest are high in prosperity as bank loans expand, and lower in times of slow business when loans reach smaller aggregates. The supply curve of funds provided by banks is to some degree interest-elastic. This curve is indicated in Figure 69 as curve M.

(4) DISINVESTMENT

Disinvestment forms another source of funds in the loan market. We shall discuss this component shortly, in connection with investment.

B. The Demand for Loanable Funds

The demand for loanable funds comes primarily from three fields: investment, hoarding, and dissaving.

(1) INVESTMENT

In normal times, the outstanding demand for funds comes from firms which borrow money for the purchase or the manufacture of new capital goods, including the building up of inventory. The reasons for enlarging inventories beyond the usual level are varied. There may be an expectation of rising costs of supplies or of higher selling prices of the output or of a general inflation. Here, as with savings, we may have in mind *ex ante* investment, or investment planned by firms on the basis of profitable prospects; or *ex post* investment, that is, investment actually materialized at the end of a period.

In dealing with investment in capital facilities we are on familiar ground. Involved are the advantage of the roundabout process of production and the negatively sloping marginal revenue productivity curve of capital. Some economists are not certain that the interest charge for the borrowed funds is generally a prominent enough cost element to sway the firm in considering a marginal investment. The position ordinarily taken by the loanable-funds theory of interest is that investment is somewhat interest-elastic. (Meaning?) The expected return from an investment is compared with the interest rate. At lower interest rates, marginal ventures can be undertaken; at higher rates, these ventures would seem prohibitive.

Individual borrowing to purchase such durable consumer goods as houses, automobiles, or vacuum cleaners may be placed alongside the businessman's borrowing for the acquisition of producer goods. At low rates there is more temptation for consumers to borrow for the purchase of durable goods so as to enjoy them sooner than would be the case if the purchase were delayed by the slow accumulation of savings. The demand for funds for investment and durable goods alike is represented by curve I in Figure 69.

Disinvestment

In some instances the opposite of investment takes place, namely the consumption of capital goods and inventories. Such consumption is called *disinvestment*. The existing stock of machines and other equipment is allowed to wear out without being replaced. Inventories are drawn down below the level of the previous period. A number of reasons account for this phenomenon. Structural changes, calling for less capital, may be taking place in an industry. A given investment may prove to be an unwise venture. In such cases the capital is allowed to depreciate, and part of the revenue from the sale of the product, instead of going into capital replacement, is flowing into the loan market. At times brisk sales deplete inventories and there is no replenishment, perhaps owing to the expectation of deflation in the prices of inventory supplies or of the firm's output.

Disinvestment is encouraged somewhat by a high rate of interest on loanable funds. When the rate is high, some of the current capital may not produce a marginal revenue product to match the rate. The firm may decide to let this capital run down and to put the depreciation fund in the loan market. Disinvestment constitutes a deduction from the demand for funds for investment and an addition to the supply of funds for borrowers. In Figure 69 the disinvestment curve DI is entered on the supply side of loanable funds.

(2) HOARDING

Previous discussion pointed out that hoarding forms a deduction from the supply of funds or functions as an explicit demand for funds to hold. We treat hoarding as a demand.

(3) DISSAVING

As was indicated in connection with the discussion of saving, dissaving reflects a demand for funds.

C. The Equilibrium Rate of Interest

SUMMARY

It is time to take stock of the components of supply and demand of loanable funds in the market. At the equilibrium rate of interest, the amount lent equals the amount borrowed: for the economy, dollar lending cannot exceed or fall short of dollar borrowing any more than the number of radios sold in a given self-contained community can be greater or smaller than the number of radios bought. As we read our account of the components, we can write the following equation:

saving (S) — dissaving (DS) — hoarding (H) +
dishoarding (DH) + new bank credit (M)
$$= \text{investment (I)} - \text{disinvestment (DI).} \tag{1}$$

Since a deduction from one side of the equation is equivalent in the effect on the interest rate to an addition to the other side, we can rewrite equation (1) as follows:

$$S + DH + DI + M = I + H + DS. \tag{2}$$

The left side of equation (2) sums up the components of the supply of loanable funds. It points to the schedules of the lenders as composed of the schedule of saving, dishoarding, disinvestment, and bank credit, all related to rates of interest. The right side of the equation sums up the schedules of demand, as the schedules of investors, hoarders, and dissavers.

The situation depicted in equation (2) can be presented graphically, as in Figure 69, to which repeated reference has already been made. In this diagram each curve symbolizes the schedule of funds bid or asked at various corresponding interest rates. Since the components of supply and demand alike are also affected by the total income, we assume that the situation in the diagram is related to one specific aggregate income. To treat income as a variable would call for a three-dimensional diagram, with the third axis measuring the incomes.

THE EQUILIBRIUM RATE OF INTEREST

In our diagram, curve L represents the final supply schedule of loanable funds, formed by the horizontal addition of the four schedules S, DH, DI, and M. Curve B reflects the total demand schedule of loanable funds. It is a composite, by horizontal addition, of the three curves I, H, and DS. The intersection of these two curves gives us the equilibrium rate of interest $Or = AE$. At this rate the funds lent equal the funds borrowed; both amount to OA.

Equation (1) or (2) can take the shape of

$$(I - DI) + (H - DH) = (S - DS) + M,$$

or

$$\text{net I} + \text{net H} = \text{net S} + M. \tag{3}$$

This new equation tells us that net investment plus net hoarding can take place in a given period when there is a corresponding rise in net savings and credit expansion in the preceding or current period. This is not all.

This equation (3) summarizes a condensed version of the loanable-funds theory, with fewer component schedules and a correspondingly simpler diagram. The total *demand* for funds becomes only the sum of net investment and net hoarding (that is, a decreased velocity of money, or a greater disposition to hold onto cash balances). The total *supply* schedule is composed only of the schedules of saving and new bank credit. The intersection of these total demand and total supply curves gives us the equilibrium rate of interest.[4]

Let us return to our diagram. The equilibrium rate Or equates total lending to total borrowing. It does not, however, necessarily equate each component on the demand side with its counterpart on the supply side. It does not of necessity equate (1) the savings of the lenders and the investment of the borrowers; nor (2) the disinvestment of lenders and the dissaving of the borrowers; nor (3) the dishoarding and the new money $(DH + M)$ on one side and the hoarding (H) on the other side. The discrepancies between these three categories of borrowings and lendings, taken together, cancel out necessarily, since the total borrowed equals the total lent.

But it does not follow that it is a matter of indifference whether or not any component of demand is in balance with the corresponding component on the supply side. For instance, it is of first importance that planned (*ex ante*) savings and planned investment be equal to each other. The economy is out of joint when this equality does not exist. In Figure 69 the equilibrium rate of interest Or is unstable, because at this rate expected saving and expected investment do not match. Curves I and S intersect at rate Or_1; at this rate of interest anticipated saving and anticipated investment are in accord. But at the rate Or, funds demanded for intended investment amount to rb whereas the savings planned by lenders come only to ra. Planned investment *exceeds* planned saving.

Such a situation is unstable and will not endure. With scheduled investment larger than scheduled saving, there is an attempt to employ more resources than are released by the intended savings. There is an upsurge in the aggregate demand for goods and services. Incomes rise, and at higher incomes intended savings mount. Also, if the supply of money is not perfectly elastic, the need for additional money to accommodate the transaction motive amid greater economic activity will tend to raise the rate of interest. In its turn, the higher rate may stimulate greater savings. Eventually the aggregate income may be pushed up to a level at which the equilibrium rate of interest may be associated with the double equality (1) of intended savings and intended investment, and (2) of total funds demanded by borrowers and total funds offered by lenders. Such an equi-

---

[4] Some writers present the loanable-funds theory in this condensed version. See G. N. Halm, *Monetary Theory* (Philadelphia, Blakiston, 1946), p. 328.

librium rate reflects a stable, full equilibrium.[5]

Similarly, with a given configuration of components of supply and demand schedules of loanable funds, we may obtain an equilibrium rate of interest which equates total borrowings and total lendings, but at which the savings planned by the lenders are greater than the investment planned by borrowing firms. Money earned in the previous period is not going fully into expenditures in the current period. This diminution of total expenditures may cause a contraction in total income. At lower incomes savings decline. Too, the smaller requirements for money for transactions may induce a lower rate of interest in the loanable-funds market. This downward process may continue until a total income is reached at which the interest rate not only equates borrowings and lendings but is also compatible with an equality between intended savings and intended investment.

SUGGESTED READINGS

Cassel, G. *The Theory of Social Economy*, chap. 6. New York, Harcourt, Brace, 1932.

Dillard, D. *The Economics of John Maynard Keynes*, chap. 8. New York, Prentice-Hall, 1948.

Enke, S. *Intermediate Economic Theory*, chaps. 11, 30. New York, Prentice-Hall, 1950.

Fisher, I. *The Theory of Interest*, Part II. New York, Macmillan, 1930.

Hansen, A. H. *A Guide to Keynes*, chaps. 6–8. New York, McGraw-Hill, 1953.

Knight, F. H. "Capital and Interest," Encyclopedia Britannica, Vol. IV, 1946, pp. 779–801. Reprinted in *Readings in the Theory of Income Distribution*, pp. 384–417.

Leigh, A. H. "Supply and Demand Analysis of Interest Rates," *American Economic Review*, Vol. XLI (September, 1951), pp. 579–602.

Robertson, D. H. "Mr. Keynes and the Rate of Interest," in *Essays in Monetary Theory*, pp. 1–38. London, King, 1940.

Somers, H. M. "Monetary Policy and the Theory of Interest," *Quarterly Journal of Economics*, Vol. LV (May, 1941), pp. 488–507. Reprinted in *Readings in the Theory of Income Distribution*, pp. 477–498.

Taussig, F. W. *Principles of Economics*, 4th ed., Vol. II, chaps. 38–40. New York, Macmillan, 1939.

Wicksell, K. *Lectures on Political Economy*, Vol. I, Part II. New York, Macmillan, 1934.

[5] This point receives more attention in Chapter XIX, section IV.

CHAPTER
XVI Rent

THE SUPPLY OF LAND

NATURAL resources are limited in supply. In relation to the food requirements of the population and in relation to the other three factors which
must collaborate with natural resources before goods can be produced,
the amount of farm land, of sites for building, of oil pools, ore deposits,
coal fields, forests, waterfalls, and stone quarries is limited. These resources
are scarce in relation to the demand for them. They are both scarce and
productive: as other factors are combined with more and more units of
a natural resource, total output rises, up to a certain critical point. The
supply of natural resources is almost entirely inelastic. There is practically
no supply price of land. When the price offered for such resources rises
or falls their amounts, even in the long run, will hardly increase or shrink
to an appreciable degree.

It may be argued, and it is true to some small extent, that natural resources are flexible in supply. Land can be reclaimed from the river, the
lake, or the sea. Swampy land can be drained. Rocks, stumps, and trees
can be removed. Irrigation ditches and dams can improve fertility. Level-
ing and grading can add to building sites. Reforestation replenishes dis-
appearing woods. Likewise, land can be diminished in amount and fertility by neglect and by erosion, or by predatory cultivation.

However, such variations in the amount of land constitute an insignificant fraction of the total quantity in existence. They do not exert enough
of an impact on the market situation to render true the assertion that land
has a supply price and that we have more of it or less of it as the price
offered for it goes up or down. Moreover, once many of the above improvements have been made on it, they become an irrevocable part of the

land. They become a sunk investment. After the rocks and trees have been cleared, after a water front has been partly turned into dry land, the land is there; it will hardly shrink in amount if real-estate prices decline. The same is true of investments in dams and many conservation measures. Furthermore, the price of land will have to rise considerably before such expensive means will be used to raise its amount.

THE CONCEPT OF RENT

Rent, meaning pure rent or economic rent, is the return to the owner for the use of natural resources in a competitive market. The essence of rent lies in the fact that it is a *surplus*, a return in excess of the amount that must be offered to the factor to induce it to stay in its current service. Why is economic rent a surplus? Because of the extreme inelasticity of its supply. Natural resources are here, available to be used. No incentive was required to have them brought into being. Natural resources are productive; but the owner cannot generally claim that he has incurred a cost, in the form of labor, capital investment, and management, to make them productive. The cost of natural resources is nearly zero; their supply price is nearly zero; their supply elasticity is nearly zero. Accordingly, the return on them is almost all rent or surplus, and not a necessary reward for their services.

Some economists apply the term rent only to the return for the use of natural resources; other economists use it to designate a surplus return to any factor, a compensation above what is necessary to keep any factor in its present occupation. A worker with superior natural aptitudes, not acquired by effort, produces more than his neighbor and in competitive conditions receives higher pay, which by such definition contains an element of rent. A rent element may also be seen in interest. Some individuals would be willing to save or to part with the liquidity of their savings at a rate of interest below the market level; but they receive the market rate. The difference may be regarded as rent. The same situation exists in relation to profit. Some entrepreneurs may obtain more profit than would suffice to induce them to stay in business and to work as hard as ever.

The economic rent that we are talking about here is not identical with the term rent or rental as used in ordinary conversation. The monthly or annual rental turned over by the tenant farmer to the landlord, or by the renting occupant of an apartment or store to the owner is a composite of several elements. It contains (1) economic rent, if there is any; (2) interest on the investment in the buildings and improvements; (3) maintenance, depreciation, and replacement of these investments; and (4) wages of management and possibly a profit to the owner for the risks involved in the venture of acquiring, improving, and leasing the properties to tenants. Economic rent, be it noticed, does not include "stumpage" paid to the owner for the timber cut nor "royalties" paid to the mine owners for the removal of such exhaustible resources as coal, oil, and ore.

Inflexible supply exists in connection with other factors than land, but ordinarily only for short periods. In our study of competitive price determination in the short run we saw that if the demand for a commodity rises, the effect is for the price to advance above average variable cost and possibly above average total cost. Certain factors are fixed in amount for the time being. The increased demand for the article is met by a more intensive use of these factors; that is, by dosing them with more and more of the variable resources, up to the level at which marginal revenue equals marginal cost. The surplus return per commodity, measured by the difference between price and the average variable cost, is the quasi-rent. The distinction between such factors and land lies in the fact that they are inelastic in supply only in the short run, whereas land is inelastic in supply in the long run as well. Quasi-rent emerges only in the short period, but rent is both a long-run and a short-run phenomenon.

I. Agricultural Rent

Our job now is to trace in some detail the appearance of rent and to see what determines its amount, first on agricultural land and then on urban sites.

Let us set ourselves straight, at the start, on the causes of rent. Scarcity of land in relation to the demand is not the only reason for rent. The phenomenon of variable proportions or *diminishing returns* shares responsibility. Let land stay fixed in quantity, but let successive applications of the variable factors to it yield consistently *proportional* outputs, and no rent will emerge. In such conditions, as the population grows and the demand for agricultural output rises, more labor and capital will be applied to land and more food and raw materials will be produced. For the scarce land, the other factors would be substituted, without diminishing returns to these substitutes. But in actuality, diminishing returns do set in, after a certain point, and rent does make an appearance.

1. RENT AS A RESIDUAL SHARE

To clarify this proposition, let us assume that there are in a country one million farms, each occupying one acre; that all farms are equally fertile and at the same distance from the market for the output; and that all farms produce one and the same crop. Table 18 illustrates the situation on each farm. In column 1 we have the successive units of variable resources applied to the farm: each unit is the best composite of a certain amount of labor, capital, and management. In column 2 are listed the corresponding total outputs. Column 3 registers the average output per unit of such a composite of variables. Column 4 measures the marginal

TABLE 18. *Diminishing Returns and Rent on a One-Acre Farm*

(1)	(2)	(3)	(4)	(5)	(6)
Units of combined variable factors	Total output (bu.)	Average output per combined unit (bu.)	Marginal output (bu.)	Returns to the combined variable factors (bu.) (4) × (1)	Total rent (bu.) (2) − (5)
1	8	8	8	8	0
2	18	9	10	20	−2
3	26	8⅔	8	24	2
4	33	8¼	7	28	5
5	39	7⅘	6	30	9
6	43	7⅙	4	24	19

physical product of these units; it measures, accordingly, the reward of each unit as more and more composite units are employed. In column 5 we have the total rewards to all the units of variables applied. Column 6 records the total rent obtained by each farm; it is arrived at by subtracting the total compensation going to the three variable factors from the total output.

Let us now make use of this table to explore the determination of rent. Assume that the country is thinly settled and has a limited amount of labor and capital, so that only 1 million composite units can turn to farming. One such unit could be applied to each of the 1 million one-acre farms, with the results as indicated in the first row of the table. But this combination would be uneconomical. Column 3 tells us that the most advantageous combination of land and variable resources is in the ratio of two units of variables to one acre of land—yielding the highest average output per unit of variables, 9 bushels.

It is better therefore to set the 1 million composite units to work on only ½ million of these farms. This combination will achieve the optimum ratio of 2 to 1, and will yield a total output of 9 million bushels: 9 bushels per unit multiplied by 1 million units. Thus by *withdrawing* 500,000 acres from cultivation we *raise* the total yield from 8 million to 9 million bushels. The marginal productivity of land is negative. Land brings no rent.

Suppose now that the population and the labor and capital resources of the country grow and more of them work on the farms. Beginning with the employment of 3 million composite units of variable factors, we enter upon the so-called second phase of the law of variable proportions, the phase of diminishing average returns. The best use of these 3 million units would be to apply them to 1½ million acres, with the optimum 2 to 1 ratio. But we have only 1 million acres; farm land is scarce. From now on the ratio will exceed 2 to 1. The attempt will be to make up for the relative scarcity of land by using more than two units of variables on each acre. During this second phase land has a positive marginal productivity. As the demand for agricultural produce rises and as the land is cultivated by more units of variables, each acre earns increasing amounts of rent (column 6).

Rent appears when the average product per unit of composite variables on each acre (column 3) rises above the marginal product of these variables (column 4). The yield per unit of variables exceeds then the reward going to these variables for their service; the total yield per acre (column 2) is greater then than the total compensation received by the variables employed on it (column 5). A surplus appears on each acre; this surplus is rent. This surplus can be defined as so much per unit of variables, column 3 minus column 4; or as a total surplus per acre, column 2 minus column 5. If 5 million composite units of variables are employed on the 1 million farms, rent per acre is 9 bushels. At a price of $2 per bushel rent per acre is $18.

To generalize the argument, as the demand for agricultural goods rises, the scarce amount of land must be cultivated with a greater quantity of variable resources. As increasing amounts of variable resources are put to a given tract of land, diminishing returns set in sooner or later, and the average product per unit of variable factors rises above the marginal product of the units. The *average* product is the yield; the *marginal* product is the reward to the variables. The difference between the two magnitudes, multiplied by the number of variable factors, is claimed by the owner of the land. Since land is costless, this total is economic rent.

2. RENT AS THE MARGINAL PRODUCT OF LAND

In the above discussion we treated rent as a residual share left after the deduction of the returns to the factors working on land. But there is nothing peculiar about rent in this regard. The return to capital or labor can also be visualized as a residual share. It depends on which factor we

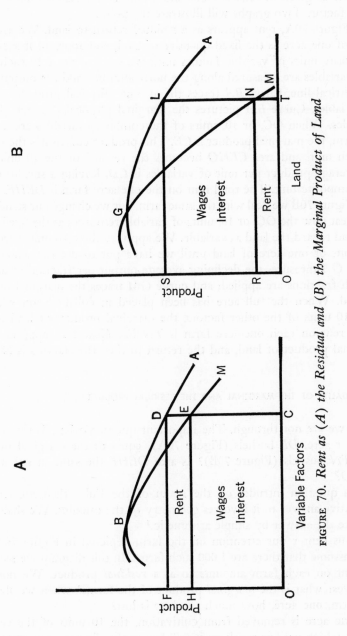

FIGURE 70. *Rent as (A) the Residual and (B) the Marginal Product of Land*

consider as given in total amount and which as a variable applied to the given factor. Two graphs will illustrate the point.

In Figure 70A, rent appears as a residual return to land. We assume a farm of one acre as the fixed quantity of land, and apply to it successive composite units of variable factors until we employ on it 10 such units. The variables are measured along the horizontal line and the output along the vertical line. Curve BA traces the average physical product per unit of variables. Curve BM pictures the marginal physical product of these variables. When OC, or 10, units of the combined variables are used on the farm, the marginal product is CE. This product constitutes the reward of each unit, and area $CEHO$ becomes the reward of the 10 units. But the average product per unit of variables is CD, leaving a surplus of DE per composite unit. The total rent on the one-acre farm is $DEHF$.

In Figure 70B we deal with the same farm, but we change our standpoint. We treat now the OC, or 10, units of variable resources as the fixed quantum and regard the land as variable. We apply to these 10 units successive fractions of one acre of land until we have put to use the whole acre. Curve GA measures the declining average output per fraction of an acre as such fractions are applied; and curve GM traces the marginal product of land. When the full acre has been placed in collaboration with the fixed 10 units of the other factors, the marginal product of land is TN. Total rent on each one-acre farm is $TNRO$. Now rent appears as the marginal product of land, and the return to the other factors is *residual*.

THE EQUALITY OF THE MARGINAL AND THE RESIDUAL PRODUCT

But we are not through. The important question arises: is the residual rent per acre, DE bushels (Figure 70A), equal to the marginal product rent, TN bushels (Figure 70B)? Is area $DEHF$ the same in size as area $TNRO$?

This question intrudes on the realm of the Euler theorem, and the affirmative answer to it involves geometry or the calculus. We shall demonstrate the answer by simple arithmetic.[1]

Let us center our attention on the farm depicted in Figure 70A and let us assume that there are 1,000 such farms. In this diagram we see what the rent on each farm amounts to as a *residual* product. We now ask ourselves: what is the *marginal* product of the farms? when we abandon one farm, one acre, how much product is lost?

If one acre is removed from cultivation, the 10 units of the variable factors which used to work on it will be evenly allocated among the 999 remaining acres. The $\frac{10}{999}$ of the composite unit, added to the old OC

[1] P. A. Samuelson, *Economics* (New York, McGraw-Hill, 1951), p. 577, n. 1.

units ($= 10$ units) working each farm, will add to the product $^{10}\!/_{999}$ of the marginal output CE. (We are dealing with small quantities, and the increment brought by these $^{10}\!/_{999}$ of a unit will be practically equal to $^{10}\!/_{999}$ of CE.)

The addition to the product of the 999 farms becomes $^{10}\!/_{999}CE \times 999$, or $10CE$, which is $OC \times CE$, or area $CEHO$. We see, then, that if we keep the abandoned acre under cultivation, it produces an output of $DCOF$; and if we keep the acre out of cultivation, the released 10 composite units of variables can produce only an output of $CEHO$. The *marginal* product of land, or the contribution of an acre, is equal to the difference between these two areas, or to the *residual* share $DCOF - CEHO = DEHF$. From Figure 70B we know that the marginal product of land is identified by area $TNRO$. It follows therefore that area $TNRO$ equals area $DEHF$.

THE EULER THEOREM

This arithmetic may serve as a substitute for the higher mathematics of the Euler theorem,[2] developed by the Swiss mathematician Leonhard Euler. The theorem states that if P is a linear homogeneous function (what this means will be explained presently) of $A, B, C, \cdots$, that is, if $P = f$ $(A, B, C, \cdots)$, the following equation will hold:

$$P = A\frac{\partial P}{\partial A} + B\frac{\partial P}{\partial B} + C\frac{\partial P}{\partial C} + \cdots.$$

Economists saw in this theorem grist for their mill. Let A, B, and C refer respectively to land, labor, and capital, and let P stand for the total physical output produced by these factors. Then $\partial P/\partial A$ is the marginal product of land, and $A\, \partial P/\partial A$ represents the return going to the whole amount of land used in producing P. Similarly $B\, \partial P/\partial B$ and $C\, \partial P/\partial C$ symbolize the shares of labor and capital. The above equation tells us, then, something significant in economics; namely, that if, as under competition, we pay each factor the equivalent of its marginal product, the total product is exhausted. The output of the collaborating factors is distributed to them entirely; no residue is left. Thus we showed that the residual rent $DEHF$ is the same as the marginal-product rent $TNRO$. Accordingly, if the payments to land and to the variable factors are governed by their marginal productivity, the total product, or area $DCOF$, is exhausted.

As was mentioned, this theorem applies only to linear homogeneous functions. In mathematics this means that if $a + b = x$, $2a + 2b = 2x$; or more generalized, if $x = f(a, b)$, then $mx = f(ma, mb)$. In economics

[2] This topic can be omitted by those unacquainted with the calculus.

this means that the production function is of linear homogeneity; that as each input, each factor-service, is increased by a certain percentage, the output rises by the same percentage. There are no net economies or diseconomies of scale; the industry is a constant-cost industry.

RENT AND DIFFERENCES IN LAND

So far our discussion of rent was based on the two simplifying assumptions that all land is homogeneous, or of the same productive capacity, and second, that it all raised only one kind of crop. We shall now approximate reality more closely by dropping the first assumption.

Tracts of land vary in quality and the variation is reflected in differences in the unit costs of production, excluding rent from the costs. The physical qualities of the soil, the rainfall, temperature, humidity, drainage, and topography render one plot of land superior to another, so that it costs less to produce a given output on one plot than on another. Nearness to the market is another differentiating factor. The market price is the same for the products of all the farms in the region, and the farm located close to the market or enjoying good roads has lower unit transportation costs than the farm not so well situated in these respects.

The adoption of the premise of different grades of land does not introduce new angles into the theory of rent. The only element affected relates to the amount of rent emerging on the various parcels of land. The superior parcel will reap more rent than the plot of lower grade and the poorest plot in use will fetch no rent at all.

Assume three grades of land all raising one particular commodity, say, wheat. The analysis will proceed more conveniently by the aid of the diagrams in Figure 71. We are dealing with three typical farms. Grade A is the best in productivity, or else is best located with respect to the market. Grade B is of lower productivity or of poorer location; and grade C is poorest.

To vary the aspect of the analysis, we shall deal now with monetary costs and price, instead of marginal outputs in bushels, as we have done in previous examples. In each diagram the horizontal line measures the output and the vertical distances indicate the price of wheat or the average or marginal costs of production. In each diagram, too, AC and MC are respectively the average and the marginal cost curves, both exclusive of rent.

If the population of the country is small, the forces of supply and demand for wheat may determine a price of OP_1 per bushel. In such a case only farms of grade A will be under cultivation. Each of these farms operates at the optimum competitive scale, producing OQ_1 bushels of

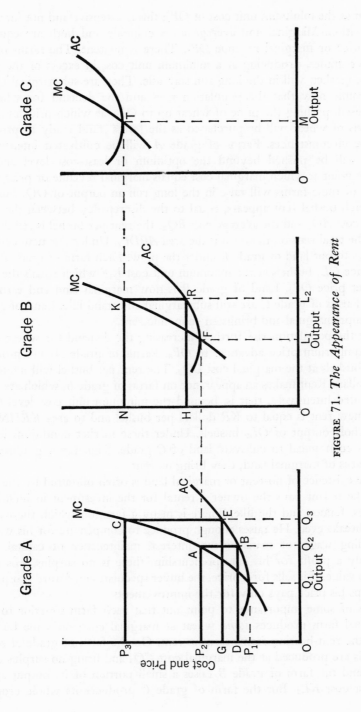

FIGURE 71. *The Appearance of Rent*

wheat at the minimum unit cost of OP_1; this is extensive and not intensive cultivation. Marginal and average costs coincide and both are equal to the price or marginal revenue OP_1. There is no rent. The farms of the poorer grades, producing at a minimum unit cost in excess of the price in the market, will in the long run stay idle. They are submarginal farms.

Assume now that the population rises and the demand for wheat is increased, pushing the price of wheat up to OP_2, at which price as many bushels of wheat will be purchased as the farms stand ready to produce in the circumstances. Farms of grade A will be cultivated intensively: they will be pushed beyond the optimum or least-cost level and up to the point at which marginal cost equals marginal revenue or price OP_2. Each of these farms will raise in the long run an output of OQ_2 bushels. On each bushel rent appears, equal to the discrepancy between the marginal cost AQ_2 and the average cost BQ_2: the rent per bushel is AB dollars and the total rent on the farm is the area $ABDP_2$. Under this new demand it pays to put land of grade B under the plow. Each farm of grade B will produce OL_1 bushels at the minimum unit cost L_1F which equals the new market price OP_2. Land of grade B is now marginal land and earns no rent. Farms of grade C are still submarginal and stand idle. Land of grade A is supramarginal and brings an economic rent.

Let the population rise further, increasing the demand for wheat until the equilibrium price advances to OP_3. Farms of grade A will produce OQ_3 bushels at the marginal cost CQ_3. The rent per bushel will mount to CE dollars. Rent makes an appearance on farms of grade B, which are now cultivated intensively, that is, beyond the minimum unit cost level OL_1. This new rent is equal to KR dollars per bushel and to area $KRHN$ for the whole output of OL_2 bushels. Under these market conditions it becomes economical to cultivate land of C grade. Such farms graduate to the status of marginal land; they bring no rent.

The existence of no-rent or marginal land is often obscured by the fact that the tenant pays the owner a rental for the investment in buildings, ditches, fences, and the like. There is many a farm on which the owner only breaks even. He raises enough produce to compensate for his wages, including wages of management, interest, maintenance of capital, and possibly a profit for his entrepreneurship; there is no surplus. His land has no value. If it sells for a price, the buyer speculates on future prospects. Perhaps his price pays only for the improvements.

It is of some importance to point out that each farm superior to the marginal farm produces *some* wheat at marginal cost; on some bushels even the rent-bearing farms earn no rent. On the farm of grade A some bushels are produced at the marginal cost CQ_3 and bring no surplus over cost; and the farm of grade B raises a small portion of its output at its highest cost KL_2. But the farm of grade C produces its whole crop at marginal cost TM. Its minimum average cost equals the price of wheat; it is the marginal farm. The marginal farm exemplifies the extensive margin. On the superior or supramarginal farms the minimum average cost is below the market price OP_3. These farms are pushed to the intensive margin OQ_3 on grade A and OL_2 on grade B.

II. Urban Rent and Other Rent Problems

By urban rent we mean the economic rent going to city sites on which buildings are used for various purposes. The rental on the building may include, in addition to the pure rent, interest on and amortization of the investment in the structure, payment for the public utilities provided by the landlord, wages to the janitor, a salary and profit to the owner. When a real-estate company develops a new residential area by improvements and advertising, much of what may later look like rent is a profit to the company for the risk of the venture and the imaginative handling of problems charged with uncertainty.

THE CONCEPT OF URBAN LOCATION

The cause or source of urban rent is basically analogous to that of agricultural rent. In agriculture the quality of the land is expressed in its fertility and nearness to the market. The quality of urban land reflects itself mainly in its location. What is meant by location in this case? The answer depends on the purpose of the buildings erected on the sites. There are categories of uses to which sites are put and subdivisions within each category. Sites are used for stores, offices, hotels, and theaters; for apartment houses and one- or two-family dwellings; for warehouses, material yards, and light and heavy manufacturing; and for the unsightly dwellings of the poor.

A good location for retail stores is a region where people with money in their pockets have a tendency to congregate. In such a location a store may do a large volume of business and may face a low unit cost in disposing of its merchandise. A drugstore on a crowded street corner will earn more money than a drugstore away from the dense traffic, although the management is of the same quality in both stores and the prices charged are identical. A desirable location for a factory is marked by the availability of power, efficient freight-carrying facilities, and acceptable means of transportation for the workers. Business sites offer productivity, residential sites offer utility. A good residential district is away from the noise of the business sections and sufficiently near schools and churches. It is within easy reach of the bus or subway. It must also be in a respectable or fashionable neighborhood. In all these respects locations along the railway track or near the gas house will not qualify.

In retail stores a rent emerges, in some cases, not so much because of the low unit cost induced by the large volume of business, as because of the large revenue from the higher prices that can be charged. Certain shopping districts have prestige value to the customers. People of means like to be seen shopping there. For example, those who choose to buy jewelry or clothes on Fifth Avenue, New York, are willing to pay a high price for their purchases. Since they exclude customers unable or unwilling to pay such prices, these places become "exclusive." They charge customers for the satisfaction of being served on high-toned premises. A store with the same management, the same appointments, and the same goods and service will earn less and pay less rent on Third Avenue than on Fifth Avenue. It hardly needs to be stressed that the returns due to the prestige and reputation of a firm *built up* by management policy and distinctive service are not in the nature of rent; they are wages, interest, and profit.

THE CAUSE OR SOURCE OF URBAN RENT

If desirable sites were plentiful in relation to the demand for them, there would be no rent on them and they would command no price. But good sites, like fertile land, are scarce. And, like fertile land, urban sites, especially business sites, are used intensively: an effort is made to substitute labor and capital for land in order to economize land space. But here, as in agriculture, eventual diminishing returns in the application of labor and capital to land set a limit to the substitution. As more stories are built on a given site the cost rises progressively. More solid foundations, stronger frames and walls, and more expensive elevators are required. Sooner or later the point is reached at which the marginal revenue product from the building facilities equals the marginal cost of producing the facilities. But the average cost of producing a unit of floor space stands below the marginal cost: such is the mathematics, and the economics, too, of the case where marginal costs are rising. The gap between the two costs is the surplus. The annual revenue or price obtained by the owner for the use of the space in the building exceeds the calculated annual cost of the building. But whether or not the site is used intensively, the advantageous location, for business or residence, brings in more revenue than the same building in a poor location; and the revenue exceeds the cost of the investment in the building and of the services going with it. The residual amount is economic rent.

Another way of looking at urban rent is to consider the productivity of a good location. Labor and capital applied, say, to the selling of an article in a good location will be productive of a greater volume of business and greater revenue than when used without benefit of such a location. Withdraw from use a relatively small tract of land in a crowded area and spread the released labor and capital—formerly used in business on the now abandoned piece of land—over the remaining space in the district. There will be a drop in the productivity of the total labor and capital in the area. There is thus marginal productivity in urban land as there is in agricultural land. In a competitive market for sites, the rivalry of the owners of buildings will bring the pure rent contained in the contractual rental down to the tenant's surplus or down to marginal productivity of the space rented; and the rivalry of businessmen seeking the surplus or earnings of good sites will push the pure rent up to this surplus or marginal productivity.[3]

RENT AND COST

Whether rent enters as an element of cost and determines the price of the article, or whether it is to be considered a resultant of price depends on the angle of vision. It depends on whether we view rent through the lenses of the economy, the particular industry, or the firm.

From the point of view of the *economy* as a whole rent is a consequence of the price as formed in the competitive market; rent does not function as a component of the price of the commodity produced by land or sold in a given location. As far as society is concerned, land is limited in quantity. Land in all its variety of quality and location comes close to having no cost and no supply price. Accordingly, when rent appears, it appears as a consequence of the long-run demand situation with regard to the final good or service produced on the land. An increased demand will induce the intensive use of the land and the price offered for the good will rise above the average cost of production. Rent becomes the consequence of the competitive price.

The situation appears different from the viewpoint of a given *industry*. If we assume, as we did heretofore, that all agricultural land has only one use, there can be no talk of industries in relation to such land. There is then only one industry; and the viewpoint of this one industry is identical with the viewpoint of the economy in general: rent is the result and not

---

[3] For an emphasis on the monopoly aspects in urban rents, see E. H. Chamberlin, *The Theory of Monopolistic Competition* (Cambridge, Harvard University Press, 1948), 6th ed., pp. 112–113 and Appendix D.

the cause of price.

But we shall now drop this assumption and adopt the premise, in conformity to reality, that land is heterogeneous, that different plots of land can be put to different uses, and that, moreover, many a piece of land can be put to alternative uses. Land producing wheat can produce barley or corn; land that can raise oranges can be turned to truck gardening; and a site for a shoe store can serve for a furniture or a clothing store.

From the angle of this realistic premise we can see that if the supply of land is extremely inelastic for the whole economy it does not follow that the supply of land is also extremely inelastic for a given purpose, for a given industry. For example, if the price of wheat rises, land given to raising barley will be transferred to wheat: with the rising price of wheat, and therefore of land raising wheat, more land becomes available for wheat. If furniture stores become scarce in relation to the demand, sites used for selling groceries may be shifted to use for furniture stores. The supply of land for a particular use is not almost a vertical line but a curve sloping upward to the right.

In the circumstances, the rent obtained from a plot of land in one use or industry becomes a cost, a supply price, for the same plot when transferred to an alternative use. If the land tilled for barley brings $10 pure rent per acre and it is turned to raising wheat because the demand for wheat has risen, the $10 rent will be considered a cost of producing the additional wheat. The price of wheat will have to be high enough to give the owner of the barley acres, now transferred to wheat, an income equal to $10 per acre above the cost of raising wheat. The $10 rent on the wheat acres appears as an opportunity cost of raising the additional wheat. The new price of wheat must cover this cost component. If the surplus earnings of a farm formerly given to barley but now raising wheat amount to $18 per acre, the price-determined rent on this farm is only $8; the other $10 of rent is a price-determining cost.

Should the demand for barley become so intense that it would pay to retransfer some land from wheat back to barley, and should the surplus on the re-established barley farm be $20 per acre, the rent on the barley farm as a "noncost" and price-determined return is only $2. The other $18 rent constitutes the opportunity cost of shifting from wheat to barley. We may generalize that the "noncost" and price-determined rent on land with alternative uses is the surplus obtained in the given use less the lower surplus which could be earned in the next best use.

As far as the individual *firm* is concerned, rent is a cost to be met by it like any other cost. In a competitive market the firm must pay the rent which other firms are expected and ready to pay. If the owning firm uses the land itself, it must earn the rent in addition to the other earnings. If it does not, it will do better to hire out the land and receive the full rent from the tenant.

Rent is a cost to the firm because the firm will not obtain the services of the land if it does not turn over to the owner the surplus appearing above expenses on the other factors used in collaboration with the land to make or sell the product. Farmers or businessmen will compete with one another for the use of the land or of the urban site, until the price paid for it is the equivalent of the surplus or the productivity for which it is responsible. In the long run the rent is an opportunity cost to the owner; when he leases the land to one tenant he will charge him as much as he would obtain from another tenant. Since the rent has to be paid, it has to be earned. The firm is compelled to charge a price which, in view of the volume of sales, will cover the cost of production, including the rent. The rent becomes a price-determining element.

RENT AND THE ALLOCATION OF LAND

Like the wage rate and interest, rent is the price for a factor-service. Like any other price, it functions to ration the service. Rent serves to allocate the employment of agricultural land among the many agricultural products, and to distribute the use of urban sites: first, among the large categories of uses, such as stores, factories, shops, and residences; and second, among the varieties of uses under each category. It governs the allocation of land between crop raising and sheep grazing, between the hardware store and the candy store, and between the beauty parlor and the barbershop. On the outskirts of a city rent is arbiter in the contest for the land between residential purposes and market gardening.

The apportionment proceeds primarily in conformity with consumer desires as expressed by the demand schedule. The rent is controlled by the price and the amount of the product raised or sold on the land. When consumers want an article badly enough, they will offer a good price for it and will buy more of it too, with the effect that the producer of it can offer a higher rent for the use of land. Land will be bid away from other uses not favored so strongly by consumers. Shifts in the demand for goods, persisting for long periods, will create shifts in the uses to which plots of land are put.

If land is scarce in relation to the demand for it, it will be economized. Its rent will rise and it will be employed for the most essential ends. What is an essential end is told the producer by the demand schedule of the consumer. If taverns and bowling alleys bring more rent, free private enterprise will stud the locality with such commercial structures instead of the "much needed" apartment houses. If housing is scarce and rentals advance, because of the high pure rent, house sites will be used more sparingly. Families which formerly occupied five rooms will have to do with four rooms; and some who lived in desirable locations will move to less attractive neighborhoods. Moreover, the high rents ordinarily serve as a corrective for the "short supply" by encouragement to housebuilding. Thus a new market equilibrium for housing is established. Whether the crowding and the shifts are desirable from the standpoint of politics, child psychology, criminology, and social ethics is another problem.

It is reasonable to expect that, if we should dispense with rent as a guide to the allocation of land, confusion and hardship might result. Experience shows that when rent is above or below equilibrium levels, land is used wastefully. In the days gone by, in various European countries the landlords burdened their farm tenants with excessive rentals. The abused tenants allowed the land to deteriorate. The soil was robbed of its fertility; land was rack-rented.

After World War II rent ceilings were instituted in many a community. Rents, too low, were no longer an adequate rationing agency. The law provided no substitute method of house rationing. The result was frequent allocation of housing by favoritism or chance. The persistent hunters found better quarters than those whom long hours of work kept from the diligent search. Various tricks of raising the rentals were practiced. Families with children had a hard time finding dwelling space. Because of the low rents, many people occupied more rooms than they would have otherwise; and signs "furnished room for rent" became scarce. However, these assertions are not meant to deny that in extreme emergency wise rent control may mitigate the hardships of rent gouging. We are dealing with a many-sided problem.

RENT AND THE VALUE OF LAND

In Chapters IX to XII we examined the problem of value, the pricing of goods in the various types of markets. The approach outlined there is valid for the analysis of the price of most commodities. But there is one unique class of commodities in the pricing of which that approach is inadequate. As we saw in those chapters, the price of goods is governed by the relation of marginal cost to marginal revenue. We come, however, upon certain types of goods where there is no marginal cost to consider, for the simple reason that they do not involve a cost of production. There is seldom a cost of producing land. Over the short period the cost of such long-lived capital facilities as machines or buildings is irrelevant to their price: their amount is fixed for the time being whatever happens to the demand for their services; they have no supply price, in the short run.

Some other principle is required for the price determination of land in the long and short run alike, and of machines and buildings in the short run only. The principle is based on the *capitalization* of the earnings of these agents, of their rents or quasi-rents. When a person buys a piece of land, he is paying for the succession of annual rents which he expects to receive from the land as the years roll on. The price which he is offering is based on the present value of these future rents, on the sum of the discounted future returns. This sum can be found in the strict mathematical way by summing a convergent series. But it can also be found simply by dividing the average annual rent by the rate of interest. If a piece of land is expected to bring an annual rent of $100 and if the rate of interest on relatively safe investments is 4%, the value of the piece of land is

$$\$100 + \frac{\$100}{1.04} + \frac{\$100}{(1.04)^2} + \frac{\$100}{(1.04)^3} + \cdots = \frac{\$100}{.04} = \$2,500.$$

The same formula gives us the price of machines and buildings over the short period. The average annual quasi-rent is divided by the appropriate rate of interest.

If the demand for sites in a given city is on the increase, the rents on the sites will advance and so will the quasi-rents on the buildings, apart from the sites. In the short run the value of the land will rise and so will the value of the buildings. But over the long period the high site values will endure, whereas the value of the buildings will go down until it conforms to their cost of production. The initial high quasi-rents of the buildings will invite greater construction activity until the large number of buildings will bring down their price. In the case of an enduring decreased demand for sites and buildings, the low earnings on buildings will discourage replacement as old buildings wear out, until the price of buildings rises to match the cost of construction. But the low site rents will occasion low land values, permanently.

SUGGESTED READINGS

Buchanan, D. H. "The Historical Approach to Rent and Price Theory," *Economica*, Vol. IX (June, 1929), pp. 123–155. Reprinted in *Readings in the Theory of Income Distribution*, pp. 599–637.

Bye, C. R. *Development and Issues in the Theory of Rent*. New York, Columbia University Press, 1940.

Chamberlin, E. H. *The Theory of Monopolistic Competition*, 6th ed., Appendix D. Cambridge, Harvard University Press, 1948.

Enke, S. *Intermediate Economic Theory*, chap. 29. New York, Prentice-Hall, 1950.

Marshall, A. *Principles of Economics*, 8th ed., Book VI, chap. 9. New York, Macmillan, 1927.

Ogilvie, F. W. "Marshall on Rent," *Economic Journal*, Vol. XL (March, 1930), pp. 1–24. M. T. Hollond, "Marshall on Rent: A Reply to Prof. Ogilvie," *ibid*. (September, 1930), pp. 369–383.

Robinson, Joan. *The Economics of Imperfect Competition*, chap. 8. London, Macmillan, 1948.

CHAPTER
XVII Profits

PERHAPS the most symbolic description of our economic order is contained in the statement that it is a profit system. The prospect of a profit is the moving force of economic activity and economic progress. Most of what is desirable, and much of what can be criticized, in our economic organization may be due to the pursuit of profit. The profit motive sets in motion policies for the expansion of firms and industries, providing increased employment and income; it launches the testing of new ideas which raise the efficiency of production; it stimulates improvements in old varieties of goods and the introduction of new varieties; and it induces efforts for the expansion of demand and the widening of markets. The prospect of low or nonexistent profits will slow down economic activity; and if the dismal prospect is widespread, the economy is paralyzed and the working population is swept out of the factories into the streets.

I. The Concept of Profit

It is the purpose of this chapter to examine the nature of profit, to look into the causes or sources of profit, and to inquire into who precisely does the job for which profit is a return.

THE MEANING OF PROFIT

Talked about as it is, profit does not stand for a simple concept with a universally accepted meaning. We shall not catalogue the variety of usages of this term, but shall explain one idea of it which is frequently and perhaps generally accepted in economic discussion.

The idea of profit in the businessman's mind differs from the idea often held in economics. To the businessman profit is what is left to him after he has paid all the expenses of production to the factors the services of which he hired, borrowed, or leased—after he has met all his contractual payments. In this view, profit includes the implicit or imputed interest on the capital which he owns in the business, rent on his land used in the business, and the wages or salary earned by him for work which could commonly be done by a hired manager.

Bent on exploring the unique character of profit, the economist is inclined to isolate and cast away what is not unique in this phenomenon. Wages, interest, and rent are shares of the nation's income per unit of time accruing for the services of labor, capital, and land. If we seek the distinctive earmarks of profit, we want to abstract from the businessman's income the other shares, so that we can take a look at profit itself. The interest on the capital contributed by the entrepreneur is no more an element of his profit than is the interest on this very capital if it were owned by somebody else and lent to the enterprise. Similarly with wages and rent, whether the services of labor and land are supplied by the businessman himself or are hired by him.

Accordingly to many an economist profit—true profit, economic profit, or pure profit—stands for the return to the entrepreneur, exclusive of the implicit returns or opportunity costs; exclusive, that is, of the income which he could earn if the money or land which he owns and uses in his business were lent or leased to another business, and exclusive of such wages of management as he could earn if he hired out his services to another firm to do the work of ordinary management. Profit is the residue left from the sale of goods after the deduction of all wages, interest, and rent. It is the revenue obtained in the output market minus the cost incurred in the factor market. Profit can be positive or negative.

Suppose an entrepreneur uses in his business some real estate of his own which if leased to another concern would bring a rental of $3,000 a year; and that he owns some of the capital on which he could collect $1,000 in annual interest if he had it invested in government bonds. Suppose, too, that the work which he puts in as manager is worth $5,000 a year in the labor market. Assume now that this businessman nets $8,000 a year after all his contractual disbursements to hired, leased, and borrowed resources. In the businessman's view, this entrepreneur makes a profit of $8,000. But the economist sees in his case a $1,000 loss. The opportunity cost to this entrepreneur is $9,000. This is what he could earn if he hired out as a manager, lent his money, and leased his real estate. By staying in business for himself and using these owned resources in his firm he suffers a loss of $1,000.

PREVIEW OF THE THEORY OF PROFIT

When we survey the various situations in which profit appears, the conclusion comes to our minds that the underlying causes of profit cannot easily be reduced to one significant common denominator. Not one but two sets of circumstances seem to account for the phenomenon. Accordingly the theory of profit set forth in this chapter is eclectic or dualistic. In presenting this theory, in the next section, we shall explore these two causes in their various aspects. But it may be advisable to get our bearings first and form a conception of the woods before we examine the trees, by making a preliminary statement of the thesis to be developed.

(1) The prime source or cause of profits is *uncertainty*. The entrepreneur cannot predict with certainty the outcome of his decisions. Circumstances beyond his control and not susceptible of accurate determination may change the conditions of supply and demand by the time his product is sold; so that the revenue left after wages, interest, and rent departs from the anticipated amount. The primary reason for uncertainty lies in the fact that we live in a dynamic business world. Basic conditions affecting supply and demand keep on changing. Some of the changes are induced by the entrepreneur himself, mainly through innovations. But the outside world does not keep still, either; many changes external to the firm impinge on the business and force risk-laden choices on the entrepreneur.

(2) A second source or cause of profit can be traced to the *position of advantage* which some firms enjoy in the market, so that the price they set is above marginal cost. At once comes to mind the advantage of monopoly. But there are other circumstances as well which put a firm in a privileged position with respect to supply and demand for its commodity.

NO PROFIT IN A COMPETITIVE AND STATIC ECONOMY

Before we begin a discussion of these two determinants of profit it is well to consider the conditions under which profit is absent. This may help us sharpen our concept of profit.

The forgoing advance statement of the causes of profit suggests that profit does not emerge when these causes are absent; that is, when conditions are not dynamic and when a unique advantage of a firm in regard to supply and demand for his product is ruled out. Positively stated, profit does not exist in a static and competitive order. Such an economy experiences no change in the conditions of demand. The size and the age and sex composition of the population stay constant; so do the tastes of consumers. There are likewise no changes in the forces back of supply. The price of the resources used and the method of production maintain a fixed pattern. Both buyers and sellers are familiar with the data needed for rational conduct. Production consists of a succession of routine processes. For good measure, we assume under static conditions the absence of such disturbances as wars, floods, and unusual weather; such occurrences would upset the supply and demand functions. Moreover, in a static and competitive economy there is no monopoly advantage and no other peculiarly favorable situation for one firm or another.

The essentials of the picture are no different if changes do occur, provided they take place gradually, or periodically, or even irregularly but according to a known law. Such changes—in population or capital accumulation, for instance—can be taken into account in the routine calculations of the firm; orderly adjustments to them can be made in the daily work of management. Predictable and measurable changes do not violate the routine nature of the static order and of the processes going on in the firm.

In such a system, or in such a model, there is no job for the entrepreneur. There is no uncertainty and there are no decisions charged with hazard. There is superintendence over the usual performance of the factors in unchanging combinations; there are the run-of-the-mine daily decisions in producing the familiar goods for familiar markets. For this work the manager is rewarded with wages of management. It is difficult to visualize the processes of a static economic world; so we cannot be sure about the level of capacity needed by such a manager. Perhaps his will still be high-grade work. If it will, we can put him in the upper group among the noncompeting groups discussed in the chapter on wages.

NO PROFIT IN THE AC CURVE

In our exploration of price formation in the four types of markets (Chapters IX to XII), the vital element of average cost, short-run and long-run, and the corresponding curves, AC and LAC, were often and necessarily brought into play. These cost curves do not contain profit as a constituent; they refer to unit cost as compounded of interest, rent, and wages, including wages of management. The reason is not far to seek.

In the analysis of price, as in the examination of any other set of causal relations, we vary only *one* element; we assume a change in demand or a change in supply. We keep all other things equal. In other words, we analyze the situation against a background of static conditions. When we draw an AC curve we imply, moreover, competitive circumstances and the absence of a position of exclusive advantage. Under such conditions profit does not exist.

Again, profit is derived from the sale of goods, in a market affected by dynamic change or in a monopoly market, at a price above marginal cost. In dynamic circumstances the price to be charged for goods cannot be anticipated. Profit is generally the resultant of the price as it actually materializes; profit is not a *determining* component of price. Accordingly, even in dynamic conditions profit cannot be set down, beforehand, as a constituent of cost. The derivative of price, profit cannot function as the cause of price in the form of a cost element in average or marginal costs and cost curves.

II. The Theory of Profit

The aim of this section is to examine the sources or causes of profit. We shall explore (A) the roles of uncertainty attending the outcome of the entrepreneur's decisions, and of the dynamic conditions as the causal background of uncertainty; and (B) the role of the position of advantage occupied by some firms.

A. Uncertainty

THE FUNCTION OF CONTROL

At the top of a business concern there must be somebody who assumes final responsibility for what is going on inside the firm. Somebody integrates into a coherent unit the many processes, the land and capital resources, and the prominent personnel as well as the anonymous rank and file of workers. Somebody makes final choices in the everyday problems of running a business, shapes the long-run policies of the enterprise, and occasionally plans something new.

The list of decisions that may arise is very long and only a few can be mentioned. These may concern: from whom to buy materials and equipment and on what terms; changes in the price and quality of the product; whether to produce additional varieties of the product or to drop some lines; when to work the plant part time, full time, or overtime; how much to allow for the depreciation of the equipment; how much of the earnings to plow back into the business; the nature and extent of the research program; a change in the financial structure of the enterprise; how to raise new capital; negotiations with labor about wages and working conditions; whether to enter into agreements with rivals; and whether general economic conditions are promising or threatening.

THE NATURE OF UNCERTAINTY

Inherent in such choices is the uncertainty of the outcome; uncertainty with respect to the conditions of supply and demand as they will prevail at the time when the product is offered for sale. Decision making in business, and elsewhere, is the fruit of, and is necessitated by, uncertainty. If the result of the step planned were reasonably known in advance, the step would be an ordinary matter; and the steering of a business would reduce itself to the ordinary or high-level tasks which could be performed by hired salaried persons. As things are in our dynamic world, the top-level policies are carriers of uncertainty. The entrepreneur must take a leap in the dark. Actual net revenue, after the deduction of the contractual payments to hired factors and after allowance for the earnings of the owned resources, may depart from the expected magnitude. The contractual payments and the earnings of the owned resources are set in advance, as formed in the wage, the interest, and the rent markets. The entrepreneur takes what is left. The amount left becomes certain only when uncertainty ends: when the goods are sold.[1]

The basic uncertainty facing the entrepreneur relates to supply and demand. On the supply side, he has to contend with possible changes introduced by rivals in the methods of production, with the appearance of new rival producers, and with changes in the amounts of resources available and in their prices. A strike in a firm which sells supplies or a poor crop in produce which provides raw materials may change the cost picture. On the demand side, a change in consumer tastes may develop (as an occurrence explainable in terms of broad social factors or as a result induced by the promotions of other firms); a shift may come in the level and in the relative distribution of income, with a turn in the phase of the business cycle; or new variants of commodities may make an appearance and become close substitutes for the given firm's product.

In the roundabout process of production, an extended interval of time

---

[1] The uncertainty theory of profit finds classic expression in its best-known proponent, F. H. Knight. See his *Risk, Uncertainty and Profit* (Boston, Houghton Mifflin, 1921).

commonly elapses between the beginning stage of production and the appearance of the article on the market. There is room for the margin of error, all the more so because production is often for imperfectly known customers. Also, in the case of pure competition and monopolistic competition, where numerous firms produce independently the same commodity or the variants of a differentiated commodity, the individual entrepreneur cannot be certain that the aggregate output seeking an outlet in response to a changed demand will not be so large as to depress the price below a profitable level. What we are apt to forget is that the ebb and flow of adjustments by the firms to changing conditions, harmless as words and graphs on the page or on the blackboard, reflect painful processes and anxious, hesitant, or bold entrepreneurial choices, potential of distressing consequences to the business.

At the heart of the entrepreneur's decisions is uncertainty; at the heart of uncertainty is ignorance of the future. Entrepreneurship and errors are inseparable. For knowledge of the future the businessman must substitute inference from experience, analysis of possibilities, judgment, and the ability to go ahead and act. In attempting to estimate future supply and demand conditions, he may err on the optimistic or on the pessimistic side. In the first instance he will pay out too much to hired factors; in the second instance too little. There may be negative and positive profits respectively.

The function of uncertainty-bearing seems to be diffused among the personnel at the various levels of operations. At each level an official makes decisions, whether it is the foreman, the manager of a department, or the vice-president in charge of production, finance, or marketing. A subordinate above the rank and file of workers does not run to his immediate superior with each problem that emerges. However, we must not lose sight of the fact that in all these gradations of risk-taking the focus of final risk and responsibility is set in the entrepreneur. He hires the top-flight executives who bear responsibility for themselves and those under them. He delegates decision-making functions, but he stands accountable for those to whom he delegates these functions. Uncertainty-bearing, seemingly diffused, is concentrated in the entrepreneur at the helm of the business.

UNINSURABLE RISKS

When we refer to uncertainty and risk as the earmark of the entrepreneur's controlling decisions, we mean to exclude insurable risks or risks which can be shifted to the professional speculator, as in hedging. Certain risks are measurable. The observation of a large number of them produces generalizations about them, so that the probability of their occurrence can be computed by the mathematical laws of large numbers. Examples of insurable risks are the hazards of fire, theft of merchandise, accidents to employees or customers, and the death of a key person on the staff. The individual firm can scarcely undertake its own insuring in such cases, since it does not deal with enough instances of its own for adequate actuarial estimates. But the insurance company can relieve the firm of such risks. These risks are not *shouldered* by the insurance agency: they are reduced or eliminated by the agency, inasmuch as it handles numerous cases. There is safety in numbers.

On the other hand, certain types of risks are unique. The lack of uniformity prevents their being herded into large aggregates permitting the computation of the probability of their occurrence. Changes in the supply and demand conditions for a commodity belong in this category. In the uniqueness of business ventures, the mathematics of probability is not of much help. Business ventures are therefore laden with uncertainty. They are in the nature of a gamble.

DEMAND AND SUPPLY

Uncertainty-bearing or risk-taking is a function of overshadowing importance in our dynamic economy. It is essential that somebody hire factors at stipulated prices, undertake the venture of producing goods and services, and shoulder the financial consequences. In a static economy there is no job for the entrepreneur. In a dynamic economy somebody must take a calculated risk.

This risk-bearing function raises the productivity of the economy; with fewer people to perform this function, total output would be smaller. But it is the quality of uncertainty characterizing the entrepreneur's functions which *dissolves* the connection between the contribution of the entrepreneur and his profit. The relation between the effort of the entrepreneur and his profit is erratic and unpredictable. We can hardly compose a marginal revenue productivity schedule, or a demand curve, for the entrepreneur's services.

Nor can a supply curve be drawn which correlates the amounts of profit received or expected with the amounts of entrepreneurial activity forthcoming. Within broad limits, however, some connection does seem to exist between profit and risk-taking. If there were a certainty that in a given enterprise gains and losses would in the long run cancel out, few businessmen would be tempted to enter it. Such an enterprise would stagnate with routine activity. Where uncertainty dominates, the psychology of gambling prevails. What counts is not the reality of profit but the potentiality of profit; the chance of making money is the lure. The first desire of a businessman is to make money; his second desire is to make more money. Ordinarily what attracts an entrepreneur into the uncertainties of running a business is the small chance of a large gain, a good probability of substantial profits, and a small hazard of suffering a loss. The knowledge that many a business makes good money and some businesses occasionally reap an extraordinary gain is stimulating to the entrepreneur. The total gains and losses of the same enterprise over a long period, say a century, or the total profits and losses of the whole system of firms may cancel out to zero. But the eye of the venturing entrepreneur is on the prospects of his individual case. The fascination of a gamble, the desire to be his own boss in a small business, and emotional elements also play a part.

In a general and imprecise way, the anticipation of a profit may be regarded as the supply price of entrepreneurial uncertainty-bearing. We face here the interesting paradox of an economy propelled and vitalized by the profit drive, but with profit possessing no more status than the illusory and elusive attribute of a gamble. Our economy is largely built on and thrives on profit-inspired venturing.

THE ENTREPRENEUR IN OTHER FIELDS

The industrialist, the merchandiser, the farmer, and the small employer generally do not exhaust the examples of entrepreneurship. We find business risks in aspects of the work of professional persons and of various other self-employed people, ranging from the lawyer and the piano teacher to the independent plumber and the adolescent bootblack who sets up in business for himself. The income for the services of such agents is a compound of wages, wages of management, and profit, in addition to rent and interest on owned resources.

Consider the physician. His daily work with patients commands a wage, or fee, suitable to the top rank of the noncompeting groups. Part of his work relates to management (the purchase of equipment and supplies and the hiring, supervision, and co-ordination of nurses and assistants). For such a function he receives wages of management. But some of his income relates to decisions stamped with uncertainty. He has to choose the town in which to practice, the location of the office in the town of his choice, and the type of clientele to which he will cater. He invests in equipment some of which may become obsolete, and he decides about adopting newer types of medical supplies appearing on the market and urged on him by visiting salesmen. He may expand his activity by organizing a clinic, with partners or with his subordinate assistants only. He takes chances on shifts in the population of his locality; on changes in the incomes of his patients; on fluctuations in collections moving with the phases of the business cycle; and on the appearance of rival doctors with a more effective bedside manner. He makes choices against the backdrop of expectations of the demand for and the supply of his services; and the expectations may be falsified by the event.

CAUSES OF UNCERTAINTY

The breeder of uncertainty is change, or imperfectly predicted change, in supply and demand. The types of change involved fall into two categories: (1) innovations, induced by the entrepreneurs themselves, and (2) external changes which spring up apart from the initiative of the entrepreneur.

1. *Innovations*

We witness an innovation when a new idea has been put to practice by a firm, with the hope of gaining a profit. If the new idea is definitely fruitful of clearly estimated earnings, the inventor or discoverer will obtain the full price for it. The price would be arrived at by the capitalization of the additional annual earnings yielded by the innovation. But implicit in a new idea in business is the uncertainty of how it will work out in the market. A patent may be bought at a price; but the purchasing firm cannot be sure about the new earnings. Many a bright idea embodied in blueprints and models has turned sour when embodied in goods offered for sale.

Innovation implies a variety of things. It means a new method of production or an improvement in the old method. It may consist of the introduction of a new commodity like television sets or of a new make of an old product like yet another brand of soap. Innovation may refer to the discovery of new materials, fresh sources of old materials, or new uses for materials or final goods. It also embraces the cultivation of new markets, by recruiting new customers at home and abroad. Innovation may take the form of new techniques in the way of administration, finance, merchandising, or human relations inside the plant and public relations outside. It is involved when new forms of business organization are instituted, such as chain stores, the supermarket, the merger of several establishments, or a monopolistic agreement among sellers.

Every innovation is a substitution, of capital or land for labor or of labor for land or capital; or of one kind of labor, capital, or land for another kind. An innovation means a new combination of factors, a new production function, a new marginal productivity curve. Innovations are introduced to affect supply or demand or both; to shift the cost curve downward and the sales curve upward. Cost is reduced by a better way of doing things; sales are raised by an improvement, real or fancied, in the product or in the art of persuading the consumer.

Innovation, almost by definition, implies uncertainty. It means a change in the data going into the profit calculations of the businessman. A new method involves rearrangements, repercussions, and unanticipated difficulties. Many an innovation, far from being narrowly localized within a corner of the plant, propagates changes across the board. The use of new materials or of a new technique of production may call for new skills, new tools, processes, containers as well as for a recasting of salesmanship. The innovator does not deal with a given cost and sales situation; it is his intention to *upset* the cost and sales situation. Without meaning to offend, we may call the innovating businessman an economic revolutionary.

INNOVATION IN THE FOUR MARKET STRUCTURES

Innovation is a prominent phenomenon in each of the four types of markets in which goods are priced. Under *pure competition* the profit incentive stimulates the search for greater efficiency in production. If successful, the improvement puts the pioneer in a preferred position, for a while at least. Imitation by the other producers is not expected to be instantaneous. Before the new method becomes a commonplace, the leader may sell at the industry price and reap a profit from his lower cost.

But the originator is not certain of ultimate results. The innovation may prove disappointing in reducing costs. Imitation may spread more quickly than expected; the consequent price reduction in the whole market may come too soon for the pioneer to benefit. The imitators may add details of their own to the initial improvement. It is easier for the imitator to surpass the leader than for the leader to conceive of the improvement and venture the introduction of it.

Be that as it may, we must realize that if pure competition embraces many *small* firms we cannot expect innovations as a matter of course. Without government aid, agriculture would hardly impress us as the mother of inventions.

A high degree of uncertainty attends innovation affecting cost and demand in *monopolistic competition*. The firm is convinced that if the price of the given variant of the article can be reduced, the product becomes more appealing to customers; and the gap between it and the closest substitute is widened. The firm also strives to widen this gap by innovation in any of the phases of a commodity which form the focus in non-price competition: style, color, service, and the like. In both cases the firm expects to acquire temporarily a greater degree of monopoly power over its product. Before imitation and free entry permit the appearance of new and closer substitutes, the originating concern hopes to have its sales curve pushed to the right of where it was before, and counts on a monopoly profit as a reward.

But it may not work out this way. The new idea in method or product may not be a success in the market. A patent does not give complete protection to the leader. A minor variation by the imitator may in many an instance provide immunity from a successful charge of infringement. The imitator's creation may be more appealing than the originator's. The innovation has to be advertised and the promotional cost may be heavier than expected. The rivals may decide to advertise more intensively to prevent the loss of custom to the innovator; an advertising tug-of-war may be precipitated with damaging effect to profits.

There is also the chance that product improvements will be introduced by several other firms at about the same time; this event will spoil the honeymoon of the pioneer. Then no firm gains as much as it anticipated: there is apt to be little detaching of trade from competitors when many of them come out with something new and each one shouts about his novelty. None may succeed in raising the demand curve for his article, but all have incurred the expense of innovation and promotion. True, the product improvement and the intensified advertising may elicit a rise in the industry demand, by inducing customers to shift expenditures away from entirely different commodities. But the extra revenue may be unimpressive in face of the extra costs incurred.

In *oligopoly* innovation is likewise permeated with uncertainty. If there is strong collusion on price, technique, product, and promotion, the situation closely resembles that of monopoly; expectations may then not be greatly affected by hazard. But if there is independence of behavior by the individual firms, or a weak collusive arrangement, or ineffective barriers to entry, uncertainty is inseparable from innovation. Uncertainty may also abound in differentiated oligopoly marked by loose agreements or by unity of policy on price alone. The emphasis is then centered on nonprice competition. Sharp rivalry may spring up in product variation or in claims to product variation, particularly in high-powered salesmanship. If successful, the improvement, genuine or fictitious, may win customers and may strengthen the position of the initiating establishment, whether it has an eye on enlarging its share of the market, on working its way to the role of price leader, or on having a stronger voice at the conference table at which schemes of co-operation are hatched. Accordingly the move of one firm has a penetrating impact on the fortunes of the few other firms. They must respond with steps of their own.

We are touching here on the unique characteristic of oligopoly: interdependence of the constituent firms. Unlike the innovator in competition, pure or monopolistic, the innovator in the oligopoly market is ordinarily protected, by barriers to entry, from having to contend with new firms. But the risk of the reaction of the established firms is particularly strong. The innovation is undertaken in a context of interdependence of firms which compels retaliatory or defensive action by the rivals. They may hasten to adopt changes of their own or they may expand the promotional program for their unchanged products. Such action may impair the chance of success of the leading innovator. The innovations of the followers may even render obsolescent the new equipment of the initiator of the change, since, to repeat, it is possible for the follower to improve on the leader. Thus to the uncertainty of the reaction of the consumer is added the uncertainty of the nature, the time lag, and the effectiveness of the reaction of the rival producers.

Single-firm *monopoly* presents a different case. Like the firms in any of the other markets, the monopolistic firm is ready to adopt a profit-making change. But the amount of risk attached to the decision is less than in the other market structures. There are no established rival firms and there is generally little fear of the intrusion of new firms. The profit from a successful innovation promises to be lasting. Furthermore, whereas under competition the innovator feels compelled to adopt the new idea quickly and make premature use of the scrap heap, the monopolist can take his time. He will persist in the old ways until the stage is reached at which the average *total* cost of production with the innovation is less than the average *variable* cost with the old methods and the old equipment embodying fixed costs (why?).

Innovation in monopoly may carry relatively little uncertainty. Innovation in monopoly may accordingly be less a source of profit and more a function for which the return is wages of management. This proposition underlines the conception that in monopoly or in a close-knit oligopoly profit is not so much the fruit of uncertainty as it is the exemplification of the second source of profit, namely advantage of position, which we examine a few pages further on in this chapter.

2. External changes

There is a second category of dynamic variations which, like innovations, impart the character of uncertainty to the work of the entrepreneur. This type of change arises outside the firm and not at the instance of the businessman affected. In the case of innovation the entrepreneur produces the change; in this second case he adapts himself to the change.

Foremost in this type of dynamics is the influence of *trade fluctuations*. We refer to the business cycle, to the periods of depression, revival, boom, and recession; to the short cycles running their course in nearly three years and to the longer cycles which last, irregularly, from seven to eleven years. Such changes are filled with uncertainty to the firm; and only an example or two will be cited. If the demand for a commodity rises, the firm faces the all-important question: does the rise reflect an accidental irregularity or the beginning of a new short or long upward turn of the business cycle? The pattern of adjustments by the firm will vary with the answer. Next, to the uncertainty regarding the duration of the new demand is added the uncertainty relative to the size of the firm's output required to meet the new demand. In the wave of optimism, a compounding of errors can develop which may lead to an excessive total production in relation to the demand, with the accompanying disappointment in anticipated profits. Only a monopoly or a monopolistically behaving oligopoly is relatively safe from such a contingency. So impressive is the possible cumulation of such errors of firms to A. C. Pigou that he makes it the cornerstone of his theory of business cycles.[2]

Business fluctuations likewise induce uncertainty with respect to prospective costs. In prosperity, costs may rise on account of an advance in wage rates, in interest and rent charges, and in the price of materials. A host of questions arise: with regard to the relative rise of the costs of the various resources; with regard to the best substitutions and combinations of resources in anticipation of these relative changes in costs—in so far as the substitutions and combinations are practicable in the short run; and with regard to the possible appearance of bottlenecks. Each phase of the business cycle breeds difficult questions.

Then there are the familiar *irregular* changes which may upset the calculations and the production functions of firms. In many an instance they also tend to place a concern in a favorable position with respect to demand and supply.

Some of these changes have been mentioned: good and bad crops and their many-sided impacts on the economy; fires, tornadoes, and floods, which cause the firms untold trouble despite the insurance company's compensation for the damage; strikes and other labor difficulties; inflation and deflation; wayward changes in the tastes of consumers; a merger movement, a new government project in public utilities, or a railroad in a new region; the intrusion of rival products and new inventions; big and small wars; political upsets in one country or another; legislation on minimum wages, on working conditions inside the factory, on freight charges, tariffs, or taxes; changes in banking policy—these and other foreseen and unforeseen events come with unbroken frequency and inescapable impacts. In this category also belong structural changes which transform prominent phases of our economy if not the whole economy; for example, a change in the rate of growth of the population or the industrial use of

[2] *Industrial Fluctuations* (New York, Macmillan, 1927), Part I, chaps. VI and VII.

atomic power. Much of the daily guidance of an enterprise is tied up with such dynamic circumstances. When setting afoot the processes of production the entrepreneur is not in a position to solve the equations of their impact on the cost and demand conditions for his output.

A NOTE ON SCHUMPETER

We shall close this part of the discussion of profit with a few words about the economist whose name is prominently linked with the study of innovations, the late J. A. Schumpeter. This distinguished economist regarded innovation as the necessary and sufficient function of the entrepreneur. Without innovation there is no entrepreneurship and no profit. Profit is the incentive and the symbol of the economic progress in which capitalistic society takes pride.[3]

Schumpeter does not, however, elevate uncertainty to a place of importance in the concept of innovation and does not treat profit as a return associated with uncertainty. Profit to him is compensation for a successful innovation, for the adoption of a new combination of factor-services.[4] But, as the forgoing pages argue, innovation without the element of uncertainty is a function resembling the contributions of the other factors, the reward being governed by marginal revenue productivity: the reward is a wage of management and not a profit. Schumpeter probably has in mind that the return to the innovator is in the nature of a temporary monopoly profit.[5]

B. Advantage of Position

Uncertainty and the dynamic forces which foster it do not account for all the situations in which profit exists. In some circumstances profit may persist when conditions are static. In such instances the second cause of profits is visible; namely the fact that for long or for a while the firm enjoys a peculiar advantage with respect to demand or cost. It can deliberately charge a price above marginal cost, or else it has the benefit of a cost below the going price in the market. For one reason or another the entry of firms is hindered, so that the favorable position of the given firm or firms is not removed. By the same token we encounter disadvantage

[3] *The Theory of Economic Development*, translated from the German by Redvers Opie (Cambridge, Harvard University Press, 1934).
[4] *Ibid.*, pp. 75, 137, 147, 153.
[5] D. Warriner, "Schumpeter and the Conception of Static Equilibrium," *Economic Journal*, Vol. XLI (March, 1931), p. 43.

of position. In the face of a slumping demand, rapid exit or rapid shrinkage of output is impracticable and negative profit unavoidable.

MONOPOLY

A prominent category of such cases is exemplified in monopoly. Pure monopoly and oligopoly [6] are formed by various conditions and devices which give the firm the leverage to regulate the supply of the article and to bring profits into being. The profit is derived from the power possessed by the firm to command a profit-bearing price.

In some instances the monopoly profit can be definitely imputed to a clearly defined medium, such as the franchise or the possession of a patent or of a strategic material. Such instruments are valuable assets; they can be sold, sometimes separately but often together with the business. The buyer will pay the capitalized value of the imputed annual earnings of such an asset. To the buyer, the subsequent extra returns no longer appear as a profit but merely as interest on his investment. But from the social point of view, the extra return remains a surplus brought into existence by the valuable instrument—precisely as rent does not cease to assert itself on a piece of land purchased at the capitalized value of its annual rents, although the rent appears to the new owner as interest on the purchase price.

Attention may be directed to two differences between the two causes of profit. *First,* uncertainty results in profit as a residual not subject to accurate prediction. Only when the uncertainty is ended, as the product is sold, will an ascertainable amount materialize above or below the cost incurred. The situation is different, to an important extent, with firms in a preferred position. True, they cannot predetermine such variables as the vagaries of consumer attitudes to the product nor the cost of resources as fashioned in the factor markets under fluctuating conditions. But they are not compelled to contend with such variables as are injected into the equation by the conduct of rivals with respect to price, product, method, or promotion. The preferred-position firms are more in command of the situation and more certain of their calculations. In estimating their profits they are subject to a smaller margin of error.

Second, uncertainty and the dynamic conditions back of it are associated with a function, and commonly a socially desirable function, on the part of the entrepreneur. It is important to introduce new ways of doing business, to cope with the dynamics of our economy, and to shoulder the risks involved. There is productivity in such performances. But the exercise of monopoly power, especially when won by expedients other

---

[6] We do not mention monopolistic competition, since in the long run this market generally provides no pure profit.

than innovation, in charging a price above marginal cost confers no benefit on anyone but the monopolist. There is no productivity in this power; it is generally the power of creating scarcity. The profit of this power was labeled by Adam Smith as an "absurd tax."

We stressed uncertainty in our discussion of innovation. But uncertainty is not the only source of the profit of innovation. We can also discern in innovation the search for the privileged position as the key to profits. In a market characterized by pure or monopolistic competition, a firm strives for innovation because it knows that the next firm strives for innovation. Why does the "next" firm strain for new ideas? Largely because it desires to set itself apart from the other firms. The originator hopes to gain a head start on his companions and enjoy, before they catch up with him, either increased sales at his lower prices or the advantage of lower cost on sales at the going price. In each market with several or many independent producers, the individual establishment seeks the sheltered advantage of a gap, or of a wider gap, between its product and the substitute product, between its cost and the competitor's cost. The entrepreneur, when he can do so, seeks a state of affairs with respect to demand or cost to which other firms have no entry, temporarily or for long. As Walter Lippmann said: "Competition is something of which producers have only as much as they cannot eliminate." [7]

From the angle of profits, innovation bears a number of aspects. It involves uncertainty of outcome, therefore a residual revenue. If successful, it often involves also the monopoly power to charge a price above marginal cost. At the same time, the fact stands out that innovation embodies a useful function which calls for qualities of originality and daring and which brings benefits to workers and consumers alike. Thus the monopoly of innovation bears a different stamp from the monopoly of contrived scarcity.

WINDFALL PROFITS

In addition to monopoly there is a large family of circumstances, accidental and short lived, which place some firms in a favorable spot to make money. The extra returns resulting may be called windfall profits.

A strike by coal miners in the winter diminishes the demand for groceries and drinks in the mining towns, and raises the demand for electric heaters and oil-heating installations over a wide area. If the strike is won and coal rises in price, the concerns using coal are upset in their previous cost calculations. The strike brings profit to some firms and losses to others. In 1941 many a lumberyard was cluttered with lumber for lack

[7] Quoted by Professor T. J. Kreps, in *Hearings before the Temporary National Economic Committee*, Part 25 (Cartels), p. 13085.

of buyers. When the war reached us, the lumber turned into its weight in gold (almost). Of course the lumber dealers could not tell how long the war would last; there was the hazard of getting caught with high-cost lumber when peace came. A concern may be insured against fire and flood. But when the disaster destroys or damages the building, equipment, and goods, the insurance company can make good the financial loss but cannot restore the properties overnight. The affected establishment has to rebuild; in the meantime orders and customers may be lost to other establishments. The same disaster, on the other hand, may enrich the local or neighboring building trades. A shift in population constitutes an un-insurable hazard to real estate and retail trade in the losing area, and a bonanza to housing and stores in the receiving area.

Many such accidental occurrences are also marked by the uncertainty attending dynamic changes. In some instances the accident, chance, or luck brings the mixture of uncertainty and the position of exclusive advantage to the same concern. In other instances it brings windfall profits to some and only the risk of loss to others. The essence of windfall profit dwells in the circumstance that the favored position is not removed by the instantaneous entry of new firms; and accidental losses are not arrested by the immediate exit of firms. It is the inflexibility of supply that accounts for windfall profits. It may be added in closing that in a broad sense restricted entry and exit or inflexibilities of supply seem to be associated with profit in all cases in which they appear—in cases of *uncertainty*, whether fostered by innovation or other changes, and in cases of a *favored position*, whether created by monopoly or accident.

III. Who Is the Entrepreneur?

This question does not apply to business units organized as individual proprietorships or partnerships. In such businesses the owners are the entrepreneurs. This is the situation with the four million farmers in our country and with the four million industrial and retailing establishments, exemplified in the small shop and store managed by the one owner or by a group of partners. Nor does this question raise difficulties when relating to the majority of the 500,000-odd corporations in the country which have no more than five stockholders.

THE ENTREPRENEUR IN THE LARGE CORPORATION

But the question causes embarrassment when it is centered on the large corporations, which play an enormous part in our economy and dominate transportation, public utilities, motor vehicles, oil refining, steel, electrical equipment, machinery, and the supermarket. The separation of ownership and control in the modern corporation has introduced a cleavage between the performance of entrepreneurial functions on the one hand and the assumption of financial risks on the other hand.

There are two possible extremes in this connection. At one extreme we may conceive of corporations whose stockholders know nothing and do not care to know anything about the business which they own, and never choose to vote on the election of the board of directors or on the policies of the corporation. They throw the ballots and the proxies into the waste-basket. They receive dividends when the business prospers and suffer the loss in the value of their shares when the business is not doing well. In addition, the board of directors may consist of relative outsiders busy with their own affairs or with the affairs of several other corporations. The entrepreneurial management in such cases may rest almost exclusively in the hands of the hired top executive officer, the president.

At the other extreme is the relatively small corporation the stockholders of which take an interest in the affairs of the enterprise, elect from among themselves both the directors and the chief executive, and attend the meetings at which they decide on the basic policies of the firm. In such a corporation the functions of the entrepreneur are united in the stockholders.

Between these two extremes are variations. The large stockholders, or some of them, may take a keen interest in the corporate problems and may exercise an active voice in policy formation. The board of directors may be composed of prominent stockholders, retired or active officers, all well acquainted with the business; or it may consist largely of ornamental names, without a financial interest in the corporation and too busy with too many things. The board may assume active supervision of developments in the firm or it may meet ordinarily for the routine endorsement of the program proposed by the hired president. The chief executives—the president and the battery of vice-presidents in charge of such main divisions as production, personnel, marketing, and finance—may or may not have substantial stockholdings, and may receive only a stated salary or may in addition be entitled to a bonus graded to the annual earnings. In some instances the board of directors do much of the exploring of recurrent problems, sometimes through committees, and do much of the policy shaping; in other instances the hired executive officers overshadow in these matters boards and shareholders alike.

In practice, among large corporations, such mixed cases are abundant. The entrepreneurial tasks are shared in varying proportions among the stockholders and the hired executives, who are often stockholders themselves and who in addition to a stated salary receive fluctuating increments. As is often the case, the facts of reality exhibit diversities which defy the classification of uniformities essential to the framing of a generalization.

The question that is the theme of this section (who is the entrepreneur?) is of great importance. The profit motive is the mainspring of our economic order. It would be embarrassing to economic analysis if the large corporation, which represents outstanding sectors of economic activity, were to exhibit a feeble connection between entrepreneurial function and profit as the reward; if a set of persons who did not participate in the conduct of the corporate business were to receive a profit, whereas another set that framed the policies of the company were to be rewarded with a fixed salary.

1. THE STOCKHOLDERS AS THE ENTREPRENEURS

Two answers may be given to the question regarding the location of entrepreneurship, neither completely satisfactory.

One answer may state that entrepreneurship resides in the stockholders, even in those who do not bother themselves with the problems of the corporation. The line of reasoning may be as follows: The stockholder who does not take the trouble to sign and mail a proxy is inactive, but inactivity in this case *is* a policy. Doing nothing reflects acquiescence in the current state of the affairs of the company. The indifferent stockholder is willing to let other stockholders sign proxies or go to the meetings, elect the directors and shape the fortunes of the corporation. The indifference of inactive stockholders may be viewed as the expression of a deliberate choice to let others attend to the business. And it is not an empty choice, inasmuch as it is associated with responsibility for the financial consequences. Be it noted that the absentee stockholder has no way of escaping the financial consequences if the corporation is doing poorly. He can sell the stock; but the price of the stock will be low. The stockholder suffers then, first because of the poor or nonexistent dividends and next because of the loss of the capital value of his shares.

Thus the surface indifference of the inactive stockholder may nonetheless be expressive of entrepreneurship in the form of the ultimate choice and risk of allowing others to run the business. Inactive stockholders may have the thought that if the dividend checks become scarce they can bestir themselves and become active. In the view of those satisfied with this first answer, the stockholders, active and inactive, are not only entrepreneurs; they are the only entrepreneurs. They are the ones who make the ultimate decision and back it up with *financial* responsibility. The hired executive may receive a bonus, so that his returns may fluctuate with the state of the enterprise. Yet the executive, apart from his status as a stock-holder, may not be regarded as the entrepreneur. His bonus may not function as a profit but as an incentive payment to stimulate him to do his best.

This first answer puts the highlight on the basic question of what constitutes the minimum core of the entrepreneur's functions. Must a person, to be an entrepreneur, perform all the functions that we talk about in this chapter, namely, solving the daily uncertainty-bearing problems, initiating a change, coping with other dynamic situations, and assuming the financial consequences? What is entrepreneurship in its irreducible quantum?

Some economists would answer as follows.[8] Assume that Mr. A borrows all the capital required in a given business, so that he owns nothing in it. Assume further that he hires Mr. B to manage this business, at a stated salary, without interference from Mr. A. Assume finally that Mr. A is financially responsible for the results of Mr. B's management; that he alone pockets the profits and suffers the losses. Mr. A is the entrepreneur. Mr. A is doing here two things. He exercises his best judgment in selecting B as the head of the enterprise. This is a decision of penetrating importance. Says Professor Knight: "The *crucial* decision is the selection of men to make decisions." [9] Second, Mr. A suffers if Mr. B proves a poor choice, and benefits if the choice is good.

To be sure, our uninterested stockholders resemble Mr. A only in that they bear the burden of financial responsibility. But, unlike Mr. A, they do not directly select the executive officer. They make the choice of letting other stockholders vote on the board which appoints the president.

2. ENTREPRENEURSHIP IS SHARED

There is a *second* answer to the question concerning the location of entrepreneurship in the large corporation: the entrepreneurship is shared by some of the stockholders and the chief executive officer. In nearly every large corporation there is an inside circle of stockholders, usually with relatively large holdings of shares, who exercise active leadership in the corporation. They have a voice in the framing of policy and in the election of the board of directors and top officers. Some of them are elected to serve on the board or on board committees. Frequently they occupy executive posts, or else are familiar with the personalities and the detailed business conduct of the president and the vice-presidents.

---

[8] *Cf.* F. H. Knight, *Risk, Uncertainty and Profit* (Boston, Houghton Mifflin, 1921), p. 300.

[9] *Ibid.*, p. 297. Italics in the original.

Entrepreneurship is lodged in the group composed of such shareholders *and* the executive officials.

There are two flaws in this second way of looking at this problem. One is the role of the inactive stockholders. Like the active stockholders, they receive profits and sustain losses; yet they are dismissed as entrepreneurs. The second flaw relates to the seemingly fixed reward of the executive and the lack of correspondence between his function and his return.

However, this second flaw is often more apparent than real. Even if the president's salary is fixed, his long-run reward is not without fluctuations geared to the fortunes of the business. If the enterprise does badly under his guidance, he risks his high salary, his reputation, his general position in business circles, and his prospects of building a career for himself. He also suffers as a stockholder. On the other hand, if he does well for the corporation, his prospects for income and advancement are bright.

But, typically, his return is not a prescribed fixed magnitude. To begin with, a well-entrenched executive often sets his own salary, usually with the acquiescence of the board and to the occasional dissatisfaction of the stockholders. There are cases on record of suits brought to court by stockholders against exorbitant salaries of corporation officers. Then there is frequently the varying bonus, in cash or stock, in addition to the salary. There is also the opportunity given the top executives to build up their shareholdings by purchase at bargain prices. There are, finally, arrangements for retirement pensions.

Furthermore, we should not lose sight of the psychic income of the entrepreneur. There is satisfaction and prestige in managing a prospering firm; in the responsibility for the well-being of numerous workers, stockholders, and consumers; in the sense of public service; and in the standing in the business and social world. The hired executive is commonly motivated alike by the possibilities of financial gain and nonmaterial rewards. In many instances, entrepreneurs find enough incentive in seeking to maximize the profits of the business. In many other instances the primary incentive is to assure a continued existence to the firm to which they have grown attached, to enable it to maintain or to improve its relative position in the market, and to see to it that it writes a record of a high level of steady profits.

Thus the amibtious wide-awake executive usually succeeds in putting himself in a position to benefit from the success of his work, either by a long-term contract with his employers or by the acquisition of voting stock or by bonuses and pensions. He will try to maximize his income or his prestige or both. With the fluctuating fortunes of the corporation goes a corresponding variation in his own fortune as well as in the fortunes of both the active and the quiescent stockholders. In sum, very often the hired top executive has a compelling stake in the earnings of the business in the steering of which he plays his part.

SUGGESTED READINGS

Bain, J. S. *Pricing, Distribution, and Employment*, revised ed., pp. 714–721. New York, Holt, 1953.

Bernstein, P. L. "Profit Theory—Where Do We Go from Here?" *Quarterly Journal of Economics*, Vol. LXVII (August, 1953), pp. 407–422.

Coase, R. H. "The Nature of the Firm," *Economica*, New Series, Vol. IV (November, 1937), pp. 386–405. Reprinted in *Readings in Price Theory*, pp. 331–351.

Gordon, R. A. "Enterprise, Profit, and the Modern Corporation," *Explorations in Economics*, pp. 306–316. New York, McGraw-Hill, 1936. Reprinted in *Readings in the Theory of Income Distribution*, pp. 558–570.

Hart, A. G. *Anticipations, Uncertainty, and Dynamic Planning*. Chicago, University of Chicago Press, 1940.

Knight, F. H. *Risk, Uncertainty and Profit*, chaps. 2, 8–11. Boston, Houghton Mifflin, 1921.

Knight, F. H. "Profit," *Encyclopedia of the Social Sciences*, Vol. XII, pp. 480–486. Reprinted in *Readings in the Theory of Income Distribution*, pp. 533–546.

Marshall, A. *Principles of Economics*, 8th ed., Book VI, chaps. 7, 8. New York, Macmillan, 1927.

Schumpeter, J. A. *The Theory of Economic Development*. Cambridge, Harvard University Press, 1934.

Triffin, R. *Monopolistic Competition and General Equilibrium Theory*, chap. 5. Cambridge, Harvard University Press, 1940.

Weston, J. F. "A Generalized Uncertainty Theory of Profit," *American Economic Review*, Vol. XL (March, 1950), pp. 40–60.

XVIII Aggregate Income: Concepts

THE PRECEDING chapters have examined how the price system solves two outstanding problems of our economy, namely: (1) the allocation of the resources for the production of the many commodities; and (2) the distribution of this total output, which forms the nation's income, among the factors of production for their contribution to the volume of production. We studied, that is, the composition of the national pie and how it is shared by those who make it. We now turn to a third problem: What governs the size of the pie and what makes for fluctuations in the size? The first problem deals with the *types* of production; the third problem, with the *volume* of production.

This problem of aggregate income is of overwhelming importance. It engages the attention of government officials, business heads, labor leaders, and informed citizens generally. The total income and the movement of its components from year to year function as strategic barometers of the condition of the national economy. The relevant data record the performance of the system, measure the standard of living attained, reveal developing strength and weakness, and warn of a coming rise or fall in employment and income. Whether the purpose is the framing of business policy in adaptation to changing conditions or the formation of government policy to modify the economic situation, income data are of enormous significance.

We are entering the province of macroeconomics, the study of national aggregates and income equilibrium. Income analysis is a tool of recent vintage, hardly over three decades old. Its evolution owes much to J. M.

Keynes. Indeed, the framework of analysis in the next chapter and nearly all the conceptions discussed there reflect alike Keynesian theory.

In this chapter we shall explore the various concepts or phases of the total income of a nation. We shall follow the definitions of the Department of Commerce.[1] In the next chapter we shall investigate the determinants of the size of the total income.

I. The Five Concepts of Total Income

The broad concept of aggregate income per unit of time splits into five variants: gross national product, net national product, national income, personal income, and disposable income. We shall discuss each of these concepts.

1. GROSS NATIONAL PRODUCT (GNP)

By the GNP we mean the total output of *final* goods and services in a given period, valued at their market prices. What are final goods? There are *intermediate* goods, such as raw materials, fuel, and semifinished goods, used in further stages of production. And there are *final* goods, ready for the ultimate consumer, such as a loaf of bread or a radio in the retailer's store, waiting for the final buyer. Flour sold to the housewife is a final good; flour sold to the baker is an intermediate good. An intermediate product is resold by the purchaser; a final product is not resold, it is enjoyed by the consumer.

To avoid counting the same item several times, only the value of the final goods and services are incorporated in the GNP. If we count a thousand dollars' worth of cotton cloth each time as it moves from the textile mill to the maker of cotton dresses, then to the wholesaler of dresses, then to the retailer, and finally to the consumer, we count the cloth four times and raise the total product by $4,000 and not by $1,000. But when we include only the market price of the dresses made of this amount of cloth, the effect is of counting the cloth only once. As a separate item, the cloth drops out of account, as do the other intermediary goods used in making these dresses: electricity, buttons, frills.

An alternative, and equivalent, way of adding up the value of all output without double or multiple counting is to include in total production only the *value added* by each firm. The added value can be obtained when

[1] *National Income: Supplement to Survey of Current Business*, July, 1947, and July, 1951.

from the dollar value of the output of each business concern we deduct the value of materials and other intermediate products purchased from other firms and used up in making the output.

Standing for the total expenditure on final output, the GNP ranks as a central element in our economy. It constitutes the total demand for goods and services; it exercises a major influence over the firm's decisions affecting production, employment, and prices. Spending on goods and services, and only such spending, generates employment and income. A dollar spent is a dollar received; a dollar received is a dollar income. These expenditures can be regarded as the sum total of four constituent expenditures: by consumers or households; by firms; by foreigners; and by the government (federal, state, and local). A few notes on each of these expenditures will clarify the concept GNP and will highlight some of the difficulties in dealing with the data involved.

First are expenditures on *consumption*. Included here are personal services, like those of barbers and physicians; goods sold by government business enterprises, such as postal service and water supplies; the rental value of homes occupied by their owners; and of course the usual consumer goods. Excluded are the services of housewives; the value of noncommercial gardens; consumer goods retained by the manufacturers for their own use; auto repairs made by the hands of their owners—all because of the difficulties of tracking down the necessary figures. The Department of Commerce excludes all illegal activity, like gambling and smuggling; it does, however, include the burglar's gun and the gambler's dice.

In normal times this type of expenditure forms the lion's share of the GNP, usually more than 60% of it. In Table 20, in section II of this chapter, we find that in 1959 households spent $313.8 billion out of a GNP of $482 billion.

Next comes the purchase of new capital goods by firms. These expenditures constitute gross private *domestic investment*; gross, because the amounts include allowance for depreciation and obsolescence.

This item embraces the spending on the many kinds of new capital facilities, such as machines, tractors, and locomotives. Also included are all business buildings as well as houses built for rent or for owner occupation. The purchase of a home is regarded as a capital investment, which offsets saving as much as does the purchase of a factory building. However, because of the difficulties of computation, consumer purchases of radios and other durable goods are excluded; they are classified as consumer expenditures. Excluded also, as we saw, are raw materials and other intermediate goods, to avoid multiple counting. Investment expenditures contain, finally, additions to *inventory*. The excess of the stock of goods on hand at the end of the year over the stock at the beginning of the same year measures the newly acquired inventory.

Investment in capital goods, dependent as it is on profit expectations of businessmen, is a fluctuating magnitude, large in prosperity and small in dull times. It has enormous effect on employment and output. In prosperity it absorbs 12% or more of the GNP; in periods of slow business, 2 to 3%.[2]

The *third* type of expenditure is net *foreign investment*. This item consists of two parts.

One part refers to the excess of exports of goods and services over imports, including the flow of monetary gold stocks. This excess indicates the size of the United States investment abroad, which creates claims on foreign goods and services. Exports financed by gifts from the United States government or from individual Americans are not included in this accounting. Exports under the Marshall Plan, for instance, are considered simply as government expenditure, discussed presently.

The second part consists of the excess of earnings due Americans from abroad over the earnings of foreigners in the United States. This excess stands for the difference between the U.S. contribution to foreign production and the foreigners' contribution to U.S. production. It is measured by the excess of receipts of dividends and interest on foreign corporate securities held by Americans over corresponding payments sent out of the United States.

Net foreign investment is ordinarily a minor item. It can be a negative quantity, indicating a net import of goods and services.

The *fourth* kind of spending is embodied in *government purchases* of goods and services. As we saw, the outright government business enterprises, like the postoffice, are classed among the expenditures on consumption. The remaining government expenditures may be grouped under three heads. *First,* the government buys certain goods directly from private enterprise: desks, typewriters, police cars, office buildings, and transportation service are examples. *Second* are the varieties of government services, ranging from defense and police protection to education, road building, research reports, and stocking the streams with fish. Since these services are, generally, free to the public, they are estimated at cost.

Third are a series of government payments which are *not* counted in the GNP. They are *transfer* payments, without a counterpart of goods and services currently produced to earn these payments. They are largely transfers to Paul from taxes levied on Peter. A prominent item here is the interest paid on the national debt. The position of the Department of Commerce is that the debt was primarily incurred to finance wars and deficits incurred during depressions; that the holders of government bonds

---

[2] *National Income: Supplement to Survey of Current Business*, July, 1951, p. 150, Table 2.

are not currently rendering a service in return for interest received, as are holders of bonds issued by business firms to obtain capital goods which are currently productive. The other transfer payments comprise social-security benefits and direct relief, and pensions to veterans.

Objections are raised to the wholesale treatment of interest on the government debt as a transfer quantity. Counting interest on the national debt as a mere transfer seems defensible enough in so far as the debt reflects war financing and borrowings for government expenditures in a depression. But interest on bonds which financed the building of water supplies, sewers, roads, and schools seems to be a different proposition. Interest payment in such instances mirrors the value of the services rendered by these public works no less than does the interest payment by a private water company or a private hospital on its bonds. The interest paid by a private company is embodied in the GNP. It seems odd that the interest paid on the bonds of public works is not.

All government services are treated as final products. Some government services are used by businessmen in production—such as research reports on raising hogs, or the roads used for trucking business materials —and are intermediary in nature. But they are treated as final goods inasmuch as it is difficult to distinguish government services which satisfy final consumer's wants, as when the roads are used for pleasure driving, from those used in production.

Government expenditures composed around 15% of the GNP in the 1930's. They rose to 45% in some of the World War II years. Since 1946 they have been high enough but have begun to oscillate again around 15%.[3]

To sum up, the GNP is a composite of the expenditures of three agencies: the households, the business units, and the government. It is composed of consumer goods, or gross investment, and of government services. It indicates the revenue from the sales of business firms, and from the services of the government at cost value. The GNP is a useful measure of the country's full productive powers when our interest centers on a short period, as when we want to know the total productive capacity of the system in time of war.

2. THE NET NATIONAL PRODUCT (NNP)

Not all of the GNP is available for consumption or as a net addition to capital. Buildings, machinery, and other equipment wear out as productive activity goes on during the year. Also, with the appearance of an invention many an old machine, still in good physical shape, becomes obsolete and must be replaced by the new facilities if the firm is to stay in

[3] *Ibid.*, p. 150, Table 2.

the competitive game. Included in such capital consumption are losses from fires, floods, and tornadoes. The consumed capital has to be replenished or industrial efficiency will be fatally injured. Part of current production, part of the GNP, is therefore used to replace worn-out or obsolete capital. This part is not available for consumption, nor does it function an increment to the capital stock.

Deduct depreciation and obsolescence from the GNP and we get the NNP. Since firms cannot make precise estimates of annual depreciation and since different firms use different methods of calculation, the NNP is, as a rule, less accurate than the GNP. The essential difference between these two aggregates lies in the fact that the GNP includes gross investment whereas the NNP includes only net investment. The NNP for the year points to the flow of goods and services that can be consumed without impairing the productive capacity of the economy.

3. NATIONAL INCOME
(a) THE PRODUCT APPROACH

The first two measures of total income are focused on the value of the total output. We are now interested in the income accruing to the factors which produced the output. The term national income refers to such a concept. "National income," or as it is sometimes called, and more revealingly, "national income at factor cost" or "national factor income," has a specific meaning. It stands for the net national product at factor prices, or, which is the same thing, for all the incomes earned by the factors of production in making the NNP.

We can look at national income, so conceived, from two angles. We can see it as the money value of the complex of final goods and services produced in a unit of time. Or we can treat it as the sum of the wages, interest, rent, and profits earned by the factors in making these goods and services. These two approaches are the two sides of the same coin. The first approach tells us from where the income came; the second approach indicates to whom the income went.

Accordingly the national income can be computed in two ways: (1) by the *product* approach, by making adjustments in the NNP, to get the output at factor cost; and (2) by the *income* approach, or by adding directly all the wages, interest, rent, and profits derived from the production of this net output. We shall discuss both methods.

First, let us derive the national income from the NNP. The NNP is output valued at *market* prices; national income is the NNP valued at *factor* prices. This difference in the valuation of the net national product creates a substantial divergence of the two totals. At least four adjustments are to be made in the NNP before we arrive at the national income.

The *first* adjustment involves *indirect business taxes*, like business-property taxes, customs duties, sales taxes, and excise taxes, as well as *nontax liabilities*, like licenses, fees, and fines. Sales taxes are imposed on the turnover of goods. They are paid by the consumer and are transferred by the retailer to the government. Excise taxes are levied on the manufacturer of articles such as cigarettes, liquor, jewelry, and luggage. To derive the national income, we subtract these payments from the NNP. Else we should engage in double counting.

The reason for this deduction requires an explanation, in which an example may help. Suppose a firm produces fur coats that could be sold for $11 million. The government puts $4 million of excise taxes on this output. The firm sells the coats for $15 million. Let the depreciation allowance amount to $1 million. Of this sum of $15 million the firm paid to factors, including the profit to itself, only $10 million: we are considering *net* output (NNP) and therefore deduct the $1 million depreciation. The $4 million tax was turned over to the government. With this tax revenue the government rendered services amounting to $4 million, and paid out this sum to the government-employed factors which helped produce these services. These government services are included in the NNP. We value the fur coats sold by our firm at market prices; and their sale adds to the NNP the sum of $14 million. In addition to including in the NNP the $4 million of government service, we include the same $4 million in the sales of the firm (as part of the $14 million); thus we count the $4 million twice. It is legitimate to include the $4 million twice in the NNP: we use the market value of the fur coats ($14 million) plus the government services at cost ($4 million) and get $18 million. But as far as *factor* income is concerned, our coat firm paid the factors only $10 million. For the other $4 million the firm merely served as a tax collector from the purchasers of the coats. To avoid counting the $4 million twice as a payment to factors, we subtract this sum from the NNP.

The national income account as affected by the transactions in this example can be presented as follows:

	Millions
Sales by the firm	$15
Government purchases of services	4
Equals: GNP	19
Less: Depreciation allowances	1
Equals: NNP	18
Less: Indirect business tax	4
Equals: National income	$14
Earned by factors in coat industry	$10
Earned by government employees	4

The *second* adjustment of the NNP to obtain national income is occasioned by government *subsidies* to business and agriculture and by the *surplus*, or profit, from the sales by government enterprises. The market value of the product of a subsidized industry does not incorporate the subsidy: what the government gives to the firm, the firm does not have to obtain from the consumer. But the subsidy is paid out by the firm to the factors which it employs. The subsidy is not included in the NNP because it is not a component of the market price; but the subsidy is a component of the national income. The subsidy is therefore added to the NNP. Contrariwise, the surplus gained by the government when it sells goods and services above cost is registered in the market price, therefore in the NNP, but it does not represent a payment to government employees—or there would be no surplus. Surplus is accordingly deducted from the NNP. It is the practice of the Department of Commerce to add to the NNP one item: the excess of subsidies over surplus.

A *third* adjustment involves the subtraction from NNP of *business transfer payments*, such as gifts to individuals, hospitals, or colleges. These donations are derived from the market price charged and are components of the NNP; but they are not ingredients of the payments (by business) to the factors. In similar fashion, bad debts of customers are treated like gifts to the consumer and are deducted from the NNP.

Finally comes the adjustment under the heading of *statistical discrepancy*. In computing the national income some countries use the NNP method, with the adjustments sketched above; other countries use the direct method of totaling the incomes, the method we discuss below. In the United States figures are available for both methods; and the results of the product approach and the income approach can serve as a check on one another. Because of the many complications in the laborious computations, a difference usually develops between the two results. The discrepancy, which amounts to the excess (positive or negative) of the result of the first method over the result of the second method, is deducted, algebraically, from the NNP.

Let us sum up the relation between the NNP and the national income. National income equals NNP *minus* indirect business taxes, *plus* government subsidies minus surplus from government sales, *minus* business transfer payments and bad debts, *minus* the statistical discrepancy. In Table 20, items 7 to 12 begin with NNP at $441.6 billion and arrive at a national income of $399.6 billion, for 1959.

(b) THE INCOME APPROACH

This approach centers attention on the flow of income to the owners of the four types of factor-services. The job is to collect and add the data on wages, interest, rent, and profit.

From this angle, the national income is a composite of the following magnitudes: (1) wages, salaries, and such supplements to employees' compensations as employers' contributions to social security and payments in case of injury in the plant; (2) interest received from bonds and other lendings, exclusive of government bonds; (3) rentals received by persons (not corporations, which enter this item as a profit) from tenants, including the estimated rentals of self-occupied homes; (4) corporate profit before taxes, whether distributed as dividends or retained in the business; and (5) the mixed earnings of unincorporated concerns such as single proprietorships, partnerships, farms, and the offices of doctors or lawyers.

In the treatment of these magnitudes one adjustment invites comment; it concerns inventory valuation. If the corporation makes a profit on its inventory on account of an advance in prices, the gain is to be deducted from corporate profits. Increases in inventory values do not represent factor earnings. Likewise, a decline in inventory value does not reflect a corresponding decline in the earnings of the factors which produced the inventory. Since in the computation of its profit the corporation deducted the loss on inventory, this loss is added. Table 19 summarizes the national income in 1959.

TABLE 19. *National Income, 1959*

Type of income	Billions of dollars
Compensation of employees:	
Wages and salaries	$258.2
Supplements	19.6
Income of unincorporated enterprises	46.5
Rental income of persons	12.4
Corporate profits:	
Corporate profits tax liability	23.2
Dividends	13.4
Undistributed profits	10.5
Inventory valuation adjustment	−0.5
Net interest	16.4
National income	399.6

Source: *Survey of Current Business*, July, 1960.
Note: Totals may not add up because of rounding.

In the ebb and flow of income in good years and bad the most constant component, percentagewise, is wages and salaries, which almost invariably fluctuate around 65% of the national income. At the other extreme is profit, the most volatile quantity. Rising to substantial heights in prosperity, it may sink to a negative figure in a depression. Corporate profits after taxes were as high as $20.7 billion in 1948 and as low as —$3.4 billion in 1932. Between these two extreme shares are the comparatively small magnitudes of rentals and interest.[4]

4. PERSONAL INCOME

For a variety of important reasons and purposes it becomes essential to know the size of the total personal income, the volume of purchasing power actually received by households from firms and the government. National income and personal income are two separate things because income currently *earned* and income currently *received* are not identical. To make the transition from the one to the other, two sets of adjustments are needed. It is necessary to deduct from national income the sums withheld from the factors; and it is necessary to add the amounts paid out to individuals who have not earned them in the current year, if ever.

Following are the chief *deductions* from national income. *First* are the income taxes and the excess-profits taxes transferred by the corporations to the government. *Second* are undistributed corporate profits. (What is left of profits after taxes may not be fully declared as dividends. Part may be saved by the corporations.) It is clear enough that the undistributed profits of single proprietorships and partnerships should also be subtracted, but they are not; the data for such firms are hard to dig up. *Third* are the contributions by employers toward the social-security funds.

Lastly comes the adjustment due to a change in the valuation of corporate *inventory*. As was already remarked, corporations include in their profits the gain or loss from a rise or fall in the price of inventory. Such a gain or loss is not a component of the GNP, NNP, and national income; but it does affect personal income and ought to be included in it. Accordingly, when we derive personal income from national income the advance in the price of inventory above the cost to the firm is to be added to national income in the year in which the inventory is disposed of. Likewise, in a period of falling prices personal income is pushed down below national income by the inventory loss in the year in which the inventory is liquidated. The loss is subtracted from national income.

The chief magnitudes *added* to national income for the derivation of personal income are in the nature of transfer payments. Here belong the interest payments on the national debt; pensions and disability

[4] *Survey of Current Business*, July, 1952, p. 12.

benefits to veterans, social-insurance disbursements to the aged, the sick, and the unemployed; and business transfers to employees under private schemes of insurance.

All the adjustments in the transition from national to personal income are summed up in Table 20, items 12 to 21.

TABLE 20. *The Relation of the GNP, NNP, and National, Personal, and Disposable Income, 1939 and 1959* (*in billions of dollars*)

Number of item		Item	1939	1959
1		Consumption expenditure	67.5	313.8
2		Gross private domestic investment	9.9	72.0
3		Net foreign investment	.9	−1.0
4		Government expenditure	13.1	97.1
5	*Equals:*	GNP	91.3	482.1
6	Less:	Capital-consumption allowances	8.1	40.5
7	*Equals:*	NNP	83.2	441.6
8	Plus:	Subsidies minus surplus on government enterprises	.5	0.6
9	Less:	Indirect business taxes and nontax liability	9.4	42.6
10		Business transfer payments	.5	1.8
11		Statistical discrepancy	1.4	−1.8
12	*Equals:*	National income	72.5	399.6
13	Less:	Undistributed corporate profit	1.2	10.5
14		Corporate profits tax liability	1.5	23.2
15		Corporate inventory valuation adjustment	−.7	−0.5
16		Contributions for social insurance	2.1	17.3
17		Excess of wage accruals over disbursements	0	0.0
18	Plus:	Net interest paid by government	1.2	7.1
19		Government transfer payments	2.5	25.2
20		Business transfer payments	.5	1.8
21	*Equals:*	Personal income	72.6	383.3
22	Less:	Personal tax and nontax payments	2.4	46.0
23	*Equals:*	Disposable personal income	70.2	337.3
24	Less:	Personal consumption expenditure	65.5	313.8
25		Personal saving	2.7	23.4
26	*Equals:*		0	0

Source: *Survey of Current Business,* July, 1960.
Note: Totals may not add up because of rounding.

5. DISPOSABLE INCOME

Not all the personal income is purchasing power at the disposal of the recipient. Part of it is turned over to the government as taxes—income, death, gift, and automobile taxes. The remainder is called disposable income. The major segment of disposable income is spent on consumption goods. Consumption accounts for about 95% of the disposable income in prosperity and for more than this in a depression. (Why?) What is not consumed is saved, in the form of life insurance, deposits in savings banks, bank balances, stocks, bonds, and cash in hiding places. At all times individual households may dissave, by dipping into the savings of a previous year. But only in a depression may aggregate savings become negative; dissaving may then take the form of using up inventories, for instance. Be it noted that the savings recorded in income data refer not to intended (*ex ante*) savings but to realized (*ex post*) savings.

II. Some Crucial Interrelations

After the scrutiny of the five concepts of aggregate income, we can turn our attention to significant interconnections between some measurements related to these concepts.

THE SUMMARIZING TABLE

First of all, it is useful to examine Table 20, which presents a summary of the determination of each of the five types of total income and which will serve as a frame of reference for our discussion.

The items in this table may be classified into two groups: the first five items, up to and including the GNP, into one group; and the remaining items into the other group. The first group lists the component expenditures which generate the GNP. It is these expenditures which, as we know, set in motion the beehive of economic activity. The second group of items indicates what disposition is made of the proceeds from the sale of the GNP. We learn, for example, that so much is used to replace worn-out capital, so much is paid out in taxes, and so on. The title of Table 20 could well be: Expenditures on the GNP and the Allocation of the Proceeds from the GNP, 1939 and 1959.

We are familiar with the items in this table. We note that one quantity "Business transfer payments" appears twice, as item 10 and 20. The GNP and the NNP alike include this item; national income excludes it. To derive national income, we deduct this quantity from NNP. By the same token, we add this magnitude to national income in order to arrive at personal income.

In Table 20 we can move up as well as down; when moving up we change "Plus" to "Less" and "Less" to "Plus." For example, to make the transition from personal income to national income, we subtract net interest paid by the government, as well as the transfer payments, and add undistributed corporate profits and the succeeding four items.

As we see, Table 20 derives the national income (not in the technical sense) by the product approach; Table 19 derives it from the income standpoint. The GNP, too, can be derived in two ways. One method is indicated in the first five items in Table 20. The other method takes us first to Table 19. There we obtain the national income as the final total. Our problem is now to make the transition from national income to GNP. We set out with national income as given in item 12, Table 20, and move up to GNP, making the indicated and familiar adjustments—only with "Plus" for "Less" and vice-versa.

SOME CRUCIAL RELATIONSHIPS

The relations between some of the items in Table 20 are of strategic significance to the flow of income. Spending generates income; saving and taxes shrink it. If income is to be maintained undiminished, savings and taxes must be channeled into the spending stream. The relation between savings and taxes, on the one hand, and the agencies which spend the savings and taxes, on the other hand, is therefore of the first importance in income analysis. The study of this relation is our objective now.

Let us rearrange the data in Table 20. Let us put in one group (identified as I below) the components of the GNP and add to them all the items marked "Plus." We omit "Business transfer payments," item 10, inasmuch as it cancels out with itself, as item 20. We note that the items marked "Plus" are government transfer payments. Let us put in the other group (II and III below) all the measurements designated as "Less." With a few minor adjustments the two groups give identical totals, as we should expect. The first sum traces the sources of the GNP and also contains the transfers; the second sum outlines the allocation of these expenditures.

When the second group has been subdivided into two smaller groups, we get the following basic elements:

I. Consumption expenditure + Gross investment, private domestic and net foreign + Government expenditures, including transfer payments

II. Consumption expenditures + Capital-consumption allowances + Undistributed profit + Adjustment for inventory valuation + Personal saving

III. Indirect business tax + Corporate tax + Social insurance contributions + Personal tax + Adjustments (= Statistical discrepancy + Wage accruals unpaid)

In these groupings we perceive the equality

$$I = II + III.$$

Group I shows that the sums available for payments consists of the GNP *plus* transfer payments, including subsidies *minus* surplus on government enterprises. Groups II and III show what disposition is made of these sums. Thus group II indicates that part is consumed and part is saved, by firms and individuals; group III shows that part is siphoned off as business and personal taxes. Ignoring the minor adjustments, we get the following equation:

$$\text{GNP} + \text{Transfer payments}$$
$$= \text{Consumption} + \text{Gross saving} + \text{Taxes.} \qquad (1)$$

To see these relations more concretely, let us translate the above three groups of items into the actual magnitudes for 1959. The figures underneath the dollar quantities refer to the numbers of the items in Table 20. We get the following:

I. $\left\{ \underset{(1)}{\$313.8} + \underset{(2+3)}{\$71.0} + \underset{(4+8+18+19)}{\$130.0} \right\} = \$514.8,$

II. $\left\{ \underset{(24)}{\$313.8} + \underset{(6)}{\$40.5} + \underset{(13-15)}{\$10.0} + \underset{(25)}{\$23.4} \right\} = \$387.7,$ and

III. $\left\{ \begin{array}{l} \underset{(9)}{\$42.6} + \underset{(14)}{\$23.2} + \underset{(16)}{\$17.3} + \underset{(22)}{\$46.0} + \underset{(11)}{(-\$1.8)} + \underset{(17)}{\$0.0} \\ \hspace{7cm} \text{Adjustments} \end{array} \right\} = \$127.3.$

And within the latitudes consistent with the approximation and rounding, we find that

$$I = II + III \quad \text{or} \quad \$514.8 = \$387.7 + \$127.3.$$

In equation (1) above we can substitute for GNP its components, namely Consumption, Gross investment, and Government expenditures; then we can merge Government transfers with Government expenditures. Equation (1) becomes then:

Consumption + Gross investment + Government expenditures
$$= \text{Consumption} + \text{Gross saving} + \text{Taxes}. \qquad (2)$$

Deduct Consumption from both sides, and we get

Gross investment + Government expenditures
$$= \text{Gross saving} + \text{Taxes}. \qquad (3)$$

Equation (3) generalizes the truth that saving and taxes can be channeled into spending in two ways: by private investment and government expenditures. Equation (3) can be rewritten to read

Gross saving = Gross investment +
(Government expenditures — Taxes).

This means that

Gross saving = Gross investment + Government *deficit*;

or that

Saving = Investment + Government *deficit*.

The savings of a nation can return to the spending stream by going into investment and into lending to the government when it runs at a *deficit*. Ignoring deficits, we reach the very important conclusion that if income is to flow undiminished, saving and investment must be in equality. Saving may well be out of balance with investment; this problem will interest us in the next chapter.

THE NATION'S ECONOMIC BUDGET

As we know, four groups are affected in income accounting: the households, the business firms, the foreigners, and the government. Each of these groups is involved in receipts and expenditures; and for each group receipts and expenditures may well diverge. However, since total receipts equal total expenditures, the differences between the receipts and the expenditures of the four groups cancel out to zero.

The account of these four groups by receipts and expenditures is called the National Economic Budget. This important account is reported by the President to Congress. Table 21 gives the budget for 1959. From this table we can see once more the equality of realized savings, on the one hand, and realized private investment plus the government deficit, on the other hand.

Hardly any comments are needed on the entries in Table 21. It is sufficient to observe that since all receipts and all spending add up to the

GNP, and since the GNP does not include government transfer payments, we deduct, in the adjustments, this item of $34.5 billion from receipts and expenditures alike.

TABLE 21. *The Nation's Economic Budget*, 1959
(*in billions of dollars*)

Economic group	Receipts	Expenditures	Excess of receipts (+) or expenditures (−)
Households:			
Disposable income	337.2		
Consumption expenditures		313.8	
Personal saving			+23.4
Business:			
Corporate undistributed profits	10.5		
Capital-consumption allowances	40.5		
Corporate inventory valuation adjustment	− .5		
Excess of wage accruals over disbursements	0		
Gross domestic investment		72.0	−21.6
International:			
Net foreign investment		−1.0	+1.0
Government:			
Tax receipts, including social-security contributions	130.6		
Purchases of goods and services		97.1	
Transfer payments (interest, transfers, subsidies net of surplus)		34.5	
Excess of receipts over payments			−1.0
Adjustments:			
Transfer payments	−34.5	−34.5	
Statistical discrepancy	−1.8		−1.8
Gross National Product	482.1	482.1	0

Note: Totals may not add up because of rounding.
Source: *Survey of Current Business*, July, 1960.

DIFFICULTIES OF INTERPRETATION

In studying income accounts for a succession of years or for two widely separated years, it is necessary to be aware of certain difficulties for a proper perspective in the interpretation and comparison of the data. The *first* difficulty comes from changes in the *price level*. We notice in Table 20 that national income rose considerably more than fivefold between 1939 and 1959. But this hardly suggests that people had proportionately more goods to enjoy in 1959. The dollar national income of 1959 must be deflated before the totals for these two years become comparable. It is not easy, however, to construct an adequate price index. The prices of the many components in each of the principal categories of goods and services, such as foodstuffs, chemicals, metals, printing, and construction, move up and down with much dispersion. In addition, proper weighting has to be devised to register the relative importance of aggregates and their components.

Second, we must bear in mind the change in *population*. The national income in 1959, even when presented in constant dollars, has to be adjusted for the rise in the population since 1939 if we are to obtain comparable per capita data for both years. *Third*, the *composition* of the national income as far as goods are concerned presents a puzzling question. Military expenditures in 1939 were under $2 billion, in 1959 over $46 billion. Even in a democratic country, where such expenditures reflect, more or less, the choice of the people, it is stretching the point to assert that the greater defense spendings in 1959 express a proportionately greater aggregate utility. We can hardly put guns and tanks on par with houses and radio programs as far as satisfaction is concerned.

A *fourth* difficulty springs from shifts in the *quality* of goods in the total output. No difficulty would develop if the changes in quality were paralleled by changes in the prices charged. In such a case a rise in the quality of goods would communicate itself to the total output in the form of somewhat new commodities valued at higher market prices. But changes in quality and in prices do not invariably move together. Industries keep on improving their products, often without raising the price at all or commensurately. Allowing for the general decline in the value of money, a man can enjoy a better car now than in 1920 and pay a lower price for it. Similarly with refrigerators between 1930 and today, with television sets between 1960 and 1970 (very likely), and with many other goods.

It is scarcely inappropriate to close this chapter with Table 22, indicating the march of four categories of expenditure for over a quarter of a century.

It is instructive, and painful, to scan the table and notice the upswing of expenditures on omnivorous wars, to point to one phenomenon.

TABLE 22. *Gross National Product or Expenditure, 1929–1959*
(in billions of dollars)

Year	Gross national product	Personal consumption expenditures	Gross private domestic investment	Net foreign investment	Government purchases of goods and services
1929	104.4	79.0	16.2	0.8	8.5
1930	91.1	71.0	10.3	0.7	9.2
1931	76.3	61.3	5.5	0.2	9.2
1932	58.5	49.3	0.9	0.2	8.1
1933	56.0	46.4	1.4	0.2	8.0
1934	65.0	51.9	2.9	0.4	9.8
1935	72.5	56.3	6.3	−0.1	10.0
1936	82.7	62.6	8.4	−0.1	11.8
1937	90.8	67.3	11.7	0.1	11.7
1938	85.2	64.6	6.7	1.1	12.8
1939	91.1	67.6	9.3	0.9	13.3
1940	100.6	71.9	13.2	1.5	14.1
1941	125.8	81.9	18.1	1.1	24.8
1942	159.1	89.7	9.9	−0.2	59.7
1943	192.5	100.5	5.6	−2.2	88.6
1944	211.4	109.8	7.1	−2.1	96.5
1945	213.6	121.7	10.4	−1.4	82.9
1946	210.7	147.1	28.1	4.9	30.5
1947	234.3	165.4	31.5	9.0	28.4
1948	259.4	178.3	43.1	3.5	34.5
1949	258.1	181.2	33.0	3.8	40.2
1950	284.6	195.0	50.0	0.6	39.0
1951	329.0	209.8	56.3	2.4	60.5
1952	347.0	219.8	49.9	1.3	76.0
1953	365.4	232.6	50.3	−0.4	82.8
1954	363.1	238.0	48.9	1.0	75.3
1955	397.5	256.9	63.8	1.1	75.6
1956	419.2	269.9	67.4	2.9	79.0
1957	442.8	285.2	66.1	4.9	86.5
1958	444.2	293.5	56.0	1.2	93.5
1959	482.1	313.8	72.0	−1.0	97.1

Source: *Economic Report of the President*, Transmitted to Congress, January 18, 1961, p. 127.
Note: Totals may not add up because of rounding.

SUGGESTED READINGS

Gordon, R. A. *Business Fluctuations*, chap. 3. New York, Harper, 1952.

Hansen, A. H. *Business Cycles and National Income*, chaps. 6, 7. New York, Norton, 1951.

Kuznets, S. *National Income: A Summary of Findings*. New York, National Bureau of Economic Research, 1946.

Ruggles, R. *An Introduction to National Income and Income Analysis*, Part I. New York, McGraw-Hill, 1949.

Shoup, C. S. *Principles of National Income Analysis*, chaps. 5–7. Boston, Houghton Mifflin, 1947.

U. S. Department of Commerce. *National Income: Supplement to Survey of Current Business*, July, 1947 and July, 1951.

Weintraub, S. *Income and Employment Analysis*, Part I. New York, Pitman, 1951.

XIX Aggregate Income: Determination

WHEN THE demand for the product of a firm rises, the firm extends its production. The expenditures of the consumers on the product are translated by the firm into expenditures on income to the factors of production. This relation is true also of the economy as a whole. If the total demand for goods and services rises, if the public spends more money, the economy responds with greater productive activity; there is more employment, output, and income. Only under full employment will a rise in aggregate demand lead, not to greater employment and more income, but to higher prices.

The single firm produces an output because it anticipates a demand for its product which will cover costs and provide a profit besides. The entire economy is guided by the same calculations. It will generally employ resources as long as total proceeds from sales are expected to cover total costs and bring a profit. Economic activity is geared to expectations of aggregate demand; economic activity fluctuates with the total volume of realized and expected expenditures.

In our study of national income we saw that there are two types of things to which total spending is directed: (1) consumption goods and (2) capital, or investment, goods. We also saw that those who do the spending can be grouped into three divisions: households, which typically spend on consumer goods; business firms, which invest in capital at home and abroad; and the government, which engages in both types of expenditures as well as on such things as tanks and bullets. All the expenditures, on these two types of goods and by these three agencies, corresponding to various levels of total income, constitute aggregate demand. Aggregate demand plays the primary role in forming the size of the total income. If we are to investigate the determination of total income, we have to examine first of all the behavior of consumption and investment in our economy.

I. The Consumption Function

The amount which a household will spend on consumption in a year and the amount which it will save depend on a number of considerations, the principal one of which is the size of the disposable income. Similarly, the total expenditure on consumption hinges on the total disposable income of all the individuals. The schedule relating the total consumption expenditures with corresponding total incomes is called the propensity to consume, the consumption function, or the consumption-income schedule. This concept was introduced and stressed by J. M. Keynes.

AVERAGE AND MARGINAL PROPENSITY TO CONSUME

Let us examine the consumption function. In Figure 72, the horizontal scale measures the aggregate disposable income and the vertical scale in-

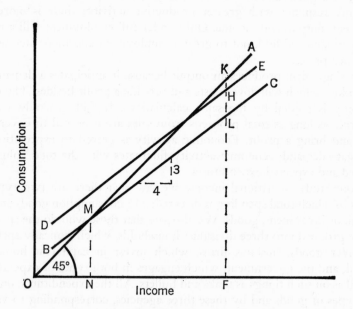

FIGURE 72. *The Consumption Function*

dicates total spending on consumption. Let OA, drawn through the origin at an angle of 45°, represent a consumption-income schedule. On a line like this every point is equidistant from both axes. In a country with a consumption schedule exemplified by OA, each income is wholly spent on consumption; consumption (C) equals income (Y). As income rises by a certain amount consumption advances by the same amount; no saving as yet. The *average* propensity to consume, or the ratio of total consumption to total income, is unity:

$$\frac{C}{Y} = 1.$$

By *marginal* propensity to consume we mean the ratio of an increment in consumption induced by a given increment in income, or $\Delta C/\Delta Y$. If total income rises from $300 billion a year to $310 billion and consumption expenditures rise from $270 billion to $275 billion, we get

$$\frac{\Delta C}{\Delta Y} = \frac{275 - 270}{310 - 300} = \frac{5}{10} = 50\%.$$

With schedule OA, the marginal propensity to consume is again unity: each dollar increment in income evokes a dollar increment in consumption. This marginal propensity to consume is indicated by the slope of schedule OA. Since the slope of a straight line is constant, the marginal propensity to consume represented by OA is unity throughout, as is the average propensity to consume for this schedule.

The average and marginal propensity to consume display a different set of characteristics for a consumption function depicted by schedule BC. On this line only one point (M) is at the same distance from both axes. The average propensity to consume, far from being a constant magnitude, changes from point to point; that is, from income to income. To the left of point M the average propensity to consume is greater than unity: for any income up to ON total consumption exceeds total income. The distance between points on OM and the corresponding points on BM reflects the excess of total consumption over total income. Such is the case when aggregate income runs at very low levels. Individuals live on their past savings or on credit accounts in the stores. The economy as a whole draws down its inventories and eats up its capital by failing to replace it as it wears out: the economy is dissaving and disinvesting. At point M income is equaled by consumption, and the average propensity to consume is unity. But to the right of M, on BC, the average propensity to consume is less than unity: for every income beyond ON consumption falls short of income. When total income reaches certain levels the economy begins to save; and the larger the income the greater the saving. The gap between CM and AM (and this gap indicates total savings) widens.

The slope of line BC is smaller than the slope of OA; BC is flatter than OA. As the dotted triangle indicates, on BC we go 4 distances to the right and move up only 3 distances; on line OA we would move up 4 distances. The marginal propensity to consume, constant throughout, is ¾; and the marginal propensity to save is ¼. Every $4 billion rise in income is associated with a $3 billion rise in consumption expenditure plus a $1 billion rise in savings.

Schedule DE describes a leftward and upward shift in the propensity to consume. Of each total income, more is consumed than according to schedule BC. These two lines are parallel and have the same slopes. The marginal propensity to consume is identical for both of these consumption functions. But the average propensity to consume is consistently greater—although by diminishing margins—on DE than along BC: each total income has as its corollary a greater volume of consumption, greater by the constant vertical distance between the two lines.[1]

The idea of the marginal propensity to consume (MPC) is one of the foundation stones of J. M. Keynes' system. To some scholars MPC is of pre-eminent significance. For a better acquaintance with the principle of marginal propensity to consume, let us sum up some of the properties and connections of this concept:

1. $MPC = $ slope of consumption line $OA = \Delta C / \Delta Y$ where C is total consumption and Y is total income of the community;
2. $MPC = 1$ where it touches line OA (why?);
3. $MPC > 1$ is on a line steeper than OA;
4. $MPC < 1$ is flatter than OA;
5. MPC shifts upward above OA for the following reasons:
    (a) greater equality among the people in a country, therefore greater total consumption;
    (b) progressive income tax: it diminishes inequality, therefore aggregate consumption may reach higher levels;
    (c) higher wage rates: "mass purchasing power" that trade-union leaders have insisted on for many a decade;
    (d) the weakening of the motives to save for old age, uninsured accidents, and so forth;
    (e) social instability; rumors of war; therefore disinclination to save.
    (f) the spending spree after a war with its restrictive regulations of consumption and its enforced saving.

More points on the MPC will be presented on pages to come.

[1] The relations indicated in these paragraphs give general ideas. They omit arithmetical subtleties depending on whether the line picturing the consumption function goes through the origin at an angle other than 45° and on whether such a line is or is not parallel to OA.

GENERAL OBSERVATIONS

The preceding paragraphs are not an idle exercise in geometry. The consumption function is a concept and an analytical tool of fruitful importance. It studies how much is spent at various incomes and how much is saved. If a given total income is to continue through the years, the savings of the households must be offset by an equivalent expenditure, either through investment by firms or through loan-financed government spending. For instance, with a consumption schedule OA (Figure 72), if a disposable income OF is to be maintained, the aggregate spending must be as large as FK; and FK the expenditure will be. But suppose the consumption schedule is BC. Only FL will be spent then by consumers, and the continuance of the income OF will be contingent on a total investment of LK to offset this amount of savings. If the consumption function is DE, the maintenance of income OF will be relatively easier to achieve, since savings will be only HK and the required offsetting investment will be smaller than LK.

The consumption function is governed by a variety of factors. Among them are social institutions which mold our habits of spending and thrift; accustomed standards of living; the tax structure; availability of consumer credit; the age composition of the population; expectations regarding changes in prices and incomes; and the distribution of income: the well-to-do have generally a lower propensity to consume than those in the lower income brackets. In the view of J. M. Keynes and his followers, the significant feature of the propensity to consume in our economy is (1) that as total income is rising the ratio of increase in consumption to increase in income is declining; or (2) that, at least, the absolute size of consumption rises less (and the absolute size of savings rises more) than the absolute size of income. The graph for (1) would be a curve rising to the right and flattening out toward the top; the graph for (2) would be a rising straight line with a slope less than one, like line BC or DE, but not OA. The implication is underscored that if a high total income is to be maintained new channels of investment must be found as an offset to the growing savings.

It would be helpful to know the shape of actual consumption-income schedules, and a number of empirical studies have been made.[2] But no definitive generalizations can be distilled from them. The following more or less tentative propositions are suggestive.

[2] These studies are summarized in A. H. Hansen, *Business Cycles and National Income* (New York, W. W. Norton, 1951), pp. 148–152, 164–170; and in R. A. Gordon, *Business Fluctuations* (New York, Harper, 1952), pp. 77–87.

(1) In the long run the trend of consumption-income relations presents a straight line going through the origin, but not at an angle of 45°. This tends to indicate that as consumers gain time to adjust expenditures to rising incomes they raise their standard of expenditures and spend a more or less constant proportion of their incomes. In the long run, the average propensity to consume may stay unchanged.

(2) But the consumption function seems far from constant in the short period, especially through the fluctuations of the business cycle. As total income rises and falls, consumption moves in the same direction but in smaller proportion; consumption fluctuates less widely than income. It takes time for the households to adjust consumption to changing incomes so as to arrive at their normal or long-run propensity to consume; so as to attain an expenditure expressive of their basic habits of spending and saving. For instance, when prosperity brings a higher total income, consumer spending rises, but not correspondingly, from the lower standards of the lean years.

(3) There is also evidence that in a given set of conditions consumption and saving do not depend on the size of the current income alone but also on the relation of the new income to the highest income plane enjoyed most recently. When the income declines from its highest level people are not prone to diminish consumption abruptly, but move downward reluctantly and in the perspective of the previous peak. Similarly with the moderating influence of the lowest level of incomes on the rising expenditure accompanying a mounting income. (Evaluate: "You cannot spend yourself into prosperity.")

II. Investment

Numerically a larger component of aggregate demand than investment, consumption expenditures are in the main a passive factor in shaping aggregate income and in stimulating changes in it. Typically, expenditure on consumption adapts itself to shifts in income stirred up by other forces rather than producing income variations on its own account.[3] On the other hand, investment—that is, new spending on machinery, construction, and inventory—is an aggressive, dynamic determinant of income. Although to some extent adaptive to and induced by shifts in income and consumption, investment is predominantly governed by autonomous forces. It is, moreover, subject to wide variations; and, as we shall soon see, changes in it exert a multiplied effect on the size of income. So

[3] Note that what is said in the immediately preceding paragraphs, marked (2) and (3), tends to modify this Keynesian view.

taught J. M. Keynes. So pronounced is the influence of investment on the volume and the movement of income that some theories see in it the chief responsibility for the business cycle; and nearly all other theories of trade fluctuations give it a position of prominence in explaining the instability of our economy.

MARGINAL EFFICIENCY OF CAPITAL (MEC)

Investment is undertaken for the same reason which inspires business ventures generally: profit. The profit of an investment depends on two variables, the marginal efficiency of capital and the rate of interest on borrowed money.

Marginal efficiency of capital is essentially the same conception as the marginal revenue product of capital. It refers to the prospective net percentage return on the cost of the new investment. If an additional machine costs the firm $1,000 and each year it raises the earnings of the firm by $150 while its annual replacement cost is $100, the marginal efficiency of the investment is

$$\frac{150 - 100}{1,000} = 5\%.$$

In common with the marginal revenue productivity of any productive factor, the marginal efficiency of capital declines, other things equal, as more capital is put to use. In a given state of the arts and with given resources in land, labor, and management, as more capital is available it can be put into less profitable channels. Also, the use of more capital goods may be associated with a rising cost of producing them, so that a given absolute return may reflect a smaller percentage return on a more expensive investment. How far investment in new capital will be carried in a given period of time will depend on the rate of interest. The profit of an investment hinges on the increment of the earnings imputed to an additional capital good over and above the ruling rate of interest on borrowed funds. Firms will carry investment up to the stage at which the marginal efficiency of capital equals the going rate of interest. If the marginal efficiency is 7% and the rate of interest is 5%, it will be profitable to push investment up until its expected marginal efficiency is 5%.

To each rate of interest charged for money corresponds a given volume of profitable new investment. The schedule relating the amounts that may be invested at various corresponding rates of interest at a given time is called the marginal efficiency schedule or the investment schedule or the *demand* for capital goods. The illustration is in Figure 73. Let the horizontal line designate the volume of investment and the vertical line the rate of interest. Curve D pictures then the demand for investment or the marginal efficiency schedule for capital at a given time. At a rate of interest OC, investment can reach the size of OA, at the rate of OE, the size of OF. If innovations are developing and the prospects of profitable

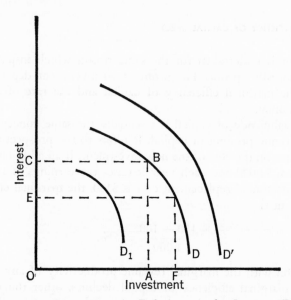

FIGURE 73. *Investment in Relation to the Interest Rate*

ventures look good, the expected marginal efficiency of capital rises and the curve shifts upward to the right, into the position of D'. At various rates of interest more investment may be undertaken than before.

VOLATILITY OF INVESTMENT

The profitability of investment is in certain circumstances more or less predictable. At times the long-run upswing in demand for some goods may be reliably foreseen; and firms are induced to raise output by enlarging fixed equipment. Examples may be found, perhaps, in the postwar demand prospects for television, housing, and children's goods. But most investments are conspicuously connected with "venture capital." The expected marginal efficiency curve of capital is not plain for all to see. Moreover, long-term investments are commonly not the fruit of cautious estimates of profit margins, but emerge as the product of enthusiastic calculations of the possibilities of such autonomous developments as shifts in the size and composition of the population, new technology, new industries and products, new resources, new markets, and new government policies. Often enough the expectations are distorted by mass enthusiasm. Of such volatile, capricious stuff are the determinants of investment made. Uncertainty dominates the scene. We discussed the point in the chapter on profit.

In a period of enthusiasm, the curve of the prospective marginal efficiency of capital swings upward to the right. Investment may be carried beyond the boundaries of planned saving; and, as we shall soon see, the operation of the multiplier expands income beyond the initial investment. Sooner or later, however, realities begin to disappoint the exuberant anticipations. For a variety of reasons, detailed in studies of the business cycle, the upward spiral of investment cannot continue. A wave of pessimism may develop which shifts the curve of the marginal efficiency of capital to the left, to the position of D_1 (Figure 73). The fluctuations in investment contribute greatly to the height and to the instability of aggregate income.

The role of consumption and investment in influencing the size of total income may be presented diagrammatically, as in Figure 74. Income and

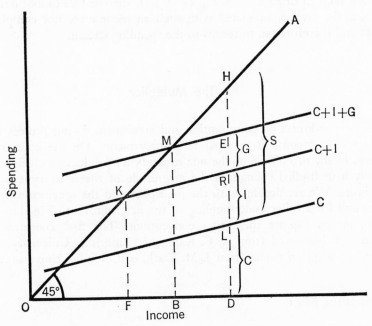

FIGURE 74. *Elements which Constitute Income*

spending are scaled respectively on the horizontal and vertical axes. Curve
C presents the consumption schedule. Curve $C + I$ traces the combined
spending on consumption (C) and private investment (I). This curve is
parallel to curve C, to indicate the assumption that investment is autonomous, constant, and insensitive to variations in total income. Curve
$C + I + G$ comprises government deficit spending as well as the other
two types of spending. Curve OA is familiar to us.

Consider a total income OF. If it is to be maintained, it must generate an
aggregate expenditure of FK. Since, as we see from curves OA and $C + I$,
such an expenditure is provided entirely by the private sector of the economy, this income could persist without benefit of government spending.
The larger income OB will also tend to maintain itself since it goes together
with the necessary spending $BM = OB$. Only in this case the government
expenditure (G), deficit-financed, is a required component because the
private sector spends, on consumption and capital, less than OB. But an
income as large as OD cannot materialize; if it happens to come about, it
will not endure. Such an income requires a total expenditure, and total
receipts by firms, equal to DH. But at income OD expenditures C, I, and
G combined make a total of only DE and fall short of DH, or OD, by
the amount EH. We can see the deficiency EH from another angle. At
income OD planned savings (S) amount to LH, whereas planned I plus G
amount only to LE; S exceeds $I + G$ by EH. Income OD cannot develop
because the savings associated with such an income are not completely
offset and therefore fail to return to the spending stream.

III. The Multiplier

The expenditures on consumption and investment do not project their
influence on income from separate compartments. On the contrary, a
change in the magnitude of the one expenditure produces a change, and
usually a multiplied change, in the magnitude of the other type of expenditure. We are dealing with the multiplier and the acceleration principle; and for a fuller understanding of the determination of income it is
important to explore these two conceptions. The first conception is
Keynesian, borrowed from R. F. Kahn, of Cambridge University. The
second conception comes from J. M. Clark, of Columbia University.

THE MULTIPLIER EFFECT

A rise in investment generates a rise in income, not an equivalent rise but
a more than proportionate rise. The change in investment produces a

magnified effect on the change in income. The ratio of the increase in income Y to the increase in investment I is called the multiplier k. Thus the definition: $k = \Delta Y / \Delta I$.

The reason for the appearance of the multiplier effect lies in the fact that the impulse of the initial investment expenditure sets going a chain reaction of spending and respending. The new investment brings additional income to the factors which produce the new capital facilities. But the process does not stop here. In time, secondary spending begins: part of this new income, governed by the marginal propensity to consume, is spent by these factors on consumption, adding now to the income of those engaged in making consumer goods. After a while these recipients of new income in turn spend a portion of it on further consumption goods; and so on. The primary expenditure on investment propagates successive waves of increases in secondary spending and respending. If the multiplier is 3, each dollar of new investment will breed a consumption expenditure of $2, in addition to the $1 of investment spending, raising the income by a total of $3.

We must make note at once of two points. *One*, the multiplier effect asserts itself, not only in the wake of a new investment, but also in response to a new government expenditure or to a rising schedule of expenditures by consumers, as when the consumption function shifts upward to the left. *Two*, the multiplier can operate in reverse. A decrease in investment will have a multiple effect in driving total income down to a lower level.

By what multiple an increase in investment will push up total income depends on the marginal propensity to consume (MPC). The higher the MPC the greater the expenditure on consumption in the various rounds of spending; and the greater the expenditure on consumption the greater the rise in income. The relation between the multiplier and the MPC can be perceived when we derive the formula for the multiplier. By definition, $k = \Delta Y / \Delta I$. Since $\Delta I = \Delta Y - \Delta C$ we can write:

$$k = \frac{\Delta Y}{\Delta Y - \Delta C}.$$

Divide both numerator and denominator by ΔY and we get

$$k = \frac{1}{1 - \dfrac{\Delta C}{\Delta Y}}. \tag{1}$$

We recognize $\Delta C / \Delta Y$ as the marginal propensity to consume. The greater the MPC the greater the multiplier. If MPC is zero, $k = 1$; there is no stimulus to consumption and to secondary spending. Income rises only by the amount of the initial investment. If MPC is $\frac{2}{3}$, $k = 3$; if MPC $= \frac{9}{10}$, $k = 10$. Since the MPC is revealed by the slope of the consumption curve, we get an idea of the strength of the multiplier from the steepness of this curve.

The multiplier is necessarily related to the marginal propensity to save. We know that consumption and saving (S) out of a given income are complementary to each other; that $Y = C + S$. Accordingly $1 - (\Delta C/\Delta Y)$ designates the marginal propensity to save. We see, then, from the formula (1) that the multiplier is the reciprocal of the marginal propensity to save. We can derive this relation in another manner. We can write

$$\Delta S = \Delta Y - \Delta C.$$

Divide both sides of this equality by ΔY. We get

$$\frac{\Delta S}{\Delta Y} = 1 - \frac{\Delta C}{\Delta Y}.$$

The right side of this equation is the same as the denominator in the formula for k. Substitute the left side for this denominator and we get

$$k = \frac{1}{\dfrac{\Delta S}{\Delta Y}}.$$

Thus when MPC $= \frac{2}{3}$ the marginal propensity to save is $\frac{1}{3}$ and $k = 3$. The greater the savings of the community the less potent the multiplier.

THE PERIOD MULTIPLIER

To clarify the workings of the multiplier, let us take advantage of some arithmetic examples. We shall assume that some time elapses, say, three months, before money received as income by individuals is (partly) spent by them and before this spending is disbursed by the retailers or the manufacturers to their factor-services, so that it becomes income to these factors. In other words, the income period, or income circuit, or income velocity of money is three months. This approach is an aspect of "period analysis" associated with the name of Professor D. H. Robertson, the brilliant economist at Cambridge University in England. We are dealing with the period multiplier in contradistinction to the simultaneous or "timeless" multiplier, usually entertained by J. M. Keynes, which assumes for analytical purposes that a new investment raises expenditures and income without a time lag.

(1) We shall examine two situations. In the first example we assume that there is *only one* new investment of $100 million and that the marginal propensity to consume is $\frac{1}{2}$ and $k = 2$. What will happen to income

from period to period?

In the first period of three months income rises by $100 million owing to the primary investment expenditure. In the second period the rise is $50 million, since only one-half of the new income is spent. In the third period, income advances by $25 million; and so on. The total increase in income presents an infinite geometric series, with the ratio of $\frac{1}{2}$, as follows:

$$100 + 50 + 25 + 12.5 + 6.25 + \cdots + 0$$

or

$$100 + 100(\tfrac{1}{2}) + 100(\tfrac{1}{2})^2 + 100(\tfrac{1}{2})^3 + \cdots + 100(\tfrac{1}{2})^\infty.$$

Algebra tells us that the sum of such a series is

$$100 \cdot \frac{1}{1 - \frac{1}{2}} = 200.$$

We note that this formula is the same as the formula for the multiplier.

Our conclusion is that (given $k = 2$) the single injection of $100 million of investment will induce a succession of falling increments to income which after a very large number of periods will add up to a rise in income of $200 million, that is, the initial increment times the multiplier. Already after five periods, or 15 months, the cumulative rise in millions of dollars of income amounts to $100 + 50 + 25 + 12.5 + 6.25 = 193.75$, which is close to the final sum. As we see, as soon as enough periods elapse to permit the multiplier nearly to play itself out, so that the increment for a period becomes negligible, the income begins to return to the old level which existed before the new investment appeared. We notice that in the fifth period the income is larger by only $6.25 million and in the next period by only $3.12 million.

(2) Let us consider a second situation. We assume now that in *each* *period* there is a new investment of $100 million. The MPC remains at $\frac{1}{2}$ and $k = 2$.

Table 23 outlines the developments. In the broad middle column are detailed the secondary induced increments of expenditures in each period, generated by previous primary (ΔI) and secondary (ΔC) increments. In the third period, for example, the secondary increments are (as indicated by the diagonals): $50 million, induced by the primary $100 million of the second period, plus $25 million, induced by the secondary $50 million in the second period, which in its turn is an echo of the $100 million of the first period. The diagonals point the way to the spending and respending.

We note that when there is a periodic increment in investment the additions to income are progressively greater, in each period beginning with the second period, than when there is the injection of but a single increment. We also note that after a certain number of periods the total increment to income (ΔY) grows in *each* period to nearly $200 million, or, practically, to $100 million multiplied by k. Already in period seven the increment is nearly $199 million.

TABLE 23. *The Multiplier Effect of a Repeated Increment of Investment*
(in millions of dollars)

Period	ΔI	Successive respending (ΔC)	Total ΔY ($= \Delta I + \Delta C$)	Total ΔS
1	100 —		100	0
2	100 50		150	50
3	100 50 25		175	75
4	100 50 25 12.5		187.50	87.50
5	100 50 25 12.5 6.25		193.75	93.75
6	100 50 25 12.5 6.25 3.12		196.88	96.88
7	100 50 25 12.5 6.25 3.12 1.56		198.44	98.44
. . .	. . .	. . .	. . .	. . .
12	100		199.95	99.95
. . .	. . .	. . .	. . . .	. . .
∞	100		200	

The last column in the table traces the cumulative increments of planned saving in the various periods. In period 1 the income obtained from the new investment of $100 million has not yet been disposed of: planned saving is zero. In period 2, with the marginal propensity to consume of $\frac{1}{2}$, out of the $100 million of period 1, $50 million is spent and $50 million constitutes planned saving. The new $100 million appearing in period 2 constitutes as yet involuntary saving. In period 3, planned saving rises to $75 million (unplanned saving becomes only $25 million): $50 million is voluntarily saved out of the $100 million income created by the ΔI of $100 million in period 2, and $25 million is voluntarily saved out of the income of $50 million appearing as the secondary expenditure in period 2.

As the periods move along, planned saving catches up with the new investment of $100 million, inasmuch as such savings cumulate from the disposal of the income generated by the spending and respending of the previous periods. Consider as early a period as the fifth. Voluntary or planned savings have risen to $93.75 million: this sum almost offsets the new investment of $100 million for this period. In period 12 the offsetting effect of designed saving is almost complete. Beyond this period ΔI is practically neutralized by ΔS; accordingly income persists at nearly $200 million, or $100 million times k.

LIMITATIONS OF THE MULTIPLIER

The career of the multiplier effect is not as precise and not as predictable as arithmetic examples seem to suggest. We have to take into account a number of diversions or "leakages" which tend to reduce the secondary spendings.

First, part of the increments of income may be used by the formerly unemployed recipients to pay off debts to banks, grocery stores, or relatives. *Next*, the revival in activity stimulated by the new investment may occasion a rise in the price of consumer products, so that the increased spending is dissipated to some extent by the offer of more money for a given volume of goods. *Third*, an increase in the primary expenditure may not always represent a net increase. The increase is especially likely not to be net when the increased spending is done by the government. Business confidence may be impaired by bigger government spending, and private investment may be discouraged. *Lastly*, the theory of the multiplier assumes a constant propensity to consume. But, as we saw, the MPC fluctuates in the short period, though it may be steady as a long-run trend. For instance, as income rises there may be a change in the pattern of the distribution of it, with a concomitant change in the MPC. Too, at higher or lower incomes there may emerge different expectations of future incomes with different expenditure responses to the new current incomes.

However, such reservations do not swallow the basic conception that when the resources of the economy are not fully employed an increased investment by business, an upsurge in consumer spending, or a greater expenditure, loan financed, by the government is very likely to produce a multiplied rise in employment and income. The multiplier explains in part the upswings in income that were corollary to railway building in the past century and to the coming of the automobile in the present century. The multiplier has given new meaning to proposals of government deficit spending as a way out of a depression.

IV. The Acceleration Principle

The acceleration principle deals with the ratio of the change in the induced output of capital goods to a change in the output of final goods which are made with the aid of these capital goods. The multiplier is concerned with the action of investment on consumption and income. The acceleration effect deals with the action of output or sales on induced investment.

ILLUSTRATION OF ACCELERATION

Let us examine Table 24. We assume that $1 of capital goods is required to produce $2 of final goods; that the capital goods last ten years and that 10% of them are accordingly replaced annually; that new equipment will therefore not require replacement before it is ten years old; and that prices do not change, so that dollar figures record faithfully the changes in the physical volumes.

TABLE 24. *Illustration of the Acceleration Principle*
(figures in millions of dollars)

Period	Output of final goods	Capital goods required	New capital goods required	Replacement	Total new capital goods required
(1)	(2)	(3) = (2) ÷ 2	(4)	(5)	(6) = (4) + (5)
1	$1,000	$500	$ 0	$50	$ 50
2	1,200	600	100	50	150
3	1,300	650	50	50	100
4	1,300	650	0	50	50
5	1,200	600	−50	50	0
6	1,100	550	−50	50	0

What goes on at a given time, say, in the first period, is indicated by the first row in the table. In the second period final output rises by $200 million and the requirement of new capital goods mounts by $100 million (column 4), from $500 million to $600 million. The total equipment required is $150 million. Thus an increase in output of 20% (from $1,000 million to $1,200 million) occasions an increase in capital goods of 200% (from $50 million to $150 million). In the third period output rises, but only by $100 million, over the preceding period; and the total call for equipment is only $100 million. In face of a rise of 8% (from $1,200 million to $1,300 million) in the output of final goods we witness a decline in the equipment industry from $150 million to $100 million. Why? Because in the output of final goods, the *absolute* increment of $200 million of the previous period has not been maintained. If the equipment industry is not to suffer a decline in output below the $150 million level attained in the second period, there must be a steady rise in the production of final goods as big as $200 million in each succeeding period.

Let us repeat that the equipment industry suffers a decline in the third period, not necessarily because the percentage increase in final output has not been maintained, but rather because the absolute increase of $200 million has not repeated itself. Maintain this $200 million increase in period 3 and the capital-goods industry will continue with a production level of $150 million, although the percentage increase would be 16% (from $1,200 to $1,400 million) and not 20%.

In the fourth period, final output remains unchanged at $1,300 million. No new equipment is required except for replacement. Production in the equipment industry drops 50%, from $100 million to $50 million. In the fifth period final output declines by $100 million and the capital-goods industry collapses. The small decline in the one industry causes a magnified decline in the other. In the sixth period the percentage decrease in final output is different from that in the preceding period. But the absolute decrease is the same, $100 million. Therefore the impact on the equipment industry is the same.

We can generalize as follows: When the absolute increment in the final output rises, the rise in the equipment industry is magnified. If the increment is maintained in the final-goods industry, the equipment industry will only manage to avoid a decline. As the increment in the final-goods industry falls, the equipment industry will suffer an absolute decline and in greater proportion. In sum, a change in the output of a product communicates a multiple change in the production of the equipment used in making the product.

ACCELERATION IN TWO OTHER CASES

The operation of the acceleration principle is not confined to the demand for consumer goods in relation to the demand for investment. The acceleration effect is also evident in two other areas: in consumer durables and in inventories.

We notice this effect in such consumer durable goods as houses, automobiles, or washing machines. Suppose that there are 30 million cars in existence and that the annual service rendered by all these cars is symbolized by $3 billion—as expenditures on gasoline, tires, and the like. If the average life of autos is 10 years, 3 million cars are produced annually as replacement. Let us fix the ratio of annual service of autos to the number of autos rendering the service as $100 of service to one auto. Then the 30 million cars are sufficient, and the 3 million cars produced for replacement constitute the total annual output of the automobile industry.

Now let the need of the service of cars rise 10%—to $3.3 billion. With the fixed ratio of $100 of service to one car, 3 million additional cars will be required. Total output rises to 6 million cars: 3 million for replacement and 3 million to fill the new orders. Thus a 10% rise in auto service necessitates a 100% rise in auto production.

The case of durable consumer goods is analogous to the preceding case of capital goods; and a table can be set up similar to Table 24. For "final goods" in Table 24 we substitute "service of autos"; for "capital goods" we substitute "autos"; and for the ratio of $1 of capital goods to $2 of final goods we substitute the ratio of $100 of the service of autos to 1 auto.

The principle also applies in every business in which goods are carried in inventory at a more or less set relation to sales. Suppose the annual sale of a certain type of towels amounts to $1.0 million and that dealers carry as much in stock. The industry produces $1.0 million worth of towels a year in order to replenish the inventory. If the call for these towels rises by $0.1 million, the industry will turn out $1.2 million worth of them, or an increase of $0.2 million worth: $0.1 million worth to satisfy larger sales and as much for additional inventory. A rise of 10% in sales is accompanied by a rise of 20% in output. The larger the ratio of inventory to sales the greater the force of acceleration.

SOME LIMITATIONS

As with the multiplier, the precision implied by the arithmetic is deceptive. In actuality the acceleration effect is neither unvarying nor definitely predictable. At least two reasons account for this.

First of all, there is in many cases no fixed relation between the change in the initial expenditure and the correlative change in the industry with the derived demand. The lags of the business cycle explain this slack. In the early stages of a business upturn use is made of the excess capacity nearly always installed in the previous boom. At this stage the quickening demand for final goods does not always cause substantial new investment. As prosperity progresses and the excess capacity is absorbed, new investment is usually made. But it is contingent on long-run prospects. If the increased demand for goods seems temporary, firms prefer to meet it by expanding the variable resources. Existing equipment is pressed into intensive service; stand-by capacity is brought into use; labor works overtime; a second shift may be introduced.

Only if prosperity promises to endure will substantial new investment be ventured. And then optimistic calculations are apt to push investment *beyond* the needs of the immediate future. Expansion policy is framed to satisfy great expectations and for the long pull. The ratio of a change in investment to a change in output is thus likely to be small before a boom develops and rather large during a boom.

The acceleration effect is equally unsteady and unpredictable when there is no general rise in demand but only a shift in the demand from commodity *A* to commodity *B*. In such a case the net dollar-value change in output of final goods may be nil; but the changes in investment may not cancel out. The durability of capital used in making commodity *A* may be different from the durability of capital used in making commodity *B*. These two industries may have different degrees of unused capacity. The acceleration effect stemming from the decreased demand for *A* can operate downward only by 100% (why?) but the upward effect on the capital-goods industry back of *B* may exceed 100%. Lastly, the net effect on investment may depend on the extent to which equipment used in making *A* is interchangeable with equipment used in producing *B*.

Nevertheless, these limitations do not hold at bay the general working of the acceleration principle. This principle stresses that current demand, output, and sales may exert a multiplied influence on investment. It helps explain the observed wide fluctuations in capital goods, in consumer durables, and in inventories. It helps throw light on why industries like steel, machine tools, railroads, or heavy electrical equipment burst into great activity when business livens up and nosedive to low levels when the tempo of final output slackens. Still, we should not forget that investment is commonly the response to autonomous profit expectations and that the acceleration effect, typifying not autonomous but induced investment, is only one factor influencing business expectations.

THE INTERACTION OF THE MULTIPLIER AND ACCELERATION

The multiplier and the acceleration effects react on each other. A change in investment multiplies the change in induced consumption; this induced change in consumption expenditure breeds in its turn a magnified change in investment. The chain of these mutual reactions can go on and on. What happens to income?

In Table 25 we assume that in *each* income period there is an autonomous investment of $100; that the marginal propensity to consume is ½; and that the accelerator, or the ratio of the increment to investment induced by an increment to consumption, is unity.

Since there is a lag of one period, the rise in investment by $100 in the first period increases income, in this period, only by this $100. In the second period the $100 income of the first period induces a rise of $50 in consumption, according to the marginal propensity to consume of ½; this $50 induces a new investment of $50, according to the accelerator of unity. Result for this period: income rises by $100 + $50 + $50 = $200. In the third period this income of $200 induces a rise in consumption of $100. Since this $100 constitutes a rise of $50 over the previous period, a new investment of $50 is induced. The increment in income is now

TABLE 25. *Interaction of the Multiplier and the Acceleration* [4]

Period	Rise in investment	Consumption induced by previous period	Induced investment	Total rise in income
(1)	(2)	(3)	(4)	(5) = (2) + (3) + (4)
1	$100	$ 0	$ 0	$100
2	100	50	50	200
3	100	100	50	250
4	100	125	25	250
5	100	125	0	225
6	100	112.5	−12.5	200
7	100	100	−12.5	187.5
8	100	93.75	−6.25	187.5
9	100	93.75	0	193.75
10	100	96.875	3.125	200

$250. In the same manner the effect on income is obtained for the succeeding periods. As we see in the last column, the advance in income in a succession of periods displays a cyclical fluctuation. It is to be noted that, with different values for the marginal propensity to consume and for the accelerator, column 5 exhibits different cycles or entirely different patterns in the series of increments in income.[5]

V. Income Equilibrium

In the exploration of the determinants of income the key idea stands out that the size of the income is governed by the size of total spending.

[4] Based on the table in P. A. Samuelson, "Interactions between the Multiplier Analysis and the Principle of Acceleration," *Review of Economic Statistics,* Vol. XXI (May, 1939), pp. 75–78. Reprinted in *Readings in Business Cycle Theory* (Chicago, Irwin, 1944), pp. 261–269.
[5] P. A. Samuelson, *op. cit.*

When households save, part of their income is not spent. If the total income is not to decline in consequence, the savings must be offset: somebody must spend an amount equal to the savings, so that aggregate demand is not impaired. As we saw in the preceding chapter, the offsetting expenditure comes in the form of business investment at home and abroad or of government expenditures financed by the sale of bonds purchased with savings or with bank credit. The final equation presented there was: *Saving = Investment + Government deficit*. Government spending fed by tax revenue does not function as an offset to saving since by saving we mean income neither spent on consumption nor siphoned off as taxes. We can lump private investment and loan-financed government investment and condense the above equation into Saving = Investment, or $S = I$.

Our object now is to examine the conditions which put income into a position of equilibrium. The question is: what relation must exist between the determinants of income to make certain that the income formed will tend to perpetuate itself?

INEQUALITY OF S AND I

The answer to this question is based on the relation between saving and investment; on whether those two crucial magnitudes are equal. We touched on saving and investment in our discussion of the loanable-funds theory of interest in Chapter XV. But now it is necessary to look at these concepts more closely. Viewed one way, S and I are always equal; viewed another way, they may part roads.

Realized (*ex post*) S and realized (*ex post*) I are always in accord with each other, for the reason that they present two aspects of the same phenomenon. Realized past S represents the excess of total income over total consumption: $S = Y - C$. Investment already made stands for the excess of the value of the net total output over the sale of consumer goods. But the net value of total output composes the national income. (We recall that national income designates net national product, NNP, at factor cost.) We have then $I = Y - C$. Since actual S and I are both equal to the same magnitude, that is, to $Y - C$, they are equal to each other. Realized S and I that appear in statistics are always equal.

It is different, however, when we look at S and I through *ex ante* spectacles. Expecting a certain aggregate income, individuals with a given propensity to consume may set out to save a given total amount. However, in the expectation of the same total income, firms may have in mind to invest a different total. Since those who plan to save and those who plan to invest are two different sets of people, the two plans may well diverge in magnitude. Intended I may exceed or fall short of intended S. Designed investment may more than offset designed saving; or else it may not quite offset designed saving. The result is an unstable total income. Income will shift up and down until an equality between S and I is established. During this shifting process, seeking to reconcile intended saving and investment, the equilibrium income is brought into being.

An inequality between S and I may appear as well if we regard these variables from the angle of "period analysis." We assume a lag of one period—a day or two, or a week—between the receipt of income and the disposal of it by consumption and saving. We shall use subscripts 0 and 1 to designate respectively the preceding period and the current or given period. The income in the current period consists of the expenditures on current consumption and current investment: $Y_1 = C_1 + I_1$. Current consumption is a function of the income of the *preceding* period: $C_1 = f(Y_0)$; and current saving is the difference between the income received in the forgoing period and current consumption: $S_1 = Y_0 - C_1$. But in the given period firms may invest more than $Y_0 - C_1$ by borrowing from banks or by using idle cash balances; or they may invest less than $Y_0 - C_1$, as when they repay debts to banks or slow down the use of cash balances. When $I_1 < S_1$, income in the current period (Y_1) will be less than in the previous period (Y_0); and when $I_1 > S_1$, income in the present period tends to exceed the income of the antecedent period.[6]

THE PROCESS LEADING TO AN EQUILIBRIUM INCOME

Let us trace the process brought into operation when the equality between saving and investment is disturbed. We shall make use of the *ex ante* line of analysis and not of the period analysis.

Assume that at the beginning of the year, in anticipation of an income of $100 billion and of certain profit prospects, the business world plans to produce $95 billion in consumer goods and $5 billion in new capital goods. Assume that the public, anticipating a total income of the same magnitude, is guided by its propensity to consume to an intended consumption of $90 billion and an intended saving of $10 billion. Planned investment falls short of planned saving. Aggregate demand proves smaller than the firms expected. Total spending on both consumption and investment begins to grow less than the cost of aggregate output turned out by the firms on the basis of their initial expectations. In other words, firms are taking in less revenue from total expenditure than they are paying out to the factors as income. Prices begin to fall, losses are incurred, and inventories accumulate.

It is well to pause here to make note of the following point. As the

---

[6] Neither the *ex post* and *ex ante* analysis nor the period analysis has been directly developed by J. M. Keynes.

public *actually* (*ex post*) saves more, the firms involuntarily invest more, by having inventories grow on their hands: investment, we recall, includes inventories. Realized investment, including inventories, rises above intended investment; realized investment matches the realized high savings.

But to return to the argument. To diminish losses and to bring down idle inventories, firms dismiss labor and curtail production. In face of declining incomes individuals save less; corporations dip into surplus to pay interest and dividends. The downward movement continues until an income level is reached at which the amount that people plan to save is brought down to the amount which firms plan to invest. When *ex ante* saving and *ex ante* investment are in accord, income is in equilibrium. We witness here the paradox of thrift. When many individuals desire to better themselves and plan to raise their savings total, income may fall as a consequence: actual total savings, instead of rising, may go down.

The downward movement of income is aided and abetted by the acceleration effect. As sales fall off, induced investment declines. Income drops more sharply than it would in the absence of acceleration. As investment recedes, the downward pressure on income is all the greater, before planned saving finally evens up with planned investment. For this reason, and others, this equality may be reached when both S and I are negative; when net dissaving equals net disinvestment.

The opposite developments tend to take place when scheduled investment exceeds planned saving. Assume that firms, spurred by expectations of profitable opportunities, decide to raise their investments, whereas the planned savings of households remain unchanged. Businessmen invest more than is saved by obtaining credit from commercial banks and by the use of idle cash balances, and thus put workers and other resources to the formation of new capital. New income is obtained by these factors and they spend it in accordance with their propensity to consume. With spending and respending, the multiplier influence contributes to the mounting income. Actual income outruns the previously expected income; voluntary savings begin to rise. The expansion of activity will continue until income rises to a scale which stimulates a volume of planned saving matching the level of planned investment.

In equilibrium, planned S and I and actual S and I are equal. Before equilibrium is established, actual S is not the desired S and realized I is not the planned I, with the consequence that total spending or aggregate demand is either not sufficient to maintain the expected level of income or else is large enough to push total income to a higher level. The condition of income equilibrium rests on the equality of planned S and I. The equality of actual S and I is no guarantee of equilibrium: this equality does not preclude a divergence between planned S and I and the emerging disequilibrium.

If planned I rises above S at a time when the economy is fully employed, the outcome is an inflationary movement. The bidding for resources by the firms will drive up the price of factor-services. The bidding of the factors, implemented by larger money incomes, for the given aggregate of consumer goods will push up commodity prices. But real income and real output cannot rise. The spiraling of prices will continue until credit expansion stops or until accumulated distortions in the economy precipitate a decline or a collapse in aggregate demand.

It is difficult to illustrate in one diagram all the aspects of the process of arriving at an equilibrium income. But Figure 75 may be of some help.

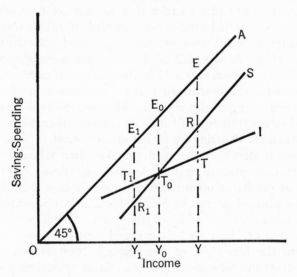

Figure 75. The Demands of Total Equilibrium

Let curves S and I represent respectively planned saving and planned investment. Curve I slopes, to show that we take into account *induced* investment: for autonomous investment the curve would be parallel to the horizontal axis, as it has been in previous figures. Assume an expected income OY. Firms pay out this amount to the factors of production. To *sustain* such an income, total spending, or revenue to the firms, or aggregate demand, must amount to EY. But intended expenditures comprise only ER on consumption and TY on investment.

$$(EY - RY(S) = C = ER.)$$

Planned saving RY is larger than planned investment TY; RT represents the deflationary gap, or the deficiency in aggregate demand. Income will shrink until it reaches the equilibrium level of OY_0, at which both planned S and I amount to T_0Y_0.

The opposite adjustment will be set going if, in the expectation of income OY_1, firms start to invest T_1Y_1 whereas the economy means to save only R_1Y_1. Aggregate demand is now E_1R_1 (consumption) plus T_1Y_1 (investment); it will exceed the firms' outlay of OY_1 by the inflationary gap T_1R_1. Income will rise until it attains the level of OY_0. If full employment is symbolized by total income OY, we have in both cases equilibrium of income at less than full employment.

When total income reaches a state of equilibrium the resources of the economy may or may not be fully employed. One of Keynes's outstanding theses is that income equilibrium may go hand in hand with unemployment. Furthermore, aggregate income fluctuates for random causes such as war, natural catastrophes, and major shifts in the government's economic policies. But more troublesome perhaps are the recurrent changes identified with the phases of the business cycles. Formally, the cyclical variations of income and employment may be translated into inequalities between saving and investment. But what breeds these inequalities?

That question is a big one. There are many complicated factors back of these inequalities and there are many intricate theories explaining them. These theories belong in the large field of business cycles, outside the range of this book.

VI. Lord Keynes and the Classicals and Neo-Classicals: Contrasts

The student of economic principles must reckon with J. M. Keynes whether he agrees with him or not. This chapter acquaints us with some of his basic ideas; to increase our knowledge of his economic theses, we may present a simple brief list of comparisons between Keynes and the classical economists, like David Ricardo and J. S. Mill, or the neo-classical economists, like Alfred Marshall, Edward Chamberlin, or Joan Robinson. In most cases, if a given proposition was explained elsewhere, the explanation is not repeated here.

1. The classicals, old and new, were interested in microeconomics and in long-run developments; Keynes's mind centers on macroeconomics and the short run. In the long run we are all dead, he would say. (Evaluate this view.)

2. The classicals worked with foundational concepts like supply and demand; marginalism; utility; cost; competition; price; profit; productivity; and monopoly. Keynes's foundation stones are: total income (Y); total consumption (C); total savings (S); total investment (I); the mul-

tiplier (k); total spending; MPC; MEC; interest; money; supply and demand. As we see, there is some overlapping between him and them.

3. To the classical economist steady unemployment is impossible in a competitive economy, inasmuch as the unemployed will compete with the employed by offering to work at a lower wage rate. Unemployment is the sequel of the inflexible monopoly wage set by the trade union, of minimum-wage laws, and of social insurance. Keynes's view is different, and we can have equilibrium of the economy with less than full employment. (Give his line of reasoning on this paramount question.)

4. As a corollary, to Keynes, advanced capitalism fails to deliver the goods and tends to degenerate into a stagnation economy. The state must go into partnership with private enterprise and undertake deficit-finance spending to give jobs to the would-be employed. To the classicals, a competitive economy has built-in adjustments for full employment, and needs no aid from the state: that government governs best which governs least, is their steady conviction.

5. To the old classicals money is neutral. Adam Smith refers to money as the mere road on which the traffic moves—the master fails to perceive that without roads traffic will be chaotic and will suffer immensely. To Keynes money is an active, causative element in our economy. In part interest depends on the volume of money, and interest in part determines investment, the volume of capital goods, and the volume of offset to aggregate saving (S). Money appears in the title of his *magnum opus*. There must be a monetary policy and not the injurious laissez faire of a gold standard.

6. To the classicals thrift is always desirable because it breeds more capital. To Keynes too much thrift (S) can hardly be offset by investment (I), with unemployment as the undesirable outcome. This unpleasant development is apt to afflict the rich capitalistic countries in which there is commonly large aggregate saving, in view of the MPC.

7. To the classicals there can be no greater economic error than taxation of profits or progressive taxation of income generally, because such levies dry up the source of savings, therefore of capital and employment. Keynes, on the other hand, favors progressive taxation in prosperous countries because such taxation mitigates inequalities of income, therefore tends to raise the MPC, to raise total expenditures on consumption, and to lower the volume of savings and the volume of necessary offsets to savings. The government ought to compound a fiscal policy with a monetary policy, both tailored to the prime objective of society, full employment.

8. Lastly we come to J. B. Say's *law of markets*. A hundred and fifty years ago this French economist concluded that free enterprise does not make possible long-run overproduction nor underproduction. The following explanation is easier to grasp than his own explanation: We start with

the proposition that in a given society everybody is employed. The simple but overpowering fact must be stressed that nobody works gratis. Each of the four factors receives pay for its contribution to production. This total pay equals the total cost of all the goods, equals the price of goods times the total of each type of good: the striking simple fact is that production provides us not only with goods but also with the money to buy these goods! We are living in the best of all possible worlds.

What of saving instead of spending? The classical would state that all savings are invested in capital goods: the market rate of interest sees to that by equating supply and demand of capital goods. If the market rate of interest rises, more is saved and more capital goods and fewer consumption goods are produced: the production on consumer goods and capital goods together provide full employment. What is not produced for consumption is produced for production. Supply creates demand, demand creates supply: no lasting discrepancy can be thrust into our economy.

Keynes is not impressed by the words of the *prince de la science*, as Karl Marx contemptuously refers to J. B. Say. While a full-dress critique of Lord Keynes can hardly be undertaken here, a few remarks may not be out of place. Keynes and his followers have an excessively broad concept of the functions of the state. The list of state activities, specified in their writings and referred to as built-in stabilizers and as promoters of high national incomes, seems to call for a change in our economic and social structure. The list includes rural electrification; social security programs; social medicine; aid to collective bargaining; the progressive income tax; farm programs; guaranteed bank deposits; lending, insuring, slum-clearing, and housing programs; and aid to education at all levels.

The more or less cautious economist wonders about the long-range harmful potentialities and social transformations implicit in policies suggested by this list. One towering fact stands out: three policies, considered eminently desirable by Keynesians, are incompatible: (1) the growth of trade unions (insisting on high-monopoly wages), (2) full employment, and (3) stable prices. Any two of these can go together but not all three of them. We can have (1) and (2) but at the expense of fluctuating and rising prices thrust into the economy by the high costs of trade union wage dictatorship and by the requirements of full employment. Likewise (1) and (3) are possible, but the high wages of trade unionism, accompanied by rising costs and prices, will preclude full employment, especially under the condition of (3) stable prices. Similarly (2) and (3) can go together. But to achieve full employment and stable prices, labor will have to be docile (or intelligent enough) about downward adjustments of wages, a contingency traditionally repugnant to labor and labor leaders. Even the comparatively conservative Samuel Gompers would so pronounce in his speeches: "What does labor want? Labor wants more and more and more!"

We are not living in the best of all possible worlds. We studied first the price of goods (Chapters III–XII); then the price of factors (Chapters XIII–XVII); then the size of the total income of the community (Chapters XVIII–XIX). In the first area the defect is the *monopoly* element, as vexing as it is ineradicable; in the second area the social shortcoming is embedded in too large a degree of *inequality;* in the third area the distressing element stems from the fluctuations of income from prosperity to depression, from boom to bust.

SUGGESTED READINGS

Dillard, D. *The Economics of John Maynard Keynes*, chap. 3. New York, Prentice-Hall, 1948.

Enke, S. *Intermediate Economic Theory*, chaps. 7–10. New York, Prentice-Hall, 1950.

Gordon, R. A. *Business Fluctuations*, chaps. 4, 5. New York, Harper, 1952.

Hansen, A. H. *Business Cycles and National Income*, chaps. 8–12. New York, Norton, 1951.

Hansen, A. H. *A Guide to Keynes*. New York, McGraw-Hill, 1953.

Keynes, J. M. *The General Theory of Employment, Interest and Money*, chap. 18. New York, Harcourt, Brace, 1936.

Morgan, T. *Income and Employment*, 2nd ed. New York, Prentice-Hall, 1952.

Ruggles, R. *An Introduction to National Income and Income Analysis*, chaps. 9–11. New York, McGraw-Hill, 1949.

Weintraub, S. *Income and Employment Analysis*, chaps. 5–11. New York, Pitman, 1951.

CHAPTER

XX Equilibrium

I. The Nature of Equilibrium

IN THE LAST CHAPTER in a book like this it may be permissible to wind up with a nonconventional economic problem or with some new approach away from the beaten path. There is no scarcity of new approaches and new problems in modern economics. The following list of possible studies is far from complete: activity analysis; welfare economics; games—useful to economic theory but uninviting on account of the higher mathematics required; linear programming; underdeveloped economies—a subject of vital interest in this age of urging governments of backward communities to hold the line against communism; the economics of growth; post-Keynesism—forging ahead beyond the master's system; equilibrium, particular and general.

We choose equilibrium. Equilibrium does not isolate itself from the typical analysis of economic questions. It helps tie together important concepts and problems. It helps us in getting a bird's-eye view of an economy and its dominant features.

DEFINITIONS AND IMPORTANCE OF THE CONCEPT

Some definitions come first. By *equilibrium* we mean that a variety of forces cluster around an object, some pressing in one direction, others tending in the opposite direction. As a result, the object does not move. It is at "rest." This idea applies in economics as well as in physics: "as well as in physics" claims too much. Economics is a social science and suffers from disabilities unknown to the physicist. The indispensable feature of equilibrium is the fact that, in the circumstances, a departure from the equilibrium magnitude would not result in a better situation for the agent making the change. Assume an equilibrium wage for semi-skilled labor in a given country, under competitive conditions in the labor market —that is, the wage tends to match the marginal value product (MVP) of this type of labor. If these workers organize and force a higher wage rate, the tendency may be for some of them to lose their jobs because their wage is above the MVP; or else, the cost of the product or of the service of this labor may go up and the price with it. This very labor, as a consumer of these goods, is worse off. J. M. Keynes would reason differently, in this case.

There is stable equilibrium and unstable equilibrium. *Stable* equilibrium implies that a change in an element in the pattern of attributes of an economic situation may induce the reaction, of a personal and objective nature, which will tend to push the deranged element into its *original* type of equilibrium. If an employer "succeeds" in scaling down the market wage of his labor, forces will be set in motion to redress the former equilibrium wage: his labor force will melt away little by little until the *former* wage rate is re-established.

Unstable equilibrium suggests that the existing equilibrium wage, for example, of a given kind of labor, far from expressing the proper wage rate in the light of MVP, is rather the result of maneuverings of the employers or of temporary artificial intrusions, like rumors of war, an expected depression or increased government interference. Unstable equilibrium suggests that somebody or some circumstance must have been manipulating the variables into a forced artificial relation; and as soon as the manipulating ceased, the variables snapped into the economic equilibrium proper to them (what is meant by "proper"?), and the previous equilibrium is no more.

It is necessary to indicate what equilibrium is not. Equilibrium is not a tool of *analysis*, a principle of cause and effect. It is rather an indicator of the direction which analysis must take. In the scrutiny of an economic problem we keep an eye on the forces that act and react; on the elements that move in a given direction. The solution of a problem is commonly so framed as to start the elements moving toward equilibrium.

Equilibrium is not charged with *moral* sentiment. Equilibrium is an objective framework. For example, the wage for a worker may be set at the MRP (marginal revenue product) level. The concept of equilibrium stresses that the worker receiving such a wage, under competitive conditions, may not better himself in the long run by compelling his trade union to force a higher money wage. The question of ethics is excluded; force is exalted.

Equilibrium does not imply that *all* the agencies involved are happy about it. In monopoly equilibrium, the consuming public is not happy. In monopsony equilibrium, labor is exploited. The aggressive trade union, with the power to paralyze an industry with spectacular strikes, may thrust wage levels into our economy which set off disruptive chain reactions in many areas.

Equilibrium may not imply beneficence to *any* economic agency. J. M. Keynes sees a possible over-all equilibrium in face of considerable unemployment. The equilibrium of an economic regime may go hand-in-hand with enduring poverty of the major part of the population. In India, in China, in Africa, and elsewhere, for centuries there had been no record of general prosperity, no autonomous economic movement or disturbance, which might have induced a reformation of the economic foundations of the country. What people saw or read about was comparative acquiescence to regimes of degrading poverty and stultifying ignorance. Custom, habit, tradition, and family worship combined to produce a society with institutions and practices steadily running in the same grooves. Even the cyclical fluctuations are foreign to the structure of such simple communities. Depressions alternating with prosperity are known in "capitalistic" countries. The normal state in these underdeveloped countries is the perennial depression with its low level of income and consumption. We have a cyclical economy, they have a depression economy.

The idea of equilibrium was presented in the introductory chapters of this book, and it was suggested that the reader keep it in mind as the principles and problems unfolded themselves over the subsequent pages. So meaningful and so compelling is equilibrium as a directive principle that it is regarded by many as a precondition of economic analysis. Where there can be no tendency toward equilibrium, it makes little sense to analyze an economic situation. Assume, for instance, that for some consumers the marginal utility of peanuts is always rising or is constant, instead of diminishing after a critical point of consumption. A bizarre situation develops. A *rising* marginal desirability of peanuts precludes analysis, as we know it, of price, output, cost, substitution, supply and demand, and monopoly power if any. If the marginal utility of peanuts has a positive slope, how many peanuts will the industry produce? at what cost? Suppose other individuals are "bitten" by a desire for oranges and cannot have "enough" of them. What will be the behavior of these two sets of consumers toward each other? toward other consumers generally? No relative scarcity, no equilibrium, and no price analysis, at least as we know it.

FROM DISEQUILIBRIUM TOWARD EQUILIBRIUM

The dynamic character of our economy breeds disequilibrium and misallocation of resources. There is constant change in one or more fields:

in supply, demand; consumer tastes, utility; in results of research; in government policies as to tariffs, taxation, subsidies to industry and agriculture, and the elasticity of the supply of money; in costs of factor services; in the composition of the population as to age, sex, and income; in social legislation; and in other important elements. Result: there is a constant *tendency* toward equilibrium of the price of goods and of factor services and of other parts of our economy, but almost never the achievement of perfect equilibrium. As Marx says: "nothing is constant but change: *mors immortalis*."

We are dealing with a far-flung problem and only some aspects can be touched on here. The tendency toward equilibrium can be looked at in the short run and the long run; as among firms in the same industry; as among the submarkets of a given industry in various areas; as among separate industries embracing the whole economy, and so on. The adjustments in one sector of the economy affects other sectors, even as a rock thrown into a pool forms ever-widening concentric circles of diminishing force.

Assume that in the paper-making industry semi-skilled labor in the South is getting a lower wage rate than similar labor in Wisconsin, after allowing for legitimate differences in wage rates, such as are due to the lower cost of living in a milder climate. The industry is in disequilibrium. If only economic considerations dominate economic behavior, there will tend to develop a two-fold movement of adjustments. *One*, this semi-skilled labor, lured by the higher wage rate in Wisconsin paper mills, will tend to move to these greener pastures, where the wage is closer to the marginal value product (MVP) of this labor, thus tending to produce about the same wage in both places. *Two*, to take advantage of the higher profit in the South (brought in by "cheaper" labor, milder taxation, and more conservative legislation) Wisconsin paper mills tend to establish branches in the inviting area—if not to abandon Wisconsin for the South altogether. This second type of adjustment raises the demand for labor in the South, and in time the MVP of labor will be about the same in both locations—higher than before in the South, lower than before in Wisconsin; and the wage will tend to parallel the equalized marginal value product (MVP).

To take another example. Assume that the wage level of carpenters exceeds the wage level of plumbers and, in the opinion of labor and businessmen, promises to stay so for many years. There is no equilibrium in these two industries, members in the same noncompeting groups, as far as the status of labor is concerned—we discussed this phenomenon in Chapter XIV. In the long run, labor will *move* from plumbing to carpentry until the marginal value product (MVP) of labor is equalized in both industries, by dropping in carpentry and rising in plumbing. In both examples, the march toward equilibrium is achieved by the mobility of resources. By mobility we do not mean, of course, that a fifty-year-old plumber turns apprentice in carpentry. We mean that young men graduating from public school prefer to adopt the trade of the carpenter. Dynamic conditions cause disequilibrium; the mobility of resources (land, labor, capital, the entrepreneur) tends to change the data of resource prices, to induce an old or a new equilibrium.

The attainment of equilibrium in a given market does not imply that the theory behind the discussion is prescribed, that only one given set of principles harbors the potential of equilibrium. Equilibrium in the relation between total employment and a reduction in wage rates across the board has no monopoly on a particular theory informing the discussion. Different assumptions and viewpoints prevail in many economic problems, and they give different answers and different kinds of equilibrium: there is seldom just one solution, one principle in partnership with one corresponding equilibrium. If wages are reduced there is more employment; this is the approach of the traditional economist. As we saw in the last topic in Chapter XIV on wages, J. M. Keynes offers a different theory and a different equilibrium. There is a third approach possible to this wage and employment problem: assume (1) that consumption is independent of the *value* of the cash balance of consumers (lower wages and lower prices have the tendency of raising the value of a cash balance); (2) that the supply of money is perfectly elastic; (3) that wages and prices are perfectly flexible; and (4) that the workers' marginal propensity to consume equals unity (no saving). The result is that the fall in total receipts (in wages) will equal the fall in total cost; the wage cut will leave employment unchanged: the *previous* equilibrium in employment remains. And yet another view may compete for consideration: Suppose that the wage reduction in the whole economy results in a smaller aggregate expenditure on consumption, inasmuch as the wages of the working masses constitute by far the major source of total expenditures on consumption, and their marginal propensity to consume is higher than with the well-to-do. Effective demand would drop and employment with it.

In the various chapters of this book the repeated theme is equilibrium. After the two introductory chapters, *three* large problems were claiming our study: the price of goods, in Chapters III–XII; the price of factor-resources, in Chapters XIII–XVII; and the size of the total income of a nation, in Chapters XVIII–XIX. In the first area we studied consumer equilibrium and the equilibrium price in the four market structures: pure competition, monopoly and monopsony, monopolistic competition, and oligopoly. In the second type of problem we studied the equilibrium in the four resource markets: in *wages*, under competition, under employer monopsony, and briefly, in bilateral monopoly; in the three theories of *interest*; in the phenomenon of economic *rent* on land (natural resources);

and in *profits*. In the chapter on profit there was more talk or implication of disequilibrium or of unstable equilibrium: the nature of profit is vagrant, dynamic, uncertain, and volatile. Finally, in the preceding two chapters we discussed *income* equilibrium, with and without full employment: in this discussion the dominant figure was Lord Keynes.

II. Particular Equilibrium

We are by now acquainted with the character of equilibrium. But we want to elaborate on this concept a little more. Our starting point is the division, often blurred, between particular equilibrium and general equilibrium.

By *particular* equilibrium or particular analysis we mean, roughly, a one-sided rather than a many-sided orientation. We are not hunting for all possible situations in which the impact of equilibrium, weak or strong, is brought in as a necessary step in our exposition. The earmark of particular equilibrium is that we confine the discussion to one or two variables or unknowns. We abstract all kinds of *relevant* sequences, interrelations, and combinations. We cast them out of consideration by "all other things equal," by "*ceteris paribus*." The person associated with such an attitude is Alfred Marshall. It may be mentioned that this attitude was in the past described as "partial" equilibrium. But the word "partial" may suggest that only part of the job has been done, whereas this word is meant to describe an equilibrium by the adjustment of only one or two variables.

ALFRED MARSHALL ON EQUILIBRIUM

Alfred Marshall knew enough mathematics to sponsor a body of economic theory based on mathematics. For evidence one can turn to the extensive mathematical appendix to his *Principles of Economics*.[1] But to him particular equilibrium is more comprehensible and more effective; it enunciates simpler propositions and a simpler analysis than would result if the economist were anxious to take full advantage of his knowledge of this new and powerful instrument, mathematics. Marshall did not regard mathematics as an integral and indispensable part of economic exploration. One thing at a time. In Chapter IX, for instance, we study the ultimate effect of an increased demand for a commodity in the market of pure competition. The procedure is to deal with only two or three variables. The steppingstones in that study are, as we know, the short-run effect of

[1] *Principles of Economics* (New York, Macmillan, 1927).

the new *price* on the *quantities* offered for sale; the behavior of the profit-propelled sellers in forming the new supply; the final equilibrium, depending on whether we deal with a long-run constant-cost or increasing-cost, or (perhaps) decreasing-cost industry. The analysis moves within the relatively limited area of the firm and the industry and of unit or marginal costs, rising or declining. There is no attempt to go beyond this area to scrutinize such problems as: what originates the initial increased demand for the article; what is the effect of the change in this industry on *other* industries; what income changes are set in motion in this industry and *elsewhere* in the economy; what happens to the demand for the products of other industries; what is the effect on imports and exports; and what is the effect on the scale of industries and firms, and on costs of production all over the economy.

Marshall is sensitively aware of the limitations of the human mind in the attempt to analyze every economic question from the viewpoint of every agent, consumer, laborer, and businessman. He was not sure that mathematical formulations stir new attitudes and point to new solutions—instead of paraphrasing words into symbols and sentences into equations.

According to Marshall's view, the best we can do is to examine an article from the angle of such variables as price, cost, and quantities. We cannot examine every aspect, every repercussion. Particular analysis is what economists can do best; what they can explain verbally is as vital to the knowledge of economics as the exchange of French or English for the other language, the mathematical language. To Marshall, equations, long and many, are not serviceable, because they bite off too much for thoroughgoing exploration. To start an analysis with a long series of equations and with a ready application of differential calculus and other conceptions of higher mathematics is to start out with an invited handicap, as far as many a student is concerned. Perhaps Marshall goes to extremes.

Particular equilibrium, narrow as it may be, is, however, useful and enlightening. The following incomplete and by now familiar summary of economic agents as affected by particular equilibrium may strengthen this argument.

(1) The consumer is in equilibrium when, with a given income and given commodity prices, his expenditures are so allocated among the goods which he is in the habit of purchasing that a dollar's worth of any commodity which he is buying will bring him the same satisfaction. The consumer also tends toward equilibrium as between spending and saving (how?).

(2) A given productive *resource* (labor, land, capital, and the businessman) is in equilibrium when its compensation (in the form of wages, economic rent, interest, and perhaps profit) is equal to MRP (marginal

revenue product); and when the resource has no incentive to shift its service to another comparable occupation, because it would not get there *greater* compensation.

(3) A *firm* is in short-run equilibrium when its MC = MR; it is in long-run equilibrium when $P = \text{LAC}$ (price = long-run average cost); it has no incentive to leave the industry and try its luck in another industry, producing a different product.

(4) Then we have equilibrium of the monopolist, of the firm in monopolistic competition; of the oligopolist; of the monopsonist; and of the various combinations of resources which tend to form new varieties of market structures, like monopsony-oligopoly.

(5) An *industry* is in equilibrium when there is no tendency for firms to leave the industry or to enter the industry.

(6) The equilibrium of the *economy* gives us pause. No simple brief phrase will be adequate. Nor does this case belong in the category of particular equilibrium. We shall touch on this point toward the end of this chapter. In the meantime it is to be observed that J. M. Keynes has an answer, as we learned in the previous chapter. To him $Y = C + I + G$, where, to repeat, Y is the total income of the community, C is total expenditure on consumption, I is the total investment, and G is total government spending above tax receipts. A second condition of equilibrium is the imperative that $S = I$, that the total savings be spent on investment in capital goods. As we saw, to Keynes, income equilibrium may emerge with full employment or with less than full employment.

In this book, as in any other book of the kind, particular equilibrium dominates the analysis. In pure competition, we study price and output of one commodity, one firm, and one industry. We study monopoly behavior in producing one given article; likewise in monopsony. We study one differentiated product in monopolistic competition, but not the impact of a change in its price upon other articles in other firms and other industries. Oligopoly deals with one product, homogeneous or differentiated, and perhaps one given industry, but we do not consider the effect of the monopoly power of oligopoly on the price, production, income, and shifts in other industries. In the chapters (XIII–XVII) on the pricing of the four types of resources, we studied the wage rate of labor in one noncompeting group, and not the repercussions of changes in wages on other units of the economy, say, on the income of members of other noncompeting groups, like doctors and lawyers, or the repercussions on prices, costs, generally in the other market structures. Similarly with the treatment of interest, rent, and profit.

As was mentioned before, the line between particular and general equilibrium is not of uncompromising clarity. There are gradations of equilibrium in the continuum between the particular kind and the general kind. Still it is too much to claim that pure competition represents a substantial degree of general equilibrium for the reason that, as we saw in Chapter IX, the analysis of constant, increasing, and decreasing cost does not confine itself to the firm alone but embraces the industry too. But pure competition is nonetheless a far cry from general equilibrium, although not as far a cry as the formation (perhaps) of the interest rate from the angle of time preference; or (perhaps) as wage setting in the monopsony market. General equilibrium, to repeat, draws into its orbit the analysis of all the economic elements *affected* by a given change in commodity price or by a given change in a factor-service price. On the other hand, the problem of the relation between the volume of employment and a general cut in wages, as treated by Keynes (see the last topic in Chapter XIV) seems farther away from particular equilibrium than is the customary analysis of pure competition.

What of *aggregative* equilibrium of the Keynesian system (Chapter XIX)? It is difficult to say how it compares with the other two types of equilibrium, principally because the Keynesian construction is different in purpose (total employment) and presentation, as we saw, again in the forgoing chapter. We studied there the nature and the conditions of income equilibrium, as argued by Lord Keynes. To try to compare the equilibrium of Marshall and Keynes is almost to try to compare incomparables.

III. General Equilibrium

Two restless minds are associated with the origination and elaboration of the principle of general equilibrium in economics, Léon Walras (1834–1910), professor at the University of Lausanne, Switzerland, and Wassily W. Leontief, professor at Harvard University.

A. The Walras Equilibrium

In some important respects Walras is the opposite of Marshall. Walras, the protagonist of general equilibrium, stresses the interactions of commodities, quantities, prices, costs, and other variables in a consistent totality. To him economic theory is not confined to cause and effect between two phenomena in the commodity or resource market. The price of one good, he would say, depends on, and is formed by, the prices of the other, related goods. Interaction and mutual causation govern economic phenomena. Everything depends on everything else. One economic agent acts, the other agents react. Act somewhere and there is reaction almost everywhere else.

Walras' mind is in the realm of variables and equations, representing as yet insoluble equations of prime importance in our economy. These variables may someday take on quantitative power. In the meantime the fact, the knowledge, that the system breeds as many equations as are needed to quantify prices and outputs is encouraging. In such a perspective, the variables are not vagrant, irresponsible symbols; they are entities authenticated by the quantitative attribute in them even if we cannot solve equations in order to dig out and bring to light the quantities behind the symbols.

Walras does not go to extremes. He does not intend to imply that any commodity whatsoever is in interrelation with any other commodity. For instance, he would not claim that an increased demand for cottage cheese would affect the sale of a book on Benjamin Franklin.

As an aside on the number of equations required, it may be desirable to mention that, to solve for all the unknowns, we need as many equations as there are unknowns. The equation $x + y = 0$ can be solved for neither x nor y. If one of these two is given, the other unknown can easily be found. But we need two equations to fix the magnitude of each. Let the second equation be $x - y = -10$. Now there is no degree of freedom available. Each value is fixed: $x = -5$, and $y = 5$.

Walras is not satisfied with particular equilibrium. When the demand for a product rises, it is not enough to explore the effect on the commodity that is favored with the increased demand. The whole system is affected. Some sellers are losing trade because of the shift in demand and suffer a decline in their income, therefore in their capacity to spend on their habitual commodities. We assume that the increments in purchases by those consumers who are instrumental in raising the demand are not washed out by decreases in purchases by other consumers. The effects of the shift on the behavior of those whose custom declined must be scrutinized. The impact on the cost of production must also be a concern of the investigation. It is precisely what Marshall casts out by "other things equal" that Walras insists on analyzing.

As we know, the followers of Marshall are aware of the shortcomings of their basic position. But their labors on a limited area are rewarding; whereas a multitude of far-flung equations achieve little more than to make us aware of the immensity of the problem. The followers of Marshall value two considerations: it is easier to understand Marshall's English than Walras' pages bristling with equations; too, in a rough way, many a student who masters Marshall does gain insight into economic problems to the extent of attempting a solution of them. Walras seemingly waits for the extension and perfection of knowledge before he will apply it to everyday problems. Marshall applies the admittedly imperfect knowledge to surrounding problems—he does not insist on waiting for better methods. Walras is an economist's economist. So is Marshall; but Marshall is more than this: he aims to encourage application of economics to our environment.

We cannot undertake to offer a systematic review of Walras' basic book, *Elements of Pure Economics*.[2] We shall limit ourselves to the central theme. Walras divides the whole economy of a country into four types of markets: the market for consumer goods; the market for productive resources; the market for capital goods; and the market for securities. One commodity in the consumer sector is chosen to serve as the *numéraire*, as the unit of account. The other commodities will have as many units as they contain the *numéraire*. This sector, like the other sectors, is governed by a unique set of equations.

Let us look into the first of the four markets, that for consumer goods. One of these goods is assigned the role of the unit of account, the unit by which the other goods are measured. But first some spadework for this set of equations is desirable.

(1) b, c, d represent consumer goods produced and consumed in the economy;

(2) N_b, N_c, N_d are the respective quantities of such goods;

(3) m, n, o indicate the productive factors to produce the above goods;

(4) p'_m, p'_n, p'_o stand for the price of the respective factors; and

(5) F_b, F_c, F_d are functions or relations between b, c, d, and the prices of factors or the goods. Consumer tastes and preferences govern the F's.

Following are some of the basic and highly important equations involved:

$$N_b = F_b \ (p'_m, p'_n, p'_o, \cdots, p_b, p_c, p_d, \cdots), \qquad (1)$$
$$N_c = F_c \ (p'_m, p'_n, p'_o, \cdots, p_b, p_c, p_d, \cdots), \qquad (2)$$
$$N_d = F_d \ (p'_m, p'_n, p'_o, \cdots, p_b, p_c, p_d, \cdots), \qquad (3)$$

$\cdot \ \cdot \ \cdot \ \cdot \ \cdot \ \cdot \ \cdot \ \cdot \ \cdot \ \cdot \ \cdot \ \cdot \ \cdot \ \cdot \ \cdot$

An equation is available for each article produced and consumed in the economy. The above equations for the article indicate the relation between the number (N_b, etc.) of such articles and all the prices of factor-services. In an economy like ours, say with a hundred thousand consumer goods, we shall need as many equations. In the above equations each consumer

[2] Léon Walras, *Elements of Pure Economics*, translated by William Jaffé (Irwin, Homewood, Illinois, 1954), Lessons 20 and 21.

good, each type of factor-service, each kind of capital is considered a separate entity entitled to an equation. The number of equations is enormous. Similar sets of equations apply to the other three types of markets, and again we need as many equations as there are unknowns.

In 1874 Walras presented his first, and one of his simplest, general equilibrium systems. Professor G. J. Stigler reproduces this essay on demand and supply. We shall, in our turn, try to reproduce Professor Stigler on demand alone. Because of the possible mathematical difficulties, the discussion of supply will be omitted. The assumption here is that the reader is interested in Walras' general approach and not in his mathematics.[3] First comes the list of symbols:

$x_1, x_2, \cdots, x_n$ are the products of the economy,
$p_1, p_2, \cdots, p_n$ are their prices;
$y_1, y_2, \cdots, y_m$ are the productive services,
$w_1, w_2, \cdots, w_m$ are their prices.

As usual, product x_1 is the *numéraire*, the unit of measure. Each consumer seeks to maximize his satisfaction with given income and given prices of commodities. This implies, as we know, that

$$\frac{MU_1}{p_1} = \frac{MU_2}{p_2} = \frac{MU_3}{p_3} = \cdots = \frac{MU_n}{p_n}.$$

With n commodities there are $n - 1$ such equations. (If n equations are needed, the one additional equation can be imported from other data.) The assumption is that each individual spends his whole income—no more, no less. His expenditure is therefore

$$x_1 + x_2 p_2 + \cdots + x_n p_n,$$

and this total sum represents his income. His income is also equal to the sums which he receives from the sale of his productive services, namely,

$$y_1 w_1 + y_2 w_2 + \cdots + y_m w_m.$$

Equating these last two summations, we obtain the so-called *budget equation*,

$$x_1 + x_2 p_2 + \cdots + x_n p_n = y_1 w_1 + y_2 w_2 + \cdots + y_m w_m.$$

Under certain conditions, the equality of the number of equations to the number of unknowns is sufficient to determine the quantities of the goods purchased as functions of their prices. Then we may solve these equations and obtain the demand functions:

[3] G. J. Stigler, *The Theory of Price*, revised ed. (New York, Macmillan, 1952), pp. 290-293.

$$x_2 = f_2 \ (p_2, \ p_3, \ \cdots, \ p_n; \ w_1, \ w_2, \ \cdots, \ w_m),$$
$$x_3 = f_3 \ (p_2, \ p_3, \ \cdots, \ p_n; \ w_1, \ w_2, \ \cdots, \ w_m),$$
$$\cdots \cdots \cdots \cdots \cdots \cdots$$
$$x_n = f_n \ (p_2, \ p_3, \ \cdots, \ p_n; \ w_1, \ w_2, \ \cdots, \ w_m).$$

To obtain the *market* demand functions, we add up the demand functions of the *individuals*. Thus if x_{2i} is the quantity of x_2 demanded by individual i, the equation is

$$X_2 = x_{21} + x_{22} + \cdots + x_{2k},$$

if there are k individuals. Since each of the individual's demand functions depends on prices, so also does the market demand function depend on prices.

Including the budget equation, we have n such equations of market demand and not $n - 1$ equations:

$$X_2 = F_2 \ (p_2, \ p_3, \ \cdots, \ p_n; \ w_1, \ w_2, \ \cdots, \ w_m),$$
$$X_3 = F_3 \ (p_2, \ p_3, \ \cdots, \ p_n; \ w_1, \ w_2, \ \cdots, \ w_m),$$
$$\cdots \cdots \cdots \cdots \cdots \cdots$$
$$X_n = F_n \ (p_2, \ p_3, \ \cdots, \ p_n; \ w_1, \ w_2, \ \cdots, \ w_m),$$
$$X_1 = Y_1 w_1 + Y_2 w_2 + \cdots + Y_m w_m - X_2 p_2 - X_3 p_3 - \cdots - X_n p_n.$$

B. Input-Output Analysis

This type of analysis is the outstanding variant of general equilibrium. The pioneer in this field is Professor Leontief. The backbone of this theory is the idea, or the fact, that industries are interrelated in such an invincible manner that a given industry both buys from various industries and sells to various industries materials and semifinished products in order to carry on the processes of production. It would be difficult to conjure up an industry the member firms of which can make shoes without first buying some of the things essential in making shoes. Even the cobbler of the Middle Ages could not do his work without buying the leather from the tanners. Nor did he make his own hammers and other tools. A degree of division of labor existed in many occupations many centuries ago; and division of labor fostered interrelations among production units then as it does now. Division of labor means co-operation of labor.

An important by-product of this approach is the so-called Input-Output Table, stretching in length to the size of three ordinary pages.[4] It

[4] W. D. Evans and M. Hoffenberg, "The Interindustry Relations Study for 1947," *The Review of Economics and Statistics*, May, 1952. The data are from Division of Interindustry Economics, U. S. Bureau of Labor Statistics.

reminds one of the road maps procured in gasoline stations, indicating the mileage between any two cities on the list. The Table of 1947 deals with fifty industries arrayed both horizontally and vertically, in the same order and with the same number. For example, Iron and Steel is No. 15, and it is registered twice, in the row and in the column. Because the study of industries has its statistical and analytical complications, and is enormously time consuming, in many a case the "industry" represents a group of industries. For example, we notice in the two arrays Food and Kindred Products (No. 2); Paper and Allied Products (No. 8); Stone, Clay, and Glass Products (No. 14); Coal, Gas, and Electric Power (No. 30); and Eating and Drinking Places (No. 44).

As the statistical and analytical work is progressing, fewer items will represent a group of industries, and the tables will be able to register more and more single industries. The tables may then include progressively more than fifty industries. But first a staggering number of equations will have to be solved. As we move along a given *row* we see in each square the dollar amounts *purchased* by the corresponding industry. Similarly each square in the vertical column registers *sales* in dollars by one industry to the other industries. Suppose we call No. 15 (Iron and Steel) horizontally and No. 24 (Radio) vertically. We get a blank in the square specified by row 15 and column 24. It means that in 1947 the iron and steel industry sold none of its products to the radio industry, and the radio industry sold none of its products to the iron and steel industry. When we put down No. 15 (Iron and Steel) horizontally and vertically, we expect the square where the two meet to be empty. But this is not the case. Inscribed in the square is the sum of $3,982,000. This means that *within* the iron and steel industry various companies buy and sell materials, semifinished products, and the like.

The input-output conception is of considerable importance in the economics of industry, for good or ill.

1. It can inform the businessman about the varieties and quantities of goods which his industry, that is, the other firms in the industry, buys and sells. What he learns may improve his practices, and his adjustments and his sophistication generally.

2. It is useful to learn about the interrelations among firms and industries, about possible trends toward horizontal combinations (like the trust in the traditional sense of monopoly), vertical combinations (like a type of merger), and the ramification of influence.

3. We see more clearly the waste and losses to industries occasioned by a prolonged strike, by tariff walls, and by preparations for war. A strike in the economic empire of the iron and steel industry may have serious repercussions nearly all over the industrial map.

4. The input-output construction can be an important factor in the

business cycle. During a revival after a depression the input-output activities energize and hasten the return to prosperity. But there is the other side of the coin. It similarly exerts a magnifying influence when a prosperous economy takes a downturn.

5. The input-output framework has its decided shortcomings. This framework thrives on equations, but thousands of revelant equations are not easily amassed. We need to ascertain first the pattern of the equations, then proceed to acquire the necessary voluminous data. To avoid some of these difficulties, simplifications are introduced. But if we simplify beyond a certain point, the results may depart too far from realities. There is a limit to abstraction. We are giving hostages to fortune—at this stage of knowledge—if we attempt to shape our policies by higher mathematics.

Walras and Leontief use mathematics, especially Walras. Can there be a *verbal* delineation of the conditions which must be satisfied if our economy is to be in equilibrium? This question has been raised from time to time, notably and recently by Professor J. S. Duesenberry.[5] What follows is in very close resemblance to his summary:

1. We shall begin with the household. It performs a number of basic functions in our economy. It is first of all the consumer of the goods and services produced per unit of time. Adam Smith emphasized long ago (in 1776) that production is for consumption. Next, the household provides factor-service in the form of labor, and its savings are turned into capital goods. When the economy is in equilibrium, the following equation is valid: Value (price times quantity) of consumption per unit of time plus savings equals the value of the services supplied by the household. In other words, the household spends and saves what it contributes as a productive resource.

2. The method of producing each commodity minimizes the cost of production. The price includes rents of all types. Also each method of production requires an input of each kind of factor-resource per unit of output of the product in question.

3. The amount of each factor required in relation to the method of production is equal to, or less than, the amount supplied.

4. The cost of producing each article equals the sum of the factor-inputs required, times their prices.

5. The cost of each product equals its price.

6. The discounted value (using the proper interest rate) of the quasi-rents (over the life of the service) of each kind of capital good equals the price of that kind of capital good. The present value of quasi-rents for a capital good therefore equals the cost of producing it.

7. The value of capital goods produced plus additions to inventory

[5] J. S. Duesenberry, *Business Cycles and Economic Growth* (New York, McGraw-Hill, 1958), pp. 16–17.

equals savings.

8. The sum of price times quantity produced per period for all commodities equals the quantity of money times income velocity of circulation per period of time.

9. Velocity is a given datum.

THE FINAL QUESTION

The economist, like any other scientist, goes through the following sequence in his pursuit of new insights and new constructions. First comes the *observation* of facts. Next, by applying his *imagination* and his *reasoning power* he composes a *hypothesis*. The next step is unique to social science: the social scientist *tests* his hypothesis by further patient and careful thinking, commonly, by the deductive analysis, and not by *experimentation* in the laboratory, as the physicist or the chemist would do. The final result may be the formulation of a new theory, or the corroboration or the modification of an older theory. Sooner or later the accumulated theories in a given field of knowledge are relevantly combined into chapters and books. In these processes the economist is objective: his aim is not to propose, not to impose, but to expose.

It is not an infraction of the principle of objectivity to raise the following question: under what conditions could our present economic order, with the given four types of resources, rise to the highest levels of productivity and thereby to the greatest total satisfaction or the greatest average of satisfaction of the population—the prime goal of an economy.

Following are the necessary conditions, each of them handled in one place or another in this book, directly or by preparing the background for it.

(1) Pure *competition* in each commodity market. This involves many firms (in each industry) each one of large enough size to reap to the full internal and external economies compounded with the economies of scale, to induce least-costs of production.

(2) Enough *dynamics* of innovation in each market to assure *progress* in the arts of production and industrial organization generally—without continual chaos and turmoil drastically upsetting the more or less established equilibrium. The other extreme would be a moratorium on innovation, and this spells stagnation. In a stationary routine economy there will scarcely be a serious function for the businessman: this suggests a change in the social order of a magnitude not to be included in the answer to "the

final question." Old countries like India, China, and African settlements offer an object lesson.

(3) Ready *mobility* of resources from area to area, from firm to firm, from industry to industry, to *checkmate* large upsets in a market. We want limited dynamics.

In such an economy each economic agent benefits, but not to the exclusion or at the expense of other economic agents. Placed at the end of the book, these propositions need no repetition of explanations and discussions.

But such a desirable economic model is not destined to be. Following is a partial list of causes for such a conclusion. Our economy is pock-marked with varying degrees of seemingly ineradicable *monopoly* elements. The actual *dynamics* of our economy do not move with measured step, but go at times to painful extremes. The mechanization of industry and agriculture did more than hurt the horse-and-buggy trade. The rise of the automobile adversely affected the bicycle industry, the railroads, but the resultant homicide on the highways has brought larger earnings to funeral parlors and life insurance companies. The *mobility* of resources is not very sensitive to greener pastures elsewhere; man is tied down by custom, habit, and the fear of the unknown. The play of *psychological* and sociological forces upset or retard equilibrium. David Ricardo mentions in his *Principles of Political Economy and Taxation* (1817) that people would rather hold domestic bonds at a low rate of interest than foreign bonds at a higher rate. Add other causes: rigidity in price markets, ignorance, lack of adequate information about ways of bettering one's self, and confusion of the consumer induced or aggravated by advertising a dozen brands of cigarettes, of beer, of laxatives for young men and elderly women, many ways of losing dandruff, bad breath, and so on and so on. As Thoreau said, we cultivate improved means toward unimproved ends.

However, we must keep in mind that our modified free enterprise economy, despite shortcomings, has added a new page to human history, telling us that in his struggle with nature, man has finally achieved an extremely high standard of living for a community of 180-odd millions of people.

The questions raised on the first page of this book receive an answer by the time we reach this last page.

SUGGESTED READINGS

Cassel, G. *Theory of Social Economy*, Book I, chap. IV. New York, Harcourt, Brace, 1932.

Dorfman, R. "The Nature and Significance of Input-Output," *Review of Economics and Statistics,* Vol. XXXVI (May, 1954), pp. 121–33.

Hicks, J. R. *Value and Capital.* 2nd ed., chaps. IV–VI. Oxford, England, Clarendon Press, 1946.

Knight, F. H. "A Suggestion for Simplifying the Statement of the General Theory of Price," *Journal of Political Economy,* XXXVI (June, 1928), pp. 353–370.

Leftwich, R. H. *The Price System and Resource Allocation,* revised ed., chap. XVII. New York, Holt, Rinehart and Winston, 1960.

Leontief, W. W. *The Structure of American Economy, 1919–1939.* New York, Oxford University Press, 1951.

Leontief, W. W. *Studies in the Structure of the American Economy.* New York, 1953.

Smith, Adam. *The Wealth of Nations.* Edwin Cannan, ed., chaps. VI and VII. New York, The Modern Library, 1937.

Stigler, G. J. *The Theory of Price,* revised ed., chap. 16. New York, Macmillan, 1952.

Walras, L. *Elements of Pure Economics,* translated by William Jaffé. Homewood, Illinois, Irwin, 1954.

Index